LATIN AMERICAN CIVILIZATION
THE COLONIAL ORIGINS

LATIN AMERICAN CIVILIZATION

The Colonial Origins

Volume I Third Edition

Edited by

BENJAMIN KEEN
Northern Illinois University

HOUGHTON MIFFLIN COMPANY BOSTON
Atlanta Dallas Geneva, Illinois
Hopewell, New Jersey Palo Alto London

Copyright © 1974 by Houghton Mifflin Company.
Copyright © 1967 by Benjamin Keen as *Readings in Latin-
American Civilization*. Copyright 1955 by Benjamin Keen
as *Readings in Latin-American Civilization*.

Printed in the U.S.A.
Library of Congress Catalog Card Number: 73-9415
ISBN: 0-395-17582-8

✛ Preface

The publisher's decision, based on recommendations of many past users, to issue *Latin American Civilization* in a new two-volume format has given me an opportunity to revise the sections on the colonial and revolutionary periods, now combined in the first volume. I have reviewed and, where necessary, revised section and chapter introductions to reflect the most recent scholarship. (Except for a few additions, I have left the readings basically intact.) The readings were carefully selected for their factual value, readability, and the insight they offered into contemporary modes of thought, and seem to have lost none of their utility.

One of the principal novelties of this volume is the concluding chapter, "Spain's Work in America: For and Against." Recently the ancient dispute about the character and results of the Spanish Conquest and the Spanish colonial process has been revived. The problem has acquired a new relevance because of its connection with the anticolonial struggles of our own time. The new chapter, bringing together old and new viewpoints on Spain's work in America, illuminates the issues in a controversy of seemingly inexhaustible interest.

Benjamin Keen
DeKalb, Illinois
1973

✤ Contents

ANCIENT AMERICA

Advances in science and archaeology of the past quarter-century have radically changed our notions concerning American prehistory. The radiocarbon dating technique, in use since 1949, establishes a much greater antiquity for the American Indian culture than was commonly assigned to it before that date. Although the earliest definite evidence of man in the New World dates from about 10,000 B.C., it seems likely that the first Americans came from Asia by way of the Bering Strait no less than 20,000 to 25,000 years ago. These first comers must have brought with them a very small stock of primitive culture.

In the course of several thousands of years the Indians spread over both the American continents and eventually developed a wide range of cultural types, ranging from nomadic groups of hunters and food gatherers to the elaborate empires of the Aztec and the Inca. There was some correspondence — but by no means absolute — between physical environment and the level of cultural achievement. The semiarid conditions of the Mexican and Peruvian highlands, for example, facilitated cultural development, because the land was easily tilled by digging-stick and irrigation farming. The Aztec and Inca empires arose in such environments. On the other hand, the brilliant Maya civilization flowered in a tropical rain forest environment on a base of slash-and-burn agriculture.

The concept of "Nuclear America" — that is, the area com-

prising central and southern Mexico, Central America, the northern Andes, and Peru — has come into wide use among students of American prehistory. "This," says Gordon R. Willey, "is the axis of aboriginal high culture in the Americas and, as such, the major center of prehistoric diffusion in the Western hemisphere." The Aztec, Maya, and Inca civilizations arose in this heartland of ancient America. These three civilizations had certain features in common. All three were based on intensive farming that made possible the development of a large sedentary population and considerable division of labor. These civilizations, however, also evolved along distinctive lines. Maya culture was distinguished by impressive achievements in writing, calendrical science, mathematics, and architecture. The Aztecs were mighty warriors, and a distinctive feature of their religion was the stupendous scale of human sacrifice. The Inca were the greatest empire builders of ancient America, and they made a systematic and largely successful effort to unify the institutions and language of their extensive empire.

Advances in archaeological research and methodology in recent decades have made it possible to trace the development of the ancient civilizations of America in broad outline. This scheme is tentative in detail, with considerable variation in the time span allotted to each developmental stage from area to area. The sequence of stages, on which specialists are largely agreed, is as follows: (1) an archaic stage, which lasted from about 7000 B.C. to 2000 B.C., characterized by a gradual shift in subsistence from hunting and gathering to agriculture; (2) a formative era, from about 2000 B.C. to 1 A.D., featured by the establishment of stable agricultural communities, steady technological advance, increase of population, and the emergence of stratified society and the state; (3) a classic stage, from about 1 A.D. to 1000 A.D., marked by the rise of regional states and a flowering of culture in all directions, based on a dense population, intensive division of labor, and the directing role of a powerful priesthood; (4) a climactic or postclassic era, from about 1000 A.D. to the coming of the Spaniards, characterized by chronic warfare, the rise of empires, and a growth of urbanism and — in some areas — of trade. The Aztec and Inca empires typify this stage.

The Aztec, Maya, and Inca civilizations pose some intriguing problems of evolution in history. These civilizations display some striking resemblances in development and culture to those of ancient Mesopotamia, Egypt, and China. How can these resemblances be explained? By diffusion, by migration, or by independent evolution? The fate of the Aztec and Inca empires poses another provocative question. What would have become of these high civilizations of Nuclear America if their development had not been interrupted by white conquerors armed with guns, swords, and a superior social organization?

1 ✣ The Aztecs of Mexico

The Aztecs were latecomers in a region that had been civilized for almost a thousand years before their arrival. The first high civilization of ancient Mexico arose between the time of Christ and A.D. 250; its seat was the great city of Teotihuacán, situated about twenty-eight miles from modern Mexico City. Teotihuacán perished at the hands of foes who burned it between 650 and 800 A.D. On its ruins arose the Toltec Empire, founded by a Nahua-speaking barbarian or semi-barbarian tribe that invaded the Valley of Mexico in the eighth century and established its capital at Tula, about forty miles north of Mexico City. The Toltec Empire, having attained a peak of splendor under the great priest-king Quetzalcóatl, entered on a period of social and economic crisis that ended in its collapse in the twelfth century.

In the period that followed the passing of Toltec supremacy, a number of other Nahua-speaking groups invaded the Valley of Mexico and settled in the lake country at its bottom. They borrowed freely from the rich civilization of their Toltec predecessors. Among the last tribes to arrive in the valley were the Aztecs or Mexica. Finding the most desirable sites occupied by other groups, they were compelled to take refuge on marshy lands in Lake Texcoco. Here, probably in 1344 or 1345, they began to build the town of Tenochtitlán. The Aztecs gradually improved their economic position and perfected their military organization. In 1430, in alliance with the city-state of

Texcoco and the smaller town of Tlacopan, they attacked and defeated Atzcapotzalco, then the dominant power in the lake country. This victory led to the rise of a Triple Alliance for the conquest, first of the valley, then of much of the Middle American world. By degrees the balance of power within the alliance shifted to the aggressive Aztec state; Texcoco became a junior partner, and Tlacopan was reduced to a satellite. When the ill-fated Montezuma came to rule in 1503, the Triple Alliance levied tribute on scores of towns, large and small, from the fringes of the arid northern plateau to the lowlands of Tehuantepec, and from the Atlantic to the Pacific.

The economic basis of life in the Aztec Empire was an intensive agriculture based on irrigation and the slash-and-burn method of cultivation. A numerous class of artisans produced a wide variety of manufactured products. Advances in regional division of labor and the increase in the market for luxury goods also led to the emergence of a merchant class organized in a very powerful guild. By the time of the Conquest, Aztec society was definitely stratified. A "chief of men" chosen from a single family stood at the head of a ruling class of nobles and priests that was maintained in economic idleness by the labor of free commoners, serfs, and slaves.

The principal divinities worshipped in Tenochtitlán were the War and Rain Gods. Artistic and technical progress was most marked in architecture, sculpture, gold and silver work, and the delicate craft of featherwork. The cultural center of the Aztec Empire was Texcoco, where the remarkable Nezahualcoyotl (1379–1472), king, religious reformer, and philosopher, had his brilliant court, fostered literary and artistic activity, and established himself as a major poet in his own right.

1. AZTEC WARFARE

Warfare was the basis of Aztec existence, and warriors shared with priests the places of greatest honor and influence in Aztec society. Warriors who consistently distinguished themselves in battle were rewarded by admission into military orders, like the Knights of the Eagle or of the Tiger, which performed special dances and rituals. The successful warrior might also be rewarded by the grant of tribal land, worked by laborers attached to the soil; such grants often became hereditary estates. An important object of warfare was the procurement of captives to be sacrificed on the altars of the gods whose goodwill brought victory to the Aztec banners. Thus, in the words of the late Dr. George C. Vaillant, "war led to sacrifice and sacrifice led

back to war, in ever-widening cycles." Our principal source of information concerning Aztec life and customs is the monumental work of the Spanish friar Bernardino de Sahagún (1499–1590), who carefully recorded a vast store of material obtained from native informants. His great General History *of the* Things of New Spain *contains the following native account of an Aztec military campaign.*[1]

✦✦✦✦ The ruler was known as the lord of men. His charge was war. Hence, he determined, disposed, and arranged how war would be made.

First he commanded masters of the youths and seasoned warriors to scan the [enemy] city and to study all the roads — where [they were] difficult, where entry could be made through them. This done, the ruler first determined, by means of a painted [plan], how was placed the city which they were to destroy. Then the chief noted all the roads — where [they were] difficult, and in what places entry could be made.

Then he summoned the general and the commanding general, and the brave warriors, and he commanded them how they were to take the road, what places the warriors were to enter, for how many days they would march, and how they would arrange the battle. And he commanded that these would announce war and send forth all the men dexterous in war to be arrayed, and to be supplied with provisions for war and insignia.

The ruler then consulted with all the majordomos — the men of the Petlacalco and of the Aztacalco, the majordomos of Quauhnauac and Uaxtepec, and [those] of Cuetlaxtlan, Tochpan, Tziuhcoac, Tepequacuilco, Uapan, Coatlixthauacan, Tlappan, Tlachco, Matlatzinco, Ocuillan, Xilotepec, Atotonilco, Axocopan, Itzcuincuitlapilco, Atocpan, and Ayotzintepec. He ordered them to take out all their [goods held in] storage, the tributes, costly articles — insignia of gold, and with quetzal feathers, and all the shields of great price.

And when the majordomos had delivered all the costly devices, the ruler then adorned and presented with insignia all the princes who were already able in war, and all the brave warriors, the men [at arms], the seasoned warriors, the fearless warriors, the Otomí, and the noblemen who dwelt in the young men's houses.

And when it had come to pass that the ruler adorned them, when he had done this to the brave warriors, then the ruler ordered all

[1] Drs. Arthur J. O. Anderson and Charles E. Dibble, translators and editors of the *Florentine Codex* (Fray Bernardino de Sahagún, *General History of the Things of New Spain*) (Santa Fe, School of American Research and University of Utah, 1950–   ), kindly permitted me to use this excerpt from the galley proofs of Book VIII of the *Florentine Codex*. B.K.

the majordomos to bear their goods, all the costly devices, and all the valuable capes there to battle, that the ruler might offer and endow with favors all the [other] rulers, and the noblemen, and the brave warriors, the men [at arms] who were about to go to war, who were to be extended as if made into a wall of men dexterous with arms. And the ruler forthwith called upon the rulers of Texcoco and Tlacopan and the rulers in all the swamp lands, and notified them to proclaim war in order to destroy a [certain] city. He presented them all with costly capes, and he gave them all insignia of great price. Then he also ordered the common folk to rise to go forth to war. Before them would go marching the brave warriors, the men [at arms], the lord general, and the commanding general.

The lords of the sun, it was said, took charge and directed in war. All the priests, the keepers of the gods, took the lead; they bore their gods upon their backs, and, by the space of one day, marched ahead of all the brave warriors and the seasoned warriors. These also marched one day ahead of all the men of Acolhuacan, who likewise marched one day ahead of all the Tepaneca, who similarly marched one day ahead of the men of Xilotepec; and these also marched one day ahead of all the so-called Quaquata. In like manner the [men of] other cities were disposed. They followed the road slowly and carefully.

And when the warlike lands were reached, the brave warrior generals and commanding generals then showed the others the way and arranged them in order. No one might break ranks or crowd in among the others; they would then and there slay or beat whoever would bring confusion or crowd in among the others. All the warriors were extended there, until the moment that Yacauitztli, [god of] the night, would descend — that darkness would fall. And when they already were to rise against the city to destroy it, first was awaited tensely the moment when fire flared up — when the priests brought [new] fire — and for the blowing of shell trumpets, when the priests blew them.

And when the fire flared up, then as one arose all the warriors. War cries were raised; there was fighting. They shot fiery arrows into the temples.

And when they first took a captive, one fated to die, forthwith they slew him there before the gods; they slashed his breast open with a flint knife.

And when the city had been overcome, thereupon were counted as many captives as there were, and as many Mexicans and Tlatilulcans as had died. Then they apprised the ruler that they had been orphaned for the sake of Uitzilopochtli; that men had been taken captive and been slain. And the ruler then commanded the high judges to go to tell and inform all in the homes of those who had gone to die in

war, that there might be weeping in the homes of those who had gone
to war to die. And they informed those in the homes of as many as
had gone to take captives in war that they had received honors there
because of their valor. And they were rewarded according to their
merits; the ruler accorded favors to all — costly capes, breech clouts,
chocolate, food, and devices, and lip rods and ear plugs. Even more
did the ruler accord favors to the princes if they had taken captives.
He gave them the offices of stewards, and all wealth without price —
honor, fame, renown.

And if some had done wrong in battle, they then and there
slew them on the battlefield; they beat them, they stoned them.

And if several claimed one captive, and one man said, "He is
my captive," and another man also said, "He is my captive": if no man
verified it, and also if no one saw how they had taken the captive, the
lord of the sun decided between them. If neither had an advantage of
the two who claimed the captive, then those who had taken four
captives, the masters of the captives, decided that to neither one would
the captive belong. He was dedicated to the Uitzcalco [or] they left
him to the tribal temple, the house of the devil.

And when the city which they had destroyed was attained, at
once was set the tribute, the impost. [To the ruler who had conquered them] they gave that which was there made. And likewise,
forthwith a steward was placed in office, who would watch over and
levy the tribute.

2. THE BATTLE OF ATZCAPOTZALCO

*A major turning point in the fortunes of the Aztec nation was
the victory achieved in 1429, in alliance with the men of Texcoco, over the dominant power in the lake region, the Tepanecs
of Atzcapotzalco. The Codex Ramirez, an important source of
information on Aztec history, written by an unidentified native
soon after the Spanish Conquest, contains a spirited account of
this affair. Written from an intensely partisan point of view,
the narrative completely omits the contribution of the Texcocan
allies to the outcome of the struggle, and in other respects dis-
torts the actual course of events. Its chief interest consists in
the insight it gives into Aztec psychology and social relations.*[2]

[2] The *Codex Ramirez*, in Paul Radin, "Sources and Authenticity of the History
of the Ancient Mexicans," University of California *Publications in American
Archaeology and Ethnology*, Vol. 17, Berkeley, Cal., University of California
Press, 1920, pp. 98–99. Originally published by the University of California Press;
reprinted by permission of the Regents of the University of California.

✠✠✠✠ Then they began to march against Atzcapotzalco in perfect order and precision to the place to which the king and the brave Atlacaellel, the commander-in-chief, led them. When they approached the Atzcapotzalcans the latter descried them and immediately came down in good order for the encounter. The latter were loaded down with great riches, gold, silver, jewels, and feathers; they had rich devices on their shields and weapons as became a powerful people who at that time held sway over all that country. The Mexicans, although poorly dressed, were full of courage and confidence in the valor and subtlety of their general.

The brave Atlacaellel, seeing that the enemy was advancing with such vehemence, before they actually came to blows, ordered that all the captains and the leaders and young men who showed great intrepidity and desire for battle be put in the wings of the army and that when the signal was given these were to rush upon the enemy, while the common people and soldiers of lesser courage should remain where they were (in the center), the king placing himself at the head of them for the time being. If the enemy were defeated these latter should not break rank but together in one mass they were to enter the city of Atzcapotzalco.

The enemy was quite near as he said this, so (those specially selected) placed themselves in the wings as Atlacaellel had ordered and the king Itzcohuatl struck a small drum suspended from his shoulders and as he thus gave the signal the Mexican army sprang forward with such great shouts and shrieks that the enemy was seized with fear. Then, attacking with impetuosity and with an invincible spirit, striking desperately to right and left, in no particular order, they began to shout, "Mexico! Mexico!" and so greatly did this disconcert the people of Atzcapotzalco that they began to lose their order and were defeated, many of the common people being killed. The Mexicans, keeping up their courage, captured great prizes and showed remarkable dexterity in wounding and killing the enemy.

The people of Atzcapotzalco began to retreat to their city and the Mexicans, gaining upon them, followed them. The Mexicans had exhibited no fear throughout the fighting and now when they saw themselves victorious they rushed with great boldness upon the enemy. Then the Mexican king, seeing this, urged on his forces, the king of Atzcapotzalco doing the same. However, the Mexicans were so fired with enthusiasm that the people of Atzcapotzalco could not resist them, and fleeing from the field they retired to their city.

Then the spirited Atlacaellel, the general of the Mexican army, let loose tremendous shouts of "Victory! Victory!" and closing in upon the enemy killed and wounded them most piteously. The king, Itzcohuatl, then ordered that part of the army under him to pillage the

city, burn the houses and sack whatever they found there, and to spare neither man nor woman, young nor old. This was done pitilessly and mercilessly and not an object was left standing upright nor a person alive, except those who succeeded in escaping and who fled to the mountains. Even these the Mexicans did not spare, for they followed them like wild lions raging with fury and anger and even pursued them to the most inaccessible parts of the *sierras*. Then the people of Atzcapotzalco prostrated themselves, surrendered their weapons and promised to give (the Mexicans) their lands, to work on their houses and plantations, to pay tribute to them forever and even to supply them with stone, lime, and wood for their houses. They also promised to give them all necessary seeds and vegetables for their support. The general, Atlacaellel, taking pity upon them, ordered the pursuit to cease and gathering his people together he made the Atzcapotzalcans swear that they would fulfill what they had promised. Then the Mexicans returned victorious and happy to their city, laden with great riches and spoils which they had found in Atzcapotzalco, for since it had been the court, all the wealth of the Tepanecan nation had centered there.

On the following day King Itzcohuatl of Mexico ordered all his chiefs to come together and told them that they no doubt remembered that the common people had obligated themselves to perpetual service if the Mexicans were victorious, and that therefore it might be well to call them and ask them to fulfill their promise. He put this proposition before the common people assembled there, and the latter admitted that they had promised all this; that the lords and leaders by their great bravery and valor had indeed merited victory and for that reason they were quite willing to accept their fate and keep their promise. So there they took the oath binding themselves to all the conditions mentioned before. And this was kept from that time on.

Then they went into the city of Atzcapotzalco, where they divided the lands among themselves, giving the largest and the best portion to the royal crown; the next, to the captain-general Atlacaellel, and the remainder to the other leaders and nobles of Mexico, each one receiving land according to the manner in which he had distinguished himself in battle. To the common people they gave no land, except to those few who had shown spirit and courage. To the others they paid no attention at all and reviled them for their cowardice and their lack of courage, telling them that they were people who lacked the imagination to look ahead of them. Finally they gave land to the *barrios* so that they might use what they harvested from these lands for the service of their gods and the embellishment of their temples. This is the method to which they ever after adhered in apportioning lands gained by conquest.

3. THE UNVANQUISHED

To the east of the Valley of Mexico, but still within the central plateau, lived the warlike tribe of the Tlaxcalans. Although they claimed a common origin with the Aztecs, the Tlaxcalans stubbornly resisted Aztec aggression, and they were still enjoying full independence when Cortés and his men landed on the Mexican coast. Like the clash between Rome and Carthage, the prolonged strife between Aztecs and Tlaxcalans had an important element of commercial rivalry. The mestizo *historian Muñoz Camargo (1528?–1599) describes the curiously modern technique of economic blockade used by the Aztecs against their enemies.*[3]

✤✤✤✤ When the lords of Tlaxcala learned of the growing might and prosperity of the Mexican realm . . . , they determined to arm and be on guard against any attack from such a great power as this; and so they watched over the frontiers of their lands and sought to keep the peace with all as they had always done. But all their precautions and prudence went for naught, for the men of Huexotzinco, Cholula, and other provinces subject to the Mexicans, moved by mortal envy, sought by their wiles and craft to obstruct the trade of the Tlaxcalans wherever they could and to force them to withdraw into their own lands. And in order to incite the Mexicans all the more and move them to greater wrath, these subject peoples spoke mischievously against the Tlaxcalans, saying that by making friendships and by their trade they were gradually winning over provinces that the Mexicans had gained for themselves. . . .

The Tlaxcalans, seeing the great enmity of the Mexicans toward them, defended their interests as best they could, but since the power of the Mexicans was greater than their own, little by little they were forced to retreat to their own lands, losing the trade that they had once enjoyed. Engaged in this strife, they sent ambassadors to the Mexican princes, asking why they made war upon them, since they had given no cause for hostilities or for the maltreatment of their people, with whose commerce the Mexicans were interfering, seizing their wares and committing other outrages and injuries. To which the Mexicans replied that the great lord of Mexico was the lord of the whole world, to whom all men were vassals; that he would conquer them and force them to acknowledge him for their master; and whoever would not yield obedience unto him, them would he destroy and raze their towns

[3] Diego Muñoz Camargo, *Historia de Tlaxcala*, México, 1947, pp. 119–123. (Excerpt translated by the editor.)

THE HALLS OF MONTEZUMA 13

to their foundations, settling them with new people. Let them therefore acknowledge him for their lord and yield themselves unto him, paying tribute as other provinces and realms were wont to do, for otherwise they would fall upon them. To which the ambassadors of Tlaxcala replied: "Most powerful lords, Tlaxcala is no vassal of yours; furthermore, not since they came out of the seven caves have the Tlaxcalans paid tribute or tax to any king or prince in the world, for they have always retained their freedom, and being unaccustomed to such service they will not obey you, for they would rather die than consent to such a thing. And know that what you demand of them they will require of you, and in this affair they will shed as much blood as the Chichimeca of Poyautlau shed in the war of Poyautlau that they fought with your ancestors.[4] And so we return with the reply that you have given us."

Learning of the arrogant reply of the Mexicans, the people of Tlaxcala thenceforth lived on their guard against whatever misfortune might befall them; and since the Mexicans had conquered the greater part of this New World and there remained nothing more for them to acquire from the one sea to the other, they thought that they could easily seize the province of Tlaxcala and subjugate it as they had done with the others. And so they fell upon the Tlaxcalans and engaged them in so many clashes and skirmishes that within a few years they had forced them back into their own lands and provinces. They kept the Tlaxcalans encircled for more than sixty years, depriving them of all their human wants, for they had no cotton with which to clothe themselves, nor gold and silver for their adornment, nor green plumes (which they favor most for their emblems and plumages), nor plumes of any other color for their festivals, nor cocoa to drink, nor salt for their food. All these and other things they lacked during the more than sixty years that they were encircled. They became so accustomed to eating no salt that to this day they have no taste for it and attach no worth to it, and even their children who have been reared among us use very little salt, although in view of its present abundance they have begun to form a liking for it.

4. THE HALLS OF MONTEZUMA

The political organization of the Aztec state on the eve of the Spanish Conquest represented a mixture of tribal democracy, theocracy, and royal absolutism, with the scanty vestiges of

---

[4] A reference to a legendary affray between the Aztecs and the Tlaxcalans when the latter still inhabited the Valley of Mexico. B.K.

*tribal democracy. The barbaric splendor and elaborate cere-
monial that marked the household of the great war chief Montezuma are vividly described by an eyewitness, the conquistador
and historian Bernal Díaz del Castillo (1492–1581?).*[5]

✠✠✠✠ The Great Montezuma was about forty years old, of good
height and well proportioned, slender, and spare of flesh, not very
swarthy, but of the natural colour and shade of an Indian. He did not
wear his hair long, but so as just to cover his ears, his scanty black
beard was well shaped and thin. His face was somewhat long, but
cheerful, and he had good eyes and showed in his appearance and
manner both tenderness and when necessary, gravity. He was very
neat and clean and bathed once every day in the afternoon. He had
many women as mistresses, daughters of Chieftains, and he had two
great Cacicas as his legitimate wives. He was free from unnatural
offences. The clothes that he wore one day, he did not put on again
until four days later. He had over two hundred chieftains in his guard,
in other rooms close to his own, not that all were meant to converse
with him, but only one or another, and when they went to speak to
him they were obliged to take off their rich mantles and put on others
of little worth, but they had to be clean, and they had to enter barefoot with their eyes lowered to the ground, and not to look up in his
face. And they made him three obeisances, and said: "Lord, my Lord,
my Great Lord," before they came up to him, and then they made
their report and with a few words he dismissed them, and on taking
leave they did not turn their backs, but kept their faces towards him
with their eyes to the ground, and they did not turn their backs until
they left the room. I noticed another thing, that when other great
chiefs came from distant lands about disputes or business, when they
reached the apartments of the Great Montezuma, they had to come
barefoot and with poor mantles, and they might not enter directly into
the Palace, but had to loiter about a little on one side of the Palace
door, for to enter hurriedly was considered to be disrespectful.

For each meal, over thirty different dishes were prepared by
his cooks according to their ways and usage, and they placed small
pottery braziers beneath the dishes so that they should not get cold.
They prepared more than three hundred plates of the food that Montezuma was going to eat, and more than a thousand for the guard. When
he was going to eat, Montezuma would sometimes go out with his
chiefs and stewards, and they would point out to him which dish was
best, and of what birds and other things it was composed, and as they

[5] Bernal Díaz del Castillo, *The True History of the Conquest of New Spain,*
translated and edited by A. P. Maudsley, London, the Hakluyt Society, Cambridge University Press, 1908–1916, 5 vols., II, pp. 60–63.

advised him, so he would eat, but it was not often that he would go
out to see the food, and then merely as a pastime. . . .

Let us cease speaking of this and return to the way things were
served to him at meal times. It was in this way: if it was cold they
made up a large fire of live coals of a firewood made from the bark
of trees which did not give off any smoke, and the scent of the bark
from which the fire was made was very fragrant, and so that it should
not give off more heat than he required, they placed in front of it a
sort of screen adorned with figures of idols worked in gold. He was
seated on a low stool, soft and richly worked, and the table, which
was also low, was made in the same style as the seats, and on it they
placed the table cloths of white cloth and some rather long napkins of
the same material. Four very beautiful cleanly women brought water
for his hands in a sort of deep basin which they call *xicales*, and they
held others like plates below to catch the water, and they brought him
towels. And two other women brought him tortilla bread, and as soon
as he began to eat they placed before him a sort of wooden screen
painted over with gold, so that no one should watch him eating. Then
the four women stood aside, and four great chieftains who were old
men came and stood beside them, and with these Montezuma now and
then conversed, and asked them questions, and as a great favour he
would give to each of these elders a dish of what to him tasted best.
They say that these elders were his near relations, and were his coun-
sellors and judges of law suits, and the dishes and food which Montezuma gave them they ate standing up with much reverence and
without looking at his face. He was served on Cholula earthenware
either red or black. While he was at his meal the men of his guard
who were in the rooms near to that of Montezuma, never dreamed
of making any noise or speaking aloud. They brought him fruit of
all the different kinds that the land produced, but he ate very little of
it. From time to time they brought him, in cup-shaped vessels of pure
gold, a certain drink made from cacao, and the women served this
drink to him with great reverence.

Sometimes at meal-times there were present some very ugly
humpbacks, very small of stature and their bodies almost broken in
half, who are their jesters, and other Indians, who must have been
buffoons, who told him witty sayings, and others who sang and
danced, for Montezuma was fond of pleasure and song, and to these he
ordered to be given what was left of the food and the jugs of cacao.
Then the same four women removed the table cloths, and with much
ceremony they brought water for his hands. And Montezuma talked
with those four old chieftains about things that interested him, and
they took leave of him with the great reverence in which they held
him, and he remained to repose.

5. AZTEC INDUSTRY AND COMMERCE

Division of labor and perfection of craftsmanship among the Aztecs attained perhaps the highest point of development compatible with what was essentially an U̲p̲p̲e̲r̲ ̲S̲t̲o̲n̲e̲ ̲A̲g̲e̲ *technology. The relatively vast scale on which the general exchange of goods and services was carried on is shown by the immense activity at the great market at Tenochtitlán, as described below[6] by Cortés in a letter to the Emperor Charles V. Trade was not confined to Aztec territory. The extension of intertribal contacts through war and diplomacy, and the rise of an aristocracy with luxurious tastes and the means to satisfy them, led to the development of a* m̲e̲r̲c̲h̲a̲n̲t̲ ̲c̲l̲a̲s̲s̲ *whose members traveled all over Mexico and beyond, exchanging the obsidian, cloth, and rope produced in the valley for shells, tropical feathers, jade, cacao, and many other articles. The second[7] of the two readings given below is a native account of the life of the Aztec trader.*

✸✸✸✸ The city has many squares where markets are held, and trading is carried on. There is one square, twice as large as that of Salamanca, all surrounded by arcades, where there are daily more than sixty thousand souls, buying and selling, and where are found all the kinds of merchandise produced in these countries, including food products, jewels of gold and silver, lead, brass, copper, zinc, stone, bones, shells, and feathers. Stones are sold, hewn and unhewn, adobe bricks, wood, both in the rough and manufactured in various ways. There is a street for game, where they sell every sort of bird, such as chickens, partridges, quails, wild ducks, flycatchers, widgeons, turtle-doves, pigeons, reed-birds, parrots, owls, eaglets, owlets, falcons, sparrow-hawks and kestrels, and they sell the skin of some of these birds of prey with their feathers, heads, beaks, and claws. They sell rabbits, hares, and small dogs which they castrate, and raise for the purpose of eating.

There is a street set apart for the sale of herbs, where can be found every sort of root and medical herb which grows in the country. There are houses like apothecary shops, where prepared medicines are

---

[6] *The Letters of Cortés to Charles V*, translated and edited by Francis A. McNutt, New York, 1908, 2 vols., I, pp. 257–259. Reprinted by permission of the publishers, the Arthur H. Clark Company from Francis A. McNutt's *Fernando Cortés, His Five Letters of Relation to the Emperor Charles V*.

[7] Arthur J. O. Anderson and Charles E. Dibble, *Florentine Codex* (Fray Bernardino de Sahagún, *General History of the Things of New Spain*), Book I, *The Gods* (Santa Fe, School of American Research and University of Utah, 1950), pp. 17–20. Reprinted by permission of the translators and the School of American Research.

sold, as well as liquids, ointments, and plasters. There are places like our barber shops, where they wash and shave their heads. There are houses where they supply food and drink for payment. There are men, such as in Castile are called porters, who carry burdens. There is much wood, charcoal, braziers, made of earthenware, and mats of divers kinds for beds, and others, very thin, used as cushions, and for carpeting halls, and bed-rooms. There are all sorts of vegetables, and especially onions, leeks, garlic, borage, nasturtion, water-cresses, sorrel, thistles, and artichokes. There are many kinds of fruits, amongst others cherries, and prunes, like the Spanish ones. They sell bees-honey and wax, and honey made of corn stalks, which is as sweet and syrup-like as that of sugar, also honey of a plant called maguey, which is better than most; from these same plants they make sugar and wine, which they also sell.

They also sell skeins of different kinds of spun cotton, in all colours, so that it seems quite like one of the silk markets of Granada, although it is on a greater scale; also as many different colours for painters as can be found in Spain and of as excellent hues. They sell deer skins with all the hair turned on them, and of different colours; much earthenware, exceedingly good, many sorts of pots, large and small, pitchers, large tiles, an infinite variety of vases, all of very singular clay, and most of them glazed and painted. They sell maize, both in the grain and made into bread, which is very superior in its quality to that of the other islands and mainland; pies of birds, and fish, also much fish, fresh, salted, cooked and raw, eggs of hens, and geese, and other birds in great quantity, and cakes made of eggs.

Finally, besides those things I have mentioned, they sell in the city markets everything else which is found in the whole country and which on account of the profusion and number, do not occur to my memory, and which also I do not tell of, because I do not know their names.

Each kind of merchandise is sold in its respective street; and they do not mix their kinds of merchandise of any species; thus they preserve perfect order. Everything is sold by a kind of measure, and, until now, we have not seen anything sold by weight.

There is in this square a very large building, like a court of justice, where there are always ten or twelve persons, sitting as judges, and delivering their decisions upon all cases which arise in the markets. There are other persons in the same square who go about continually among the people, observing what is sold, and the measures used in selling, and they have been seen to break some which were false.

[YIACATECUTLI] was the god of the merchants. Greatly they esteemed him, arraying in paper the stout traveling staves with which they journeyed. Wheresoever they slept, there they set them up; before them they did penances, they drew [their] blood, they offered

incense that they might be favored by their god, Yiacatecutli — thus they begged and implored his favor.

All manner of places they came to and entered. And hence they were named "the merchants who lead." They took their name from their god, Yiacatecutli.

These vanguard merchants went into the coast-lands, looking well for whatever goods there might be; they stretched over the southern coast-lands, they circled around the coast-lands.

They traveled exhausted by the heat and the winds; weakened, tired in the heat, they walked in great affliction. Their foreheads burned; they shaded the sun's heat with their hands [as] they plodded [under] its rays.

They betook themselves into the deserts; they climbed up and down canyons and mountains — all places. On elbow, on knee, they thus sped, they thus took much time.

Greatly were they wearied, much did they suffer, that they might find precious green stones, emeralds, turquoise, amber, gold; [and] feathers of all manner of birds — the [long tail feathers of the] quetzal and its black and green head and breast feathers; the red spoonbill; the blue cotinga; the parrot; the trupial; the eagle; and the skins of fierce animals, of ocelots.

And [they brought] vases, and incense-burners, and jars made of calabashes, spoons for stirring cacao, and stoppers for jars.

When they entered lands with which they were at war, and went among people who were far distant, they became like their enemies in their garments, their hair-dress, their speech, [that they might] mimic the natives.

And if they came to an evil pass, if they were discovered, then they were slain in ambush and served up with chili sauce. [But if] any — even one, even two — escaped alive, [such a one] informed Montezuma.

This one then gave him a gift, and decked him with his amber lip-plug. He did him honor, singling him out as a valiant warrior, thus making him a man of consequence.

And when those who returned arrived home, when they had come back, when they had reached and had contentment in their land, they feasted all, [especially] the merchants and the principal men, that they might make themselves celebrated.

It was called "the washing of the feet." They paid great honor to the cane, to the walking staff, of Yiacatecutli.

In the tribal temple they set it upright. They offered it an offering first, when they laid a feast. And when they summoned people to a banquet, they always offered it an offering when they ate.

And when they ceremoniously bathed and slew a man as a sacrifice, he whom they offered was the likeness of their god Yiaca-

tecutli; or else one of [the following gods], or all of them, whom they worshipped — Chiconquiauitl, or Chalmecaciuatl, Axcomoquil, and Naxcitl, Cochimetl, Yacapitzauac. No one determined, [for] it was of their own free will, whether they should offer up one or two men.

They bought them there at the slave market at Atzcaputzalco; they sorted and arranged them, turning them around many times, examining them, buying the good ones — those of good bodies, without blemish, the best men, in good health, sick in no degree, who were marked by no marks on the body.

Such as these they slew on the feast-day, Panquetzaliztli, when the feast of Uitzilopochtli was celebrated.

Thereupon they garbed them in trappings like those of Yiacatecutli, which were assigned to them.

And before they slew them, first they let them be seen by the people. It was said: "They save them up [like gods]." Thus it was made known to the people that they would be offered up as sacrifices.

At this time they gave gifts and had a feast.

And their victims they set up in a good place, all in costly mantles which had been placed upon them. [And] they made them dance upon the roof-tops or in the market place. [And] they went singing, ending their song mocking death.

6. THE CONDITION OF THE AZTEC PEASANTRY

Among the Aztecs, as among many other peoples of ancient Mexico, the basic social unit was a kinship group called the calpulli (pl. calpultin), which was a territorial as well as a kinship organization. At the head of each calpulli stood a council of elders who administered the group's affairs; by the time of the Conquest these positions seem to have become hereditary in certain families. Each calpulli possessed a ceremonial center and council house where members gathered for communal activities. Each farming calpulli held carefully mapped lands, some of which were set aside to be cultivated in common for the support of the group's officials, the temples, and the crown. The remainder was assigned in lots to the heads of families. Most accounts assert that these lots could not be transferred or sold. The Aztec clans seem not to have been of the egalitarian, democratic type, but were strongly stratified internally and in relation to each other. The calpulli offered its members a certain collective security and other advantages, but the life of the Aztec free commoners was probably a fairly hard one. Besides working on communal lands, they had to labor on the con-

struction and maintenance of _dikes, temples, and other public works_. Compulsory offerings to the gods placed another heavy burden on commoners. Even harder was the lot of serfs (_mayeque_) attached to the private estates of Aztec nobles. The royal chronicler of the Indies, Gonzalo Fernández de Oviedo y Valdés (_1478–1557_), took a dim view of the condition of the Aztec common man before the Conquest. Oviedo was doubtless influenced by a desire to demonstrate the advantages of the new Spanish order, but his unvarnished picture of poverty and oppression is probably truer to life than the idealized conceptions of later writers.[8]

✠✠✠✠ The Indians of New Spain, I have been told by reliable persons who gained their information from Spaniards who fought with Hernando Cortés in the conquest of that land, are the poorest of the many nations that live in the Indies at the present time. In their homes they have no furnishings or clothing other than the poor garments which they wear on their persons, one or two stones for grinding maize, some pots in which to cook the maize, and a sleeping mat. Their meals consist chiefly of vegetables cooked with chili, and bread. They eat little — not that they would not eat more if they could get it, for the soil is very fertile and yields bountiful harvests, but the common people and plebeians suffer under the tyranny of their Indian lords, who tax away the greater part of their produce in a manner that I shall describe. Only the lords and their relatives, and some principal men and merchants, have estates and lands of their own; they sell and gamble with their lands as they please, and they sow and harvest them but pay no tribute. Nor is any tribute paid by artisans, such as masons, carpenters, feather-workers, or silversmiths, or by singers and kettle-drummers (for every Indian lord has musicians in his household, each according to his station). But such persons render personal service when it is required, and none of them is paid for his labor.

Each Indian lord assigns to the common folk who come from other parts of the country to settle on his land (and to those who are already settled there) specific fields, that each may know the land that he is to sow. And the majority of them have their homes on their land; and between twenty and thirty, or forty and fifty houses have over them an Indian head who is called _tiquitlato_, which in the Castilian tongue means "the finder (or seeker) of tribute." At harvest time this _tiquitlato_ inspects the cornfield and observes what each one reaps, and when the reaping is done they show him the harvest, and he counts the ears of corn that each has reaped, and the number of

[8] Gonzalo Fernández de Oviedo y Valdés, _Historia general y natural de las Indias_, Asunción, Paraguay, 1944–45, 14 vols., X, pp. 110–114. (Excerpt translated by the editor.)

wives and children that each of the vassals in his charge possesses. And with the harvest before him he calculates how many ears of corn each person in that household will require till the next harvest, and these he gives to the Indian head of that house; and he does the same with the other produce, namely kidney beans, which are a kind of small beans, and chili, which is their pepper; and *chia*, which is as fine as mustard seed, and which in warm weather they drink, ground and made into a solution in water and used for medicine, roasted and ground; and cocoa, which is a kind of almond that they use as money, and which they grind, make into a solution, and drink; and cotton, in those places where it is raised, which is in the hot lands and not the cold; and pulque, which is their wine; and all the various products obtained from the maguey plant, from which they obtain food and drink and footwear and clothing. This plant grows in the cold regions, and the leaves resemble those of the cinnamon tree, but are much larger. Of all these and other products they leave the vassal only enough to sustain him for a year. And in addition the vassal must earn enough to pay the tribute of mantles, gold, silver, honey, wax, lime, wood, or whatever products it is customary to pay as tribute in that country. They pay this tribute every forty, sixty, seventy, or ninety days, according to the terms of the agreement. This tribute also the *tiquitlato* receives and carries to his Indian lord.

Ten days before the close of the sixty or hundred days, or whatever is the period appointed for the payment of tribute, they take to the house of the Indian lord the produce brought by the *tiquitlatos;* and if some poor Indian should prove unable to pay his share of tribute, whether for reasons of health or poverty, or lack of work, the *tiquitlato* tells the lord that such-and-such will not pay the proportion of the tribute that had been assigned to him; then the lord tells the *tiquitlato* to take the recalcitrant vassal to a *tianguez* or market, which they hold every five days in all the towns of the land, and there sell him into slavery, applying the proceeds of the sale to the payment of his tribute. . . .

All the towns have their own lands, long ago assigned for the provision of the *orchilobos* or *ques* or temples where they kept their idols; and these lands were and are the best of all. And they have this custom: At seeding time all would go forth at the summons of the town council to sow these fields, and to weed them at the proper time, and to cultivate the grain and harvest it and carry it to a house in which lived the pope and the *teupisques, pioches, exputhles* and *piltoutles* (or, as we would say, the bishops, archbishops, and canons and prebendaries, and even choristers, for each major temple had these five classes of officials). And they supported themselves from this harvest, and the Indians also raised chickens for them to eat.

In all the towns Montezuma had his designated lands, which

they sowed for him in the same way as the temple lands; and if no garrison was stationed in their towns, they would carry the crops on their backs to the great city of Temestitan [Tenochtitlán]; but in the garrison towns the grain was eaten by Montezuma's soldiers, and if the town did not sow the land, it had to supply the garrison with food, and also give them chickens and all other needful provisions.

7. RELIGION AND RITUAL

The Aztec inhabited a frightening universe peopled by numerous gods and goddesses endowed with vast powers and capricious tempers. The divinities held in highest honor and most actively worshiped in Tenochtitlán were the War God, Huitzilopochtli, and the Rain God, Tlaloc, whose favor was considered essential to survival on the semiarid Mexican plateau. An imposing hierarchy of priests, said to have numbered five thousand in Tenochtitlán alone, acted as intermediaries between gods and men. Human sacrifice on an immense scale played an important part in Aztec religion and ritual. The following selection is a native account of the awesome ceremonies that attended the spring festival held in the second month of the Aztec year. The wearing of human skins symbolized the renewal of vegetation.[9]

✦✦✦✦ Tlacaxipeualiztli. This feast came and was thus celebrated; [it was] when all the captives died, all those taken in war — the men, the women, the children.

Those who had taken captives, when, on the morrow, their prisoners were to die, then began the captives' dance, when the sun had passed noon. And they held an all-night vigil for their prisoners there in the tribal temple. And they placed [the captives] before the fire and took hair from the top of the captives' heads, when half the night had passed and when they made offerings of blood from the ear.

And when the dawn came, then they made them leave, that they might go to die, they who were to die appropriately to this feast day. For during the entire festival they were all flayed. Hence they called [the feast] Tlacaxipeualiztli.

And the captives were called *xipeme* and *tototecti*. Those who

[9] Arthur J. O. Anderson and Charles E. Dibble, *Florentine Codex*, Book II, *The Ceremonies* (Santa Fe, School of American Research and University of Utah, 1951), pp. 46–53. Reprinted by permission of the translators and the School of American Research.

slew them were the priests. Those who had taken them captive did not kill them; they only brought them as tribute, only delivered them as offerings; [the priests] went laying hold of their heads, and seizing [the hair of] their heads. Thus they went leading them up to the top of the temple.

And when some captive faltered, fainted, or went throwing himself upon the ground, they dragged him.

And when one showed himself strong, not acting like a woman, he went with a man's fortitude; he bore himself like a man; he went speaking in manly fashion; he went exerting himself; he went strong of heart and shouting, not without courage nor stumbling, but honoring and praising his city.

He went with a firm heart, speaking as he went: "Already here I come! You will speak of me there in my home land!"

And so they were brought up [the pyramid temple steps] before [the sanctuary] of Uitzilopochtli.

Thereupon they stretched them, one at a time, down on the sacrificial stone; then they delivered them into the hands of six priests, who threw them upon their backs, and cut open their breasts with a wide-bladed flint knife.

And they named the hearts of the captives "precious eagle-cactus fruit." They lifted them up to the sun, the turquoise prince, the soaring eagle. They offered it to him; they nourished him with it.

And when it had been offered, they placed it in the eagle-vessel. And those captives who had died they called "eagle men."

Afterwards they rolled them over; they bounced them down; they came tumbling down head over heels, and end over end, rolling over and over; thus they reached the terrace at the base of the pyramid.

And here they took them up.

And the old men, the *quaquacuilti,* the old men of the tribal temples, carried them there to their tribal temples, where the captor had promised, undertaken, and vowed [to take a captive].

There they took [the slain captive] up, in order to carry him to the house [of the captor], so that they might eat him. There they portioned him out, cutting him to pieces and dividing him. First of all they reserved for Montezuma a thigh and set forth to take it to him.

And [as for] the captor, they there applied the down of birds to his head and gave him gifts. And he summoned his blood relations, he assembled them, that they might go to eat at the house of him who had taken the captive.

And here they cooked each one a bowl of stew of dried *maize,* called *tlacatlaolli,* which they set before each, and in each was a piece of the flesh of the captive.

They named [the captor] the sun, white earth, the feather, because [he was] as one whitened with chalk and decked with feathers.

The pasting on of feathers was done to the captor because he had not died there in the war, but was yet to die, and would pay his debt [in war or by sacrifice]. Hence his blood relations greeted him with tears and encouraged him.

And on the morrow, the gladiatorial sacrifice was made. Until early morning, until dawn, they made them hold vigil, all night, until the dawn was ended. Thus did the captives, those to be sacrificed, pass the whole night until dawn. . . .

Thereupon began the gladiatorial sacrifice. The captives were spread out in order; the captors stood arranging and accompanying them. Then also the striped ones came forth; swiftly the ocelot [-costumed] warrior led and guided them; he came quickly to meet [the captives], displaying his shield and war club and lifting them up toward the sun [in dedication].

Then he turned back, retreated, turned to the rear; once again he went back.

In the same manner there then followed him, coming second, the eagle [-costumed warrior], who similarly lifted up [as an offering] to the sun his shield and his war club.

Once again emerged another ocelot [-costumed warrior], who came out as third, doing the same as he quickly came out.

Yet again an eagle [-costumed warrior] came out, doing just as had been done. All four [acted as if] fighting. They raised their shields and war clubs [as offerings] to the sun.

Now no longer did they delay, by turning back. When they came out, they came out dancing, they went in order. As if lying down on the ground, as if crawling along, flat on the ground, they went looking from side to side; they went up leaping and fighting.

And thereafter the Youallauan came forth, garbed like Totec; only he came last, after the others, behind the four great eagle and ocelot [warriors]; they lifted up their shields and war clubs, offering and dedicating them to the sun.

Then all the impersonators, the proxies, of all the gods emerged in order, ahead of all. They were called the lieutenants, the delegates, the images.

Similarly, they proceeded; they came in order; they came together. All came down. They came hence, from Iopico, from the very top of the [pyramid] Temple of Iopitli.

And when they had come down below, on the ground, on the earth, they gathered around the circular, flat, sacrificial stone; they seated themselves according to rank on large chairs called *quecholicpalli*.

And when they were seated, when they were arranged according to their importance, again the first in order was the chief priest, the Youallauan; because it was his right, his office, that he should slay,

offer as sacrifice, [that] with his hands he should destroy — with his hands hack open each of the captives destined for sacrifice.

When this was done, then trumpets were sounded; conch shells, large sea shells, were blown; men put their fingers in their mouths and whistled, and there was singing. With singing of songs and blowing of trumpets they arrived. The Cozcateca placed themselves in order, their shoulders decked with feather banners, and they encircled the offering-stone.

One [of the captors] quickly seized a captive. The captor, he who owned the captive, seized him by the head to bring him to the offering-stone.

When he had brought him there, he offered him wine; and the captive raised the wine four times [as an offering], and afterwards drank it with a long hollow gourd.

Then still another man, [a priest] came out and cut the throat of a quail for the captive, him who was to be offered as a sacrifice; and when he had beheaded the quail, he raised [to the sun] the captive's shield, and cast the quail away, behind him.

Having done this, then they made [the captive] climb upon the round sacrificial stone; and when they had lifted him on the offering-stone, the wolf [priest] came up to him, representing [a wolf], and known as "Old Wolf." [He came forth] as the uncle of the captive destined for the sacrifice.

Then he took the rope holding the captive, which reached and was attached to the center [of the stone]; then he tied it about the waist of the captive. And he gave him a war club, decked with feathers and not set with obsidian blades.

And he placed before him four pine cudgels, his missiles, with which to lay about him, with which to defend himself. And the captor when he had left his prisoner on the offering-stone, thereupon went away [to the place where] he had stood [before]. He stood dancing, looking upon, and studying, his captive.

Then [the fight] was begun; the contest [was started]. Carefully they studied where they would smite him in a dangerous place, and cut him — perchance the calf of the leg, or the thigh, or his head, or his middle.

And if some captive was valiant and courageous, with great difficulty he surpassed [his adversary]. He met and fought all four of the ocelot and eagle [warriors]. And if they could not weaken him, then came one who was left-handed. He then wounded his arm and threw him flat upon the surface. This one appeared as [the god] Opochtli. And although the captive might falter and faint, yet he acquitted himself as a man.

And when one went faltering, sinking down on all fours, reeling and overcome in the fray, uselessly and vainly holding the war club,

which they snatched from him, thus his adversaries contended with him. And this useless one could now no longer do more; no more could he use his hands; no longer make himself do anything. No longer did he move; he did not speak. Then, faltering and fainting, he fell upon the surface, tumbling as if dead. He wished that he might stop breathing, that he might suffer [no longer], that he might perish, that he might cast off his burden of death.

And thereupon they quickly took and seized him, pushed him, and dragged him, and raised and stretched him out upon the edge of the round sacrificial stone.

And then, when the Youallauan went [forth], in the guise of Totec, he gashed [the captive's] breast, seized his heart, and raised it as an offering to the sun; and the priests placed it in the eagle vessel. And another man, a priest, carried the [hollow] eagle cane and set it in the breast of the captive, there where the heart had been; he stained it with blood; he submerged it well into the blood. Thereupon he offered [the blood] to the sun. It was said: "Thus he giveth [the sun] to drink."

And the captor thereupon took the blood of his captive into a green bowl with a feathered rim. The sacrificing priests came to pour it there. In it went the hollow cane, which also had feathers. And then the captor departed with it that he might nourish the demons. He went into and came out of all [shrines]; he omitted none; he forgot not the priests' dwellings in the tribal temples. On the lips of the stone images he placed the blood of his captive, giving them nourishment with the hollow cane. He went in festive attire.

And when he had gone to and reached all the places, then he took the insignia to the palace, and he caused his captive to be taken to the tribal quarters, where they had passed the night in vigil; here he flayed him. Afterwards he had [the flayed body] taken to his house, where they cut it up, that it might be eaten and shared, and, as was said, to bestow as a favor to others. . . .

And the captor might not eat the flesh of his captive. He said: "Shall I, then, eat my own flesh?" For when he took [the captive] he had said: "He is as my own beloved son." And the captive had said: "He is as my beloved father." And yet he might eat of someone else's captive.

And the captor kept the [captive's] skin for himself; he lent it to others. For twenty days the skin was carried by one person and another, worn for the entire feast. He who wore it gave everything given him, all that he had collected, to the captor. Afterwards [the captor] divided up [the gifts] among [all of] them. Thus he made use of his skin.

And when this was done, when they had finished with the gladiatorial sacrifice victims, then there was a dance and a procession

about the round sacrificial stone, by all the impersonators [of the gods] and those who had fought the victims, all going ceremonially arrayed. In this way did they who did the slaying end [the ceremony]. All severally took with them the head of a captive, a sacrificial victim, and therewith danced. This was called "the dance with severed heads."

And the old wolf man grasped the rope [which had fastened the captives to the offering-stone] and raised it [as an offering] to the four directions. He went weeping and howling, like one bereaved; he wept for those who had suffered and died.

And also from the warring cities, from beyond [the mountains], those with whom there was war, were summoned, in secret, and came within, in secret, as Moctezuma's guests, the Nonoalca, the Cozcateca, the Cempoalteca, the Mecateca. [These ceremonies] were shown to them, and they were confounded. For thus they were undone and disunited.

8. THE AZTEC LITERARY HERITAGE

Although the Aztec system of hieroglyphics was not sufficiently developed to record formal compositions, there existed an extensive body of literature which Mexican youths were required to memorize in school and in their homes. This material was later written down in the Spanish alphabet by Indian students of the mission schools established in Mexico after the Conquest. Much of it deals with the exploits and misfortunes of the great Mexican culture hero Quétzalcóatl. The Song of Quétzalcóatl tells how the enchanter Titlacáhuan destroyed the wondrous city of Tula and forced the departure of Quétzalcóatl, its yellow-bearded god and prophet. After wandering over Mexico and performing many magical feats, Quétzalcóatl at last reached the Gulf of Mexico, where he fashioned a raft of serpents that bore him over the waters to the dominions of his master the Sun. Two selections from the Song of Quétzalcóatl, rendered into English by the late John H. Cornyn, follow.[10]

[*The Splendor of the City of Tula*]

    All the glory of the godhead
Had the prophet Quétzalcóatl;
All the honor of the people.
Sanctified his name and holy;
And their prayers they offered to him

[10] John H. Cornyn, *The Song of Quétzalcóatl*, Antioch, Ohio, Antioch College Press, 1930, pp. 78–82, 107–110. Reprinted by permission of Miss Eleanor Cornyn.

In the days of ancient Tula.
There in grandeur rose his temple;
Reared aloft its mighty ramparts,
Reaching upward to the heavens.
    Wondrous stout and strong the walls were,
High the skyward-climbing stairway
With its steps so long and narrow,
With its many steps so narrow
That there scarce was room for setting,
Room for placing of the footsteps.

    And his people, they the Toltecs,
Wondrous skilled in all the trades were,
All the arts and artifices,
So that naught there was they knew not;
And as master workmen worked they,
Fashioned they the sacred emeralds;
Fashioned they the precious turquoise;
Smelted they both gold and silver.
Other arts and trades they mastered;
In all crafts and artifices
Skilled were they as wondrous workmen.
And in Quétzalcóatl all these
Arts and crafts had their beginning;
In him all were manifested.
He the master workman taught them
All their trades and artifices.

    Very rich was Quétzalcóatl.
Nothing pleasing to the palate,
Nothing helpful to the body
Ever lacked they there in Tula.
Very large there grew the squashes;
Wondrous big and stout the squashes
So that one could scarcely span them
With the outstretched arms embracing.
Very long and thick the corn ears
So that in their arms they bore them.
Stoutly grew the amaranth stocks;
Wondrous tall the amaranth stocks;
And like trees they used to climb them.
    Ready colored grew the cotton,
Red and yellow, rose and purple,
Green and bluish, verdigris,
Black and orange, gray and crimson,
Blushing like the ripening berry.

Ready colored grew the cotton
And no need was there to dye it.
  Variegated, many-colored
Were the birds in ancient Tula.
There the bluish xiútótol;
There the quétzal and zácuan;
There the red-necked tláuhquéchol;
Birds of every hue and color;
Birds that sang with wondrous sweetness
Songs that gladdened all the listeners.

  Wondrous rich were all the Toltecs;
Masters they of wealth uncounted;
Every need was satisfied them;
Nothing lacked they in their households;
Hunger never dwelt among them;
And the small corn never used they
Save to heat their thermal baths with.

[*The Necromancer Titlacáhuan Lures the
  People of Tula to Their Death*]

  And you now shall hear of other
Magic of the necromancer,
The Enchanter, Titlacáhuan,
Who adorned himself with feathers,
With the precious Tócihuitli,
And waged war on Cóatépec;
And defeated Zácatépec.
  Forth into the Place of Singing
Straightway goes the necromancer;
Goes the master priest enchanter,
To the Place of Inspiration
Where the songs come to the singer.
And he there begins composing,
Starts the weaving of his verses.
From the hill of Tzátzitépec
Loudly calls the public crier;
Shouts advising to the people;
Cries out to the Toltecs saying;
"You who hear my voice outreaching
Far o'er all the land of Tula,
Come ye here and come ye quickly!"
  And full swiftly came the Toltecs,
At the call from Tzátzitépec.
Came they forth to Téxcalápan,

To the town upon the river,
Flowing past the cliffs uprising.
All the workers, all the masses
Hastened forth to Téxcalápan.
Came the young men and the maidens;
Came they forth in swarms unnumbered,
Mighty multitudes uncounted.
    Then his song of deep enchantment
Straight began the necromancer;
Played his instrument of music,
Ever beating on his war drum;
And at once began the dancing.
    Ever tramping go the people,
Marking time unto the music,
With their feet the measure stamping.
Swiftly move they in the dancing;
Move they to the ancient measure;
Joining hands they dance together.
Joyfully they sing the chorus;
Chant the song of vanished ages.
Grandly swells the choral music
Like the waves upon the ocean,
Breaking, ever breaking shoreward
Louder, louder grows the music;
Higher, higher swells the singing
Of the song the necromancer,
In the Place of Inspiration,
There and there alone composing,
Chanted in the Place of Singing.
    As the song of the enchanter
Ever grandly swelling rises,
From his lips the people take it
And, repeating all together,
Sing they forth the magic chorus;
Chant they in the Place of Singing,
From the opening of the evening
Till the midnight wind is blowing.
    As they dancing, ever dancing;
As they stamping, ever stamping,
Round and round about go swinging,
Crushed to earth they fall and falling
O'er the precipice are thrown
Sheer into the open canyon,
Downward unto death are driven;
Hurled to death are hosts unnumbered;

Straightway into cliffs converted.
   And the others there remaining,
Forward moving, ever forward,
Press across the yawning canyon,
From whose depths the boulders rising
Cover all the gorge's pathway.
Straightway then the necromancer,
He the wondrous priest enchanter,
Breaks the bridge of stone asunder;
Hurls the struggling masses downward
Sheer into the moving water
Rushing underneath the roadway;
Into rocks forthwith converts them.
   And so powerful was the magic
Of the wondrous priest enchanter
That the ever-dancing Toltecs
Nothing knew of all that happened;
Nothing knew of what befell them.
And thus to the place of singing,
Many times to Téxcalápan
Came they pressing ever forward;
Straight to death came rushing onward.
Forthwith then the grand enchanter
Hurled them from the cliffs uprising
Sheer into the yawning canyon.
And the Toltecs veiled their faces
That they might not view the corpses
Where they lay below extended;
See the many dead and dying.

2 ✤ The Maya of Central America

The ancient Maya occupied a territory formed by portions of southern Mexico, almost all of Guatemala, the western part of Honduras, and all of British Honduras. Maya civilization attained its highest development in the jungle lowland area whose core is the Petén region of Guatemala, at the base of the Yucatan Peninsula. The economic basis of Maya civilization was an agricultural system that consisted essentially in felling the forest, burning the dried trees and brush, and planting maize in the cleared area. Priest-kings ruled small states from "cities" that were actually civic or ceremonial centers containing temples, pyramids, ritual ball courts, and the homes of nobles and priests, with the peasant population grouped into small hamlets in the surrounding countryside. Maya society was highly stratified, with a division into four classes: nobility, priests, commoners, and slaves. Ruling over all was a hereditary priest-king with civil, military, and religious functions. The principal Maya divinities represented those natural forces which most directly affected human welfare.

Maya civilization rose to great heights of cultural splendor in the Classic period, between about 300 and 800 A.D., in the lowlands of southern Yucatan. The ensuing decline of the Classic Maya is not well understood. The explanations advanced for this decline include a variety of natural disasters (epidemic disease, drought, plagues of

insects and the like), invasion of the area by grasslands which could not be cultivated with Indian equipment, and peasant revolts caused by the excessive tribute demands of priestly rulers. Over a long period of time the great ceremonial centers in this region were abandoned. The primary center of Maya civilization now became the dry limestone plateau of northern Yucatan, which had been occupied by the Maya fully as long as the south. In the tenth century the area was invaded by Toltec warriors who gave a strong Mexican flavor to the architecture and religion of northern Yucatan.

Maya culture experienced a revival in its new homeland in the eleventh and twelfth centuries. The outbreak of strife between two leading city-states brought this renaissance to a close. By the time of the coming of the Spaniards all the larger ceremonial centers had been abandoned, and Yucatan was divided among numerous petty states that constantly warred with each other. These conditions paved the way for the Spanish conquest of the Maya and the fulfillment of an ancient native prophecy:

On that day, a strong man seizes the land,
On that day, things fall to ruin,
On that day, the tender leaf is destroyed,
On that day, the dying eyes are closed,
On that day, three generations hang there,
On that day, the battle flag is raised,
And they are scattered afar in the forest.

I. MAYA INDUSTRY, COMMERCE, AND AGRICULTURE

The Spanish Bishop Diego de Landa (1524–1579) is remembered by students of Maya culture for two achievements of very different types. One is his consignment to the flames of twenty-seven Maya hieroglyphic rolls as "works of the devil," the other his authorship of the famous Relation of the Things of Yucatan, *our principal source of information on the native way of life in northern Yucatan before and after the Conquest. In the following extract from Landa, mention of the use of foreign trade, money, and credit points to the existence among the ancient Maya of a fairly complex economy, in which exchange played a significant part. The references to cooperative effort in agriculture, hunting, and fishing suggest the importance of the communal element in Maya life.*[1]

[1] Alfred M. Tozzer, "Landa's *Relación de las cosas de Yucatan,*" *Papers of the Peabody Museum of American Archeology and Ethnology,* Harvard Univer-

✦✦✦ The trades of the Indians were making pottery and carpentering. They earned a great deal by making idols out of clay and wood, with many fasts and observances. There were also surgeons, or, to be more accurate, sorcerers, who cured with herbs and many superstitious rites. And so it was with all the other professions. The occupation to which they had the greatest inclination was trade, carrying salt and cloth and slaves to the lands of Ulua and Tabasco, exchanging all they had for cacao and stone beads, which were their money; and with this they were accustomed to buy slaves, or other beads, because they were fine and good, which their chiefs wore as jewels in their feasts; and they had others made of certain red shells for money, and as jewels to adorn their persons; and they carried it in purses of net, which they had, and at their markets they traded in everything which there was in that country. They gave credit, lent and paid courteously and without usury. And the greatest number were the cultivators and men who apply themselves to harvesting the maize and other grains, which they keep in fine underground places and granaries, so as to be able to sell (their crops) at the proper time. Their mules and oxen are the people themselves. For each married man with his wife, they are accustomed to sow a space of four hundred feet, which they call a "hun uinic," measured with a rod of twenty feet, twenty feet wide and twenty feet long.

The Indians have the good habit of helping each other in all their labors. At the time of sowing those who do not have their own people to do their work, join together in groups of twenty, or more or less, and all together they do the work of all of them (each doing) his assigned share, and they do not leave it until everyone's is done. The lands today are common property, and so he who first occupies them becomes the possessor of them. They sow in a great number of places, so that if one part fails, another may supply its place. In cultivating the land they do nothing except collect together the refuse and burn it in order to sow it afterwards. They cultivate the land from the middle of January up to April, and they sow in the rainy season. They do this by carrying a little bag on their shoulders, and with a pointed stick they made a hole in the ground, and they drop there five or six grains, which they cover over with the same stick. It is a wonder how things grow, when it rains. They also joined together for hunting in companies of fifty more or less, and they roast the flesh of the deer on gridirons, so that it shall not be wasted, and when they reach the town, they make their presents to their lord and distribute the rest as among friends. And they do the same in their fishing.

sity, Vol. 18, Cambridge, Mass., Harvard University Press, 1941, pp. 94–97. Reprinted by permission of the author and the Peabody Museum.

2. THE SOCIAL ORDER

Ancient Maya society was highly stratified, with a fourfold division into classes: nobility, priesthood, commoners, and slaves, and over all a hereditary ruler with civil, religious, and military functions. The hierarchical order of society was reflected in the pattern of settlement in the Maya towns, where the homes of the nobles, priests, and the wealthy were clustered around the ceremonial center and the huts of the peasantry lay on the outskirts. For this, as for other aspects of Maya life, Bishop Landa's Relación *is our chief source.*[2]

✤✤✤✤ After the departure of Kukulcan, the nobles agreed, in order that the government should endure, that the house of the Cocoms should have the chief power; because it was the most ancient or the richest family, or because at this time he who was at the head of it was a man of the greatest worth. This being done, since within the enclosure there were only temples and houses for the lords and the high priest, they ordered that other houses should be constructed outside, where each one of them could keep some servants, and to which the people from their towns could repair, when they came to the city on business. Each one then established in these houses his mayordomo, who bore for his badge of office a short and thick stick, and they called him *caluac*. He kept account with the towns and with those who ruled them; and to them was sent notice of what was needed in the house of their lord, such as birds, maize, honey, salt, fish, game, cloth and other things, and the *caluac* always went to the house of his lord, in order to see what was wanted and provided it immediately, since his house was, as it were, the office of his lord.

It was the custom to seek in the towns for the maimed and blind, and they supplied their needs.

The lords appointed the governors, and if they were acceptable confirmed their sons in the offices, and they charged them with the kind treatment of the poor people, the peace of the town and to occupy themselves in their work of supporting themselves and the lords.

All the lords were careful to respect, visit and to entertain the Cocom, accompanying him, making feasts in his honor and repairing to him with important business, and they lived in peace with each other amusing themselves with their accustomed pastimes of dancing, feasts and hunting. . . .

Before the Spaniards had conquered that country, the natives

[2] Tozzer, "Landa's *Relación*," pp. 26, 62, 85–87. Reprinted by permission of the author and the Peabody Museum.

lived together in towns in a very civilized fashion. They kept the land well cleared and free from weeds, and planted very good trees. Their dwelling place was as follows: — in the middle of the town were their temples with beautiful plazas, and all around the temples stood the houses of the lords and the priests, and then (those of) the most important people. Then came the houses of the richest and of those who were held in the highest estimation nearest to these, and at the outskirts of the town were the houses of the lower class. And the Wells, if there were but few of them, were near the houses of the lords; and they had their improved lands planted with wine trees and they sowed cotton, pepper and maize, and they lived thus close together for fear of their enemies, who took them captive, and it was owing to the wars of the Spaniards that they scattered in the woods.
. . .

Beyond the house, all the town did their sowing for the nobles; they also cultivated them (the fields) and harvested what was necessary for him and his household. And when there was hunting or fishing, or when it was time to get their salt, they always gave the lord his share, since these things they always did as a community. If the lord died, although it was the oldest son who succeeded him, the other children were very much respected and assisted and regarded as lords themselves. And they aided the other *principales* inferior to the lord in all these ways, according to whom he was and the favor which he enjoyed with his lord. The priests got their living from their offices and from offerings. The lords governed the town, settling disputes, ordering and settling the affairs of their republics, all of which they did by the hands of leading men, who were very well obeyed and highly esteemed, especially the rich, whom they visited, and they held court in their houses, where they settled their affairs and business usually at night. And if the lords went out of their town, they took with them a great many people, and it was the same way when they went out of their homes.

3. THE RELIGIOUS LIFE

The great object of Maya religion and worship was, as Landa concisely puts it, "that they [the gods] should give them health, life, and sustenance." The principal divinities in the Maya pantheon represented those natural forces and objects that most directly affected the temporal welfare of the people. Such were the God of Rain; the God of the Heavens (who in one or another of his manifestations was the sun-god, the god

of medicine, and the divine inventor of writing and books); the God of Corn; and the much-feared God of Death. The priesthood owed their influence to their assumed intimacy and power of intercession with the divine beings. Human sacrifice, vividly described below, was practiced from a very early period, but it did not assume mass proportions among the Maya until the tenth century, as a result of growing Mexican influence.[3]

✠✠✠✠ The natives of Yucatan were as attentive to the matters of religion as to those of government, and they had a high priest whom they called *Ah Kin* Mai and by another name *Ahau Can* Mai, which means the Priest Mai, or the High-Priest Mai. He was very much respected by the lords and had no *repartimiento* of Indians, but besides the offerings, the lords made him presents and all the priests of the towns brought contributions to him, and his sons or his nearest relatives succeeded him in his office. In him was the key of their learning and it was to these matters that they dedicated themselves mostly; and they gave advice to the lords and replies to their questions. He seldom dealt with matters pertaining to the sacrifices except at the time of the principal feasts or in very important matters of business. They provided priests for the towns when they were needed, examining them in the sciences and ceremonies, and committed to them the duties of their office, and the good example to people and provided them with books and sent them forth. And they employed themselves in the duties of the temples and in teaching their sciences as well as in writing books about them.

They taught the sons of the other priests and the second sons of the lords who brought them for this purpose from their infancy, if they saw that they had an inclination for this profession.

The sciences which they taught were the computation of the years, months and days, the festivals and ceremonies, the administration of the sacraments, the fateful days and seasons, their methods of divination and their prophecies, events and the cures for diseases, and their antiquities and how to read and write with the letters and characters, with which they wrote, and drawings which illustrate the meaning of the writings.

Their books were written on a large sheet doubled in folds, which was enclosed entirely between two boards which they decorated, and they wrote on both sides in columns following the order of the folds. And they made this paper of the roots of a tree and gave it a white gloss upon which it was easy to write. And some of

[3] Tozzer, "Landa's *Relación*," pp. 27–28, 108–113, 115–120. Reprinted by permission of the author and the Peabody Museum.

the principal lords learned about these sciences from curiosity and were very highly thought of on this account although they never made use of them publicly. . . .

They had a very great number of idols and of temples, which were magnificent in their own fashion. And besides the community temples, the lords, priests and the leading men had also oratories and idols in their houses, where they made their prayers and offerings in private. And they held Cozumel and the well of Chichen Itza in the same veneration as we have for pilgrimages to Jerusalem and Rome, and so they used to go to visit these places and to offer presents there, especially to Cozumel, as we do to holy places; and if they did not go themselves, they always sent their offerings, and those who went there were in the habit of entering the abandoned temples also, as they passed by them, to offer prayers there and to burn copal. They had such a great quantity of idols that even those of their gods were not enough; for there was not an animal or insect of which they did not make a statue, and they made all these in the image of their gods and goddesses. They had some idols of stone, but very few, and others of wood, and carved but of small size but not as many as those of clay. The wooden idols were so much esteemed that they were considered as heirlooms and were (considered) as the most important part of the inherited property. They possessed no idols of metal, since there was no metal there. They knew well that the idols were the works of their hands, dead and without a divine nature; but they held them in reverence on account of what they represented, and because they had made them with so many ceremonies, especially the wooden ones. The greatest idolaters were the priests, *Chilans*, the sorcerers and physicians, *Chacs*, and *Nacoms*. The office of the priest was to discuss and to teach their sciences, to make known their needs and the remedies for them, to preach and to publish the festival days, to offer sacrifices and to administer their sacraments. The duty of the *Chilans* was to give the replies of the gods to the people, and so much respect was shown to them that they carried them on their shoulders. The sorcerers and physicians performed their cures by bleedings of the parts which gave pain to the sick man; and they cast lots so as to know the future in their own duties and in other things. The *Chacs* were four old men who were always chosen anew for each occasion, to aid the priest in carrying on the festivals well and thoroughly. The *Nacoms* were two officers; the first was perpetual and did not bring much honor with it, since it was he that opened the breasts of the human victims whom they sacrificed. The second was a choice made of a captain for war and for other feasts. His duties lasted three years, and he was held in high honor. . . .

Besides the festivals in which they sacrificed persons in accordance with their solemnity, the priest or *Chilan*, on account of some

misfortune or necessity, ordered them to sacrifice human beings, and everyone contributed to this, that slaves should be bought, or some in their devotion gave their little children, who were made much of, and feasted up to the day (of the festival), and they were well guarded, so that they should not run away or pollute themselves with any carnal sin. And in the meanwhile they led them from town to town with dancing, while the priests, Chilans and other officers fasted. And when the day arrived, they all came together in the court of the temple, and if the victim was to be sacrificed with arrows, they stripped him naked, and anointed his body with a blue color, and put a *coroza* on his head. When they had reached the victim, all, armed with bows and arrows, danced a solemn dance with him around the stake, and while dancing they put him up on it and bound him to it, all of them keeping on dancing and gazing at him. The foul priest in vestments went up and wounded the victim with an arrow in the parts of shame, whether it was a man or woman, and drew blood and came down and anointed the faces of the idols with it. And making a certain sign to the dancers, they began one after another to shoot, as they passed rapidly before him, still dancing, at his heart, which had been marked beforehand with a white mark. And in this way they made his whole chest one point like a hedgehog of arrows. If the heart of the victim was to be taken out, they led him with a great show and company of people of the temple, and having smeared him with blue and put on a *coroza*, they brought him up to the round altar, which was the place of sacrifice, and after the priest and his officials had anointed the stone with a blue color, and by purifying the temple drove out the evil spirit, the *Chacs* seized the poor victim, and placed him very quickly on his back upon that stone, and all four held him by the legs and arms, so that they divided him in the middle. At this came the executioner, the *Nacom*, with a knife of stone, and struck him with great skill and cruelty a blow between the ribs of his left side under the nipple, and he at once plunged his hand in there and seized the heart like a raging tiger and snatched it out alive and, having placed it upon a plate, he gave it to the priest, who went very quickly and anointed the faces of the idols with that fresh blood. Sometimes they made this sacrifice on the stone and high altar of the temple, and then they threw the body, now dead, rolling down the steps. The officials below took it and flayed it whole, taking off all the skin with the exception of the feet and hands, and the priest, all bare, covered himself, stripped naked as he was, with that skin, and the others danced with him. And this was considered as a thing of great solemnity amongst them. The custom was usually to bury in the court of the temple those whom they had sacrificed, or else they ate them, dividing him among those who had arrived (first) and the lords, and the hands, feet and head were reserved for the priest and

his officials, and they considered those who were sacrificed as holy. If the victims were slaves captured in war, their master took their bones, to use them as a trophy in their dances as tokens of victory. Sometimes they threw living victims into the well of Chichen Itza, believing that they would come out on the third day, although they never appeared again.

4. A MAYA LEGEND OF THE CREATION OF THE FIRST MEN

The Quiché of Guatemala, a branch of the great Maya nation and the most powerful and cultured group inhabiting the Guatemalan highlands in pre-Spanish times, had a Sacred Book or "Book of the People," that contained their mythology, religious beliefs, and traditional history. This book, the Popol Vuh, *was first written in the Quiché language, but in Latin script, by an unknown native who drew on the oral traditions of his people; it was translated into Spanish by Father Francisco Ximénez of the Dominican Order early in the eighteenth century, and was first published in Spanish in 1857. Authorities of the stature of Hubert H. Bancroft and Sylvanus G. Morley have praised it highly as "one of the rarest relics of aboriginal thought" and "the most distinguished example of native American literature that has survived the passing centuries." In contrast with the account in the* Popol Vuh *of the creation of the earth, which bears a suspicious resemblance to the Biblical story of Genesis, the following legend of the creation of the first men and their destruction has a strong and enjoyable indigenous flavor.*[4]

✤✤✤✤ And instantly the figures were made of wood. They looked like men, talked like men, and populated the surface of the earth.

They existed and multiplied; they had daughters, they had sons, these wooden figures; but they did not have souls, nor minds, they did not remember their Creator, their Maker; they walked on all fours, aimlessly.

They no longer remembered the Heart of Heaven and therefore they fell out of favor. It was merely a trial, an attempt at man. At first they spoke, but their face was without expression; their feet and hands had no strength; they had no blood, nor substance, nor

[4] Reprinted from Adrian Recinos, *Popol Vuh, the Sacred Book of the Ancient Quiché Maya* (pp. 89–93), copyright 1952, by the University of Oklahoma Press. Reprinted by kind permission of the publisher.

moisture, nor flesh; their cheeks were dry, their feet and hands were dry, and their flesh was yellow.

Therefore, they no longer thought of their Creator nor their Maker, nor of those who made them and cared for them.

These were the first men who existed in great numbers on the face of the earth. . . .

Immediately the wooden figures were annihilated, destroyed, broken up, and killed.

A flood was brought about by the Heart of Heaven; a great flood was formed which fell on the heads of the wooden creatures.

Of tzite [wood], the flesh of man was made, but when woman was fashioned by the Creator and the Maker, her flesh was made of rushes. These were the materials the Creator and the Maker wanted to use in making them.

But those that they had made, that they had created, did not think, did not speak with their Creator, their Maker. And for this reason they were killed, they were deluged. A heavy resin fell from the sky. The one called Xecotcovach came and gouged out their eyes; Camalotz came and cut off their heads; Cotzbalam came and devoured their flesh. Tucumbalam[5] came, too, and broke and mangled their homes and their nerves, and ground and crumbled their bones.

This was to punish them because they had not thought of their mother, nor their father, the Heart of Heaven, called Hurac'an. And for this reason the face of the earth was darkened and a black rain began to fall, by day and by night.

Then came the small animals and the large animals, and sticks and stones struck their faces. And all began to speak: their earthen jars, their griddles, their plates, their pots, their grinding stones, all rose up and struck their faces.

"You have done us much harm; you ate us, and now we shall kill you," said their dogs and birds of the barnyard.

And the grinding stones said: "We were tormented by you; every day, every day, at night, at dawn, all the time our faces went *holi, holi, huqui, huqui*, because of you. This was the tribute we paid you. But now that you are no longer men, you shall feel our strength. We shall grind and tear your flesh to pieces," said their grinding stones.

And then their dogs spoke and said: "Why did you give us

---

[5] It is difficult to interpret the names of these enemies of man. Ximénez says that *Xecotcovach* was a bird, probably an eagle (*cot*) or sparrow hawk. The *Camalotz* which cut off men's heads was evidently the large vampire (*nima chicop*) *Camazotz*, bat of death. . . . *Cotzbalam* may be interpreted as the jaguar who lies in wait for his prey. *Tucumbalam* is another name for the danta or tapir.

nothing to eat? You scarcely looked at us, but you chased us and threw us out. You always had a stick ready to strike us while you were eating.

"Thus it was that you treated us. You did not speak to us. Perhaps we shall not kill you now; but why did you not look ahead, why did you not think about yourselves? Now we shall destroy you, now you shall feel the teeth of our mouths; we shall devour you," said the dogs, and then they destroyed their faces.

And at the same time, their griddles and pots spoke: "Pain and suffering you have caused us. Our mouths and our faces were blackened with soot; we were always put on the fire and you burned us as though we felt no pain. Now you shall feel it, we shall burn you," said their pots, and they all destroyed their [the wooden men's] faces. The stones of the hearth, which were heaped together, hurled themselves straight from the fire against their heads, causing them pain.

The desperate ones [the men of wood] ran as quickly as they could; they wanted to climb to the tops of the houses, and the houses fell down and threw them to the ground; they wanted to climb to the treetops, and the trees cast them far away; they wanted to enter the caverns, and the caverns repelled them.

So was the ruin of the men who had been created and formed, the men made to be destroyed and annihilated; the mouths and faces of all of them were mangled.

And it is said that their descendants are the monkeys which now live in the forests; these are all that remain of them because their flesh was made only of wood by the Creator and the Maker.

And therefore the monkey looks like man, and is an example of a generation of men which were created and made but were only wooden figures.

5. THE MAGICAL FEATS OF TWO MAYA HEROES

The Popol Vuh *concerns, among other matters, the adventures of the heroic twins Hunahpú and Xbalanqué, who set out for the gloomy land of Xibalba, a kind of Quiché underworld, to avenge the deaths of their father and uncle. Put to a series of grueling tests by the sardonic lords of Xibalba, including a trial of their skill at a strenuous kind of Mayan basketball, the brothers escape all the traps set for them by their enemies, and in a climactic scene overcome them by their magical prowess. The twins then ascend into heaven to become the sun and the moon. This Maya tale of high adventure is remarkable for its sustained dramatic interest, poetic fantasy, and touches of*

grim, barbaric humor. The following extract suggests the delight of the Maya in song, dance, and the art of juggling.[6]

❖❖❖❖ And the following day, two poor men presented themselves with old-looking faces and of miserable appearance, [and] ragged clothes, whose countenances did not commend them. So they were seen by all those of Xibalba.

And what they did was very little. They only performed the dance of the *puhuy* [owl or churn-owl], the dance of the *cux* [weasel], and the dance of the *iboy* [armadillo], and they also danced the *xtzul* [centipede] and the *chitic* [that walks on stilts].

Furthermore, they worked many miracles. They burned houses as though they really were burning and instantly they were as they had been before. Many of those of Xibalba watched them in wonder.

Presently they cut themselves into bits; they killed each other; the first one whom they had killed stretched out as though he were dead, and instantly the other brought him back to life. Those of Xibalba looked on in amazement at all they did, and they performed it, as the beginning of their triumph over those of Xibalba.

Presently word of their dances came to the ears of the lords Hun-Camé and Vucub-Camé. Upon hearing it they exclaimed: "Who are these two orphans? Do they really give you so much pleasure?"

"Surely their dances are very beautiful, and all that they do," answered he who had brought the news to the lords.

Happy to hear this, the [lords] then sent their messengers to call [the boys] with flattery. "Tell them to come here, tell them to come so that we may see what they do; that we may admire them and regard them with wonder," this the lords said. "So you shall say unto them," this was told to the messengers.

They arrived at once before the dancers and gave them the message of the lords.

"We do not wish to," the [boys] answered, "because, frankly, we are ashamed. How could we not but be ashamed to appear in the house of the lords with our ugly countenances, our eyes which are so big, and our poor appearance? Do you not see that we are nothing more than some [poor] dancers? What shall we tell our companions in poverty who have come with us and wish to see our dances and be entertained by them? How could we do our dances before the lords? For that reason, then, we do not want to go, oh, messengers," said Hunahpú and Xbalanqué.

Finally, with downcast faces and with reluctance and sorrow

[6] *Popol Vuh*, pp. 156–160, copyright 1952, by the University of Oklahoma Press. Reprinted by kind permission of the publisher.

they went; but for a while they did not wish to walk, and the messengers had to beat them in the face many times, when they led them to the house of the lords.

They arrived, then, before the lords, timid and with head bowed; they came prostrating themselves, making reverences and humiliating themselves. They looked feeble, ragged, and their appearance was really that of vagabonds when they arrived.

They were questioned immediately about their country and their people; they also asked them about their mother and their father. "Where do you come from?" [the lords] said.

"We do not know, Sir. We do not know the faces of our mother and father; we were small when they died," they answered, and did not say another word.

"All right. Now do [your dances] so that we may admire you. What do you want? We shall give you pay," they told them.

"We do not want anything; but really we are very much afraid," they said to the lord.

"Do not grieve, do not be afraid. Dance! And do first the part in which you kill yourselves; burn my house, do all that you know how to do. We shall marvel at you, for that is what our hearts desire. And afterwards, poor things, we shall give help for your journey," they told them.

Then they began to sing and dance. All the people of Xibalba arrived and gathered together in order to see them. Then they performed the dance of the *cux*, they danced the *puhuy*, and they danced the *iboy*.

And the lord said to them: "Cut my dog into pieces and let him be brought back to life by you," he said to them.

"Very well," they answered, and cut the dog into bits. Instantly they brought him back to life. The dog was truly full of joy when he was brought back to life, and wagged his tail when they revived him.

The lord said to them then: "Burn my house now!" Thus he said to them. Instantly they put fire to the lord's house, and although all the lords were assembled together within the house, they were not burned. Quickly it was whole again, and not for one instant was the house of Hun-Camé destroyed.

All of the lords were amazed, and in the same way the [boys'] dances gave them much pleasure.

Then they were told by the lord: "Now kill a man, sacrifice him, but do not let him die," he told them.

"Very well," they answered. And seizing a man, they quickly sacrificed him, and raising his heart on high, they held it so that all the lords could see it.

Again Hun-Camé and Vucub-Camé were amazed. A moment

afterward the man was brought back to life by them [the boys], and his heart was filled with joy when he was revived.

The lords were astounded. "Sacrifice yourselves now, let us see it! We really like your dances!" said the lords. "Very well, Sirs," they answered. And they proceeded to sacrifice each other. Hunahpú was sacrificed by Xbalanqué; one by one his arms and his legs were sliced off; his head was cut from his body and carried away; his heart was torn from his breast and thrown onto the grass. All the lords of Xibalba were fascinated. They looked on in wonder, but really it was only the dance of one man; it was Xbalanqué.

"Get up!" he said, and instantly [Hunahpú] returned to life. They [the boys] were very happy and the lords were also happy. In truth, what they did gladdened the hearts of Hun-Camé and Vucub-Camé, and the latter felt as though they themselves were dancing.

Then their hearts were filled with desire and longing by the dances of Hunahpú and Xbalanqué; and Hun-Camé and Vucub-Camé gave their commands.

"Do the same with us! Sacrifice us!" they said. "Cut us into pieces, one by one!" Hun-Camé and Vucub-Camé said to Hunahpú and Xbalanqué.

"Very well; afterward you will come back to life again. Perchance, did you not bring us here in order that we should entertain you, the lords, and your sons, and vassals?" they said to the lords.

And so it happened that they first sacrificed the one, who was the chief and [Lord of Xibalba], the one called Hun-Camé, king of Xibalba.

And when Hun-Camé was dead, they overpowered Vucub-Camé, and they did not bring either of them back to life.

The people of Xibalba fled as soon as they saw that their lords were dead and sacrificed. In an instant both were sacrificed. And this they [the boys] did in order to chastise them. Quickly the principal lord was killed. And they did not bring him back to life.

And another lord humbled himself then, and presented himself before the dancers. They had not discovered him, nor had they found him. "Have mercy on me!" he said when they found him.

All the sons and vassals of Xibalba fled to a great ravine, and all of them were crowded into this narrow, deep place. There they were crowded together and hordes of ants came and found them and dislodged them from the ravine. In this way [the ants] drove them to the road, and when they arrived [the people] prostrated themselves and gave themselves up; they humbled themselves and arrived, grieving.

In this way the Lords of Xibalba were overcome. Only by a miracle and by their [own] transformation could [the boys] have done it.

3 ✣ The Inca of Peru

The Inca, the greatest empire-builders of ancient America, began their career of conquest as one of a number of tribes that inhabited the Cuzco region in the Andean Highlands. A strong strategic situation in the Valley of Cuzco and a marked cultural superiority to most of their neighbors favored the Inca in their schemes of conquest. True imperial expansion seems to have begun in the second quarter of the fifteenth century, in the reign of the Emperor Pachacuti. By 1525 the boundary markers of the "Children of the Sun" rested on the modern frontier between Ecuador and Colombia, to the north, and on the Maule River in Chile, on the south.

The principal economic activity of the Inca was an intensive agriculture that made wide use of irrigation, terracing, and fertilizer, supplemented by the raising of the llama for its wool and meat and of the alpaca solely for its fine wool. Special classes of craftsmen, such as silversmiths, jewelers, and tapestry weavers, manufactured only for the emperor, who distributed the surplus as gifts to the nobility. A large number of metals, including tin, copper, gold, and silver, were mined with tribute labor supplied by the neighboring villages. Copper and bronze were used extensively for tools and to a lesser extent for luxury articles.

The *ayllu,* a village community composed of individuals claim-

ing descent from a common ancestor, was the unit of Inca social organization. As a result of the growth of Inca imperialism, the *ayllu* lost much of its original independence and democratic character. By the time of the Conquest a vast gulf separated the regimented and laborious life of the Inca commoner from the luxurious existence of the nobility.

The Inca worshiped a large number of divinities and an innumerable host of sacred places or objects. Most highly respected among their gods were a nameless Creator who had made all the other gods and all living creatures, and the sun, which was regarded as the divine ancestor of the Inca royal family. Their art work was marked by a high level of technical excellence. Their architecture, technically of a high order, was characteristically solid and functional, without the ornamental sculpture or relief carving found in Central American art. The Inca had no system of writing, but had developed an ingenious counting device and memory aid known as the *quipu*. Their literature consisted in the main of narrative poems dealing with mythology, history, and other subjects that were handed down from generation to generation. A melancholy and nostalgic spirit pervades many of the traditional Inca love songs, and the same plaintiveness characterizes the few examples of their music that have come down to us.

I. THE SOURCES OF INCA STRENGTH

Like the Romans and other great imperialist nations of antiquity, the Inca had a body of legends and myths that ascribed to their rulers a divine origin and afforded their soldiers a comforting assurance of supernatural favor and protection. This belief in divine favor, and in their "civilizing mission" among "the lesser breeds without the law," undoubtedly aided the Inca in their career of conquest. The Spanish lawyer and government official Polo de Ondegardo (1500?–1580?), did not believe the Inca claims of a lineage of great antiquity and miraculous origin. His report on this subject, based on exhaustive inquiry into Inca history and institutions, is remarkably sound in its chronology and shrewd in its analysis of the factors responsible for the successes of Inca imperialism. In this analysis special emphasis is placed on the cultural superiority of the Inca to all their neighbors, as shown in their agriculture, architecture, mode of warfare, and political organization.[1]

[1] *Narratives of the Rites and Laws of the Yncas,* translated by Clements R. Markham, London, the Hakluyt Society, Cambridge University Press, 1873, pp. 151–157.

✤✤✤✤ It must be understood, in the first place, that the lineage of these Yncas was divided into two branches, the one called Hanan Cuzco, and the other Hurin Cuzco. From this it may be concluded (and there is no memory of anything to the contrary) that they were natives of the Valley of Cuzco, although some pretend that they came from other parts to settle there. But no credit should be given to them, for they also say that this happened before the flood. From what can be gathered and conjectured in considering the traditions of the present time, it is not more than three hundred and fifty to four hundred years since the Yncas only possessed and ruled over the valley of Cuzco as far as Urcos, a distance of six leagues, and to the Valley of Yucay, which is not more than five leagues.

Touching the Lords that the people can remember, their recollection does not carry them back beyond the time already stated. They preserve the memory of these Lords by their *Quipus*, but if we judge by the time that each is said to have lived, the historical period cannot be placed further back than four hundred years at the earliest.

It must have been at about that period that they began to dominate and conquer in the districts around Cuzco, and, as would appear from their records, they were sometimes defeated. For, although Andahuaylas, in the province of the Chancas, is only thirty leagues from Cuzco, they did not bring it under their sway until the time of Pachacutec Yupanqui Ynca, who defeated those Chancas. . . . On the other side of Cuzco is the road of Colla-suyu; and they also retain a recollection of the time when the Canas and Canches, whose country is even nearer, were paid to go with the Yncas to the wars, and not as vassals following their lords; and this was in the same battle in which Pacachutec Ynca fought against *Usco-vilca*, Lord of the Chancas. They also recollect the time when they extended their dominion along this road to the lake of Villcañota, the point where the Collao begins. Two powerful rivers flow out of this lake, one going to the north sea, and the other to the south. The lake was worshipped by the natives, before the Yncas advanced beyond this point. It was the successor of that lord who conquered the Chancas who began to advance beyond this point, and those provinces had no peace until the time of Tupac Ynca, of the Yncas, but each province also had its registers of wars, so that, if it were necessary, we might very easily fix the time when each province was subjugated by the Yncas.

But it is enough to understand that these Yncas at first extended their conquests by violence and war. There was no general opposition to their advance, for each province merely defended its land without aid from any other; so that the only difficulty encountered by the Yncas was in the annexation of the districts around Cuzco. Afterwards all the conquered people joined them, so that they always had a vastly superior force as well as more cunning in

the art of war. Thus it was seldom that they were completely defeated, although sometimes they were obliged to retreat, and desist from a war during a year.

No province ever attempted to disturb them in their own land, only seeking to be left in quiet possession of their own territories, and this seems to me to have been a great advantage to the Yncas. There is no memory of such an attempt in their registers; but after the districts were reduced to obedience, the great natural strength of this region conduced to its security. The four roads which diverge from Cuzco are all crossed by rivers that cannot be forded at any time in the year, while the land is very rugged and strong. There cannot, therefore, be a doubt that in this, and in possessing better discipline and more knowledge, lay the advantage they had over all the other nations of this region. This superiority is shown in their edifices, bridges, farms, systems of irrigation, and in their higher moral lives. If other nations have anything good, it has all been taught them by the Yncas. The Yncas also had a different system of warfare, and were better led, so that they could not fail to become lords over the rest. Thus they continued to extend their dominions and to subjugate their neighbours.

The second thing that may be taken for granted is that having resolved to conquer and subjugate other nations, the Yncas sought some colour and pretext for prosecuting their objects. The first story that these Yncas put forward, though it was not the idea which they finally asserted, was an idea that, after the deluge, seven men and women had come out of a cave which they call *Paccari-tampu*, five leagues from Cuzco, where a window was carved in masonry in most ancient times; that these persons multiplied and spread over the world. Hence every province had a like place of worship where people came forth after the universal destruction; and these places were pointed out by their old men and wizards, who taught them why and how the Yncas venerated the cave of *Paccari-tampu*. Thus in every province these places of worship are to be found, each one with a different tale attached to it.

With this title the Yncas were for a long time unable to conquer more than the provinces bordering on Cuzco until the time of Pachacuti Ynca Yupanqui. His father had been defeated by the Chancas, and retreated to Cuzco, leaving his troops in a *Pucara* or fortress. Then the son formed an army out of the fugitives, and out of the garrison of Cuzco, and out of the men of Canes and Canches, and turned back to attack the Chancas. Before he set out his mother had a dream that the reason [for] the victory of the Chancas was that more veneration was shown for the Sun than *Pachayachachic*, who was the universal creator. Henceforward a promise was made that more sacrifices and prayers should be offered to that statue. Then

the son was promised a victory over the Chancas, and that men should be sent from Heaven to reinforce him. With that title he went forth and conquered. . . . Sacrifices of many kinds were continually invented, and all who were subjugated were taught that Cuzco was the abode and home of the gods. Throughout that city there was not a fountain, nor a well, nor a wall, which they did not say contained some mystery, as appears in the report on the places of worship in that city, where more than four hundred such places are enumerated. All this continued until the arrival of the Spaniards; and even now all the people venerate the *huacas* given them by the *Yncas*.

The third thing to be understood is that as soon as the Yncas had made themselves lords of a province they caused the natives, who had previously been widely scattered, to live in communities, with an officer over every ten, another over every hundred, another over every thousand, another over every ten thousand, and an Ynca governor over all, who reported upon the administration every year, recording the births and the deaths that had occurred among men and flocks, the yield of the crops, and all other details with great minuteness. They left Cuzco every year, and returned in February to make their report, before the festival of Raymi began, bringing with them the tribute of the whole empire. This system was advantageous and good, and it was most important in maintaining the authority of the Yncas. Every governor, how great lord soever he might be, entered Cuzco with a burden on his back. This was a ceremony that was never dispensed with, and it gave great authority to the Yncas.

The fourth thing is that in every place where a settlement or village community was formed, the land was divided in the following manner: one portion was set apart for the support of religion, being divided between the Sun and the Pachayachachic, and the thunder, which they called *Chuquilla*, and the *Pacha-mama* and their ministers, and other *huacas* and places of worship, both general and such as were peculiar to each village. It would take long to enumerate them, for they were so numerous that, if they had had nothing else to do, the sacrifices alone would have given them occupation. For each town was divided in the same way as Cuzco, and every notable thing was made an object of worship, such as springs, fountains, streams, stones, valleys and hill summits, which they called *apachetas*. Each of these things had its people, whose duty it was to perform the sacrifices, and who were taught when to sacrifice and what kind of things to offer up. Although in no part were there so many objects of worship as in Cuzco, yet the order and manner of worshipping was the same. . . .

Another share of the produce was reserved for the Ynca. This was stored in the granaries or sent to Cuzco, according to the necessities of the Government. For it was not always disposed of in the

same way. The Ynca supplied with food all his garrisons, his servants, his relations, and the chiefs who attended upon him, out of this share of the tribute, which was brought to Cuzco from all parts of the country. In time of war the provisions from some parts were sent to others, in addition to the ordinary consumption, and there was such order in these arrangements that no mistake ever occurred. Sometimes the stores were sent from the magazines in the mountains to the coast, at others from the coast to the interior, according to the exigencies of each case, and this was done with never-failing speed and exactness. When there was no demand the stores remained in the magazines, and occasionally there was an accumulation sufficient for ten years.

2. PACHACUTI: CONQUEROR AND GIVER OF LAWS

The process of Inca territorial expansion effectively began in the reign of the Inca or Emperor Pachacuti, who assumed the imperial fringe about 1438 A.D. Together with his son, Topa Inca, an equally great conqueror, Pachacuti obtained the peaceful or forced submission of many provinces by the skillful use of claims of divine favor, fair promises, threats, and naked force. About 1471 the aged Pachacuti resigned the empire to Topa Inca, and soon thereafter, according to the rather imaginative account of the chronicler Sarmiento de Gamboa, "he laid his head upon a pillow and expired, giving his soul to the devil, having lived a hundred and twenty-five years." A great organizer as well as a mighty warrior, Pachacuti is credited with many reforms and innovations, including the establishment of the territorial divisions and the elaborate administrative bureaucracy that made the wheels of the Inca Empire go round. He also appears to have established the official ascendancy of the cult of the Creator over the more traditional worship of the sun. His exploits are described by the Jesuit Father Bernabé Cobo (1582–1657) in a work that has been called "the best and most complete description of Inca culture in existence."[2]

✦✦✦✦ Pachacutic married a lady named *Mama-Anahuarque*, a native of the town of Choco, near Cuzco, and founded the lineage called Ynnaca-Panaca. This king was the most valiant and warlike, the wisest and most solicitous of the public weal, of all the Incas; for he

[2] Bernabé Cobo, *Historia del nuevo mundo*, Seville, 1890–93, 4 vols., III, pp. 156–162. (Excerpt translated by the editor.)

it was that gave to the land the order, laws, and statutes which were still in force at the time of the coming of the Spaniards. He established good order in all things; took away and added rites and ceremonies; enhanced the worship of his religion; decided with what sacrifices and solemnities the gods should be venerated; endowed the temples with magnificent edifices, rents, and a great number of priests and ministers; reformed the reckoning of time; divided the year into twelve months, attaching his name to each month, and designating the solemn festivals and sacrifices which should be held during the year. He composed many beautiful prayers with which to invoke the gods, and ordered the priests to recite these prayers when they offered their sacrifices. He was no less diligent and careful in matters touching the temporal welfare of the commonwealth, and so he showed his vassals how they should cultivate their fields and make use of the lands that were useless and barren because of their roughness and folds; he ordered the construction of terraces on the steep hillsides and the bringing of canals from the rivers to irrigate them; in fine, he overlooked nothing and established good order and harmony in everything; and that is why they gave him the name of Pachacutic, which means, "The Overturn of Time or of the World," for through his wise governance matters had so improved that the times appeared to have changed and the world to have made a turn; and so his memory was much celebrated by the Indians, and they gave him more honor in their songs and poesy than to any other of the kings who preceded or succeeded him. . . .

After having shown himself most devoted to the sun and most diligent in ensuring that all adored him as their forefathers had done, one day he fell to considering how it could be that a thing so subject to movement as the sun — which never rests or pauses for a moment, since daily it revolves about the world — should be God; and from this train of thought he inferred that it must be nothing more than a messenger sent by the Creator to visit the Universe; besides which, if it were God, it would not permit the smallest cloud to impair its splendor and prevent its rays from shining down; and if it were the Universal Creator of all things, surely some day it would rest and from some place illuminate all the land and order what it wished to be done; and so it must be that there was another and more powerful Lord, who doubtless was the *Pachayachachic*. He communicated his thoughts to the members of his council, and with their assent determined that the *Pachayachachic* should be preferred above the sun, and in the city of Cuzco he raised a special temple called *Quishuar-Cancha;* and in it he placed a likeness of the Creator of the World, *Viracocha* Pachayachachic, made of gold, of the size of a ten-year-old boy, with the appearance of a man, very resplendent, standing with the right arm upraised, the hand almost closed, and the thumb

and index fingers held up in the manner of one who gives commands. . . .

To his great wisdom Pachacutic united a great heart and enterprising spirit, with which he gained illustrious victories; so that he was equally fortunate in war and in peace. To his kingdom he added many extensive provinces which he and his captains conquered. He began his conquests in the provinces of Viticos and Vilcabamba, a land most difficult to subdue by reason of its roughness and numerous crags and dense forests. The Inca departed from Cuzco with his most valiant and select men; he entered the valley of Yucay and marched down stream as far as Tambo; he reached the valley of Amaybamba, and there was told that there was no bridge on the river by which he might proceed farther, for his foes had removed the bridge of Chuquichaca (meaning the Golden Bridge), and, confident that the Inca could not cross the river, had determined to resist him. But such was the power of the Inca that he not only had a bridge made where that one had been, but many others in such places that the men of Vilcabamba were struck with fear and amazement, confessing that only the power of the Inca could achieve such great works.

When the Inca had completed the bridges, he ordered his army to march in good order, that the enemy might not take them by surprise, and at Cocospata, some twenty-five leagues from Cuzco, there came to him ambassadors from the *caciques* of Viticos and Vilcabamba, who told him that theirs was a rough land of cliffs and bush and forest, and very unhealthful; that his Highness might fall ill if he insisted on going forward, and hence that he should say what he wanted of the Lords of that land and they would do all that he required of them. The Inca would not accept this offer, and the reply with which he sent them away was: Let them say to their *caciques* that he swore by the sun, his father, that if they did not have the roads cleared and made smooth he would sacrifice them to the sun. The ambassadors, filled with sadness, returned bearing this threat and advised the warriors of their *caciques*, who were stationed along the roads in convenient places, that they should withdraw into the interior, for the power of the Inca was so great that he would destroy the whole province.

When the ambassadors returned the *caciques* of Vilcabamba were in the plains of Pampacona, at the foot of the mountains. And being informed of the great might of the Inca, and learning from their spies that he was on the march with his army while his engineers went before to clear and open the road, they lost heart, believing that if the Inca attacked them their destruction was certain. And in order to escape harm the chiefs of Vilcabamba resorted to a cruel ruse, for they summoned their captains on some pretext and had them be-

headed in their presence. And the next day they carried the heads of their captains to the Inca and told him that they came in peace and that their only wish had been to obey him, but their captains against their will had taken up arms and advanced to obstruct the Inca's passage, for which disobedience and disrespect toward his Highness they had cut off their captains' heads, which they now offered to the Inca together with their own, to do with as he pleased. When the Inca had seen the heads of the dead captains and the good will and loyalty shown by the *caciques*, he received them affably, praised what they had done, and told them that he and the sun, his father, pardoned them and received them under their protection. The Inca did not advance beyond the plains of Pampacona; to this place came the other lords of the land to pay him homage, bringing great quantities of foodstuffs and presents for the army.

The *caciques*, for the greater pleasure of the Inca and to gain his favor, told him that they would give him an entire mountain of fine silver and some rich gold mines. The Inca was much pleased by this offering; he sent some of his people to see if it were so and to bring him some samples of gold and silver. They went with alacrity and found that the richness of the mines was much greater than had been described to the Inca, and they brought him many loads of gold and silver, whereat he rejoiced greatly. He remained there some time longer, causing a great quantity of gold and silver to be extracted. It was then that the mines of Vilcabamba began to be worked by order of Pachacutic, and his successors continued this work; and with the silver and gold that they obtained from them they assembled the riches found in Cuzco by the Spaniards. The Inca departed from Vilcabamba by the same road on which he had come, and on his arrival at Cuzco he ordered that this campaign and the discovery of the mines should be celebrated with public festivals, which lasted two months.

On their termination, word was brought to the Inca that a bastard brother of his, named Inca-Urco, was secretly conspiring to revolt and make himself tyrant over the kingdom. The Inca, without further inquiry into the matter, summoned his brother, and on the pretext of honoring him he entrusted him with the conduct of a certain war, and secretly ordered another of his captains to slay him in the heat of battle; and so it was done, and when the king received the news of the death of his brother he pretended great sorrow at it and ordered it to be observed with solemn obsequies and public lamentations.

He made another campaign in which he completed the pacification of the Charcas, who remained restless and endlessly hatched intrigues and revolts in order to throw off the Inca sway, for, believing that they were created to rule, they greatly resented being ruled

by others. And having done all they could to regain their liberty, without success, they lost all hope of returning to be lords as before. And with a strange fury and desperation, taking for their leader a valorous Indian by the name of Anco-Allo, many departed from their homeland, and embarking on rafts on an arm of the Marañón River, they plunged into the forests on the eastern slopes of the Andes, and nothing more was known of them. . . .

Having greatly enlarged his empire, this king devoted his remaining years to beautifying these provinces by erecting in their principal towns magnificent temples and palaces and some strong forts modeled on the buildings he had seen in Tiahuanaco. Among them were the edifices of Vilcas, Huarco, Lima-tambo, and the great fortress of Cuzco; in fine, the most sumptuous structures in the kingdom, whose ruins yet survive, were, according to Indian tradition, founded by King Pachacutic. This king also had a great idol, all of gold, named Inticllapa, which during his lifetime, and even down to the time of the coming of the Spaniards, was held in great veneration. They kept it in a very valuable golden litter and it is said that idol and litter, broken in pieces, were borne to Caxamarca as part of the ransom of the Inca Atahualpa, together with much more of the estate left by this Inca. The kindred of the Inca buried his body in Patallacta, whence they later moved it to Totocache, and there the licentiate Polo found it carefully guarded, and so well embalmed with a certain wax and preparation that it seemed to be alive.

3. THE WAY OF THE EMPEROR

At the time of the Conquest the Inca emperors were absolute rulers who claimed lineal descent from the sun. The elaborate formality and the atmosphere of religious awe that surrounded the emperor are well described by Cobo in his work on the Inca.[3]

❖❖❖❖ The Inca presented a very majestic appearance by reason of their grooming and apparel and the pomp with which they went about and were served at home and abroad. They had a multitude of servants in their palaces; many of these were the sons of *caciques* and lords who were raised in the royal household so that they might acquire good manners. They considered it a sign of opulence to keep many servants and have many wives and concubines; they were served with all the rare, exquisite, and precious things that the land yielded,

[3] Cobo, *Historia*, III, pp. 287–290. (Excerpt translated by the editor.)

and had them brought for their pleasure from the outermost limits of their Empire. The king ate seated on a small stool more than a *palmo* in height . . . ; it was of prettily painted wood, and was always covered with a thin mantle, even when the Inca was seated on it. The table was the floor, as with the other Indians, but there was a rich display of gold and silver plates, a multitude of dishes and delicate *chichas* or wines, and much bustling attendance of servants. The women brought him all the dishes at once in vessels of gold, silver, and clay; they were placed before him on very small thin rushes; he indicated whatever dish pleased him and it was brought to him by one of the serving women, who held it in her hand while he ate from it. When certain great festivals were held he would go out and dine in the plaza, accompanied by a noisy retinue. Everything that was salvaged from his table and everything that he had touched with his hands was kept by the Indians in chests; in one chest they would keep the rushes on which his food was placed, in another the chicken bones and meat scraps that were cleared from the table, and in another his cast-off garments. Finally, all that the Inca had ever touched was stored in a hut under the care of a principal Indian, and on a certain day of the year everything was burned; for they said that whatever had been touched by the Incas, the Children of the Sun, must be reduced to ashes and thrown to the winds, so that no one else might touch it. The king's bed was unremarkable; he slept on the floor on a large cotton mattress and covered himself with woolen blankets.

Whenever he journeyed, and frequently even in town, he was borne about on the shoulders of Indians in a litter lined with gold; it was considered a particular favor and honor to carry him. On the road he was accompanied by many *orejones*, his gentlemen and men-at-arms, for both protection and display. In advance of his litter went two or three hundred litter-bearers of the Lucana nation, dressed in livery, whose special office it was to carry him. They were changed when they grew tired, and went ahead sweeping the road. He also displayed his majesty by his leisurely rate of travel; when there was no urgent business he covered no more than four leagues a day, and wherever he made a stop they prepared him a repast as complete as if he were in his court.

The riches of these barbarian kings were so immense that they cannot easily be described. . . . The wealth that was collected in the city of Cuzco alone, as the capital and court of the empire, was incredible, for the principal houses of the dead kings were there, together with all the treasure that each had assembled in his lifetime. Since a new king never touched the estate or the fortune of his predecessor (which was applied solely to the service and worship of the deceased monarch) but instead built himself a new house and accumulated his own store of gold and silver and so forth, the treasure in this

city was immense, for each king sought to outdo his predecessors in the luxury, brilliance, and pomp of his house. There, too, were the richest and most frequented temples of the kingdom, and the principal *guacas* and gods of the provinces, together with the famous and much revered sanctuary of the Sun, called *Coricancha* (meaning the House of Gold). This edifice was one of the world's richest shrines in gold and silver, and men came to it from all regions, bringing the most precious objects that they could offer for sacrifice. For all these reasons Cuzco was the richest city that has been found in the New World.

4. HOW THE INCA FORMED A NATION

The Inca made a systematic attempt to unify the institutions and even the language of their extensive empire; that they had considerable success in the latter is shown by the fact that five-sixths of the Indians of the Andean area still speak Quechua, the official language of the empire. The Inca obtained their results with the aid of an elaborate bureaucracy that brought every inhabitant of the empire under the direct and continuous control of an official appointed by the emperor. An important factor in the success of the Inca plan of unification was the famous policy of resettlement or colonization, described below by Father Cobo.[4]

✦✦✦✦ The entire empire of the Inca, though so extensive and composed of so many diverse nations, was a single commonwealth, ruled by the same laws, statutes, and customs and observing the same religion, rites, and ceremonies. . . .

The first thing that these kings did after conquering a province was to remove six or seven thousand families, more or less, as seemed best to them, taking into account the capacity and temper of the population, and to transfer these families to the quiet, peaceful provinces, assigning them to different towns. In their stead they introduced the same number of people, taken from the places to which the former families had been sent or from such other places as seemed convenient; among these people were many nobles of royal blood. Those who were thus domiciled in new lands were called *mitimaes* — that is, newcomers or strangers, as distinct from the natives. This term applied to the new vassals as well as to the old ones who were sent in their places, since both went from their own to foreign lands; even today we use the word in this sense, calling *mitimaes* all those newcomers who have settled in the provinces of this kingdom. In these transfers of popula-

[4] Cobo, *Historia*, III, pp. 222–225. (Excerpt translated by the editor.)

tion they saw to it that the migrants, both the newly conquered persons and the others, were moved to lands whose climate and conditions were the same as, or similar to, those which they had left behind and in which they had been reared. . . .

The Incas introduced these changes of domicile in order to maintain their rule with greater ease, quiet, and security; for since the city of Cuzco, their capital, where they had their court and residence, was so distant from the provinces most lately acquired, in which there were many barbarous and warlike nations, they considered that there was no other way to keep them in peaceful submission. And since this was the principal purpose of the transfer, they ordered the majority of the *mitimaes* whom they sent to the recently conquered towns to make their homes in the provincial capitals, where they served as garrisons, not for wages or for a limited time but in perpetuity, both they and their descendants. As soldiers they received certain privileges to make them appear of nobler rank, and they were ordered always to obey the slightest commands of their captains and governors. Under this plan, if the natives revolted, the *mitimaes*, being devoted to the governors, soon reduced them to obedience to the Inca; and if the *mitimaes* rioted they were repressed and punished by the natives; thus, through this scheme of domiciling the majority of the people of some province in other parts, the king was made secure against revolts in his dominions, and the social and commercial intercourse among the different provinces was more frequent and the entire land was better supplied with all its needs. The Inca profited further by this transfer of their vassals from one part to another in that throughout the length and breadth of the Empire similarity and conformity prevailed in religion and government. All the nations learned and spoke the language of Cuzco, which thus came to be general throughout Peru; for through this change of domicile the newly conquered peoples, removed into the interior of the kingdom, learned all this quickly and without difficulty or coercion, and the old vassals who were resettled in place of the new subjects who were being pacified taught it to the natives. The Inca required everyone to absorb their language, laws, and religion, with all the beliefs about these matters that were established at Cuzco; they either partly or wholly abolished their former usages and rites and made them receive their own. In order to introduce and establish these things more effectively, in addition to transferring people they would remove the principal idol from a conquered province and set it up in Cuzco with the same attendance and worship that it had formerly had; all this was seen to by persons who had come from that province, just as they had done when they had had the idol in their own country. For this reason Indians from every province of the kingdom were at all times in residence in the capital and court, occupied in guarding and ministering to their own idols. Thus they

learned the usages and customs of the court; and when they were replaced by others according to their system of *mitas*, or turns, on their return to their own country they taught their people what they had seen and learned in the court.

5. THE VILLAGE BASIS OF INCA SOCIETY

The basic unit of Inca social organization was the ayllu, a kinship group whose members claimed descent from a common ancestor. An Inca village typically consisted of several ayllu. Each ayllu held certain lands which were assigned in lots to individual households to use and pass on to their male descendants, but these lots could not be sold or individually disposed of. In addition to cultivating their own lots, commoners were required to till certain community lands reserved for the imperial government and the Inca religion. The chronicler Garcilaso de la Vega (1539–1616), son of a Spanish noble and an Inca princess, drew an idyllic picture of Indian village life and of the relations between the Inca and their subjects. His account of a happy peasantry going forth with songs and rejoicing to labor in the service of their king is at serious variance with what is known of the chronic unrest and frequent revolts of conquered tribes against their Inca rulers.[5]

✦✦✦✦ In the matter of working and cultivating the fields they also established good order and harmony. First they worked the fields of the sun, then those of the widows and orphans and of those disabled by old age or illness: all such were regarded as poor people, and therefore the Inca ordered that their lands should be cultivated for them. In each town, or in each ward if the town was large, there were men assigned exclusively to look after the cultivation of the fields of the persons that we would call poor. These deputies were called *llactamayu*, or town councillors. It was their task, at the time of plowing, sowing, and harvesting the fields, to ascend at night towers that were made for this purpose, to blow on a trumpet or shell to attract attention, and loudly announce: "On such-and-such a day the fields of the disabled persons will be cultivated; let each betake himself to his assigned place." The people in each precinct already knew, by means of a list that had been made, to which fields they must go; these were the fields of their relatives or closest neighbors. Each one had to bring his own food, whatever he had in the house, so that the disabled persons would

[5] Garcilaso de la Vega, *Comentarios reales de los Incas*, Buenos Aires, 1943, 2 vols., I, pp. 227–229. (Excerpt translated by the editor.)

not have to provide for them. For they said that the aged, the sick, and the widows and orphans had trouble enough of their own, without being burdened with the troubles of others. If the disabled persons had no seeds they were provided from the storehouses, of which we shall have more to say hereafter. The fields of the soldiers who were away at war were also worked in common, for when their husbands were absent on army duty the wives were counted as widows. And so they performed this favor for them as for needy people. They took great care in the rearing of the children of those who were killed in the wars, until such time as they were married.

After the fields of the poor had been cultivated, each one tilled his own, and they helped each other in groups, cultivating their fields in turn. Then they tilled the fields of the *curaca*, the chief, and these were the last to be worked in each town or province. In the time of Huaina Capac, in a town of the Chacapuyas, one Indian town councillor gave precedence to the fields of the *curaca*, a relative of his, before those of a widow. He was hanged for breaking the rule that the Inca had established for the cultivation of the fields, and the gallows was set up on the land of the *curaca*. The Inca decreed that the fields of their vassals should have precedence before their own, for they said that the prosperity of his subjects was the source of good service to the king; that if they were poor and needy they could not serve well in war or in peace.

The last fields to be cultivated were those of the king. They worked them in common; all the Indians went to the fields of the king and the sun, generally with great good cheer and rejoicing, dressed in the vestments and finery that they kept for their principal festivals, adorned with gold and silver ornaments and wearing large feathered headdresses. When they plowed the land (and this was the labor that gave them the greatest pleasure), they sang many songs that they composed in praise of their Inca; thus they converted their work into merrymaking and rejoicing, because it was in the service of their God and of their kings.

6. INCA AGRICULTURE

The economic basis of Inca civilization was an intensive agriculture, which supported not only the laboring population but the large Inca armies, an enormous bureaucracy, and many other persons engaged in nonproductive activities. Garcilaso de la Vega describes Inca agricultural technique.[6]

[6] Garcilaso de la Vega, *Comentarios*, I, pp. 225–227, 230–231. (Excerpt translated by the editor.)

✤✤✤✤ After the Inca had conquered some kingdom or province and had approved the government of the villages and the place of residence of the inhabitants according to his laws and the worship of his person, he ordered the cultivated land (land that would bear maize) to be enlarged, and for this purpose he sent for engineers to construct irrigation channels. From their works, both those that have fallen into ruin and those that remain in good order, it is clear that they were superb artisans. They dug as many channels as were required, according to how much useful land needed irrigation, for since this country is generally poor in grain-bearing land, they sought to increase it as much as possible. And because this land is underneath the torrid zone it must be irrigated, and they did this very carefully, never sowing a seed of grain without irrigation. They also built channels to water the pastures when the autumn rains were belated, for they wished to benefit the pasture lands as well as the sowed fields, since they had immense flocks. These channels for the pastures fell into ruin after the Spaniards entered the country, but their remains may still be seen.

After the channels had been made, they leveled the fields and arranged them in squares, to obtain the full benefit of the water. On the hills and slopes, where there was good land, they made terraces such as may be seen today in Cuzco and throughout Peru. To make these terraces they erected three strong walls of hewed stone, one in front and two at the sides, inclining slightly inward (as all their walls do) to sustain the weight of the earth, which they fill in until it is level with the top of the walls. Having constructed this terrace, they built another smaller one above it, and farther on one that was still smaller. In this manner they gradually covered the whole hill, grading it with their terraces like a stairway, and making use of all the land that was arable and could be irrigated. Where a hillside was rocky they removed the rocks and brought earth from elsewhere to construct terraces and make the place useful, rather than let it go to waste. The first terraces were large, of sufficient width and length for sowing one, two, and three hundred *fanegas* of seed, more or less, according to the situation of the site, and the next ones were smaller, and thus they continued to diminish as they ascended until the last terraces had room for two or three rows of maize. So much industry did the Incas display in the matter of increasing the land for the sowing of maize. In many places they would continue an irrigation canal for fifteen or twenty leagues in order to water a small quantity of grain land, lest it be wasted.

Having increased the arable area, they measured all the land in that province, each village separately, and divided the land into three parts: one for the sun, another for the king, and the remaining part for the natives. In the division they always took care that the natives had enough land to sow, preferring that they have too much rather than not enough. And when the population of the town or province in-

creased, they took land from the portions of the sun and the Inca for the vassals; thus the king retained for himself and for the sun only those lands that would otherwise remain deserted, without an owner. The greater part of the terraces were allocated to the sun and to the Inca, since he had ordered their construction. Besides the cornfields that they irrigated, they divided dry, unirrigated land, where they planted other seeds and very important vegetables, such as the *papa* and *oca* and *añus*; these lands they also divided according to their system, a third part to the vassals and the same to the Sun and the Inca. And since these lands were sterile for lack of irrigation, they planted them for only one or two years, after which they distributed still other lands, letting the first ones lie fallow; in this manner they adjusted the use of their infertile lands so that they might always be productive.

The corn fields they planted every year, for they watered and fertilized them like a vegetable garden, and thus they always bore fruit. Along with corn they planted a seed that resembles rice, called *quinua*, which also grows in cold lands. . . .

They manured the land to make it fertile; in the valley of Cuzco, and nearly everywhere in the highlands, they used human manure in the cornfields, because they considered it the best. They collect it with much care and diligence, and dry and pulverize it to have it ready when the time for sowing comes. Throughout the Collao, a region more than one hundred and fifty leagues in length, where it is too cold to raise corn, they fertilize the fields sown to potatoes and other plants with the dung of llamas; they say it is more beneficial than any other manure.

On the sea coast, from below Arequipa to Tarapaca, a distance of more than two hundred leagues, they use no other manure than the droppings of sea birds, both large and small, which are to be found along the entire coast of Peru, and which fly in flocks so large as to be incredible to one who had not seen them. They breed on certain unpopulated islands along that coast, and the quantity of manure that they deposit on them is also incredible. From a distance the mounds of manure resemble snowy mountain peaks. In the time of the Inca kings they guarded these birds with such care that it was forbidden on pain of death to enter these islands during the breeding season, lest the birds should be disturbed and driven from their nests. It was similarly unlawful to kill them at any time either on the island or elsewhere, also on pain of death.

Each island, by order of the Inca, was assigned for the use of a particular province; and if the island was large they gave it to two or three provinces. They set up markers so that the people of one province would not encroach on the district of another; and they made still more minute divisions, assigning to each village its share and to

each of its inhabitants his portion, according to how much manure that he would require. The inhabitant of one village was punished with death if he took manure from the portion assigned to another, for this was regarded as theft; nor could he take more from the portion assigned to his village than had been allotted him in accordance with the requirements of his lands, and they punished the offender for his presumption in taking the excess. These bird droppings are a rich fertilizer.

7. INCA SUN WORSHIP

The chief of the Inca gods was a nameless creator, usually called Viracocha and Pachayachachic ("lord" and "instructor of the world"). First in importance after Viracocha was the Sun God, claimed by the Inca royal family as its divine ancestor. Father Cobo describes the elaborate cult of the Sun God among the Incas.[7]

✦✦✦✦ The god most respected by them after Viracocha was that most excellent of material creations, the sun; and the Inca, who boasted that they were the Children of the Sun, bent all their efforts toward exalting its authority and endowing it with a magnificent ritual, numerous priests, and frequent offerings and sacrifices. Not that much had to be done to inspire esteem for the sun among their people; they respected the objects of Nature in accord with the benefits that they obtained from them, and since the beneficial effects produced by this planet were so manifest and excellent, they held it in great regard. The authority and example of the Inca only served to make the external displays of worship more costly and elaborate. They believed that the Pachayachachic had given the sun power to create all the foods, together with the earth, whence came their regard for it as the greatest guaca of all after the Viracocha; and so they called it *Apu-Inti*, which means "My Lord Sun": they visualized it in the likeness of a man, and consequently they used to say that the moon was his wife and the stars their children.

They held the sun in such reverence throughout this kingdom of the Inca that I question whether in any other part of the world there ever prevailed a cult so respected and well served. This may be seen from the fact that to no other god did they dedicate so many and such magnificent temples; for there was not an important town where the sun did not have a temple with numerous priests and *mamaconas* and ample revenues for its maintenance. And the wealthiest and most

[7] Cobo, *Historia*, III, pp. 324–327. (Excerpt translated by the editor.)

sumptuous temple of all was that which the Inca kings had erected to the sun in their court, the temple called Coricancha, where they kept their principal and most venerated idol. It was an impressive image, called *Punchau*, which means "the day," all worked in finest gold with a wealth of precious stones, in the likeness of a human face, surrounded by rays, as we depict the sun; they placed it so that it faced the east, and when the sun rose its rays fell on it; and since it was a sheet of finest metal the rays were reflected from it so brightly that it actually seemed to be the sun. The Indians were wont to say that the sun lent this image both its light and its power. From the spoils which the Spaniards obtained in the beautiful temple of Coricancha there fell to the lot of a soldier this splendid sheet of gold, and since at that time gambling was the popular pastime he lost it one night at play; from this came the saying used in Peru about heavy gamblers: "He gambles the sun away before it rises." This soldier was named Manso Serra; he later became a leading citizen of Cuzco, where I came to know a son of his, named Juan Serra. . . .

They regarded the eclipse of the sun as a grave matter, and when it occurred they consulted the diviners about its meaning; and having been told what it denoted, they made great and costly sacrifices, offering up various gold and silver figures, and killing a large number of sheep as well as many boys and girls. The sorcerers commonly asserted that the eclipse portended the death of some prince, and that the sun had gone into mourning for the loss that the world would suffer; when this happened all the women dedicated to the sun fasted for many days, wore mourning garments, and offered frequent sacrifices. The Inca retired to a secret spot, and there, having dealings with none, he fasted many days; during all this time no fire was lighted in the whole city.

8. THE SHEPHERD AND THE VIRGIN OF THE SUN

Only a few examples of Inca literature have come down to us in unmodified form. The lack of a system of writing, and the hostility of the Spanish priesthood to the Inca religious ideas that pervaded their literature, help to explain why so little material survives. The Inca hymns and prayers that have been preserved are described by one writer as notable for "their lofty thought and beauty of expression." The famous play Ollanta, cited by Markham as proof that the Inca composed dramatic pieces, is now generally thought to have been written after the Conquest. Of the long narrative poems that dealt with Inca mythology, legends, and history, and were memorized by each

generation in turn, there remain only summaries in Spanish prose. Spanish chroniclers recorded a large number of Inca legends and fables, among them being many origin myths that explained the appearance of lakes, mountains, stones of unusual shape, and the like. In this category belongs the following tale, which describes with unaffected simplicity the tragic romance of an Andean shepherd and a Virgin of the Sun.[8]

✦✦✦✦ In the snow-clad Cordillera above the valley of Yucay, called Pitu-siray, a shepherd watched the flock of white llamas intended for the Inca to sacrifice to the Sun. He was a native of Laris, named Acoya-napa, a very well disposed and gentle youth. He strolled behind his flock, and presently began to play upon his flute very softly and sweetly, neither feeling anything of the amorous desires of youth, nor knowing anything of them.

He was carelessly playing his flute one day when two daughters of the Sun came to him. They could wander in all directions over the green meadows, and never failed to find one of their houses at night, where the guards and porters looked out that nothing came that could do them harm. Well! the two girls came to the place where the shepherd rested quite at his ease, and they asked him about his llamas.

The shepherd, who had not seen them until they spoke, was surprised, and fell on his knees, thinking that they were the embodiments of two out of the four crystalline fountains which were very famous in those parts. So he did not dare to answer them. They repeated their question about the flock, and told him not to be afraid, for they were children of the Sun, who was lord of all the land, and to give him confidence they took him by the arm. Then the shepherd stood up and kissed their hands. After talking together for some time the shepherd said that it was time for him to collect his flock, and asked their permission. The elder princess, named Chuqui-llantu, had been struck by the grace and good disposition of the shepherd. She asked him his name and of what place he was a native. He replied that his home was at Laris and that his name was Acoya-napa. While he was speaking Chuqui-llantu cast her eyes upon a plate of silver which the shepherd wore over his forehead, and which shone and glittered very prettily. Looking closer she saw on it two figures, very subtilely contrived, who were eating a heart. Chuqui-llantu asked the shepherd the name of that silver ornament, and he said it was called *utusi*. The princess returned it to the shepherd, and took leave of him, carrying well in her memory the name of the ornament and the figures, thinking with what delicacy they were drawn, almost seeming to her to be alive. She talked about it with her sister until they came to their palace.

[8] C. R. Markham, *The Incas of Peru*, London, 1910, pp. 408–415.

On entering, the doorkeeper looked to see if they brought with them anything that would do harm, because it was often found that women had brought with them, hidden in their clothes, such things as fillets and necklaces. After having looked well, the porters let them pass, and they found the women of the Sun cooking and preparing food. Chuqui-llantu said that she was very tired with her walk, and that she did not want any supper. All the rest supped with her sister, who thought that Acoya-napa was not one who could cause inquietude. But Chuqui-llantu was unable to rest owing to the great love she felt for the shepherd Acoya-napa, and she regretted that she had not shown him what was in her breast. But at last she went to sleep.

In the palace there were many richly furnished apartments in which the women of the Sun dwelt. These virgins were brought from all the four provinces which were subject to the Inca, namely Chincha-suyu, Cunti-suyu, Anti-suyu and Colla-suyu. Within, there were four fountains which flowed towards the four provinces, and in which the women bathed, each in the fountain of the province where she was born. They named the fountains in this way. That of Chincha-suyu was called *Chuclla-puquio*, that of Cunti-suyu was known as *Ocoruro-puquio*, *Sicilla-puquio* was the fountain of Anti-suyu, and *Llulucha-puquio* of Colla-suyu. The most beautiful child of the Sun, Chuqui-llantu, was wrapped in profound sleep. She had a dream. She thought she saw a bird flying from one tree to another, and singing very softly and sweetly. After having sung for some time, the bird came down and regarded the princess, saying that she should feel no sorrow, for all would be well. The princess said that she mourned for something for which there could be no remedy. The singing bird replied that it would find a remedy, and asked the princess to tell her the cause of her sorrow. At last Chuqui-llantu told the bird of the great love she felt for the shepherd boy named Acoya-napa, who guarded the white flock. Her death seemed inevitable. She could have no cure but to go to him whom she so dearly loved, and if she did her father the Sun would order her to be killed. The answer of the sing-ing bird, by name *Checollo*, was that she should arise and sit between the four fountains. There she was to sing what she had most in her memory. If the fountains repeated her words, she might then safely do what she wanted. Saying this the bird flew away, and the princess awoke. She was terrified. But she dressed very quickly and put herself between the four fountains. She began to repeat what she remembered to have seen of the two figures on the silver plate, singing:

"Micuc isutu cuyuc utusi cucim."

Presently all the fountains began to sing the same verse.

Seeing that all the fountains were very favourable, the princess went to repose for a little while, for all night she had been conversing with the *checollo* in her dream.

When the shepherd boy went to his home he called to mind the great beauty of Chuqui-llantu. She had aroused his love, but he was saddened by the thought that it must be love without hope. He took up his flute and played such heart-breaking music that it made him shed many tears, and he lamented, saying: "Ay! ay! ay! for the unlucky and sorrowful shepherd, abandoned and without hope, now approaching the day of your death, for there can be no remedy and no hope." Saying this, he also went to sleep.

The shepherd's mother lived in Laris, and she knew, by her power of divination, the cause of the extreme grief into which her son was plunged, and that he must die unless she took order for providing a remedy. So she set out for the mountains, and arrived at the shepherd's hut at sunrise. She looked in and saw her son almost moribund, with his face covered with tears. She went in and awoke him. When he saw who it was he began to tell her the cause of his grief, and she did what she could to console him. She told him not to be downhearted, because she would find a remedy within a few days. Saying this she departed and, going among the rocks, she gathered certain herbs which are believed to be cures for grief. Having collected a great quantity she began to cook them, and the cooking was not finished before two princesses appeared at the entrance of the hut. For Chuqui-llantu, when she was rested, had set out with her sister for a walk on the green slopes of the mountains, taking the direction of the hut. Her tender heart prevented her from going in any other direction. When they arrived they were tired, and sat down by the entrance. Seeing an old dame inside they saluted her, and asked her if she could give them anything to eat. The mother went down on her knees and said she had nothing but a dish of herbs. She brought it to them, and they began to eat with excellent appetites. Chuqui-llantu then walked round the hut without finding what she sought, for the shepherd's mother had made Acoya-napa lie down inside the hut, under a cloak. So the princess thought that he had gone after his flock. Then she saw the cloak and told the mother that it was a very pretty cloak, asking where it came from. The old woman told her that it was a cloak which, in ancient times, belonged to a woman beloved by Pachacamac, a deity very celebrated in the valleys on the coast. She said it had come to her by inheritance; but the princess, with many endearments, begged for it until at last the mother consented. When Chuqui-llantu took it into her hands she liked it better than before and, after staying a short time longer in the hut, she took leave of the old woman, and walked along the meadows looking about in hopes of seeing him whom she longed for.

We do not treat further of the sister, as she now drops out of the story, but only of Chuqui-llantu. She was very sad and pensive when she could see no signs of her beloved shepherd on her way back to the palace. She was in great sorrow at not having seen him, and when, as

was usual, the guards looked at what she brought, they saw nothing but the cloak. A splendid supper was provided, and when every one went to bed the princess took the cloak and placed it at her bedside. As soon as she was alone she began to weep, thinking of the shepherd. She fell asleep at last, but it was not long before the cloak was changed into the being it had been before. It began to call Chuqui-llantu by her own name. She was terribly frightened, got out of bed, and beheld the shepherd on his knees before her, shedding many tears. She was satisfied on seeing him, and inquired how he had got inside the palace. He replied that the cloak which she carried had arranged about that. Then Chuqui-llantu embraced him, and put her finely worked *lipi* mantles on him, and they slept together. When they wanted to get up in the morning, the shepherd again became the cloak. As soon as the sun rose, the princess left the palace of her father with the cloak, and when she reached a ravine in the mountains, she found herself again with her beloved shepherd, who had been changed into himself. But one of the guards had followed them, and when he saw what had happened he gave the alarm with loud shouts. The lovers fled into the mountains which are near the town of Calca. Being tired after a long journey, they climbed to the top of a rock and went to sleep. They heard a great noise in their sleep, so they arose. The princess took one shoe in her hand and kept the other on her foot. Then looking towards the town of Calca both were turned into stone. To this day the two statues may be seen between Calca and Huayllapampa.

9. TWO VIEWS OF THE INCA EMPIRE

The debate on the nature of the Inca state that began soon after its downfall continues to be waged in our own times. Successive generations of historians, consciously or unconsciously influenced by political, social, or sentimental partialities, have found in the Inca Empire whatever type of governmental system or social order they perhaps wanted to find. Some of the pros and cons of this debate are presented in the following selections, written by men who are not clearly identifiable with either of the two major schools and who are highly regarded for their honesty and objectivity. The first reading[9] *is from the* Chronicle of Peru, *written in 1551 by Cieza de León (1518–1560), a soldier who had traveled throughout the Andean region studying Indian*

[9] Pedro de Cieza de León, *Del señorio de los Incas*, Buenos Aires, 1943, pp. 34–35. (Excerpt translated by the editor.)

customs and institutions. The second[10] is from the previously cited work of Father Cobo.

✦✦✦✦ Since these kings ruled over a land of such great length and vast provinces, and in part so rugged and full of snow-capped mountains and sandy, treeless, arid plains, they had to be very prudent in governing so many nations that differed so greatly in language, law, and religion, in order to maintain them in tranquillity and keep peace and friendship with them. Therefore, although the city of Cuzco was the head of their empire, . . . they stationed deputies and governors at various points; these men were the wisest, ablest, and most courageous that could be found, and none was so young but that he was in the last third of his age. And since the natives were loyal to such a governor and none dared to rebel, and he had the *mitimaes* on his side, no one, no matter how powerful, dared to rise against him; and if such a rebellion did take place, the village in which the uprising occurred was punished and the instigators were sent to Cuzco. Hence the kings were so greatly feared that if they traveled through the kingdom and merely permitted one of the hangings on their litters to be lifted so that their vassals might see them, the people raised such a great cry as to cause the birds flying on high to fall and be captured by hand; and so great was their fear that they dared not speak ill of even the shadow that the Inca cast. And this was not all; . . . if any of his captains or servants went out to visit some part of the kingdom, the people came out to receive him on the road with many presents, never failing, even if he were alone, to comply in detail with his every order.

So greatly did they fear their princes, in this extensive land, that every village was as well organized and governed as if their lord were present in it to punish those who disobeyed him. This fear arose from the power that these lords enjoyed, and from their justice, for all knew that if they did wrong they would certainly be punished and that neither pleas nor bribes would help them. And the Incas always did good works for their subjects, not permitting them to be wronged or burdened with excessive tribute or outraged in any way. They helped those who lived in barren provinces, where their forefathers had lived in great need, to make them fertile and abundant, providing them with the things they required; and to other provinces where they had insufficient clothing, for lack of sheep, they sent flocks of sheep with great liberality. In fine, it was understood that these lords knew not only how to be served by their subjects and to obtain tribute from them but also how to keep up their lands and how to raise them from their first rude condition to a civilized state and from destitution to comfort. And through these good works and through constantly

[10] Cobo, *Historia*, III, pp. 279–281. (Excerpt translated by the editor.)

presenting their principal men with wives and jewels, they gained the extreme good will of all, and were so greatly loved that I recall with my own eyes having seen aged Indians, visiting Cuzco, gaze upon the city with tearful lamentations, as they contemplated the present time and recalled the past, when that city so long housed their natural lords, who knew how to gain their service and friendship in other ways than those used by the Spaniards.

The yoke that weighed down the necks of these miserable Indians was so heavy that I doubt if all the men in the world, joining together to invent a species of subjection and tyranny as oppressive as that in which they lived, could improve on what the Incas achieved to keep these Indians in a state of submission.

And anyone who carefully considers the system they maintained in administering and conserving their empire will find that all was directed solely toward this end. I could easily prove this by describing in detail the actions they ordered for oppressing their subjects, but it will suffice to say that these poor people were not allowed to own anything privately without the permission of the Inca or his governors, not even to slaughter a sheep or to have two suits of clothes; nor could they eat what they chose, but they had to observe the wishes of the Inca or his governors; nor could they marry whomever they pleased, and still less could they marry off their daughters at their pleasure; nor (what is worse) were they masters of their own wives and children, for the lords took away the wives of some to give them to others, and they took their children to slay them in the sacrifices.

The *caciques* made the round of their districts several times a year, to make sure that the Indians had no more than was allowed them, for they were not permitted to possess gold or silver or to wear fine clothes. They could not own a flock of more than ten animals without special permission; this privilege the Inca would grant to the *caciques*, but in a specified number, which never exceeded fifty or a hundred heads; and the *caciques* themselves could not wear fine clothes unless they received them from the Inca as a reward for some distinguished service. Daughters ordinarily were in the power of their parents until the age of ten, and thereafter they were at the disposition of the Inca. All persons, no matter how noble their rank, when entering the presence of the king took off their sandals and placed light burdens on their shoulders as a sign of homage and reverence. In speaking to the Inca they kept their eyes lowered and did not look him in the face, while he maintained a visage of notable gravity and replied with few words, spoken in such a low voice that they could scarcely be heard. Only the great lords, by special privilege, seated themselves before him.

And since the Incas had no other aim in their method of gov-

ernment than to place their vassals daily in a state of greater subjection and servitude, to please them each of their governors and *caciques*, both high and low, applied himself to the attainment of their objective, which was to exhaust the strength of the Indians until they were unable to raise their heads. And since the Incas were very capable men, they were not found wanting in the craft and skill required for the difficult task of taming nations so barbarous and indomitable. The principal method that they used for this purpose was to keep their subjects poor and continually occupied with excessive labors, so that being oppressed and abased they might lack the fire and spirit to aspire to revolt. To this end they built great fortresses, opened roads, constructed terraces on the hillsides, and compelled them to bring tribute to Cuzco from distances of three and four hundred leagues. With the same aim they introduced many cults and burdened them with many rites and sacrifices, so that when they were free from other labors and services this work alone sufficed to leave them without time to take breath or rest. . . .

Moreover, the Incas were much aided in their designs by the great esteem and respect that the Indians felt for them, through which these simple people came to believe that the Incas not only were different from other men in valor and strength but had close kinship, familiarity, and intercourse with the sun and with the *huacas*, basing this erroneous opinion on the testimony of the Incas themselves, who boasted of this relationship, and on the religious claims which the Incas always advanced in making their conquests. And by reason of these things, and because of the diligence with which the Incas propagated the worship of their religion, consuming in its honor so much wealth and so many people that it became the principal occupation of the whole land, the Indians concluded that the gods must be under a great sense of obligation and duty toward the Incas, never failing to favor their designs. They were daily confirmed in this view by the many victories that the Incas won over all kinds of nations, and by the fact that although at the outset they had been so few in number they had placed this whole great empire under their sway. And the esteem that the Indians felt for the Incas was not a little enhanced by the admirable order and harmony that they established in all matters, both in what concerned the good of the commonwealth and in the aggrandizement of the cult of their gods. To this also contributed the nonsense the Incas daily fed their subjects, as a result of which these simple people conceived the Incas to be very close to the gods and endowed with super-human wisdom, particularly when they saw the beauty and majesty with which the Incas had adorned their court, for which the Indians felt great reverence. . . .

Nevertheless, I believe that these measures would not have sufficed to establish so firmly the power of the Incas and the sub-

jection of these peoples if the Incas had not also resorted to severe measures, inflicting deaths and exemplary punishments upon those who attempted to overthrow the existing order. Actually, there were numerous revolts on the part of their subjects, who tried to regain their liberty by this means. . . . Many of these terrible chastisements are still fresh in the memories of living men, since their stories have been handed down from father to son. I will cite here two or three of these cases. In a place near Payta an Inca slew five thousand men at one time, and to strike greater fear into his subjects he ordered the hearts of the slain men to be plucked out and placed around the fortress in a circle. In the towns of Otavalo and Caranque, Guaynacapac put to death all the males (except the boys), and for this reason the inhabitants of those towns were long called Guambracuna, which means "lads." . . . From which I conclude that it was through strictness and cruelty, more than by any other means, that the Incas succeeded in breaking the spirit of their subjects, in placing them in the strict servitude in which they kept them, and in developing in them the abject submissiveness with which they were obeyed and revered. For theirs was a slavery so rigorous that it is difficult to imagine a worse one, even if we reviewed all the governments of the world of which we have any knowledge.

THE CONQUEST OF AMERICA

The peculiar course of Spain's development helps to explain her leadership in the exploration and conquest of America. Five centuries of struggle against the Moslems had made warfare almost a Spanish way of life, and had created a large class of titled fighting men who regarded manual labor and commerce with contempt. The crusading character of the Moorish Wars engendered a spirit of religious fanaticism that provided a convenient sanction for the conquest of New World pagans. Finally, Ferdinand and Isabella, the monarchs who brought the Moorish Wars to a successful conclusion, also created a unified Spain, free from internal strife, and thereby established favorable conditions for a mighty movement of overseas expansion.

The discovery of America by Columbus resulted from the search for an all-water route to the East that was promoted by the monarchs of Portugal and Spain in an effort to break the Italian monopoly of European commerce with the Orient.

From its primary base on Hispaniola the Spanish Conquest branched out to the other great Antilles (Puerto Rico, Cuba, Jamaica) and simultaneously sent out weak offshoots to the coasts of South and Central America. Slave-hunting and exploring expeditions gradually made the coasts of Central America and Mexico better known and re-

vealed Indian societies far wealthier and more advanced than those found in the West Indies.

The discovery of these societies led to the invasion of Mexico by Hernando Cortés in 1519. The superstitious fears of the Aztec war chief Montezuma enabled Cortés to enter the Indian capital without opposition, but an unprovoked aggression by his lieutenant Alvarado precipitated a mortal struggle. Guatemoc, the last Aztec ruler, surrendered only when the city lay in ruins and its native defenders were dead or starving. From Mexico the stream of conquest flowed south into Guatemala and Honduras; in Nicaragua it joined another current formed by Spaniards coming north from Darien.

The town of Panama, founded in 1519 across the isthmus from Darien, became a base for expeditions seeking another golden kingdom that was rumored to lie southwards. After repeated failures, Francisco Pizarro and his companions achieved their aim of reaching and conquering the Inca Empire. However, before the Indian resistance was entirely overcome, the conquerors fell out among themselves, and by the time that peace was restored to Peru all the leading figures in the struggle had come to violent ends.

4 ✢ The Hispanic Background

The rugged Iberian peninsula had undergone successive invasions by foreign tribes or nations from very ancient times. The Iberians and Celts, who are believed to have come from North Africa and Central Europe, respectively, were succeeded by Phoenicians, Greeks, and Carthaginians. These commercial nations established trading posts and cities on the coast but made no effort to establish control over the interior. Still later, Spain became a stake of empire in the great struggle for commercial supremacy between Rome and Carthage that ended with the decisive defeat of the latter in 201 B.C. For six centuries thereafter Rome was the dominant power in the peninsula.

Early in the fifth century the waning of Roman military power that accompanied the general crisis of the Empire made possible the invasion of Spain by a number of barbarian peoples of Germanic origin. By the last half of the century one of these groups of invaders, the Visigoths, had gained mastery over most of the peninsula. For most of its brief history the Visigothic Kingdom was plagued by internal strife; this generally arose out of disputes over the succession to the kingship, which was elective among the Germanic tribes. These divisions among the Goths played into the hands of their Moslem foes in North Africa. In A.D. 711 the latter crossed the straits and decisively defeated Roderic, the last Gothic king. Within a few years all Spain,

aside from certain small districts in the mountainous north, had fallen into Moslem hands.

The Moslems, who had inherited the accumulated cultural wealth of the ancient Mediterranean and Eastern worlds, enriched this heritage with their own magnificent contributions to science, art, and literature. But for all its noble achievements, Moslem civilization rested on insecure foundations. The Moslem world was rent by fierce political and religious feuds over control of the empire. In Spain these internal differences were complicated by conflicts between the Arabs and the North African Berbers, recent converts to Mohammedanism and more fanatically devout than their teachers. These discords enabled the small Christian kingdoms that had arisen in the North to survive, to grow strong, and eventually to launch a general advance against the Moslem power. By the opening of the fifteenth century all of Spain except the small southeastern kingdom of Granada was in Christian hands.

A turning point in peninsular history was the marriage, in 1469, of the heirs apparent to the thrones of Aragon and Castile — Ferdinand and Isabella. The "Catholic Kings," as they are known in Spanish history, broke the power of the lawless grandees by force of arms and by subtler means curbed the authority and independence of the proud Spanish towns. The crowning domestic achievement of their reign was the surrender of the city and kingdom of Granada in 1492, after a ten-year war. Unified politically and religiously, filled with martial and crusading zeal, and avid for the gold and silver that symbolized power and wealth in an age of dawning capitalism, Spain stood ready to launch the great enterprise of the Indies.

1. IN PRAISE OF SPAIN

The swift destruction of the Visigothic realm by Moslem invaders had a natural interest for early Spanish historians. According to legend, a certain Count Julian, seeking revenge for the seduction of his daughter by King Roderic, helped the Moors to enter Spain. In reality, the Moslems were invited to enter as allies of one of the parties contending for the Visigothic crown, but remained to conquer the land for themselves. The depth of feeling aroused by recollection of the disaster in a time of emergent Spanish nationalism is revealed in the following selection from the first general history of Spain, written at the behest of Alfonso the Sage of Castile (1252–1284).[1]

[1] Ramón Menéndez Pidal, ed., *Primera crónica general de España*, Madrid, 1906, 2 vols., I, pp. 310–312. (Excerpt translated by the editor.)

✦✦✦✦ And so King Roderick and the Christians were vanquished and slain, and the noble Gothic nation, which had overthrown and humbled so many kingdoms, was itself defeated and abased, and its proud banners were trampled in the dust. The Goths, who had conquered Scythia, Pontus, Asia, Greece, Macedonia, and Illyria, and had robbed and ravaged these countries and even their womenfolk; who had subjugated all the eastern territory and imprisoned the great Cyrus, king of Babylonia, Syria, Media, and Hircania, and slain him in a wineskin full of blood; the people to whom the Romans, masters of the whole world, had bent the knee in surrender; they who had burned the Emperor Valentius in a fire and to whom the great Attila, king of the Huns, yielded in the battle of the Catalonian plains; that people before whom the Alani fled, leaving the Hungarian land, and to whom the Vandals abandoned Gaul in their flight; they whose victories had terrified the whole world as loud thunder terrifies men — that Gothic nation that had once been so fiery and proud, was destroyed in a single battle by the power of Mohammed the upstart, who had only recently come to notice. Let all learn from this that no one should boast of his estate — neither the rich man of his riches, nor the powerful man of his power, nor the strong man of his strength, nor the wise man of his wisdom, nor the noble of his high rank and good fortune. . . .

All the countries of the world, and their provinces, were honored by God in diverse ways, and to each He gave His gift, but of all the lands of the West Spain was most highly favored, for God gave her all the things that men desire. For when the Goths wandered through all the countries, harassing them with wars and battles and conquering many places in the provinces of Asia and Europe, inhabiting and studying every one in order to select the most favored spot in all the world, they found Spain to be the best, and they prized it above all others as the most richly endowed. Moreover, it is completely enclosed —on one side by the Pyrenees, which run to the sea, and on the others by the Ocean Sea and the Mediterranean. . . . Then this land of Spain is like God's Paradise, for it is watered by five principal rivers, the Ebro, Duero, Tagus, Guadalquivir, and Guadiana. Each is separated from the others by great mountains and lands; the valleys and plains are broad and because of the goodness of the soil and the humor of the rivers they yield many fruits in abundance. . . .

Spain above all other lands is witty, daring, courageous in battle, light of heart, loyal to its lord, earnest in study, courtly in speech, endowed with all good things; no land in the world can match it for abundance or in number of strongholds, and few compare with it in size. Spain leads all other lands in greatness and loyalty. Ah, Spain! No tongue or intellect can recount thy good! . . . And this kingdom,

so noble, so rich, so powerful, so honored, was separated and destroyed in a single attack because of discord among its people, who turned their swords against each other, as if they had no enemies to fight; and because of this everything was lost, for all the cities of Spain were captured and destroyed by the Moors.

2. THE CID CAMPEADOR: SYMBOL OF SPANISH NATIONALITY

The heroic figure of Ruy Días de Vivar, the Cid Campeador or "Warrior Lord," as he was called by his Moslem soldiers, typifies in Spanish popular tradition the crusading era of Hispanic history. The real Cid, true to the ideals of his times, placed feudal above religious loyalties and ably served the Moslem kings of Saragossa and Valencia against not only Moorish foes but Christian princes. Furthermore, the Cid frequently displayed a chivalrous spirit in an age not remarkable for these virtues, and, in the words of the historian Altamira, "nobly personified the purest and loftiest type of the warrior nobility of his time." His greatest triumph was the seizure of the Moslem city of Valencia in the name of the king of Castile, in 1092. A thirteenth-century Spanish chronicler describes the aftermath of the victory.[2]

✤✤✤✤ That night the Cid conferred with Alvar Fañez and Pero Bermudez and the other men of his council, and they decided what policy they would adopt with the Moors. On the next day all the Moors of Valencia assembled in the castle, as the Cid had ordered. The Cid seated himself on his dais, with all his nobles around him, and said:

"All you good men of the *aliama* of Valencia, you know how well I served and aided the king of Valencia, and how many opportunities I let pass to take this city; now that God has seen fit to make me lord of Valencia, I want it for myself and for those who helped me to take it, subject only to the authority of my lord King Alfonso. You are all in my power, and I could easily take from you everything you have in the world — your persons, your wives, and your children. But I do not want to do this, and I therefore decree that the honorable men among you, who were always loyal to me, shall dwell in Valencia in their homes with their wives. However, each of you may keep only one animal — a mule — and one servant, and you may not own or use weapons unless by my order. All the others I

[2] Menéndez Pidal, *Primera crónica general*, I, pp. 591–592. (Excerpt translated by the editor.)

order to leave Valencia and go to live outside the city in the Alcudia, where I once lived. You may keep your mosques in Valencia and outside in the Alcudia, and your *alfaquis* and your own laws; and you shall have your own judges and your sheriff besides those whom I have placed over you. You may keep all your estates, but you shall give me a tithe of all you grow, and I shall have supreme charge of justice and the coinage of money. Now, those who wish to remain with me on these terms may stay; as for the others, they may now leave, taking no possessions, and I shall order that no one harm them."

When the Moors of Valencia heard this they were sad, but the times were such that they had no choice. Within the hour all the Moors, except those that the Cid had ordered to remain, began to leave the town with their wives and children; and as they left the Christians who had dwelt in the Alcudia entered. History relates that so many people left Valencia that their departure required two days. . . . This business took a full two months to complete. And thereafter the Cid was called: "My Cid Campeador, Lord of Valencia."

3. THE CATHOLIC KINGS

The joint reign of Ferdinand of Aragon and Isabella of Castile was rich in dramatic and important events. Their reign has a dual aspect. Although they were constructive in their efforts to unify Spain, subdue feudal lawlessness, and activate Spanish industry, they nevertheless helped to initiate Spain's ultimate decay through their policies of religious intolerance and systematic weakening of the autonomy and political influence of the Spanish towns. This negative aspect of their work was not apparent to the patriotic Jesuit Father Mariana (1535–1625), whose history of Spain contains a glowing tribute to the "Catholic Kings." [3]

✛✛✛✛ Truly it was they who restored justice, previously corrupted and fallen into decay, to its proper place. They made very good laws for governing the towns and settling lawsuits. They defended religion and faith and established public peace, putting an end to discords and tumults, at home as well as abroad. They extended their dominions, not only in Spain but to the farthest parts of the earth. Most laudably, they distributed rich rewards and dignities not on the basis of

[3] Juan de Mariana, *Historia de España*, Madrid, 1909, 2 vols., II, p. 239. (Excerpt translated by the editor.)

noble birth or as private favors but according to individual merit, and thus encouraged their subjects to devote their intellects to good work and literature. There is no need to describe the benefits of all this; the results speak for themselves. Truly, where in the world are to be found more learned and saintly priests and bishops, or judges of greater wisdom and rectitude? Before their day one could list very few Spaniards distinguished in science; since their time who can count the Spaniards who have gained fame as scholars?

The king and queen were of average stature and well built; they carried themselves majestically, and their facial expressions were gravely pleasant. The king's naturally fair skin had been tanned in military campaigns; he wore his chestnut hair long and shaved his beard more often than necessary. He had wide eyebrows, a smooth face, a small crimson mouth, narrow teeth, wide shoulders, a straight neck, and a sharp voice; he spoke quickly and thought clearly; his manner was smooth, courteous, and kindly. He was skilled in the art of war, unexcelled in the business of government, and so conscientious that labor seemed to relax him. He was not self-indulgent; he ate simply and dressed soberly. He was a skilful horseman; as a youth he enjoyed playing cards and dice; as he grew older he practiced hawking, and took much pleasure in the flights of herons.

The queen had a pleasant face, blonde hair, and light blue eyes; she used no cosmetics and was exceedingly dignified and modest in appearance. She was devoted to religion and fond of literature; she loved her husband, but her love was mixed with jealousy and suspicion. She knew Latin, an accomplishment that King Ferdinand lacked because he had not received a liberal education; he liked to read histories, however, and to talk with scholars. On the day of his birth, it is said, a certain saintly Carmelite friar of Naples said to King Alfonso, his uncle: "Today in the Kingdom of Aragon is born a child of thy lineage; heaven promises him new empires, great riches, and good fortune; he will be very devout, a lover of the good, and an excellent defender of Christianity." Considering human frailty, it was almost inevitable that among so many virtues there should be certain defects. The avarice that is charged against him can be excused by his lack of money and by the fact that the royal revenues were diverted from their proper use. The severe punishments that also are charged to him were occasioned by the disorder and depravity of the time. Foreign writers have implied that he was a crafty man and one who sometimes broke his word if it was to his advantage. I do not propose to discuss whether this be truth or fiction concocted out of hatred for our nation; I would only point out that malicious men often assign the name of vices to true virtues and, conversely, praise the deceitful vices that resemble virtues; for the rest, the king merely

adapted himself to the times and to the language, methods, and strategies that were then in use.

4. THE SPANISH INQUISITION

All of Spain's troubles since the time of Ferdinand and Isabella should not be laid at the door of the Spanish Inquisition, but the operations of the Holy Office unquestionably contributed to the picture of economic decay that Spain presented by the close of the sixteenth century. The blows struck by the Spanish Inquisition at the Conversos (Jewish converts and their descendants, who were frequently charged with heresy), fell on an important segment of Spain's merchant and banking class, the social group that in England and Holland was transforming economic life and preparing the way for the Industrial Revolution. As the great historian of the Spanish Inquisition, Charles Henry Lea, observed, "many causes contributed to [Spain's decline], but not the least among them was the bleeding to anemia, through centuries, of the productive classes and the insecurity which the enforcement of confiscation cast over all the operations of commerce and industry." The Santangel mentioned below was condemned by the civil court to burn at the stake, as the findings of the inquisitors required. Ironically, he was a kinsman of that Luis de Santangel, Ferdinand's treasurer, who at the last moment persuaded Isabella to support Columbus's project, and who obtained at least half the money needed for the enterprise.[4]

❖❖❖❖ It appears that the accused, the said Luis de Santangel, has openly and very clearly practiced heresy and apostasy from our holy Catholic Faith, performing and maintaining rites and ceremonies of the old law of Moses, as a true and consummate Jew, especially observing the Sabbath with entire faith and devotion, abstaining on that day from engaging in business, travel, or other lowly tasks, as much and as well as he could, keeping it a holiday with all zeal and devotion, as the Jews do, eating on that day meat and *amin* and many other Jewish foods, both those prepared in his house on Friday for use on Saturday and those brought and sent from the ghetto, getting and lighting clean candles on Friday evening in honor of the Sabbath, as the Jews do, donning a clean shirt and performing other ceremonies

[4] Cited in: Manuel Serrano y Sanz, *Orígenes de la dominación española en América*, Madrid, 1918, pp. 114-116. (Excerpt translated by the editor.)

such as the Jews on that day are wont to perform. And likewise he zealously observed the holiday of the thin bread, eating ceremonially of the said thin bread, and of no other, this bread being sent to him by Jews, and on such days he would eat from new plates and bowls, keeping and observing the said holiday as best he could. Moreover, he observed the fasts that the Jews call the Great Kippur and Haman, abstaining from food until nightfall and then breaking fast with meat, as the Jews do. Moreover, he did not observe the Christian holidays, or attend mass, or observe the fasts of the Holy Mother Church, but on the contrary he ate meat at Lent; in particular we find that he ate meat stewed in a pan on Good Friday. And that he continually prayed in the Judaic manner, his face turned to the wall, looking toward heaven through a window, bowing and reciting the psalms of David in Spanish, in the Judaic manner; and at the end of each psalm he said not *gloria patri* but instead *Adonai, Adonai*, and he had a psalter in the Spanish language that did not have *gloria patri* or the litany of the saints. And that he had faith and true hope in the said law of Moses, rather than in the evangelical law of our Lord Jesus Christ, defending the said law of Moses as superior to that of Jesus Christ; and that he gave oil for the lamps of the synagogue, and other alms to Jews; and that he had no oratory or other Christian practice. Nor did he kneel at the sounding of the orisons or at the elevation of the Corpus Christi, or cross himself, or say "Jesus." And when riding horseback, if the beast should stumble, in place of saying "Jesus" he used to say *Sadday*, and *Adonai*, as the Jews do; and he abstained from eating the foods forbidden by the law of Moses as much as he could, eating instead the meat of animals slaughtered by Jewish hands, cleansing away the tallow, salting it to draw out the blood before cooking, and removing a certain small round body from the leg. Nor did he eat the flesh of game or birds that had been strangled, but instead he had his chickens and other fowls slaughtered by Jews; and the other game that he purchased he would kill or have killed with a well-sharpened knife, in the Judaic manner.

And as we already had information of the aforementioned matters, the said Luis de Santangel, suspecting this and suspecting that orders had been issued for his seizure, came before us with lying and deceitful words, saying that he, as a good Christian, wished to submit to our justice and confess completely certain errors that he had committed against the faith, and of his own will he bound himself to the punishment of a relapsed heretic if he should not tell the whole truth, and he gave in writing a certain confession in his handwriting, in which he confessed that he had observed certain Judaic ceremonies and fasts, by which it immediately became evident that he had committed perjury and relapsed into heresy, to which charge he had ex-

posed himself of his own will; and after the above-cited confession, with the hope of being released from prison and even of having his goods returned, as we lawfully know, he made other confessions, more extensive than the first, although in none of these did he confess all the heresies that he had committed.

In fine, it appears that the said Luis de Santangel has been and is a negative, obdurate heretic, and that he came to seek reconciliation to the Holy Mother Church with a lying tale, and not in a sincere or contrite spirit, as the case required, and that he is unworthy of forgiveness or of admission to the Holy Mother Church; concerning all of which we have resolved and deliberated with learned men of good conscience, who have seen and examined the said process and the said confessions. And desiring to extirpate and eradicate completely, as by our office we are most strictly bound and held to do, in the name of the Church, all such vile, grave, and wicked errors, so that the name of Jesus Christ may be truly believed, exalted, adored, praised, and served, without any pretence, hypocrisy, or sham, and so that no one may bear the name of a Christian and the air of a lamb who is truly a Jew and has the heart of a wolf; and having before our eyes Our Lord, from whom proceed all just and righteous judgments, we find that we must pronounce and declare, as by these presents we do pronounce and declare, that the said Luis de Santangel has been and is a true heretic and apostate from the faith, negative and obdurate. . . . We moreover declare all his goods confiscated for the Treasury and exchequer of the King our lord. . . . And since the Holy Mother Church cannot and should not do anything more against the said heretic and apostate, except to withdraw from him its protection and remit him to the secular justice and arm that he may be punished and chastised according to his demerits, therefore, with the customary protestations established in canon law, we remit the said Luis de Santangel, heretic and apostate, to the excellent and virtuous Juan Garcez de Marcella, chief justice of the King our lord in this city, and to its judge and justices, that they may dispose of him as in law and justice they may decree.

5. THE FALL OF GRANADA

On January 2, 1492, the city and kingdom of Granada were surrendered to the Catholic Kings, bringing the ten-year Granadine war to a close. In the joyful procession that entered the last Moslem stronghold in Spain marched an obscure Genoese navigator named Cristoforo Colombo. The age of crusades had

ended; the age of discovery and overseas conquest was about to begin. Father Mariana describes the last days and the fall of Moslem Granada.[5]

✠✠✠ It was believed that the siege of Granada would be of long duration; accordingly, the queen and her children came to the camp, for King Ferdinand had resolved not to make peace until Granada had fallen. With this intent he ordered the surrounding countryside laid waste, in order that the inhabitants of the city should be deprived of a source of foodstuffs; and on the site of the royal camp he built a strongly fortified town, which to this day bears the name of Santa Fe. Within the walls were shops and lodgings, assigned according to the King's orders, and barracks, streets and squares, all laid out with admirable precision. Meanwhile various bands of people, sent out to plunder, clashed with the Moors who sallied from the city against them. In one skirmish the Christians advanced so far that they seized the Moorish artillery, captured many of the enemy, and compelled the rest to take refuge in the city. So great was the ardor of the Christians that they ventured to come closer than usual to the walls of the city and seized two towers that served the enemy as watch-towers and bastions and in which troops were stationed. . . . They gave the enemy no peace, although the Moors defended themselves with desperate bravery. Finally the Moors, wearying of so much harassment and seeing no prospect of relief, determined to negotiate a settlement.

Bulcacin Mulch, military governor of the city, went to the royal camp to discuss an agreement and capitulation. The King entrusted the negotiation to Gonzalo Fernández de Córdoba, later known as "The Great Captain," and to his own secretary, Hernando de Zafra. After conferring for several days they drew up an agreement, to which both parties pledged their faith on the 25th of November. The Moors were to surrender within sixty days the two castles, the towers, and the gates of the city. They were to render homage to King Ferdinand and to swear obedience and loyalty to him. All Christian captives were to be freed without ransom. As hostages for the fulfilment of these conditions, the Moors were to turn over within twelve days five hundred children of the principal citizens of Granada. They were to retain their estates, arms, and horses and surrender only their artillery. They would be permitted to keep their mosques and would have freedom to observe the ceremonies of their faith. They were to be governed according to their own laws, and to this end persons of their own nation would be designated to assist and advise the governors appointed by the king in ruling the Moors.

[5] Mariana, *Obras*, II, pp. 236, 238-240. (Excerpt translated by the editor.)

Those who wished to depart for Africa could sell their goods, and ships were to be provided for their passage at such ports as they might designate. It was also agreed that the son of Boabdil, with the other hostages that he had previously given the king, should be returned to him, since with the surrender of the city and the fulfilment of the treaty no other security or hostage was necessary.

A tumult among the Moslems of Granada, in protest against the capitulation agreement, is quelled by Boabdil, who fears new disorders. Ed.]

Boabdil, the "little king," immediately sent a letter to King Ferdinand, with a gift of two pure-blooded horses, a scimitar, and some harnesses. He told him of the rising in the city and said that speed was necessary to avoid trouble; he urged the king to come promptly, since small delays frequently brought about great changes. Since it was the will of God, he concluded, on the following day he would with good grace turn over the Alhambra and his kingdom to King Ferdinand as to a conqueror, but the king must not fail to come.

This letter reached the camp on New Year's Day, and King Ferdinand's satisfaction on reading it can easily be imagined. He ordered that everything should be made ready for the following day. . . . Changing from the mourning that he wore for the death of his son-in-law, Alonso, Prince of Portugal, to his royal vestments, the king set off for the castle with his retinue, all in formation and armed as if advancing to battle. A brilliant company and a splendid sight they were, indeed. Following them were the queen and her elder children, in sumptuous brocades and silks. When they had arrived with all this pomp and show near the fortress, Boabdil came out to meet them, accompanied by fifty men on horseback. He apparently intended to alight to kiss the hand of the conqueror, but the king would not permit it. Then, with downcast eyes and a melancholy expression, he said: "Invincible king, we are in your hands; we surrender to you this castle and kingdom; we trust that you will be fair and lenient in your dealings with us." He then placed in the king's hands the keys to the fortress. The king gave them to the queen, who gave them to the prince, her son; the latter placed them in the hands of Don Iñigo de Mendoza, Count of Tendilla, whom the king had appointed to hold the castle and be captain-general of the kingdom. . . . Surrounded by a large number of mounted men, the king then entered the city. He was followed by a group of lords and churchmen. Among the most distinguished were the prelates of Toledo and Seville, the master of the order of Santiago, the duke of Cadiz, and Fray Hernando de Talavera, lately made archbishop of Avila, of which city he had been bishop. Friar Hernando, having pronounced a prayer of thanksgiving, placed the standard of the cross that the cardinal of Toledo, as primate, carried before him, on the

highest part of the principal tower, flanked on one side by the royal banner and on the other by that of Santiago. This was greeted by joyful shouts from the soldiers and the principal people. The king, kneeling with great humility, gave thanks to God that the empire and name of that evil people had been uprooted from Spain, and that the banner of the cross had been raised in the city where impiety had so long flourished. He implored Him to continue His favor and make it enduring and perpetual. When he had concluded this prayer, the grandees and lords approached the king to felicitate him on his acquisition of a new kingdom, and in order of rank each kissed the king's hand. They did the same with the queen and with the prince, his son.

I conclude by saying that with the entrance of the kings into Granada and their taking possession of that town, by the will of God the Moors were fortunately and forever subjected to Christian rule in that part of Spain. This was in the year 1492 of our salvation, on Friday the sixth of January — in the year 897 of the Hegira, on the eighth day of the month *rahib haraba,* according to Arabic count. This day, which for Christians is the joyful and solemn holiday of the Kings and of the Epiphany, became no less joyful for all Spain by virtue of this new victory, though a day of gloom to the Moors; for by the uprooting and destruction of impiety in our land its past disgrace and injuries were atoned for, and a sizable part of Spain was reunited with the Christian community and received its government and laws — a great joy in which the other nations of Christendom shared. . . . As a token of their satisfaction, and in acknowledgment of the divine source of this favor, the Pope, the cardinals, and the people of Rome made a solemn procession to the Spanish church of Santiago. There services were held, and in a sermon on the events of the day the preacher lauded the Spanish kings and the entire Spanish nation for their feats, their bravery, and their notable victories.

6. THE SPANISH TEMPER

The great movement of the Reconquista *— the reconquest of Spain from the Moslems — left an enduring stamp on the Spanish character. The soldier of the* Reconquista *was reborn in the Conquistador of America. Centuries of struggle against the Moor made war almost a way of life and created a numerous military nobility who regarded manual labor and commerce with contempt. The noble scorn for labor infected all classes. In the Castilian scale of values, the military virtues of courage,*

endurance, and honor held the first place. Thoughtful Spaniards were aware of the dangers that this militarist psychology and disdain for labor posed for their country. In a memorial to Philip II (1558), the reformer Luis de Ortiz wrote: "Spaniards are ready to die for their religion and their king. If they cannot find a foreign war, they will fight among themselves, for the majority are by nature choleric and proud. And since most live in idleness, and possess neither learning nor any mechanical art, they are more prone to violence than any other nation." And he continued: "So great is the love of ease, so far advanced Spain's perdition, that none, whatever his state or condition, will hear of working at any craft or business, but must go to the University of Salamanca, or to the Italian Wars or the Indies, or become a notary public or attorney, all to the ruin of the commonwealth." The Italian historian and diplomat, Francesco Guicciardini (1483–1540), who represented Florence in the court of King Ferdinand, left an acid — yet often perceptive — account of the Spanish character at the opening of the sixteenth century:[6]

❖❖❖❖ The Spaniards are of melancholy and choleric disposition, dark-skinned, small in stature, and haughty by nature. They believe no other nation can compare with them; in speech they brag and puff themselves up all they can. They have little love for foreigners and are very rude to them. They are more inclined to arms, perhaps, than any other Christian nation, and that because they are extremely agile, skillful, and light in movement. In war they have a high regard for honor, and would rather suffer death than dishonor. . . .

In their wars they have begun to adopt the Swiss formation, but I question whether this conforms to their nature, for when they form a compact front or wall, in the Swiss manner, they cannot make use of their nimbleness, the quality in which they surpass all others. All Spaniards carry arms, and in the old days they took part not only in foreign wars but in domestic broils, each man siding with one faction or another. For this reason Spain formerly had more cavalrymen, and more skillful ones, than now. In the reign of Queen Isabella peace and order were restored to the kingdom, and that, in my opinion, is why Spain is less of a military power today than at any time in the past.

Spaniards are generally regarded as ingenious and astute people, but they have little taste for the mechanical or liberal arts. Almost all the artisans in the royal court are from France or some other

---

[6] Francesco Guicciardini, "Relazione di Spagna," in *Opere,* edited by Vittorio de Caprariis (Milano, 1961), pp. 29–31.

foreign country. Nor do Spaniards devote themselves to commerce, for they think it shameful, and all give themselves the airs of a hidalgo. They would rather eat the meager fare of a soldier, or serve some grandee, suffering a thousand privations and inconveniences, or — before the time of the present king — even take to the roads as a highwayman, than devote themselves to commerce or some other work. True, in certain places they have begun to pay attention to industry, and in some regions they are now producing textiles, clothing, crimson damasks, and gold embroideries. They do this in Valencia, Toledo, and Seville. In general, however, the Spaniards have no liking for industry. Thus the artisans work only when driven by necessity, and then they rest until they have used up their earnings. This is the reason why manual labor is so expensive. It is the same in the countryside, for the peasants will not work hard unless compelled by extreme need. Each one works much less land than he could, and the little land that is farmed is badly cultivated.

There is great poverty in Spain, and I believe this arises less from the quality of the country than from the nature of its people, who lack the inclination to devote themselves to industry and trade. The problem is not that Spaniards leave their country, but that they prefer to export the raw materials that the kingdom yields and buy them back in the form of finished goods; this is the case with wool and silk, which they sell to other nations and then purchase back in the form of woolen and silk cloth. From the resulting poverty arises the misery of the people. Aside from a few grandees of the realm, who live sumptuously, the Spaniards live in very straitened circumstances, and if they have some money to spend, they spend it on clothing and a mule, making a greater show in the street than at home, where they live so meanly and eat so sparingly that it is a marvel to see. Although they can manage with very little, they are not free from greed for gain. Indeed, they are very avaricious, and, since they know no trade, they are given to robbery. Formerly, when there was less rule of law in this kingdom, the whole land swarmed with assassins, a thing favored by the nature of the country, which is very mountainous and sparsely settled. Their astuteness makes them good thieves. There is a popular saying that the Frenchman makes a better lord than a Spaniard, for, although both extort from their subjects, the Frenchman immediately spends what he takes, whereas the Spaniard hoards it. For the rest, the Spaniard, being more clever, surely robs better.

They are not given to letters. One finds little knowledge of Latin among the nobility or among the rest of the population, and that among very few persons. In demonstrations and outward show they are very religious, but not in fact. They are very ceremonious, with many deep bows, great verbal humility, and much use of titles

and hand kisses. They assure everyone that he is their *señor*, that they are at his orders; but it is best to keep one's distance with them and give little credit to their words.

Dissimulation is natural to this nation, and one finds masters of this art among all classes. This is the basis of their reputation for astuteness and ingenuity; for the rest, they are not especially faithless or treacherous. In this matter of dissimulation the Andalusians surpass all others, particularly those of the ancient and famous city of Córdoba, home of the Great Captain.[7] From this dissimulation arise their ceremoniousness and their great hypocrisy.

[7] Gonzalo Fernández de Córdoba (1453–1515), Spanish general whose brilliant victories in the Italian wars won him the sobriquet of *El Gran Capitán* (The Great Captain.)

5 ✢ The Great Discoveries

Italian merchants enjoyed a virtual monopoly of European trade with the Orient in the Middle Ages. The draining of their scanty store of gold and silver into the pockets of Italian and Levantine middlemen grew intolerable to the ambitious merchants and monarchs of Western Europe. Their answer to this problem was the search for an all-water route to the East, pursued with great energy in the fifteenth and sixteenth centuries. Little Portugal took a decisive lead in the race to find a waterway to the land of spices. The famous Prince Henry, known as the Navigator, initiated and organized explorations down the west coast of Africa that brought Portugal an unequaled prosperity based on trade in slaves and gold dust. Under Alfonso V and João II the effort to round Africa and reach India was vigorously pressed; success was finally achieved when Vasco da Gama made his way to Calicut in 1498.

The discovery of America was a by-product of the search for a sea road to the East. When Columbus, in about 1484, presented to the Portuguese ruler João II his plan for reaching the Orient by sailing west, the king's maritime committee rejected it, probably on sound technical grounds. Undismayed by the Portuguese rebuff, Columbus took his idea to the Spanish court. Eight years of discouraging delays elapsed before Queen Isabella agreed to support the "Enterprise of the Indies."

The voyages of Columbus laid a solid base for Spanish empire-building through the settlement of the island of Hispaniola, to which Castilian fortune-seekers flocked in large numbers. Columbus died in 1506, still believing that he had reached the mainland of Asia. It remained for Amerigo Vespucci, a Florentine merchant and navigator who made two important voyages of exploration along the north and east coasts of South America between 1499 and 1502, to announce the existence of a new continent that formed a "fourth part of the world."

The growing shortage of Indian labor, and the general lack of economic opportunities for new settlers on Hispaniola, stimulated Spanish adventurers to explore and conquer the remaining great Antilles between 1509 and 1511. In the same period, efforts to found colonies on the coasts of present-day Colombia and Central America failed disastrously, and the remnants of two expeditions were united under the able leadership of the conquistador Balboa to form the new settlement of Darien on the Isthmus of Panama. Indian accounts of a great sea and a land of gold to the south induced Balboa to make a laborious journey with a party of sixty-seven men across the isthmus to the shores of the Pacific. The discovery of the "South Sea" supported the belief that the so-called Indies formed no part of Asia and posed the problem of finding a passage to the East across or around the American continents.

Ferdinand Magellan, a native of Portugal, was convinced that such a passage existed south of Brazil. Failing to interest the Portuguese crown in his project, Magellan turned to Spain, with greater success. The resulting voyage of circumnavigation of the globe represented an immense navigational feat and greatly increased Europe's fund of geographical knowledge. But from a practical point of view, aside from the acquisition of the Philippines for Spain, Magellan's exploit had little significance. His new route to the Orient was too long to have commercial importance. Disappointed in her dream of an easy access to the riches of the East, Spain turned with concentrated energy to the task of extending her American conquests and to the exploitation of the human and natural resources of the New World.

1. PRINCE HENRY OF PORTUGAL: ADVANCE INTO THE UNKNOWN

At the threshold of the age of discovery and exploration stands the figure of Prince Henry of Portugal (1394–1460), somewhat misleadingly known as "the Navigator," since he apparently never sailed beyond sight of land. In Prince Henry were united a medieval crusading spirit with more modern traits:

*the desire to penetrate the secrets of unknown seas and lands
and a lively appreciation of the importance of such discoveries
for the expansion of Portuguese commerce. All these motives
appear to have figured in his lifelong work of directing exploration down the west coast of Africa, but before his death the
commercial motive had clearly become uppermost. The first
of two selections from the chronicle of Gomes Eannes de Azurara (1410–1474), who enjoyed the friendship of the prince,
affectionately portrays his appearance and character; the second
describes the birth of the African slave trade with Portugal —
the first bitter fruit of European overseas expansion.*[1]

✠✠✠✠ The noble Prince was of a good height and broad frame, big
and strong of limb, the hair of his head somewhat erect, his colour
naturally fair, but by constant toil and exposure it had become dark.
His expression at first sight inspired fear in those who did not know
him, and when wroth, though such times were rare, his countenance
was harsh. He possessed strength of heart and keenness of mind to
a very excellent degree, and he was beyond comparison ambitious of
achieving great and lofty deeds. Neither lewdness nor avarice ever
found a home in his breast, for as to the former he was so restrained
that he passed all his life in purest chastity, and as a virgin the earth
received him again at his death to herself. . . .

His palace was a school of hospitality for the good and high
born of the realm and still more for strangers, and the fame of it
caused him a great increase of expense, for commonly there were to
be found in his presence men from various nations, so different from
our own that it was a marvel to well-nigh all our people; and none
of that multitude could go away without some guerdon from the
Prince.

All his days he spent in the greatest toil, for of a surety among
the nations of mankind no one existed who was a sterner master to
himself. It would be hard to tell how many nights he passed in which
his eyes knew no sleep; and his body was so transformed by absti-
nence, that it seemed as if Henry had made its nature to be different
from that of others. Such was the length of his toil and so rigorous
was it, that as the poets have feigned that Atlas the giant held up the
heavens upon his shoulders, for the great knowledge there was in him
concerning the movements of the celestial bodies, so the people of
our kingdom had a proverb that the great labours of this our prince
conquered the heights of the mountains, that is to say, the things that

[1] Gomes Eannes de Azurara, *The Chronicle of the Discovery and Conquest of
Guinea,* translated by C. R. Beazley and Edgar Prestage, London, the Hakluyt
Society, Cambridge University Press, 1896, 2 vols., I, pp. 12–15, 81–83.

seemed impossible to other men were made by his continual energy to appear light and easy.

The prince was a man of great wisdom and authority, very discreet and of good memory, but in some matters a little tardy, whether it was from the influence of the phlegm in his nature, or from the choice of his will, directed to some certain end not known to men. His bearing was calm and dignified, his speech and address gentle. He was constant in adversity, humble in prosperity. Never was hatred known to him, nor ill-will toward any man, however great the wrong done him; and such was his benignity in this respect, that wiseacres reproached him as wanting in distributive justice. And this they said, because he left unpunished some of his servants who deserted him at the siege of Tangier, which was the most perilous affair in which he ever stood before or after, not only becoming reconciled to them, but even granting them honourable advancement over others who had served him well, which in the judgment of men was far from their deserts, and this is the only shortcoming of his I have to record. The Infant drank wine only for a very small part of his life and that in his youth, but afterwards he abstained entirely from it.

He ever showed great devotion to the public affairs of this kingdom, toiling greatly for their good advancement and he much delighted in the trial of new undertakings for the profit of all, though with great expense of his own substance, and he keenly enjoyed the labour of arms, especially against the enemies of the holy Faith, while he desired peace with all Christians. Thus he was loved by all alike, for he made himself useful to all and hindered no one. His answers were always gentle and he showed great honour to the standing of every one who came to him, without any lessening of his own estate. A base or unchaste word was never heard to issue from his mouth. He was very obedient to the commands of Holy Church and heard all its offices with great devotion; aye and caused the same to be celebrated in his chapel, with no less splendour and ceremony than they could have been in the college of any Cathedral Church. . . . Well-nigh one-half of the year he spent in fasting and the hands of the poor never went away empty from his presence. . . . His heart knew not fear, save the fear of sin. . . .

On the next day, which was the 8th of the month of August, very early in the morning, by reason of the heat, the seamen began to make ready their boats, and to take out their captives and carry them on shore, as they were commanded. And these, placed altogether in that field, were a marvellous sight, for amongst them were some white enough, fair to look upon and well proportioned, others were less white like mulattoes; others again were as black as Ethiops, and so

ugly, both in features and in body, as almost to appear the images of
a lower hemisphere. But what heart could be so hard as not to be
pierced with piteous feeling to see that company? For some kept
their heads low and their faces bathed in tears, looking one upon another; others stood groaning very grievously, looking up to the height
of heaven, fixing their eyes upon it, crying out loudly, as if asking
help of the Father of Nature; others struck their faces with the palms
of their hands, throwing themselves at full length upon the ground;
others made their lamentations in the manner of a dirge, after the
custom of their country. And though we could not understand the
words of their language, the sound of it right well accorded with the
measure of their sadness. But to increase their sufferings still more,
there now arrived those who had charge of the division of the captives and who began to separate one from another in order to make
an equal partition of the fifths; and then it was needful to part fathers
from sons, husbands from wives, brothers from brothers. No respect
was shown either to friends or relations, but each fell where his lot
took him.

And who could finish that partition without very great toil,
for as often as they had placed them in one part, the sons, seeing their
fathers in another, rose with great energy and rushed over to them;
the mothers clasped their other children in their arms, and threw
themselves flat on the ground with them, receiving blows with little
pity for their own flesh, if only they might not be torn from them.

The Infant was there, mounted upon a powerful steed, and
accompanied by his retinue, making distribution of his favours, as a
man who sought to gain but small treasure from his share; for he
made a very speedy partition of the forty-six souls that fell to him
as his fifth. His chief riches lay in his purpose, and he reflected with
great pleasure upon the salvation of those souls that before were lost.
And certainly his expectation was not in vain, since, as we said before,
as soon as they understood our language, they turned Christians with
very little ado; and I who put together this history into the present
volume, saw in the town of Lagos boys and girls (the children and
grandchildren of those first captives) born in this land, as good and
true Christians as if they had directly descended, from the beginning
of the dispensation of Christ, from those who were first baptised.

2. THE MAN COLUMBUS

*Christopher Columbus, like Prince Henry of Portugal, was a
figure of transition whose thought and aspirations reflected
both the waning Middle Ages and the rising new day of ration-*

alism and capitalism. Medieval in his ardent and mystical faith, which led him to seek Scriptural authority for his enterprise of the Indies and to identify the Orinoco as one of the four rivers of Paradise, he was singularly modern in his questing, adventurous spirit and in his greed for gold and worldly honors. A major source of information about the Columbian epic is the monumental History of the Indies *of Bartolomé de Las Casas (1474–1566), whose father and uncle accompanied Columbus on his second voyage, and who was with him on Hispaniola in 1500. Las Casas describes the appearance and character of the Discoverer.*[2]

✦✦✦✦ As concerns his appearance, he was fairly tall, his face long and giving an impression of authority, his nose aquiline, his eyes blue, his complexion light and tending to bright red; his beard and hair were fair in his youth but very soon turned gray from his labors. He was witty and gay in speech and, as the aforementioned Portuguese history relates, eloquent and boastful in his negotiations. His manner was serious, but not grave; he was affable with strangers and mild and pleasant with members of his household, whom he treated with dignity, and so he easily won the love of those who saw him. In short, he had the appearance of a man of great consequence. He was sober and moderate in eating and drinking, in dress and footwear; he would often say, whether jokingly or angrily: "God take you, don't you agree to that?" or "Why did you do that?" In the matter of Christian doctrine he was a devout Catholic; nearly everything he did or said he began with: "In the name of the Holy Trinity I shall do this" or "— this will come to pass," or "— may this come to pass." And at the head of everything he wrote he put: "Jesus and Mary, attend us on our way." I have many of these writings in my possession. Sometimes his oath was: "I swear by San Fernando"; when he wanted to affirm the truth of something very important, especially when writing to the King and Queen, he said: "I swear that this is true." He kept the fasts of the Church most faithfully, confessed and took communion very often, said the canonical offices like any churchman or monk, abhorred blasphemy and vain oaths, and was most devoted to Our Lady and the Seraphic Father Saint Francis. He appeared very grateful for benefits received at the divine hand; and it was almost a proverb with him, which he repeated frequently, that God had been especially good to him, as to David. When gold or precious objects were brought to him he would enter his chapel and kneel, asking the bystanders to do the same, saying: "Let us give thanks to the Lord, who made us worthy of discovering such great wealth." He was most zealous in the service

[2] Bartolomé de Las Casas, *Historia de las Indias*, Mexico, 1951, 3 vols., I, pp. 29–30. (Excerpt translated by the editor.)

of God; he was eager to convert the Indians and to spread the faith of Jesus Christ everywhere, and was especially devoted to the hope that God would make him worthy of helping to win back the Holy Sepulcher. . . . He was a man of great spirit and lofty thoughts, naturally inclined — as appears from his life, deeds, writings, and speech — to undertake great and memorable enterprises; patient and long-suffering . . . quick to forgive injuries, and wishing nothing more than that those who offended him should come to know their error and be reconciled with him. He was most constant and forbearing amid the endless incredible hardships and misfortunes that he had to endure, and always had great faith in the Divine Providence. And as I learned from him, from my own father, who was with him when he returned to settle the island of Hispaniola in 1493, and from other persons who accompanied and served him, he was always most loyal and devoted to the King and Queen.

3. "SAINT AUGUSTINE DOUBTS . . ."

Among the numerous legends that surround the Columbus story, perhaps the most popular of all is that which portrays Columbus as seeking to convince his bigoted and dull-witted opponents of the faculty of the University of Salamanca that the earth was round. In reality, the question of the sphericity of the earth never entered the discussions between Columbus and the committee appointed by Queen Isabella to consider his claims. The main issue, as Professor Morison points out, "was the width of the ocean; and therein the opposition was right." Of pedantry and excessive deference to the authority of the ancients, however, the committee was doubtless guilty, if we may trust Las Casas' lively account of the debate, in which he reveals a warm partisanship for Columbus.[3]

❖❖❖❖ Some said that it was impossible that after so many thousands of years these Indies should be unknown, if there were such places in the world, for surely Ptolemy and the many other astronomers, geographers, and sages that had lived would have known something of them, and would have left some reference to them in writing, since they had written of many other matters; hence, they said, to affirm what Columbus affirmed was to claim to know or divine more than anyone else. Others argued this way: The world is infinitely large, and therefore in many years of navigation it would be impossible to

[3] Bartolomé de Las Casas, *Historia de las Indias*, I, pp. 157–158. (Excerpt translated by the editor.)

reach the end of Asia, as Christopher Columbus proposed to do by sailing westward. . . .

Still others, who vaunted their mathematical learnings, talked about astronomy and geography, saying that only a very small part of this inferior sphere is land, all the rest being entirely covered with water, and therefore it could only be navigated by sailing along the shores or coasts, as the Portuguese did along the coasts of Guinea; the proponents of this view had read precious few books on navigation, and had done even less sailing themselves. They added that whoever sailed directly west, as Christopher Columbus proposed to do, could never return, for supposing that the world was round, and that going westward you went downhill, then once you had left the hemisphere described by Ptolemy, on your return you must go uphill, which ships could not do — truly a subtle and profound reason, and proof that the matter was well understood! Others cited Saint Augustine, who . . . denied the existence of antipodes . . . and their refrain was: "Saint Augustine doubts." Then someone had to bring up the business of the five zones, of which three, according to many, are totally uninhabitable; this was a commonly held opinion among the ancients, who, after all, did not know very much. Others adduced still other reasons, not worth mentioning here since they came from the kind of people who disagree with everybody — who find any statement illogical, no matter how sound and clear it is, and never lack for reasons to contradict it. . . .

And so Christopher Columbus could give little satisfaction to those gentlemen whom the monarchs had convened, and therefore they pronounced his offers and promises impossible and vain and worthy of rejection. Having formed their opinion, they went to the monarchs and stated their views, persuading them that it did not become their royal authority to favor a project that was based on such weak foundations and that must appear vague and unfeasible to any sensible person, even an uneducated one, for if they sponsored it, they would lose the money that they spent on it and would weaken their own standing, with no benefit to anyone. Finally the monarchs sent a reply to Columbus, dismissing him for the time being, though not entirely depriving him of the hope of a return to the subject when their Highnesses should be less occupied with important business, as they were at that time by the War of Granada.

4. LANDFALL

Few records of navigation have the inherently dramatic quality of the straightforward log and journal kept by Columbus on his

first voyage. Las Casas incorporated an abstract of this document, which has since vanished, in his History of the Indies. *The crisis of the voyage, to which Columbus' diary evidently made only meager reference, came on October 9–10, when the discoverer was apparently forced by a threat of mutiny to promise his fearful captains and crews that they would turn about if land were not sighted in three days. Landfall was made the following day. "Never again," justly writes Samuel Eliot Morison, "may mortal men hope to recapture the amazement, the wonder, the delight of those October days in 1492 when the New World gracefully yielded her virginity to the conquering Castilians."*[4]

✠✠✠✠ Monday, Oct. 8th. Steered W.S.W. and sailed day and night eleven or twelve leagues; at times during the night, fifteen miles an hour, if the account can be depended upon. Found the sea like the river at Seville, *"thanks to God,"* says the Admiral. The air soft as that of Seville in April, and so fragrant that it was delicious to breathe it. The weeds appeared very fresh. Many land birds, one of which they took, flying towards the S.W.; also *grajaos,* ducks, and a pelican were seen.

Tuesday, Oct. 9th. Sailed S.W. five leagues, when the wind changed, and they stood W. by N. four leagues. Sailed in the whole day and night, twenty leagues and a half; reckoned to the crew seventeen. All night heard birds passing.

Wednesday, Oct. 10th. Steered W.S.W. and sailed at times ten miles an hour, at others twelve, and at others, seven; day and night made fifty-nine leagues' progress; reckoned to the crew but forty-four. Here the men lost all patience, and complained of the length of the voyage, but the Admiral encouraged them in the best manner he could, representing the profits they were about to acquire, and adding that it was to no purpose to complain, having come so far, they had nothing to do but continue on to the Indies, till with the help of our Lord, they should arrive there.

Thursday, Oct. 11th. Steered W.S.W.; and encountered a heavier sea than they had met with before in the whole voyage. Saw pardelas and a green rush near the vessel. The crew of the Pinta saw a cane and a log; they also picked up a stick which appeared to have been carved with an iron tool, a piece of cane, a plant which grows on land, and a board. The crew of the Niña saw other signs of land, and a stalk loaded with roseberries. These signs encouraged them, and they all grew cheerful. Sailed this day till sunset, twenty-seven leagues.

After sunset steered their original course W. and sailed twelve miles an hour till two hours after midnight, going ninety miles, which

[4] *Personal Narrative of the First Voyage of Columbus to America,* translated by Samuel Kettell, Boston, 1927, pp. 30–37.

are twenty-two leagues and a half; and as the Pinta was the swiftest sailer, and kept ahead of the Admiral, she discovered land and made the signals which had been ordered. The land was first seen by a sailor called Rodrigo de Triana, although the Admiral at ten o'clock that evening standing on the quarterdeck saw a light, but so small a body that he could not affirm it to be land; calling to Pero Gutierrez, groom of the King's wardrobe, he told him he saw a light, and bid him look that way, which he did and saw it; he did the same to Rodrigo Sánchez of Segovia, whom the King and Queen had sent with the squadron as comptroller, but he was unable to see it from his situation. The Admiral again perceived it once or twice, appearing like the light of a wax candle moving up and down, which some thought an indication of land. But the Admiral held it for certain that land was near; for which reason, after they had said the *Salve* which the seamen are accustomed to repeat and chant after their fashion, the Admiral directed them to keep a strict watch upon the forecastle and look out diligently for land, and to him who should first discover it he promised a silken jacket, besides the reward which the King and Queen had offered, which was an annuity of ten thousand maravedis. At two o'clock in the morning the land was discovered, at two leagues' distance; they took in sail and remained under the squaresail lying to till day, which was Friday, when they found themselves near a small island, one of the Lucayos, called in the Indian language Guanahani. Presently they descried people, naked, and the Admiral landed in the boat, which was armed, along with Martín Alonzo Pinzon, and Vincent Yañez his brother, captain of the Niña. The Admiral bore the royal standard, and the two captains each a banner of the Green Cross, which all the ships had carried; this contained the initials of the names of the King and Queen each side of the cross, and a crown over each letter. Arrived on shore, they saw trees very green, many streams of water, and divers sorts of fruits. The Admiral called upon the two Captains, and the rest of the crew who landed, as also to Rodrigo de Escovedo, notary of the fleet, and Rodrigo Sánchez, of Segovia, to bear witness that he before all others took possession (as in fact he did) of that island for the King and Queen his sovereigns, making the requisite declarations, which are more at large set down here in writing. Numbers of the people of the island straightway collected together. Here follow the precise words of the Admiral: "As I saw that they were very friendly to us, and perceived that they could be much more easily converted to our holy faith by gentle means than by force, I presented them with some red caps, and strings of beads to wear upon the neck, and many other trifles of small value, wherewith they were much delighted, and became wonderfully attached to us. Afterwards they came swimming to the boats, bringing parrots, balls of cotton thread, javelins and many other things which they exchanged for articles we gave them,

such as glass beads, and hawk's bells; which trade was carried on with the utmost good will. But they seemed on the whole to me, to be a very poor people. They all go completely naked, even the women, though I saw but one girl. All whom I saw were young, not above thirty years of age, well made, with fine shapes and faces; their hair short, and coarse like that of a horse's tail, combed toward the forehead, except a small portion which they suffer to hang down behind, and never cut. Some paint themselves with black, which makes them appear like those of the Canaries, neither black nor white; others with white, others with red, and others with such colours as they can find. Some paint the face, and some the whole body; others only the eyes, and others the nose. Weapons they have none, nor are acquainted with them, for I showed them swords which they grasped by the blades, and cut themselves through ignorance. They have no iron, their javelins being without it, and nothing more than sticks, though some have fish-bones or other things at the ends. They are all of a good size and stature, and handsomely formed. I saw some with scars of wounds upon their bodies, and demanded by signs the cause of them; they answered me in the same way, that there came people from the other islands in the neighbourhood who endeavored to make prisoners of them, and they defended themselves. I thought then, and still believe, that these were from the continent. It appears to me, that the people are ingenious, and would be good servants; and I am of opinion that they would very readily become Christians, as they appear to have no religion. They very quickly learn such words as are spoken to them. If it please our Lord, I intend at my return to carry home six of them to your Highnesses, that they may learn our language. I saw no beasts in the island, nor any sort of animals except parrots." These are the words of the Admiral.

5. AMERIGO VESPUCCI: MASTER MARINER AND HUMANIST

In one of his essays Ralph Waldo Emerson found it strange that "broad America must wear the name of a thief." For centuries the view prevailed that Amerigo Vespucci had foisted his name upon the continent by publishing accounts of a fictitious voyage in which he claimed to have reached the American mainland before Columbus. Modern research has attempted to untangle what Stefan Zweig called "the comedy of errors" surrounding the Vespucci problem. In the 1930's Alberto Magnaghi advanced the theory that the boastful documents attributed to Vespucci were forgeries in which he had no part. The controversy over Vespucci and his work con-

tinues. The indisputably authentic letters of Vespucci, describing two voyages that he made to South America in 1499 and 1501, reveal an urbane, cultivated Renaissance figure who united to his impressive talent for astronomical and geographical observation an equal capacity for lively and realistic description of the fauna, flora, and inhabitants of the New World. These qualities appear in his Lisbon letter to Lorenzo de' Medici, reporting on his voyage to Brazil, in which he almost casually announces the existence of a new continent, thus refuting Columbus's theory that the lands he had discovered were a part of Asia.[5]

✠✠✠✠ To conclude, I was on the side of the antipodes; my navigation extended through one-quarter of the world; my zenith direction there made a right angle, at the center of the earth, with the zenith direction of the inhabitants of this Northern Hemisphere in the latitude of forty degrees. This must suffice.

Let us describe the country and the inhabitants and the animals and the plants and the other things I found in their habitations which are of general usefulness to human living.

This land is very pleasing, full of an infinite number of very tall trees which never lose their leaves and throughout the year are fragrant with the sweetest aromas and yield an endless supply of fruits, many of which are good to taste and conducive to bodily health. The fields produce many herbs and flowers and most delicious and wholesome roots. Sometimes I was so wonder-struck by the fragrant smells of the herbs and flowers and the savor of the fruits and the roots that I fancied myself near the Terrestrial Paradise. What shall we say of the multitude of birds and their plumes and colors and singing and their numbers and their beauty? I am unwilling to enlarge upon this description, because I doubt if I would be believed.

What should I tell of the multitude of wild animals, the abundance of pumas, of panthers, of wild cats, not like those of Spain, but of the antipodes; of so many wolves, red deer, monkeys, and felines, marmosets of many kinds, and many large snakes? We saw so many other animals that I believe so many species could not have entered Noah's ark. We saw many wild hogs, wild goats, stags and does, hares and rabbits, but of domestic animals, not one.

Let us come to rational animals. We found the whole land inhabited by people entirely naked, the men like the women without any covering of their shame. Their bodies are very agile and well

[5] Vespucci to Lorenzo di Pier Francesco de' Medici, Lisbon, 1502, quoted in Frederick J. Pohl, *Amerigo Vespucci, Pilot Major*, New York, Columbia University Press, 1945, pp. 131–135. Reprinted by permission of the Columbia University Press.

proportioned, of light color, with long hair, and little or no beard. I strove a great deal to understand their conduct and customs. For twenty-seven days I ate and slept among them, and what I learned about them is as follows:

Having no laws and no religious faith, they live according to nature. They understand nothing of the immortality of the soul. There is no possession of private property among them, for everything is in common. They have no boundaries of kingdom or province. They have no king, nor do they obey anyone. Each one is his own master. There is no administration of justice, which is unnecessary to them, because in their code no one rules. They live in communal dwellings, built in the fashion of very large cabins. For people who have no iron or indeed any metal, one can call their cabins truly miraculous houses. For I have seen habitations which are two hundred and twenty paces long and thirty wide, ingeniously fabricated; and in one of these houses dwelt five or six hundred persons. They sleep in nets woven out of cotton, going to bed in mid-air with no other coverture. They eat squatting upon the ground. Their food is very good: an endless quantity of fish; a great abundance of sour cherries, shrimps, oysters, lobsters, crabs, and many other products of the sea. The meat which they eat most usually is what one may call human flesh à la mode. When they can get it, they eat other meat, of animals or birds, but they do not lay hold of many, for they have no dogs, and the country is a very thick jungle full of ferocious wild beasts. For this reason they are not wont to penetrate the jungle except in large parties.

The men have a custom of piercing their lips and cheeks and setting in these perforations ornaments of bone or stone; and do not suppose them small ones. Most of them have at least three holes, and some seven, and some nine, in which they set ornaments of green and white alabaster, half a palm in length and as thick as a Catalonian plum. This pagan custom is beyond description. They say they do this to make themselves look more fierce. In short, it is a brutal business.

Their marriages are not with one woman only, but they mate with whom they desire and without much ceremony. I know a man who had ten women. He was jealous of them, and if it happened that one of them was guilty, he punished her and sent her away. They are a very procreative people. They do not have heirs, because they do not have private property. When their children, that is, the females, are of age to procreate, the first who seduces one has to act as her father in place of the nearest relative. After they are thus violated, they marry.

Their women do not make any ceremony over childbirth, as

do ours, but they eat all kinds of food, and wash themselves up to the very time of delivery, and scarcely feel any pain in parturition.

They are a people of great longevity, for according to their way of attributing issue, they had known many men who had four generations of descendants. They do not know how to compute time in days, months, and years, but reckon time by lunar months. When they wished to demonstrate something involving time, they did it by placing pebbles, one for each lunar month. I found a man of advanced age who indicated to me with pebbles that he had seen seventeen hundred lunar months, which I judged to be a hundred and thirty-two years, counting thirteen moons to the year.

They are also a warlike people and very cruel to their own kind. All their weapons and the blows they strike are, as Petrarch says, "committed to the wind," for they use bows and arrows, darts, and stones. They use no shields for the body, but go into battle naked. They have no discipline in the conduct of their wars, except that they do what their old men advise. When they fight, they slaughter mercilessly. Those who remain on the field bury all the dead of their own side, but cut up and eat the bodies of their enemies. Those whom they seize as prisoners, they take for slaves to their habitations. If women sleep with a male prisoner and he is virile, they marry him with their daughters. At certain times, when a diabolical frenzy comes over them, they invite their kindred and the whole tribe, and they set before them a mother with all the children she has, and with certain ceremonies they kill them with arrow shots and eat them. They do the same thing to the above-mentioned slaves and to the children born of them. This is assuredly so, for we found in their houses human flesh hung up to smoke, and much of it. We purchased from them ten creatures, male as well as female, which they were deliberating upon for the sacrifice, or better to say, the crime. Much as we reproved them, I do not know that they amended themselves. That which made me the more astonished at their wars and cruelty was that I could not understand from them why they made war upon each other, considering that they held no private property or sovereignty of empire and kingdoms and did not know any such thing as lust for possession, that is, pillaging or a desire to rule, which appear to me to be the causes of wars and of every disorderly act. When we requested them to state the cause, they did not know how to give any other cause than that this curse upon them began in ancient times and they sought to avenge the deaths of their forefathers. In short, it is a brutal business. Indeed, one man among them confessed to me that he had shared in the eating of the flesh of more than two hundred corpses, and this I assuredly believe. It was enough for me!

As to the nature of the land, I declare it to be the most agree-

able, temperate, and healthful, for in all the time that we were in it, which was ten months, none of us died and only a few fell ill. As I have already said, the inhabitants live a long time and do not suffer from infirmity or pestilence or from any unhealthy atmosphere. Death is from natural causes or from the hand of man. In conclusion, physicians would have a wretched standing in such a place.

6. THE DISCOVERY OF THE PACIFIC

Vespucci's theory that the land mass said by Columbus to be part of Asia was really a new continent gained wide though not universal approval in the decade after 1502. If Vespucci was right, there was another ocean to cross between the New World and Asia. Confirmation of this view was forthcoming in 1513, when Balboa, standing "silent, upon a peak in Darien," looked out upon the waters of the Pacific. Although further exploration was required to dispel the lingering belief of some that the whole American land mass was a peninsula projecting from southeast Asia, after 1513 the work of discovery centered on the search for a waterway to the East through or around the American continents. The Spanish chronicler Oviedo, who came to Darien in 1514 in an official capacity, tells the story of Balboa's feat, with some mention of the exploits of his remarkable dog, Leoncico.[6]

✠✠✠✠ For four years the Christians had been in Tierra-Firme; they fought under Captain Vasco Núñez de Balboa, and had made peace with certain *caciques*, in particular with the chieftains of Careta, which lies on the west coast, twenty leagues west of Darien, and of Comogre, and both of them had been baptized. The *cacique* of Careta was called Chima, and they named him Don Fernando, and he had as many as two thousand Indian warriors; the *cacique* of Comogre was a greater lord, and his proper name was Ponquiaco, but they gave him the baptismal name of Don Carlos; he had more than three thousand warriors and ruled over more than ten thousand persons. These *caciques* had grown so peaceful that they sent messengers and canoes; they came and went to and from Darien to see the Christians and communicated with them as with friends. Vasco Núñez, filled with hope by the information that he had secretly obtained from these *caciques*, resolved to set out on Friday, the first day of September, 1513; and he departed from the town of Santa María de la Antigua

[6] Oviedo y Valdés, *Historia general*, VII, pp. 92–95. (Excerpt translated by the editor.)

with eight hundred men in a galleon and nine canoes to search out the secrets of the land, on the pretext of going to seek for mines. On the following Sunday, the fourth day of September, half of this company arrived at Careta in the canoes, and the galleon came later with the rest; there Vasco Núñez disembarked. The *cacique* Don Fernando received him and all his people very well, both those who came in the canoes and those in the galleon. After they had arrived and assembled, Captain Vasco Núñez selected those whom he wished to take with him and left there those who were to guard the galleon and the canoes, and set out for the interior on the sixth day of the month. After a two-day march over a rough, difficult, and mountainous route he approached the vicinity of the *cacique* of Ponca, only to find that he and his people had fled to the hills.

Before proceeding further, I should state that the town that the Christians now call Acla was founded in the abovementioned port of Careta. I also want to tell of a dog that belonged to Vasco Núñez, called Leoncico, a son of the dog Becerrico of the isle San Juan [Puerto Rico] and no less famous than his father. This dog gained for Vasco Núñez in this and other conquests more than a thousand gold pesos, for he received as large a share in the gold and slaves as a member of the company when the division was made. So, whenever Vasco Núñez went along, the dog was assigned wages and a share like the other captains; and he was so active that he earned his reward better than many sleepy comrades who like to gain at their ease what others reap by their toil and diligence. He was truly a marvelous dog, and could distinguish a peaceable from a wild Indian as well as I or any other who went to these wars. When Indians had been taken and rounded up, if any should escape by day or by night the dog had only to be told: "He's gone, go get him," and he would do it; and he was so keen a pointer that only by a miracle could a runaway Indian escape him. After overtaking him, if the Indian remained still the dog would seize him by the wrist or hand and would bring him back as carefully, without biting or molesting him, as a man could; but if the Indian offered resistance he would tear him to pieces. He was so much feared by the Indians that if ten Christians went with the dog they went in greater safety and accomplished more than twenty without him. I saw this dog, for when Pedrarias arrived in the following year, 1514, he was still alive, and Vasco Núñez lent him for some Indian wars that were made afterwards and gained his shares as was told above. He was a dog of middle size, reddish in color, with a black muzzle, and not elegant in appearance; but he was strong and robust, and had many wounds and scars of wounds that he had received fighting with the Indians. Later on, out of envy, someone gave the dog some poisoned food, and he died. . . .

On September 13 came the *cacique* of Ponca, reassured by

Captain Vasco Núñez, who did him much honor, gave him shirts and hatchets, and made him as comfortable as he could. Since this *cacique* found himself so well treated, he told Vasco Núñez in secret a great deal about the secrets and treasures of the land, which gratified the captain; among other things, he said that a certain number of days' journey from there was another *pechry*, which in their language means "sea"; and he presented Vasco Núñez with some very finely worked pieces of gold. . . .

On the twentieth of that month, Vasco Núñez set out from the land of this *cacique* with certain guides that Ponca assigned to go with him till they reached the land of the *cacique* Torecha, with whom Ponca was at war; and on the twenty-fourth day of that month they came by night upon the *cacique* Torecha and his people. This was ten leagues beyond the land of Ponca, and was reached by a most difficult route and by crossing rivers in rafts, at great peril to themselves. And there they took some people and some gold and pearls, and Vasco Núñez obtained more extensive information concerning the interior and the other sea, to the South. In Torecha he left some of his people, and set out with about seventy men; on the twenty-fifth of the month, the same day that he had left, he arrived at the village and seat of the *cacique* called Porque, who had absented himself; however, this did not matter to Vasco Núñez, and he went ahead, continuing his search for the other sea. And on Tuesday, the twenty-fifth of September of the year one thousand five hundred and thirteen, at ten o'clock in the morning, Captain Vasco Núñez, leading all the rest in the ascent of a certain bare mountain, saw from its peak the South Sea, before any other of his Christian companions. He joyfully turned to his men, raising his hands and eyes to the skies, praising Jesus Christ and his glorious mother the Virgin, Our Lady; then he sank on his knees and gave thanks to God for the favor that had been granted to him in allowing him to discover that sea and thereby to render such a great service to God and to the Catholic and Most Serene King of Castile, our lord. . . . And he ordered them all to kneel and give the same thanks to God for this grace, and to implore Him to let them discover and see the hoped-for great secrets and riches of that sea and coast, for the exaltation and increase of the Christian faith, for the conversion of the Indians of those southern regions, and for the greater glory and prosperity of the royal throne of Castile and its princes, both present and to come.

7. THE GREATEST VOYAGE IN HISTORY

Magellan's project for reaching the Spice Islands by way of a passage around South America was a logical sequel to the dis-

coveries of Vespucci and Balboa, and had been anticipated by the former. Its principal defect was Magellan's understandable failure to conceive of the immensity of the ocean separating America from Asia. Though limited in its practical results, in point of duration, distance covered, and hardships suffered Magellan's accomplishment easily dwarfs the more celebrated first voyage of Columbus. Only one of the five ships that left Seville returned to port with its lucrative cargo of spices, and Magellan himself died in a skirmish with natives in the Philippines. His secretary, Antonio Pigafetta, describes the horrors of the crossing of the Pacific, and the circumstances of Magellan's death.[7]

✠✠✠✠ Wednesday, November 28, 1520, we debouched from that strait, engulfing ourselves in the Pacific Sea. We were three months and twenty days without getting any kind of fresh food. We ate biscuit, which was no longer biscuit, but powder of biscuits swarming with worms, for they had eaten the good. It stank strongly of the urine of rats. We drank yellow water that had been putrid for many days. We also ate some ox hides that covered the top of the mainyard to prevent the yard from chafing the shrouds, and which had become exceedingly hard because of the sun, rain, and wind. We left them in the sea for four or five days, and then placed them for a few moments on top of the embers, and so ate them; and often we ate sawdust from boards. Rats were sold for one-half ducado apiece, and even then we could not get them. But above all the other misfortunes the following was the worst. The gums of both the lower and upper teeth of some of our men swelled, so that they could not eat under any circumstances and therefore died. Nineteen men died from that sickness, and the giant together with an Indian from the country of Verzin. Twenty-five or thirty men fell sick [during that time], in the arms, legs, or in another place, so that but few remained well. However, I, by the grace of God, suffered no sickness. We sailed about four thousand leguas during those three months and twenty days through an open stretch in that Pacific Sea. In truth it is very pacific, for during that time we did not suffer any storm. We saw no land except two desert islets, where we found nothing but birds and trees, for which we called them the Ysolle Infortunate [i.e., the Unfortunate Isles]. They are two hundred leguas apart. We found no anchorage, [but] near them saw many sharks. The first islet lies fifteen degrees of south latitude, and the other nine. Daily we made runs of fifty, sixty, or seventy leguas at the catena or at the stern. Had not God and His blessed mother given us so good weather we would all

[7] Antonio Pigafetta, *Magellan's Voyage around the World*, translated and edited by James A. Robertson, Cleveland, 1902, 2 vols., I, pp. 91–93, 171–179. Reprinted by permission of the publishers, The Arthur H. Clark Company.

have died of hunger in that exceeding vast sea. Of a verity I believe no such voyage will ever be made [again].

When we left that strait, if we had sailed continuously westward we would have circumnavigated the world without finding other land than the cape of the xi thousand Virgins. The latter is a cape of that strait at the Ocean Sea, straight east and west with Cape Deseado of the Pacific Sea. Both of these capes lie in a latitude of exactly fifty-two degrees toward the Antarctic Pole.

On Friday, April twenty-six, Zula, a chief of the island of Matan, sent one of his sons to present two goats to the captain-general, and to say that he would send him all that he had promised, but that he had not been able to send it to him because of the other chief Cilalulapu, who refused to obey the king of Spagnia. He requested the captain to send him only one boatload of men on the next night, so that they might help him and fight against the other chief. The captain-general decided to go thither with three boatloads. We begged him repeatedly not to go, but he, like a good shepherd, refused to abandon his flock. At midnight, sixty men of us set out armed with corselets and helmets, together with the Christian king, the prince, some of the chief men, and twenty or thirty balanguais. We reached Matan three hours before dawn. The captain did not wish to fight them, but sent a message to the natives by the Moro to the effect that if they would obey the king of Spagnia, recognize the Christian king as their sovereign, and pay us our tribute, he would be their friend; but that if they wished otherwise, they should wait to see how our lances sounded. They replied that if we had lances they had lances of bamboo and stakes hardened with fire. [They asked us] not to proceed to attack them at once, but to wait until morning, so that they might have more men. They said that in order to induce us to go in search of them; for they had dug certain pitholes between the houses in order that we might fall into them. When morning came forty-nine of us leaped into the water up to our thighs, and walked through water for more than two crossbow flights before we could reach the shore. The boats could not approach nearer because of certain rocks in the water. The other eleven men remained behind to guard the boats. When we reached land, those men had formed in three divisions to the number of more than one thousand five hundred persons. When they saw us, they charged down upon us with exceeding loud cries, two divisions on our flanks and the other on our front. When the captain saw that, he formed us into two divisions, and thus did we begin to fight. The musketeers and crossbowmen shot from a distance for about a half-hour, but uselessly; for the shots only passed through the shields which were made of thin wood and the arms [of the bearers]. The captain cried to them, "Cease firing! Cease firing!" but his order was not at all heeded. When the natives saw that we were shooting our muskets to

no purpose, crying out they determined to stand firm, but they re-doubled their shouts. When our muskets were discharged, the natives would never stand still, but leaped hither and thither, covering them-selves with their shields. They shot so many arrows at us and hurled so many bamboo spears (some of them tipped with iron) at the captain-general, besides pointed stakes hardened with fire, stones, and mud, that we could scarcely defend ourselves. Seeing that, the captain-general sent some men to burn their houses in order to terrify them. When they saw their houses burning, they were roused to greater fury. Two of the men were killed near the houses, while we burned twenty or thirty houses. So many of them charged down upon us that they shot the captain through the right leg with a poisoned arrow. On that account, he ordered us to retire slowly, but the men took to flight, except six or eight of us who remained with the captain. The natives shot only at our legs, for the latter were bare; and so many were the spears and stones that they hurled at us, that we could offer no resistance. The mortars in the boats could not aid us as they were too far away. So we continued to retire for more than a good cross-bow flight from the shore always fighting up to our knees in the water. The natives continued to pursue us, and picking up the same spear four or six times, hurled it at us again and again. Recognizing the captain, so many turned upon him that they knocked his helmet off his head twice, but he stood firmly like a good knight, together with some others. Thus did we fight for more than one hour, refusing to retire farther. An Indian hurled a bamboo spear into the captain's face, but the latter immediately killed him with his lance, which he left in the Indian's body. Then, trying to lay hand on sword, he could draw it out but halfway, because he had been wounded in the arm with a bamboo spear. When the natives saw that, they all hurled themselves upon him. One of them wounded him on the left leg with a large cutlass, which resembles a scimitar, only being larger. That caused the captain to fall face downward, when immediately they rushed upon him with iron and bamboo spears and with their cutlasses, until they killed our mirror, our light, our comfort, and our true guide. When they wounded him, he turned back many times to see whether we were all in the boats. Thereupon, beholding him dead, we, wounded, re-treated, as best we could, to the boats, which were already pulling off. The Christian king would have aided us, but the captain charged him before we landed, not to leave his balanghai, but to stay to see how we fought. When the king learned that the captain was dead, he wept. Had it not been for that unfortunate captain, not a single one of us would have been saved in the boats, for while he was fighting the others retired to the boats. I hope through [the efforts of] your most illustrious Lordship that the fame of so noble a captain will not become effaced in our times. Among the many virtues which he possessed, he

was more constant than ever any one else in the greatest of adversity. He endured hunger better than all the others, and more accurately than any man in the world did he understand sea charts and navigation. And that this was the truth was seen openly, for no other had had so much natural talent nor the boldness to learn how to circumnavigate the world, as he had almost done. That battle was fought on Saturday, April twenty-seven, 1521. The captain desired to fight on Saturday, because it was the day especially holy to him. Eight of our men were killed with him in that battle, and four Indians, who had become Christians and who had come afterward to aid us were killed by the mortars of the boats. Of the enemy, only fifteen were killed, while many of us were wounded.

In the afternoon the Christian king sent a message with our consent to the people of Matan, to the effect that if they would give us the captain and the other men that had been killed, we would give them as much merchandise as they wished. They answered that they would not give up such a man, as we imagined [they would do], and that they would not give him up for all the riches in the world, but that they intended to keep him as a memorial.

6 ✢ The Conquest of Mexico

In 1517 an expedition sent from Cuba under Hernández de Córdova discovered Yucatan and its Maya civilization, then in a decadent state. A second expedition, headed by Juan de Grijalva, followed the coasts of Yucatan and Mexico as far as the river Panuco, and obtained some idea of the wealth and splendor of the Aztec court. These discoveries resulted in a decision on the part of Governor Velásquez of Cuba to send still another expedition, under Hernando Cortés, to the Mexican mainland.

The thirty-four-year-old Cortés was a native of Estremadura in Spain who had come over to the Indies in 1504. In February, 1519, Cortés sailed from Cuba with a force of some six hundred men. He landed on the coast of the Mexican province of Tabasco in March of that year, defeated the local Indians in a sharp skirmish, and went on to drop anchor near the site of modern Veracruz. Becoming aware of the tributary towns' bitter discontent with Aztec rule, he decided to move upon the Mexican capital. Rich gifts of gold and other valuable objects sent by Montezuma, accompanied by warnings that the strangers should depart from Mexico, only confirmed Cortés in his determination to push into the interior.

In this crisis superstitious fears that identified the coming of Cortés with the prophesied return of the god Quetzalcoatl helped to

paralyze the wills of Montezuma and his advisers. Visualizing both real and imaginary dangers, the Aztec leader was reduced to a hopelessly indecisive state of mind. As the Spanish invaders and their Indian allies approached the Aztec capital, Montezuma virtually capitulated, and he welcomed Cortés into Tenochtitlán as a representative of the rightful lord of Mexico.

The relations between the Aztecs and their white guests grew strained as Montezuma indignantly rejected Spanish proposals to substitute Christianity for the worship of his gods. Cortés now took decisive action; with a few followers he boldly entered Montezuma's rooms and forced him to come to the Spanish quarters as his prisoner. Montezuma was soon completely broken in spirit. However, an unprovoked massacre of many leading Aztec chiefs and warriors caused a popular uprising that forced the Spaniards to retreat into their quarters. The tribal council, having deposed the imprisoned Montezuma, elected a new chief who launched heavy attacks upon the Spanish forces. Cortés, fearing a long siege and famine, determined to evacuate the city. He accomplished this exploit at a terrible cost in lives. Performing a difficult retreat, the surviving Spaniards and their Indian auxiliaries at last reached the haven of friendly Tlaxcala.

In December, 1520, Cortés, his forces strengthened by the arrival of more Spaniards and by thousands of Indians who flocked to fight against their Aztec overlords, marched again on Tenochtitlán. Ferocious fighting began in late April of 1521, and it was not until the middle of August, 1521, that Guatemoc, the last Aztec war chief, surrendered to Cortés.

From the Valley of Mexico the process of conquest was gradually extended in all directions. Guatemala was reduced by Pedro de Alvarado; Honduras, by Cortés himself. In 1527 Francisco de Montejo began the conquest of Yucatan, but as late as 1542 the Mayas rose in a last desperate revolt that was crushed with great slaughter. Meanwhile, expeditions from Darien subjugated the Indians of Nicaragua, and thus the two streams of Spanish conquest, both originally starting from Hispaniola, came together again.

1. TWILIGHT OVER TENOCHTITLÁN

The last years of the Aztec domination were troubled by growing internal tensions and by presentiments of danger from outside the country. Revolts on the part of tributary tribes, restive under the mounting exactions of their Aztec masters, became more frequent, and were put down with increasing difficulty and ferocity. Then, one day in the year 1518, the agitated

tribute-collector Pinotl arrived from the coast to inform Monte-zuma of the approach from the sea of winged towers containing men with white faces and heavy beards (Grijalva's expedition). Pinotl had spoken with the mysterious strangers, who later departed, promising to return. This event, presaging an early fulfilment of Quetzalcoatl's prophecy that he would return, caused the Aztec leaders grave misgivings. Their apprehensive frame of mind on the eve of the conquest is suggested by a native account of the "evil omens" that preceded the coming of the Spaniards.[1]

✣✣✣✣ When the Spaniards had not yet arrived, by ten years, an omen first appeared in the heavens. It was like a tongue of fire, like a flame, as if showering the light of the dawn. It appeared as if it were piercing the heavens. [It was] wide at the base and pointed [at the head]. To the very midst of the sky, to the very heart of the heavens it extended; to the very midpoint of the skies stood stretched that which was thus seen off to the east. When it arose and thus came forth, when it appeared at midnight, it looked as if day had dawned. When day broke, later, the sun destroyed it when it arose. For a full year [the sign] came forth. (It was [in the year] Twelve House that it began.) And when it appeared, there was shouting; all cried out striking the palm of the hand against the mouth. All were frightened and waited with dread.

A second omen came to pass here in Mexico: of its own accord fire broke out in the house of the demon Uitzilopochtli, and flared greatly. No one had set fire to it; only of itself it burst into flames. It was called Itepeyoc, at the place named Tlacateccan. When [the fire] appeared, already the squared, wooden pillars were blazing; from within them emerged the flames, the tongues of fire, the blaze [which] speedily ate all the house beams. Thereupon there was an outcry; [the priests] said: "O Mexicans, hasten here to put out [the fire! Bring] your earthen water jars!" And when they cast water upon it, when they sought to smother it, all the more did it flare. It could not be put out; it all burned.

A third omen: a temple was struck by a thunder bolt. It was only a straw hut, a place called Tzonmulco, Temple of Xiuhtecutli. It was raining not heavily; it only sprinkled, so that it was considered a bad omen. For, it was said, there was a mere summer flash; nor did thunder sound.

A fourth omen: there was yet sun when a comet fell. It became three parts. It departed from where the sun set and traveled toward

[1] Arthur J. O. Anderson and Charles E. Dibble, Florentine Codex, Book XII, The Conquest, Ch. I (Sahagún, *General History of the Things of New Spain*). MS. Used by kind permission of the authors.

where he came forth. As if sprinkling live coals, [so] its tail went extended a great distance. Far did its tail reach. And when it was seen, great was the uproar; like [the din of] shell rattles [the outcry] was overspread.

A fifth omen: the water [of the lake] foamed up. No wind stirred it. It was as if the water swirled, as if it boiled up with a cracking sound. Very far did it go, as it rose upward. And it reached the bases of the houses, and flooded them, and crumbled the houses. This was the great lake which stretcheth about us here in Mexico.

A sixth omen: often a woman was heard [as] she went weeping and crying out. Loudly did she call out at night. She walked about saying: "Oh my beloved sons, now we are about to go!" Sometimes she said: "O my beloved sons, whither shall I take you?"

A seventh omen: at one time the fisher folk who hunted or snared with nets took captive an ashen-hued bird like a crane. Then they went to show it to Moctezuma, [who was] in the [room] Tlillan calmecatl. It was past noon, and still day time. On its head was as it were a mirror, round, circular, and as if pierced in the middle, where were to be seen the heavens, the stars — the Fire Drill [constellation]. And Moctezuma took it as an omen of great evil when he saw the stars and the Fire Drill. And when he looked at the bird's head a second time, a little beyond [the stars] he saw people who came as if massed, who came as conquerors, girt in war array. Deer bore them on their backs. And then he summoned the soothsayers and the sages. He said to them: "Do you not know what I have seen there, which was as if people came massed?" And when they would answer him, that which they looked at vanished. They could tell [him] nothing.

An eighth omen: often were discovered men of monstrous form, having two heads [but] only one body. They took them there to the Tlillan calmecatl, where Moctezuma beheld them; but when he looked at them, they then vanished.

2. PORTRAIT OF THE CONQUEROR

Historians and biographers do not agree in their estimate of the character and actions of Hernando Cortés. Some writers, recalling his treatment of Montezuma, the massacre of Cholula, and the torture and execution of the last Aztec war chief, Guatemoc, draw his portrait in unrelievedly sombre colors. Others see in him the creator of a Mexican nationality, and they extol his bravery, his intelligence, and his varied contributions to Mexican economic and educational life. The chronicler López de Gómara (1511?–1562?), who lived in Cortés' household as his

private chaplain for some years, had no doubts concerning the righteousness of either Cortés' actions or the civilizing mission of the Spanish Conquest. His history of the conquest of Mexico, which is actually a biography of Cortés, contains an intimate and not altogether flattering description of his former patron.[2]

✦✦✦✦ Ferdinand Cortés was of good size, broad in shoulders and chest, and of sallow complexion; his beard was light-colored, and he wore his hair long. He was very strong, high-spirited, and skilled in the use of arms. As a youth he was given to adventurous pranks, but in later years he acquired a mature dignity and thus became a leader in both war and peace. He was mayor of the town of Santiago de Barucoa [in Cuba], which fact the townspeople still regard as their chief title to fame. There he acquired a reputation for the qualities that he later displayed. He was passionately attracted to women, and indulged this proclivity without regard to time or place. It was the same with games of chance; he played dice exceedingly well and with great enjoyment. Although he drank moderately he was a very hearty eater and kept an abundant table. He bore hunger with great fortitude, as he showed on the march of Higueras and on the sea to which he gave his name. He was very contentious and so was involved in more lawsuits than became his condition. He spent freely on warfare, on women, on his friends, and to satisfy his whims, but showed himself niggardly in some things; hence some people called him a "wet-weather stream," one that ran high one day and dry the next. He dressed neatly rather than richly, and kept himself scrupulously clean. He took pleasure in keeping a large house and family, with a great display of plate, both for use and for show. He bore himself like a lord, and with such gravity and discretion that it neither caused disgust nor appeared presumptuous. A story has it that as a boy he was told that he was fated to conquer many lands and become a very great lord. He was jealous of the honor of his own house but forward in the homes of others — a common trait of lustful men. He was devout and prayerful, and knew many prayers and psalms by heart; he was very charitable, and on his deathbed especially charged his son with the giving of alms. He usually gave the Church a thousand ducats a year, and sometimes he borrowed money for giving alms, saying that he redeemed his sins with the interest on the money. On his shields and coats of arms he put the motto: *Judicium Domini apprehendit eos, et fortitudo ejus corroboravit brachium meum*[3] — a text very

[2] Francisco López de Gómara, *Conquista de Méjico*, in *Historiadores primitivos de las Indias*, edited by Enrique de Vedia, Madrid, 1852–1853, 2 vols., I, pp. 454-455. (Excerpt translated by the editor.)
[3] "The judgment of the Lord overtook them; and his strength supported my arm." B.K.

appropriate to the conquest. Such was Ferdinand Cortés, Conqueror of New-Spain. . . .

3. CLASH AT TLAXCALA

A major factor in the conquest of Mexico was the alliance formed between the invaders and the tough Tlaxcalan Indians, traditional foes of the Aztec Confederacy. To win that alliance, however, the Spaniards first had to prove in battle against the Tlaxcalans their fighting capacity and the superiority of their weapons. That doughty warrior and incomparable storyteller, Díaz del Castillo, describes the last major action in the war of Tlaxcala.[4]

✦✦✦✦ The next morning, the 5th September, 1519, we mustered the horses. There was not one of the wounded men who did not come forward to join the ranks and give as much help as he could. The crossbowmen were warned to use the store of darts very cautiously, some of them loading while the others were shooting, and the musketeers were to act in the same way, and the men with sword and shield were instructed to aim their cuts and thrusts at the bowels [of their enemies] so that they would not dare to come as close to us as they did before. With our banner unfurled, and four of our comrades guarding the standard-bearer, Corral, we set out from our camp. We had not marched half a quarter of a league before we began to see the fields crowded with warriors with great feather crests and distinguishing devices, and to hear the blare of horns and trumpets.

All the plain was swarming with warriors and we stood four hundred men in number, and of those many sick and wounded. And we knew for certain that this time our foe came with the determination to leave none of us alive excepting those who would be sacrificed to their idols.

How they began to charge on us! What a hail of stones sped from their slings! As for their bowmen, the javelins lay like corn on the threshing floor; all of them barbed and fire-hardened, which would pierce any armour and would reach the vitals where there is no protection; the men with swords and shields and other arms larger than swords, such as broadswords, and lances, how they pressed on us and with what mighty shouts and yells they charged upon us! The

[4] Bernal Díaz del Castillo, *The True History of the Conquest of New Spain,* translated and edited by A. P. Maudslay, London, the Hakluyt Society, 1908–1916, 5 vols., I, pp. 237–240.

steady bearing of our artillery, musketeers, and crossbowmen, was indeed a help to us, and we did the enemy much damage, and those of them who came close to us with their swords and broadswords met with such sword play from us that they were forced back and they did not close in on us so often as in the last battle. The horsemen were so skillful and bore themselves so valiantly that, after God who protected us, they were our bulwark. However, I saw that our troops were in considerable confusion, so that neither the shouts of Cortés nor the other captains availed to make them close up their ranks, and so many Indians charged down on us that it was only by a miracle of sword play that we could make them give way so that our ranks could be reformed. One thing only saved our lives, and that was that the enemy were so numerous and so crowded one on another that the shots wrought havoc among them, and in addition to this they were not well commanded, for all the captains with their forces could not come into action and from what we knew, since the last battle had been fought, there had been disputes and quarrels between the Captain Xicotenga and another captain the son of Chichimecatecle, over what the one had said to the other, that he had not fought well in the previous battle; to this the son of Chichimecatecle replied that he had fought better than Xicotenga, and was ready to prove it by personal combat. So in this battle Chichimectecle and his men would not help Xicotenga, and we knew for a certainty that he had also called on the company of Huexotzinco to abstain from fighting. Besides this, ever since the last battle they were afraid of the horses and the musketry, and the swords and crossbows, and our hard fighting; above all was the mercy of God which gave us strength to endure. So Xicotenga was not obeyed by two of the commanders, and we were doing great damage to his men, for we were killing many of them, and this they tried to conceal; for as they were so numerous, whenever one of their men was wounded, they immediately bound him up and carried him off on their shoulders, so that in this battle, as in the last, we never saw a dead man.

The enemy was already losing heart, and knowing that the followers of the other two captains whom I have already named, would not come to their assistance, they began to give way. It seems that in that battle we had killed one very important captain, and the enemy began to retreat in good order, our horsemen following them at a hard gallop for a short distance, for they could not sit their horses for fatigue, and when we found ourselves free from that multitude of warriors, we gave thanks to God.

In this engagement, one soldier was killed, and sixty were wounded, and all the horses were wounded as well. They gave me two wounds, one in the head with a stone, and one in the thigh with an arrow; but this did not prevent me from fighting and keeping watch,

and helping our soldiers, and all the soldiers who were wounded did the same; for if the wounds were not very dangerous, we had to fight and keep guard, wounded as we were, for few of us remained unwounded.

Then we returned to our camp, well contented, and giving thanks to God. We buried the dead in one of those houses which the Indians had built underground, so that the enemy should not see that we were mortals, but should believe that, as they said, we were Teules. We threw much earth over the top of the house, so that they should not smell the bodies, then we doctored all the wounded with the fat of an Indian. It was cold comfort to be even without salt or oil with which to cure the wounded. There was another want from which we suffered, and it was a severe one — and that was clothes with which to cover ourselves, for such a cold wind came from the snow mountains, that it made us shiver, for our lances and muskets and crossbows made a poor covering. That night we slept with more tranquillity than on the night before, when we had so much duty to do, with scouting, spies, watchmen and patrols.

4. THE SORCERERS' VISION

As the invaders, with their thousands of Indian auxiliaries, moved steadily up the sierra and across the Mexican plateau toward Tenochtitlán, the panicky Montezuma sent ambassadors who offered Cortés rich gifts, but simultaneously urged him to turn about and go home. This tactic failing, Montezuma sent a band of sorcerers and necromancers to conjure away the mysterious strangers. Their spells likewise failed to halt the irresistible advance of Cortés' army. A native history of the conquest elaborates the episode of the magicians into an impressive legend, in which the destruction of Tenochtitlán appears as the judgment of the gods upon the Aztecs for their crimes of imperialism and mass killings.[5]

❋❋❋❋ And Moctezuma thereupon sent and charged the princes, when Tziuacpopocatzin led, and many others besides of his henchmen, to go to meet [Cortés] between Iztactepetl and Popocatepetl, there in Quauhtechcac. They laid before them golden streamers, quetzal feather streamers, and golden necklaces.

[5] Arthur J. O. Anderson and Charles E. Dibble, Florentine Codex, Book XII, The Conquest, Chs. 12 and 13 (Sahagún, *General History of the Things of New Spain*). MS. Used by kind permission of the authors.

And when they had given them the gifts, they appeared to smile, rejoice exceedingly, and take great pleasure. Like monkeys they seized upon the gold. It was as if then they were satisfied, sated, and gladdened. For in truth they thirsted mightily for gold; they stuffed themselves with it, and hungered and lusted for it like pigs.

And they went about moving the golden streamer back and forth, and showed it to one another, all the while babbling; what they said was gibberish.

And when they saw Tziuacpopocatzin, they said: "Is this one perchance Moctezuma?" They spoke to those who came with them, their spies, those of Tlaxcala and Cempoalla. Thus in secret they questioned them. [These] said: "Not he, O our lords." This one was Tziuacpopocatzin, who was appearing in place of Moctezuma.

[The Spaniards] said to him: "Art thou perchance Moctezuma?" He replied: "I am your henchman; I am Moctezuma."

And these said to him: "Go thou hence. Why dost thou lie to us? Whom dost thou take us to be? Thou canst not fool us; thou canst not mock us. Thou canst not make us stupid, nor flatter us, nor become our eyes, nor trick us, nor misdirect our gaze, nor turn us back, nor destroy us, nor dazzle us, nor cast mud into our eyes, nor place a muddy hand over our faces. Thou art not [Moctezuma]. Now Moctezuma cannot hide from us. He cannot take refuge. Where can he go? [Is he] perchance a bird that he can fly? Or can he set out on his way under the earth? Is there somewhere a mountain pierced by a hole that he may enter? For we shall see him; for we shall listen to that [which cometh] from his lips."

Thus they only despised and belittled him. Thus came only to nothing still another of their welcomes and greetings.

Then they hurried straight and took the road direct [to Moctezuma].

And another company of messengers, who were soothsayers and sorcerers, and fire priests, also went and made their way to contend with them. But they could do nothing. They could not cast a spell on them; no more could they contend against and exert power over them. No longer could they succeed.

For a drunkard came along the way. They came up against him and stopped, stunned. They beheld him as one from Chalco, for so was he arrayed. He was dressed as a man from Chalco; he acted as a Chalcan. Like one besotted, he bore himself and acted like one who is drunk. With eight grass ropes was he bound about the chest. He accosted them, having come ahead of the outposts of the Spaniards.

And he rose up against them and said: "What do you come to do here again? What do you now wish? What would Moctezuma yet wish to do? Hath he perchance now come to his senses? Is he now filled with a great fear? For he hath committed a fault. He hath

abandoned the common folk; he hath destroyed men. People have been struck upon the head; they have been bound [in wrappings for the dead]. He hath laughed at and deceived them!"

And when they had thus seen this, when they had heard his words, to no purpose did they give him attention, praying humbly to him and quickly setting up his earth pyramid, to keep him upon, and his straw bed. On no account would he look at it; vain was its erection. To no purpose had they made the earth pyramid.

Just as if they had plunged him into his rage, he then chid and abused them, and spoke harshly. He said to them:

"Why do you vainly stand there? No longer will there be a Mexico; [it is gone] forever. Go hence; it no more existeth. Turn about; look at what befalleth Mexico — what thus already cometh to pass!"

Then they look there; they quickly turned there to see. They beheld that already all the temples, the tribal temples, the priests' dwellings, and all the houses in Mexico burned; and [it looked] as if already there were fighting.

And when the soothsayers had seen this, it was as if they had lost heart; they could say nothing; it was as if they had been made to swallow something.

They said: "This is not for us to see; it must needs be that Moctezuma see what we have seen. For this is no common being; this is the youth Tezcatlipoca."

Then he vanished, and they saw him no more.

And so the messengers went no further to encounter [the Spaniards]; they no longer pressed on toward them. From there the soothsayers and fire priests turned back and came to tell Moctezuma. There they and those who earlier [had gone with] Tziuacpopocatzin saw one another.

And when these messengers had come to arrive, just so they related to Moctezuma how this had come to pass and how they had beheld it. Moctezuma, when he heard it, only bowed his head; he stood with head downcast. He did not then speak, but only remained full of woe for a long time as if beside himself.

Finally he thus answered them, and said: "What can we do? What can be done? For we are finished; we have taken the [bitter] medicine. Shall we perhaps climb a mountain? Should we perhaps flee? For we are Mexicans. Shall we in truth perhaps enslave the Mexican domain? Unlucky are the poor old men and old women! And the children, who have no understanding — where may they be taken? What can be done? Where, in truth, can one go? For now we have taken the [bitter] medicine. Come what may, in whatsoever way it may befall, we shall marvel at it!"

5. THE MEETING OF CORTÉS AND MONTEZUMA

Few incidents in history have the romantic quality of the meeting between Cortés and Montezuma at the entrance to Tenochtitlán. Two worlds of culture met in the persons of the Indian chieftain and the Spanish conquistador. The remarkable speech of welcome made by Montezuma, as reported by Cortés, supports the view that Montezuma regarded the conqueror as an emissary of the departed Quetzalcoatl, about to return to his Mexican realm.[6]

✤✤✤✤ I followed the said causeway for about half a league before I came to the city proper of Temixtitan. I found at the junction of another causeway, which joins this one from the mainland, another strong fortification, with two towers, surrounded by walls, twelve feet high with castellated tops. This commands the two roads, and has only two gates, by one of which they enter, and from the other they come out. About one thousand of the principal citizens came out to meet me, and speak to me, all richly dressed alike according to their fashion; and when they had come, each one in approaching me, and before speaking, would use a ceremony which is very common amongst them, putting his hand on the ground, and afterward kissing it, so that I was kept waiting almost an hour, until each had performed his ceremony. There is a wooden bridge, ten paces broad, in the very outskirts of the city, across an opening in the causeway, where the water may flow in and out as it rises and falls. This bridge is also for defense, for they remove and replace the long broad wooden beams, of which the bridge is made, whenever they wish; and there are many of these bridges in the city, as Your Highness will see in the account which I shall make of its affairs.

Having passed this bridge, we were received by that lord, Montezuma, with about two hundred chiefs, all barefooted and dressed in a kind of livery, very rich, according to their custom, and some more so than others. They approached in two processions near the walls of the street, which is very broad, and straight, and beautiful, and very uniform from one end to the other, being about two thirds of a league long, and having, on both sides, very large houses, both dwelling places, and mosques. Montezuma came in the middle of the street, with two lords, one on the right side, and the other on the left, one of whom was the same great lord, who, as I said, came in that litter to speak with me, and the other was the brother of Montezuma, lord of that city Iztapala-

[6] *The Letters of Cortés to Charles V*, translated and edited by F. A. McNutt, I, pp. 232–236.

pan, whence I had come that day. All were dressed in the same manner, except that Montezuma was shod, and the other lords were barefooted. Each supported him below his arms, and as we approached each other, I descended from my horse, and was about to embrace him, but the two lords in attendance prevented me, with their hands, that I might not touch him, and they, and he also, made the ceremony of kissing the ground. This done, he ordered his brother who came with him, to remain with me, and take me by the arm, and the other attendant walked a little ahead of us. After he had spoken to me, all the other lords, who formed the two processions, also saluted me, one after the other, and then returned to the procession. When I approached to speak to Montezuma, I took off a collar of pearls and glass diamonds, that I wore, and put it on his neck, and, after we had gone through some of the streets, one of his servants came with two collars, wrapped in a cloth, which were made of coloured shells. These they esteem very much; and from each of the collars hung eight golden shrimps executed with great perfection and a span long. When he received them, he turned towards me, and put them on my neck, and again went on through the streets, as I have already indicated, until we came to a large and handsome house, which he had prepared for our reception. There he took me by the hand, and led me into a spacious room, in front of the court where we had entered, where he made me sit on a very rich platform, which had been ordered to be made for him, and told me to wait there; and then he went away.

After a little while, when all the people of my company were distributed to their quarter, he returned with many valuables of gold and silver work, and five or six thousand pieces of rich cotton stuffs, woven, and embroidered in divers ways. After he had given them to me, he sat down on another platform, which they immediately prepared near the one where I was seated, and being seated he spoke in the following manner:

"We have known for a long time, from the chronicles of our forefathers, that neither I, nor those who inhabit this country, are descendants from the aborigines of it, but from strangers who came to it from very distant parts; and we also hold, that our race was brought to these parts by a lord, whose vassals they all were, and who returned to his native country, and had many descendants, and had built towns where they were living; when, therefore, he wished to take them away with him they would not go, nor still less receive him as their ruler, so he departed. And we have always held that those who descended from him would come to subjugate this country and us, as his vassals; and according to the direction from which you say you come, which is where the sun rises, and from what you tell us of your great lord, or king, who has sent you here, we believe, and hold for certain,

that he is our rightful sovereign, especially as you tell us that since many days he has had news of us. Hence you may be sure, that we shall obey you, and hold you as the representative of this great lord of whom you speak, and that in this there will be no lack or deception; and throughout the whole country you may command at your will (I speak of what I possess in my dominions), because you will be obeyed, and recognized, and all we possess is at your disposal.

"Since you are in your rightful place, and in your own homes, rejoice and rest, free from all the trouble of the journey, and wars which you have had, for I am well aware of all that has happened to you, between Puntunchan and here, and I know very well, that the people of Cempoal, and Tascaltecal, have told you many evil things respecting me. Do not believe more than you see with your own eyes, especially from those who are my enemies, and were my vassals, yet rebelled against me on your coming (as they say), in order to help you. I know they have told you also that I have houses, with walls of gold, and that the furniture of my halls, and other things of my service, were also of gold, and that I am, or make myself, a god, and many other things. The houses you have seen are of lime and stone and earth." And then he held up his robes, and showing me his body he said to me, "Look at me, and see that I am flesh and bones, the same as you, and everybody, and that I am mortal, and tangible." And touching his arms and body with his hands, "Look how they have lied to you! It is true indeed that I have some things of gold, which have been left to me by my forefathers. All that I possess, you may have whenever you wish.

"I shall now go to other houses where I live; but you will be provided here with everything necessary for you and your people, and you shall suffer no annoyance, for you are in your own house and country."

I answered to all he said, certifying that which seemed to be suitable, especially in confirming his belief that it was Your Majesty whom they were expecting. After this, he took his leave, and, when he had gone, we were well provided with chickens, and bread, and fruits, and other necessities, especially such as were required for the service of our quarters. Thus I passed six days well provided with everything necessary, and visited by many of the lords.

6. ALVARADO UNLEASHES THE STORM

Cortés' brilliantly conceived and executed plan for a bloodless seizure of power in Tenochtitlán-Mexico, with the captive

Montezuma acting as his mouthpiece, appeared to have every prospect of success. The broken-spirited Montezuma, together with the principal Mexican chiefs, took a solemn oath of allegiance to the Spanish emperor and even connived at the seizure and imprisonment of his own rebellious brother and nephew. But Cortés had not taken into account the Aztec nation, increasingly resentful of the actions of the arrogant white strangers and increasingly doubtful of their divine attributes. Pedro de Alvarado's wanton attack on the celebrants of a great Aztec religious festival unleashed the storm that would probably have broken sooner or later.[7]

✦✦✦✦ All hastened and ran, as they made their way toward the temple courtyard, in order there to dance the winding dance. And when all had assembled, then the start was made; then began the chanting and the winding dance. And those who had fasted twenty days, and those who had fasted a year, stood aside facing the others. Those who hemmed in [the dancers had] their pine cudgels; whomsoever tried to leave [the dance] they menaced with the pine cudgels. But one who would [leave to] urinate took off his net cape and his forked, heron feather head ornament. But one who did not at once obey, who would not be excluded, or who was mischievous, they soundly beat his back therefor, [or] his thighs, [or] his shoulders, and thrust him outside. They cast him out by force; they threw him on his face — he went falling on his face; he fell forth on his ear. No one in their hold took his leave.

The elder brothers of Uitzilcpochtli — those who had fasted for a year — were much feared, looked upon with terror and awe, and dreaded. And those at the head, the great leaders, the participants, might leave; they did not detain them. Yet all the small boys, those with the lock of hair at the back of the head, with back lock of hair, and those with the jar-shaped hair dress — they who had taken a captive with others' help — the leaders, those called leaders of young men, who were unmarried, who had gone [to war] to take one or two [captives], they also held away. They said to them: "Go along there, knaves! You shall give a good example! Appear not before us!"

And after this, when already the feast was taking place, all were dancing and singing; there was song with dance, and the song resounded like the dashing of waves.

When now it was time, and the moment was opportune for the

---

[7] Arthur J. O. Anderson and Charles E. Dibble, Florentine Codex, Book XII, The Conquest, Chs. 19 and 20 (Sahagún, *General History of the Things of New Spain*). Used by kind permission of the authors.

Spaniards to slay them, then they issued forth girt for battle; they came
to block everywhere the ways leading out and in — the Eagle Gate,
the Little Palace, the Point of Reeds, and the Mirror Serpent. And
when they had closed them off and also various other places, [the
people] were contained, so that nowhere could they get out.

And this having been done, they then entered the Temple
Courtyard to slay them. They whose task it was to kill them went
only afoot, each with [his] leather shield, some with their iron-studded
shields, and each with iron sword. Then they surrounded those who
danced, whereupon they went among the drums. Then they struck
the arms of the one who beat the drums; they severed both his hands,
and afterwards struck his neck, [so that] his neck [and head] flew off,
falling far away. Then they pierced them all with iron lances, and they
struck each with the iron swords. Of some they slashed open the back,
and then their entrails gushed out. Of some, they split the head; they
hacked the heads to pieces; their heads were completely cut up. And
of some they hit the shoulder; they split open and cut their bodies to
pieces. Some they struck on the shank; some on the thigh. Of some,
they struck the belly, and then their entrails streamed forth. And
when one in vain would run, he would only drag his entrails like something raw, as he tried to flee. Nowhere could he go. And one who
tried to go out, there they struck and pierced him.

But some climbed the wall, and so succeeded in taking flight.
Some entered the various tribal temples, and there escaped. And some
eluded [the Spaniards] among [the dead]; they went in among those
who had died, only feigning death, and were able to escape. But one
who stirred, when they saw him, they pierced.

And the blood of the chieftains ran like water; it spread out
slippery, and a foul odor rose from the blood. And the entrails lay as
if dragged out. And the Spaniards walked everywhere, searching in
the tribal temples; they went making thrusts everywhere in case someone were hidden there. Everywhere they went, ransacking every tribal
temple as they hunted.

And when [all this] became known, there then was a shout:
"O chieftains! O Mexicans! Hasten here! Let all prepare the devices,
shields, and arrows! Come! Hasten here! Already the chieftains have
died; they have been put to death, destroyed, shattered, O Mexicans,
O Chieftains!" Thereupon there was an outcry, a shouting, a shrieking
with hands striking the lips. Quickly the chieftains marshalled themselves; as if working with a will they brought the arrows and shields.
Then the fray was joined. They shot at them with barbed arrows,
spears, and tridents, and they loosed darts with broad, obsidian points
at them. It was as if a [mass of] deep yellow reeds spread over the
Spaniards.

7. THE FALL OF TENOCHTITLÁN

For three months the Aztec nation fought for its independence with incredible valor and fortitude. Not until a great part of the city was in ruins, and the streets and canals were choked with corpses, did the gallant Guatemoc, the last Aztec war chief, surrender in the name of his people. An Aztec account of the fall of Tenochtitlán conveys with simple eloquence the pathos of the surrender and the terrible aftermath of the Conquest.[8]

✣✣✣✣ And when night had fallen, then it rained and sprinkled at intervals. Late at night the flame become visible; just so was it seen, just so it emerged as if it came from the heavens. Like a whirlwind it went spinning around and revolving; it was as if embers burst out of it — some very large, some very small, some like sparks. Like a coppery wind it arose, crackling, snapping, and exploding loudly. Then it circled the dike and traveled toward Coyonacazco; then it went into the middle of the lake there to be lost.

None shouted; none spoke aloud.

And on the next day, nothing more happened. All remained quiet, and also our foes [so] remained.

But the Captain [Cortés] was watching from a roof-top at Amaxac — from the roof-top of [the house of] Aztauatzin — under a canopy. It was a many-colored canopy. He looked toward [us] common folk; the Spaniards crowded about him and took counsel among themselves.

And [on our side] were Quauhtemoc and the other noblemen — the vice ruler Tlacotzin, the lords' judge Petlauhtzin, the captain of the armies Motelchiuhtzin; the constable of Mexico; and the lord priest; and also the noblemen of Tlatilulco — the general Coyoueuetzin; the commanding general Temilotzin; the army commander Topantemoctzin; the chief justice Auelitoctzin; the captain of the armies Uitziliuitzin; and the courtier Uitzitzin. All of these noblemen were assembled at Tolmayecan; they appeared to consult among themselves how to do that which we were to undertake and how we should yield to [the Spaniards].

Thereafter only two [men] took Quauhtemoc in a boat. The two who took him and went with him were the seasoned warrior Teputzitoloc, and Yaztachimal, Quauhtemoc's page. And the one who poled [the boat] was named Cenyaotl.

And when they carried Quauhtemoc off, then there was weep-

[8] Arthur J. O. Anderson and Charles E. Dibble, Florentine Codex, Book XII, The Conquest, Chs. 39 and 40 (Sahagún, *General History of the Things of New Spain*). MS. Used by kind permission of the authors.

ing among all the common folk. They said: "Now goeth the young lord Quauhtemoc; now he goeth to deliver himself to the gods, the Spaniards!"

And when they had betaken themselves to bring and disembark him, thereupon all the Spaniards came to see. They drew him along; the Spaniards took him by the hand. After that they took him up to the roof-top, where they went to stand him before the Captain, the war leader. And when they had proceeded to stand him before [Cortés], they looked at Quauhtemoc, made much of him, and stroked his hair. Then they seated him with [Cortés] and fired the guns. They hit no one with them, but only made them go off above, [so that] they passed over the heads of the common folk. Then [some Mexicans] only fled. With this the war reached its end.

Then there was shouting; they said: "Enough! Let it end! Eat greens!" When they heard this, the common folk thereupon issued forth. On this, they went, even into the lagoon.

And as they departed, leaving by the great road, once more they there slew some, wherefore the Spaniards were wroth that still some again had taken up their obsidian-bladed swords and their shields. Those who dwelt in house clusters went straightway to Amaxac; they went direct to where the ways divide. There the common folk separated. So many went toward Tepeyacac, so many toward Xoxouiltitlan, so many toward Nonoalco. But toward Xolloco and toward Macatzintamal no one went.

And all who lived in boats and [in houses] on poles, and those at Tolmayecan, went into the water. On some, the water reached to the stomach; some, to the chest; and on some it reached to the neck. And some were all submerged, there in the deeps. Little children were carried on the backs [of their elders]; cries of weeping arose. Some went on happy and rejoicing as they traveled crowding on the road. And those who owned boats, all the boatmen, left by night, and even [continued to] leave all day. It was as if they pushed and crowded one another as they set out.

And everywhere the Spaniards were seizing and robbing the people. They sought gold; as nothing did they value the green stone, quetzal feathers and turquoise [which] was everywhere in the bosoms or in the skirts of the women. And as for us men, it was everywhere in [our] breech clouts and in [our] mouths.

And [the Spaniards] seized and set apart the pretty women — those of light bodies, the fair [-skinned] ones. And some women, when they were robbed, covered their face with mud and put on old, mended shirts and rags for their shifts. They put all rags on themselves.

And also some of us men were singled out — those who were strong, grown to manhood, and next the young boys, of whom they would make messengers, who would be their runners, and who were

known as their servers. And on some they burned [brand marks] on their cheeks; on some they put paint on their cheeks; on some they put paint on their lips.

And when the shield was laid down, when we gave way, it was the year count Three House and the day count was One Serpent.

8. THE SUN-GOD IN GUATEMALA

After his victory over the Aztecs, Cortés sent Pedro de Alvarado, called "Tunatiuh," the sun, by the Indians because of his yellow hair and ruddy complexion, to conquer the mountainous land of Guatemala, inhabited by powerful tribes of Maya stock. Alvarado's devastating progress through northern Central America is commemorated in the so-called Annals of the Cakchiquels, written in the Cakchiquel language by educated natives, probably during the early half of the seventeenth century.[9]

✠✠✠✠ It was on the day I Hunahpu when the Castilians arrived at Iximche with their chief, Tunatiuh. The people went forth to meet Tunatiuh with the chiefs Belehe Qat and Cahi Ymox. Good was the heart of Tunatiuh when he entered the city with the chiefs. There was no fighting and Tunatiuh rejoiced when he entered Iximche. Thus did the Castilians enter of yore, O my children; but it was a fearful thing when they entered; their faces were strange, and the chiefs took them for gods. We, even we, your father, saw them when they first set foot in Iximche, at the palace of Tzupam where Tunatiuh slept. The chief came forth, and truly he frightened the warriors; he came from his chamber and called the rulers: "Why do you make war with me, when I also can make it?" said he. "Not at all. Why should so many warriors find their death? Do you see any pitfalls among them?" So replied the chiefs, and he went to the house of the chief Chicbal.

Then Tunatiuh agreed to join the chiefs in their wars, and the chiefs said to him: "O thou God, we have two wars, one with the Tzutuhils, one at Panatacat." Thus spake the chiefs. Only five days after, Tunatiuh went forth from the capital. Then the Tzutuhils were conquered by the Castilians. It was the day 7 Camey that the Tzutuhils were destroyed by the Castilians.

Twenty-five days afterwards Tunatiuh went forth from the capital to Cuzcatan, going there to destroy Atacat. On the day 2

[9] Pedro de Alvarado, *An Account of the Conquest of Guatemala*, edited by Sedley J. Mackie, New York, The Cortés Society, 1924, Appendix I, pp. 93-98.

Queh, Atacat was slain by the Castilians, with all his warriors. There went with Tunatiuh all his Mexicans to this battle.

On the day 10 Hunahpu he returned from Cuzcatan. He had been absent only forty days to make the conquest at Cuzcatan when he returned to the capital. Then Tunatiuh asked for a daughter of one of the chiefs, and she was given to Tunatiuh by the chiefs.

A Demand for Money is Made

Then Tunatiuh began to ask the chiefs for money. He wished that they should give him jars full of precious metals, and even their drinking cups and crowns. Not receiving anything, Tunatiuh became angry and said to the chiefs: "Why have you not given me the metal? If you do not bring me the precious metal in all your towns, choose then, for I shall burn you alive and hang you." Thus did he speak to the chiefs.

Then Tunatiuh cut from three of them the gold ornaments they wore in their ears. The chiefs suffered keenly from this violence, and wept before him. But Tunatiuh was not troubled, and said: "I tell you that I want the gold here within five days. Woe to you if you do not give it. I know my heart." So said he to the chiefs. The word was then given. The chiefs gathered together all their metals, those of the parents and children of the king, and all that the chiefs could get from the people.

While they were gathering the gold for Tunatiuh, a priest of the Demon showed himself. "I am the lightning; I will destroy the Castilians." So said he to the chiefs. "I will destroy them by fire. When I beat the drum let the chiefs come forth and go to the other bank of the river. This I shall do on the day 7 Ahmak." Thus did this priest of the Demon speak to the chiefs. Truly the chiefs thought that they should trust in the words of this man. It was when they were gathering the gold that we went forth.

How We Went Forth from the City

The day 7 Ahmak was that of the going forth. They deserted the city of Iximche on account of the priest of the Demon, and the chiefs left it. "Yes, truly, Tunatiuh shall die," said they. "There is no more war in the heart of Tunatiuh, as he now rejoices in the gold given him." Thus it was that our city was abandoned on the day 7 Ahmak on account of a priest of the Demon, O my children.

But what the chiefs did was soon known to Tunatiuh. Ten days after we had left the city, war was begun by Tunatiuh. On the day 4 Camey began our destruction. Then began our misery. We scattered in the forests; all our towns were taken, O my children; we were slaughtered by Tunatiuh. The Castilians entered the city and they arrived as to a deserted spot. From that time the Castilians were

hated by the Cakchiquels. They made trenches, they dug pitfalls, that the horses might be killed, and war was waged by their men. Many men of the Castilians were slain, and many horses killed in the pitfalls. The Quichés and Tzutuhils were destroyed and all their villages ruined by the Cakchiquels. Only thus did the Castilians let them live, and only thus were they let live by all the villagers. One hundred and eighty days after the desertion of the city of Iximche was completed the ninth year (of the second cycle).

On the day 2 Ah was completed the 29th year after the Revolt.

During the tenth year the war continued with the Castilians. But the Castilians having received aid in this tenth year at Xepau, carried on the war with such vigor that they destroyed the forces of the nation.

Tunatiuh then went forth from Xepau, and so harassed us that the people would not come before him. There were lacking one hundred and twenty days to complete two years since we had abandoned the capital, now deserted, when Tunatiuh came there on his march in order to set fire to the city. On the day 4 Camey, two years less six months after the beginning of the war, he set fire to the capital and returned.

On the day 12 Ah was completed the 30th year after the Revolt.

7 ✣ The Conquest of Peru

The epic conquest of Mexico challenged other Spaniards to match the exploits of Cortés and his companions. The work of discovering a golden kingdom reported to lie beyond the "South Sea" was undertaken by Francisco Pizarro, an illiterate Spanish soldier of fortune of whose early history little is known. Pizarro recruited two partners for his Peruvian venture: Diego Almagro, an adventurer of equally obscure antecedents, and Hernando de Luque, a priest who acted as financial agent for the trio. Two preliminary expeditions, fitted out from Panama in 1524 and 1526, yielded enough finds of gold and silver to confirm the existence of the elusive kingdom.

In December, 1531, Pizarro again sailed from Panama for the south with a force of some 200 men, and landed in the spring on the Peruvian coast. On their arrival the Spaniards learned that civil war was raging in the Inca Empire. Atahualpa, an illegitimate son of the late emperor, had risen against the lawful heir to the throne, had defeated him in a war marked by great slaughter, and had made him prisoner. Atahualpa was advancing toward the imperial capital of Cuzco when messengers brought him news of the arrival of the white strangers. After an exchange of messages and gifts between the leaders, the two armies advanced to a meeting at Cajamarca, high in the mountains.

There, in a famous scene, the priest Valverde stepped forward to harangue the bewildered Inca concerning his obligations to the Christian God and the Spanish king until the angry monarch threw down a Bible which Valverde had handed him. At a signal from Pizarro his ambushed soldiers, supported by cavalry and artillery, rushed forward to slay hundreds of the terrified Indians and take the Inca prisoner. Later, after a farcical trial, the Inca was found guilty of polygamy, idolatry, the murder of his brother Huascar, and was condemned to burn at the stake, a sentence commuted to strangling on his acceptance of baptism.

Pizarro, posing as a defender of the legitimate Inca line, now proclaimed Huascar's brother Manco the new Inca. But Manco was not content to play the part of a Quisling. A formidable native insurrection, organized and led by Manco himself, broke out in many sections of the empire. Defeated at last by a force under the command of Almagro, just returned from an unprofitable expedition to Chile, the Inca retreated to a remote part of the mountains, where he and his successors maintained a shadowy court for many years.

Indian resistance had not yet ended when the Spaniards began fighting among themselves. Claiming that Cuzco was rightfully his, Almagro seized the city and made war on the Pizarro brothers. Before the civil wars in Peru had run their course, four of the Pizarro "brothers of doom" had met violent deaths; the Almagros, father and son, had died on the block; a royal viceroy, Blasco Núñez de Vela, had been slain in battle, and numberless others had lost their lives. Peace and order were not solidly established in the country until the administration of the Viceroy Francisco de Toledo, who came out in 1569, a quarter-century after the beginning of the great civil wars.

1. RENDEZVOUS IN CAJAMARCA

As the conquest of Peru unfolded, it repeated in a number of important ways the sequence of events in Mexico. Perhaps in direct imitation of Cortés, Pizarro sought to win a quick and relatively bloodless victory by seizing the person of the Inca Atahualpa, through whom he may have hoped to rule the country, much as Cortés had done with Montezuma. In one important respect, however, the Peruvian story differs from that of Mexico. If Montezuma's undoing was his passive acceptance of the divinity of the invaders and their inevitable triumph, Atahualpa erred disastrously in his serious underestimation of the massed striking power of the small Spanish forces. He had been led to believe that the swords were no more dangerous

than women's weaving battens, that the firearms were capable of firing only two shots, and that the horses were powerless at night. This last illusion apparently led to his delayed entry into Cajamarca at dusk, instead of at noon, as Pizarro had been told to expect. Francisco de Jérez (1504–?), secretary to Pizarro and an active participant in the conquest, describes the fateful meeting at Cajamarca.[1]

✠✠✠✠ When the Governor saw that it was near sunset, and that Ataliba did not move from the place to which he had repaired, although troops still kept issuing out of his camp, he sent a Spaniard to ask him to come into the square to see him before it was dark. As soon as the messenger came before Atabaliba, he made an obeisance to him, and made signs that he should come to where the Governor waited. Presently he and his troops began to move, and the Spaniard returned and reported that they were coming, and that the men in front carried arms concealed under their clothes, which were strong tunics of cotton, beneath which were stones and bags and slings; all of which made it appear that they had a treacherous design. Soon the van of the enemy began to enter the open space. First came a squadron of Indians dressed in a livery of different colours, like a chess board. They advanced, removing the straws from the ground, and sweeping the road. Next came three squadrons in different dresses, dancing and singing. Then came a number of men with armour, large metal plates, and crowns of gold and silver. Among them was Atabaliba in a litter lined with plumes of macaws' feathers, of many colours and adorned with plates of gold and silver. Many Indians carried it on their shoulders on high. Next came two other litters and two hammocks, in which were some principal chiefs; and lastly, several squadrons of Indians with crowns of gold and silver.

As soon as the first entered the open space they moved aside and gave space to the others. On reaching the centre of the open space, Atabaliba remained in his litter on high, and the others with him, while his troops did not cease to enter. A captain then came to the front and, ascending the fortress near the open space, where the artillery was posted, raised his lance twice, as for a signal. Seeing this, the Governor asked the Father Friar Vicente if he wished to go and speak to Atabaliba, with an interpreter? He replied that he did wish it, and he advanced, with a cross in one hand and the Bible in the other, and going amongst them: "I am a Priest of God, and I teach Christians the things of God, and in like manner I come to teach you. What I teach is that which God says to us in this Book. Therefore, on the part of God and of the Christians, I beseech you to be their

---

[1] *Reports on the Discovery of Peru*, translated by C. R. Markham, London, the Hakluyt Society, Cambridge University Press, 1872, pp. 52–56.

friend, for such is God's will, and it will be for your good. Go and speak to the Governor, who waits for you."

Atabaliba asked for the Book, that he might look at it, and the Priest gave it to him closed. Atabaliba did not know how to open it, and the Priest was extending his arm to do so, when Atabaliba, in great anger, gave him a blow on the arm, not wishing that it should be opened. Then he opened it himself, and, without any astonishment at the letters and paper, as had been shown by other Indians, he threw it away from him five or six paces, and, to the words which the monk had spoken to him through the interpreter, he answered with much scorn, saying: "I know well how you have behaved on the road, how you have treated my Chiefs, and taken the cloth from my storehouses." The monk replied: "The Christians have not done this, but some Indians took the cloth without the knowledge of the Governor, and he ordered it to be restored." Atabaliba said: "I will not leave this place until they bring it all to me." The monk returned with this reply to the Governor. Atabaliba stood up on the top of the litter, addressing his troops and ordering them to be prepared. The monk told the Governor what had passed between him and Atabaliba, and that he had thrown the Scriptures to the ground. Then the Governor put on a jacket of cotton, took his sword and dagger, and, with the Spaniards who were with him, entered amongst the Indians most valiantly; and, with only four men who were able to follow him, he came to the litter where Atabaliba was, and fearlessly seized him by the arm, crying out *Santiago*. Then the guns were fired off, the trumpets were sounded, and the troops, both horse and foot, sallied forth.

On seeing the horses charge, many of the Indians who were in the open space fled, and such was the force with which they ran that they broke down part of the wall surrounding it, and many fell over each other. The horsemen rode them down, killing and wounding, and following in pursuit. The infantry made so good an assault upon those that remained that in a short time most of them were put to the sword. The Governor still held Atabaliba by the arm, not being able to pull him out of the litter because he was raised so high. Then the Spaniards made such a slaughter amongst those who carried the litter that they fell to the ground, and, if the Governor had not protected Atabaliba, that proud man would there have paid for all the cruelties he had committed.

The Governor, in protecting Atabaliba, received a slight wound in the hand. During the whole time no Indian raised his arms against a Spaniard. So great was the terror of the Indians at seeing the Governor force his way through them, at hearing the fire of the artillery, and beholding the charging of the horses, a thing never before heard of, that they thought more of flying to save their lives

than of fighting. All those who bore the litter of Atabaliba appeared to be principal chiefs. They were all killed, as well as those who were carried in the other litters and hammocks. One of them was the page of Atabaliba, and a great lord, and the others were lords of many vassals, and his Councillors. The chief of Caxamalca was also killed, and others; but, the number being very great, no account was taken of them, for all who came in attendance on Atabaliba were great lords. The Governor went to his lodging, with his prisoner Atabaliba, despoiled of his robes, which the Spaniards had torn off in pulling him out of the litter. It was a very wonderful thing to see so great a lord, who came in such power, taken prisoner in so short a time.

2. DEATH OF A HERO

Pizarro, suspecting that Atahualpa planned to lead a revolt against Spanish rule, presided over a grotesque trial which ended in the execution of the Inca for his alleged crimes. The Spaniards proclaimed a new puppet Inca in the person of the youthful Manco, brother of the murdered Huascar. Three years after his inaugural, taking advantage of growing discontent with Spanish rule, Manco led and directed a nationwide uprising against the invaders. A large Indian army laid siege to Cuzco for ten months, but failed by a narrow margin to take the city. Defeated at last by superior Spanish weapons and tactics, and by food shortages in his army, Manco retreated to a fastness in the Andean mountains, where he and his successors maintained a kind of Inca government-in-exile until 1572, when a Spanish military expedition entered the mountains, broke up the imperial court, and captured the last Inca, Tupac Amaru, who was beheaded in a solemn ceremony at Cuzco. Pedro Pizarro (1514–1571?), a first cousin of the conqueror of Peru and a participant in the defense of Cuzco, relates an incident of the siege, the Spanish capture of the key Inca fortress of Sacsahuaman.[2]

❖❖❖❖ When Hernando Pizarro arrived [at the fortress] it had already dawned, and we were all of this day and the next fighting with the Indians who had collected together on the two topmost levels, which could only be gained by means of thirst, awaiting the time when their water should give out, and so it happened that we were

[2] Pedro Pizarro, *Relation of the Discovery and Conquest of the Kingdoms of Peru*, translated and edited by Philip A. Means, New York, The Cortés Society, 1921, 2 vols., II, pp. 313–317.

here two or three days until their water came to an end, and when it had given out, they hurled themselves from the highest walls, some in order to flee, and others in order to kill themselves, and others surrendered, and in this way they began to lose courage, and so was gained one level.

And we arrived at the last level [which] had as its captain an *orejon* so valiant that the same might be written of him as has been written of some Romans. This *orejon* bore a shield upon his arms and a sword in his hand and a cudgel in the shield-hand and a morion upon his head. These arms this man had taken from Spaniards who had perished upon the roads, as well as many others which the Indians had in their possession. This *orejon*, then, marched like a lion from one end to another of the highest level of all, preventing the Spaniards who wished to mount with ladders from doing so, and killing the Indians who surrendered, for I understand that he killed more than thirty Indians because they [tried] to surrender and to glide down from the level, and he attacked them with blows upon the head from the cudgel which he carried in his hand. Whenever one of his men warned him that some Spaniard was climbing up in some place, he rushed at him like a lion, with his sword and grasping his shield.

Seeing this, Hernando Pizarro commanded that three or four ladders be set up, so that while he was rushing to one point, they might climb up at another, for the Indians which this *orejon* had with him were all now either surrendered or lacking in courage, and it was he alone who was fighting. And Hernando Pizarro ordered those Spaniards who climbed up not to kill this Indian but to take him alive, swearing that he would not kill him if he had him alive. Then, climbing up at two or three places, the Spaniards won the level. This *orejon*, perceiving that they had conquered him and had taken his stronghold at two or three points, threw down his arms, covered his head and face with his mantle and threw himself down from the level to a spot more than one hundred *estados* below, where he was shattered. Hernando Pizarro was much grieved that they had not taken him alive.

Having won this fortress, Hernando Pizarro stationed here fifty infantrymen with a captain named Juan Ortiz, a native of Toledo, providing them with many vessels in which they had water and food, and fortifying the part where they were to be. And he left them some crossbows and arquebuses, and we went down to Cuzco. And the taking of the fortress was the reason why the Indians withdrew a little, giving up the part of the city which they had gained. In this manner we were on the alert during more than two months, tearing down some *andenes* by night so that the horsemen might go up by that route, because the Indians always withdrew at night to the strong-

est and most secure place, and this withdrawal was always to some strong *andenes*.

3. THE KNIGHTS OF THE CLOAK

A heavy atmosphere of intrigue, broken by recurrent cycles of murderous violence, hung over Peru in the time of the great civil wars. The last Indian resistance had not yet ended when fighting began between one group of the conquerors, headed by the Pizarro brothers, and another led by Diego de Almagro, over possession of the city of Cuzco. Defeated in battle, Almagro suffered death on the block, but left behind him a large group of supporters who brooded over their poverty and supposed wrongs. Twelve of them, contemptuously dubbed by Pizarro's secretary "the knights of the cape" because they allegedly had only one cloak among them, planned and carried out the assassination of the conqueror of Peru. The Spanish chronicler and official Agustín de Zárate (1520?–?), who came to Peru in 1543 with the Viceroy Blasco Núñez Vela, gives a detailed account of the episode.[3]

✠✠✠✠ It was so widely known in Lima that a plot was afoot to slay the Marquis that many told him of it. He replied that the heads of the others were surety for his own; and to those who advised him to go about attended by guards, he said that he would not have it appear that he was on guard against the judge that his majesty was sending to Peru.

One day Juan de Herrada complained to the Marquis, saying that it was bruited about that he (Pizarro) meant to slay the men of Chile. The Marquis swore that he never had such a design. Juan de Herrada said that this was hard to believe, when they saw him buying many lances and other arms. When the Marquis heard this he reassured them affectionately, saying that the lances were not bought for use against them. And he took some oranges, which were highly prized, being the first grown in that country, and gave them to Juan de Herrada, and whispered that if he had need of anything, he (Pizarro) would provide it. Juan de Herrada kissed his hands for this favor, and, leaving the Marquis secure and confident, he departed for his house, where he, together with the most important men of his

---

[3] Agustín de Zárate, *Historia del descubrimiento y conquista del Perú, in Historiadores primitivos de las Indias*, II, pp. 496–498. (Excerpt translated by the editor.)

faction, agreed to kill the Marquis the following Sunday, since they had not done so on Saint John's Day, as they had planned. . . .

On Saturday of that week, one of them revealed the plot in confession to the priest of the great church, and that night the priest went to tell the story to Antonio Picado, secretary to the Marquis, and asked him to take him to his master. The secretary took him to the house of Francisco Martín, brother of the Marquis, where he was dining with his children. When the priest told him what he had learned, Pizarro changed countenance somewhat, but later on he told his secretary that he believed nothing of the sort, because a few days previously Juan de Herrada had come to speak to him very humbly, and the man who had told that story to the priest must want to ask some favor of him, and had invented that tale to place him (Pizarro) under obligation.

Nevertheless, Pizarro sent for Doctor Juan Velásquez, his lieutenant, and because an indisposition kept the doctor from coming, the Marquis went to his house that night, accompanied only by his secretary and two or three others, by the light of a torch. Finding his lieutenant in bed, he related all that had happened. The lieutenant reassured him, saying that his lordship should not fear; that as long as he had his judge's wand in his hand no one would dare revolt. In which it seems that he kept his word, for when he later fled (as will presently be told) when they came to kill the Marquis, he let himself down from a window into the garden, holding the wand between his teeth.

For all these assurances, the Marquis was so uneasy that on Sunday he did not go to hear Mass at church, but ordered Mass said in his house, for greater security. And when Doctor Juan Velásquez and Captain Francisco de Chaves (who was at that time the leading man in the country, after the Marquis) came out of Mass, they went with many others to the house of the Marquis. When his closest neighbors had paid their respects they returned to their houses, and the doctor and Francisco de Chaves remained to dine with the Marquis. After they had eaten, which must have been between eleven and one o'clock in the afternoon, knowing that all the townspeople were quiet and that the servants of the Marquis had gone to eat, Juan de Herrada and some eleven or twelve others sallied from his house, which must have been more than 300 steps from that of the Marquis, because between them lay the whole length of the square and a good part of the street. And as soon as they came out they unsheathed their swords and shouted as they went along: "Death to the tyrant and traitor who has caused the death of the judge sent by the king!" . . .

Arrived at the house of the Marquis, they left one of their number at the door with a naked sword (which he had blooded in a sheep that was in the yard), crying out: "The tyrant is dead! The

tyrant is dead!" Some citizens wanted to offer aid, but when they heard this they returned to their homes, believing it to be the truth. So Juan de Herrada and his men stormed upstairs. Meanwhile the Marquis, who had been warned of their coming by some Indians at the door, had ordered Francisco de Chaves to close the doors of his room and the large hall, while he went in to arm himself. But Chaves became so excited that without closing any doors he ran out to the stairs, asking "What was that noise?" One of them gave Chaves a sword thrust; and he, seeing himself wounded, put his hand to his sword saying: "What! Do you slay your friends too?" Whereupon all the others gave him many wounds.

So, leaving him dead, they ran toward the hall of the Marquis, at which more than twelve Spaniards who were there fled, jumping from some windows into the garden, and among them Doctor Juan Velásquez, with his judge's wand between his teeth, as was told above, in order to let himself down from the window. And the Marquis, who was arming in his chamber, with his brother Francisco Martín and two other gentlemen, and two grown pages, one named Juan de Vargas, son of Gómez de Tordoya, and the other named Escandón, seeing their enemies so close, without waiting to tie the straps of their cuirasses, ran with sword and shield to the door, where Pizarro and his men defended themselves so valiantly that for a long time they prevented their entry, the Marquis crying: "At them, brother, death to the traitors!"

The men of Chile fought until they slew Francisco Martín, and one of the pages took his place. After a while they realized that Pizarro's group were defending themselves so well that there might be time for help to arrive, and they might be thus surrounded and easily killed. So they determined to end the business quickly by putting forward one of their best-armed men, who gave the Marquis such trouble in killing him that the rest were able to get through the door. Then they all fell upon him with such fury that he was exhausted and could no longer brandish his sword. Then they slew him with a thrust in the throat. As he fell to the floor he called for confession; and as his life ebbed away he made the sign of a cross on the floor and kissed it, and so yielded up his soul to God. His two pages also died; of the men of Chile four died, and others were wounded.

4. HOW THE NEW LAWS WERE RECEIVED IN PERU

The assassins of Pizarro proclaimed Almagro's halfbreed son, commonly known as "Almagro the lad," governor of Peru. But their triumph was of short duration. From Spain came a

judge, Vaca de Castro, sent by Charles V to advise Pizarro concerning the government of his province. Assuring himself of the loyalty of Pizarro's principal captains, Castro made war on Almagro the lad, defeated his army on the "bloody plains of Chupas," and promptly had him tried and beheaded as a traitor to the king. Presently fresh troubles arose. Early in 1544 a new viceroy, Blasco Núñez Vela, arrived in Lima to proclaim the edicts known as the "New Laws of the Indies." These laws, the fruit of years of devoted labor on the part of Father Bartolomé de las Casas to save the Indians from destruction, evoked outraged cries and appeals for their suspension from the Spanish landowners in Peru. When these pleas failed, the desperate conquistadores rose in revolt and found a leader in Gonzalo Pizarro, brother of the murdered Marquis. The chronicler Gómara describes the reception accorded the New Laws in Peru.[4]

✠✠✠✠ Blasco Núñez entered Trujillo amid great gloom on the part of the Spaniards; he publicly proclaimed the New Laws, regulating the Indian tributes, freeing the Indians, and forbidding their use as carriers against their will and without pay. He took away as many vassals as these laws permitted, and vested them in the crown. The people and the town council petitioned for repeal of these ordinances, except for those which regulated Indian tribute and prohibited the use of Indians as carriers; of these provisions they approved. He did not grant their appeal, but instead set very heavy penalties for those judges who should fail to execute the laws, saying that he brought an express order of the emperor for their enforcement, without hearing or granting any appeal. He told them, however, that they had reason to complain of the ordinances; that they should take their case to the emperor; and that he would write to the king that he had been badly informed to order those laws.

When the citizens perceived the severity behind his soft words, they began to curse. Some said that they would leave their wives. Actually, some were ready to leave them for any reason, good or bad, since many had married their lady-loves or camp-followers only on account of an order that stripped them of their estates if they did not do so. Others said that it would be much better not to have a wife and children to maintain, if they were to lose the slaves who supported them by their labors in mines, fields, and other pursuits; others demanded payment for the slaves that were being taken from them, since they had bought them from the crown fifth[5] and they bore the royal brand and mark. Still others said that they were ill-requited for

---

[4] Gómara, *Historia de las Indias*, in *Historiadores primitivos de las Indias*, I, p. 251. (Excerpt translated by the editor.)
[5] The *quinto*, or royal share of the spoils of war. B.K.

THE PLEASANTRIES OF CARBAJAL 143

their labors and services, if in their declining years they were to have no one to serve them; these showed their teeth, decayed from eating toasted corn in the conquest of Peru; others displayed many wounds, bruises, and great lizard bites; the conquerors complained that after wasting their estates and shedding their blood in gaining Peru for the emperor, he was depriving them of the few vassals that he had given them. The soldiers said that they would not go to conquer other lands, since they were denied the hope of holding vassals, but instead would rob right and left all they could; the royal lieutenants and officials complained bitterly of the loss of their allotments of Indians, though they had not maltreated them, and held them not by virtue of their officers but in return for their labors and services.

The priests and friars also declared that they could not support themselves nor serve their churches if they were deprived of their Indian towns; the one who spoke most shamelessly against the viceroy and even against the king was Fray Pedro Múñoz, of the Mercedarian Order, saying how badly the king rewarded those who had served him so well, and that the New Laws smelled of calculation rather than of saintliness, for the king was taking away the slaves that he had sold without returning the money received for them, and that he was taking away Indian towns from monasteries, churches, hospitals, and the conquistadores who had gained them; and, what was worse, they were laying a double tribute and tax on the Indians whom they took away in this fashion and vested in the crown, and that the Indians themselves were weeping over this. There was bad blood between this friar and the viceroy because the latter had stabbed the friar one evening in Málaga, when the viceroy was *corregidor* there.

5. THE PLEASANTRIES OF CARBAJAL

The first phase of the great revolt in Peru ended auspiciously for Gonzalo Pizarro with the defeat and death of the Viceroy Núñez Vela in a battle near Quito. Pizarro now became the uncrowned king of the country. The rebel leader owed much of his initial military success to the resourcefulness and demoniac energy of his eighty-year-old field commander and principal adviser, Francisco de Carbajal. To these qualities Carbajal united an inhuman cruelty that became legendary in Peru. Garcilaso de la Vega, who as a youth witnessed the terrors of Carbajal's regime in Cuzco, gives some examples of the curious wit and humor of Francisco de Carbajal.[6]

[6] Garcilaso de la Vega, *Historia general del Perú*, Buenos Aires, 1944, 3 vols., II, pp. 269-274. (Excerpt translated by the editor.)

✢✢✢✢ The master of the camp, Francisco de Carbajal, priding himself on his soldierly appearance, almost invariably wore, in place of a cape, a Moorish cloak of purple color, with a border and a hood; I saw him in this dress many times. On his head he wore a hat lined with black taffeta and a very plain silk braid; he trimmed the hat with numerous black and white hen feathers, crossed to form the figure X. He wore this finery to set an example to his soldiers; one of the things he most earnestly urged upon them was to wear plumes, no matter of what kind; for he said that plumes were the proper adornment and device of soldiers, and not of civilians, for in the latter it indicated frivolity, whereas in the former it was a mark of gallantry. . . .

Francisco de Carbajal had a fund of diverting stories that he would tell on all occasions. I wish I remembered them all and could write them down here, for they were amusing. I shall tell those that I remember of the more decent kind, lest the freedom of his language (which was very great) give offense.

In pursuing Diego Centeno, one day Carbajal captured three soldiers of the kind that he called "weavers," who changed sides as their advantage required. Since he never pardoned such men when he caught them, he ordered these to be hanged. After two had been hanged, the third, seeking some pretext for a pardon, called out: "Pardon me, your worship, for I have eaten your bread!" And actually, as his soldier, he had often eaten at his table. To which Carbajal replied: "A curse on bread that had such evil use!" And turning to the hangman, he said: "Since this gentleman has eaten of my bread, hang him over there, on the highest branch of all. . . ."

Earlier, I mentioned that Francisco de Carbajal strangled Doña María Calderón and hung her from a window of her house. . . . I shall now relate what I omitted before. Doña María Calderón, though in the power of her enemies, spoke quite openly against Gonzalo Pizarro and his tyranny, and in ordinary conversation could say nothing but evil of him. Carbajal, who learned of it, sent her one, two, and more warnings to desist from such remarks, on the basis that they were neither discreet nor good for her health. She received the same warning from other persons who feared that harm would come to her. Doña María Calderón, instead of curbing her speech and mending her ways, henceforth spoke with even greater freedom and disrespect, which obliged Carbajal to come to her house in order to correct the situation. There he said to her: "Fellow godparent" (which she was, in reality), "do you know that I have come to strangle you?" She, in her usual debonair way, thinking that Carbajal was joking, replied: "Go to the Devil, you crazy drunk, I don't care to listen to your jokes." Carbajal said: "I am not joking, really, for I have come to twist your neck so that your ladyship may not speak so much evil; and to prove it to your ladyship, I order these African soldiers to strangle you,"

signaling to three or four Negroes that he always took with him for such exploits. They immediately strangled her and hung her from a window that looked out upon the street. Carbajal, passing below her, raised his eyes and said, "For the life of me, fellow godparent, I don't know what I shall do if you don't learn a lesson from this."

6. THE MAN WHO WOULD BE KING

After his victory over the viceroy Vela, Carbajal and other advisers urged Pizarro to proclaim himself King of Peru. But Pizarro, a weaker man than his iron-willed lieutenant, hesitated to avow the revolutionary meaning of his actions. The arrival of a smooth-tongued envoy of the crown, La Gasca, who announced suspension of the New Laws and offered pardons and rewards to all repentant rebels, caused a trickle of desertions from Pizarro's ranks that in time became a flood. As his army melted away, Carbajal is said to have hummed the words of an old Spanish song: "These my hairs, mother, two by two the breeze carries them away." In the sequel the rebellion collapsed almost without a struggle, and its leaders ended on the gallows or the block. Garcilaso de la Vega describes the execution of Gonzalo Pizarro.[7]

✠✠✠✠ It remains only for me to tell of the pitiful death of Gonzalo Pizarro. He spent all of his last day in confession. . . . The ministers of justice, coming and going, sought to hasten the execution of his sentence. One of the gravest of them, angered by the delay, said loudly: "Well! Are they not done with the fellow yet?" All the soldiers who heard him took offense at his disrespect and hurled a thousand oaths and insults at him, but though I remember many of them and knew the man, I will not set them down here nor give his name. He went without saying a word, before it came to blows, something he had reason to fear in view of the indignation and annoyance that the soldiers displayed at his rudeness. A little later Gonzalo Pizarro came out and mounted a saddled mule that was held ready for him. He was covered with a cape; although one author says that his hands were tied, it was not so. They threw one end of a halter over the neck of the mule, in compliance with the law. In his hands he bore an image of Our Lady, to whom he was most devoted. He continually implored her to intercede for his soul. Halfway along he asked for a crucifix. A priest, one of the twelve that accompanied him, gave him

[7] Garcilaso de la Vega, *Historia general del Perú*, II, pp. 276–277. (Excerpt translated by the editor.)

one. Gonzalo Pizarro took it and gave the priest the image of Our Lady, kissing with great affection the hem of the dress of the image. With the crucifix in his hands, never taking his eyes from it, he came up to the platform that had been made for his execution. This he ascended, and, standing at one side, he spoke to the people who were watching him. Among them were all the men of Peru, soldiers and citizens, excepting only the grandees who had turned against him — and even some of them were there, disguised and muffled up. He said in a loud voice:

"Gentlemen, your worships know well that my brothers and I gained this empire. Many of your worships hold *repartimientos* of Indians that the Marquis, my brother, gave you; many others hold them from me. Moreover, many of your worships owe me money that you borrowed from me; many others have received money from me as free gift. I die so poor that even the clothes I wear belong to the executioner who will cut off my head. I have nothing with which to ensure the good of my soul. Therefore I appeal to those of your worships who owe me money, as well as those who do not, to grant me the alms and charity of having as many masses as possible said for my soul, for I place hopes in God that by the blood and passion of Our Lord Jesus Christ, His Son, and through the alms that your worships grant me, He will have pity of me and will pardon my sins. And may your worships remain with God."

Before he had finished his plea for alms, there arose a general lament, with great moans and sobs and tears, from those who heard his pitiful words. Gonzalo Pizarro kneeled before the crucifix that he bore, and which was placed on a table on the platform. The executioner, who was named Juan Enríquez, came up to place a bandage over his eyes. Gonzalo Pizarro said to him: "I do not need it." And when he saw that Enríquez was raising the sword to cut off his head, he said: "Do your task well, brother Juan." He meant that he should do the job cleanly, and not prolong the agony, as frequently happens. The executioner replied: "I promise it to your Lordship." Saying this, with his left hand he raised his beard, which was long, about eight inches, and round, for it was not the fashion in those days to clip beards. And with one back stroke he cut off his head as easily as if it were a lettuce leaf and held it in his hand, and the body fell slowly to the ground. Such was the end of this good gentleman. The executioner, true to his trade, wanted to despoil him of his clothing, but Diego Centeno, who had come to inter the body safely, forbade him to approach it and promised him a good sum of money for the clothing. And so they bore the body to Cuzco; they buried Pizarro in his clothes, for there was no one to offer him a burial shroud. They buried him in the Convent of Nuestra Señora de las Mercedes, in the same chapel where were buried the two Don Diegos de Almagro, father and son, in order

that they might be equal and comrades in all things — in their common conquest of the land, in the common death of all three on the executioner's block, and in the pauper's burial of all three in a common grave, as if they even lacked earth enough to cover each one separately. Fortune made them equal in all things, as if to prevent any one of them from lording it over the others and as if to prevent all three from setting themselves above the Marquis Francisco Pizarro, who was brother of the one and comrade of the other and who was likewise slain and buried in a pauper's grave, as was told above. Thus all four were brothers and comrades in all and for all. Such is the way of the world (as those remarked who viewed these matters dispassionately) with those who serve it most and best, for such was the end of those who won that empire called Peru.

8 ✦ The Quest for El Dorado

From its original base in the West Indies, and from the two new centers of Mexico and Peru, the great movement of Spanish expansion radiated in all directions.

The North American mainland early attracted the attention of Spanish gold-seekers and slave-hunters based in the West Indies. In 1513 Ponce de León, governor of Puerto Rico, sailed west and discovered a subtropical land to which he gave the name La Florida. In the 1520's another expedition, ineptly led by Pánfilo de Narváez, met with disaster in the vast, indefinite expanse then called La Florida. Only four survivors of the venture, among them its future chronicler, Cabeza de Vaca, reached safety in Mexico after a lengthy, circuitous trek over the plains of Texas. Cabeza de Vaca's tales of adventure, with their hints of populous cities just beyond the horizon, inspired the conquistador Hernando de Soto to try his fortune in La Florida. After three years of unprofitable wanderings and struggles with Indians in the great area between South Carolina and Arkansas, the discoverer of the Mississippi died in the wilderness of a fever.

The glowing account of a certain Fray Marcos, who claimed to have seen in the distant northern lands one of the legendary Seven Cities of Cibola, induced Viceroy Antonio de Mendoza to send an expedition there under the command of Francisco Vásquez de Coro-

nado. Coronado, disillusioned by the humble reality of the Zuñi pueblos of Arizona, the original of the Cibola myth, went on to discover the Grand Canyon of the Colorado, and then pushed east in search of still another El Dorado, this time called Quivira. In the spring of 1542 Coronado, much chagrined at his failure to find any treasure, returned to Mexico.

The golden will-o'-the-wisp that lured Spanish knights into the deserts of the Southwest also beckoned to them from South American jungles and mountains. From the town of Santa Marta, on the coast of present-day Colombia, an expedition led by Jiménez de Quesada departed in 1539 on a difficult pilgrimage through jungles and mountains in search of a legendary Gilded Chieftain; they suffered incredible hardships before they finally emerged on the cool plateau of Bogotá. There they met and conquered the Chibchas — the last advanced Indian culture discovered by the Spaniards.

In the southern reaches of the continent, which contained little gold or silver, new agricultural and pastoral settlements arose. Pedro de Valdivia, a captain under Pizarro, laid the foundations of the colony of Chile in struggle with the tough Araucanian Indians, losing his life in battle in 1553. In the same period Buenos Aires was founded on the Plate estuary by Pedro de Mendoza, but was soon abandoned by its famished inhabitants, who moved upstream to the newly risen town of Asunción in Paraguay. Not until 1580 was Buenos Aires permanently refounded by colonists coming downstream from Asunción.

1. ADVICE TO A WOULD-BE CONQUEROR

The conquest of America, like similar enterprises before and after, or like our own gold rushes, attracted a wide variety of types. A common figure in the conquest was the adventurer, who frequently had a military background and not infrequently a past that he preferred to forget; such, assuredly, were the "fine-feathered birds and great talkers" that Oviedo warns against below. But there were other thousands of young and high-spirited hidalgos, "men of good family who were not reared behind the plow," who sailed in the ships bound for the Indies. In the matter of motives, it is probably safe to assume that of the trinity of motives usually assigned to the Spanish conquistador ("God, Gold, and Glory"), the second was uppermost in the minds of most.[1]

---

[1] Gonzalo Fernández de Oviedo y Valdés, *Historia general*, V, pp. 213–218. (Excerpt translated by the editor.)

✠✠✠✠ Sir captain: Understand me and understand yourself. When you make up a company to go to the Indies, and especially in Seville (for it is there, on the steps of the cathedral, that the soldiers are wont to gather), you should first examine the face of each; having scrutinized the face, you will see part of the evil beneath. But because the outward aspect may deceive you in the choice of a soldier, you should make secret inquiry concerning his habits, his mode of life, his skills, and his nationality; for even in that sacred place[2] there are some who will lie about their countries and even their own names for the sake of going to the Indies. And do not attach much importance to his height and his well-combed beard, but rather try to find out whether he is of good character and family, and a frank and modest man. And if he tells you that he was in the battle of Ravenna, dismiss him, if he is a Spaniard, since he remained alive or was not taken prisoner; and do the same if he speaks of the battle of Pavia; and dismiss him if he tells you that he was in the sack of Genoa or Rome, since he did not get rich; and if he was there, and gambled his wealth away or lost it, do not trust him. Those slashed hose and shoes will not do at all for such lands as the Indies, full of ambushes and thick with trees and hawthorns, where there are so many rivers to swim and so many swamps and bogs to cross.

The dress and the person should conform to your needs; above all do not take a man whose faith is suspect, or one less than twenty-five or more than fifty years old. And do not take such fine-feathered birds and great talkers as those I mentioned above, for in the many years that I have seen them in the Indies, and before that in Europe, I have found that few turn out well. As long as there is gold, or they suspect that they will get it through your hands, they will serve you diligently; but be careful, for the minute that things do not go their way they will either slay you or sell you or forsake you, when they find that you promised them more in Spain than you can produce. . . .

And before you begin this examination, examine yourself, and make sure that your aim is to serve God and your king by converting the Indians and treating them well, and by finding a way to lead them to the Republic of Christ. Do not enslave them without cause, or stain your hands with blood without cause or justice, or rob them or remove them from the lands where God created them; he gave them life

---

[2] The first chronicler of the Indies alludes here to the immemorial custom of meeting at the cathedral of Seville to arrange all manner of contracts, which gave rise likewise to the practice of hiring and negotiating with soldiers bound for the Indies, who usually were found on the steps, in the yard, lined with orange trees, and at the gates of the cathedral. . . . The soldiers awaited outside the church the results of the conferences that the merchants and captains held within; from these conferences commonly developed the great American enterprises and expeditions. [José Amador de los Ríos.]

and humanity not to help you carry out any evil design but in order to save them. . . . And do not say that you are going to the Indies to serve the king and to employ your time as a brave man and an *hidalgo* should; for you know that the truth is just the opposite; you are going solely because you want to have a larger fortune than your father and your neighbors. However, you can do everything you want to do without hurting others or jeopardizing your soul. And do not seek any estate or treasure that might cost you such a price, if in so doing you lose that invaluable treasure by which you were redeemed and God freed you from Hell. . . .

Comrade and friend: If you decide to go to the Indies, when you are in Seville ascertain first of all whether the captain with whom you are going is a man who will fulfill what he promises, and learn on the basis of what word or guaranty you are entrusting your life and person to his will — because many of these captains promise what they do not have, know, or understand; and they pay for your person with words that are worth less than feathers; because feathers, though the wind bear them away, at least have some substance and you know their purpose, which is to float in the air aimlessly; but the words of a liar are without substance and, having been said, are invisible and vanish like air. . . . Do you not see that he speaks of what is yet to come, and promises what he neither has nor understands? And once you are free of the perils of the sea and the land, which are innumerable, and come to the Indies, if he should succeed, he neither knows nor rewards you; and if you fall ill, he does not heal you; and if you should die, he will not bury you. . . . And if he gives you an allotment of Indians, he does not care to ascertain whether you are competent to teach them or whether you yourself have more need of a teacher than of governing others, in order that both your consciences may be at rest. And since these estates are acquired unjustly, God permits them to be lost, and you with them. . . .

I observe that for every man who has made his fortune in these parts and has returned to Castile with or without it, an incomparably larger number have lost both their fortunes and their lives. You will say: What should I do? Shall I hold back from going to the Indies, where so many go and return rich — men who were formerly poor and do not measure up to me in ability, merit, or capacity for work? Is it fitting that for lack of courage I should fail to do what so many have done who are older than I and not of such good health and presence? I do not counsel you not to go to the Indies, nor to go there; but I do counsel you, whether you come or not, first to justify yourself with God and to commend yourself to Him. I am aware that it is proper and necessary to seek one's fortune, especially for men of good family who were not reared behind the plow; but let the under-

taking be well thought out, and once you have determined upon it, never let greed turn you aside from the loyalty that you owe, and never let necessity give occasion for you to be considered an ingrate or to tarnish your good name; for if you only set your mind to it, in the Indies as elsewhere you can live without offense to your fellowmen.

2. THE ADVENTURES OF CABEZA DE VACA

Few chronicles of exploration have the charm and interest of the narrative of Cabeza de Vaca (?–1557), one of the four survivors of Narváez's disastrous expedition to the land of Florida. In refreshing contrast to other Spanish accounts of the Conquest, Cabeza de Vaca's has few scenes of bloodshed and destruction, for, like Robinson Crusoe, it is essentially an absorbing tale of how one individual managed to survive and even prosper modestly in a strange and difficult environment. Honest and humane, Cabeza de Vaca fared reasonably well at the hands of the Indians, who often fed him from their own pitifully meager stocks; in time he achieved an exalted reputation among them as a medicine-man of great powers. In the last stage of his great trek over the Texan plains, Cabeza de Vaca was followed by thousands of adoring Indians, "clouds of witnesses" to his healing arts.[3]

✦✦✦✦ Those who there received us, after they had touched us went running to their houses and directly returned, and did not stop running, going and coming, to bring us in this manner many things for support on the way. They fetched a man to me and stated that a long time since he had been wounded by an arrow in the right shoulder, and that the point of the shaft was lodged above his heart, which, he said, gave him much pain, and in consequence, he was always sick. Probing the wound I felt the arrowhead, and found it had passed through the cartilage. With a knife I carried, I opened the breast to the place, and saw the point was aslant and troublesome to take out. I continued to cut, and, putting in the point of the knife, at last with great difficulty I drew the head forth. It was very large. With the bone of a deer, and by virtue of my calling, I made two stitches that threw the blood over me, and with hair from a skin I stanched the flow. They asked me for the arrow-head after I had

3 "The Narrative of Álvar Núñez Cabeza de Vaca," edited by Frederick W. Hodge, in *Spanish Explorers in the Southern United States*, New York, 1907, pp. 96–99, 109–110. Reprinted by permission of the publishers, Charles Scribner's Sons.

taken it out, which I gave, when the whole town came to look at it. They sent it into the back country that the people there might view it. In consequence of this operation they had many of their customary dances and festivities. The next day I cut the two stitches and the Indian was well. The wound I made appeared only like a seam in the palm of the hand. He said he felt no pain or sensitiveness in it whatsoever. This cure gave us control throughout the country in all that the inhabitants had power, or deemed of any value, or cherished. . . .

We left there, and travelled through so many sorts of people, of such diverse languages, the memory fails to recall them. . . . We drew so many followers that we had not use for their services. While on our way through these vales, every Indian carried a club three palms in length, and kept on the alert. On raising a hare, which animals are abundant, they surround it directly and throw numerous clubs at it with astonishing precision. Thus they cause it to run from one to another; so that, according to my thinking, it is the most pleasing sport which can be imagined, as oftentimes the animal runs into the hand. So many did they give us that at night when we stopped we had eight or ten back-loads apiece. Those having bows were not with us; they dispersed about the ridge in pursuit of deer; and at dark came bringing five or six for each of us, besides quail, and other game. Indeed, whatever they either killed or found, was put before us, without themselves daring to take anything until we had blessed it, though they should be expiring of hunger, they having so established the rule, since marching with us.

The women carried many mats, of which the men made us houses, each of us having a separate one, with all his attendants. After these were put up, we ordered the deer and hares to be roasted, with the rest that had been taken. This was done by means of certain ovens made for the purpose. Of each we took a little and the remainder we gave to the principal personage of the people coming with us, directing him to divide it among the rest. Every one brought his portion to us, that we might breathe upon and give it our benediction; for not until then did they dare eat any of it. Frequently we were accompanied by three or four thousand persons, and as we had to breathe upon and sanctify the food and drink for each, and grant permission to do the many things they would come to ask, it may be seen how great was the annoyance. The women first brought us prickly pears, spiders, worms, and whatever else they could gather; for even were they famishing, they would eat nothing unless we gave it to them.

In company with these, we crossed a great river coming from the north, and passing over some plains thirty leagues in extent, we found many persons coming a long distance to receive us, who met us

on the road over which we were to travel, and welcomed us in the manner of those we had left. . . .

We passed through many territories and found them all vacant: their inhabitants wandered fleeing among the mountains, without daring to have houses or till the earth for fear of Christians. The sight was one of infinite pain to us, a land very fertile and beautiful, abounding in springs and streams, the hamlets deserted and burned, the people thin and weak, all fleeing or in concealment. As they did not plant, they appeased their keen hunger by eating roots and the bark of trees. We bore a share in the famine along the whole way; for poorly could these unfortunates provide for us, themselves being so reduced they looked as though they would willingly die. They brought shawls of those they had concealed because of the Christians, presenting them to us; and they related how the Christians at other times had come through the lands, destroying and burning the towns, carrying away half the men, and all the women and the boys, while those who had been able to escape were wandering about fugitives. We found them so alarmed they dared not remain anywhere. They would not nor could they till the earth, but preferred to die rather than live in dread of such cruel usage as they received. Although these showed themselves greatly delighted with us, we feared that on our arrival among those who held the frontier, and fought against the Christians, they would treat us badly and revenge upon us the conduct of their enemies; but, when God our Lord was pleased to bring us there, they began to dread and respect us as the others had done, and even somewhat more, at which we no little wondered. Thence it may at once be seen that, to bring all these people to be Christians and to the obedience of the Imperial Majesty, they must be won by kindness, which is a way certain, and no other is.

3. THE PRAIRIE AND THE BUFFALO

The strange tales told by Cabeza de Vaca and his three companions on their arrival in Mexico in 1536, and the even stranger story told by a certain Fray Marcos, who claimed to have seen in the far north one of the Seven Golden Cities of Cibola (from a great distance, it was true), persuaded Viceroy Antonio de Mendoza to send there an expedition commanded by Francisco Vásquez de Coronado. For two years Spanish knights in armor pursued the elusive realm of gold through the future states of Arizona, New Mexico, Colorado, Oklahoma, Kansas, and possibly Nebraska. Intruders in the great plains that left no trace of their passage, the Spaniards were only repelled by their

immensity, and returned home bitterly disappointed with their failure to find treasure. Pedro de Castañeda, a soldier in Coronado's army of whose life very little is known, describes the prairie and its curious denizen — the American buffalo.[4]

✸✸✸✸ Who could believe that 1,000 horses and 500 of our cows and more than 5,000 rams and ewes and more than 1,500 friendly Indians and servants, in travelling over those plains, would leave no more trace where they had passed than if nothing had been there — nothing — so that it was necessary to make piles of bones and cow-dung now and then, so that the rear guard could follow the army. The grass never failed to become erect after it had been trodden down, and, although it was short, it was as fresh and straight as before.

Another thing was a heap of cow bones, a crossbow shot long, or a very little less, almost twice a man's height in places, and some eighteen feet or more wide, which was found on the edge of a salt lake in the southern part, and this in a region where there are no people who could have made it. The only explanation of this which could be suggested was that the waves which the north winds must make in the lake had piled up the bones of the cattle which had died in the lake, when the old and weak ones who went into the water were unable to get out. The noticeable thing is the number of cattle that would be necessary to make such a pile of bones.

Now that I wish to describe the appearance of the bulls, it is to be noticed first that there was not one of the horses that did not take flight when he saw them first, for they have a narrow, short face, the brow two palms across from eye to eye, the eyes sticking out at the side, so that, when they are running, they can see who is following them. They have very long beards, like goats, and when they are running they throw their heads back with the beard dragging on the ground. There is a sort of girdle round the middle of the body. The hair is very wooly, like a sheep's, very fine, and in front of the girdle the hair is very long and rough like a lion's. They have a great hump, larger than a camel's. The horns are short and thick, so that they are not seen much above the hair. In May they change the hair in the middle of the body for a down, which makes perfect lions of them. They rub against the small trees in the little ravines to shed their hair, and they continue this until only the down is left, as a snake changes his skin. They have a short tail, with a bunch of hair at the end. When they run, they carry it erect like a scorpion. It is worth noticing that the little calves are red and just like ours, but they change their color and appearance with time and age.

[4] "The Narrative of the Expedition of Coronado, by Pedro de Castañeda," edited by F. W. Hodge, in *Spanish Explorers in the Southern United States*, pp. 382–384. Reprinted by permission of the publishers, Charles Scribner's Sons.

Another strange thing was that all the bulls that were killed had their left ears slit, although these were whole when young. The reason for this was a puzzle that could not be guessed. The wool ought to make good cloth on account of its fineness, although the color is not good, because it is the color of buriel.[5]

Another thing worth noticing is that the bulls travelled without cows in such large numbers that nobody could have counted them, and so far away from the cows that it was more than forty leagues from where we began to see the bulls to the place where we began to see the cows. The country they travelled over was level and smooth that if one looked at them the sky could be seen between their legs, so that if some of them were at a distance they looked like smooth-trunked pines whose tops joined, and if there was only one bull it looked as if there were four pines. When one was near them, it was impossible to see the ground on the other side of them. The reason for all this was that the country seemed as round as if a man should imagine himself in a three-pint measure, and could see the sky at the edge of it, about a crossbow shot from him, and even if a man only lay down on his back he lost sight of the ground.

I have not written about other things which were seen nor made any mention of them, because they were not of so much importance, although it does not seem right for me to remain silent concerning the fact that they venerate the sign of the cross in the region where the settlements have high houses. For at a spring which was in the plain near Acuco they had a cross two palms high and as thick as a finger, made of wood with a big square twig for its crosspiece, and many little sticks decorated with feathers around it, and numerous withered flowers, which were the offerings. In a graveyard outside the village at Tutahaco there appeared to have been a recent burial. Near the head there was another cross made of two little sticks tied with cotton thread, and dry withered flowers. It certainly seems to me that in some way they must have received some light from the cross of Our Redeemer, Christ, and it may have come by way of India, from whence they proceeded.

4. IN THE LAND OF AMAZONS

The dream of spices played its part in inspiring the saga of Spanish exploration and conquest. Attracted by accounts of an eastern land where cinnamon trees grew in profusion, in 1539 Gonzalo Pizarro led an expedition from Quito across the Andes

---

[5] The kersey, or coarse woollen cloth out of which the habits of the Franciscan friars were made. Hence the name Grey Friars.

and down the forested eastern slopes of the mountains. Cinnamon was found, but in disappointingly small quantity. Lured on by the customary Indian tall tales of rich kingdoms somewhere beyond the horizon, the treasure-hunters plunged deep into the Amazonian wilderness. Gonzalo's lieutenant Orellana, sent with a party down a certain stream in search of food, found the current too strong to return, and went on to enter a great river whose course he followed in two makeshift boats for a distance of eighteen hundred leagues, eventually emerging from its mouth to reach Spanish settlements in Venezuela in safety. On the banks of the great stream Orellana battled hostile Indians whose womenfolk joined in the fray, on which account he gave the river its Spanish name of Amazonas. Father Gaspar de Carvajal (1504?-1584), whose narrative is the principal source of information on the expedition, describes its encounter with the "Amazons" — an excellent illustration of the myth-making process among the Spaniards of the Conquest.[6]

✢✢✢ On the following Thursday we passed by other villages of medium size, and we made no attempt to stop there. All these villages are the dwellings of fishermen from the interior of the country. In this manner we were proceeding on our way searching for a peaceful spot to celebrate and to gladden the feast of the blessed Saint John the Baptist, herald of Christ, when God willed that, on rounding a bend which the river made, we should see on the shore ahead many villages, and very large ones, which shone white. Here we came suddenly upon the excellent land and dominion of the Amazons. These said villages had been forewarned and knew of our coming, in consequence whereof they [i.e., the inhabitants] came out on the water to meet us, in no friendly mood, and, when they had come close to the Captain, he would have liked to induce them to accept peace, and so he began to speak to them and call them, but they laughed, and mocked us and came up close to us and told us to keep on going and [added] that down below they were waiting for us, and that there they were to seize us all and take us to the Amazons.

The Captain, angered at the arrogance of the Indians, gave orders to shoot at them with the crossbows and arquebuses, so that they might reflect and become aware that we had wherewith to assail them; and in this way damage was inflicted on them and they turned about towards the village to give the news of what they had seen; as for us, we did not fail to proceed and to draw close to the village, and before we were within half a league of putting in, there were along the edge

[6] *The Discovery of the Amazon*, translated by Bertram T. Lee and edited by H. C. Heaton, New York, American Geographical Society, 1934, pp. 212-214. Reprinted by permission of the American Geographical Society.

of the water, at intervals, many squadrons of Indians, and, in proportion as we kept on going ahead, they gradually came together and drew close to their living quarters.

There was in the center of this village a very great horde of fighters, formed in a good squadron, and the Captain gave the order to have the brigantines beached right there where these men were, in order to go look for food, and so it came about that, as we began to come in close to land, the Indians started to defend their village and to shoot arrows at us, and as the fighters were in great numbers it seemed as if it rained arrows; but our arquebusiers and crossbowmen were not idle, because they did nothing but shoot, and although they killed many, they [i.e. the Indians] did not become aware of this, for in spite of the damage that was being done to them they kept it up, some fighting and others dancing: and here we all came very close to perishing, because as there were so many arrows our companions had all they could do to protect themselves from them, without being able to row, in consequence whereof they did [so much] damage to us that before we could jump out on land they had wounded five of us, of whom I was one, for they hit me in one side with an arrow, which went in as far as the hollow region, and, if it had not been for [the thickness of] my clothes, that would have been the end of me.

In view of the danger that we were in, the Captain began to cheer up the men at the oars and urge them to make haste to beach the brigantines, and so, although with hard work, we succeeded in beaching the boats and our companions jumped into the water, which came up to their chests: here there was fought a very serious and hazardous battle, because the Indians were there mixed in among our Spaniards, who defended themselves so courageously that it was a marvelous thing to behold. More than an hour was taken up by this fight, for the Indians did not lose spirit, rather it seemed as if it was being doubled in them, although they saw many of their own number killed, and they passed over them [i.e. their bodies], and they merely kept retreating and coming back again.

I want it to be known what the reason was why these Indians defended themselves in this manner. It must be explained that they are the subjects of, and tributaries to, the Amazons, and, our coming having been made known to them, they went to them to ask help, and there came as many as ten or twelve of them, for we ourselves saw these women, who were there fighting in front of all the Indian men as women captains, and these latter fought so courageously that the Indian men did not dare to turn their backs, and anyone who did turn his back they killed with clubs right there before us, and this is the reason why the Indians kept up their defense for so long. These women are very white and tall, and have hair very long and braided and wound about the head, and they are very robust and go about

naked, [but] with their privy parts covered, with their bows and arrows in their hands, doing as much fighting as ten Indian men, and indeed there was one woman among these who shot an arrow a span deep into one of the brigantines, and others less deep, so that our brigantines looked like porcupines.

5. THE EL DORADO OF SIR WALTER RALEIGH

The life and death of Sir Walter Raleigh, courtier, poet, historian, and promoter of colonial enterprise, are curiously linked to the quest for El Dorado. In 1594 Raleigh came into possession of captured Spanish papers containing a fantastic story of a golden kingdom supposed to be located near the headwaters of the Caroni River, a tributary of the Orinoco. So vast was the capital city of the kingdom that one had to walk through its golden streets for two days in order to reach the center. In 1595 Raleigh, as credulous as any Spanish conquistador, outfitted an expedition to search for the golden city of Manoa. He traveled up the Orinoco to its junction with the Caroni, but decided that his force was too small to attempt further exploration and returned to England to publish a glowing account of the mythical kingdom. In the reign of the pro-Spanish James I Raleigh fell out of favor with the crown and was sentenced to death on charges of conspiracy, but was reprieved without annulment of the sentence. After spending twelve years in the Tower he was released in 1616 on the basis of his assurances that he would bring the king a great store of El Dorado treasure. His second expedition to Guiana was a dismal failure, and on his return to England, Raleigh, aged sixty-six, was beheaded by order of the king. Raleigh's description of the "Rich and Beautiful Empire of Guiana" incorporates just about all the elements that ever entered into the legend of El Dorado, including the themes of lost Inca treasure, the Gilded Chieftain, and a warlike tribe of women.[7]

✦✦✦✦ The empire of Guiana is directly east from Peru towards the sea, and lieth under the equinoctial line, and it hath more abundance of gold than any part of Peru, and as many or more great cities than ever Peru had when it flourished most. It is governed by the same laws, and the emperor and people observe the same religion and the same form and policies in government as was used in Peru, not differing in any

[7] Sir Walter Raleigh, *The Discovery of Guiana*, London, 1887, pp. 24, 32–33, 41–45, 142–143.

part; and as I have been assured by such of the Spaniards as have seen Manoa, the imperial city of Guiana, which the Spaniards call El Dorado, that for the greatness, for the riches, and for the excellent seat, it far exceedeth any of the world, at least of so much of the world as is known to the Spanish nation; it is founded upon a lake of salt water of two hundred leagues long, like unto *mare caspiu*.[8] . . .

[The] Guianians, and also the borderers, and all others in that tract which I have seen, are marvellous great drunkards, in which vice I think no nation can compare with them; and at the times of their solemn feasts, when the Emperor carouseth with his captains, tributaries, and governors, the manner is thus: All those that pledge him are first stripped naked, and their bodies anointed all over with a kind of white balsam (by them called Curai), of which there is great plenty, and yet very dear, amongst them, and it is of all others the most precious, whereof we have had good experience: when they are anointed all over, certain servants of the Emperor having prepared gold made into fine powder, blow it through hollow canes upon their naked bodies, until they be all shining from the foot to the head, and in this sort they sit drinking by twenties and hundreds, and continue in drunkenness sometimes six or seven days together; the same is also confirmed by a letter written into Spain which was intercepted, which Master Robert Dudley told me he had seen. . . .

Undoubtedly those that trade with the Amazons return much gold, which (as is aforesaid) cometh by trade from Guiana, by some branch of a river that falleth from the country into the Amazons, and either it is by the river which passeth by the nations called Tisnados, or by Carepuna. I made inquiries amongst the most ancient and best travelled of the Orinocoponi, and I had knowledge of all the rivers between Orinoco and Amazons, and was very desirous to understand the truth of those warlike women, because of some it is believed, of others not: and though I digress from my purpose, yet I will set down what hath been delivered me for truth of those women; and I spoke with a cazique, or lord of people, that told me he had been in the river, and beyond it also.

The nations of these women are on the south side of the river, in the provinces of Topago, and their chiefest strengths and retreats are in the islands situated on the south side of the entrance, some sixty leagues within the mouth of the said river. The memories of the like women are very ancient as well in Africa as in Asia; in Africa those that had Medusa for queen, others in Scythia, near the rivers of Tanais and Thermadon; we find also that Lampedo and Marthesia were queens of the Amazons; in many histories they are verified to have been, and in divers ages and provinces; but they which are not far from Guiana

---

[8] The Caspian Sea. B.K.

do accompany with men but once in a year, and for the time of one month, which I gather by their relation to be in April.

At that time all the kings of the borders assemble, and the queens of the Amazons, and after the queens have chosen, the rest cast lots for their valentines. This one month they feast, dance, and drink of their wines in abundance, and the moon being done, they all depart to their own provinces. If they conceive and be delivered of a son, they return him to the father, if of a daughter, they nourish it and retain it; and as many as have daughters send unto the begetters a present, all being desirous to increase their own sex and kind; but that they cut off the right dug of the breast I do not find to be true.

It was further told me that if in the wars they took any prisoners that they used to accompany with those also at what time soever, but in the end for certain they put them to death; for they are said to be very cruel and bloodthirsty, especially to such as offer to invade their territories. These Amazons have likewise great store of these plates of gold, which they recover by exchange chiefly for a kind of green stone, which the Spaniards call Piedras Hijadas, and we use for spleen stones, and for the disease of the stone we also esteem them: of these I saw divers in Guiana, and commonly every king or cazique hath one, which their wives for the most part wear, and they esteem them as great jewels. . . .

To conclude, Guiana is a country that hath yet her maidenhead, never sacked, turned, nor wrought, the face of the earth hath not been torn, nor the virtue and salt of the soil spent by manuring, the graves have not been opened for gold, the mines not broken with sledges, nor their images pulled down out of their temples. It hath never been entered by any army of strength, and never conquered or possessed by any Christian prince. It is besides so defensible, that if two forts be built in one of the provinces which I have seen the flood setteth in so near the bank, where the channel also lieth, that no ship can pass up but within a pike's length of the artillery, first of the one, and afterwards of the other; which two forts will be sufficient guard both to the Empire of Inga, and to a hundred other several kingdoms lying within the said river, even to the city of Quito in Peru.

6. JOURNEY'S END

Of the many bold captains who rode under the banner of Castile to the conquest of America, few lived to enjoy in peace and security the fruits of their valor, their sufferings, and their cruelties. "He that killeth with the sword must be killed with the sword," recalled the old conquistador Oviedo. Certainly

there was a kind of poetic justice about the ends met by such notorious and hardened Indian slave-catchers and tormentors as Balboa, Ponce de León, and Pedro de Alvarado. But fortune was little kinder to the humane and thoughtful Cabeza de Vaca, who spent his last years in the shadow of poverty and imprisonment; or to Hernando de Soto, who protested against the farcical trial and execution of Atahualpa and later died brokenhearted on the shores of the Mississippi. Oviedo presents a partial roll-call of the great adelantados, *or leaders of conquering expeditions, and relates the ends to which they came.*[9]

✠✠✠✠ I do not like the title of *adelantado*, for actually that honor and title is an evil omen in the Indies, and many who bore it have come to a pitiable end. So it was with Don Bartholomew Columbus, the first adelantado in the Indies, brother of the first admiral, who left behind him neither heirs nor any other enduring thing. Look at Ponce de León, adelantado of Florida, slain by the Indians; the adelantado Rodrigo de Bastidas, treacherously slain by the dagger blows of his own soldiers; the adelantado Diego Velásquez, who spent infinite sums on the discovery of New Spain, only to see another enjoy it and himself disappointed. Consider Vasco Núñez de Balboa, adelantado of the South Sea, and its first discoverer, who was beheaded as a traitor, and others with him, although they were all innocent of treason; the adelantado Lucas Vásquez de Ayllón, his Majesty's judge on the Royal Audience that sits here in Santo Domingo, who spent his estate and died in the discovery of a certain province that was given him in the northern regions, and whose body was flung in the sea; Francisco de Garay, adelantado of Panuco, who wasted his substance in arming and going to settle a land he knew nothing of, and who lost everything and finally died, although some say he was poisoned.

Antonio Sedeño spent much money on the conquest of Trinidad and Meta, and in the end was ruined and died disastrously; Diego de Ordaz, somewhat madder than the others, left and lost all he had and sought to settle the River Marañón, and in the end, departing for Spain, died and was cast in the sea; the adelantado Hernando de Soto, governor of the isle of Cuba, after returning to Spain loaded with gold, went to settle the mainland [of North America] and died there, leaving no trace or memory of himself. The adelantado Simón de Alcazaba was treacherously slain by his soldiers; the adelantado Diego de Almagro died a good and Catholic death; and, finally, his comrade Francisco Pizarro and his brothers, especially Hernando Pizarro, were slain against all reason and justice by those who were not their judges — but there is another world after this.

[9] Gonzalo Fernández de Oviedo y Valdés, *Historia general*, V, pp. 150–152. (Excerpt translated by the editor.)

PART III

The adelantado Francisco Pizarro, later a marquis, was wickedly slain by his enemies and soldiers; the adelantado Pedro de Heredia, governor of Cartagena, is still alive, and no one can tell how he will end; a worse fate than others befell the adelantado Francisco de Orellana, who went to the River Marañón in search of the tribe of the Amazons — or, to put it better, in search of death, although he did not know it — and so met his end at the mouth of the river. . . . The adelantado Pedro de Mendoza went to the River Plate and wasted and lost all he had, and sailing for Spain, died and was cast into the sea; the adelantado Pánfilo de Narváez and his followers suffered an even worse fate, for some were eaten by their fellows, and of six hundred men only three escaped, while Narváez drowned in the sea; the adelantado Pedro de Alvarado lived and died violently, for his horse rolled down a steep hill, with him helplessly entangled underneath, and dragged him from cliff to cliff, leaving him in such a state that he died soon after, but not before receiving the Sacraments like a good Catholic. . . .

And thus, prudent reader, you may see what sort of title is that of adelantado, that leaves in such conditions those who have held it in the Indies; and it seems to me that after what I have said of the adelantados named above, no man of sound sense will seek to obtain this title in that part of the world.

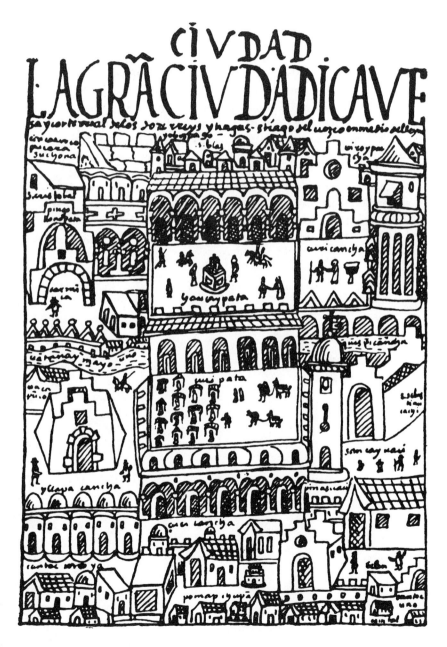

THE FOUNDATIONS OF COLONIAL LIFE

The Spanish monarchs early had to contend with the problem of devising a workable Indian labor policy for the colonies. Left to themselves, the conquistadores would obviously bring about the speedy extinction of the natives or become great feudal barons independent of royal authority. Royal intervention resulted in the abolition of Indian slavery and helped to stabilize the chaotic labor situation in the colonies. Nevertheless, the economic life of the Indies continued to be based on Indian forced labor, whether this took the form of the *encomienda*, the *repartimiento*, or peonage.

Agriculture, the principal economic activity of the Spanish colonies, was aided by the introduction of new European plants and animals. Although the silver and gold mines employed only a tiny proportion of the total colonial labor force, they yielded enormous revenues to the crown and to the fortunate Spaniards who "struck it rich." The most widely-developed manufacturing industry was that of textiles; this was carried on in the home or in workshops everywhere in the colonies.

The Spanish commercial system was restrictive and exclusive to an extreme degree. Colonial discontent with the resulting régime of scarcity and intolerably high prices stimulated the growth of a contra-

band trade that eventually surpassed the legal traffic in volume and importance.

Social status in the colonies was nominally based on the criteria of race, family, and occupation. The Indians (save for the favored descendants of native ruling houses and nobility) and the Negroes constituted hereditary servile castes, subject to numerous restrictions and burdens. In practice, racial lines were not so strictly drawn. Wealth, rather than gentle birth or racial purity, was the distinguishing characteristic of the colonial aristocracy.

The supreme governing authority for the Indies was the Council of the Indies. In consultation with the king, this body framed laws for the colonies, nominated all high colonial officials, and acted as a court of last resort in cases appealed from colonial tribunals. In particular, it named the viceroys, powerful officials who ruled over vast jurisdictions from their capitals at Mexico City, Lima, Bogotá, and Buenos Aires.

Next to the crown, with which it was indissolubly united, the Church was the most powerful institution in the Indies. The friars or regular clergy were the first priests to come to the Indies; later an ecclesiastical organization patterned on that of Spain, complete with bishoprics and archbishoprics, was erected. In addition to their religious duties, the clergy established and maintained schools, hospitals, and asylums of various kinds. Other clerics worked to convert and domesticate the wild Indians of the desert and jungle; the most celebrated of these mission establishments was that of the Jesuits in Paraguay. As in Spain, the colonial Inquisition was active in ferreting out and punishing heresy, as well as many minor offenses.

9 ✤ The Evolution of Spain's Indian Policy

The central problem of Spain's Indian policy was that of devising a workable labor system for the American colonies. The first decade of colonial experience demonstrated that the Indians, left to the tender mercies of the conquistadores, would either become an extinct race, as actually happened on the once densely-populated island of Hispaniola, or would rise in revolts that might threaten the very existence of the Spanish Empire in America. The crown naturally regarded these alternatives with distaste.

The situation created on the island of Hispaniola by the arrival of Columbus's second expedition has been aptly summed up in the phrase "Hell on Hispaniola." Columbus, anxious to prove to the crown the value of his discoveries, resorted to the expedient of compelling the natives to bring in a daily tribute of gold dust. When the Indians revolted they were hunted down, and hundreds were sent to Spain as slaves. Later, yielding to the pressure of rebellious settlers, Columbus divided the lands of the island among them in *repartimientos*, or shares, with the grantee enjoying the right to use the forced labor of the Indians living on his land. This system, formalized under the administration of Governor Ovando and sanctioned by the crown, became the *encomienda*.

In operation, the *encomienda* in the West Indies became a hideous slavery. The first voices raised against this state of affairs were those of a company of Dominican friars who arrived in Hispaniola in 1510. Their spokesman was Father Antonio Montesino, who on Advent Sunday, 1511, ascended the church pulpit to threaten the Spaniards of the island with damnation for their offenses against the Indians.

The agitation begun by the Dominicans raised the larger question of the legality of Spain's claim to the Indies. To satisfy the royal conscience, a distinguished jurist, Doctor Palacios Rubios, drew up a document, the *requerimiento*, which was supposed to be read by all conquistadores to the Indians before making war upon them. This document called upon the natives to acknowledge the supremacy of the Church and the Pope and the sovereignty of the Spanish monarchs over their lands by virtue of the papal donation of 1493, on pain of suffering the disasters of war and enslavement.

The famous Father Bartolomé de Las Casas now entered the lists against Indian slavery and the doctrines of Palacios Rubios. He argued that the papal grant of America to the Spanish crown had been made solely for the purpose of conversion, and carried with it no temporal power or possession. Love, reason, and persuasion, he insisted, were the only ways to lead the Indians to the true faith.

Las Casas appeared to have won a brilliant but largely illusive victory in the promulgation of the New Laws of 1542. Faced with revolt in Peru and the threat of revolt elsewhere, the Spanish crown offered the colonists a compromise. The laws forbidding enslavement and forced personal service by *encomienda* Indians were reaffirmed, but the right of *encomenderos* to continue collecting fixed amounts of tribute from the natives was confirmed. In Yucatan and Chile the *encomienda* survived till the last quarter of the eighteenth century.

Indian forced labor, legally separated from the *encomienda*, soon appeared in another guise. The demand of the colonists for cheap labor on their estates, in mines, and in domestic service was satisfied by legal conscription of Indians, working in shifts or relays. There also emerged a pattern of Indian debt servitude or peonage. A class of free, paid laborers also existed at an early date and came into fairly wide use in mining areas.

1. WANTED: A LABOR POLICY

From the first days of the conquest the Spanish crown faced a problem of harmonizing the demand of the conquistadores for cheap Indian labor, frequently employed in a wasteful and destructive manner, with the interest of the crown in the preserva-

tion of a large, contented, and productive native population and with the requirements of the Christian ethic. The pious Isabella, first to face the problem, resolved its contradictions in a way that became typical of Spanish legislation on the subject. The Indians were to be forced to labor, but as free men. This verbal reconciliation of opposites is well illustrated by the important order of December 20, 1503, which laid the basis for the encomienda system.[1]

✠✠✠✠ Medina del Campo, Dec. 20, 1503. Isabella, by the Grace of God, Queen of Castile, etc. In as much as the King, my Lord, and I, in the instruction we commanded given to Don Fray Nicholas de Ovando, Comendador mayor of Alcantara, at the time when he went to the islands and mainland of the Ocean Sea, decreed that the Indian inhabitants and residents of the island of Española, are free and not subject . . . and as now we are informed that because of the excessive liberty enjoyed by the said Indians they avoid contact and community with the Spaniards to such an extent that they will not even work for wages, but wander about idle, and cannot be had by the Christians to convert to the Holy Catholic Faith; and in order that the Christians of the said island . . . may not lack people to work their holdings for their maintenance, and may be able to take out what gold there is on the island . . . and because we desire that the said Indians be converted to our Holy Catholic Faith and taught in its doctrines; and because this can better be done by having the Indians living in community with the Christians of the island, and by having them go among them and associate with them, by which means they will help each other to cultivate and settle and increase the fruits of the island and take the gold which may be there and bring profit to my kingdom and subjects:

I have commanded this my letter to be issued on the matter, in which I command you, our said Governor, that beginning from the day you receive my letter you will compel and force the said Indians to associate with the Christians of the island and to work on their buildings, and to gather and mine the gold and other metals, and to till the fields and produce food for the Christian inhabitants and dwellers of the said island; and you are to have each one paid on the day he works the wage and maintenance which you think he should have . . . and you are to order each cacique to take charge of a certain number of the said Indians so that you may make them work wherever necessary, and so that on feast days and such days as you think proper they may be gathered to hear and be taught in matters of the Faith. . . . This

---

[1] Quoted in Lesley B. Simpson, *The Encomienda in New Spain*, Berkeley, Calif., University of California Press, 1929, pp. 30–31. Originally published by the University of California Press; reprinted by permission of the Regents of the University of California.

the Indians shall perform as free people, which they are, and not as slaves. And see to it that the said Indians are well treated, those who become Christians better than the others, and do not consent or allow that any person do them any harm or oppress them.

I, THE QUEEN

2. THE STRANGE SERMON OF FATHER MONTESINO

The struggle for justice for the Indians was begun by a small group of Dominican friars, who were horrified by the sights that they daily saw on the island of Hispaniola. They delegated one of their number, Father Antonio Montesino, to preach a sermon that would drive home to the Spanish settlers the wickedness of their deeds. Father Antonio's tremendous denunciation produced much dismay and anger among his listeners, but apparently not a single conversion. In the sequel, the infuriated townspeople called upon the Dominicans to retract their sentiments in next Sunday's sermon; otherwise the friars should pack up and get ready to sail for home. (This would not have been at all difficult, observes Las Casas, with quiet humor, for all they had on earth would have gone into two small trunks.) In reply, Father Montesino mounted the pulpit the following Sunday and let loose a second and even more terrible blast against Spanish mistreatment of the Indians. Las Casas describes the opening round in the great controversy over Spain's Indian policy.[2]

✦✦✦✦ Sunday having arrived, and the time for preaching, Father Antonio Montesino rose in the pulpit, and took for the text of his sermon, which was written down and signed by the other friars, "I am the voice of one crying in the wilderness." Having made his introduction and said something about the Advent season, he began to speak of the sterile desert of the consciences of the Spaniards on this isle, and of the blindness in which they lived, going about in great danger of damnation and utterly heedless of the grave sins in which they lived and died.

Then he returned to his theme, saying: "In order to make your sins known to you I have mounted this pulpit, I who am the voice of Christ crying in the wilderness of this island; and therefore it behooves you to listen to me, not with indifference but with all your heart and senses; for this voice will be the strangest, the harshest and

[2] Las Casas, *Historia de las Indias*, II, pp. 441–442. (Excerpt translated by the editor.)

hardest, the most terrifying that you ever heard or expected to hear."

He went on in this vein for a good while, using cutting words that made his hearers' flesh creep and made them feel that they were already experiencing the divine judgment. . . . He went on to state the contents of his message.

"This voice," said he, "declares that you are in mortal sin, and live and die therein by reason of the cruelty and tyranny that you practice on these innocent people. Tell me, by what right or justice do you hold these Indians in such cruel and horrible slavery? By what right do you wage such detestable wars on these people who lived mildly and peacefully in their own lands, where you have consumed infinite numbers of them with unheard-of murders and desolations? Why do you so greatly oppress and fatigue them, not giving them enough to eat or caring for them when they fall ill from excessive labors, so that they die or rather are slain by you, so that you may extract and acquire gold every day? And what care do you take that they receive religious instruction and come to know their God and creator, or that they be baptized, hear mass, or observe holidays and Sundays?

"Are they not men? Do they not have rational souls? Are you not bound to love them as you love yourselves? How can you lie in such profound and lethargic slumber? Be sure that in your present state you can no more be saved than the Moors or Turks who do not have and do not want the faith of Jesus Christ."

Thus he delivered the message he had promised, leaving his hearers astounded. Many were stunned, others appeared more callous than before, and a few were somewhat moved; but not one, from what I could later learn, was converted.

When he had concluded his sermon he descended from the pulpit, his head held high, for he was not a man to show fear, of which indeed he was totally free; nor did he care about the displeasure of his listeners, and instead did and said what seemed best according to God. With his companion he went to their straw-thatched house, where, very likely, their entire dinner was cabbage soup, unflavored with olive oil. . . . After he had left, the church was so full of murmurs that . . . they could hardly complete the celebration of the mass.

3. THE LAUGHTER OF DOCTOR PALACIOS RUBIOS

The dispute over Indian policy that had begun on the island of Hispaniola and was carried to Spain by the contending parties stimulated discussion of a fundamental question: By what right did Spain claim to rule over America and wage war on its native

peoples? The strong tradition of legalism in Spanish life and history, as well as the pious professions of the Catholic Kings, required that a satisfactory reply be devised to this query. King Ferdinand, who is not particularly remembered by historians for scrupulosity in dealing with his fellow European monarchs, summoned a committee of theologians to deliberate on the matter. The fruit of their discussions was the famous requerimiento, drawn up by Doctor Palacios Rubios. This document called upon the Indians to acknowledge the supremacy of the Church, the Pope, and the Spanish kings and to permit the faith to be preached to them. Not until they had rejected these demands, which would be made known to them by interpreters, could war be legally waged on them. The chronicler Oviedo, who accompanied the expedition of Pedrarias Dávila to the South American mainland in 1514, records in his great history the first use made of the Requirement, and the ironic laughter of Doctor Palacios Rubios as he listened to Oviedo's account of his experience with this curious manifesto.[3]

✦✦✦✦ After crossing this river we entered a village of some twenty huts; we found it deserted, and the general entered one of the houses, accompanied by all the captains who were there, by the licentiate Espinosa, who was the royal comptroller, factor, and governor, and by his lieutenant Juan de Ayora, and in the presence of all I said to him:

"Sir, it seems to me that these Indians do not care to hear the theology of this requirement, nor do you have anyone who can make them understand it. Your worship had better put this paper away until we have caught an Indian and put him in a cage, where he can gradually master its meaning, and the bishop can help to make it clear to him."

And I gave the general the requirement, and he took it, amid the hearty laughter of all who were there. While we were all resting in those huts, waiting for the sun to go down, our sentinels gave the alarm at about two o'clock in the afternoon. And down a very wide and handsome road, bordered with many trees that had been planted for adornment, came more than a thousand Indian bowmen, with much noise and blowing on certain large shells which are called *cobos* and are heard at a great distance. . . .

The general quickly left the village to meet the Indians on the road and arrayed his men in battle formation, each line separated from the other by a distance of two hundred paces. He also ordered a bronze cannon of about two hundred pounds to be loaded. Two greyhounds, highly praised by their masters, were to be placed on our

[3] Gonzalo Fernández de Oviedo y Valdés, *Historia general*, VII, pp. 131-132. (Excerpt translated by the editor.)

wings; we were to fire when he gave the signal; and at that instant the dogs should be loosed and we were all to fall upon the enemy and conduct ourselves like valiant men.

I should have preferred to have that requirement explained to the Indians first, but no effort was made to do so, apparently because it was considered superfluous or inappropriate. And just as our general on this expedition failed to carry out this pious proceeding with the Indians, as he was supposed to do before attacking them, the captains of many later expeditions also neglected the procedure and did even worse things, as will be seen. Later, in 1516, I asked Doctor Palacios Rubios (who had written that proclamation) if the consciences of the Christians were satisfied with that requirement, and he said yes, if it were done as the proclamation required. But I recall that he often laughed when I told him of that campaign and of others that various captains later made. I could laugh much harder at him and his learning (for he was reputed to be a great man, and as such had a seat on the Royal Council of Castile), if he thought that the Indians were going to understand the meaning of that requirement until many years had passed.

4. BARTOLOMÉ DE LAS CASAS: GOD'S ANGRY MAN

Among the many personalities who intervened in the great controversy over Spain's Indian policy, the figure of Bartolomé de Las Casas (1474–1566) has perhaps grown most in stature with the passing of the centuries. By scholars he is most highly regarded for his monumental History of the Indies, *which is indispensable to every student of the first phase of the Spanish conquest. The world generally knows him best for his flaming tract against Spanish cruelty to the Indians, the* Brief Account of the Destruction of the Indies *(1552), a work soon translated into most of the languages of Europe and joyously used by Spain's imperialist rivals to discredit her colonial enterprise. Opponents of Las Casas have severely criticized his statements concerning the size of Indian populations and the numbers slain by the Spaniards, overlooking, perhaps, what John Fiske pointed out long ago: that "the arithmetic of Las Casas is . . . no worse than that of all the Spanish historians of that age. With every one of them the nine digits seem to have gone on a glorious spree." Moreover, recent studies in the social history of colonial Latin America tend to confirm Las Casas' claims of large pre-conquest Indian populations and his thesis of a catastrophic population decline under the impact of the Conquest. Typical*

of the tone and contents of the Brief Account *is its description of the Spanish conquest of Cuba.*[4]

✠✠✠✠ In the year 1511 the Spaniards passed over to the island of Cuba, which as I said, is as long as from Valladolid to Rome, and where there were great and populous provinces. They began and ended in the above manner, only with incomparably greater cruelty. Here many notable things occurred.

A very high prince and lord, named Hatuey, who had fled with many of his people from Hispaniola to Cuba, to escape the calamity and inhuman operations of the Christians, having received news from some Indians that the Christians were crossing over, assembled many or all of his people, and addressed them thus.

"You already know that it is said the Christians are coming here; and you have experience of how they have treated the lords so and so and those people of Hayti (which is Hispaniola); they come to do the same here. Do you know perhaps why they do it?" The people answered no; except that they were by nature cruel and wicked. "They do it," said he, "not alone for this, but because they have a God whom they greatly adore and love; and to make us adore Him they strive to subjugate us and take our lives." He had near him a basket full of gold and jewels and he said: "Behold here is the God of the Christians, let us perform *Areytos* before Him, if you will (these are dances in concert and singly); and perhaps we shall please Him, and He will command that they do us no harm."

All exclaimed: it is well! it is well! They danced before it, till they were all tired, after which the lord Hatuey said: "Note well that in any event if we preserve the gold, they will finally have to kill us to take it from us: let us throw it into this river." They all agreed to this proposal, and they threw the gold into a great river in that place.

This prince and lord continued retreating before the Christians when they arrived at the island of Cuba, because he knew them, but when he encountered them he defended himself; and at last they took him. And merely because he fled from such iniquitous and cruel people, and defended himself against those who wished to kill and oppress him, with all his people and offspring until death, they burnt him alive.

When he was tied to the stake, a Franciscan monk, a holy man, who was there, spoke as much as he could to him, in the little time that the executioner granted them, about God and some of the teachings of our faith, of which he had never before heard; he told him that if he would believe what was told him, he would go to heaven where there was glory and eternal rest; and if not, that he would go to hell, to

---

[4] "The Brevíssima Relación," in Francis A. McNutt, *Bartholomew de Las Casas*, New York, 1909, Appendix I, pp. 328–332. Reprinted by permission of the publishers, G. P. Putnam's Sons.

suffer perpetual torments and punishment. After thinking a little, Hatuey asked the monk whether the Christians went to heaven; the monk answered that those who were good went there. The prince at once said, without anymore thought, that he did not wish to go there, but rather to hell so as not to be where Spaniards were, nor to see such cruel people. This is the renown and honour, that God and our faith have acquired by means of the Christians who have gone to the Indies.

On one occasion they came out ten leagues from a great settlement to meet us, bringing provisions and gifts, and when we met them, they gave us a great quantity of fish and bread and other victuals, with everything they could supply. All of a sudden the devil entered into the bodies of the Christians, and in my presence they put to the sword, without any motive or cause whatsoever, more than three thousand persons, men, women, and children, who were seated before us. Here I beheld such great cruelty as living man has never seen nor thought to see.

Once I sent messengers to all the lords of the province of Havana, assuring them that if they would not absent themselves but come to receive us, no harm should be done them; all the country was terrorized because of the past slaughter, and I did this by the captain's advice. When we arrived in the province, twenty-one princes and lords came to receive us; and at once the captain violated the safe conduct I had given them and took them prisoners. The following day he wished to burn them alive, saying it was better so because those lords would some time or other do us harm. I had the greatest difficulty to deliver them from the flames but finally I saved them.

After all the Indians of this island were reduced to servitude and misfortune like those of Hispaniola, and when they saw they were perishing inevitably, some began to flee to the mountains; others to hang themselves, together with their children, and through the cruelty of one very tyrannical Spaniard whom I knew, more than two hundred Indians hanged themselves. In this way numberless people perished.

There was an officer of the King in this island, to whose share three hundred Indians fell; and by the end of the three months he had, through labour in the mines, caused the death of two hundred and seventy; so that he had only thirty left, which was the tenth part. The authorities afterwards gave him as many again, and again he killed them: and they continued to give, and he to kill, until he came to die, and the devil carried away his soul.

In three or four months, I being present, more than seven thousand children died of hunger, their fathers and mothers having been taken to the mines. Other dreadful things did I see.

Afterwards the Spaniards resolved to go and hunt the Indians who were in the mountains, where they perpetrated marvellous massacres. Thus they ruined and depopulated all this island which we be-

held not long ago; and it excites pity, and great anguish to see it deserted, and reduced to a solitude.

5. ALL MANKIND IS ONE

What was perhaps Las Casas' finest hour came in 1550, when he rose to answer the eminent humanist Juan Ginés de Sepúlveda (1490?–1572?), author of a treatise which sought to prove that wars against the Indians were just. The background of the great debate, held before a junta of theologians summoned by Charles V to decide the matter, was a general reaction in the Spanish court against Las Casas' liberal views, signalized by the partial repeal of the New Laws of 1542. All further conquests in the New World were ordered suspended while the great battle of words raged in Valladolid. Sepúlveda, a disciple of Aristotle, invoked his theory that some men are slaves by nature and thus made to serve others in order to show that the Indians must be made to serve the Spaniards for their own good as well as for that of their masters. Furthermore, the spread of the faith would be served by their subjugation. The highest point of Las Casas' argument was his eloquent affirmation of the equality of all races, the essential oneness of mankind. The outcome of the debate was inconclusive, with the judges finding themselves unable to reach agreement. The first[5] of the following extracts is from Sepúlveda's treatise on the subject of Indian wars; the second[6] is taken from Las Casas' Apological History of the Indies.

✦✦✦✦ Now compare these [Spanish] traits of prudence, intelligence, magnanimity, moderation, humanity, and religion with the qualities of these little men in whom you will scarcely find even vestiges of humanity; who not only are devoid of learning but do not even have a written language; who preserve no monuments of their history, aside from some vague and obscure reminiscense of past events, represented by means of certain paintings; and who have no written laws but only barbaric customs and institutions. And if we are to speak of virtues, what moderation or mildness can you expect of men who are given to all kinds of intemperance and wicked lusts, and who eat human flesh?

[5] Juan Ginés de Sepúlveda, *Tratado sobre las justas causas de la guerra contra los indios*, México, 1941, pp. 105–113. (Excerpt translated by the editor.)
[6] Las Casas, *Apologética historia de las Indias*, Madrid, 1909, pp. 128–129. (Excerpt translated by the editor.)

And do not believe that before the coming of the Christians they lived in that peaceful reign of Saturn that the poets describe; on the contrary, they waged continuous and ferocious war against each other, with such fury that they considered a victory hardly worth while if they did not glut their monstrous hunger with the flesh of their enemies, a ferocity all the more repellent since it was not joined to the invincible valor of the Scythians, who also ate human flesh. For the rest, these Indians are so cowardly that they almost run at the sight of our soldiers, and frequently thousands of them have fled like women before a very few Spaniards, numbering less than a hundred. . . .

Could one give more convincing proof of the superiority of some men to others in intelligence, spirit, and valor, and of the fact that such people are slaves by nature? For although some of them display a certain talent for craftsmanship this is not proof of human intelligence, for we know that animals, birds, and spiders do certain work that no human industry can completely imitate. And as regards the mode of life of the inhabitants of New Spain and the province of Mexico, I have already said that they are considered the most civilized of all. They themselves boast of their public institutions, for they have cities constructed in an orderly fashion, and kings, not hereditary but elected by popular vote; and they carry on commerce among themselves in the manner of civilized people.

But see how they deceive themselves, and how much I disagree with their opinion, for in these same institutions I see proof on the contrary of the rudeness, the barbarism, and the inherently slavish nature of these people. For the possession of habitations, of a fairly rational mode of life, and of a kind of commerce is something that natural necessity itself induces, and only serves to prove that they are not bears or monkeys and are not completely devoid of reason. But on the other hand, they have no private property in their state, and they cannot dispose of or bequeath to their heirs their houses or fields, since they are all in the power of their lords, whom they improperly call kings, at whose pleasure, rather than at their own, they live, attentive to their will and caprice rather than to their own freedom. And the fact that they do all this in a voluntary and spontaneous manner and are not constrained by force of arms is certain proof of the servile and abased spirit of these barbarians. . . .

Such, in sum, are the disposition and customs of these little men — barbarous, uncivilized, and inhumane; and we know that they were like this before the coming of the Spaniards. We have not yet spoken of their impious religion and of the wicked sacrifices in which they worshiped the devil as their God, believing that they could offer no better tribute than human hearts. . . . How can we doubt that these peoples, so uncivilized, so barbarous, contaminated with so many

infidelities and vices, have been justly conquered by such an excellent, pious, and just king as the late Ferdinand the Catholic, and the present Emperor Charles, and by a nation that is most humane and excels in every kind of virtue?

From these examples, both ancient and modern, it is clear that no nation exists, no matter how rude and uncivilized, barbarous, gross, savage or almost brutal it may be, that cannot be persuaded into a good way of life and made domestic, mild, and tractable — provided that diligence and skill are employed, and provided that the method that is proper and natural to men is used: namely, love and gentleness and kindness. . . .

For all the peoples of the world are men, and the definition of all men, collectively and severally, is one: that they are rational beings. All possess understanding and volition, being formed in the image and likeness of God; all have the five exterior senses and the four interior senses, and are moved by the objects of these; all have the natural capacity or faculties to understand and master the knowledge that they do not have; and this is true not only of those that are inclined toward good but of those that by reason of their depraved customs are bad; all take pleasure in goodness and in happy and pleasant things; and all abhor evil and reject what offends or grieves them. . . .

Thus all mankind is one, and all men are alike in what concerns their creation and all natural things, and no one is born enlightened. From this it follows that all of us must be guided and aided at first by those who were born before us. And the savage peoples of the earth may be compared to uncultivated soil that readily brings forth weeds and useless thorns, but has within itself such natural virtue that by labor and cultivation it may be made to yield sound and beneficial fruits.

6. INDIAN FORCED LABOR IN GUATEMALA

Las Casas died in 1566, at the great age of ninety-two, in a convent outside Madrid. Three Spanish kings had listened respectfully to his advice on Indian affairs, had sometimes acted upon that advice, and in their Indian legislation gave pious lip-service to the principles he advocated. But the realities of colonial existence overruled the voice of morality and religion. Legal slavery and personal service under the encomienda *system had largely disappeared by 1700, but their place had been effectively taken by a system of labor conscription under which all adult male Indians were required to give a certain amount of*

their time to work in mines and factories and on farms, ranches, and public works, receiving a small wage for their labor. In New Spain this institution was known as the repartimiento. *Its operation in this area is described by Thomas Gage (1600?– 1656), an observant though highly biased Englishman who spent twelve years as a priest in Guatemala before turning apostate and coming home to write an anti-Spanish book about his experiences. Frequent references in Gage's book to Indians who had grown rich by farming and trading testify that not all natives shared in the general misery of their race; in one town he found an Indian "who alone had bestowed upon the church five thousand ducats."*[7]

✠✠✠✠ The miserable condition of the Indians of that country is such that though the Kings of Spain have never yielded to what some would have, that they should be slaves, yet their lives are as full of bitterness as is the life of a slave. For which I have known myself some of them that have come home from toiling and moiling with Spaniards, after many blows, some wounds, and little or no wages, who have sullenly and stubbornly lain down upon their beds, resolving to die rather than to live any longer a life so slavish, and have refused to take either meat or drink or anything else comfortable and nourishing, which their wives have offered unto them, that so by pining and starving they might consume themselves. Some I have by good persuasions encouraged to life rather than to a voluntary and wilful death; others there have been that would not be persuaded, but in that wilful way have died.

The Spaniards that live about that country (especially the farmers of the Valley of Mixco, Pinola, Petapa, Amatitlan, and those of the Sacatepequez) allege that all their trading and farming is for the good of the commonwealth, and therefore whereas there are not Spaniards enough for so ample and large a country to do all their work, and all are not able to buy slaves and blackamoors, they stand in need of the Indians' help to serve them for their pay and hire; whereupon it hath been considered that a partition of Indian labourers be made every Monday, or Sunday in the afternoon to the Spaniards, according to the farms they occupy, or according to their several employments, calling, and trading with mules, or any other way. So that for such and such a district there is named an officer, who is called *juez repartidor*, who according to a list made of every farm, house, and person, is to give so many Indians by the week. And here is a door opened to the President of Guatemala, and to the judges, to provide well for their menial servants, whom they commonly ap-

[7] Thomas Gage, *The English-American: A New Survey of the West Indies,* edited by A. P. Newton, London, 1946, pp. 230–233.

point for this office, which is thus performed by them. They name
the town and place of their meeting upon Sunday or Monday, to the
which themselves and the Spaniards of that district do resort. The
Indians of the several towns are to have in a readiness so many labourers as the Court of Guatemala hath appointed to be weekly taken
out of such a town, who are conducted by an Indian officer to the
town of general meeting; and when they come thither with their
tools, their spades, shovels, bills, or axes, with their provision of victuals for a week (which are commonly some dry cakes of maize,
puddings of *frijoles,* or French beans, and a little chilli or biting long
pepper, or a bit of cold meat for the first day or two) and with beds
on their backs (which is only a coarse woolen mantle to wrap about
them when they lie on the bare ground) then are they shut up in
the townhouse, some with blows, some with spurnings, some with
boxes on the ear, if presently they go not in.

Now all being gathered together, and the house filled with
them, the *juez repartidor,* or officer, calls by the order of the list
such and such a Spaniard, and also calls out of the house so many
Indians as by the Court are commanded to be given him (some are
allowed three, some four, some ten, some fifteen, some twenty, according to their employments) and delivereth unto the Spaniard his
Indians, and so to all the rest, till they be all served; who when they
receive their Indians, take from them a tool, or their mantles, to secure them that they run not away; and for every Indian delivered
unto them, they give unto the *juez repartidor,* or officer, half a real,
which is three-pence an Indian for his fees, which mounteth yearly
to him to a great deal of money; for some officers make a partition
or distribution of four hundred, some of two hundred, some of three
hundred Indians every week, and carrieth home with him so many half
hundred reals for one, or half a day's work. If complaint be made by
any Spaniard that such and such an Indian did run away from him,
and served him not the week part, the Indian must be brought, and
surely tied to a post by his hands in the marketplace, and there be
whipped upon his bare back. But if the poor Indian complain that the
Spaniards cozened and cheated him of his shovel, axe, bill, mantle, or
wages, no justice shall be executed against the cheating Spaniard,
neither shall the Indian be righted, though it is true the order runs
equally in favour of both Indian and Spaniard. Thus are the poor Indians sold for threepence apiece for a whole week's slavery, not
permitted to go home at nights unto their wives, though their work
lie not above a mile from the town where they live; nay some are carried ten or twelve miles from their home, who must not return till
Saturday night late, and must that week do whatsoever their master
pleaseth to command them. The wages appointed them will scarce
find them meat and drink, for they are not allowed a real a day, which

is but sixpence, and with that they are to find themselves, but for six days' work and diet they are to have five reals, which is half a crown. This same order is observed in the city of Guatemala, and towns of Spaniards, where to every family that wants the service of an Indian or Indians, though it be but to fetch water and wood on their backs, or to go of errands, is allowed the like from the nearest Indian towns.

7. INDIAN FORCED LABOR IN PERU

Indian forced labor in Peru, commonly known as the mita, *produced even greater evils there than in New Spain. The situation was most disastrous in the highland areas, with the silver mines of Potosí and the Huancavelica mercury mine enjoying particular notoriety as death traps for Indian laborers. To the operations of the* mita, *Spanish observers frequently attributed the depopulation of Indian villages that is frequently mentioned in seventeenth- and eighteenth-century accounts. Vásquez de Espinosa (?–1630), a Carmelite friar who traveled widely in the Indies between 1612 and 1620, gives a restrained description of labor conditions in the Potosí mines at that period.*[8]

❖❖❖❖ According to His Majesty's warrant, the mine owners on this massive range have a right to the *mita* of 13,300 Indians in the working and exploitation of the mines, both those which have been discovered, those now discovered, and those which shall be discovered. It is the duty of the Corregidor of Potosí to have them rounded up and to see that they come in from all the provinces between Cuzco over the whole of El Collao and as far as the frontiers of Jarija and Tomina; this Potosí Corregidor has power and authority over all the Corregidors in those provinces mentioned; for if they do not fill the Indian *mita* allotment assigned each one of them in accordance with the capacity of their provinces as indicated to them, he can send them, and does, salaried inspectors to report upon it, and when the remissness is great or remarkable, he can suspend them, notifying the Viceroy of the fact.

These Indians are sent out every year under a captain whom they choose in each village or tribe, for him to take them and oversee them for the year each has to serve; every year they have a new election, for as some go out, others come in. This works out very

[8] Antonio Vásquez de Espinosa, *Compendium and Description of the West Indies,* translated by C. U. Clark, Washington, the Smithsonian Institution, 1942, pp. 623–625.

badly, with great losses and gaps in the quotas of Indians, the villages being depopulated; and this gives rise to great extortions and abuses on the part of the inspectors toward the poor Indians, ruining them and thus depriving the caciques and chief Indians of their property and carrying them off in chains because they do not fill out the *mita* assignment, which they cannot do, for the reasons given and for others which I do not bring forward.

These 13,300 are divided up every 4 months into 3 *mitas*, each consisting of 4,433 Indians, to work in the mines on the range and in the 120 smelters in the Potosí and Tarapaya areas; it is a good league between the two. These *mita* Indians earn each day, or there is paid each one for his labor, 4 reals. Besides these there are others not under obligation, who are *mingados* or hire themselves out voluntarily: these each get from 12 to 16 reals, and some up to 24, according to their reputation of wielding the pick and knowing how to get the ore out. These *mingados* will be over 4,000 in number. They and the *mita* Indians go up every Monday morning to the locality of Guayna Potosí which is at the foot of the range; the Corregidor arrives with all the provincial captains or chiefs who have charge of the Indians assigned them, and he there checks off and reports to each mine and smelter owner the number of Indians assigned him for his mine or smelter; that keeps him busy till 1 P.M., by which time the Indians are already turned over to these mine and smelter owners.

After each has eaten his ration, they climb up the hill, each to his mine, and go in, staying there from that hour until Saturday evening without coming out of the mines; their wives bring them food, but they stay constantly underground, excavating and carrying out the ore from which they get the silver. They all have tallow candles, lighted day and night; that is the light they work with, for as they are underground, they have need of it all the time. The mere cost of these candles used in the mines on this range will amount every year to more than 3,000,000 pesos, even though tallow is cheap in that country, being abundant; but this is a very great expense, and it is almost incredible, how much is spent for candles in the operation of breaking down and getting out the ore.

These Indians have different functions in the handling of the silver ore; some break it up with bar or pick, and dig down in, following the vein in the mine; others bring it up; others up above keep separating the good and the poor in piles; others are occupied in taking it down from the range to the mills on herds of llamas; every day they bring up more than 8,000 of these native beasts of burden for this task. These teamsters who carry the metal do not belong to the *mita*, but are *mingados* — hired.

10 ✢ The Economic Foundations of Colonial Life

The economic life of the Spanish-American colonies reflected both New and Old World influences. Side by side with the subsistence-and-tribute economy of the Indians, there arose a Spanish commercial agriculture producing food stuffs or raw materials for sale in local or distant markets. To some extent this agriculture served internal markets, as in the mining areas of Mexico and Peru, or intercolonial trade, as in the case of the wine industry of Peru, but its dominant trait, which became more pronounced with the passage of time, was that of production for export to European markets. Spain imposed certain restrictions on colonial agriculture, in the mercantilist spirit of the age, but this legislation was largely ineffective.

Stock-raising was another important economic activity in the colonies. The introduction of domestic animals represented a major Spanish contribution to American economic life, since ancient America, aside from a limited region of the Andes, had no domestic animals for use as food or in transportation. By 1600 the export of hides from Hispaniola to Spain had assumed large proportions, and meat had become so abundant on the island that the flesh of slain wild cattle was generally left to rot. The export of hides also became important during the seventeenth century in the Plate area.

Mining, as the principal source of royal revenue, received the special attention and protection of the crown. Silver, rather than gold, was the principal product of the American mines. The great mine of Potosí in Upper Peru was discovered in 1545; the rich mines of Zacatecas and Guanajuato in New Spain were opened up in 1548 and 1558 respectively. Silver mining was greatly stimulated in 1556 by the introduction of the *patio* process for separating silver from the ore with quicksilver. As in other times and places, the mining industry brought prosperity to a few and either failure or small success to the great majority.

The Spaniards found a flourishing handicrafts industry in the advanced culture areas of Mexico, Central America, and Peru. Throughout the colonial period the majority of the natives continued to supply their own needs for pottery, clothing, and other household requirements. With the coming of the Spaniards new manufacturing industries arose in the towns, stimulated by the high prices of imported Spanish goods. The artisans were organized in guilds (from which Indians were excluded as masters), which included silversmiths, goldbeaters, weavers, and the like.

The period up to 1700 also witnessed a remarkable growth of factory-type establishments (*obrajes*) that produced cheap cotton and woolen goods for popular consumption. A number of towns in New Spain (Puebla, Guadalajara, Cholula, and others) were centers of the textile industry. Other factory-type establishments produced soap, chinaware, leather, and other products. Internal and intercolonial trade, based on regional specialization and particularly on the rise of mining centers that consumed large quantities of agricultural produce and manufactures, steadily increased in the sixteenth and seventeenth centuries.

1. THE INDIAN AGRICULTURAL HERITAGE

The Indian contributions to colonial and world agriculture were extremely rich and varied. A partial list includes such important products as maize, the potato and sweet potato, pineapple, peanut, cultivated strawberry, lima and kidney beans, squash and pumpkin, cacao, rubber, and tobacco. To Europeans of the era of colonization, some of the new American plants appeared to have strange and possibly supernatural qualities. The learned Jesuit José de Acosta (1539?–1600) sought to satisfy Spanish curiosity about the natural productions of the New World in his scientific and historical work, the Natural and Moral History of the Indies *(1590). Among the plants described*

by Father Acosta are maize, the Indian staff of life; cacao, source of the refreshing chocolate drink first used by the Mayas; coca, the magic plant that imparted endurance to the weary frame of the Peruvian Indian; and maguey, the Mexican tree of wonders.[1]

✦✦✦✦ Turning to plants, I shall speak first of those which are more peculiar to the Indies and afterwards of those which are common both to those lands and to Europe. And because plants were created principally for the maintenance of man, and man sustains himself above all by bread, I should speak first of their bread. . . . The Indians have their own words to signify bread, which in Peru is called *tanta* and in other parts is given other names. But the quality and substance of the bread the Indians use is very different from ours, for they have no kind of wheat, barley, millet, panic grass, or any grain such as is used in Europe to make bread. Instead they have other kinds of grains and roots, among which maize, called Indian wheat in Castile and Turkey grain in Italy, holds the first place.

And just as wheat is the grain most commonly used by man in the regions of the Old World, which are Europe, Asia, and Africa, so in the New World the most widely used grain is maize, which is found in almost all the kingdoms of the West Indies; in Peru, New Spain, the New Kingdom of Granada, Guatemala, Chile, and in all the Tierra Firme.[2] In the Windward Isles, which are Cuba, Hispaniola, Jamaica, Puerto Rico, it does not seem to have been used in earlier times; to this day they prefer to use yucca and cassava, of which more later. I do not think that maize is at all inferior to our wheat in strength and nourishment; but it is stouter and hotter and engenders more blood, so that if people who are not accustomed to it eat it in excess they swell up and get the itch.

Maize grows on canes or reeds; each one bears one or two ears, to which the grains are fastened, and though the grains are big they hold a large number of them, and some contain seven hundred grains. The seeds are planted one by one. Maize likes a hot and humid soil. It grows in many parts of the Indies in great abundance; a yield of three hundred *fanegas* from a sowing is not uncommon. There are various kinds of maize, as of wheat; one is large and nourishing; another, called *moroche*, is small and dry. The leaves of the maize and the green cane are a choice fodder for their beasts of burden, and when dry are also used as straw. The grain gives more nourishment to horses than barley, and therefore it is customary in those countries to water their horses before giving them maize to eat, for

---

[1] José de Acosta, *Historia natural y moral de las Indias*, México, 1940, pp. 265–266, 285–289. (Excerpt translated by the editor.)
[2] The northern coast of South America. B.K.

if they drank after feeding they would swell up and have gripes, as they do when they eat wheat.

Maize is the Indian bread, and they commonly eat it boiled in the grain, hot, when it is called *mote* . . . ; sometimes they eat it toasted. There is a large and round maize, like that of the Lucanas, which the Spaniards eat as a delicacy; it has better flavor than toasted chickpeas. There is another and more pleasing way of preparing it, which consists in grinding the maize and making the flour into pancakes, which are put on the fire and are later placed on the table and eaten piping hot; in some places they call them *arepas*. . . .

Maize is used by the Indians to make not only their bread but also their wine; from it they make beverages which produce drunkenness more quickly than wine made of grapes. They make this maize wine in various ways, calling it *azua* in Peru and more generally throughout the Indies *chicha*. The strongest sort is made like beer, steeping the grains of maize until they begin to break, after which they boil the juice in a certain way, which makes it so strong that a few drinks will produce intoxication. In Peru, where it is called *sora*, its use is forbidden by law because of the terrific drinking it occasions. But the law is little observed, for they use it anyway, and stay up whole days and nights, dancing and drinking. . . .

The cacao tree is most esteemed in Mexico and coca is favored in Peru; both trees are surrounded with considerable superstition. Cacao is a bean smaller and fattier than the almond, and when roasted has not a bad flavor. It is so much esteemed by the Indians, and even by the Spaniards, that it is the object of one of the richest and largest lines of trade of New Spain; since it is a dry fruit, and one that keeps a long time without spoiling, they send whole ships loaded with it from the province of Guatemala. Last year an English corsair burned in the port of Guatulco, in New Spain, more than one hundred thousand *cargas* of cacao. They also use it as money, for five cacao beans will buy one thing, thirty another, and one hundred still another, and no objections are made to its use. They also use it as alms to give to the poor.

The chief use of this cacao is to make a drink that they call chocolate, which they greatly cherish in that country. But those who have not formed a taste for it dislike it, for it has a froth at the top and an effervescence like that formed in wine by dregs, so that one must really have great faith in it to tolerate it. In fine, it is the favorite drink of Indians and Spaniards alike, and they regale visitors to their country with it; the Spanish women of that land are particularly fond of the dark chocolate. They prepare it in various ways: hot, cold, and lukewarm. They usually put spices and much chili in it; they also make a paste of it, and they say that it is good for the chest

and the stomach, and also for colds. Be that as it may, those who have not formed a taste for it do not like it.

The tree on which this fruit grows is of middling size and well-made, with a beautiful top; it is so delicate that to protect it from the burning rays of the sun they plant near it another large tree, which serves only to shade it; this is called the mother of the cacao. There are cacao plantations where it is raised as are the vine and the olive in Spain. The province of Guatemala is where they carry on the greatest commerce in this fruit.

The cacao does not grow in Peru; instead they have the coca, which is surrounded with even greater superstition and really seems fabulous. In Potosí alone the commerce in coca amounts to more than 5,000,000 pesos, with a consumption of from 90 to 100,000 hampers, and in the year 1583 it was 100,000. . . . This coca that they so greatly cherish is a little green leaf which grows upon shrubs about one *estado* high; it grows in very warm and humid lands and produces this leaf, which they call *trasmitas*, every four months. Being a very delicate plant, it requires a great deal of attention during cultivation and even more after it has been picked. They pack it with great care in long, narrow hampers and load it on the sheep of that country, which carry this merchandise in droves, bearing one, two, and three thousand hampers. It is commonly brought from the Andes, from valleys of insufferable heat, where it rains the greater part of the year, and it costs the Indians much labor and takes many lives, for they must leave their highlands and cold climates in order to cultivate it and carry it away. Hence there have been great disputes among lawyers and wise men about whether the coca plantations should be done away with or no — but there they still are.

The Indians prize it beyond measure, and in the time of the Inca kings plebeians were forbidden to use coca without the permission of the Inca or his governor. Their custom is to hold it in their mouths, chewing and sucking it; they do not swallow it; they say that it gives them great strength and is a great comfort to them. Many serious men say that this is pure superstition and imagination. To tell the truth, I do not think so; I believe that it really does lend strength and endurance to the Indians, for one sees effects that cannot be attributed to imagination, such as their ability to journey two whole days on a handful of coca, eating nothing else, and similar feats. . . . All would be well, except that its cultivation and commerce endanger and occupy so many people. . . .

The maguey is the tree of wonders, to which the newly-come Spaniards, or *chapetones* (as they call them in the Indies), attribute miracles, saying that it yields water and wine, oil and vinegar, honey, syrup, thread, needles, and a thousand other things. The Indians of

New Spain value it greatly, and they commonly have one or several of these trees near their homes to supply their needs. It grows in the fields, and there they cultivate it. Its leaves are wide and thick, with strong, sharp points which they use as fastening pins or sewing needles; they also draw a certain fibre or thread from the leaves.

They cut through the thick trunk when it is tender; there is a large cavity inside, where the sap rises from the roots; it is a liquor which they drink like water, since it is fresh and sweet. When this liquor is boiled it turns into a kind of wine, and if it is left to sour it becomes vinegar. But when boiled for a longer time it becomes like honey, and cooked half as long it turns into a healthful syrup of good flavor, superior in my judgment to syrup made of grapes. Thus they boil different substances from this sap, which they obtain in great quantity, for at a certain season they extract several *azumbres* a day.

2. SPAIN'S CONTRIBUTIONS TO NEW WORLD AGRICULTURE

The colonial era saw a notable exchange of agricultural gifts between the Old and the New Worlds. The Spanish crown displayed much solicitude for the agricultural development of the Indies, and paid particular attention to the shipping of trees, plants, seeds, and agricultural implements of all kinds. Father Acosta gives an account of the transit of Spanish plants to America and of the rapid rise there of a commercial agriculture producing wine, wheat, sugar, and other products.[3]

❖❖❖❖ The Indies have been better repaid in the matter of plants than in any other kind of merchandise; for those few that have been carried from the Indies into Spain do badly there, whereas the many that have come over from Spain prosper in their new homes. I do not know whether to attribute this to the excellence of the plants that go from here or to the bounty of the soil over there. Nearly every good thing grown in Spain is found there; in some regions they do better than in others. They include wheat, barley, garden produce and greens and vegetables of all kinds, such as lettuce, cabbage, radishes, onions, garlic, parsley, turnips, carrots, eggplants, endive, salt-wort, spinach, chickpeas, beans, and lentils — in short, whatever grows well here, for those who have gone to the Indies have been careful to take with them seeds of every description. . . .

The trees that have fared best there are the orange, lemon, citron, and others of that sort. In some parts there are already whole

---

[3] Acosta, *Historia natural de las Indias*, pp. 311–315. (Excerpt translated by the editor.)

forests and groves of orange trees. Marvelling at this, I asked on a certain island who had planted so many orange trees in the fields. To which they replied that it might have happened that some oranges fell to the ground and rotted, whereupon the seeds germinated, and, some being borne by the waters to different parts, gave rise to these dense groves. This seemed a likely reason. I said before that orange trees have generally done well in the Indies, for nowhere have I found a place where oranges were not to be found; this is because everywhere in the Indies the soil is hot and humid, which is what this tree most needs. It does not grow in the highlands; oranges are transported there from the valleys or the coast. The orange preserve which is made in the islands is the best I have ever seen, here or there.

Peaches and apricots also have done well, although the latter have fared better in New Spain. . . . Apples and pears are grown, but in moderate yields; plums give sparingly; figs are abundant, chiefly in Peru. Quinces are found everywhere, and in New Spain they are so plentiful that we received fifty choice ones for half a *real*. Pomegranates are found in abundance, but they are all sweet, for the people do not like the sharp variety. The melons are very good in some regions, as in Tierra Firme and Peru. Cherries, both wild and cultivated, have not so far prospered in the Indies. . . . In conclusion, I find that hardly any of the finer fruits is lacking in those parts. As for nuts, they have no acorns or chestnuts, nor, as far as I know, have any been grown over there until now. Almonds grow there, but sparingly. Almonds, walnuts, and filberts are shipped there from Spain for the tables of epicures. I have not seen any medlars or services, but those do not matter. . . .

By profitable plants I mean those plants which not only yield fruit but bring money to their owners. The most important of these is the vine, which gives wine, vinegar, grapes, raisins, verjuice, and syrup — but the wine is the chief concern. Wine and grapes are not products of the islands or of Tierra Firme; in New Spain there are vines which bear grapes but do not yield wine. The reason must be that the grapes do not ripen completely because of the rains which come in July and August and hinder their ripening; they are good only for eating. Wine is shipped from Spain and the Canary Islands to all parts of the Indies, except Peru and Chile, where they have vineyards and make very good wine. This industry is expanding continually, not only because of the goodness of the soil, but because they have a better knowledge of winemaking.

The vineyards of Peru are commonly found in warm valleys where they have water channels; they are watered by hand, because rain never falls in the coastal plains, and the rains in the mountains do not come at the proper time. . . . The vineyards have increased so far that because of them the tithes of the churches are now five and

six times what they were twenty years ago. The valleys most fertile in vines are Victor, near Arequipa; Yca, hard by Lima; and Caracaro, close to Chuquiavo. The wine that is made there is shipped to Potosí and Cuzco and various other parts, and it is sold in great quantities, because since it is produced so abundantly it sells at five or six ducats the jug, or *arroba,* whereas Spanish wine (which always arrives with the fleets) sells for ten and twelve. . . . The wine trade is no small affair, but does not exceed the limits of the province.

The silk which is made in New Spain goes to other provinces — to Peru, for example. There was no silk industry before the Spaniards came; the mulberry trees were brought from Spain, and they grow well, especially in the province called Misteca, where they raise silkworms and make good taffetas; they do not yet make damasks, satins, or velvets, however.

The sugar industry is even wider in scope, for the sugar not only is consumed in the Indies but is shipped in quantity to Spain. Sugar cane grows remarkably well in various parts of the Indies. In the islands, in Mexico, in Peru, and elsewhere they have built sugar mills that do a large business. I was told that the Nasca [Peru] sugar mill earned more than thirty thousand pesos a year. The mill at Chicama, near Trujillo [Peru], was also a big enterprise, and those of New Spain are no smaller, for the consumption of sugar and preserves in the Indies is simply fantastic. From the island of Santo Domingo, in the fleet in which I came, they brought eight hundred and ninety-eight chests and boxes of sugar. I happened to see the sugar loaded at the port of Puerto Rico, and it seemed to me that each box must contain eight *arrobas.* The sugar industry is the principal business of those islands — such a taste have men developed for sweets!

Olives and olive trees are also found in the Indies, in Mexico, and in Peru, but up to now they have not set up any mills to make olive oil. Actually, it is not made at all, for they prefer to eat the olives, seasoning them well. They find it unprofitable to make olive oil, and so all their oil comes from Spain.

3. THE RISE OF THE CATTLE INDUSTRY

The Spanish introduction of all kinds of domestic animals made possible a large increase in the food supply of the Americas and in the productivity of American agriculture. Their increase in this land of almost infinite pasturage soon outstripped potential demand and utilization, and herds of wild cattle became a common phenomenon in some parts of the Spanish colonies. Although the salting process and the preparation of

jerked beef (meat cut into strips and dried in the sun) were used on a limited scale before 1700, exports of cattle products before that time were largely limited to hides and tallow.[4]

✺✺✺✺ I find three kinds of animals in the Indies: some were brought there by the Spaniards; others are of the same kind we have in Europe but were not brought over by Spaniards; and still others are indigenous to the Indies and are not found in Spain. In the first category are sheep, cows, goats, pigs, horses, donkeys, dogs, cats, and the like, for all these species are found in the Indies. The sheep have greatly multiplied, and if their wool could profitably be exported to Europe it would be one of the greatest sources of wealth in the Indies, for the flocks have immense pastures, and in some places the grass never gets parched. So great is the extent of pasture land in Peru that there are no private pastures; everyone pastures his flocks where he pleases. For this reason there is usually an abundance of cheap meat there, as well as of the other products of sheep, such as cheese, milk, and the like. For a time the wool went entirely to waste, until they set up workshops in which they make cloth and blankets. This industry has greatly helped the poor people of that land, since the cloth of Castile is very expensive.

There are a variety of workshops in Peru, but a much greater number in New Spain. Nevertheless, either because the wool is inferior or because the workmen are less expert, the cloth that comes from Spain is much finer than what is made here. There used to be men who owned seventy and even a hundred thousand head of sheep, and even today some men have herds nearly as large. In Europe this would be a great fortune, but there it is only modest wealth. In most parts of the Indies, sheep do not do very well, because the grass is so high and the soil so overgrown that only the cattle can graze there.

There are two kinds of cattle. Some are domesticated and wander in herds, as in Charcas and other provinces of Peru, and in all New Spain. They use these tame cattle as do the Spaniards — for their meat, butter, and calves, and as oxen for tilling the ground. The other kind runs wild in the woods and hills, and because of the wildness and density of the forests, and also because of the great number of these cattle, they have no brands or masters; as with any other wild game, whoever kills an animal is its owner. The cattle have multiplied so greatly in Santo Domingo, and in other islands of that region, that they wander by the thousands through the forests and fields, all masterless. They hunt these beasts only for their hides; whites and Negroes go out on horseback, equipped with a kind of hooked knife, to chase the cattle, and any animal that falls to their

[4] Acosta, *Historia natural de las Indias*, pp. 317–318. (Excerpt translated by the editor.)

knives is theirs. They kill it and carry the hide home, leaving the flesh to rot — no one wants it, since meat is so plentiful. They told me in Santo Domingo that in some parts an infection has been caused by the rotting of so much flesh.

The export of hides to Spain forms one of the principal industries of the islands and New Spain. The fleet that came in 1587 brought 35,444 hides from Santo Domingo. From New Spain came 74,350 hides, valued at 96,532 pesos. When one of these fleets discharges, it is a wonderful thing to see the river at Seville, and the sandbar where they unload so many hides and so much merchandise.

There are also large numbers of goats, which in addition to the usual products — kids, milk, and so forth — yield the lucrative tallow, which rich and poor alike commonly use for lighting, because its abundance makes it cheaper than oil. . . . Tanned goat hides are also used to make footwear, but I do not believe them to be as good as those which are brought from Castile.

4. THE PROMISE OF THE PAMPA

Buenos Aires, situated on the edge of a large plain of marvelous fertility, and the natural outlet for the trade of the vast region drained by the Paraná River and its affluents, remained a provincial village or town of little importance for the greater part of the colonial period. Spanish prohibition of any seaborne commerce with the outside world, only occasionally relieved by grudging permission to send licensed vessels to Spain or Brazil, hampered the development of the teeming livestock resources of the region. In the seventeenth century the aggressive drive of Dutch, English, and other foreign merchants to break into the Spanish-American markets brought a marked growth of clandestine trade in the Plate area, and some economic relief to its inhabitants. A Frenchman by the name of Acarette, of whom very little is known, left an interesting and on the whole reliable account of his visit to Buenos Aires in 1657. However, an Argentine editor of Acarette's book questions his enthusiastic estimates of the number of cattle on the pampa at that date. The same editor doubts the truth of Acarette's story that herds of wild cattle were used to prevent hostile landings, and suggests that the traveler was the victim of a joke of fun-loving porteños (citizens of Buenos Aires).[5]

[5] Acarette, *Relación de un viaje al Rio de la Plata* . . . , edited by Julio Cesar González, Buenos Aires, 1943, pp. 45–46. (Excerpt translated by the editor.)

✠✠✠✠ All the wealth of these inhabitants consists in livestock, which multiply so prodigiously in this province that the plains are almost completely covered with them — particularly bulls, cows, sheep, horses, mares, donkeys, pigs, deer, and others — to such an extent that if it were not for the vast number of dogs that devour the calves and other young animals they would devastate the country. The people make such great profits from the skins and hides of these animals that a single example will suffice to show how it could be increased in good hands. Each of the twenty-two Dutch ships that we found in Buenos Aires was loaded with 13 to 14,000 bull hides, whose value was at least 300,000 *livres* or 33,500 pounds sterling. These hides were bought by the Dutch at seven or eight *reales* apiece — that is, less than an English crown — and were sold in Europe for at least twenty-five English shillings.

When I expressed my surprise at the sight of such an infinite number of heads of cattle, they told me of a stratagem that they use when they fear the landing of some enemy: They drive such a multitude of bulls, cows, horses, and other animals toward the beach that it becomes impossible for any number of men, though they have no fear of the fury of the animals, to open a way for themselves through such an immense assemblage of beasts.

The first inhabitants of this place put their personal brands on the animals that they could trap and put in enclosures, but they multiplied so rapidly that they had to let them go, and now they merely kill as many as they need when they have occasion to sell a considerable number of hides. At present they only brand those horses and mules that they catch to break in and train for their own use. Some individuals carry on a large business sending these draft animals to Peru, where a pair brings fifty *patacones*, or eleven pounds, thirteen shillings, and four pence. The majority of the cattle-dealers are very rich, but of all the merchants, those who trade in European goods are most important, and many of them are reputed to be worth from 200 to 300,000 crowns, or 67,000 pounds sterling. By these standards a merchant who is not worth more than 15 or 20,000 crowns is considered a mere retailer.

5. THE POTOSÍ MINE

Spain's proudest possession in the New World was the great silver mine of Potosí in Upper Peru (present-day Bolivia), whose flow of treasure attained gigantic proportions between 1579 and 1635. More than any other colonial resource, the fantastic wealth of Potosí captivated the Spanish imagination. The

following selection gives some account of this wealth and of mining practices in the late sixteenth century.[6]

✠✠✠✠ It appears from the royal accounts of the House of Trade of Potosí, and it is affirmed by venerable and trustworthy men, that during the time of the government of the licentiate Polo, which was many years after the discovery of the hill, silver was registered every Saturday to the value of 150 to 200,000 pesos, of which the King's fifth (*quintos*) came to 30 to 40,000 pesos, making a yearly total of about 1,500,000 pesos. According to this calculation, the value of the daily output of the mine was 30,000 pesos, of which the King's share amounted to 6,000 pesos. One more thing should be noted in estimating the wealth of Potosí; namely, that accounts have been kept of only the silver that was marked and taxed. But it is well known in Peru that for a long time the people of that country used the silver called "current," which was neither marked nor taxed. And those who know the mines well conclude that at that time the bulk of the silver mined at Potosí paid no tax, and that this included all the silver in circulation among the Indians, and much of that in use among the Spaniards, as I could observe during my stay in that country. This leads me to believe that a third — if not one half — of the silver production of Potosí was neither registered nor taxed. . . . [It should also be noted that] although the mines of Potosí have been dug to a depth of two hundred *estados*, the miners have never encountered water, which is the greatest possible obstacle to profitable operations, whereas the mines of Porco, so rich in silver ore, have been abandoned because of the great quantity of water. For there are two intolerable burdens connected with the search for silver: the labor of digging and breaking the rock, and that of getting out the water — and the first of these is more than enough. In fine, at the present time His Catholic Majesty receives on the average a million pesos a year from his fifth of the silver of Potosí, not counting the considerable revenue he derives from quicksilver and other royal perquisites. . . .

The hill of Potosí contains four principal veins: the Rich vein, that of Centeno, the vein called "of Tin," and that of Mendieta. All these veins are in the eastern part of the hill, as if facing the sunrise; there is no vein to the west. These veins run from north to south, or from pole to pole. They measure six feet at their greatest width, and a *palmo* at the narrowest point. From these veins issue others, as smaller branches grow out of the arms of trees. Each vein has different mines that have been claimed and divided among different owners, whose names they usually bear. The largest mine is eighty yards in size, the legal maximum; the smallest is four yards. By now all these

[6] Acosta, *Historia natural de las Indias*, pp. 238-243. (Excerpt translated by the editor.)

mines are very deep. In the Rich vein there are seventy-eight mines; they are as deep as one hundred and eighty and even two hundred *estados* in some places. In the Centeno vein there are twenty-four mines. Such are as much as sixty and even eighty *estados* deep, and the same is true of the other veins and mines of that hill. In order to work the mines at such great depths, tunnels (*socavones*) were devised; these are caves, made at the foot of the mountain, that cross it until they meet the veins. Although the veins run north to south, they descend from the top to the foot of the mountain — a distance calculated at more than 1200 *estados*. And by this calculation, although the mines run so deep it is six times as far again to their root and bottom, which some believe must be extremely rich, being the trunk and source of all the veins. But so far experience has proven the contrary, for the higher the vein the richer it is, and the deeper it runs the poorer the yield. Be that as it may, in order to work the mines with less cost, labor, and risk, they invented the tunnels, by means of which they can easily enter and leave the mines. They are eight feet wide and one *estado* high, and are closed off with doors. With the aid of these tunnels they get out the silver ore without difficulty, paying the owner of the tunnel a fifth of all the metal that is obtained. Nine tunnels have already been made, and others are being dug. A tunnel called "of the Poison" (*del Veneno*), which enters the Rich vein, was twenty-nine years in the making, for it was begun in 1556 (eleven years after the discovery of those mines) and was completed on April 11, 1585. This tunnel crossed the vein at a point thirty-five *estados* from its root or source, and from there to the mouth of the mine was 135 *estados;* such was the depth of that they had to descend to work those mines. This tunnel (called the *Crucero*) is 250 yards in length, and its construction took twenty-nine years; this shows how much effort men will make to get silver from the bowels of the earth. They labor there in perpetual darkness, not knowing day from night; and since the sun never penetrates these places, they are not only always dark but very cold, and the air is very thick and alien to the nature of men. And that is why those who enter there for the first time get seasick, as it were, being seized with nausea and stomach cramps, as I was. The miners always carry candles, and they divide their labor so that some work by day and rest by night and others work at night and rest during the day. The silver ore is generally of a flinty hardness, and they break it up with bars. Then they carry the ore on their backs up ladders made of three cords of twisted cowhide, joined by pieces of wood that serve as rungs, so that one man can climb up and another come down at the same time. These ladders are ten *estados* long, and at the top and bottom of each there is a wooden platform where the men may rest, because there are so many ladders to climb. Each man usually carries on his back a load of two *arrobas* of silver ore tied in a cloth, knapsack

fashion; thus they ascend, three at a time. The one who goes first carries a candle tied to his thumb, because, as I mentioned, they receive no light from above; thus, holding with both hands, they climb that great distance, often more than 150 *estados* — a fearful thing, the mere thought of which inspires dread. So great is the love of silver, which men suffer such great pains to obtain.

6. THE COLONIAL FACTORY

The Mexican city of Puebla was a leading industrial center in the colonial period, with numerous workshops (obrajes) *producing cotton, woolen, and silk cloth, hats, chinaware, and glass. The Englishman Gage, who visited Puebla not many years after the visit described below, observed that "the cloth which is made in it . . . is sent far and near, and [is] judged now to be as good as the cloth of Segovia, which is the best that is made in Spain." It is noteworthy that many of the factory owners, who treated their native employees so mercilessly, were themselves Indians or* mestizos.[7]

✠✠✠✠ There are in this city large woolen mills in which they weave quantities of fine cloth, serge, and grogram, from which they make handsome profits, this being an important business in this country. . . . To keep their mills supplied with labor for the production of cloth and grogram, they maintain individuals who are engaged and hired to ensnare poor innocents; seeing some Indian who is a stranger to the town, with some trickery or pretext, such as hiring him to carry something, like a porter, and paying him cash, they get him into the mill; once inside, they drop the deception, and the poor fellow never again gets outside that prison until he dies and they carry him out for burial. In this way they have gathered in and duped many married Indians with families, who have passed into oblivion here for 20 years, or longer, or their whole lives, without their wives or children knowing anything about them; for even if they want to get out, they cannot, thanks to the great watchfulness with which the doormen guard the exits. These Indians are occupied in carding, spinning, weaving, and the other operations of making cloth and grogram; and thus the owners make their profits by these unjust and unlawful means.

And although the Royal Council of the Indies, with the holy zeal which animates it for the service of God our Lord, of His Majesty, and of the Indians' welfare, has tried to remedy this evil with warrants

[7] Vásquez de Espinosa, *Description of the West Indies*, translated by C. U. Clark, pp. 133–134.

and ordinances, which it constantly has sent and keeps sending, for the proper administration and the amelioration of this great hardship and enslavement of the Indians, and the Viceroy of New Spain appoints mill inspectors to visit them and remedy such matters, nevertheless, since most of those who set out on such commissions, aim rather at their own enrichment, however much it may weigh upon their consciences, than at the relief of the Indians, and since the mill owners pay them well, they leave the wretched Indians in the same slavery; and even if some of them are fired with holy zeal to remedy such abuses when they visit the mills, the mill owners keep places provided in the mills in which they hide the wretched Indians against their will, so that they do not see or find them, and the poor fellows cannot complain about their wrongs. This is the usual state of affairs in all the mills of this city and jurisdiction, and that of Mexico City; the mill owners and those who have the mills under their supervision, do this without scruple, as if it were not a most serious mortal sin.

11 ✛ Commerce, Smuggling, and Piracy

Spain's colonial commercial system was unusually restrictive, exclusive, and regimented in character, even by the mercantilist standards of that day. Control over all colonial trade, under the Royal Council of the Indies, was vested in the *Casa de Contratación*, or House of Trade, established in 1503. Trade with the colonies was restricted until the eighteenth century to the wealthier merchants of Seville and Cadiz, who were organized in a guild that exercised great influence in all matters relating to colonial trade. With the aim of safeguarding the Seville monopoly and preventing contraband trade, only three American ports, Veracruz in New Spain, Cartagena in New Granada, and Nombre de Dios (later Portobello) on the Isthmus of Panama, were licensed to receive the Spanish merchant fleets. Inevitably the system generated colonial discontent and stimulated the growth of contraband trade.

The Spanish kings, on the basis of the papal donation of 1493 and the treaty of Tordesillas with Portugal of the following year, laid claim to all America except that portion which belonged to Portugal. By virtue of this title, all foreigners were forbidden to navigate American waters or trade on American coasts, on pain of destruction of ships and crews. The rising merchant classes and ambitious monarchs of northern Europe were unwilling to accept these pretensions. French, Dutch, and English mariners participated in the mounting offensive

against Spain's monopoly in the New World, but England soon emerged as the principal threat to Spain's empire in America. Slave-trading, smuggling, and outright banditry were the various forms of the British offensive against the Spanish empire in America. "No peace beyond the line" was the formula that described the chronic warfare that raged in American waters east of the meridian of the Azores and south of the Tropic of Cancer, even while peace prevailed in Europe.

In the seventeenth century piracy and contraband were supplemented by efforts to found foreign colonies in the forbidden waters of the Spanish Main. The net result of a century of colony-building and attempts to wrest territory from Spain measured in square miles was meager: England held the large island of Jamaica, and divided with Holland and France possession of a number of small islands in the Lesser Antilles. In this period piracy became a highly-organized and large-scale activity. Piracy entered on a decline after the signing of the treaty of Madrid (1670) between England and Spain, by which the English government agreed to aid in suppressing the corsairs in return for Spanish recognition of its sovereignty over the British West Indian islands.

Contraband trade attained even larger proportions in the course of the sixteenth and seventeenth centuries. Buenos Aires became a funnel through which foreign traders poured immense quantities of merchandise that penetrated as far as Peru. The European establishments in Jamaica and the Lesser Antilles formed another focus of forbidden trade with the Spanish colonies. This traffic, to which the colonists were driven by their unsatisfied needs, and to which the venality of local officials materially contributed, did untold damage to Spanish royal and private interests.

1. ON THE SEA-ROAD TO THE INDIES

Throughout the sixteenth century men and goods were carried to the colonies in much the same tiny vessels as those with which Columbus had made his memorable discovery. Danger and hardship attended the long voyage to the Indies from the time a ship left Seville to thread its careful way down the shoal-ridden Guadalquivir to the Mediterranean. Father Tomás de la Torre, one of a number of Dominican friars who accompanied Bishop Bartolomé de las Casas when the Protector of the Indians came to Mexico in 1544, describes the trials of an Atlantic crossing in the days of the Galleons.[1]

[1] Fray Tomás de la Torre, *Desde Salamanca, España, hasta Ciudad Real, Chiapas, Diario del viaje, 1544–1545,* edited by Frans Blom, México, 1945, pp. 70–73. (Excerpt translated by the editor.)

✠✠✠ After boarding our ship we passed the day there, exposed to a burning sun. On the following day (July 10) we hoisted sails with a very feeble wind, because the sailors said that once on the high seas we could navigate with any kind of wind. That day all the other ships got off that difficult and dangerous sandbar at San Lucar. Only ours remained in the middle of the bar and its dangers. They put the blame on the land pilot; but it was really the fault of our sailors, who had ballasted the ship badly, loading all the cargo above deck. That day the fleet moved three leagues out, while we remained on the bar in front of the town, enduring miseries that made a good beginning to our labors and perils.

When the townspeople saw that the ship remained there they thought that something had happened, and the Duke [of Alba] sent a boat to express the regrets of himself and his lady, and to say that if boats were needed to get the ship off the bar he would send them. But the crazy sailors, very haughty about all that concerned their business, wanted no help. The captain of the fleet sent a small vessel to let us know that he would wait for us only a day or two. . . . The pilot and master of the ship, named Pedro de Ibarra, went to give an account of himself and to complain of the land pilot, who, in accordance with prevailing custom, is supposed to take the ships off the bar. . . .

The following day, which was Friday, July 11, we raised sails and with perfectly dry eyes lost sight of our Spain. The wind was good but weak. The sea quickly gave us to understand that it was not meant to be the habitation of men, and we all became so deathly sick that nothing in the world could move us from where we lay. Only the Father Vicar and three others managed to keep their feet, but these three were so ill that they could do nothing for us; the Father Vicar alone served us all, placing basins and bowls before us so that we could bring up our scanty meals, which did us no good at all. There were four or five neophytes in our company, on their way to serve God in the Indies, who usually took care of us, but they also became sick and had to be nursed themselves. We could not swallow a mouthful of food, although we were quite faint, but our thirst was intense.

One could not imagine a dirtier hospital, or one that resounded with more lamentations, than ours. Some men went below deck, where they were cooked alive; others roasted in the sun on deck, where they lay about, trampled upon, humiliated, and indescribably filthy; and although after several days some of them had recovered, they were not well enough to serve those who were still sick. His Lordship the Bishop donated his own hens to the sick, for we had not brought any, and a priest who was going as a schoolteacher to Chiapa helped the Father Vicar. . . . We were a pitiful sight indeed, and there was no one to console us, since nearly everyone was in the same condition.

When we left Spain the war with France was at its height, so we departed in great fear of the enemy. On the afternoon of that day those who could raise their heads saw sixteen sails. They feared that they were Frenchmen, and all that night the fleet was much alarmed, although the enemy had greater reason to fear us, because of our superior numbers. But in the morning nothing could be seen, so we decided it was a fleet coming from the Indies. . . . In the evening our stomachs quieted down and we did not vomit, but the heat, especially below deck, was intolerable.

Saturday morning we saw a large boat, and, thinking that it was a French spy, a ship went after it. The bark began to escape, when the ship fired a shot, whereupon the bark lowered its sails, was recognized as Spanish, and was permitted to go in peace. The crews of the vessels that heard the shot thought that we had run into Frenchmen and that the ships were firing at each other. When we below deck heard the noise of arms being got ready, we were alarmed and suddenly recovered enough to say a litany; some even confessed themselves. Others made a joke of the whole affair. When we learned it was nothing at all, we returned to our former supine misery. After this there was no more disturbance.

So that those who do not know the sea may understand the suffering one endures there, especially at the beginning of a voyage, I shall describe some things that are well known to anyone who has sailed on it. First, a ship is a secure prison, from which no one may escape, even though he wears neither shackles nor irons; so cruel is this prison that it makes no distinctions among its inmates but makes them all suffer alike. The heat, the stuffiness, and the sense of confinement are sometimes overpowering. The bed is ordinarily the floor. Some bring a few small mattresses; ours were very poor, small, and hard, stuffed with dog hairs; to cover us we had some extremely poor blankets of goat's wool. Add to this the general nausea and poor health; most passengers go about as if out of their minds and in great torment — some longer than others, and a few for the entire voyage. There is very little desire to eat, and sweet things do not go down well; there is an incredible thirst, sharpened by a diet of hardtack and salt beef. The water ration is half an *azumbre* daily; if you want wine you must bring your own. There are infinite numbers of lice, which eat men alive, and you cannot wash clothing because the sea water shrinks it. There is an evil stink, especially below deck, that becomes intolerable throughout the ship when the pump is working — and it is going more or less constantly, depending on how the ship sails. On a good day the pump runs four or five times, to drain the foul-smelling bilge water.

These and other hardships are common on board ship, but we felt them more because they were so foreign to our usual way of living. Furthermore, even when you are enjoying good health there is

no place where you can study or withdraw for a little while, and you have to sit all the time, because there is no room to walk about. . . . The most disturbing thing of all is to have death constantly staring you in the face; you are separated from it by only the thickness of one board joined to another with pitch.

2. THE PATTERN OF COLONIAL TRADE

The Spanish colonial trade system was restrictive and exclusive to a degree unusual even in that age of mercantilist policies. But Spanish industry, handicapped by its guild organization and technical backwardness, was unable to supply cheap and abundant manufactures in return for colonial foodstuffs and raw materials, as required by the implied terms of the mercantilist bargain. Nor was it in the interest of the merchant monopolists of Seville, who throve on a régime of scarcity and high prices, to permit an abundant flow of manufactures to the colonies. Inevitably the more advanced industrial nations of northern Europe sought to enter by force or guile into the large and unsatisfied Spanish-American markets. Foreign interest in the commercial possibilities of Spanish America gave rise to a considerable body of pamphlets and books dealing with that part of the world. John Campbell (1708–1775), a popular writer on politics and history, composed one of the best-informed works of this type. His book went through numerous editions in the eighteenth century, suggesting the strong interest that Englishmen took in its subject. Here Campbell discusses the operation of the Spanish fleet system.[2]

✦✦✦✦ It has been always the ruling maxim in the Spanish councils to preserve by all means possible the commerce with the West Indies, not only to the Spanish nation, but to the crown of Spain. On this principle they restrained, with great punctuality, all strangers from passing into their American dominions; and though there have been formerly some instances of foreigners passing through the Spanish settlements, and even residing in them, yet they are so rare, and attended with such extraordinary circumstances, that instead of admiring that such things have happened, we ought rather to wonder that they have not happened more frequently, considering the strong passion that strangers have always had for penetrating unknown countries, especially such countries as Mexico and Peru, rich in themselves, and repre-

[2] John Campbell, *The Spanish Empire in America*, London, 1747, pp. 279–286.

sented much richer than they were. . . . Thus we see that the lawful commerce between Europe and Spanish America is entirely in the hands of the Spaniards, and absolutely subject to the direction of the crown.

The method in which this trade is carried on is well enough known in general, but few enter far enough into its particulars. In order to give as distinct an account of this matter as possible, we shall speak of the Galleons, the Flota, the Flotilla, Register-Ships, and Guardas Costas; and when we have done this, the reader will perfectly comprehend the mystery of the Spanish policy in this point.

A Galleon is, properly speaking, a very large man-of-war, of three or four decks, built in a manner now altogether out of fashion, except in Spain, and the reason why it is still used there, is, that it affords a great deal of room for merchandise, with which the king's ships are generally so much crowded, as to be in no condition of defending themselves. That fleet which we call the Galleons, consists of eight such men-of-war. Of these there are three very large ones, styled *la Capitana, la Almiranta,* and *el Gobierno;* two others which are less, *la Patacha,* and *la Margarita,* each of fifty guns; and an advice frigate of forty. The merchant-men which sail with this fleet, and purchase their licences at a very high rate, are in number from twelve to sixteen, and burthen at least a third part bigger than is expressed in their respective schedules. These ships are intended to carry all that is necessary, either of warlike stores, or merchandise for Peru: and this is the specific difference between this fleet and the Flota, which is intended for Mexico. In time of peace, the Galleons sail regularly once a year from Cadiz, at no set time, but according to the king's pleasure, and the convenience of the merchants. From Cadiz the Galleons steer directly for the Canaries, where, if the Flota sailed with them, as it sometimes does, they anchor together in the haven of Gomera. Thence they bear away for the Antilles, and when they arrive at that height, the Flota separates, and the Galleons bear away for Cartagena. As soon as they double Cape de la Vela, and appear before the mouth of Rio de la Hacha, advice is sent to all parts, that every thing may be got ready for their reception. In the harbour of Cartagena they remain a month, and land there all the goods designed for the Audience of the Terra Firma. Then they sail to Porto Bello, where they continue during the fair, which lasts five or six weeks; and having landed the merchandise intended for Peru, and received the treasure and rich commodities sent from thence on board, they sail again to Cartagena, where they remain till they return to Spain, which is usually within the space of two years. When they have orders to return, they sail first to the Havana, and having there joined the Flota, and what other ships are returning to Europe, they steer through the gulf of Florida, and so to the height of Carolina, where meeting with the western winds, they

shape their course then for the Azores. They take in fresh water and provisions at Tercera, and thence continue their voyage to Cadiz.

The Flota consists, as well as the Galleons, of a certain number of men-of-war, and of a certain number of merchant ships. The former are seldom more than three, la Capitana, la Almiranta, and la Patacha. The latter are usually about sixteen, in burthen between five hundred and a thousand tons. This fleet sails about the month of August, that by the favour of the winds which reign about November, they may the more easily pursue their voyage to Vera Cruz. In their passage they call at Puerto Rico, to take in fresh water and provisions, then pass in sight of Hispaniola, Jamaica, and Cuba; and, according to the season of the year, and the nature of the winds, pass either by the coast of Yucatan, or higher thro' the gulf of Vera Cruz, two hundred and sixty leagues in twelve days, or thereabouts; in all eighteen hundred and ten leagues in about sixty-two days. As the Flota is designed to furnish not only Mexico, but the Philippine Islands also, as we have before remarked in speaking of the trade of Acapulco, with European goods, they are obliged to remain there for a considerable space; and, when it is necessary, they winter in that port. The cargo with which they return, is not so rich as that of the Galleons; but some writers say, that it increases annually in its value, which must be owing to the progress made in settling what the Spaniards call the Kingdom of New Mexico.

It is usually in the month of May that the Flota leaves Vera Cruz, though sometimes it is detained in that harbour till August. Then the ships that compose it, sail for the Havana; for though the Galleons and the Flota seldom leave Spain, yet they generally return, together. As soon as they are safely arrived in the Havana, they detach a few of the lightest and cleanest ships to Europe, who, besides money and merchandise, carry also an exact account of the contents both of the Galleons and Flota. These ships are called by the Spaniards, with propriety enough, the Flotilla, i.e. the little fleet. The principal reason for sending them in this manner into Spain, is to give the court of Madrid an opportunity of judging what convoy may be necessary, in case of any alteration of affairs, to be sent to escort the grand fleet, as also to regulate the Indulto which may be levied on the merchants in proportion to their interest in the Galleons and Flota. But the reader may possibly incline to enquire what obliges this great fleet to remain so long at the Havana? To which two causes may be assigned, viz. waiting for a wind, or for the register-ships which they are to convoy home.

A register-ship is so called, from its being registered with all the effects embarked in Spain, in the books kept for that purpose in the Chamber of Seville. As this general account will not probably appear satisfactory, I shall endeavor to state the matter more fully. A company of merchants having, as they conceive, just grounds to imagine

that European goods are greatly wanted at some particular ports in the West Indies, they draw up a memorial or petition, containing these reasons in the clearest and concisest terms, and lay it before the Council of the Indies. The prayer of this petition is, that they may have leave to send a ship of three hundred ton burthen, or under, to the port they mention. When leave is obtained, they pay a certain sum to the crown, which is generally between thirty and fifty thousand pieces of eight, besides presents, and those no small ones, to the king's officers, from the greatest to the last. That this however may not induce any suspicion of fraud, they register their ship and cargo, that it may appear consistent with their petition and licence, and yet (such a fatality there attends on all custom-house actions) this ship of under three hundred tons generally carries upwards of six hundred tons of goods, and affords accommodation for passengers besides. Copies from the register are transmitted to the governor and royal officers at the port, to which the register-ship is bound; and such is their diligence, such their integrity, that when the ship comes to an anchor in the port, they make a very narrow enquiry, and yet there is seldom or never any fraud discovered, but, on the contrary, this ship of six or seven hundred tons returns into Europe with an authentic certificate from all the King of Spain's officers, that she does not carry quite three hundred, together with a bill of lading in the same strain of computation. By these register-ships there is sometimes a gain of two, or three hundred per cent, which enables the owners to pay so bountifully for cheating the King, having first got the money by robbing his subjects.

3. THE GREAT FAIR AT PORTOBELLO

After 1584 the chief port of entry for the legal commerce with South America was the little town of Portobello on the Isthmus of Panama. For a few weeks during the year a brisk trade, strictly supervised by royal officials, was plied in the town square. In the 1730's, when the Portobello fair was visited by two youthful Spanish scientists and naval officers, Jorge Juan (1713–1773), and Antonio Ulloa (1716–1795), it had long passed its heyday, principally because of the growing influx of foreign interlopers into colonial trade, but it still presented a scene of considerable business activity.[3]

✠✠✠✠ The town of Porto Bello, so thinly inhabited, by reason of its noxious air, the scarcity of provisions, and the soil, becomes, at the

[3] George Juan and Antonio de Ulloa, *A Voyage to South America*, London, 1772, 2 vols., I, pp. 103–105.

time of the galleons, one of the most populous places in all South America. Its situation on the isthmus betwixt the south and north sea, the goodness of its harbour, and its small distance from Panama, have given it the preference for the rendezvous of the joint commerce of Spain and Peru, at its fair.

On advice being received at Carthagena, that the Peru fleet had unloaded at Panama, the galleons make the best of their way to Porto Bello, in order to avoid the distempers which have their source from idleness. The concourse of people, on this occasion, is such, as to raise the rent of lodging to an excessive degree; a middling chamber, with a closet, lets, during the fair, for a thousand crowns, and some large houses for four, five, or six thousand.

The ships are no sooner moored in the harbour, than the first work is, to erect, in the square, a tent made of the ship's sails, for receiving its cargo; at which the proprietors of the goods are present, in order to find their bales, by the marks which distinguish them. These bales are drawn on sledges, to their respective places by the crew of every ship, and the money given them is proportionally divided.

Whilst the seamen and European traders are thus employed, the land is covered with droves of mules from Panama, each drove consisting of above an hundred, loaded with chests of gold and silver, on account of the merchants of Peru. Some unload them at the exchange, others in the middle of the square; yet, amidst the hurry and confusion of such crowds, no theft, loss, or disturbance, is ever known. He who has seen this place during the *tiempo muerto*, or dead time, solitary, poor, and a perpetual silence reigning everywhere; the harbour quite empty, and every place wearing a melancholy aspect; must be filled with astonishment at the sudden change, to see the bustling multitudes, every house crowded, the square and streets encumbered with bales and chests of gold and silver of all kinds; the harbour full of ships and vessels, some bringing by the way of Rio de Chape the goods of Peru, as cacao, quinquina, or Jesuit's bark, Vicuña wool, and bezoar stones; others coming from Carthagena, loaded with provisions; and thus a spot, at all other times detested for its deleterious qualities, becomes the staple of the riches of the old and new world, and the scene of one of the most considerable branches of commerce in the whole earth.

The ships being unloaded, and the merchants of Peru, together with the president of Panama, arrived, the fair comes under deliberation. And for this purpose the deputies of the several parties repair on board the commodore of the galleons, where, in presence of the commodore, and the president of Panama; the former, as patron of the Europeans, and the latter, of the Peruvians; the prices of the several kinds of merchandizes are settled; and all preliminaries being adjusted in three or four meetings, the contracts are signed, and made public, that every one may conform himself to them in the sale of his effects.

Thus all fraud is precluded. The purchases and sales, as likewise the exchanges of money, are transacted by brokers, both from Spain and Peru. After this, every one begins to dispose of his goods; the Spanish brokers embarking their chests of money, and those of Peru sending away the goods they have purchased, in vessels called chatas and bongos, up the river Chagre. And thus the fair of Porto Bello ends.

Formerly this fair was limited to no particular time; but as a long stay, in such a sickly place, extremely affected the health of the traders, his Catholic majesty transmitted an order, that the fair should not last above forty days, reckoning from that in which the ships came to an anchor in the harbour; and that, if in this space of time the merchants could not agree in their rates, those of Spain should be allowed to carry their goods up the country to Peru; and accordingly the commodore of the galleons has orders to reimbark them, and return to Carthagena; but otherwise, by virtue of a compact between the merchants of both kingdoms, and ratified by the king, no Spanish trader is to send his goods, on his own account, beyond Porto Bello: and, on the contrary, those of Peru cannot send remittances to Spain, for purchasing goods there.

4. JOHN HAWKINS: MERCHANT ADVENTURER

The famous trading voyage of John Hawkins to Hispaniola in 1563 opened the great struggle between England and Spain for world supremacy. Half honest trader, half corsair, Hawkins came to the Indies heavily armed and ready to compel the colonists to deal with him at cannon point, but he showed himself scrupulously correct in his business dealings with the Spaniards, even to the point of paying the royal license and customs dues. Hawkins owed the success of his first two American voyages to the needs of the Spanish settlers, who were ready to trade with a Lutheran heretic or the Devil himself to satisfy their desperate need for slave labor and European goods. To cover up these violations of Spanish law, the venal local officials made a thin pretense of enforcement. But by 1567 the pretense had worn too thin, the Spanish government had taken alarm, and angry orders went out to drive the English contra- bandists away. An official report describes the reception ac- corded to Hawkins on his third voyage, at the town of Rio de la Hacha on the Venezuelan coast.[4]

---

[4] *Spanish Documents Concerning English Voyages to the Caribbean, 1527–1568,* translated and edited by Irene A. Wright, London, the Hakluyt Society, Cam- bridge University Press, 1929, pp. 120–123.

✠✠✠✠ On June 10 of the current year John Hawkins, English corsair, arrived off the port of this city. He came in command of ten very handsome ships, which he said belonged to the queen of England, his mistress. As soon as he had arrived off this port he sent me a letter in which he offered me great gifts, if I would permit him to trade; and if I would not, he made great threats. I answered him what your majesty has ordered and provided in your majesty's royal orders and provisions, and that I would by no means yield a single point from the tenor of those commands.

In view of my determination, after much argument, he landed his forces three-quarters of a league down the coast, beyond all my defences and bulwarks, and out of range of the artillery which in your majesty's service I have placed here. Seeing this, I went out with all the men there were in this town to see if I could manage to prevent him from landing; although inasmuch as the enemy's number was so overwhelming and we were so few, it seemed to me to be madness to attempt to oppose the attack of such superior forces.

The Englishman having landed his party, with what few persons were available in the place I manned a fort which is built on the road by which he must advance, and there disputed his passage as fully as I was able. From that work I inflicted serious damage on him, but because of his superior numbers we were unable to prevent him from taking the fort, for from his pinnaces and shallops he played so many guns on the fort, not a man dared to remain in any part of it. When he had taken the fort, he also took the town.

I assembled the people of the place in as good order as possible and retired to a point from which I could prevent his advance, although my force was badly cut up. My hope was to keep a fighting body together that the enemy might not forget himself and begin to capture the women, children, aged and ill, who were scattered over the adjacent countryside.

When he had taken the town the Englishman again sent word to permit trade, saying that unless I did so he would burn and destroy the town and invade the interior and capture and steal whatever he might find. I answered him to do as he pleased, since I preferred to lose my worldly goods rather than to yield a jot of your majesty's commands. Immediately upon the messenger's arrival there he began to fire the town and that day he burned about half of it.

The next day in the morning he set out with as many as four hundred men and his field artillery, to invade the land. I opposed him with the few men I had. Wherever he turned I preceded him, doing what damage I could to his men, and burning and destroying the fields and food crops and farmhouses belonging to the people of the town. Seeing that their very owners were destroying their own houses and estates, the Englishman returned to the town in very desperate humour

and burned the government house and another large portion of the town. Excepting only certain houses he needed to shelter his men, he left no others standing. He spared about one-third of the town and burned two-thirds of it.

That night a negro and mulatto, slaves of mine, deserted to the enemy and told him they would lead him to the place, seven leagues from this city, where I had buried your majesty's royal treasure-chest, and that night they fell on a tent where I had all my goods, and where some poor and sick people and some women were in hiding. They seized these and robbed their poverty and stole everything I had, and threatened them that unless they were ransomed they would be killed. They released a prisoner that he might come to tell me the pitiable lamentations of the rest. In order that such grievous cruelty might not be carried out, for 4000 *pesos* gold I redeemed them and what remained to be burned of the town, including its holy church, on condition that they deliver to me the mulatto and the negro aforesaid.

I paid over the 4000 *pesos* and the enemy released the prisoners. Although they promised to restore the property that had been taken from them, they did not fulfil this promise. On the contrary, they stole it and carried it off. They reembarked and delivered to me the mulatto and the negro and I handed them over to your majesty's royal law that they might be punished and made an example to all the rest on this coast, and so the mulatto was hung and the negro quartered.

Before they cleared, after this ransom had been arranged, because they were unable to feed them, the English set a certain number of negroes ashore rather than throw them overboard. Some were children not over six years of age, and some were old males and old females (over a hundred years). Although the Englishman left them in recompense for the damage he did the town, acting with the royal officials I took possession of them all for your majesty and delivered them to a certain person to feed them through two or three months and so put them into condition that they might be worth something. We are now selling them off little by little despite the fact that the burghers demand them, alleging that the Englishman left them to pay for the damage done the town. I assure your majesty that had he left as many again it would not cover the damage he did here.

5. "NO PEACE BEYOND THE LINE"

Returning from his third voyage to the Indies, Hawkins encountered storms in the Florida channel that forced him to seek refuge in the port of Veracruz in September, 1568. There he was attacked by a large Spanish fleet bringing the new viceroy

of Mexico, Don Martín Enriquez. Only two of the English ships managed to get away; one was commanded by Hawkins, the other by his cousin, Francis Drake. Four years later Drake left England with four small ships, bound for the Isthmus of Panama. In actions marked by audacity and careful planning he stormed and plundered the town of Nombre de Dios, escaping at dawn; later he made the most lucrative haul in the history of piracy by capturing the pack-train carrying Peruvian silver from the Pacific side of the isthmus to Nombre de Dios. In 1577 Drake set sail again on an expedition that had the secret sponsorship and support of Queen Elizabeth. Its objects were to "singe the King of Spain's beard" by seizing his treasure-ships and ravaging his colonial towns; to explore the whole Pacific coast of America, taking possession of the regions beyond the limits of Spanish occupation; and to display English maritime prowess through a second circumnavigation of the globe. Drake achieved these ends without shedding the blood of a single Spaniard. The involuntary respect and liking that he inspired even in a Spanish enemy appear in the following letter from Don Francisco de Zárate to Viceroy Enriquez of New Spain, describing his captivity on board the Golden Hind.[5]

✠✠✠✠ On the following day, which was Sunday, in the morning, he dressed and decked himself very finely and had his galleon decorated with all its flags and banners. He also ordered that all the men on our ship be passed to another one of his, which he had taken on this same coast, and which had served for this purpose since he reached the coast of Chile, where he had on his hands a ship laden with a large quantity of gold and many others laden with silver. He had entered the port of Callao de Lima and cut the cables of all the ships that were in port. As the wind was from the land, they all went out to sea, where he had time to sack them at his will. Before he proceeded to do the same to ours he said to me: "Let one of your pages come with me to show me your apparel." He went from his galleon at about nine in the morning and remained until towards dusk, examining everything contained in the bales and chests. Of that which belonged to me he took but little. Indeed he was quite courteous about it. Certain trifles of mine having taken his fancy, he had them brought to his ship and gave me, in exchange for them, a falchion and a small brazier of silver, and I can assure Your Excellency that he lost nothing by the bargain. On his return to his vessel he asked me to pardon him for taking the trifles, but that they were for his wife. He said that I could depart the

⁵ *New Light on Drake*, translated and edited by Zella Nuttall, London, the Hakluyt Society, Cambridge University Press, 1914, pp. 204–208.

next morning, when the breeze would rise, for which I gave him thanks. . . .

This general of the Englishmen is a nephew* of John Hawkins, and is the same who, about five years ago, took the port of Nombre de Dios. He is called Francisco Drac, and is a man about 35 years of age, low of stature, with a fair beard, and is one of the greatest mariners that sails the seas, both as a navigator and as a commander. His vessel is a galleon of nearly four hundred tons, and is a perfect sailor. She is manned with a hundred men, all of service, and of an age for warfare, and all are as practised therein as old soldiers from Italy could be. Each one takes particular pains to keep his arquebuse clean. He treats them with affection, and they treat him with respect. He carries with him nine or ten cavaliers, cadets of English noblemen. These form a part of his council which he calls together for even the most trivial matter, although he takes advice from no one. But he enjoys hearing what they say and afterwards issues his orders. He has no favourite.

The aforesaid gentlemen sit at his table, as well as a Portuguese pilot, whom he brought from England, who spoke not a word during all the time I was on board. He is served on silver dishes with gold borders and gilded garlands, on which are his arms. He carries all possible dainties and perfumed waters. He said that many of these had been given him by the Queen.

None of these gentlemen took a seat or covered his head before him until he repeatedly urged him to do so. This galleon of his carries about thirty heavy pieces of artillery and a great quantity of firearms with the requisite ammunition and lead. He dines and sups to the music of viols. He carries trained carpenters and artisans, so as to be able to careen the ship at any time. Besides being new, the ship has double lining. I understood that all the men he carries with him receive wages, because, when our ship was sacked, no man dared take anything without his orders. He shows them great favour, but punishes the least fault. He also carries painters who paint for him pictures of the coast in its exact colours. This I was most grieved to see, for each thing is so naturally depicted that no one who guides himself according to these paintings can possibly go astray. I understood from him that he had sailed from his country with five vessels, four sloops (of the long kind) and that half of the armada belonged to the Queen.

6. THE BROTHERHOOD OF THE COAST

The seventeenth century saw a marked increase in privateering and piratical activity in Spanish-American waters. Chronic war-

* Zárate was mistaken, Drake was Hawkins' cousin. B.K.

fare between Spain and her European rivals, and Spain's stubborn refusal to concede the right of other powers to trade or navigate in the waters "beyond the line," provided these powers with a convenient pretext for tolerating and even fomenting piratical enterprise against Spanish colonial shipping and coastal towns. Jamaica, captured by the British in 1655; the western end of the island of Hispaniola; and the neighboring island of Tortuga became the principal lairs of the buccaneers. The typical pirate captain of the latter half of the seventeenth century was quite free of patriotic or religious zeal, and plied his trade in the calculating spirit of a businessman engaged in a likely speculation. John Esquemeling, a Dutch ex-corsair who wrote a valuable account of the exploits of the leading pirates of his time, describes the mode of operation of the "Brethren of the Coast," the name the buccaneers commonly gave to themselves.[6]

✠✠✠✠ Before the Pirates go out to sea, they give notice to every one that goes upon the voyage, of the day on which they ought precisely to embark, intimating also to them their obligation of bringing each man in particular so many pounds of powder and bullets as they think necessary for that expedition. Being all come on board, they join together in council, concerning what place they ought first to go to wherein to get provisions — especially of flesh, seeing that they scarce eat anything else. And of this the most common sort among them is pork. The next food is tortoises, which they are accustomed to salt a little. Sometimes they resolve to rob such or such hog-yards, wherein the Spaniards often have a thousand heads of swine together. They come to these places in the dark of the night, and having beset the keeper's lodge, they force him to rise, and give them as many heads as they desire, threatening withal to kill him in case he disobeys their commands or makes any noise. Yea, these menaces are oftentimes put in execution, without giving any quarter to the miserable swine-keepers, or any other person that endeavours to hinder their robberies.

Having got provisions of flesh sufficient for their voyage, they return to their ship. Here their allowance, twice a day to every one, is as much as he can eat, without either weight or measure. Neither does the steward of the vessel give any greater proportion of flesh, or anything else to the captain than to the meanest mariner. The ship being well victualled, they call another council, to deliberate towards what place they shall go, to seek their desperate fortunes. In this council, likewise, they agree upon certain Articles, which are put in writing, by way of bond or obligation, which every one is bound to observe, and all of them, or the chief, set their hands to it. Herein they

[6] John Esquemeling, *The Buccaneers of America*, London, 1893, pp. 58–60.

specify, and set down very distinctly, what sums of money each particular person ought to have for that voyage, the fund of all the payments being the common stock of what is gotten by the whole expedition; for otherwise it is the same law, among these people, as with other Pirates, *No prey, no pay*. In the first place, therefore, they mention how much the Captain ought to have for his ship. Next the salary of the carpenter, or shipwright, who careened, mended and rigged the vessel. This commonly amounts to one hundred or an hundred and fifty pieces of eight, being, according to the agreement, more or less. Afterwards for provisions and victualling they draw out of the same common stock about two hundred pieces of eight. Also a competent salary for the surgeon and his chest of medicaments, which usually is rated at two hundred or two hundred and fifty pieces of eight. Lastly they stipulate in writing what recompense or reward each one ought to have, that is either wounded or maimed in his body, suffering the loss of any limb, by that voyage. Thus they order for the loss of a right arm six hundred pieces of eight, or six slaves; for the loss of a left arm five hundred pieces of eight, or five slaves; for a right leg five hundred pieces of eight, or five slaves; for the left leg four hundred pieces of eight, or four slaves; for an eye one hundred pieces of eight, or one slave; for a finger of the hand the same reward as for the eye. All which sums of money, as I have said before, are taken out of the capital sum or common stock of what is got by their piracy. For a very exact and equal dividend is made of the remainder among them all. Yet herein they have also regard to qualities and places. Thus the Captain, or chief Commander, is allotted five or six portions to what the ordinary seamen have; the Master's Mate only two; and other Officers proportionate to their employment. After whom they draw equal parts from the highest even to the lowest mariner, the boys not being omitted. For even these draw half a share, by reason that, when they happen to take a better vessel than their own, it is the duty of the boys to set fire to the ship or boat wherein they are, and then retire to the prize which they have taken.

They observe among themselves very good orders. For in the prizes they take, it is severely prohibited to every one to usurp anything in particular to themselves. Hence all they take is equally divided, accordingly to what has been said before. Yea, they make a solemn oath to each other not to abscond, or conceal the least thing they find amongst the pray. If afterwards any one is found unfaithful, who has contravened the said oath, immediately he is separated and turned out of the society. Among themselves they are very civil and charitable to each other. Insomuch that if any wants what another has, with great liberality they give it one to another. As soon as these Pirates have taken any prize of ship or boat, the first thing they endeavour is to set on shore the prisoners, detaining only some few for their own help and

service, to whom also they give their liberty after the space of two or three years. They put in very frequently for refreshment at one island or another; but more especially into those which lie on the Southern side of the Isle of Cuba. Here they careen their vessels, and in the meantime some of them go to hunt, others to cruize upon the seas in canoes, seeking their fortune. Many times they take the poor fishermen of tortoises, and, carrying them to their habitations, they make them work so long as the Pirates are pleased.

7. DOING BUSINESS IN THE SMUGGLING WAY

Smuggling was the principal weapon employed by the rising industrial powers of Europe to batter down the wall of commercial monopoly that surrounded Spain's American possessions. Colonial merchants and consumers alike were glad of the opportunity to buy cheap foreign wares and dispose of their own surplus products. The royal officials in the colonies, corrupt almost to a man, most often connived with local merchants at the introduction of contraband goods. A useful survey of the subject appears in Campbell's work on the Spanish empire in America.[7]

✤✤✤✤ The methods taken by his most Catholic Majesty for effectually securing the commerce of his American dominions to the inhabitants of Old Spain, is the grand source of the little respect paid him in the Indies, and of the great weakness of his government at home. The inhabitants of the Spanish America consider gold and silver as commodities, which they have, and would willingly barter for some other commodities, which they have not, and which would be more useful to them than large heaps of either of those metals. It seems therefore to these people a great hardship, that either proper care is not taken to furnish them with what they want from Spain, or that they should not be allowed to supply themselves some other way. The native Spaniards, who have the government of the Indies entirely in their hands, treat such complaints with haughtiness natural to that nation, which renders them universally odious and insupportable. . . .

When folks are in such a situation, there need be no wonder at their endeavouring to carry on a clandestine trade, as, on the other hand, one cannot think it strange that their neighbours, who live under better governments, who have at cheap rates all that these Spaniards want, and yet stand in need of the silver and gold with which they abound, should be very willing to commence such an intercourse as

[7] John Campbell, *The Spanish Empire in America*, pp. 306–310, 315–319.

might take away all their wants. Sometimes governors have winked at this, not from a principle of avarice only, that they might share in the profits resulting from such a trade, but also from a sense of the necessity of dispensing with laws so ill executed as to deserve no respect. For, to be sure, that rule of justice, which connects the Spanish plantations to Spain, requires that the government of Spain should have a reciprocal regard for those plantations; and a neglect on one part infers licence on the other. Upon this principle it was, that before the treaty of Utrecht the English at Jamaica furnished the Spaniards at Porto Bello with Negroes, with the knowledge at least, if not by the permission of the governors. The inhabitants of Peru never could be without slaves. The government of Old Spain never could, indeed never attempted to supply them, but permitted sometimes the Genoese, sometimes the French to carry on this trade; and when they did not do it effectually, the deficiency was made good by such a commerce as I before mentioned with the English, though without any formal licence, but by a connivance, the less criminal for its being absolutely necessary.

The situation of the island of Jamaica, together with the conveniences of building and freighting sloops from thence, engaged the inhabitants in this, and in other branches of traffic. Such as settle themselves in these distant parts of the world, do it generally from a spirit of getting and therefore the grand point with them is always how to get most. They therefore for a long tract of time, and by various methods, not necessary to be insisted on here, supplied the Spaniards at Carthagena, Porto Bello, Rio de la Hacha, and other places with European commodities of all sorts, notwithstanding the mighty hazard they ran in the management of so dangerous a business, their own lives, and those of their customers, being alike exposed, and frequently forfeited to what the Spaniards call justice. They likewise carried on a trade with the Indians of Darien, to their great profit, but with equal risk, for the Spaniards were wont to shew no mercy either to English or Indians that fell into their hands; which is so much the harder, since the latter never were their subjects, nor ever will have any intercourse with them. By degrees the gains by this commerce tempted so many persons to be concerned in it, and the ships made use of were so well manned, and of such force, that the Spaniards grew less timorous than formerly; so that at last the commerce by the Galleons was greatly affected; for, knowing where to buy goods cheaper, the merchants would not give the prices usually demanded at the fairs of Carthagena and Porto Bello. . . .

The little island of St. Thomas, which lies in the North Seas, about fourteen leagues off Porto Rico, is the sole colony possessed by the Danes in the West Indies; nor would it be worth the keeping, but as it serves to maintain an illicit trade with the Spanish islands in its neighbourhood. We may form some idea of the vast advantages flow-

ing from this contraband commerce, from this very particular, especially if we consider that the Hamburgers have likewise a factory in this little isle purely on the same score. In order to maintain this correspondence, they transport from the Danish colonies in Africa a considerable number of slaves for the supply of Porto Rico, and sometimes of the Spanish part of the island of St. Domingo. Under color of this trade, a commerce in European goods is carried on; and we may easily discern how hard the Spaniards are to it for the necessaries, or at least the conveniences of life, when we find them trading to a place which is a free port to privateers and pirates of all nations, who there vend openly, and in the very sight of the Spaniards, what they have taken from them in the basest and most barbarous manner possible, and yet so tame are they, that they not only bear this with patience, but will even purchase commodities from these very buccaneers. Of late years other nations have made an advantage of this free port, and keep warehouses there of all sorts of commodities, for the service of such customers, as will run the hazard of coming at them; and in time of war the privateers never want a market in this place.

The Portuguese at Rio Janeiro entertain also a very beneficial correspondence with their Spanish neighbours. The goods with which they supply them, are sugars, indigo, tobacco, wines, brandies, and rums, with some European goods, and sometimes slaves. The inhabitants of this colony are far more industrious than the rest of the Brazil planters; and this gives them an opportunity of gaining considerably by the inhabitants of Buenos Ayres, and other places on the River of Plate. . . .

Besides these methods of trading, which we have hitherto spoken of, there is another common to all nations, with the mention of which we shall conclude. Ships frequently approach the Spanish coasts under pretence of wanting water, wood, provisions, or more commonly, in order to stop a leak. The first thing that is done in such a case, is to give notice to the governor of their great distress, and, as a full proof thereof, to send a very considerable present. By this means leave is obtained to come on shore, to erect a warehouse, and to unlade the ship, but then all this is performed under the eye of the king's officers, and the goods are regularly entered in a register as they are brought into the warehouse, which when full is shut up, and the doors sealed. All these precautions taken, the business is effectually carried on in the night by a back-door, and the European goods being taken out, indigo, cochineal, vinellos, tobacco, and above all bars of silver and pieces of eight are very exactly packed in the same cases, and placed as they stood before. But then, that such as have bought may be able to sell publicly, a new scheme takes place. A petition is presented to the governor, setting forth the stranger's want of money to pay for provisions, building the warehouse, timber for repairing the

ship, and a proportionable number of such like items; in consideration of all which, leave is desired to dispose of some small part of their cargo, in order to discharge these debts. This being obtained in the usual manner, something of each sort of goods which had been privately sold, is now publicly brought to market, and purchased by those persons respectively who had larger quantities in their warehouses before. Thus the whole of this scene of iniquity is transacted with all the formal solemnity which could attend an act of justice and compassion.

8. A FOREIGN VIEW OF THE SPANISH COMMERCIAL SYSTEM

By the opening of the eighteenth century it was apparent to thoughtful Spaniards and foreign observers alike that the Spanish commercial policy in the colonies was a dismal failure from the point of view of the general interests of the mother country. The English publicist Campbell offered a shrewd analysis of the reasons for this failure. Historians generally concur in his argument that it sprang not from any want of intelligence or industry in such able rulers as Charles V and Philip II, but from an incorrect policy that neglected the development of domestic commerce and industry and squandered the vast revenues obtained from the colonies in ruinous European wars aiming at the achievement of "universal empire."[8]

✠✠✠✠ There is nothing more common than to hear Spain compared to a sieve, which, whatever it receives, is never the fuller. How common soever the comparison may be, most certainly it is a very true one; but the means by which all this immense wealth, or at least the far greatest part of it is drawn from the Spaniards, and conveyed to other nations, and in what proportions, is neither so well, nor so generally understood. To account for this shall be our present task. . . .

If after the discovery of the New World, as the Spaniards justly enough called it, the government had encouraged trade or manufactures, there is great probability that the supreme direction of the affairs of Europe would have fallen into the hands of the Catholic Kings. For, if all the subjects of Spain, without restraint, had traded to these far distant regions, this must have created such a maritime force, as no other nation could have withstood. Or, supposing the trade had been restrained as it is at present, yet, if manufactures had been encouraged, so as that the greatest part of the trade of the West

[8] Campbell, *The Spanish Empire in America*, pp. 291–299.

Indies had been driven without having recourse to foreigners, such prodigious sums of money must have rested in Spain, as would have enabled its monarchs to have given law to all their neighbours. But, by neglecting these obvious, and yet certain rules for establishing solid and extensive at least, if not universal dominion, her kings had recourse to those refinements in policy, which, however excellent they may seem in theory, have never yet been found to answer in practice. They were for fixing their commerce by constraint, and for establishing power by the sword; the first, experience has shewn to be impracticable, and the latter, perhaps was the only method whereby they could have missed that end they used it to obtain. In short, by repeated endeavours to secure the wealth of the Indies to Spain absolutely, they scattered it throughout Europe, and, by openly grasping at universal monarchy, they alarmed those they might have subdued; so that in process of time, some of those they intended for slaves became their equals and allies, and some their masters.

Yet the princes that took these steps were not either rash and hasty, or voluptuous and profuse, but, on the contrary, were esteemed by all the world the wisest monarchs of their respective times, and, in many things deserved to be so esteemed. They erred, not through want of capacity, or want of application, as their successors did, but for want of considering things in a right light, occasioned purely by their fixing their eyes on that dazzling meteor, universal empire. . . .

From what has been said it is evident, that however wise, however penetrating these princes might be, they certainly overshot themselves in their schemes concerning the Western Indies. Instead of looking upon it as an estate, they seemed to think it only a farm, of which they were to make presently the most they could. In doing this, it must be owned, they acted with skill and vigour, for they drew immense sums from thence, which they wasted in Europe to disturb others, and in the end to destroy their own state. Mr. Lewis Roberts, author of the *Map of Commerce*, an excellent book for the time in which it was written, tells us, that it appeared by the records in the custom-house of Seville, that in the space of seventy-four years, computing backwards from the time in which he wrote, the kings of Spain had drawn into that country from America, two hundred and fifty millions of gold, which make about ninety-one millions sterling. He also observes that . . . Philip II . . . spent more in his reign than all his predecessors in the whole of their respective reigns; though no less than 62 kings had reigned before him. Yet this cunning, this ambitious monarch left his subjects in a manner quite exhausted, and, by establishing a most pernicious system of politics, left the total ruining of his dominions by way of legacy to his successors, a point which with wonderful obstinacy they have pursued ever since.

All who are in any degree acquainted with the history of Europe know, that for a long course of years Spain maintained wars in Flanders, Germany, Italy, and sometimes in Ireland, which created a prodigious expense of treasure and of troops; neither of which from the death of Charles V they were in any condition to spare. As families were reduced by the expense of serving in the army, they were inclined to seek new fortunes in the West Indies: and thus numbers went over thither, not to cultivate the country, or to improve trade, but to strip and plunder those who were there before them. Other great families again concurred with the measures of the crown, in hopes of vice-royalties, and other valuable offices in its conquests: but if ever their schemes were beneficial to their families, which may admit of doubt, certain it is that they contributed more and more to the ruin of the Spanish nation. For, though his Catholic Majesty once possessed Naples, Sicily, Sardinia, Milan, with other territories in Italy, besides all the Low Countries, and some other provinces which are now lost; yet, for want of attending to commerce, and by having no sort of economy, all this turned to his prejudice; and it plainly appeared towards the close of the last century, that with all their boasted sagacity and firmness, the Spaniards had ruined themselves by acquiring too great power, and rendered themselves beggars by misusing their immense riches. With swelling titles and wide dominions, they were despicably weak, and scarce any but copper money was to be seen in a country, which received above twenty millions annually from its plantations.

Before I quit this topic, I must take notice of another thing, which is certainly very extraordinary. This wrong turn in the Spanish policy had a wonderful effect; it made all the enemies of that nation rich, and all its friends poor. Everybody knows that the United Provinces not only made themselves free and independent, but rich and powerful also, by their long war with Spain. Our maritime power was owing to the same cause. If Philip II had not disturbed Queen Elizabeth, our fleet might have been as inconsiderable at the close of her reign as it was at the beginning, when we were pestered with pirates even in the narrow seas. Our plantations abroad were in a great measure owing to expeditions against the Spaniard. Our manufactures at home were the consequence of affording refuge to the king of Spain's protestant subjects. When Queen Elizabeth's successor closed with Spain, he suffered by it, while France, the only country then at war with Spain, was a gainer. I say nothing of Cromwell's breach with Spain, and the advantages he drew from it, because the world seems well enough apprized of all I could say on that subject already. . . .

By so long a series of mismanagement the Spaniards have brought their affairs into so wretched a situation, that they neither

have, nor can have any very great benefit from their vast dominions in America. They are said to be stewards for the rest of Europe; their Galleons bring the silver into Spain, but neither wisdom nor power can keep it there; it runs out as fast as it comes in, nay, and faster; insomuch that the little Canton of Bern is really richer, and has more credit, than the king of Spain, notwithstanding his Indies. At first sight this seems to be strange and incredible; but when we come to examine it, the mystery is by no means impenetrable. The silver and rich commodities which come from the Indies come not for nothing (the king's duties excepted) and very little of the goods or manufactures for which they come, belong to the subjects of the crown of Spain. It is evident, therefore, that the Spanish merchants are but factors, and that the greatest part of the returns from the West Indies belong to those foreigners for whom they negotiate.

12 ✢ Class and Caste in the Spanish Colonies

The social order that arose in the Spanish colonies on the ruins of the old Indian societies was based, like that of Spain, on feudal principles. All agricultural and mechanical labor was regarded as degrading. The various races and racial mixtures were carefully distinguished, and a trace of Negro or Indian blood legally sufficed to deprive an individual of the right to hold public office or enter the professions and of the other rights and privileges of white men. In practice, racial lines were not so strictly drawn. For a stipulated sum a wealthy *mestizo* or mulatto could often purchase from the Spanish crown a certificate placing him in the category of whites.

Wealth, not gentle birth or racial purity, was the true distinguishing characteristic of the colonial aristocracy. Legally, the Creoles and peninsular Spaniards were equal. In practice, during most of the colonial period the former suffered from a system of discrimination that denied them employment in the highest church and government posts and in large-scale commerce. In the first half of the eighteenth century their situation improved, and Creoles came to dominate the prestigious *audiencias* of Mexico City and Lima. But in the second half of the century a reaction took place, and high-ranking creoles were removed from positions in the imperial administration. The cleavage in the colonial upper class grew wider with the passage

of time and must be considered a major cause of the Creole Wars of Independence.

The mestizo caste had its main origin in a multitude of irregular unions between Spaniards and native women, although mixed marriages were not uncommon, especially in the early period. The mass of mixed-bloods were consigned to an inferior social status by their poverty and illegitimate birth. The mestizo caste tended to become a lower middle class of artisans, overseers, shopkeepers, and the like.

By contrast with the mestizo, no ambiguity marked the position of the Indian in the social scale. Aside from a small and privileged group of hereditary chiefs and their families, the Indians formed a distinct servile class, burdened with many tribute and labor obligations. They lived apart from the whites, in their own communities of pre-Conquest origin, or in towns established by the Spaniards. In many regions they preserved quite intact their ancestral social organization, language, and other culture traits. On numerous occasions they rose against their oppressors in revolts that were generally crushed with great severity.

The virtual disappearance of the native population of the Antilles, and the rapid growth of sugar-cane cultivation in the islands, created an insistent demand on the part of the colonists for Negro slave labor. A numerous Negro and mixed population came into being in the regions of plantation culture, notably in the West Indies and on the coasts of Mexico and Venezuela; smaller numbers were found in all the large colonial towns, where they were chiefly used as household servants.

Negro slavery in the Spanish colonies has been described as patriarchal and humane by comparison with the operations of the system in the English and French colonies, but this judgment, based in considerable part on the Spanish eighteenth-century slave code, has recently been subjected to sharp criticism. Emancipation was legally possible, and occurred with some frequency during the colonial period. Whether slaves or freemen, Negroes occupied the lowest position in the social scale. Unless redeemed by wealth or singular talents, mulattoes and other racial mixtures containing Negro blood shared this disfavor. Many found employment in the mines, in the mechanical trades, as confidential servants, and in the colonial militia, where they formed separate units under the command of white officers.

I. THE STRUCTURE OF CLASS AND CASTE

The population of the Spanish colonies formed a melting pot of races, white, red, and black. Their progressive amalgama-

tion was retarded but not halted by a caste system that assigned different social values to the respective races and mixtures. A white skin was a symbol of social superiority, but not all whites belonged to the privileged economic group. The Spaniard compelled by poverty to choose his mate from the colored races generally doomed his descendants to an inferior economic and social status. On the other hand, the mestizo or mulatto son of a wealthy Spanish landowner, if acknowledged and made his father's legal heir, as occasionally happened, could often purchase from the crown a certificate of white blood or even a title of nobility. The Spanish travelers, Juan and Ulloa, describe the complicated structure of class and caste of a colonial town — the Caribbean port of Cartagena.[1]

✤✤✤✤ The inhabitants may be divided into different castes or tribes, who derive their origin from a coalition of Whites, Negroes, and Indians. Of each of these we shall treat particularly.

The Whites may be divided into two classes, the Europeans, and Creoles, or Whites born in the country. The former are commonly called *Chapetones*, but are not numerous; most of them either return into Spain after acquiring a competent fortune, or remove up into inland provinces in order to increase it. Those who are settled at Carthagena, carry on the whole trade of that place, and live in opulence; whilst the other inhabitants are indigent, and reduced to have recourse to mean and hard labour for subsistence. The families of the White Creoles compose the landed interest; some of them have large estates, and are highly respected, because their ancestors came into the country invested with honourable posts, bringing their families with them when they settled here. Some of these families, in order to keep up their original dignity, have either married their children to their equals in the country, or sent them as officers on board the galleons; but others have greatly declined. Besides these, there are other Whites, in mean circumstances, who either owe their origin to Indian families, or at least to an intermarriage with them, so that there is some mixture in their blood; but when this is not discoverable by their colour, the conceit of being Whites alleviates the pressure of every other calamity.

Among the other tribes which are derived from an intermarriage of the Whites with the Negroes, the first are the Mulattoes. Next to these the *Tercerones*, produced from a White and a Mulatto, with some approximation to the former, but not so near as to obliterate their origin. After these follow the *Quarterones*, proceeding from a White and a *Terceron*. The last are the *Quinterones*, who owe their origin to a White and *Quarteron*. This is the last gradation,

[1] George Juan and Antonio de Ulloa, *Voyage to South America*, I, pp. 29–32.

there being no visible difference between them and the Whites, either in colour or features; nay they are often fairer than the Spaniards. The children of a White and *Quinteron* are also called Spaniards, and consider themselves as free from all taint of the Negro race. Every person is so jealous of the order of their tribe or cast, that if, through inadvertence, you call them by a degree lower than what they actually are, they are highly offended, never suffering themselves to be deprived of so valuable a gift of fortune.

Before they attain the class of the *Quinterones*, there are several intervening circumstances which throw them back; for between the Mulatto and the Negro, there is an intermediate race, which they call *Sambos*, owing their origin to a mixture between one of these with an Indian, or among themselves. They are also distinguished according to the class their fathers were of. Betwixt the *Tercerones* and the Mulattoes, the *Quarterones* and the *Tercerones*, etc. are those called *Tente en el Ayre*, suspended in the air, because they neither advance nor recede. Children, whose parents are a *Quarteron* or *Quinteron*, and a Mullatto or *Terceron*, are *Salto atras* retrogrades; because, instead of advancing towards being Whites, they have gone backwards towards the Negro race. The children between a Negro and *Quinteron* are called *Sambos de Negro, de Mulatto, de Terceron*, etc.

These are the most known and common tribes or Castas; there are indeed several others proceeding from their intermarriages; but, being so various, even they themselves cannot easily distinguish them; and these are the only people one sees in the city, the *estancias*, and the villages; for if any White, especially women, are met with, it is only accidental, these generally residing in their houses; at least, if they are of any rank or character.

These casts, from the Mulattoes, all affect the Spanish dress, but wear very slight stuffs on account of the heat of the climate. These are the mechanics of the city; the Whites, whether Creoles or *Chapetones*, disdaining such a mean occupation follow nothing below merchandise. But it being impossible for all to succeed, great numbers not being able to procure sufficient credit, they become poor and miserable from their aversion to those trades they follow in Europe, and, instead of the riches which they flattered themselves with possessing in the Indies, they experience the most complicated wretchedness.

The class of Negroes is not the least numerous, and is divided into two parts; the free and the slaves. These [last] are again subdivided into Creoles and *Bozales*, part of which are employed in the cultivation of the *haciendas* or *estancias*. Those in the city are obliged to perform the most laborious services, and pay out of their wages a certain quota to their masters, subsisting themselves on the small re-

mainder. The violence of the heat not permitting them to wear any cloaths, their only covering is a small piece of cotton stuff about their waist; the female slaves go in the same manner. Some of these live at the *estancias,* being married to the slaves who work there; while those in the city sell in the markets all kind of eatables, and cry fruits, sweet-meats, cakes made of the maize, and cassava, and several other things about the streets. Those who have children sucking at their breast, which is the case of the generality, carry them on their shoulders, in order to have their arms at liberty; and when the infants are hungry, they give them the breast either under the arm or over the shoulder, without taking them from their backs. This will perhaps appear incredible; but their breasts, being left to grow without any pressure on them often hang down to their very waist, and are not therefore difficult to turn over their shoulders for the convenience of the infant.

2. THE COLONIAL CITY: MEXICO

Mexico City and Lima were the two great centers of urban civilization in colonial Spanish America. In each an uncrossable chasm separated the world of the white upper class, flaunting its wealth in gay apparel, richly ornamented dwellings, and colorful pageants, from that of the sullen Indian, Negro, and mixed-blood proletariat, living in wretched huts amid incredible squalor. In the sixteenth and seventeenth centuries a spirit of violence pervaded the life of the colonial city. Brawls, duels, and murders were commonplace among the gentry as well as the lower classes; and occasionally the latter erupted in blindly destructive tumults against el mal gobierno (*the rotten government*). *The renegade English priest Thomas Gage paints a vivid picture of Mexico City in 1625.*[2]

❦❦❦❦ At the rebuilding of this city there was a great difference betwixt an inhabitant of Mexico, and a Conqueror; for a Conqueror was a name of honour, and had lands and rents given him and to his posterity by the King of Spain, and the inhabitant or only dweller paid rent for his house. And this hath filled all those parts of America with proud Dons and gentlemen to this day; for every one will call himself a descendant from a Conqueror, though he be as poor as Job; and ask him what is become of his estate and fortune; he will answer that fortune hath taken it away, which shall never take away

---

[2] Thomas Gage, *The English-American,* pp. 89–92.

a Don from him. Nay, a poor cobbler, or carrier that runs about the country far and near getting his living with half-a-dozen mules, if he be called Mendoza, or Guzman, will swear that he descended from those dukes' houses in Spain, and that his grandfather came from thence to conquer, and subdued whole countries to the Crown of Spain, though now fortune have frowned upon him, and covered his rags with a threadbare cloak.

When Mexico was rebuilt, and judges, aldermen, attorneys, town-clerks, notaries, scavengers, and serjeants with all other officers necessary for the commonwealth of a city were appointed, the fame of Cortez and majesty of the city was blown abroad into far provinces, by means whereof it was soon replenished with Indians again, and with Spaniards from Spain, who soon conquered above four hundred leagues of land, being all governed by the princely seat of Mexico. But since that first rebuilding, I may say it is now rebuilt the second time by Spaniards, who have consumed most of the Indians; so that now I will not dare to say there are a hundred thousand houses which soon after the Conquest were built up, for most of them were of Indians.

Now the Indians that live there, live in the suburbs of the city, and their situation is called Guadalupe. In the year 1625, when I went to those parts, this suburb was judged to contain five thousand inhabitants; but since most of them have been consumed by the Spaniards' hard usage and the work of the lake. So that now there may not be above two thousand inhabitants of mere Indians, and a thousand of such as they call there mestizoes, who are of a mixed nature of Spaniards and Indians, for many poor Spaniards marry with Indian women, and others that marry them not but hate their husbands, find many tricks to convey away an innocent Uriah to enjoy his Bathsheba. The Spaniards daily cozen them of the small plot of ground where their houses stand, and of three or four houses of Indians built up one good and fair house after the Spanish fashion with gardens and orchards. And so is almost all Mexico new built with very fair and spacious houses with gardens of recreation.

Their buildings are with stone, and brick very strong, but not high, by reason of the many earthquakes, which would endanger their houses if they were above three storeys high. The streets are very broad, in the narrowest of them three coaches may go, and in the broader six may go in the breadth of them, which makes the city seem a great deal bigger than it is. In my time it was thought to be of between thirty and forty thousand inhabitants — Spaniards, who are so proud and rich that half the city was judged to keep coaches, for it was a most credible report that in Mexico in my time there were above fifteen thousand coaches. It is a byword that at Mexico there are four things fair, that is to say, the women, the apparel, the

horses, and the streets. But to this I may add the beauty of some of the coaches of the gentry, which do exceed in cost the best of the Court of Madrid and other parts of Christendom; for there they spare no silver, nor gold, nor precious stones, nor cloth of gold, nor the best silks from China to enrich them. And to the gallantry of their horses the pride of some doth add the cost of bridles and shoes of silver.

The streets of Christendom must not compare with those in breadth and cleanness, but especially in the riches of the shops which do adorn them. Above all, the goldsmiths' shops and works are to be admired. The Indians, and the people of China that have been made Christians and every year come thither, have perfected the Spaniards in that trade. The Viceroy that went thither the year 1625 caused a popinjay to be made of silver, gold, and precious stones with the perfect colours of the popinjay's feathers (a bird bigger than a pheasant), with such exquisite art and perfection, to present unto the King of Spain, that it was prized to be worth in riches and workmanship half a million of ducats. There is in the cloister of the Dominicans a lamp hanging in the church with three hundred branches wrought in silver to hold so many candles, besides a hundred little lamps for oil set in it, every one being made with several workmanship so exquisitely that it is valued to be worth four hundred thousand ducats; and with such-like curious works are many streets made more rich and beautiful from the shops of goldsmiths.

To the by-word touching the beauty of the women I must add the liberty they enjoy for gaming, which is such that the day and night is too short for them to end a primera when once it is begun; nay gaming is so common to them that they invite gentlemen to their houses for no other end. To myself it happened that passing along the streets in company with a friar that came with me that year from Spain, a gentlewoman of great birth knowing us to be *chapetons* (so they call the first year those that come from Spain), from her window called unto us, and after two or three slight questions concerning Spain asked us if we would come in and play with her a game at primera.

Both men and women are excessive in their apparel, using more silks than stuffs and cloth. Precious stones and pearls further much their vain ostentation; a hat-band and rose made of diamonds in a gentleman's hat is common, and a hat-band of pearls is ordinary in a tradesman; nay a blackamoor or tawny young maid and slave will make hard shift but she will be in fashion with her neck-chain and bracelets of pearls, and her ear-bobs of some considerable jewels. The attire of this baser sort of people of blackamoors and mulattoes (which are of a mixed nature, of Spaniards and blackamoors) is so light, and their carriage so enticing, that many Spaniards even of the

better sort (who are too too prone to venery) disdain their wives for them.

Their clothing is a petticoat of silk or cloth, with many silver or golden laces, with a very broad double ribbon of some light colour with long silver or golden tags hanging down before, the whole length of their petticoat to the ground, and the like behind; their waistcoats made like bodices, with skirts, laced likewise with gold or silver, without sleeves, and a girdle about their body of great price stuck with pearls and knots of gold (if they be any ways well esteemed of), their sleeves are broad and open at the end, of holland or fine China linen, wrought some with coloured silks, some with silk and gold, some with silk and silver, hanging down almost unto the ground; the locks of their heads are covered with some wrought coif, and over it another of network of silk bound with a fair silk, or silver, or golden ribbon which crosseth the upper part of their forehead, and hath commonly worked out in letters some light and foolish love posy; their bare, black, and tawny breasts are covered with bobs hanging from their chains of pearls.

And when they go abroad, they use a white mantle of lawn or cambric rounded with a broad lace, which some put over their heads, the breadth reaching only to their middle behind, that their girdle and ribbons may be seen, and two ends before reaching to the ground almost; others cast their mantles only upon their shoulders, and swaggers-like, cast the one end over the left shoulder that they may the better jog the right arm, and shew their broad sleeve as they walk along; others instead of this mantle use some rich silk petticoat to hang upon their left shoulder, while with their right arm they support the lower part of it, more like roaring boys than honest civil maids. Their shoes are high and of many soles, the outside whereof of the profaner sort are plated with a list of silver, which is fastened with small nails of broad silver heads.

Most of these are or have been slaves, though love have set them loose at liberty to enslave souls to sin and Satan. And there are so many of this kind both men and women grown to a height of pride and vanity, that many times the Spaniards have feared they would rise up and mutiny against them. And for the looseness of their lives, and public scandals committed by them and the better sort of the Spaniards, I have heard them say often who have professed more religion and fear of God, they verily thought God would destroy that city, and give up the country into the power of some other nation. . . .

Great alms and liberality towards religious houses in that city commonly are coupled with great and scandalous wickedness. They wallow in the bed of riches and wealth, and make their alms the coverlet to cover their loose and lascivious lives. From hence are the churches so fairly built and adorned. There are not above fifty

churches and chapels, cloisters and nunneries, and parish churches in that city; but those that are there are the fairest that ever my eyes beheld, the roofs and beams being in many of them all daubed with gold, and many altars with sundry marble pillars, and others with brazil-wood stays standing one above another with tabernacles for several saints richly wrought with golden colours, so that twenty thousand ducats is a common price of many of them. These cause admiration in the common sort of people, and admiration brings on daily adoration in them to those glorious spectacles and images of saints.

Besides these beautiful buildings, the inward riches belonging to the altars are infinite in price and value, such as copes, canopies, hangings, altar cloths, candlesticks, jewels belonging to the saints, and crowns of gold and silver, and tabernacles of gold and crystal to carry about their sacrament in procession, all which would mount to the worth of a reasonable mine of silver, and would be a rich prey for any nation that could make better use of wealth and riches. I will not speak much of the lives of the friars and nuns of that city, but only that there they enjoy more liberty than in the parts of Europe (where yet they have too much) and that surely the scandals committed by them do cry up to Heaven for vengeance, judgment, and destruction.

In my time in the cloister of the Mercenarian friars which is entitled for the Redemption of Captives, there chanced to be an election of a Provincial to rule over them, to the which all the priors and heads of the cloisters about the country had resorted, and such was their various and factious difference that upon the sudden all the convent was in an uproar, their canonical election was turned to mutiny and strife, knives were drawn, many wounded, the scandal and danger of murder so great, that the Viceroy was fain to interpose his authority and to sit amongst them and guard the cloister until their Provincial was elected.

It is ordinary for the friars to visit their devoted nuns, and to spend whole days with them, hearing their music, feeding on their sweetmeats, and for this purpose they have many chambers which they call *locutorios*, to talk in, with wooden bars between the nuns and them, and in these chambers are tables for the friars to dine at; and while they dine the nuns recreate them with their voices. Gentlemen and citizens give their daughters to be brought up in these nunneries, where they are taught to make all sorts of conserves and preserves, all sorts of needlework, all sorts of music, which is so exquisite in that city that I dare be bold to say that the people are drawn to their churches more for the delight of the music than for any delight in the service of God. More, they teach these young children to act like players, and to entice the people to their churches

make these children to act short dialogues in their choirs, richly attiring them with men's and women's apparel, especially upon Mid-
summer Day, and the eight days before their Christmas, which is so
gallantly performed that many factious strifes and single combats
have been, and some were in my time, for defending which of these
nunneries most excelled in music and in the training up of children.
No delights are wanting in that city abroad in the world, nor in their
churches, which should be the house of God, and the soul's, not the
sense's delight.

The chief place in the city is the market-place, which though
it be not as spacious as in Montezuma his time, yet is at this day
very fair and wide, built all with arches on the one side where people
may walk dry in time of rain, and there are shops of merchants furnished with all sorts of stuffs and silks, and before them sit women
selling all manner of fruits and herbs; over against these shops and
arches is the Viceroy his palace, which taketh up almost the whole
length of the market with the walls of the house and of the gardens
belonging to it. At the end of the Viceroy his palace is the chief
prison, which is strong of stone work. Next to this is the beautiful
street called *La Plateria*, or Goldsmiths Street, where a man's eyes may
behold in less than an hour many millions' worth of gold, silver, pearls,
and jewels. The street of St. Austin is rich and comely, where live
all that trade in silks; but one of the longest and broadest streets is
the street called Tacuba, where almost all the shops are of iron-
mongers, and of such as deal in brass and steel, which is joining to
those arches whereon the water is conveyed into the city, and is so
called for that it is the way out of the city to a town called Tacuba;
and this street is mentioned far and near, not so much for the length
and breadth of it, as for a small commodity of needles which are made
there, and for proof are the best of all those parts. For stately buildings the street called *del Aquila*, the Street of the Eagle, exceeds the
rest, where live gentlemen, and courtiers, and judges belonging to the
Chancery, and is the palace of the Marques del Valle from the line
of Ferdinando Cortez; this street is so called from an old idol an
eagle of stone which from the Conquest lieth in a corner of that
street, and is twice as big as London stone.

The gallants of this city shew themselves daily, some on horseback, and most in coaches, about four of the clock in the afternoon
in a pleasant shady field called *la Alameda*, full of trees and walks,
somewhat like unto our Moorfields, where do meet as constantly as
the merchants upon our exchange about two thousand coaches, full
of gallants, ladies, and citizens, to see and to be seen, to court and to
be courted, the gentlemen having their train of blackamoor slaves
some a dozen, some half a dozen waiting on them, in brave and gallant
liveries, heavy with gold and silver lace, with silk stockings on their

black legs, and roses on their feet, and swords by their sides; the ladies also carry their train by their coach's side of such jetlike damsels as before have been mentioned for their light apparel, who with their bravery and white mantles over them seem to be, as the Spaniard saith, *mosca en leche*, a fly in milk. But the train of the Viceroy who often goeth to this place is wonderful stately, which some say is as great as the train of his master the King of Spain. At this meeting are carried about many sorts of sweetmeats and papers of comfits to be sold, for to relish a cup of cool water, which is cried about in curious glasses, to cool the blood of those love-hot gallants. But many times these their meetings sweetened with conserves and comfits have sour sauce at the end, for jealousy will not suffer a lady to be courted, no nor sometimes to be spoken to, but puts fury into the violent hand to draw a sword or dagger and to stab or murder whom he was jealous of, and when one sword is drawn thousands are presently drawn, some to right the party wounded or murdered; others to defend the party murdering, whose friends will not permit him to be apprehended, but will guard him with drawn swords until they have conveyed him to the sanctuary of some church, from whence the Viceroy his power is not able to take him for a legal trial.

3. THE COLONIAL CITY: LIMA

A little more than a hundred years after the Englishman Gage visited Mexico City, the young Spanish scientists Juan and Ulloa came to Lima, proud capital of the viceroyalty of Peru, and the seat of the most corrupt, sophisticated, and extravagant society in the Americas. The upper class, following the lead of Spain, where French manners were winning ascendancy, had acquired an urbanity and polish foreign to the early conquistadores. Pleasure and dissipation were the order of the day, with cockfighting, bullfights, gambling, balls, and the theater among the principal amusements. The women of the city enjoyed a reputation for beauty, gala dress, captivating manners, and a passion for intrigue. Juan and Ulloa offer their impressions of life and manners in eighteenth-century Lima.[3]

✸✸✸✸ The inhabitants of Lima are composed of whites, or Spaniards, Negroes, Indians, Mestizos, and other casts, proceeding from the mixture of all three.

The Spanish families are very numerous; Lima according to the

[3] Juan and Ulloa, *A Voyage to South America*, II, pp. 53–60.

lowest computation, containing sixteen or eighteen thousand whites. Among these are reckoned a third or fourth part of the most distinguished nobility of Peru; and many of these dignified with the stile of ancient or modern Castilians, among which are no less than 45 counts and marquises. The number of knights belonging to the several military orders is also very considerable. Besides these are many families no less respectable and living in equal splendor; particularly 24 gentlemen of large estates, but without titles, tho' most of them have ancient seats, a proof of the antiquity of their families. One of these traces, with undeniable certainty, his descent from the Incas. The name of this family is Ampuero, so called from one of the Spanish commanders at the conquest of this country, who married a Coya, or daughter of the Inca. To this family the kings of Spain have been pleased to grant several distinguishing honours and privileges, as marks of its great quality: and many of the most eminent families in the city have desired intermarriages with it.

All those families live in a manner becoming their rank, having estates equal to their generous dispositions, keeping a great number of slaves and other domestics, and those who affect making the greatest figure, have coaches, while others content themselves with calashes or chaises, which are here so common, that no family of any substance is without one. It must be owned that these carriages are more necessary here than in other cities, on account of the numberless droves of mules which continually pass thro' Lima, and cover the streets with their dung, which being soon dried by the sun and the wind, turns to a nauseous dust, scarce supportable to those who walk on foot. These chaises, which are drawn by a mule, and guided by a driver, have only two wheels, with two seats opposite to each other, so that on occasion they will hold four persons. They are very slight and airy; but on account of the gildings and other decorations, sometimes cost eight hundred or a thousand crowns. The number of them is said to amount to 5 or 6000; and that of coaches is also very considerable, tho' not equal to the former.

The funds to support these expenses, which in other parts would ruin families, are their large estates and plantations, civil and military employments or commerce, which is here accounted no derogation to families of the greatest distinction; but by this commerce is not to be understood the buying and selling by retail or in shops, every one trading proportional to his character and substance. Hence families are preserved from those disasters too common in Spain, where titles are frequently found without a fortune capable of supporting their dignity. Commerce is so far from being considered as a disgrace at Lima, that the greatest fortunes have been raised by it; those on the contrary, being rather despised, who not being blessed with a sufficient estate, through indolence, neglect to have recourse

to it for improving their fortunes. This custom, or resource, which was established there without any determinate end, being introduced by a vain desire of the first Spaniards to acquire wealth, is now the real support of that splendor in which those families live; and whatever repugnance these military gentlemen might originally have to commerce, it was immediately removed by a royal proclamation, by which it was declared that commerce in the Indies should not exclude from nobility or the military orders; a very wise measure, and of which Spain would be still more sensible, were it extended to all its dependencies.

At Lima, as at Quito, and all Spanish America, some of the eminent families have been long since settled there, whilst the prosperity of others is of a later date; for being the center of the whole commerce of Peru, a greater number of Europeans resort to it, than to any other city; some for trade, and others, from being invested in Spain with considerable employments: among both are persons of the greatest merit; and tho' many after they have finished their respective affairs, return home, yet the major part induced by the fertility of the soil, and goodness of the climate, remain at Lima, and marry young ladies remarkable equally for the gifts of fortune as those of nature, and thus new families are continually settled.

The Negroes, Mulattoes, and their descendants, form the greater number of the inhabitants; and of these are the greatest part of the mechanics; tho' here the Europeans also follow the same occupations, which are not at Lima reckoned disgraceful to them, as they are at Quito; for gain being here the universal passion, the inhabitants pursue it by means of any trade, without regard to its being followed by Mulattoes, interest here preponderating against any other consideration.

The third, and last class of inhabitants are the Indians and Mestizos, but these are very small in proportion to the largeness of the city, and the multitudes of the second class. They are employed in agriculture, in making earthen ware, and bringing all kinds of provisions to market, domestic services being performed by Negroes and Mulattoes, either slaves or free, though generally by the former.

The usual dress of the men differs very little from that worn in Spain, nor is the distinction between the several classes very great; for the use of all sorts of cloth being allowed, every one wears what he can purchase. So that it is not uncommon to see a Mulatto, or any other mechanic dressed in a tissue, equal to any thing that can be worn by a more opulent person. They all greatly affect fine cloaths, and it may be said without exaggeration, that the finest stuffs made in countries, where industry is always inventing something new, are more generally seen at Lima than in any other place; vanity and ostentation not being restrained by custom or law. Thus the great

quantities brought in the galleons and register ships notwithstanding they sell here prodigiously above their prime cost in Europe, the richest of them are used as cloaths, and worn with a carelessness little suitable to their extravagant price; but in this article the men are greatly exceeded by the women, whose passion for dress is such as to deserve a more particular account.

In the choice of laces, the women carry their taste to a prodigious excess; nor is this an emulation confined to persons of quality, but has spread thro' all ranks, except the lowest class of Negroes. The laces are sewed to their linen, which is of the finest sort, though very little of it is seen, the greatest part of it, especially in some dresses, being always covered with lace; so that the little which appears seems rather for ornament than use. These laces too must be all of Flanders manufacture, no woman of rank condescending to look on any other.

Their dress is very different from the European, which the custom of the country alone can render excusable; indeed to Spaniards at their first coming over it appears extremely indecent. Their dress consists of a pair of shoes, a shift, a petticoat of dimity, an open petticoat, and a jacket, which in summer, is of linen, in winter of stuff. To this some add a mantellette, that the former may hang loose. The difference between this dress and that worn at Quito, though consisting of the same pieces is, that at Lima it is much shorter, the petticoat which is usually tied below the waist, not reaching lower than the calf of the leg, from whence, nearly to the ankle, hangs a border of very fine lace, sewed to the bottom of the under petticoat; through which the ends of their garters are discovered, embroidered with gold or silver, and sometimes set with pearls; but the latter is not common. The upper petticoat, which is of velvet, or some rich stuff, is fringed all round, and not less crowded with ornaments, than those described in the first volume of this work. But be the ornaments what they will, whether of fringe, lace, or ribbands, they are always exquisitely fine. The shift's sleeves, which are a yard and a half in length, and two yards in width, when worn for ornament, are covered with rolls of laces, variegated in such a manner as to render the whole truly elegant. Over the shift is worn the jacket, the sleeves of which are excessively large, of a circular figure, and consist of rows of lace, or slips of cambrick or lawn, with lace disposed betwixt each, as are also the shift sleeves, even of those who do not affect extraordinary ornament. The body of the jacket is tied on the shoulders with ribbands fastened to the back of their stays; and the round sleeves of it being tucked up to the shoulders, are so disposed together with those of the shift, as to form what may be term'd four wings. If the jacket be not buttoned or clasped before, it is agreeably fastened on the shoulders; and indeed the whole dress makes a most elegant figure. They who use a close vest, fasten it with clasps, but wear over it the

loose jacket, already described. In the summer they have a kind of veil, the stuff and fashion of which is like that of the shift and body of the vest, of the finest cambrick or lawn, richly laced: But in winter the veil worn in their houses is of baize; when they go abroad full dressed, it is adorned like the sleeves. They also use brown baize, finely laced and fringed, and bordered with slips of black velvet. Over the petticoat is an apron of the same stuff as the sleeves of the jacket, hanging down to the bottom of it. From hence some idea may be formed of the expense of a dress, where the much greater part of the stuff is merely for ornament; nor will it appear strange, that the marriage shift should cost a thousand crowns, and sometimes more.

One particular on which the women here extremely value themselves, is the size of their feet, a small foot being esteemed one of the chief beauties; and this is the principal fault they find with the Spanish ladies, who have much larger feet than those of Lima. From their infancy they are accustomed to wear straight shoes, that their feet may not grow beyond the size of which they esteem beautiful; some of them do not exceed five inches and a half, or six inches in length, and in women of a small stature they are still less. Their shoes have little or no sole, one piece of Cordovan serving both for that and the upper leather, and of an equal breadth and roundness at the toe and heel, so as to form a sort of long figure of eight; but the foot not complying with this figure, brings it to a greater regularity. These shoes are always fastened with diamond buckles, or something very brilliant in proportion to the ability of the wearer, being worn less for use than ornament; for the shoes are made in such a manner, that they never loosen of themselves, nor do the buckles hinder their being taken off. It is unusual to set these buckles with pearls, a particular to be accounted for, only from their being so lavish of them in the other ornaments of dress, as to consider them as of too little value. The shoemakers, who are no strangers to the foible of the sex, take great care to make them in a manner very little calculated for service. The usual price is three half crowns a pair, those embroidered with gold or silver cost from eight to ten crowns. The latter, however, are but little worn, the encumbrance of embroidery being suited rather to enlarge than diminish the appearance of a small foot.

They are fond of white silk stockings, made extremely thin, that the leg may appear the more shapely; the greatest part of which is exposed to view. These trifles often afford very sprightly sallies of wit in their animadversions on the dress of others.

Hitherto we have considered only the more common dress of these ladies; the reader will conceive a still higher idea of their magnificence, when he is informed of the ornaments with which they are decorated in their visits, and upon public occasions. We shall begin with their manner of dressing the hair, which being naturally black,

and capable of reaching below their waists, they dispose in such a manner as to appear perfectly graceful. They tie it up behind in six braided locks, through which a golden bodkin a little bent is inserted, and having a cluster of diamonds at each end. On this the locks are suspended so as to touch the shoulder. On the front and upper part of the head they wear diamond egrets, and the hair is formed into little curls, hanging from the forehead to the middle of the ear, with a large black patch of velvet on each temple. Their earrings are of brilliants, intermixed with tuffs of black silk, covered with pearls, resembling those already described in the first volume. These are so common an ornament, that besides their necklaces, they also wear about their necks rosaries, the beads of which are of pearls, either separate or set in clusters to the size of a large filbert; and those which form the cross are still larger.

Besides diamond rings, necklaces, girdles, and bracelets, all very curious both with regard to water and size, many ladies wear other jewels set in gold, or for singularity sake, in tombac [an alloy consisting essentially of copper and zinc]. Lastly, from their girdle before is suspended a large round jewel enriched with diamonds; much more superb than their bracelets, or other ornaments. A lady covered with the most expensive lace instead of linen, and glittering from head to foot with jewels, is supposed to be dressed at the expense of not less than thirty or forty thousand crowns. A splendor still the more astonishing, as it is so very common.

A fondness for expense in these people, does not confine itself to rich apparel; it appears no less in the strange neglect, and the small value they seem to set upon them, by wearing them in a manner the most careless, and by that means bringing upon themselves fresh expenses in repairing the old or purchasing new jewels; especially pearls on account of their fragility.

The most common of the two kinds of dresses worn when they go abroad, is the veil and long petticoat; the other is a round petticoat and mantelet. The former for church, the latter for taking the air, and diversions; but both in the prevailing taste for expense, being richly embroidered with silver or gold.

The long petticoat is particularly worn on holy Thursday; as on that day they visit the churches, attended by two or three female Negro or mulatto slaves, dressed in an uniform like pages.

4. THE MESTIZO: SEED OF TOMORROW

The mestizo arose from a process of racial fusion that began in the first days of the Spanish Conquest and has continued

down to the present. The Spanish jurist Juan de Solórzano Pereira (1575–1655) discusses the status of the mestizo in colonial law and opinion.[4]

✤✤✤✤ Turning now to the persons called mestizos and mulattoes, of whom there are great numbers in the Indies, first let me say that the name mestizo was assigned to the former because they represent a mixture of blood and nationality. . . .

As for the mulattoes, although for the same reason they belong in the class of mestizos, yet as the offspring of Negro women and white men, or the reverse, which is the most strange and repulsive mixture of all, they bear this specific name which compares them to the species of the mule. . . .

If these men were born of legitimate wedlock and had no other vices or defects, they could be regarded as citizens of those provinces and could be admitted to honor and office in them, as is argued by Victoria and Zapata. I am of the opinion that such an intention was the basis of certain royal decrees that permit mestizos to take holy orders and mestizas to become nuns, and admit mestizos to municipal offices and notaryships.

But because they are most often born out of adultery or other illicit unions, since few Spaniards of honorable position will marry Indian or Negro women . . . , they bear the taint of illegitimacy and other vices which they take in, as it were, with their milk. And these men, I find by many other decrees, are forbidden to hold any responsible public office, whether it is that of Protector of the Indians, councilman, or notary public, unless they acknowledge this defect at the time of application and receive special dispensation from it; and those who have gained office in any other way are not allowed to keep it.

There are other decrees that forbid them to take holy orders, unless by special dispensation.

I shall content myself for the present with saying that if these mestizos (especially those in the Indies) possess recognized and assured virtue, and sufficient ability and learning, they could be extremely useful in matters relating to the Indians, being, as it were, their countrymen, and knowing their languages and customs. . . .

But returning to the question of curacies, although for the reason given above it would be convenient to entrust them to mestizos, great care must be taken with this, for we see that the majority of them come from a vicious and depraved environment, and it is they who do the most harm to the Indians. . . . And for this reason many decrees forbid them to visit or live in the Indian towns, and compel

[4] Juan de Solórzano Pereira, *Política indiana*, Madrid, 1930, 5 vols., I, pp. 445–448. (Excerpt translated by the editor.)

them to live in the Spanish towns, or in such towns as may be formed and populated by mestizos and mulattoes. These same decrees order that mestizas married to Spaniards, if charged with adultery, shall be tried and punished like Spanish women.

There are other decrees, of later date, issued in 1600 and 1608, directed to the viceroys of Peru Don Luis de Velasco and the marquis of Montes Claros, saying that the king had learned that the number of mestizos, mulattoes, and *zambahigos* (the children of Negro men and Indian women, or the reverse) was increasing sharply, and ordering them to take appropriate measures that men of such mixtures, vicious in their majority, should not cause injury and disturbances in that kingdom — a thing always to be feared from such people, especially if to the sins that arise from their evil birth are added those that spring from idleness and poor upbringing.

For this reason, although by the ordinances of the viceroy of Peru, Don Francisco de Toledo, they are exempt from paying tribute, by later decrees of the years 1600, 1612, 1619, by the celebrated decrees concerning personal service of 1601 and 1609, and by many others that have been successively promulgated, it is ordered that they pay tribute. And the same decrees command the viceroys to see that the mestizos and mulattoes, like the Indians, are made to labor in the mines and fields. . . .

For it does not appear just that this labor [of the mines], which requires such physical strength . . . , should be assigned entirely to the wretched Indians, while the mestizos and mulattoes, who are of such evil caste, race, and character, are left to idleness; this contravenes the rule that lewdness should not be more favored than chastity, and that the offspring of legitimate marriage should be more privileged than the illegitimate, as is taught by Saint Thomas and other authorities. . . .

From this abuse results the fact that many Indian women desert their Indian husbands and neglect the children that they have by them, seeing them subject to tribute-payments and personal services, and desire, love, and spoil the children that they have out of wedlock by Spaniards or even by Negroes, because they are free and exempt from all burdens — a condition that plainly should not be permitted in any well-governed state.

5. THE INDIAN TOWN

Among the various races and mixtures that composed the population of the Spanish empire in America, the Indians formed a nation apart. Most of them lived in their own self-governing

communities, in which Spaniards other than the village priest were forbidden to reside. In many regions they maintained intact their ancient clan or tribal organization, language, dress, and customs. Thomas Gage, who spent twelve years as a priest in Guatemala and amassed a tidy fortune from the piety and credulity of his native parishioners, describes the life of the Indian town.[5]

✦✦✦✦ Their ordinary clothing is a pair of linen or woollen drawers broad and open at the knees, without shoes (though in their journeys some will put on leathern sandals to keep the soles of their feet) or stockings, without any doublet, a short coarse shirt, which reacheth a little below their waist, and serves more for a doublet than for a shirt, and for a cloak a woollen or linen mantle (called *aiate*) tied with a knot over one shoulder, hanging down on the other side almost to the ground, with a twelvepenny or two shilling hat, which after one good shower of rain like paper falls about their necks and eyes; their bed they carry sometime about them, which is that woollen mantle wherewith they wrap themselves about at night, taking off their shirt and drawers, which they lay under their head for a pillow; some will carry with them a short, slight, and light mat to lie, but those that carry it not with them, if they cannot borrow one of a neighbour, lie as willingly in their mantle upon the bare ground as a gentleman in England upon a soft down-bed, and thus do they soundly sleep, and loudly snort after a day's work, or after a day's journey with a hundred-weight upon their backs.

Those that are of the better sort, and richer, and who are not employed as *tamemez* to carry burdens, or as labourers to work for Spaniards, but keep at home following their own farms, or following their own mules about the country, or following their trades and callings in their shops, or governing the towns, as *alcaldes*, or *alguaziles*, officers of justice, may go a little better apparelled, but after the same manner. For some will have their drawers with a lace at the bottom, or wrought with some coloured silk or crewel, so likewise the mantle about them shall have either a lace, or some work of birds on it; some will wear a cut linen doublet, others shoes, but very few stockings or bands about their necks; and for their beds, the best Indian Governor or the richest, who may be worth four or five thousand ducats, will have little more than the poor *tamemez;* for they lie upon boards, or canes bound together, and raised from the ground, whereon they lay a board and handsome mat, and at their heads for man and wife two little stumps of wood for bolsters, whereon they lay their shirts and mantles and other clothes for pillows, covering

[5] Thomas Gage, *The English-American*, pp. 234–247.

themselves with a broader blanket than is their mantle, and thus hardly would Don Bernabé de Guzman the Governor of Petapa lie, and so do all the best of them.

The women's attire is cheap and soon put on; for most of them also go barefoot, the richer and better sort wear shoes, with broad ribbons for shoe-strings, and for a petticoat, they tie about their waist a woollen mantle, which in the better sort is wrought with divers colors, but not sewed at all, pleated, or gathered in, but as they tie it with a list about them; they wear no shift next their body, but cover their nakedness with a kind of surplice (which they call *guaipil*) which hangs loose from their shoulders down a little below their waist, with open short sleeves, which cover half their arms; this *guaipil* is curiously wrought, especially in the bosom, with cotton, or feathers. The richer sort of them wear bracelets and bobs about their waists and necks; their hair is gathered up with fillets, without any coif or covering, except it be the better sort. When they go to church or abroad, they put upon their heads a veil of linen, which hangeth almost to the ground, and this is that which costs them most of all their attire, for that commonly it is of Holland or some good linen brought from Spain, or fine linen brought from China, which the better sort wear with a lace about. When they are at home at work they commonly take off their *guaipil*, or surplice, discovering the nakedness of their breasts and body. They lie also in their beds as do their husbands, wrapped up only with a mantle, or with a blanket.

Their houses are but poor thatched cottages, without any upper rooms, but commonly one or two only rooms below, in the one they dress their meat in the middle of it, making a compass for fire, with two or three stones, without any other chimney to convey the smoke away, which spreading itself about the room filleth the thatch and the rafters so with soot that all the room seemeth to be a chimney. The next unto it is not free from smoke and blackness, where sometimes are four or five beds according to the family. The poorer sort have but one room, where they eat, dress their meat, and sleep. Few there are that set any locks upon their doors, for they fear no robbing nor stealing, neither have they in their houses much to lose, earthen pots, and pans, and dishes, and cups to drink their chocolate being the chief commodities in their house. There is scarce any house which hath not also in the yard a stew, wherein they bathe themselves with hot water, which is their chief physic when they feel themselves distempered.

Among themselves they are in every town divided into tribes, which have one chief head, to whom all that belong unto that tribe do resort in any difficult matters, who is bound to aid, protect, defend, counsel, and appear for the rest of his tribe before the officers of justice in any wrong that is like to be done unto them. When any

is to be married, the father of the son that is to take a wife out of another tribe goeth unto the head of his tribe to give him warning of his son's marriage with such a maid. Then that head meets with the head of the maid's tribe, and they confer about it. The business commonly is in debate a quarter of a year; all which time the parents of the youth or man are with gifts to buy the maid; they are to be at the charges of all that is spent in eating and drinking when the heads of the two tribes do meet with the rest of the kindred of each side, who sometimes sit in conference a whole day, or most part of a night. After many days and nights thus spent, and a full trial being made of the one and other side's affection, if they chance to disagree about the marriage, then is the tribe and parents of the maid to restore back all that the other side hath spent and given. They give no portions with their daughters, but when they die their goods and lands are equally divided among their sons. If anyone want a house to live in or will repair and thatch his house anew, notice is given to the heads of the tribes, who warn all the town to come to help in the work, and everyone is to bring a bundle of straw, and other materials, so that in one day with the help of many they finish a house, without any charges more than of chocolate, which they minister in great cups as big as will hold above a pint, not putting in any costly materials, as do the Spaniards, but only a little aniseed, and chilli, or Indian pepper; or else they half fill the cup with *atole*, and pour upon it as much chocolate as will fill the cup and colour it.

In their diet the poorer sort are limited many times to a dish of *frijoles*, or Turkey beans, either black or white (which are there in very great abundance, and are kept dry for all the year) boiled with chilli; and if they can have this, they hold themselves well satisfied; with these beans, they make also dumplings, first boiling the bean a little, and then mingling it with a mass of maize, as we do mingle currents in our cakes, and so boil again the *frijoles* with the dumpling of maize mass, and so eat it hot, or keep it cold; but this and all whatsoever else they eat, they either eat it with green biting chilli, or else they dip it in water and salt, wherein is bruised some of that chilli. But if their means will not reach to *frijoles*, their ordinary fare and diet is their *tortillas* (so they call thin round cakes made of the dough and mass of maize) which they eat hot from an earthen pan, whereon they are soon baked with one turning over the fire; and these they eat alone either with chilli and salt, and dipping them in water and salt with a little bruised chilli. When their maize is green and tender, they boil some of those whole stalks or clusters, whereon the maize groweth with the leaf about, and so casting a little salt about it, they eat it. I have often eat of this, and found it as dainty as our young green peas, and very nourishing, but it much increaseth the blood. Also of this green and tender maize they make a furmety, boiling the

maize in some of the milk which they have first taken out of it by bruising it. The poorest Indian never wants this diet, and is well satisfied as long as his belly is thoroughly filled.

But the poorest that live in such towns where flesh meat is sold will make a hard shift but that when they come from work on Saturday night they will buy one half real, or a real worth of fresh meat to eat on the Lord's day. Some will buy a good deal at once, and keep it long by dressing it into *tasajos*, which are bundles of flesh, rolled up and tied fast, which they do when, for example's sake, they have from a leg of beef sliced off from the bone all the flesh with the knife, after the length, form, and thinness of a line, or rope. Then they take the flesh and salt it (which being sliced and thinly cut, soon takes salt) and hang it up in their yards like a line from post to post, or from tree to tree, to the wind for a whole week, and then they hang it in the smoke another week, and after roll it up in small bundles, which become as hard as a stone, and so as they need it they wash it, boil it and eat it. This is America's powdered beef, which they call *tasajo*. . . .

As for drinking, the Indians generally are much given unto it; and drink if they have nothing else of their poor and simple chocolate, without sugar or many compounds, or of *atole*, until their bellies be ready to burst. But if they can get any drink that will make them mad drunk, they will not give it over as long as a drop is left, or a penny remains in their purse to purchase it. Among themselves they use to make such drinks as are in operation far stronger than wine; and these they confection in such great jars as come from Spain, wherein they put some little quantity of water, and fill up the jar with some molasses or juice of the sugar-cane, or some honey for to sweeten it; then for the strengthening of it, they put roots and leaves of tobacco, with other kind of roots which grow there, and they know to be strong in operation, and in some places I have known where they have put in a live toad, and so closed up the jar for a fortnight, or month's space, till all that they have put in him be thoroughly steeped and the toad consumed, and the drink well strengthened, then they open it and call their friends to the drinking of it (which commonly they do in the night time, lest their priest in the town should have notice of them in the day), which they never leave off until they be mad and raging drunk. This drink they call *chicha*, which stinketh most filthily, and certainly is the cause of many Indians' death, especially where they use the toad's poison with it. . . .

And thus having spoken of apparel, houses, eating and drinking, it remains that I say somewhat of their civility, and religion of those who lived under the government of the Spaniards. From the Spaniards they have borrowed their civil government, and in all towns they have one, or two, *alcaldes*, with more or less *regidores* (who

are as aldermen or jurats amongst us) and some *alguaziles*, more or less, who are as constables, to execute the orders of the *alcalde* (who is a mayor) with his brethren. In towns of three or four hundred families, or upwards, there are commonly two *alcaldes*, six *regidores*, two *alguaziles mayores*, and six under, or petty, *alguaziles*. And some towns are privileged with an Indian Governor, who is above the *alcaldes* and all the rest of the officers. These are changed every year by new election, and are chosen by the Indians themselves, who take their turns by the tribes or kindreds, whereby they are divided. Their offices begin on New Year's Day, and after that day their election is carried to the city of Guatemala (if in that district it be made) or else to the heads of justice, or Spanish governors of the several provinces, who confirm the new election, and take account of the last year's expenses made by the other officers, who carry with them their townbook of accounts; and therefore for this purpose every town hath a clerk, or scrivener, called *escribano* who commonly continueth many years in his office, by reason of the paucity and unfitness of Indian scriveners who are able to bear such a charge. This clerk hath many fees for his writings and informations, and accounts, as have the Spaniards, though not so much money or bribes, but a small matter, according to the poverty of the Indians. The Governor is also commonly continued many years, being some chief man among the Indians, except for his misdemeanours he be complained of, or the Indians in general do all stomach him.

Thus they being settled in a civil way of government they may execute justice upon all such Indians of their town as do notoriously and scandalously offend. They may imprison, fine, whip, and banish, but hang and quarter they may not; but must remit such cases to the Spanish governor. So likewise if a Spaniard passing by the town, or living in it, do trouble the peace, and misdemean himself, they may lay hold on him, and send him to the next Spanish justice, with a full information of his offence, but fine him, or keep him about one night in prison they may not. This order they have against Spaniards, but they dare not execute it, for a whole town standeth in awe of one Spaniard, and though he never so heinously offend, and be unruly, with oaths, threatenings, and drawing of his sword, he maketh them quake and tremble, and not presume to touch him; for they know if they do they shall have the worst, either by blows, or by some misinformation which he will give against them. . . .

Amongst themselves, if any complaint be made against any Indian, they dare not meddle with him until they call all his kindred, and especially the head of that tribe to which he belongeth; who if he and the rest together find him to deserve imprisonment, or whipping, or any other punishment, then the officers of justices, the *alcaldes* or mayors, and their brethren the jurats inflict upon him that punishment

which all shall agree upon. But yet after judgment and sentence given, they have another, which is their last appeal, if they please, and that is to their priest and friar, who liveth in their town, by whom they will sometimes be judged, and undergo what punishment he shall think fittest.

13 ✛ The Political Institutions of the Indies

To Columbus, Cortés, Pizarro, and other conquistadores, the Spanish kings granted sweeping political powers that made these men practically sovereign in the territories that they had won or proposed to subdue. But royal jealousy of the great expeditionary leaders was quick to show itself. Their authority was soon revoked or strictly limited, and the institutions that had been employed in Spain to achieve centralized political control were transferred to America for the same end.

The Council of the Indies, chartered in 1524, stood at the head of the Spanish imperial administration almost to the close of the colonial period. Under the king (active royal participation in its work varied from monarch to monarch) it was the supreme legislative, judicial, and executive institution of colonial government. One of its most important functions was the nomination of all high colonial officials to the king. It also framed a vast body of legislation for the colonies — the famous Laws of the Indies.

The principal royal agents in the colonies were the viceroys, the captains-general, and the *audiencias*. The viceroys and captains-general had essentially the same functions, differing only in the greater importance and extent of the territory assigned to the jurisdiction of the former. At the end of the Hapsburg era in 1700 there were two

great American viceroyalties. The viceroyalty of New Spain, with its capital at Mexico City, included all the Spanish possessions north of the isthmus of Panama; that of Peru, with its capital at Lima, embraced all of Spanish South America, except for the coast of Venezuela. Captains-general, theoretically subordinate to the viceroys but in practice virtually independent of them, governed subdivisions of these vast political jurisdictions.

Each viceroy or captain-general was assisted in the performance of his duties by an audiencia which was the highest court of appeal in its district and also served as the viceroy's council of state. Although the viceroy had supreme executive and administrative powers and was not legally obligated to heed the advice of the audiencia, its immense prestige and its right to correspond directly with the Council of the Indies made it a potential check on the viceregal authority.

Provincial administration in the Indies was entrusted to royal officials who governed districts of varying size and importance from their chief towns and who were most commonly styled *corregidores*. One of their principal duties was to protect the Indians from fraudulent or extortionate practices on the part of the whites, but there is ample testimony that the corregidor was himself the worst offender in this respect.

All royal officials in the Indies, from the viceroy down, faced a *residencia* or judicial review of their conduct at the end of their terms of office. As a general rule, however, the judicious use of bribery and influence could get an erring governor over this last hurdle.

The only political institution in the Indies that at all satisfied local aspirations to self-government was the town council, generally known in the colonies as the *cabildo*. Despite its undemocratic character, inefficiency, and waning prestige and autonomy, the cabildo was not devoid of potential significance. As the only political institution in which the creoles were largely represented, and upon which popular pressure could be in some measure exerted, it was destined to play an important part in the creole seizure of power in the coming age of revolution.

1. THE STRUCTURE OF COLONIAL GOVERNMENT

The shifting pattern of Spain's administration of the Indies in the sixteenth century reflected the steady growth of centralized rule in Spain itself and the application of a trial-and-error method to the problems of colonial government. By the middle of the century the political organization of the Indies had assumed the definitive form that it was to retain, with slight variations, until

late in the eighteenth century. The Mexican historian and states-man Lucas Alamán (1792–1853) included an informative sketch of colonial governmental institutions in his classic History of Mexico. *His account, somewhat abstract and idealized, suggests Alamán's sympathy with the old Spanish regime, but gains much value from his familiarity with the colonial climate of opinion in which he passed his youth and early manhood.*[1]

✸✸✸✸Among the many kingdoms and lordships that were united in the kings of Spain by inheritance, marriage, and conquest were included the *East and West Indies, islands, and Tierra firme of the Ocean Sea,* the name given to the immense possessions that these kings held on the continent of America and adjacent islands, the Philippine Islands, and others in the eastern seas. These vast dominions were ruled by special laws promulgated in various times and circumstances and later brought together in a code called the *Compilation of Laws of the Kingdoms of the Indies,* authorized by King Charles II on May 18, 1680. At the same time the monarch ordered that all the decrees and orders given to the audiencias that did not contravene the compiled laws should continue in force, and that where these laws did not suffice those of Castile, known as the Laws of Toro, should apply.

The discovery and conquest of America coincided with the changes that Charles V made in the fundamental laws of Castile and that his son Philip completed by destroying the *fueros* [privileges] of Aragón. The *cortes* of Castile, Aragón, Valencia, and Catalonia, which formerly had met separately, were transformed and gradually declined in importance until they were reduced to a meeting in Madrid of some representatives or deputies of a few cities of Castile and Aragón, solely for the ceremony of acknowledging and taking the oath of allegiance to the heirs to the throne. All the high functions of government, both legislative and administrative, were vested in the councils, of which there were established in Madrid as many as the monarchy had parts. These councils were in no way dependent upon each other, and had no other relation to each other than that of being under a single monarch. Thus there was the Council of Castile, which was called "royal and supreme" and which the kings had always maintained, though in different forms, to aid them with its advice, and with whose concurrence the dispositions of the monarch had the force of laws, *as if they were proclaimed in the cortes,* a phrase that filled the gap caused by the disappearance of these bodies.

There were also Councils of Aragón, Flanders, and Italy, in addition to those which had jurisdiction over particular departments, such as the Council of the Inquisition, over matters of faith; the Council

[1] Lucas Alamán, *Historia de Méjico,* México, 1849–52, 5 vols., I, pp. 31–34, 40–43. (Excerpt translated by the editor.)

of the Orders, for the towns that belonged to the military orders of knighthood; and that of the *Mesta*, for the problems arising from the migratory herds of sheep. When, at the beginning of the eighteenth century, the monarchy was reduced in Europe by the War of the Spanish Succession to the Spanish peninsula and adjacent islands, the first three councils were suppressed. Although these councils were endowed with great powers, they derived their authority entirely from that of the monarch, in whose name they performed all their acts and who was the fountainhead and first principle of all power.

Although the Indies were incorporated in the crown of Castile, "from which they could not be alienated totally or in part, under any condition, or in favor of any person," its government was not on that account made at all dependent on the council established for that kingdom; on the contrary, particular care was taken to establish for the colonies a government entirely independent and separate from the Council of Castile. In 1542 was created "the Council of the Indies," to which were assigned the same exemptions and privileges enjoyed by that of Castile; the same power of making laws in consultation with the king; and the same supreme jurisdiction in the East and West Indies and over their natives, even though resident in Castile, subjecting to it the audiencia of the commerce of Seville and expressly forbidding all the councils and tribunals of Spain, except that of the Inquisition, to take cognizance of any question relating to the Indies.

The Council of the Indies, then, was the legislative body in which were framed the laws that governed those vast dominions, it being declared that no law or provision should be obeyed in the colonies that had not passed through the council and had not been communicated by it; it was the supreme court, to which were brought all suits that by reason of the large sums involved could be appealed to this last resort; and, finally, it was the consultative branch of the government in all the weighty matters in which it was judged fitting to hear the Council's opinion. It was also charged with the duty of submitting to the king, through its chamber composed of five councilors, lists of . . . candidates from which were filled the vacant bishoprics, canonates, and judgeships of the audiencias. In order to enable it to perform this task more adequately, the viceroys were required to inform the council privately, at stated intervals, concerning residents of the territory under their command who might be worthy of filling these posts. . . .

The first governors [in the colonies] were the conquistadores themselves, either under the terms of their capitulations or agreements with the king, as in the case of Pizarro in Peru, or by choice of their soldiers, later confirmed by the crown, as happened with Cortés in New Spain. Later the governmental authority was transferred to the same bodies that were appointed to administer justice, called audiencias.

Finally the Emperor Charles V created in Barcelona on November 20, 1542, the two viceroyalties of Mexico and Peru, to which were added in the eighteenth century those of Santa Fe and Buenos Aires, the other provinces remaining under captains-general and presidents, who exercised the same functions as the viceroys and differed from them only in title.

The authority of these high functionaries varied greatly according to the times. In the epoch of the creation of the first viceroyalties it was almost without limits, for the king declared: "In all the cases and affairs that may arise, they may do whatever appears fitting to them, and they can do and dispose just as we would do and dispose . . . in the provinces in their charge . . . saving only what is expressly forbidden them to do. . . ."

In the period we are discussing the power of the viceroys was moderated by prudent compromises, reflected in the participation of other bodies in the different branches of government, although the viceroys retained all the glitter and pomp of their supreme authority. In the arduous and important tasks of public administration . . . they were obliged to consult with the *real acuerdo,* the name given to a sitting of the audiencia when it acted as the viceroy's council, although he was not bound to accept the advice of the *oidores* or judges. . . . The viceroy was also subject to the *residencia,* which was a judicial review held immediately at the end of his term of office, and to which the judge who was appointed for this purpose summoned all who desired to complain of some offense or injustice.

From the decision of this judge there was no appeal except to the Council of the Indies. But although all these restrictions had a very laudable object — to limit and bring within the scope of the laws an authority that bordered on the royal — distance and the very extent of that authority frequently made these precautions illusory. A viceroy of Mexico . . . said in this connection: "If he who comes to govern (this kingdom) does not repeatedly remind himself that the most rigorous *residencia* is that which the viceroy must face when he is judged by the divine majesty, he can be more sovereign than the Grand Turk, for there is no evil action that he may contrive for which he will not find encouragement, nor any tyranny that he may practice which will not be tolerated. . . ."

The period of time that a viceroy could remain in office was at first indefinite, and the first two viceroys of New Spain retained their positions for many years. It was later fixed at a period of three years, which was commonly renewed for those who distinguished themselves by their services, or for those who were the objects of the king's favor; finally it was increased to five years. . . . The salary also varied, and in Mexico, from the time of the Marquis de Croix in 1766, it was 60,000 pesos a year. . . .

The authority exercised by the audiencias in their respective districts may be likened to that enjoyed by the council over all the Indies. These bodies were held in much respect, not only because they possessed great powers, acted as councils to the viceroys with the name of *acuerdo,* and were supreme tribunals from which there was no appeal (save in particular cases, to the Council of the Indies) but also because of their members' reputation for honesty, their discreet conduct and bearing, and even their distinctive attire on public occasions. . . .

This combination of circumstances made these posts very desirable and their holders objects of envy. Appointments were made according to an established scale, with the judges progressing from less important audiencias to those of higher rank.

In order that these magistrates might be entirely independent and devote themselves to the administration of justice without relations of interest, friendship, or kinship in the place where they exercised their functions, they were strictly forbidden to engage in any kind of commerce or business; to borrow or lend money; to own lands, whether vegetable gardens or estates; to pay visits or attend betrothals and baptisms; to associate with merchants; to receive gifts of any kind; or to attend pleasure or gambling parties. These prohibitions also extended to their wives and children. In order to marry they had to obtain a license from the king, on pain of loss of their positions; and if such a license was granted they were generally transferred to another audiencia. The number of *oidores* varied according to the rank of the audiencia. These tribunals were found not only in the viceregal capitals but wherever else they were necessary.

Such was the general system of government of the kingdoms or large divisions of the Indies.

2. A VICEROY ENTERS LIMA

A colonial viceroy was regarded as the very image of his royal master. He enjoyed an immense delegated authority, which was augmented by the distance that separated him from Spain and by the frequently spineless or venal nature of lesser officials. A court modeled on that of Spain, a numerous retinue, and the constant display of pomp and circumstance bore witness to his exalted status. The Spanish travellers, Juan and Ulloa, describe the elaborate and colorful ceremonies that attended the entrance of such an official into Lima, capital of the viceroyalty of Peru.[2]

[2] Juan and Ulloa, *Voyage to South America,* II, pp. 46–52.

✠✠✠✠ On the landing of the viceroy at Paita, two hundred and four leagues from Lima, he sends a person of great distinction, generally some officer of his retinue, to Lima, with the character of an ambassador; and, by a memoir, informs his predecessor of his arrival, in conformity to his majesty's orders, who had been pleased to confer on him the government of that kingdom. On this ambassador's arrival at Lima, the late viceroy sends a messenger to compliment him on his safe arrival; and on dismissing the ambassador, presents him with some jewel of great value, and a jurisdiction or two which happen at that time to be vacant, together with an indulgence of officiating by deputy, if most agreeable to him. The corregidor of Piura receives the new viceroy at Paita, and provides litters, mules, and every other necessary for the viceroy and his retinue, as far as the next jurisdiction. He also orders booths to be built at the halting-places in the deserts; attends him in person, and defrays all the expences, till relieved by the next corregidor. Being at length arrived at Lima, he proceeds, as it were incognito, through the city to Callao, about two leagues and a half distant. In this place he is received and acknowledged by one of the ordinary alcaldes of Lima, appointed for that purpose, and also by the military officers. He is lodged in the viceroy's palace, which on this occasion is adorned with astonishing magnificence. The next day, all the courts, secular and ecclesiastical, wait on him from Lima, and he receives them under a canopy in the following order: The audiencia, the chamber of accounts, the cathedral chapter, the magistracy, the consulado, the inquisition, the tribunal de Cruzada, the superiors of the religious orders, the colleges, and other persons of eminence. On this day the judges attend the viceroy to an entertainment given by the alcalde; and all persons of note take a pride in doing the like to his attendants. At night there is a play, to which the ladies are admitted veiled, and in their usual dress, to see the new viceroy.

The second day after his arrival at Callao, he goes in a coach provided for him by the city, to the chapel de la Legua, so called from its being about-half-way between Callao and Lima, where he is met by the late viceroy, and both alighting from their coaches, the latter delivers to him a truncheon as the ensign of the government of the kingdom. After this, and the usual compliments, they separate.

If the new viceroy intends to make his public entry into Lima in a few days, he returns to Callao, where he stays till the day appointed; but as a longer space is generally allowed for the many preparatives necessary to such a ceremony, he continues his journey to Lima, and takes up his residence in his palace, the fitting up of which on this occasion is committed to the junior auditor, and the ordinary alcalde.

On the day of public entry, the streets are cleaned, and hung with tapestry, and magnificent triumphal arches erected at proper distances. At two in the afternoon the viceroy goes privately to the

church belonging to the monastery of Montserrat, which is separated by an arch and a gate from the street, where the cavalcade is to begin. As soon as all who are to assist in the procession are assembled, the viceroy and his retinue mount on horses, provided by the city for this ceremony, and the gates being thrown open, the procession begins in the following order:

The militia; the colleges; the university with the professors in their proper habits; the chamber of accounts; the audiencia on horses with trappings; the magistracy, in crimson velvet robes, lined with brocade of the same colour, and a particular kind of caps on their heads, a dress only used on this occasion. Some members of the corporation who walk on foot, support the canopy over the viceroy; and the two ordinary alcaldes, which are in the same dress, and walk in the procession, act as equerries, holding the bridle of his horse. This part of the ceremony, though prohibited by the laws of the Indies, is still performed in the manner I have described; for the custom being of great antiquity, the magistrates have not thought proper to alter it, that the respect to the viceroy might not suffer any diminution, and no person has yet ventured to be the first in refusing to comply with it.

This procession is of considerable length, the viceroy passing through several streets till he comes to the great square, in which the whole company draw up facing the cathedral, where he alights, and is received by the archbishop and chapter. Te Deum is then sung before the viceroy, and the officers placed in their respective seats; after which he again mounts his horse and proceeds to the palace-gate, where he is received by the audiencia, and conducted to an apartment in which a splendid collation is provided, as are also others for the nobility in the anti-chambers.

On the morning of the following day, he returns to the cathedral in his coach, with the retinue and pomp usual in solemn festivals, and public ceremonies. He is preceded by the whole troop of horse-guards, the members of the several tribunals in their coaches, and after them the viceroy himself with his family, the company of halberdiers bringing up the rear. On this occasion all the riches and ornaments of the church are displayed; the archbishop celebrates in his pontifical robes the mass of thanksgiving; and the sermon is preached by one of the best orators of the chapter. From hence the viceroy returns to the palace attended by all the nobility, who omit nothing to make a splendid figure on these occasions. In the evening of this, and the two following days, the collations are repeated, with all the plenty and delicacy imaginable. To increase the festivity, all women of credit have free access to the halls, galleries, and gardens of the palace, when they are fond of shewing the dispositions of their genius, either by the vivacity of repartees, or spirited conversations, in which they often silence strangers of very ready wit.

This shew and ceremony is succeeded by bull-feasts at the city's expense, which continue five days; the three first for the viceroy, and the two latter in compliment of the ambassador who brought advice of his arrival, and the great honour conferred on him by the sovereign in the government of this kingdom.

This ambassador, who, as I before observed, is always a person of eminent quality, makes also a public entrance into Lima on horseback on the day of his arrival, and the nobility being informed of his approach, go out to receive and conduct him to the palace, from whence they carry him to the lodgings prepared for him. This ceremony used to be immediately followed by feasts and public diversions; but in order to avoid that inconvenience, just when the city is everywhere busied in preparing for the reception of the viceroy, they are deferred, and given at one and the same time as above recited.

The bull-feasts are succeeded by that ceremony, in which the university, the colleges, the convents and nunneries acknowledge him as their vice-royal protector. This is also accompanied with great splendour, and valuable prizes are bestowed on those who make the most ingenious compositions in his praise. These ceremonies, which greatly heighten the magnificence of this city, are so little known in Europe, that I shall be excused for enlarging on them.

They are begun by the university, and the rector prepares a poetical contest, adapted to display either the wit or learning of the competitors. After publishing the themes, and the prizes to be given to those who best handle the subjects they have chosen, he waits on the viceroy to know when he will be pleased to honour the university with his presence; and, the time being fixed, every part of the principal court is adorned with the utmost magnificence. The prizes which are placed in order distinguish themselves by their richness, while the pillars and columns are hung with emblematical devices, or pertinent apothegms on polished shields, surrounded by the most beautiful mouldings.

The reception is in the following order. On the viceroy's entering the court he is conducted to the rectorial chair, which, on this occasion, glitters with the magnificence of an Eastern throne. Opposite to it sits the rector, or, in his absence, one of the most eminent members of that learned body, who makes a speech, in which he expresses the satisfaction the whole university feels in such a patron. After this the viceroy returns to his palace, where, the day following, the rector presents him with a book, containing the poetical contest, bound in velvet, and plated at the corners with gold, accompanied with some elegant piece of furniture, whose value is never less than eight hundred or a thousand crowns.

The principal end of the university in this ceremony being to ingratiate itself with the viceroy and his family, the rector contrives

that the poetical pieces which gain the prizes, be made in the name of the principal persons of his family, and accordingly the most distinguished prizes are presented to them; and there being 12 subjects in the contest, there are three prizes for each, of which the two inferior fall to those members, whose compositions are most approved of. These prizes are pieces of plate, valuable both for their weight and workmanship.

The university is followed by the colleges of St. Philip and St. Martin, with the same ceremonies, except the poetical contest.

Next follow the religious orders, according to the antiquity of their foundation in the Indies. These present to the viceroy the best theses maintained by students at the public acts.

The viceroy is present at them all, and each disputant pays him some elegant compliment, before he enters on his subject.

The superiors of the nunneries send him their congratulatory compliments, and when he is pleased in return to visit them, they entertain him with a very fine concert of musick, of which the vocal parts are truly charming: and at his retiring they present him with some of the chief curiosities which their respective institutes allow to be made by them.

Besides these festivities and ceremonies, which are indeed the most remarkable; there are also others, some of which are annual, in which the riches and liberality of the inhabitants are no less conspicuous. Particularly on new-year's day, at the election of alcaldes, who being afterwards confirmed by the viceroy, appear publickly on horseback the same evening, and ride on each side of him, in very magnificent habits ornamented with jewels, and the furniture of their horses perfectly answerable. This cavalcade is very pompous, being preceded by the two companies of horse-guards, the halberdiers, followed by the members of the tribunals in their coaches, the viceroy's retinue, and the nobility of both sexes.

On twelfth-day in the morning, and the preceding evening, the viceroy rides on horseback through the town, with the royal standard carried in great pomp before him. This is performed in commemoration of the building of the city, which, as we have already observed, was begun on this day; solemn vespers are sung in the cathedral, and a mass celebrated; and the ceremony is concluded with a cavalcade, like that on new-year's day.

The alcaldes chosen for the current year, give public entertainments in their houses, each three nights successively; but that the feasts of one might not interfere with those of another, and occasion resentments, they agree for one to hold his feasts the three days immediately succeeding the election, and the other on twelfth-day and the two following. Thus each has a great number of guests, and the entertainments are more splendid and sumptuous. The other feasts

in the course of the year, are not inferior to these either with regard to numbers or expense; at least the number of them must excite a high idea of the wealth and magnificence of Lima.

3. "I HAVE SEEN CORRUPTION BOIL AND BUBBLE . . . "[3]

Corruption became structural in the government of the Indies in the seventeenth century. Colonial officials, high and low, prostituted their trusts in innumerable and ingenious ways. An audacious adventurer who had an intimate knowledge of conditions in the colonies, Gabriel Fernández de Villalobos, Marquis of Varinas (1642?-?), showered Charles II with memorials in which he sought to guide the monarch through the bewildering thicket of official misdeeds and warned him that failure to remedy the situation must lead to the loss of the Indies. He was rewarded for his pains by imprisonment in a North African fortress. The following extract from one of his memorials illuminates the technique of a grafting viceroy.[4]

✠✠✠✠ I shall assume that your Majesty has everywhere excellent ministers, conscientious and learned, and that the Indies are today and have often before been governed by viceroys and *oidores* of notable piety and integrity. . . . And certainly some were distinguished by all the virtues; there was one, in particular, of such zeal and integrity that on departing from Mexico City after completing his term of office he received with kindness an Indian who offered him a bouquet of flowers, saying: "This is the first gift I have received in this kingdom." A great viceroy was this, my lord, who died so poor that King Philip II (may he be with God) paid his debts out of the royal treasury. And it may be that these virtues (in addition to the merits of his family) later won for his sons the favor of Philip IV, your Majesty's father.

There were viceroys before and after him who worked in the same righteous spirit. For that reason, in this discourse I shall neither name names nor accuse anyone in particular; I shall speak instead of the evils that I have seen and of the remedies that are necessary. . . .

Your Majesty may assume that a high official driven by an immoderate desire to make his fortune will operate in the following manner:

[3] Shakespeare, *Measure for Measure*, Act V, Scene I.
[4] *Colección de documentos inéditos . . . de las antiguas posesiones españolas de Ultramar*, Madrid, 1885-1932, 25 vols., XII, pp. 226-231. (Excerpt translated by the editor.)

First, he will utilize or sell (to put it more precisely), for his own profit and at high prices, every kind of judicial office, *alcaldías mayores*, *corregimientos*, commissions, and *residencias*.

Second, he will also sell the rights to *encomiendas*, licenses, and concessions — authorizations to do various things that are forbidden by the laws and ordinances but that the viceroy may allow.

Third, he will dispose in the same way of all kinds of military positions, such as the titles and commissions of lieutenants, captains, generals, recruiting officers, garrison commanders, constables, and many non-existent posts.

Fourth, he will do the same with all that relates to the public finances, selling drafts on the royal treasury (which is the ruin of your Majesty's estate) and disposing of the offices of revenue collectors, of judges appointed to make various investigations, of officials charged with collecting the royal fifth and making financial settlements, of inspectors of the mines and lands, of *alcaldes* with jurisdiction over water rights, and so forth. . . .

Such, my lord, are the articles of faith that your ministers of the Indies observe most diligently.

The minister who does these things, my lord, clearly will be guided not by reason but by his own convenience, and therefore he will surround himself with individuals who will advance his interests; and will encourage these men to commit excesses, while he will always persecute and humiliate the just and virtuous, for these are the only ones he fears.

Such a minister must also seek the good will of superiors as well as inferiors, and share his spoils with them, so that they will write favorably of him to Spain and so that his trickery will be concealed. He must also try to persuade the tribunals to close their eyes to his actions, sometimes through terrorizing them, sometimes by bribing them. . . .

Such viceroys and presidents must also go about in fear and distrust of the people, who see what goes on and murmur, complain, denounce it publicly, and compose satires and squibs. . . .

All these things together, and each one separately, contribute to the total destruction of the Indies, for every item is a source of political offenses and scandalous crimes that cause infinite miseries.

4. THE CORREGIDOR: ENEMY OF THE PEOPLE

The provincial governor — or corregidor, the title he most commonly bore — occupied a key position in the political hierarchy of the Indies. His supreme authority on the local level, under

the viceroy, from whom he usually bought his position, gave him immense power for good or evil. By common consent, he generally employed that power for bad ends. The worst abuse of his authority arose in connection with the practice of reparti-miento, the mandatory purchase of goods for the corregidor by the Indians of his district. The Marquis of Varinas describes in vivid detail the operations of the repartimiento.[5]

✤✤✤✤ This corregidor or governor, president or *alcalde mayor,* whose office cost him 10 or 12,000 pesos, must acquire a stock of goods worth 20,000 pesos to sell in his province, in order to make a profit on the money he has expended. . . . He sells this merchandise to his poor subjects at six or eight times its true value, and buys up the products of the Indians and Spaniards at four or five times below the current price of the country, using force and threats . . . to enrich himself and slake his unnatural thirst for money, as soon as he takes up the tasks of government. . . .

The goods that this official receives from the merchants who outfit him, he purchases at steep prices; and he must increase their cost to the Indians accordingly. So the unhappy judge, dragging the chains of his many debts, arrives in his district, which he finds filled with naked Indians and impoverished Spaniards burdened with children and obligations, whose total possessions, if put up at public auction, would not yield 6,000 pesos. Withal, this judge must squeeze out of them more than 30,000 pesos in two years in order to pay his debts, and half as much again if he wishes to make a profit from his office. And if he cannot do this he is beyond salvation (as they say in the Indies), since he is considering only his temporal welfare and forgetting that such a policy may consign him to eternal perdition, as will inevitably ensue if he does not make restitution.

When this judge enters upon his office, his sole concern is to find means of paying off his large debts and to make a profit from his employment; and since time is short, his needs immense, the land exhausted, and his vassals poor, he must use violence and cruelty to attain what equity, moderation, and kindness will not secure.

To this end he must monopolize the products of the land, compelling his miserable vassals to sell all their fruits to him, who, rod in hand, is judge and inspector, merchant, corregidor, and interpreter of his own contract. . . .

Let your Majesty's ministers of the Council of the Indies, and your Majesty's confessor, take note that the distribution of goods by the corregidor, made to enable him to buy the products of the district, is never carried out by arrangement with the Indians who have to buy

[5] *Colección de documentos inéditos,* XII, pp. 237–239, 245–246, 249–256. (Excerpt translated by the editor.)

this merchandise. The customary practice is for the Spanish governor to turn the goods over to the Indian *alcaldes* and bosses and to fix prices in collusion with them. . . . The Indian bosses never object to the high prices, for they do not have to buy anything; their principal concern is to avoid having to shoulder any part of the burden and to ingratiate themselves with the corregidores, so that they may keep their jobs.

Having agreed on prices and received the goods, the Indian bosses, who are stupid and heartless, count the people living in each town; they make no exception of the widows or of the poor, sick, and aged, but treat all alike, and assign to them by heads the payment they must make for these goods. They take the merchandise, according to the assessment made by the corregidor, to each one's house, place it before him, and tell him the reckoning; he must pay this in the allotted time or else go to rot in prison. As a clear example of the injustice of this distribution, the Indians are often seen wearing scapularies of various colors . . . which fell to their lot in the distribution and of which they can make no other use. . . .

Your Majesty may imagine from these and similar facts how these Indians fear prison, the threat of which compels the Indian bosses and commoners to submit to their governors; and no wonder, for the Indian prison is a fearful thing. It is a small dark room, without windows or other vent than a very small door. There they must perform their bodily functions, chained by the feet; there are no beds; and as the Indians are brought from other towns, they generally forget to give them any food. They suffer from hunger and thirst and a terrible stench; and since these unhappy beings have been raised in the open country they consider imprisonment worse than death, and therefore many prefer to take their own lives. . . .

At the conclusion of one year, the period for which his office is granted (with a second year possible by way of extension), the judge makes another deal with the superior officer who appointed him, and adds another 1 or 2,000 pesos to the original price, unless this sum was included in the original agreement. If he did not do this he would be completely ruined, for in the first year he was occupied with the distribution of his goods . . . and he must have the second year to collect payment for his merchandise. . . . In any case the judge almost always ends "over-extended" (as they say), with the district owing him for the goods that he distributed — and these debts represent not only the profit that he hoped to make but the sums that he must pay out. On this account the judge resorts to the following expedients, which are all new and greater injustices and injuries to the service of God and of your Majesty:

First, seeing that the end of his term of office and the arrival of a successor are near, the corregidor tries to collect payment from

Your Majesty's vassals in four days . . . for goods that he had sold on credit for a much longer period.

Second, after his successor has been named he makes a deal with him (if he is the judge of residence), paying him a certain sum; if he is not the judge, he uses this money to have a judge appointed who will absolve him of all guilt.

Third, in any case he will try to obtain a pledge from his successor that he will not permit any inhabitant to lodge any complaints or charges against him in the *residencia*, making it clear to him that whatever befalls the old judge will happen to the new one, since he must of necessity manage his affairs in the same way as his predecessor.

Fourth, since the debt with which he began his term of office — of 10, 12, and 200,000 pesos, with interest added — is so large that his subjects, though exploited with such great severity, simply cannot furnish this sum of money . . . , he must choose one of two courses of action. He may remain in the vicinity until he has collected all that is owed him — which is his profit — all the rest having gone to pay his outfitters, his creditors, the official who appointed him, and the judge of residence. In this case Your Majesty's vassals, and the judge who succeeds him, are saddled with a very burdensome and offensive guest who not only obstructs their industry but impoverishes them with his collections. Or he may sell his debts to his successor, taking a partial loss; and since these obligations grow with the passage of time, they come to form an unbearable burden on the Spanish and Indian settlements, so that the people become impoverished and leave their homes, and the district is soon depopulated through these intolerable injuries.

Fifth, the evil ministers often resort to the following expedient: Sometimes, in order to leave no debts outstanding when they quit office, they sell or hire the Indians to owners of workshops to satisfy their debts, using trivial offenses as pretexts. . . . At other times they use for pretexts the arrears in the tribute they owe Your Majesty. In other places they commit still greater offenses and violence for the same cause, compelling the Indians to cultivate fields for them, which gives rise to a mass of injuries more numerous than the seeds of grain gathered from the land, for with this pretext fifty Indians are forced to pay the tributes of five hundred. So these Indians must pass their lives in endless labor, lacking food, clothing, or time in which to plant for themselves and their families. They go about continually harassed — men, women, the aged, boys, widows, young girls, and married women, sowing and plowing with their own hands, unaided by oxen or other animals, and threshing the grain with their feet, all without recompense. . . .

Sixth, since the first question put in the *residencia* asks the witnesses under oath whether the judge engaged in any business deal-

ings on his own account, it becomes necessary to keep from the judge of residence what everybody else knows. Hence, by one means or another — threats or pleas for mercy, or bad conscience — all are made to swear that the corregidor engaged in no business dealings, either personally or through intermediaries; and this is sworn to by the same persons to whom the judge forcibly sold and distributed the steers, mules, and other merchandise in which he traded during his term of office, and whose grain and other supplies he monopolized. . . .

Thus, through such perjury and sins of sacrilege on the part of the persons he suborned, the corregidor obtains an acquittal and quits his office — one which he secured through bribery and fraud, which he entered with usury and oppression, whose duties he performed with violence and injury, and which he left committing sacrilege, bearing false witness before God concerning his actions.

5. CITY GOVERNMENT IN THE INDIES

The birth of the colonial city coincided with the passing of the freedom and authority of the communes or towns of Spain. Under the circumstances it was inconceivable that Spain's rulers should permit any development of municipal democracy or autonomy in the colonies. From the outset the right of the king to appoint municipal officials was accepted without question. Philip II began the practice — which later became general —of selling posts in the town councils to the highest bidders, with the right of resale or bequest, on condition that a certain part of their value be paid to the crown at each transfer. Inevitably, this system caused such an office to be regarded as a source of social prestige or profit, rather than as a public trust for which the holder was answerable to the citizenry. Gonzalo Gómez de Cervantes, a leading citizen of Mexico, of whose life little is known, criticized the practice and suggested its reform in a memorial addressed to a member of the Council of the Indies, dated 1599.[6]

✦✦✦✦ It is well known and understood that Mexico is the head of all this kingdom and that all the other cities, towns, and places of this New Spain acknowledge it as such. All the more reason, then, that its *regidores* (councilmen) should be outstanding men, of quality, experience, and mature judgment. And the lack of such men has been

[6] Gonzalo Gómez de Cervantes, *La vida económica y social de Nueva España al finalizar el siglo XVI*, edited by Alberto María Carreño, México, 1944, pp. 93–94. (Excerpt translated by the editor.)

a cause of many different things, that show a serious weakness. The proof of this is that the majority of the regidores are youths who even twenty years from now will not have enough experience to govern a city; and it is a sorry thing to see those who have not yet left off being children, already made city fathers.

This evil arises from the permission granted by His Majesty for the sale of these offices — whereby they go to those who can pay the most for them, and not to those who would render the best honor and service to the commonweal. It is shameful that such youths should be preferred for the posts of regidores and other important positions over mature and eminent men who should occupy those offices. Truly, it would redound much more to the service of His Majesty and to the increase of his kingdom, if he gave these council seats to qualified persons, descendants of conquistadores, and others who have served him; they would regard their king and country with greater love, if His Majesty rewarded them for their merits and services, and would be inspired to serve him still more.

It is not seemly that those who yesterday were shopkeepers or tavern-keepers, or engaged in other base pursuits, should today hold the best offices in the country while gentlemen and descendants of those who conquered and won the land go about poor, dejected, degraded, and neglected. And it is the city that suffers most from this injustice, because the fixing of market prices, the supervision of weights and measures in the markets, and other very important matters are in a state of great disorder. It would be a very efficacious remedy, if his Majesty were to add a dozen council seats and give them to men of quality, maturity, wisdom, and merit — not by way of sale, but as gifts — and if he were to do the same with the seats that fall vacant. If such a policy were adopted, everything pertaining to his royal estate and the preservation of this realm would be greatly served and advanced.

14 ✢ The Church in the Indies

The controlling influence of the Catholic Church in the social and spiritual life of the colonies was deeply rooted in the Spanish past. During the long centuries of struggle against the Moslems, the Church, in whose name the Wars of Reconquest were waged, acquired immense wealth and an authority second only to that of the crown. The Catholic Kings, Ferdinand and Isabella, particularly favored the clergy and the spread of its influence as a means of achieving their ideals of national unity and royal absolutism. The Spanish Inquisition, founded by them in 1480, had political as well as religious uses, and under their great-grandson Philip II it became "the strongest bulwark of the omnipotence of the crown."

Royal control over ecclesiastical affairs, in both Spain and the Indies, was solidly founded on the institution of the *patronato real* (royal patronage). As applied to the colonies, this consisted in the absolute right of the Spanish kings to nominate all church officials, collect ecclesiastical tithes, and found churches and monasteries in America. The Spanish monarchs regarded the patronage of the Church as their most cherished prerogative, and reacted sharply to all encroachments upon it.

Beginning with Columbus's second voyage, one or more clergymen accompanied every expedition that sailed for the Indies, and

they came in swelling numbers to the subjugated territories. They converted prodigious numbers of natives, who as a rule willingly accepted the new and more powerful divinities of the invaders; frequently they championed the rights of the Indians against their Spanish oppressors. Unfortunately, some lost their apostolic fervor as the high religious excitement of the first strenuous years dissolved; many of the later arrivals preferred ease and profit to a life of austerity and service. From first to last, the colonies were a scene of unedifying strife between regular and secular clergy over their fields of jurisdiction.

The missionary impulse of the first friars survived longest on the frontier, "the Rim of Christendom." The most notable instance of successful missionary effort, at least from an economic point of view, was that of the Jesuit establishments in Paraguay.

The Inquisition was established in the Indies by Philip II in 1569. Its great privileges, its independence of other courts, the secrecy of its proceedings, and the dread with which the charge of heresy was generally regarded by Spaniards made the Inquisition an effective check on "dangerous thoughts," whether religious, political, or philosophical. The great mass of cases tried by its tribunals, however, had to do with offenses against morality or minor deviations from orthodox religious conduct.

By the first decades of the eighteenth century the morals of the clergy had declined to a condition that the Mexican historian Lucas Alamán, himself a leader of the clerical party in the period of independence, could only characterize as "scandalous." Yet the power of the Church, founded upon its immense wealth, its many bonds with the state, and the fanaticism of the masses, was not significantly diminished by the moral decline of many of the clergy. It was destined to survive the wreck of the Spanish colonial system and to play an important role in the life of the new Spanish-American republics.

I. THE ROYAL PATRONAGE

The privilege of the patronato real *was to some extent implied in the papal grant of the newly-discovered western lands to the king of Castile in 1493, "with free, full, and absolute power, authority, and jurisdiction." By later bulls, issued in 1501 and 1508, the Papacy conceded to King Ferdinand and his successors the exclusive right of patronage over the Church in the New World. The following decree of Philip II, dated July 10, 1574, fully defines that right, and claims it not only on the basis of the papal concessions but on the ground that the Indies*

had been discovered and acquired at the expense of the crown of Castile.[1]

✤✤✤✤ The king, to our viceroy of the provinces of Peru, or to any other person or persons who for the time may be in charge of the government of that country. As you know, the right of ecclesiastical patronage, throughout the whole dominion of the Indies, belongs to us, not only because it was at our expense and that of the Catholic sovereigns, our predecessors, that that part of the world was discovered and acquired, and that churches and monasteries were built and endowed therein, but also because that right was granted to us by bulls issued by the supreme pontiffs, of their own accord; and in order to preserve it, and maintain our just title thereto, we order and command that said right of patronage, one and undivided throughout the whole dominion of the Indies, may always remain preserved to us and to our royal Crown, without any possibility of our losing it, either wholly or in part, and that we may never be understood as conceding the right of patronage by favour or disfavour, by statute or by any other action that we ourselves, or the sovereigns our successors, may take.

And, moreover, that neither by custom, nor by prescription, nor by any other title, shall any person or persons, or ecclesiastical or secular communities, churches, or monasteries, be able to use the right of patronage, except the person who in our name and with our authority and power shall exercise it; and that no person, be he a layman or an ecclesiastic, no order, convent, religion, community, of whatever state, condition, quality and rank it may be, may dare to intermeddle on any occasion or by any reason whatever, either judicially or extrajudicially, in any affair that may concern our royal patronage, neither to prejudice us respecting it, nor to appoint to any church or benefice, or ecclesiastical office, nor to accept such appointment when made in any part of the dominion of the Indies, without our nomination or the nomination of the person whom we by law or by patent shall have authorized; and whoever shall act contrary to this, shall, in case of being a layman, incur a loss of the privileges which he shall hold from us in the whole dominion of the Indies, and he shall be incompetent to hold others, and shall be for ever banished from all our kingdoms and dominions, and in case of being an ecclesiastic, he shall be regarded as a stranger and an alien in all our kingdoms and dominions, and shall not be able to hold any benefice or ecclesiastical office therein, and shall, moreover, incur the other penalties established against such acts by the laws of these kingdoms; and our viceroys, audiencias, and royal justices shall proceed with all

[1] Quoted in Bernard Moses, *The Spanish Dependencies in South America*, New York, 1914, 2 vols., II, pp. 219–221.

rigour against those who shall so stand or act in opposition to our right of patronage, proceeding on the charge or demand of our fiscals, or of any party whatsoever who may ask for such prosecution; and great diligence shall be observed in the conduct of the case. We wish and command that there shall not be erected, instituted, founded, or constituted any cathedral or parochial church, monastery, hospital, votive church, or any other pious or religious place without our express consent, or that of the person who shall have our authority and commission for this purpose. And again, that there shall not be instituted or established any archbishopric, dignity, canonry, prebend, benefice, either simple or parochial, or any other benefice, or ecclesiastical or religious office, without our express permission, or that of the person on whom we shall have conferred full power and authority for the purpose.

2. THE COMING OF THE FRIARS

Hard on the heels of the conquistador came the priest. Even before all fighting in Mexico had ceased, Cortés wrote to the Emperor Charles V urgently asking that missionaries be sent from Spain. In June, 1524, twelve Franciscan friars, led by Father Martín de Valencia, landed on the shores of Mexico and began their barefooted pilgrimage toward the capital. There Cortés received them with a humility that confounded the Indian chiefs summoned for the occasion. Father Gerónimo de Mendieta (1525–1604), a Franciscan friar who passed many years of his life in New Spain, where he wrote an important ecclesiastical history of the colony, records the arrival of the first friars in Mexico.[2]

✠✠✠✠ When the Governor, Don Fernando Cortés, learned of the arrival of these friars, whose coming he had so greatly desired and worked for, he was very joyful and gave thanks to God for this mercy. Then he ordered some of his servants to go out on the road to meet them, to receive them in his name, and to look after them. He did this so that they might not lack anything, and so that they might suffer no mishap, for the affairs of the country were not entirely settled, since it had been conquered only recently, and the few Spaniards in it were collected in Mexico City, and feared new disturbances. One of these servants was Juan de Villagomez, who told me the story that I write down here.

[2] Gerónimo de Mendieta, *Historia eclesiástica indiana*, México, 1945, 4 vols., II, pp. 51–55. (Excerpt translated by the editor.)

While these friars journeyed toward Mexico City (which lies sixty leagues from their port of debarkation) on foot and unshod, and wanting no special care for themselves, the governor summoned all the Indian caciques and principal men of the largest towns around Mexico City, so that they might all join him in receiving the ministers of God who came to teach them His law, show them His will, and guide them along the road of salvation.

These servants of God, passing through Tlascala, stopped there for a few days to rest from their journey and to view the city, which was famed for its size. They remained there till market day, when most of the people of that province are wont to gather to obtain provisions for their families. And they marveled to see such a multitude of souls, a greater throng than they had ever seen before. They praised God with great joy to see such a plentiful harvest placed before them. And though they could not speak to them in their language, they made signs (like mutes), pointing to heaven, to convey that they came to teach them the treasures and wonders that were to be found on high.

The Indians trailed behind them (like boys following someone who is performing a novel trick), and wondered to see their threadbare garments, so different from the gallant attire of the Spanish soldiers. And they said to each other: "Who are these men that look so poor? What kind of clothing are they wearing? They are not like the other Christians of Castile." And they frequently uttered a word in their language, saying: "*motolinea, motolinea.*" One of the fathers, named Fray Toribio de Benavente, asked a Spaniard the meaning of this word that they used so frequently. The Spaniard replied, "Father, *motolinea* means poor." Then Fray Toribio said: "That shall be my name as long as I live"; thereafter he always signed himself Fray Toribio Motolinea.

When they had arrived at Mexico, the governor, accompanied by all the Spanish gentlemen and the leading Indians who were assembled for that purpose, came out to receive them; he went from one to another, kneeling before each and kissing his hands. The same was done by Don Pedro de Alvarado and the other Spanish captains and gentlemen. The Indians, seeing this, imitated the Spaniards and also kissed the hands of the fathers. Such is the power of example when given by superiors. . . .

When the governor had shown the new guests to their lodgings and had seen to their needs, he returned to the Indian caciques and principal men (who stood as if stunned by this unusual event) and said to them:

"Do not marvel that I, who am captain-general, governor, and lieutenant of the Emperor of the World, should render obedience and submission to these shabbily dressed men who have come to us from

Spain. For the power that governors enjoy . . . extends only to the bodies and estates of men, which are the outward and visible part that is perishable and corruptible on this earth. But the dominion that these men wield is over men's immortal souls, each of which has greater worth and price than all the gold or silver or precious stones in the world, or than the heavens themselves. For God has endowed them with power to guide men's souls to heaven to enjoy eternal glory, if they will accept their aid. But if they reject it, they are damned and must go to Hell to suffer eternal torments, as happened to all your forebears for lack of ministers to teach them knowledge of the God who created us. . . .

"And so that the same may not happen to you, and lest through ignorance you go where your fathers and grandfathers went before you, these priests of God, whom you call *teopixques,* have come to show you the way of salvation. Regard them, therefore, with much esteem and reverence as the guides of your souls, messengers of the most high God, and your spiritual fathers. Listen to their teachings and heed their advice and commands, and see to it that all the rest obey them, for such is my will and that of the Emperor our Lord, and of God himself . . . , who sent them to this land."

3. DIALOGUE IN YUCATAN

Some of the early friars in the Indies were saintly and cour-
ageous men who preached not only the gospel of Christ but
the message of justice to the Indians. Their zeal in this cause
won them the hatred of Spanish encomenderos *and mine own-*
ers and the gratitude of the natives. Objectively their altruism
served the long-range interests of Spanish imperialism, for it
helped to overcome the spiritual resistance of the Indians to
their conquerors and aided in stabilizing the social and eco-
nomic life of the colonies. But their sincerity and good will
cannot be questioned. Their point of view is well expressed in
a dialogue overheard in a Yucatan village by Father La Torre,
one of the Dominican friars who accompanied Las Casas when
the great fighter for Indian rights came to southern Mexico as
Bishop of Chiapas in 1544.[3]

✠✠✠✠ The sun had already set when we came to a clean-looking little church, decorated with branches. We were much pleased and greatly heartened, believing that where these signs appeared we were certain

[3] F. Tomás de la Torre, *Desde Salamanca . . . hasta . . . Chiapas,* pp. 150–152. (Excerpt translated by the editor.)

to find charity. After saying a prayer we continued on our way as if spellbound, for we knew nothing of these people and did not know how to talk to them. This was our first encounter with the Indians, who certainly could do as they pleased with us without fear of resistance; it was we who were afraid of them.

So we came to a village where many Indians were sitting about. When they saw us they rose and gave us seats, which were small stools, no larger than the distance between the extended thumb and forefinger of one hand. . . . The father vicar said, "Let us stay here this night, for God has prepared this lodging for us." The Indians, seeing how miserable we were, owing to the cold of the lagoon, made a great bonfire, the first that we had needed since leaving Spain. Then the chief came with half a pumpkin shell filled with water; he washed our feet, and they gave us each two tortillas and a piece of fresh fish and another of sweet potato. We ate and felt much better, and were filled with devotion and wonder to see the charity of these Indians, who the Spaniards claimed were so bestial.

At night came Ximénes, who knew their language, and through him we asked them why they had treated us so kindly. They replied that on the road an Indian had seen us and realized that we were thirsty and had told them so, and for that reason they had sent that pumpkin shell of water and accorded us that hospitality, because they knew that we came from Castile for their good. We took great pleasure in the reply of these barbarians.

That night there arrived a peasant who came with the bishop [Las Casas], Zamora by name, and after we had all lain down to sleep, some on boards and others on small mats that the Indians make of rushes . . . , Zamora, the recently-arrived peasant from Castile, and Ximénes, an oldtimer in the country and a conqueror of Yucatan, began to talk, and because their conversation was very diverting I shall set down here what I remember of it.

Said Ximénes to Zamora:

"You chose a poor place to stable that beast of yours for the night; the Indians will surely take it and eat it."

Said Zamora:

"Let them eat it, by God; we Christians owe them a good deal more than that."

Ximénes:

"What the devil do you mean by that?"

Zamora:

"I mean that you've robbed them of their property and taken their sons from them and made them slaves in their own land."

Ximénes:

"They owe us more than that, for we are Christians."

Zamora:

"Christians? A Christian is known by his works."

Ximénes:

"We are Christians, and we came to this land to make Christians of them."

Zamora:

"I'll bet you came over here because your deviltries made Spain too hot a place for you, or else you would not have left your own country. I swear to God that no one comes to the Indies for any other reason, and myself first of all."

Ximénes:

"God alone knows why each man came over; but the main thing is that we conquered this country."

Zamora:

"And that is why you expect the Indians to give you their food and property — because you murdered them in their own houses! Good friends you proved to be, indeed!"

Ximénes:

"You would not say that if you had shed your blood in the war."

Zamora:

"I dare say that even if they had killed you they would not go to Hell, because you made war on them."

Ximénes:

"They are dogs, and will not believe in God."

Zamora:

"And very good preachers they had in you, for certain."

Ximénes:

"Surely, Zamora, you will not go back to Castile."

Zamora:

"The devil take me if I carry away a cent that I did not earn with my spade; the Indians owe me nothing."

While this dialogue went on the rest of us kept quiet, lying in the dark, but we could hardly keep from laughing at the humor of Zamora's remarks. On the other hand, we were confounded by the clarity and simplicity of the judgments of this illiterate peasant, who said only what his reason dictated. . . .

4. THE JESUIT MISSION EMPIRE

In the wilderness of eastern Paraguay, a region favored by a genial climate and fertile soil, two Jesuit priests, Joseph Cataldino and Simon Mazetta, began missionary work among the Guarani Indians in 1609. Eventually more than thirty missions

or reductions had arisen in the area; they formed the principal field of Jesuit activity in America until their expulsion in 1767. Their strict discipline, centralized organization, and absolute control over the labor of thousands of docile Indians enabled the Jesuits to turn their missions into a highly profitable business enterprise. The self-imposed isolation of the Jesuit mission empire aroused the curiosity of European philosophers and literati; Voltaire gave an ironic and fanciful description of it in his witty satire on the follies and vices of the age, Candide. Félix de Azara (1742–1804), a distinguished Spanish soldier and scientist who came to Paraguay on an official assignment in 1781, fourteen years after the expulsion of the Jesuits, describes the life and government of the missions.[4]

✠✠✠✠ Having spoken of the towns founded by the Jesuit fathers, and of the manner in which they were founded, I shall discuss the government which they established in them. . . .

In the town of Candelaria there was a father, a kind of provincial, named *Superior of the Missions,* who had authority from the Pope to confirm the Indians and was the chief of all the curacies or towns. In each one resided two priests, a curate and a sub-curate, who had certain assigned functions. The sub-curate was charged with all the spiritual tasks, and the curate with every kind of temporal responsibility. Since the latter required much knowledge and experience, the curates were always priests of notable gravity, who had earlier been provincials or rectors of their colleges; whether or not they knew the language of the Indians was not considered important. Their predecessors in office left them copious diaries, with directions for the management of labor, workshops, and so forth. The curates, in sum, were masters of all. Although each town had its Indian *corregidor, alcaldes,* and *regidores,* who comprised a municipal council like that of a Spanish town, they had no jurisdiction, and were in effect nothing more than the executors of the orders of the curate, who invariably handed down mild judgments in all cases, civil and criminal, but did not permit an appeal to other Spanish judges or *audiencias.*

The curate allowed no one to work for personal gain; he compelled everyone, without distinction of age or sex, to work for the community, and he himself saw to it that all were equally fed and dressed. For this purpose the curates placed in storehouses all the fruits of agriculture and the products of industry, selling in the Spanish towns their surplus of cotton, cloth, tobacco, vegetables, skins,

[4] Félix de Azara, *Descripción y historia del Paraguay y del Rio de la Plata,* Asunción, Paraguay, 1896, 2 vols., I, pp. 338–352. (Excerpt translated by the editor.)

yerba maté, and wood, transporting them in their own boats down the nearest rivers, and returning with implements and whatever else was required.

From the foregoing one may infer that the curates disposed of the surplus funds of the Indian towns, and that no Indian could aspire to own private property. This deprived them of any incentive to use reason or talent, since the most industrious, able, and worthy person had the same food, clothing, and pleasures as the most wicked, dull, and indolent. It also follows that although this form of government was well designed to enrich the communities it also caused the Indian to work at a languid pace, since the wealth of his community was of no concern to him. . . .

It must be said that although the fathers were supreme in all respects, they employed their authority with a mildness and restraint that command admiration. They supplied everyone with abundant food and clothing. They compelled the men to work only half a day, and did not drive them to produce more. Even their labor was given a festive air, for they went in procession to the fields, to the sound of music and carrying a little image in a litter, for which they always constructed a bower; and the music did not cease until they had returned in the same way they had set out. They gave them many holidays, dances, and tournaments, dressing the actors and the members of the municipal councils in gold or silver tissue and the most costly European garments, but they permitted the women to act only as spectators.

They likewise forbade the women to sew; this occupation was restricted to the musicians, sacristans, and acolytes. But they made them spin cotton; and the cloth that the Indians wove, after satisfying their own needs, they sold together with the surplus cotton in the Spanish towns, as they did with the tobacco, vegetables, yerba maté, wood, and skins. The curate and his companion, or sub-curate, had their own plain dwellings, and they never left them except to take the air in the great enclosed yard of their college. They never walked through the streets of the town or entered the house of any Indian or let themselves be seen by any woman — or, indeed, by any man, except for those indispensable few through whom they issued their orders. If some ailing person required spiritual aid, they brought him from his miserable dwelling to a clean room near the college that was set apart for that purpose, and the sub-curate, carried in a sedan with great pomp, administered the holy sacraments to him there.

When they appeared in the church, although it was only to say mass, it was with the greatest ceremony, wearing costly garments, surrounded and assisted by about a hundred sacristans, acolytes, and musicians. All their churches were the largest and most magnificent in that part of the world, filled with great altars, pictures, and gilding;

the ornaments could not be better or more costly in Madrid or Toledo. All this is convincing evidence that the Jesuits spent on churches
and their accessories, and in attiring the actors and municipal officers
on festival days, the vast sums that they could have appropriated for
themselves if they had been ambitious.

The streets of their towns were five paces wide. The buildings
were one-story structures, each consisting of a long hall that originally
housed all the subjects of a chieftain; they were later divided into
little rooms, each seven *varas* long, one to each family. These rooms
had no window, chimney, or kitchen, and their entire furnishings
consisted of a cotton hammock, for the master of the house; the
others slept on skins on the floor, without any partitions between
them. The food of the Indians cost the priests little or nothing, since
they had a surplus of meat from the increase of the herds on their
estates. For clothing they gave each man a cap, a shirt, stockings, and
a poncho, all made of cotton cloth, a thick, coarse, light-colored
material. They made them shave their hair, and did not permit them
to wear anything on their feet. The women also went barefooted,
and their only garment was a *tipos* or sleeveless shirt of the same
material as was described above, girdled at the waist. . . .

From what I could learn, in visiting all the towns, none of the
Indians understood Spanish, nor could they read or write, except for
a few who were taught to read and write in Guarani in order to keep
accounts of what was taken into and out of the storehouses and so
forth. They had no scientific knowledge and only a few crafts, since
they only wove cloth for their own garments and for slaves or very
poor people; but some were taught the trades of ironsmith and silver-
smith and painting, sculpture, music, dancing, and so forth, in which
they were instructed by Jesuits brought especially for this purpose.

All were batpized and knew how to say their prayers, which
all the boys and unmarried girls had to recite in a chorus under the
portico of the church at dawn. Yet those who have replaced the
Jesuits assert that there was little true religion among the Indians.
This is not strange, in view of the fact that the Indians themselves
say that there were few Jesuit curates capable of preaching the gospel in Guarani. . . . As a partial remedy for this deficiency, the Jesuits
had certain clever Indians learn a few sermons, which they preached
in the town square after some festival or tournament; I have heard
some of these, and they contained a good deal of nonsense which
the orator drew out of his head. . . .

In the year 1769, the Jesuits turned their towns over to an
equal number of friars; but theirs was only the spiritual power, while
the temporal power formerly enjoyed by the Jesuit curate was entrusted to a secular administrator. There was also established a military governor of all the missions of the Parana and Uruguay rivers.

It could be said that these towns only changed hands, but the Jesuits were more able, moderate, and frugal, and regarded their towns as their own handiwork and private possession, and so loved them and worked for their good. The secular governors, on the other hand, and the administrators whom they appointed, not only lacked the intelligence of the Jesuits but regarded the wealth of the communities as a mine which was theirs to exploit for a short time. It is not strange, therefore, that the towns have grown poor, and that the Indians are compelled to work harder and are more poorly fed and clothed.

5. IN THE HANDS OF THE INQUISITION

Among the first victims of the Inquisition in Spanish America were a number of English mariners who were set on the Mexican shore by Sir John Hawkins, at their own request, after Hawkins had escaped with two battered ships from a severe naval defeat at Spanish hands in the harbor of Veracruz. After a residence of some six years in the country, during which time they were fairly well treated by the colonists, the Englishmen were rounded up and brought to Mexico City to be tried for heresy by the Inquisition. Miles Philips, one who lived to return to England and tell the tale, recorded his ordeal in a narrative first published by Richard Hakluyt (1552?–1616?) in his great documentary collection dealing with English voyages. Modern archival research has confirmed the essential reliability of this and other accounts in Hakluyt of the experiences of Englishmen in Mexico during the sixteenth century.[5]

✠✠✠✠ Now after that six years were fully expired after our first coming into the Indies, in which time we had been imprisoned and served in the said countries as is before truly declared, in the year of our Lord one thousand five hundred seventy four, the Inquisition began to be established in the Indies very much against the minds of the Spaniards themselves. For never until this time since their first conquering and planting in the Indies, were they subject to that bloody and cruel Inquisition.

The chief Inquisitor was named Don Pedro Moya de Contreras, and John de Bovilla his companion, and John Sanchez the fiscal, and Pedro de los Rios, the secretary. They being come and settled,

---

[5] "The Voyage of Miles Philips . . . ," in Richard Hakluyt, *The Principal Navigations, Voyages, Traffiques and Discoveries of the English Nation*, London, n.d., 8 vols., VI, pp. 318–323.

and placed in a very fair house near unto the white friars, considering with themselves that they must make an entrance and beginning of that their most detestable Inquisition here in Mexico, to the terror of the whole country, thought it best to call us that were Englishmen first in question, and so much the rather, for that they had perfect knowledge and intelligence that many of us were become very rich, as has been already declared, and therefore we were a very good booty and prey to the Inquisitors.

So that now again began our sorrows afresh, for we were sent for, and sought out in all places of the country, and proclamation made upon pain of losing of goods and excommunication, that no man should hide or keep secret any Englishman or any part of their goods. By means whereof we were all soon apprehended in all places, and all our goods seized and taken for the Inquisitor's use, and so from all parts of the country we were conveyed and sent as prisoners to the city of Mexico, and there committed to prison in sundry dark dungeons, where we could not see but by candle light, and were never past two together in one place, so that we saw not one another, neither could one of us tell what was become of another.

Thus we remained close imprisoned for the space of a year and a half, and others for some less time, for they came to prison ever as they were apprehended. During which time of our imprisonment, at the first beginning we were often called before the Inquisitors alone, and there severely examined of our faith, and commanded to say the Pater Noster, the Ave Maria, and the Creed in Latin, which God knows a great number of us could not say, otherwise than in the English tongue. And having the said Robert Sweeting who was our friend at Tescuco always present with them for an interpreter, he made report for us, that in our own country speech we could say them perfectly, although not word for word as they were in Latin.

Then did they proceed to demand of us upon our oaths what we did believe of the Sacrament, and whether there did remain any bread or wine after the words of consecration, yea or no, and whether we did not believe that the host of bread which the priest did hold up over his head, and the wine that was in his chalice, was the very true and perfect body and blood of our Savior Christ, yea or no. To which if we answered not yea, then was there no way but death. Then they would demand of us what we did remember of ourselves, what opinions we had held, or had been taught to hold contrary to the same while we were in England. To which we for the safety of our lives were constrained to say, that never we did believe, nor had been taught otherwise than . . . before we had said.

Then would they charge us that we did not tell them the truth, that they knew the contrary, and therefore we should call ourselves to

remembrance, and make them a better answer at the next time, or else we should be racked, and made to confess the truth whether we would or no. And so coming again before them the next time, we were still demanded of our belief while we were in England, and how we had been taught, and also what we thought or did know of such our own company as they did name unto us, so that we could never be free from such demands, and at other times they would promise us, that if we would tell them truth, then we should have favor and be set at liberty, although we very well knew their fair speeches were but means to entrap us to the hazard and loss of our lives.

Howbeit God so mercifully wrought for us by a secret means that we had, that we kept us still to our first answer, and would still say that we had told the truth unto them, and knew no more by ourselves nor any other of our fellows than as we had declared, and that for our sins and offenses in England against God and our Lady, or any of his blessed Saints, we were heartily sorry for the same, and did cry God mercy, and besought the Inquisitors for God's sake, considering that we came into those countries by force of weather, and against our wills, and that never in our lives we had either spoken or done anything contrary to their laws, and therefore they would have mercy upon us.

Yet all this would not serve; for still from time to time we were called upon to confess, and about the space of three months before they proceeded to their severe judgment, we were all racked, and some enforced to utter that against themselves, which afterwards cost them their lives. And thus having gotten from our own mouths matter sufficient for them to proceed in judgment against us, they caused a large scaffold to be made in the middle of the market place in Mexico right over against the head church, and fourteen or fifteen days before the day of their judgment, with the sound of a trumpet, and the noise of their *atabales*, which are a kind of drums, they did assemble the people in all parts of the city. Before whom it was then solemnly proclaimed, that whosoever would upon such a day repair to the market place, they should hear the sentence of the holy Inquisition against the English heretics, Lutherans, and also see the same put in execution.

Which being done, and the time approaching of this cruel judgment, the night before they came to the prison where we were, with certain officers of that holy hellish house, bringing with them certain fool's coats which they had prepared for us, being called in their language San Benitos, which coats were made of yellow cotton and red crosses upon them, both before and behind. They were so busied in putting on their coats about us, and bringing us out into

a large yard, and placing and pointing us in what order we should go to the scaffold or place of judgment upon the morrow, that they did not once suffer us to sleep all that night long.

The next morning being come, there was given to every one of us for our breakfast a cup of wine, and a slice of bread fried in honey and so about eight of the clock in the morning, we set forth of the prison, every man alone in his yellow coat, and a rope about his neck, and a great green wax candle in his hand unlighted, having a Spaniard appointed to go upon either side of every one of us. And so marching in this order and manner toward the scaffold in the market place, which was a bow shoot distant or thereabouts, we found a great assembly of people all the way, and such a throng, that certain of the Inquisitors officers on horseback were constrained to make way, and so coming to the scaffold, we went up by a pair of stairs, and found seats ready made and prepared for us to sit down on, every man in order as he should be called to receive his judgment.

We being thus set down as we were appointed, presently the Inquisitors came up another pair of stairs, and the viceroy and all the chief justices with them. When they were set down and placed under the cloth of estate agreeing to their degrees and calling, then came up also a great number of friars, white, black, and gray, about the number of 300 persons, they being set in the places for them appointed. Then was there a solemn Oyes made, and silence commanded, and then presently began their severe and cruel judgment.

The first man that was called was one Roger the chief armorer of the *Jesus,* and he had judgment to have three hundred stripes on horseback, and after condemned to the galleys as a slave for ten years.

After him were called John Gray, John Brown, John Rider, John Moon, James Collier, and one Thomas Brown. These were adjudged to have 200 stripes on horseback, and after to be committed to the galleys for the space of eight years.

Then was called John Keyes, and was adjudged to have 100 stripes on horseback, and condemned to serve in the galleys for the space of six years.

Then were severally called the number of fifty-three one after another, and every man had his several judgment, some to have 200 stripes on horseback, and some 100, and condemned for slaves to the galleys, some for six years, some for eight and some for ten.

And then was I Miles Philips called, and was adjudged to serve in a monastery for five years, without any stripes, and to wear a fool's coat, or San Benito, during all that time.

Then were called John Storie, Richard Williams, Robert Cook, Paul Horsewell and Thomas Hull. The six were condemned to serve in monasteries without stripes, some for three years and some for

four, and to wear the San Benito during all the said time. Which being done, and it now drawing toward night, George Rively, Peter Momfrie, and Cornelius the Irishman were called and had their judgment to be burned to ashes, and so were presently sent away to the place of execution in the market place but a little from the scaffold, where they were quickly burned and consumed. And as for us that had received our judgment, being sixty-eight in number; we were carried back that night to prison again.

And the next day in the morning being Good Friday, the year of our Lord 1575, we were all brought into a court of the inquisitors' palace, where we found a horse in a readiness for everyone of our men which were condemned to have stripes, and to be committed to the galleys, which were in number sixty and so they being enforced to mount up on horseback naked from the middle upward, were carried to be showed as a spectacle for all the people to behold throughout the chief and principal streets of the city, and had the number of stripes to everyone of them appointed, most cruelly laid upon their naked bodies with long whips by sundry men appointed to be the executioners thereof. And before our men there went a couple of criers which cried as they went: "Behold these English dogs, Lutherans, enemies to God,"and all the way as they went there were some of the Inquisitors themselves, and of the familiars of that rakehell order, that cried to the executioners, "Strike, lay on those English heretics, Lutherans, God's enemies."

And so this horrible spectacle being showed round about the city, they returned to the Inquisitors' house, with their backs all gore blood, and swollen with great bumps, and were then taken from their horses, and carried again to prison, where they remained until they were sent into Spain to the galleys, there to receive the rest of their martyrdom. And I and the six other with me which had judgment, and were condemned amongst the rest to serve an apprenticeship in the monastery, were taken presently and sent to certain religious houses appointed for the purpose.

6. THE SOURCES OF CATHOLIC POWER

By the last decades of the colonial era the discipline of the clergy had become seriously relaxed, and the unity of the Church was rent by unseemly squabbles between regular and secular clergy and between creole and peninsular priests. Yet the influence of the Church in colonial society, except among a tiny handful of converts to the new materialistic doctrines of the encyclopedists, remained undiminished. In the follow-

ing excerpt the Mexican historian Alamán explains the sources of Catholic power.[6]

✣✣✣✣ The immense influence of the Church rested on three foundation-stones: respect for religion, remembrance of its great benefactions, and its immense wealth. The people, poorly instructed in the essentials of religion, tended to identify it in large part with ceremonial pomp; they found relief from the tedium of their lives in the religious functions, which, especially during Holy Week, represented in numerous processions the most venerated mysteries of the redemption. The festivals of the Church, which should have been entirely spiritual, were thus transformed into so many profane performances, marked by displays of fireworks, dances, plays, bullfights and cockfights, and even such forbidden diversions as cards and the like, in order to celebrate at great cost the festivals of the patron saints of the towns, into which the Indians poured the greater part of the fruits of their labor. It was this vain pomp, attended by little true piety, that led the viceroy whom I have frequently cited [the Duke of Linares] to remark that "in this realm all is outward show, and though their lives are steeped in vices, the majority think that by wearing a rosary about their necks and kissing the hand of the priest they are made Catholics, and that the Ten Commandments can be replaced by ceremonies."

The Indians continued to regard the regular clergy with the respect that the first missionaries had justly gained by protecting them against the oppression and violence of the conquistadores and by instructing them not only in religion but in the arts necessary for subsistence. This respect, which grew to be a fanatical veneration, presented no dangers as long as it was accorded to men of admirable virtue, and the government, to which they were very devoted and obedient, found in these exemplary ecclesiastics its firmest support; but it could become highly dangerous if a clergy of debased morals wished to abuse this influence for its own ends. This danger to the government was made still greater by the very precaution that Archbishop Haro had advised to avoid it, for since the high Church positions were intrusted to Europeans, the Americans, who generally enjoyed only the less important posts and benefices, exerted greater influence over the people with whom they were placed in more immediate contact.

The wealth of the clergy consisted not so much in the estates that it possessed, numerous though they were (especially the urban properties in the principal cities like Mexico City, Puebla, and others), as in capital invested in quitrent mortgages on the property of indi-

[6] Alamán, *Historia de Méjico*, I, pp. 64–70. (Extract translated by the editor.)

viduals; the traffic in mortgages and the collection of interest made of every chaplaincy and religious brotherhood a sort of bank. The total property of the clergy, both secular and regular, in estates and loans of this kind, certainly was not less than half of the total value of the real estate of the country.

The town council of Mexico City, seeing the multitude of monasteries and nunneries that were being founded, and the large number of persons destined for the ecclesiastical profession, together with the great sums devised to pious foundations, petitioned King Philip IV in 1644 "that no more convents of nuns or monks be established, since the number of the former was excessive, and the number of their woman servants even greater; that limits be placed upon the estates of the convents and that they be forbidden to acquire new holdings, complaining that the greater part of the landed property of the land had come into the hands of the religious by way of donations or purchases, and that if steps were not taken to remedy the situation they would soon be masters of all; that no more religious be sent from Spain, and that the bishops be charged not to ordain any more clerics, since there were already more than six thousand in all the bishoprics without any occupation, ordained on the basis of tenuous chaplaincies; and, finally, that there should be a reform in the excessive number of festivals, which increased idleness and gave rise to other evils." The *cortes* assembled in Madrid at that period petitioned the king to the same effect, and similar reforms were earlier proposed by the Council of Castile, but nothing was done, and things continued in the same state. . . .

In addition to the revenues derived from these estates and loans, the secular clergy had the tithes, which in all the bishoprics of New Spain amounted to some 1,800,000 pesos annually, although the government received a part of this sum. . . . In the bishopric of Michoacán the tithes were farmed out; this made their collection more rigorous and oppressive, since private interest devised a thousand expedients to burden even the least important products of agriculture with this assessment.

The clergy had a privileged jurisdiction, with special tribunals, and a personal *fuero* which in former times had been very extensive but had greatly diminished with the intervention of the royal judges in criminal cases and with the declaration that the secular courts had jurisdiction in cases involving both principal and interest of the funds of the chaplaincies and pious foundations. The viceroy decided conflicts between ecclesiastical and civil courts, and this prerogative was one of those that gave the greatest luster to his authority.

From the instructions of the Duke of Linares to his successor and from the secret report made by Don Jorge Juan and Don Antonio Ulloa to King Ferdinand VI, it appears that the customs of the clergy

had declined at the beginning of the eighteenth century to a point of scandalous corruption, especially among the friars charged with the administration of the curacies or doctrines. In the epoch of which I speak this corruption was particularly notable in the capitals of some bishoprics and in smaller places, but in the capital of the realm the presence of the superior authorities enforced more decorum. Everywhere, it should also be said, there were truly exemplary ecclesiastics, and in this respect certain religious orders stood out. The Jesuits, above all others, were remarkable for the purity of their customs and for their religious zeal, a notable contrast, appearing in the above-cited work by Juan and Ulloa between their comments on the Jesuits and their references to other orders. Their expulsion left a great void, not only in the missions among the barbarians whom they had in charge but in the matter of the instruction and moral training of the people. . . . No less commendable were the friars of the order of Saint James, those of the order of Saint Philip, whose oratories had largely replaced those of the Jesuits, and among the hospitaller orders the Bethlehemites, who devoted themselves to primary education and the care of hospitals.

Into these religious orders the rivalry of birth had also penetrated, excepting always the Jesuits, who had no chapters or tumultuous elections and whose prelates were named in Rome by the general of the order, with regard only to the merit and virtue of individuals. Not only did there prevail in some of them the strife between "*gachupines* and creoles*," but there were entire communities composed almost exclusively of one or the other element.

THE SPANISH COLONIES IN THE EIGHTEENTH CENTURY

In the eighteenth century Spanish America felt the influence of the vast changes that were ushering in the modern world. The Industrial Revolution, greatly increasing the demand for Latin-American raw materials, helped to create a wealthy class of creole landlords, mineowners, and merchants. The Enlightenment, teaching creole youth to reason and to question, prepared them intellectually for the coming struggle for independence. And Spain herself, in which the new Bourbon dynasty was engaged in a supreme effort to modernize Spanish economic and political life, stimulated progressive change in the colonies through her reform policies.

The colonial policy of the Bourbon kings had two principal aims: to regain for Spain a major share of the trade of her colonies, wrested from her by English and other foreign contrabandists, and to increase the royal revenues from the colonies. To achieve the first of these aims the Bourbons gradually abolished the system of fleets and fairs, while preserving the principle of peninsular monopoly. Between the stimulus given by this and other commercial reforms and that offered by the increasing European market for Spanish-American staples, the colonial economy experienced a marked expansion in the eighteenth century.

The second Bourbon ambition, that of increasing the royal revenues from the colonies, was to be achieved by making their administration more efficient. Accordingly the intendant system of government, borrowed from France, was introduced in the colonies. Many of the viceroys and intendants of the reform era were men of great diligence and enlightened views, but the intendants' subordinates, the subdelegates, generally continued the evil practices of the *corregidor*.

Spanish-American colonial culture was basically on extension of the richer culture of the mother country. The Church enjoyed a virtual monopoly of education, which was restricted with few exceptions to the Indian aristocracy and the children of well-to-do Spaniards. Colonial writing, born in the twilight of the Golden Age of Spanish literature, produced only one truly great figure, the Mexican poetess Sor Juana Inés de la Cruz. Largely isolated from foreign influences and vigilantly watched over by the Inquisition, most colonial political and religious thought was expressed within the limits approved by Church and State.

In the eighteenth century the Enlightenment made a cautious entrance into the colonies. Under official auspices, efforts were made to establish schools of a more modern and useful type. The first true colonial newspapers and reviews appeared, promoting the rise of a secular and critical spirit through their articles on economic and scientific subjects. The forbidden writings of the French Encyclopedists and other European writers circulated among the educated classes in increasing quantity.

The creole upper class enjoyed greater opportunities for material and cultural enrichment in the Bourbon era, but the same was not true of Indians, mestizos, and other laboring groups. The intolerable conditions of the common people led to major revolutionary outbreaks in Peru, Bolivia, and Colombia (1780–1783) that were sternly suppressed by Spanish arms.

15 ✢ The Bourbon Reforms and Spanish America

Spain made a remarkable recovery in the eighteenth century from the state of abject weakness into which she had fallen under the last Hapsburg kings. This revival is associated with the reigns of three princes of the Houses of Bourbon: Philip V (1700–1746), grandson of Louis XIV of France, and his two sons, Ferdinand VI (1746–1759) and Charles III (1759–1788).

The work of national reconstruction reached its maximum under Charles III. During his reign Spanish industry, agriculture, and trade made marked gains. Clerical influence suffered a setback as a result of the expulsion of the Jesuits in 1767 and of decrees restricting the authority of the Inquisition. Under the cleansing influence of able and honest ministers, a new spirit of austerity and service began to appear among public officials.

In the field of colonial reform the Bourbons moved slowly and cautiously, as was natural in view of the fact that powerful vested interests were identified with the old order of things. The *Casa de Contratación*, or House of Trade, was gradually reduced in importance until it finally disappeared in 1790. A similar fate overtook the venerable Council of the Indies, although it was not abolished until 1854.

Most of its duties were entrusted to a colonial minister appointed by the king. The Bourbons alternately suspended and tried to rehabilitate the fleet system of sailing, but in the end it was abandoned, the Portobello fleet disappearing in 1740, the Veracruz fleet in 1789. The Portobello and Veracruz fairs vanished contemporaneously. In the same period the trading monopoly of Cadiz was gradually eliminated. The success of the "free trade" policy was reflected in a spectacular increase in the value of Spain's commerce with Spanish America.

The eighteenth century witnessed a steady growth of agricultural, pastoral, and mining production in Spanish America. By contrast with these signs of progress, the once-flourishing colonial handicrafts industry declined, owing to the influx of cheap European wares with which the native products could not compete. Contraband trade, never completely eliminated under the Bourbons, reached vast proportions during the frequent intervals of warfare in which British naval power swept Spanish shipping from the seas.

The most important Bourbon political reform was the transfer to the colonies, between 1782 and 1790, of the intendant system, already introduced in Spain from France. The intendants were expected to relieve the over-burdened viceroys of many of their duties, especially in financial matters, and to develop agriculture, industry, and commerce and generally to promote the welfare of their respective districts. Many of the viceroys and intendants of the reform period were able and progressive men, devoted to the interests of the crown and their subjects. But the same cannot be said of the majority of their subordinates, who, like their predecessors, the *corregidores,* soon became notorious for their oppressive practices. Following the triumph of reaction in Spain after 1788, the familiar evils of administrative corruption, mismanagement, and indifference to the public interest reappeared on a large scale in the colonies as in the mother country.

1. CHARLES III: REFORMER-KING

Gaspar Melchor de Jovellanos (1744–1811) was a leading collaborator of Charles III in the work of reform. Of noble birth, broadly cultured, abreast of the most advanced thought of his time, Jovellanos devoted himself principally to the improvement of Spanish agriculture. His report on this subject, vigorously attacking the evils of entailed estates and mortmain, is a classic of Spanish economic literature. His eulogy of Charles III, presented before the Economic Society of Madrid on November 8, 1788, not only depicts the many-sided battle of the great king

against peninsular backwardness but reveals the basic premises of the intellectual vanguard of the reform movement.[1]

✦✦✦✦ The enumeration of the measures and establishments with which this beneficent monarch won our love and gratitude has already been the object of more eloquent discourse. My design barely permits me to mention them. The founding of new agricultural colonies, the division of the communal lands, the reduction of the privileges of the stock raisers, the abolition of price-fixing and the free circulation of grain, by which he improved the state of agriculture; the encouragement of technical training, the reform of the guild system, the increase of industrial establishments, and the generous provision of privileges and exemptions in favor of industry; the breaking of the ancient chains that bound our internal commerce, the opening of new ports to foreign trade, the establishment of peace in the Mediterranean and of periodic communication and free trade with our overseas colonies in the interest of commerce . . . , and above all, the founding of those patriotic and model groups [the Economic Societies], to whose consideration he submitted all that concerned the common weal: What ample and glorious cause is this for eulogizing Charles III, and for calling him the Father of His Country!

But let us not deceive ourselves: The path of reform would have brought Charles III a highly transient glory if his vigilance had not sought to perpetuate in his dominions the good to which he aspired. His wisdom enabled him to perceive that the best-meditated laws do not as a rule suffice to bring prosperity to a nation, much less to maintain it. . . . Charles understood that he could do nothing for his people if he did not first prepare it to receive these reforms — if he did not infuse into it that spirit upon which their perfection and stability completely depend.

You, gentlemen, you who are cooperating with such zeal for the achievement of his paternal designs, are aware of the spirit that the nation lacked. Useful sciences, economic principles, a general spirit of enlightenment — that is what Spain owes to the reign of Charles III. . . .

At the opening of the eighteenth century the first Bourbon prince passed over the Pyrenees, and amid the horrors of a war as just as it was sanguinary he from time to time turned his eyes to the people, which fought generously for its rights. Philip, knowing that he could not make his people happy if he did not instruct it, founded academies, erected seminaries, established libraries, and subsidized literature and

[1] Gaspar Melchor de Jovellanos, *Obras escogidas*, Madrid, 1940, 5 vols., III, pp. 64–82. (Excerpt translated by the editor.)

literary men; in a reign of almost half a century he taught Spain the value of enlightenment.

Ferdinand, in a shorter but more prosperous and peaceful reign, followed in the footsteps of his father; he developed the merchant marine, stimulated industry, promoted internal trade, housed and rewarded the fine arts, and protected talent; and in order to augment more rapidly the sum total of useful knowledge, at the same time that he sent many promising youths through Europe to acquire this precious commodity he received with favor foreign savants and artisans and rewarded their brilliance with prizes and pensions. Thus he prepared the road that Charles III later trod so gloriously.

This pious sovereign, determined to admit light into his dominions, began by removing the obstacles that could hinder its progress. This was his first care. Ignorance yet held out in its trenches, but Charles would completely smash them. Truth battled on his side, and at its sight all the shadows would vanish.

For long centuries the philosophy of Aristotle had tyrannized over the republic of letters, and though scorned and expelled from almost all Europe it was still revered in our schools. Of little utility in itself, since it was based entirely on speculation and not at all on experience and had been garbled in the versions of the Arabs, to whom Spain owed this unfortunate gift, it was completely corrupted by the ignorance of its commentators.

Its sectaries, divided into bands, had obscured it among us with new subtleties, invented to support the empire of each sect . . . Charles dissipated, destroyed, annihilated at one blow those parties, and by admitting freedom of philosophy into our academic halls he attracted to them a treasure-trove of philosophic knowledge, which already circulates in the minds of our youth and begins to restore the sway of reason. Nowadays one rarely hears among us those barbarous words, those obscure judgments, those vain and subtle reasonings that were once the glory of the peripatetic philosopher [Aristotle] and the delight of his believers; and, finally, even the very names of Thomists, Scotists, Suarists, have fled from our schools, together with the names of Froilan, González, and Losada, their leaders, once so celebrated and now neglected and forgotten. . . .

Charles began by promoting the study of the exact sciences, without whose aid little or no progress can be made in the investigation of the truths of nature. Madrid, Seville, Salamanca, and Alcalá saw the rebirth of their ancient schools of mathematics, Barcelona, Valencia, Zaragoza, Santiago, and nearly all the universities established mathematical studies anew. The force of demonstration replaced the subtlety of syllogisms. The study of physics, based on experiment and calculation, was perfected; together with it arose the other sciences

within its jurisdiction: chemistry, mineralogy, metallurgy, natural history, botany. . . .

But still another science was necessary to make profitable use of all the others. . . . Hardly had Charles ascended the throne when the spirit of examination and reform surveyed all aspects of the public economy. The activity of the government aroused the curiosity of the citizens. Then was born the study of this science, which at that time attracted the major attention of European thinkers. Spain read the most celebrated writers in the field, examined their ideas, analyzed their works. There was discussion, controversy, writing; and Spain began to have economists.

2. THE BOURBON COMMERCIAL REFORMS

The Bourbon reforms in the field of colonial trade represented a supreme effort to recover for Spain a dominant position in the markets of Spanish America. The reform program provided for a stricter enforcement of the laws against contraband; more importantly, it included a series of measures designed to liberalize the commerce between Spain and her colonies while retaining the principle of peninsular trade monopoly. The fundamental reasons for the ultimate failure of this well-conceived program were, first, Spain's industrial weakness, which the best efforts of the Bourbons were unable to overcome, and, second, her closely related inability to keep her sea-lanes to America open in time of war with England, when foreign traders again swarmed in Spanish-American ports. Yet the Bourbon reforms, combined with a rising European demand for Spanish-American products, helped to produce a remarkable expansion of colonial trade and prosperity in the last half of the eighteenth century. The Mexican historian Alamán surveys the beneficial effects of these reforms on the commerce of New Spain.[2]

✠✠✠✠ Commerce with Spain, the only one that was permitted, was restricted until 1778 to the port of Cadiz, where were assembled, under the inspection of the *audiencia* and the House of Trade of Seville, all the goods bound for America. They were carried there in the fleets, which departed each year and whose routes were minutely prescribed by the laws, and in the interval there was no other communication than that of the dispatch boats and the storeships coming with quicksilver.

[2] Alamán, *Historia de Méjico*, I, pp. 110–113, 109–110. (Excerpt translated by the editor.)

On the arrival of the fleets a great fair was held at Panama, for all South America, and another in Jalapa for New Spain, whence this town acquired the name of Jalapa of the Fair.

This order of things gave rise to a double monopoly: that enjoyed by the houses of Cadiz and Seville which made up the cargoes and that which was secured at the fairs by the American merchants, who made agreements among themselves whereby particular merchants acquired complete control over certain lines of goods. Since the supply of these goods was not renewed for a long time, it was in their power to raise prices at will, whence arose the high prices of some commodities, especially when maritime war prevented the arrival of the fleets for several years. This condition gave occasion for the arbitrary measures of certain viceroys in fixing retail prices in favor of the consumer, as was done by the second Duke of Albuquerque in 1703.

Commerce with Asia was reduced to a single vessel, known as the "China-ship," which was sent once a year from Manila and, passing in sight of San Blas, arrived at Acapulco, to which came the buyers for the fair that was held there; after the fair it sailed again, carrying the cash proceeds of the sale of the goods that it had brought, the subvention with which the royal treasury of Mexico aided that of Manila, the criminals condemned to serve time in those islands, and those dissipated youths whom their families had consigned to this kind of exile as a disciplinary measure, called "being sent to China." Commerce between New Spain and Peru, Guatemala, and New Granada by way of the Pacific was prohibited for a variety of reasons.

By the ordinance of October 12, 1778, all this system of commerce with Europe was changed. The fleets ceased to come, the last being the one that arrived at Vera Cruz in January of that year, under the command of Don Antonio de Ulloa, so celebrated for his voyage to Peru and his secret report to the king on the state of that kingdom. Commerce thus became free for all Spanish ships sailing from habilitated ports in the peninsula, but it could only be carried on in New Spain through the port of Vera Cruz, and European goods could not be introduced from Havana or any other American place but must be brought directly from Spain.

The results of this change were very important, not only because of the abundance of goods and price reductions that it yielded but also because it ended the monopoly and the vast profits acquired with little labor by the *flotistas*, the name given to the monopolists. These men, finding it impossible to continue their former practices, retired from commerce and invested their capital in agriculture and mining, which they greatly stimulated, especially the latter. Their places were taken by a larger number of individuals, who in order to prosper had to display much activity, and thus instead of a few large

capitals there arose many small ones, which, distributed among all the towns, contributed largely to their betterment.

In this same period were lifted the odious restrictions on commerce among the provinces or kingdoms of America; and a royal decree of January 17, 1774, promulgated in the Prado, conceded freedom of trade in the Pacific, though only in the goods and productions of the respective provinces. Later declarations broadened this freedom, removing the restrictions imposed by the aforementioned order in regard to European and Asiatic goods. . . .

The exclusive colonial system of Spain provided great and valuable compensations for the prohibitions that it imposed. If one glances at the balance of trade of Vera Cruz, the only port habilitated in that period for trade with Europe and the West Indies, for the year 1803, one of the last years of peace with England, it will be seen that of the total exports to Spain, worth 12,000,000 pesos, more than a third, or 4,500,000, were in the form of produce, including not only 27,000 *arrobas* of cochineal of a value of 2,200,000 pesos but also 150,000 pounds of indigo, worth 260,000 pesos, and 500,000 *arrobas* of sugar of the value of 1,500,000 pesos, besides 26,600 *quintales* of logwood and 17,000 *quintales* of cotton. Among the exports to various points in America one notes 20,000 *tercios* of flour, 14,700 *varas* of coarse frieze, 1,300 *varas* of baize, 1,760 boxes of soap, and 700 boxes of ordinary Puebla chinaware; all this, with other minor articles, comes to a value of more than 600,000 pesos a year.

The effect of these exports was to give a great value to the sugarcane plantations, while the flour of Puebla, flowing down to Vera Cruz to satisfy not only the needs of that place but also those of Havana, the other islands, and Yucatan, left the provisioning of the markets of Mexico City to the wheatfields of Querétaro and Guanajuato, adding to their value and bringing prosperity to the wheat farmers of those provinces. All this active traffic infused animation and life into our internal commerce. Mexican agriculture today would gladly exchange the sterile freedom to cultivate vines and olives for an exportation of 500,000 *arrobas* of sugar and 20,000 *tercios* of flour.

3. THE EXPANSION OF AGRICULTURE

Stimulated by the Bourbon commercial reforms, and perhaps even more by the growing European demand for sugar, tobacco, coffee, hides, and other American staples, colonial agricultural and pastoral production rose sharply in the last half of the eighteenth century. Contrary to a common belief, by the end of the

colonial period the value of this production considerably exceeded that of the precious metals. This increase, however, was made possible by more extensive use of land and labor rather than by employment of improved implements or techniques. Agricultural progress was also held back by the growing concentration of land in a few hands, with much arable land being kept idle. The great Prussian scientist Alexander von Humboldt (1769–1859), who spent the years 1799–1804 in travel through Mexico and northern South America, describes the condition of Mexican agriculture.[3]

✦✦✦✦ The produce of the earth is the sole basis of permanent opulence. It is consolatory to see that the labour of man for half a century, has been more directed toward this fertile and inexhaustible source, than towards the working of mines, of which the wealth has not so direct an influence on the public prosperity, and merely changes the nominal value of the annual produce of the earth. The territorial impost levied by the clergy, under the name of tenth, or tithe, measures the quantity of that produce, and indicates with precision the progress of agricultural industry, if we compare the periods, in the intervals of which the price of commodities has undergone no sensible variation. The following is a view of the value of these tithes; taking for example two series of years, from 1771 to 1780, and 1780 to 1789:

Names of dioceses	Periods	Value of tithes in piastres	Periods	Value of tithes in piastres
Mexico	1771–1780	4,132,630	1781–1790	7,082,879
Puebla de los Angeles	1770–1779	2,965,601	1780–1789	3,508,884
Valladolid de Mechoacan	1770–1779	2,710,200	1780–1789	3,239,400
Oaxaca	1771–1780	715,974	1781–1790	863,237
Guadalaxara	1771–1780	1,889,724	1781–1790	2,579,108
Durango	1770–1779	913,028	1780–1789	1,080,313

The result of this view is, that the tithes of New Spain have amounted in these six dioceses:

Double Piastres, or pezzos fuertes.

From 1771 to 1779 — to 13,357,157
From 1779 to 1789 — to 18,353,821

[3] Alexander von Humboldt, *Political Essay on the Kingdom of New Spain*, London, 1822–1823, 4 vols., III, pp. 95–101.

Consequently the total augmentation has been, in the last ten years, five millions of piastres, or two-fifths of the total produce. The same data also indicate the rapidity of the progress of agriculture, in the intendancies of Mexico, Guadalaxara, Puebla, and Valladolid, compared with the provinces of Oaxaca and New Biscay. The tithes have been nearly doubled in the archbishopric of Mexico; for those which were levied during the ten years anterior to 1780, were to those levied ten years afterwards, in the proportion of 10 to 17. In the intendancy of Durango or New Biscay, this augmentation has been only in the proportion of 10 to 11.

The celebrated author of the *Wealth of Nations*, estimates the territorial produce of Great Britain, from the produce of the landtax. In the political view of New Spain, which I presented to the court of Madrid in 1803, I had hazarded a similar valuation, from the value of the tithes payable to the clergy. The result of this operation was, that the annual produce of the land amounted at least, to 24 millions of piastres. The results, which I came to in drawing up my first view, have been discussed with much sagacity, in a memoir presented by the municipal body of the town of Valladolid de Mechoacan, to the king, in the month of October 1805, on the occasion of passing an edict, relative to the property of the clergy. According to this memoir, a copy of which I have before me, we must add to these 24 millions of piastres, three millions for the produce of cochineal, vanilla, jalap, pimento of Tabasco, sarsaparilla which pay no tithes; and 2 millions for sugar and indigo, which yield only to the clergy a duty of 4 per cent. If we adopt these data, we shall find that the total agricultural produce amounts annually to 29 millions of piastres, or to more than 145 millions of francs, which, reducing them to a natural measure, and taking for basis the actual price of wheat in Mexico, 15 francs for 10 myriagrammes of wheat, are equal to 96 millions of myriagrammes of wheat. The mass of precious metals annually extracted from the mines of the kingdom of New Spain, scarcely represent 74 millions of myriagrammes of wheat, which proves the interesting fact, that the value of the gold and silver of the Mexican mines is less, by almost a fourth, than the value of the territorial produce.

The cultivation of the soil, notwithstanding the fetters with which it is everywhere shackled, has lately made a more considerable progress, on account of the immense capitals laid out in land, by families enriched either by the commerce of Vera Cruz and Acapulco, or by the working of the mines. The Mexican clergy scarcely possess land (*bienes raíces*) to the value of two or three millions of piastres; but the capitals which convents, chapters, religious societies, and hospitals have laid out in lands, amount to the sum of 44½ millions of piastres, or more than 222 millions of livres tournois.

. . . When we read the excellent work on agrarian laws, pre-

sented to the council of Castille in 1795, we perceive that notwithstanding the difference of climate and other local circumstances, Mexican agriculture is fettered by the same political causes which have impeded the progress of industry in the Peninsula. All the vices of the feudal government have passed from the one hemisphere to the other; and in Mexico these abuses have been so much the more difficult to the supreme authority to remedy the evil, and display its energy at an immense distance. The property of New Spain, like that of Old Spain, is in a great measure in the hands of a few powerful families, who have gradually absorbed the smaller estates. In America, as well as Europe, large commons are condemned to the pasturage of cattle, and to perpetual sterility.

4. THE REVIVAL OF MINING

The eighteenth century saw a marked revival of the silver mining industry in the Spanish colonies. Peru and Mexico both shared in this advance, but the Mexican mines, whose production had been rising quite consistently since the sixteenth century, forged far ahead of their Peruvian rivals in the Bourbon era. As in the case of agriculture, the increase in production was primarily due not to improved technique but rather to the opening of many new as well as old mines and the growth of the labor force. Although the Bourbon kings and their colonial agents exerted themselves to overcome the backwardness of the mining industry, their efforts were largely frustrated by the traditionalism of the mineowners and by lack of capital to finance necessary changes.[4]

✠✠✠✠ When we take a general view of the mining operations of New Spain, and compare them with those of the mines of Freiberg, the Hartz, and Schemnitz, we are surprised at still finding in its infancy, an art which has been practised in America for these three centuries, and on which, according to the vulgar prejudice, the prosperity of these ultramarine establishments depends. The causes of this phenomenon cannot escape those who, after visiting Spain, France, and the western parts of Germany, have seen that mountainous countries still exist in the centre of civilized Europe, in which the mining operations partake of all the barbarity of the middle ages. The art of mining cannot make great progress, where the mines are dispersed over a great extent of ground, where the government allows to the proprietors the full liberty of directing the operations without control, and of

[4] Humboldt, *Political Essay on the Kingdom of New Spain*, III, pp. 231–246.

tearing the minerals from the bowels of the earth, without any consideration of the future. Since the brilliant period of the reign of Charles the 5th, Spanish America has been separated from Europe, with respect to the communication of discoveries useful to society. The imperfect knowledge which was possessed in the 16th century relative to mining and smelting, in Germany, Biscay, and the Belgic provinces, rapidly passed into Mexico and Peru, on the first colonization of these countries; but since that period, to the reign of Charles the third, the American miners have learned hardly anything from the Europeans, but the blowing up with powder those rocks which resist the *pointrole*. This King and his successor have shown a praiseworthy desire of imparting to the colonies all the advantages derived by Europe from the improvement in machinery, the progress of chemical science, and their application to metallurgy. German miners have been sent at the expense of the court to Mexico, Peru, and the kingdom of new Granada; but their knowledge has been of no utility, because the mines of Mexico are considered as the property of the individuals, who direct the operations, without the government being allowed to exercise the smallest influence. . . .

After the picture which we have just drawn of the actual state of the mining operations, and of the bad economy which prevails in the administration of the mines of New Spain, we ought not to be astonished at seeing works, which for a long time have been most productive, abandoned whenever they have reached a considerable depth, or whenever the veins have appeared less abundant in metals. We have already observed, that in the famous mine of Valenciana, the annual expenses rose in the space of fifteen years from two millions of francs to four millions and a half. Indeed, if there be much water in this mine, and if it require a number of horse baritels to draw it off, the profit must, to the proprietors, be little or nothing. The greatest part of the defects in the management which I have been pointing out, have been long known to a respectable and enlightened body, the *Tribunal de Mineria* of Mexico, to the professors of the school of mines, and even to several of the native miners, who without having ever quitted their country, know the imperfection of the old methods; but we must repeat here, that changes can only take place very slowly among a people who are not fond of innovations, and in a country where the government possesses so little influence on the works which are generally the property of individuals, and not of shareholders. It is a prejudice to imagine, that the mines of New Spain on account of their wealth, do not require in their management the same intelligence and the same economy which are necessary to the preservation of the mines of Saxony and the Hartz. We must not confound the abundance of ores with their intrinsic value. The most part of the minerals of Mexico being very poor, as we have already proved, and as all those who do not allow themselves to be dazzled by false calculations very

well known, an enormous quantity of gangue impregnated with metals must be extracted, in order to produce two millions and a half of marcs of silver. Now it is easy to conceive that in mines of which the different works are badly disposed, and without any communication with one another, the expense of extraction must be increased in an alarming manner, in proportion as the shifts (*pozos*) increasing in depth, and the galleries (*cañones*) become more extended.

The labour of a miner is entirely free throughout the whole kingdom of New Spain; and no Indian or Mestizo can be forced to dedicate themselves to the working of mines. It is absolutely false, though the assertion has been repeated in works of the greatest estimation, that the court of Madrid sends out galley slaves to America, to work in the gold and silver mines. The mines of Siberia have been peopled by Russian malefactors; but in the Spanish colonies this species of punishment has been fortunately unknown for centuries. The Mexican miner is the best paid of all miners; he gains at the least from 25 to 30 francs per week of six days, while the wages of labourers who work in the open air, husbandmen for example, are seven livres sixteen sous, on the central table land, and nine livres twelve sous near the coast. The miners, *tenateros* and *faeneros* occupied in transporting the minerals to the place of assemblage (*despachos*) frequently gain more than six francs per day, of six hours. Honesty is by no means so common among the Mexican as among the German or Swedish miners; and they make use of a thousand tricks to steal very rich specimens of ores. As they are almost naked, and are searched on leaving the mine in the most indecent manner, they conceal small morsels of native silver, or red sulphuret and muriate of silver in their hair, under their arm-pits, and in their mouths; and they even lodge in their anus, cylinders of clay which contain the metal. These cylinders are called *longanas*, and they are sometimes found of the length of thirteen centimetres, (five inches). It is a most shocking spectacle to see in the large mines of Mexico, hundreds of workmen, among whom there are a great number of very respectable men, all compelled to allow themselves to be searched on leaving the pit or the gallery. A register is kept of the minerals found in the hair, in the mouth, or other parts of the miners' bodies. In the mine of Valenciana at Guanaxuato, the value of these stolen minerals, of which a great part was composed of the *longanas*, amounted between 1774 and 1787, to the sum of 900,000 francs.

5. COLONIAL INDUSTRY IN DECLINE

In the last half of the eighteenth century, colonial manufactur-ing, after experiencing a long and steady growth, began to de-

cline because of the influx of cheap European wares with which the domestic products could not compete. The textile and wine industries of western Argentina fell into decay as they lost their markets in Buenos Aires and Montevideo to lower-priced foreign wines and cloth. The textile producers of the province of Quito in Ecuador complained of injury from the same cause. In the Mexican manufacturing center of Puebla, production of china-ware, of which the city had long been a leading center, slumped catastrophically between 1793 and 1802. Industrial decadence was accompanied by a falling-off of internal trade in some areas as Spanish-American economic life became increasingly geared to the export of agricultural and pastoral products and the im-port of European finished goods. Humboldt's account of his visits to Mexican manufacturing centers clearly reveals the weak-ness and backwardness of colonial industry.[5]

✦✦✦✦ The oldest cloth manufactories of Mexico are those of Tezcuco. They were in great part established in 1592 by the viceroy Don Louis de Velasco II, the son of the celebrated constable of Castille, who was second viceroy of New Spain. By degrees, this branch of national in-dustry passed entirely into the hands of the Indians and Mestizos of Querétaro and Puebla. I visited the manufactories of Querétaro in the month of August 1803. They distinguish there the great manu-factories, which they call *obrajes*, from the small, which go by the name of *trapiches*. There were 20 *obrajes*, and more than 300 *trapiches* at that time, who altogether wrought up 63,900 *arrobas* of Mexican sheepwool. According to accurate lists, drawn up in 1793, there were at that period at Querétaro, in the *obrajes* alone, 215 looms, and 1500 workmen who manufactured 6,042 pieces, or 226,522 *varas* of cloth (*paños*); 287 pieces, or 39,718 *varas* of ordinary woollens (*xerguatillas*); 207 pieces, or 15,369 *varas* of baize (*bayetas*); and 161 pieces, or 17,960 *varas* of serge (*xergas*). In this manufacture they consumed 46,270 *arrobas* of wool, the price of which only amounted to 161,945 piastres. They reckon in general seven *arrobas* to one piece of *xerguatilla*, and five *arrobas* to one piece of *xerga*. The value of the cloths and woollen stuffs of the *obrajes* and *trapiches* of Querétaro at present amounts to more than 600,000 piastres, or three millions of francs per annum.

On visiting these workshops, a traveller is disagreeably struck, not only with the great imperfection of the technical process in the preparation for dyeing, but in a particular manner also with the un-healthiness of the situation, and the bad treatment to which the work-men are exposed. Free men, Indians, and people of colour, are con-founded with the criminals distributed by justice among the manu-

[5] Humboldt, *Political Essay on the Kingdom of New Spain*, III, pp. 462–469.

factories, in order to be compelled to work. All appear half naked, covered with rags, meagre, and deformed. Every workshop resembles a dark prison. The doors, which are double, remain constantly shut, and the workmen are not permitted to quit the house. Those who are married are only allowed to see their families on Sunday. All are unmercifully flogged, if they commit the smallest trespass on the order established in the manufactory.

We have difficulty in conceiving how the proprietors of the *obrajes* can act in this manner with free men, as well as how the Indian workman can submit to the same treatment with the galley slaves. These pretended rights are in reality acquired by stratagem. The manufacturers of Querétaro employ the same trick, which is made use of in several of the cloth manufactories of Quito, and in the plantations, where from a want of slaves, labourers are extremely rare. They choose from among the Indians the most miserable, but such as show an aptitude for the work, and they advance them a small sum of money. The Indian, who loves to get intoxicated, spends it in a few days, and having become the debtor of the master, he is shut up in the workshop, under the pretence of paying off the debt by the work of his hands. They allow him only a real and a half, or 20 sous tournois per day of wages; but in place of paying it in ready money, they take care to supply him with meat, brandy, and clothes, on which the manufacturer gains from fifty to sixty per cent; and in this way the most industrious workman is forever in debt, and the same rights are exercised over him which are believed to be acquired over a purchased slave. I knew many persons in Querétaro, who lamented with me the existence of these enormous abuses. Let us hope that a government friendly to the people, will turn their attention to a species of oppression so contrary to humanity, the laws of the country, and the progress of Mexican industry.

With the exception of a few stuffs of cotton mixed with silk, the manufacture of silks is at present next to nothing in Mexico. In the time of Acosta, towards the conclusion of the sixteenth century, silk worms brought from Europe were cultivated near Panuco, and in la Misteca, and excellent taffeta was there manufactured with Mexican silk.

On my passage through Querétaro, I visited the great manufactory of cegars (*fábrica de puros y cigarros*), in which 3000 people, including 1900 women, are employed. The halls are very neat, but badly aired, very small, and consequently excessively warm. They consume daily in this manufacture 130 reams (*resmas*) of paper, and 2770 pounds of tobacco leaf. In the course of the month of July, 1803, there was manufactured to the amount of 185,288 piastres; viz. 2,654,820 small chests (*caxillas*) of cegars, which sell for 165,926 piastres, and 289,799 chests of *puros* or cegars, which are not enveloped

in paper. The expense of manufacture of the month of July alone, amounted to 31,789 piastres. It appears that the royal manufactory of Querétaro annually produces more than 2,200,000 piastres, in *puros* and *cigarros*.

The manufacture of hard soap is a considerable object of commerce at Puebla, Mexico, and Guadalaxara. The first of these towns produces nearly 200,000 *arrobas* per annum; and in the intendancy of Guadalaxara, the quantity manufactured is computed at 1,300,000 *livres tournois*. The abundance of soda which we find almost everywhere at elevations of 2000 or 2500 metres, in the interior table land of Mexico, is highly favourable to this manufacture. . . .

The town of Puebla was formerly celebrated for its fine manufactories of delf ware (*loza*) and hats. We have already observed that, till the commencement of the eighteenth century, these two branches of industry enlivened the commerce between Acapulco and Peru. At present there is little or no communication between Puebla and Lima, and the delf manufactories have fallen so much off, on account of the low price of the stone ware and porcelain of Europe imported at Vera Cruz, that of 46 manufactories which were still existing in 1793, there were in 1802 only sixteen remaining of delf ware, and two of glass.

6. POLITICAL REFORM: THE INTENDANT SYSTEM

The intendant reform was made by Charles III in the interests of greater administrative efficiency and increased royal revenues from the colonies. Among their many duties, the intendants were expected to further the economic development of their districts by promoting the cultivation of new crops, the improvement of mining, the building of roads and bridges, and the establishment of consulados (*chambers of commerce*) *and Economic Societies. At the height of the reform era many of these officials were capable and cultivated men who earnestly sought to foster the material and cultural welfare of the regions in their charge. The historian Alamán gives a glowing account of the favorable consequences of the establishment of the intendant system in New Spain and of the accomplishments of two model intendants.*[6]

✠✠✠✠ The principal source of profit of the *alcaldes mayores* consisted in the traffic they carried on under the pretext of getting the Indians

[6] Alamán, *Historia de Méjico*, I, pp. 73–76. (Excerpt translated by the editor.)

to work, as was recommended by the laws. They assigned them certain tasks and purchased the product at low prices, paying for it in necessary articles of dress and food that were overpriced. Having all authority in their hands, they compelled the Indians to fulfill these contracts with great punctuality, and reaped large profits thereby. This was particularly true in those districts where there was some valuable product, such as cochineal in Oaxaca, which constituted a monopoly for those officers and for the merchants who equipped them with capital and goods. Meanwhile the Indians were cruelly oppressed. A miserable system of administration was this, in which the pecuniary advantage of the governors was rooted in the oppression and misery of the governed! The Duke of Linares, in his vigorous and concise style, characterized it in a few words: "Although the jurisdiction of the *alcaldes mayores* is most extensive, I can define it very briefly, for it amounts to this: They are faithless to God from the time they enter upon their employment, by breaking the oath they have taken; they are faithless to their king, because of the *repartimientos* they engage in; and they sin against the common Indians, by tyrannizing over them as they do."

The whole order of things, so unjust and oppressive, ceased with the promulgation of the Ordinance of Intendants, published by Minister [José de] Gálvez on December 4, 1786, and limited at that time to New Spain alone, but later extended, with appropriate modifications, to all Spanish America. In it, under the titles of "the four departments of justice, police, finance, and war," were set forth the most comprehensive rules for the administration of the country in these spheres and for the encouragement of agriculture, industry, and mining. The whole territory of the vice-royalty, including Yucatán and the *provincias internas*, was divided into twelve intendancies, which took the names of their capitals. The corregimiento of Querétaro was retained for civil and judicial matters, but it was made financially dependent on the intendancy of Mexico. To the posts of intendants were appointed men of integrity and intelligence in the performance of their functions. Among those who distinguished themselves by their special merit were the intendants of Guanajuato and Puebla.

Minister Gálvez, at the time when he was in power, sought to place all his relatives in high posts, and their actions justified this preference. Don Matías, his brother, and Don Bernardo, his nephew, succeeded each other as viceroys of Mexico; the latter married in New Orleans, while in command of the expedition that reconquered the Floridas, Doña Felicitas Saint-Maxent, whose two sisters, Doña Victoria and Doña Mariana, married Don Juan Antonio de Riaño and Don Manuel de Flon, respectively. At the time of the creation of the intendancies, the former was assigned that of Valladolid, where

he remained only a short time, being transferred immediately to the more important one of Guanajuato; and Flon was placed over that of Puebla.

The strict and honorable Flon reformed great abuses, encouraged all the branches of industry in his province, and notably beautified its capital. Riaño, of equal integrity but of a mild and affable disposition, had served in the royal navy, and to a knowledge of mathematics and astronomy, natural in that profession, united a taste for literature and the fine arts. These interests, and in particular his delight in architecture, he introduced to Guanajuato; through his influence there were erected, not only in the capital but in all the province, magnificent structures, whose building he himself supervised, even instructing the stonecutters in the art of hewing stone. He promoted the study of the Latin classics and of the best Spanish writers; it was owing to his influence that the young men of Guanajuato devoted themselves to the study of the Castilian tongue and to its correct pronunciation.

French, the native tongue of his wife, was spoken in their home, and he introduced among the youth of the provincial capital a taste for that language and its literature, together with an elegance of manners unknown in other cities of the province. He was also responsible for the development of interest in drawing and music and for the cultivation of mathematics, physics, and chemistry in the school that had formerly been maintained by the Jesuits. To that end he zealously patronized Don José Antonio Rojas, professor of mathematics in that school and a graduate of the School of Mines. He also established a theater, promoted the cultivation of olives and vines, and diligently fostered the mining industry, the chief wealth of that province, by encouraging the rich citizens of Guanajuato to form companies for the exploitation of old and abandoned mines as well as new ones.

7. "THE MORE IT CHANGES . . . "

Plus ça change, plus c'est la même chose *could be fairly applied to Spain's Indian policy. The Ordinance of Intendants, by abolishing the offices of* corregidor *and* alcalde mayor *and forbidding their successors, the subdelegates, to engage in the infamous* repartimiento, *promised to inaugurate a new and better day for the Indian. Despite the complacent observation of Alamán (see the previous selection) that the old order of things, "so unjust and oppressive, ceased with the promulgation of the Ordinance of Intendants," other observers came to dif-*

ferent conclusions. In Peru, the intendant Demetrio O'Higgins asserted in an official report that the subdelegates continued to force the Indians to trade with them, in violation of the laws; that the curates oppressed the natives in the many ways described by Juan and Ulloa half a century before; and that the wretched Indians were being despoiled of their lands by the Spaniards. And in Mexico an enlightened prelate, Bishop Manuel Abad Queipo of Michoacán, denounced the entire system of subjection and segregation of the Indians and mixed castes and flatly stated that the natives were worse off than they had been before the intendant reform.[7]

✤✤✤✤ The population of New Spain is composed of some four and a half million inhabitants, who can be divided into three classes: Spaniards, Indians, and castes. The Spaniards number one tenth of the total population but possess almost the entire property or wealth of the kingdom. The other two classes, forming the other nine tenths, can be divided into two parts castes, the other part pure Indians. The Indians and castes are employed in domestic service, agricultural labors, and the ordinary tasks of commerce and industry — that is to say, they are servants and day-laborers for the Spaniards. Consequently there arises between them and the Spaniards that opposition of interests and views that is typical of those who have nothing and those who have everything — between superiors and inferiors. Envy, theft, and unwilling service are the traits of the latter; arrogance, exploitation, and harsh treatment, the qualities of the former. These evils are to a certain extent common to all the world. But in America they are immeasurably greater because there are no gradations or intermediate states: all are either rich or wretched, noble or infamous.

In effect, the two classes of Indians and castes are sunk in the greatest abasement and degradation. The color, ignorance, and misery of the Indians places them at an infinite distance from a Spaniard. The ostensible privileges which the laws accord them do them little good and in most respects injure them greatly. Shut up in a narrow space of six hundred *varas*, assigned by law to the Indian towns, they possess no individual property and are obliged to work the communal lands. This cultivation is made all the more hateful by the fact that in recent years it has become increasingly difficult for them to enjoy any of the fruits of their labor. Under the new intendant system they cannot draw on the communal funds [*caja de comunidad*] without special permission from the office of the royal exchequer [*junta superior de la real hacienda*] in Mexico City.

Forbidden by law to commingle with the other castes, they

---

[7] José María Luis Mora, *Obras sueltas*, Paris, 1837, 2 vols., I, pp. 55–57. (Excerpt translated by the editor.)

are deprived of the instruction and assistance that they should receive from contact with these and other people. They are isolated by their language, and by a useless, tyrannical form of government. In each town there are found eight or ten old Indians who live in idleness at the expense of their fellows and artfully try to perpetuate their ancient customs, usages, and gross superstitions, ruling them like despots. Incapable, by law, of making a binding contract or of running into debt to the extent of more than five pesos — in a word, of any dealings at all — they cannot learn anything or better their fortune or in any way raise themselves above their wretched condition. Solorzano, Fraso, and other Spanish authors have wondered why the privileges granted them have redounded to their injury; but it is greater cause for wonder that such men as these should have failed to understand that the source of the evil lies in these very privileges. They are an offensive weapon employed by the white class against the Indians, and never serve to defend the latter. This combination of causes makes the Indians indifferent to their future and to all that does not excite the passions of the moment.

The castes are declared infamous by law, as descendants of Negro slaves. They are subject to the payment of tribute, which is punctiliously recorded; as a result, this obligation has become a brand of slavery which neither the passage of time nor the mixture of successive generations can ever obliterate. There are many of these who in their color, physiognomy, and conduct could pass for Spaniards if it were not for this impediment, which reduces them all to the same state. . . .

The Indians as well as the castes are governed directly by magistrates of districts [*justicias territoriales*] whose conduct has measurably contributed to the situation in which they find themselves. The *alcaldes mayores* considered themselves not so much justices as merchants, endowed with the exclusive privilege . . . of trading in their province and of extracting from it in a five-year term of office from thirty to two hundred thousand pesos. Their usurious and arbitrary *repartimientos* caused great injuries. But despite this state of affairs two favorable circumstances commonly resulted, one being that they administered justice with impartiality and rectitude in cases in which they were not parties, the other being that they fostered agriculture and industry, in their own interests.

The Spanish government undertook to put an end to these abuses by replacing the *alcaldes mayores* with the subdelegates. But since the latter were not assigned any fixed salary, the remedy proved much worse than the evil. If they adhere to the schedule of fees, among a wretched folk who litigate only against each other, they will inevitably perish of hunger. They must of necessity prostitute their posts, swindle the poor, and traffic in justice. For the same rea-

son it is extremely difficult for the intendants to find suitable individuals to fill these posts. They are sought, therefore, only by bank-
rupts or by those whose conduct and talents unfit them for success
in the other walks of life. Under these conditions, what benefits, what
protection, can these ministers of law dispense to the abovementioned
two classes? How can they attract their good-will and respect, when
extortion and injustice are virtually their livelihood?

16 ✤ Colonial Culture and the Enlightenment

Colonial culture in all its aspects was a projection of contemporaneous Spanish culture and only faintly reflected native American influences. Colonial culture thus suffered from all the infirmities of its parent but inevitably lacked the breadth and vitality of Spanish literature and art, the product of a much older and more mature civilization.

The Church enjoyed a virtual monopoly of colonial education on all levels. Poverty condemned the great majority of the natives and mixed castes to illiteracy. The Universities of Lima and Mexico City, both chartered in 1551, were the first permanent institutions of higher learning. Since they were modeled on the Spanish University of Salamanca, their organization, curricula, and methods of instruction were alike medieval.

Within the limits imposed by official censorship and their own backgrounds, colonial scholars, especially those of the sixteenth and early seventeenth centuries, were able to make impressive contributions in the fields of history, anthropology, linguistics, geography, and natural history. The second half of the seventeenth century saw a decline in the quantity and quality of scholarly production. Nevertheless, in this period two remarkable men, Carlos Sigüenza y Gón-

gora, in Mexico, and Pedro de Peralta Barnuevo, in Peru, foreshadowed the eighteenth-century enlightenment by the universality of their interests and by their concern with the practical uses of science.

Colonial literature, with some notable exceptions, was a pallid reflection of prevailing literary trends in the mother country. Among a multitude of poetasters towered a strange and rare genius, one of the greatest poets of the New World, Sor Juana Inés de la Cruz. Sor Juana could not escape the pressures of her environment. Rebuked by the Bishop of Puebla for her worldly interests, she ultimately gave up her books and scientific instruments and devoted the remainder of her brief life to religious devotions and charitable works.

Colonial art drew its principal inspiration from Spanish sources, but Indian influence was visible, particularly in sculpture and architecture. As might be expected, religious motifs dominated the sculpture and painting. In architecture the colonies followed Spanish examples, with the severely classical style of the sixteenth century giving way in the seventeenth to the highly ornamented baroque, and in the eighteenth to the even more ornate churrigueresque.

In the eighteenth century Spanish America began to awake from its medieval sleep. A lively contraband in unorthodox ideas accompanied the growing trade between the colonies and non-Spanish lands. Spain, now under the sway of the enlightened Bourbon kings, herself contributed to the intellectual renovation of the colonies. Spanish or foreign scientific expeditions to Spanish America, authorized and sometimes financed by the crown, stimulated the growth of scientific interests. The expulsion of the Jesuits (1767) removed from the scene the ablest exponents of scholasticism and cleared the way for modest projects of educational reform. But the most significant cultural activity took place outside academic halls — in the Economic Societies, organized for the promotion of useful knowledge; in private gatherings and coffee houses, where young men ardently discussed the advantages of free trade and the rights of men; and in the colonial press, in which the new secular and critical spirit found articulate expression.

1. THE COLONIAL UNIVERSITY

The colonial university was patterned on similar institutions in Spain and faithfully reproduced their medieval organization, curricula, and methods of instruction. Indifference to practical or scientific studies, slavish respect for the authority of the Bible, Aristotle, the Church Fathers, and certain medieval

schoolmen, and a passion for hair-splitting debate of fine points of theological or metaphysical doctrine were among the features of colonial academic life. "In ordinary circumstances," writes Professor Lanning, "the regimen produced men of stupendous rote memory, along with imposing but inappropriate and artificial allusions to the ancients and the myths." In the following selection a Spanish friar describes the University of Lima in the first quarter of the seventeenth century.[1]

✠✠✠✠ The university and Royal Schools are so distinguished that they need envy no other in the world, since they were established by the Emperor Charles V, and later by Philip II, both of glorious memory; they enlarged, ennobled and enriched them, with the same privileges as the University of Salamanca; they endowed the professorial chairs of Prime with 1,000 assay pesos, and those of Vespers with 600, per annum. The Prime chairs are in Theology, Scholastics, Scripture, Law, and Canons; the Vespers, in the Institutes, the Code, the Decretals, three in Philosophy, one in the Indian language for the training of the priests who are to be parish priests or doctrineros; before they are commissioned, they have to be examined and certificated by the Professor of the language.

The Professors are in major part natives of the Indies and especially of this city, where it would appear that the skies, as usually in the Indies, train outstanding and unusual intellects in subtlety and facility, so that in general they are very able and keen witted; this is obvious from the professorial positions which they occupy and the pulpits, where remarkable men distinguish themselves in their mastery of science and oratory; but they are unfortunate in living far from the eyes of His Majesty. For after all their labors, since there are so few professorial chairs and so many candidates, and there cannot be many lawyers, after having drudged and done brilliantly, and having spent in attaining the degrees of Licentiate and Doctor, 3,500 pesos, they lose heart, unless they have private means, at seeing themselves unrewarded; so the clerics take benefices and Indian curacies in order to live, and many abandon their books and studies, and never take their degrees.

This University's faculty is important, for it comprises more than 80 Doctors and Masters; the members of the Circuit Court join them, for at the end of the year the fees amount to many ducats. The lecture halls in the schools are excellent, and the chapel very fine, but the most remarkable feature is the amphitheater, where [are held] the public functions and commencements; it is very large and impos-

1 Vásquez de Espinosa, *Description of the West Indies*, translated by C. V. Clark, pp. 444–446.

ing; the display at the granting of whatever degrees are given, is also imposing. They [the faculty] invite the city's nobility as an escort, and meet at the house of the Doctor-to-be in a blare of trumpets, flageolets, and bugles, with a banner which hangs from a window of the house over a canopy on crimson velvet cushions and has the arms of the University and of the graduating Doctor; these are likewise set up in the theater erected in the Cathedral under the royal arms; they remind and notify the invited guests and doctors, who form an escort the evening before; the nobility follow the banner, then the Beadles with their silver maces, then the Masters and Doctors with their insignia, in order of age, closing with the Dean of the faculty and the graduating Doctor; and in this order they repair to the Rector's house, where the members of the Circuit Court await them; with the Rector in their center, they continue in the procession, in order of age. And in this same order the following day they parade till they arrive at the Cathedral, where the theater and the stage have been decorated and provided with seats; Mass is said for them, and at its close after leaving the Cathedral, the newest Doctor of the faculty delivers his burlesque invective, and the Chancellor gives him his degree, just as is done at Salamanca.

2. THE TENTH MUSE

The conditions of colonial life did not favor the development of a rich literature. Isolation from foreign influences, the strict censorship of all reading matter, and the limited audience for writing of every kind made literary creation difficult. "A narrow and dwarfed world," the discouraged Mexican poet Bernardo Balbuena (1568–1627) called the province of New Spain. To make matters worse, in the seventeenth century colonial literature succumbed to the Spanish literary fad of Gongorismo (so called after the poet Luis de Góngora) — the cult of an obscure, involved, and artificial style. Amid "a flock of jangling magpies," as one literary historian describes the Gongorist versifiers of the seventeenth century, appeared an incomparable songbird, known to her admiring contemporaries as "the tenth muse" — Sor Juana Inés de la Cruz (1651–1695). English and American translators have tried, without great success, to capture the "curious light music" of her poems, "the most gentle and delicate that have ever come from the pen of a woman." Rebuked by the Bishop of Puebla, who wrote under the pseudonym of "Sor Filotea," for her interest in secular learning, Sor Juana replied in a letter that is both an important

autobiographical document and an eloquent defense of the rights of women to education and intellectual activity.[2]

✳✳✳✳ I was less than three years old when my mother sent an older sister to be taught reading at a school for small children, of the kind called *Amigas*. Moved by sisterly affection and by a mischievous spirit, I followed her; and seeing her receive instruction, I formed such a strong desire to learn to read that I tried to deceive the schoolmistress, telling her that *my mother wanted her to give me lessons*. She did not believe me, since it was incredible; but to humor me she acquiesced. I continued to come and she to teach me, no longer in jest but in earnest; and I learned so quickly that I already knew how to read by the time my mother heard about the lessons from the teacher, who had kept them secret in order to break the pleasant news to her and receive her reward all at once. I had concealed it from my mother for fear that I would be whipped for acting without permission. The lady who taught me still lives — God keep her — and can testify to this.

I remember that at that time, although I had the healthy appetite of most children of that age, I would not eat cheese because I heard that it made one dull-witted, and the desire to learn prevailed more with me than hunger, so powerful in children. Later, at the age of six or seven, when I already knew how to read and write, as well as to sew and do other women's tasks, I heard that in Mexico City there was a university, and schools where the sciences were taught. No sooner had I heard this than I began to badger my mother with pleas that she let me put on men's clothing and go to Mexico City, where I could live with some relatives and attend the university. She would not do it, and quite rightly, too, but I satisfied my desire by reading in a large number of books that belonged to my grandfather, and neither punishments nor rebukes could stop me. Hence when I came to Mexico City men wondered not so much at my intelligence as at my memory and knowledge, at an age when it seemed I would do well to know how to talk.

I began to study Latin, in which I had barely twenty lessons; and so intense was my application that although women (especially in the flower of their youth) naturally cherish the adornment of their hair, I would cut it off four or six fingers' length, making it a rule that if I had not mastered a certain subject by the time it grew back, I would cut it off again . . . , for it did not seem right to me that a head so empty of knowledge, which is the most desirable adornment of all, should be crowned with hair. I became a nun, for although I knew that the religious state imposed obligations (I speak of inciden-

[2] Sor Juana, *Carta atenagórica, Respuesta a Sor Filotea*, edited by E. Abreu Gómez, México, 1934, pp. 54–58, 66–70. (Excerpt translated by the editor.)

tals and not of the fundamentals) most repugnant to my temperament, nevertheless, in view of my total disinclination to marriage, it was the most becoming and proper condition that I could choose to ensure my salvation. To achieve this I had to repress my wayward spirit, which wished to live alone, without any obligatory occupation that might interfere with the freedom of my studies or any conventional bustle that might disturb the restful quiet of my books. These desires made me waver in my decision, until, having been told by learned persons that it was temptation, with divine favor I conquered and entered the state which I so unworthily occupy. I thought that I had fled from myself, but - wretched me! — I brought myself with me and so brought my grea.est enemy, that thirst for learning which Heaven gave me — I know not whether as a favor or chastisement, for repress it as I might with all the exercise that the conventual state offers, it would burst forth like gunpowder; and it was verified in me that *privatio est causa appetitus* [deprivation is the cause of appetite].

I renewed or rather continued (for I never truly ceased) my labors (which were my rest in all the leisure time that my duties left me) of reading and more reading, of studying and more studying, with no other teacher than the books themselves. You will readily comprehend how difficult it is to study from these lifeless letters, denied the living voice and explanation of a teacher, but I joyfully endured all this labor for love of learning. Ah, if it had been for love of God, as was fitting, how worthy it would have been! True, I sought to direct it as much as possible to His service, for my aspiration was to study theology, since it seemed a notable defect to me, as a Catholic, not to know all that can be learned in this life about the Divine Mysteries; and since I was a nun, and not a lay person, it seemed to me an obligation of my state to study literature. . . . So I reasoned, and convinced myself — though it could well be that I was only justifying what I already wanted to do. And so, as I have said, I directed the steps of my studying toward the heights of Sacred Theology; it seemed to me that in order to arrive there I should climb the stairway of the human sciences and arts; for how should I understand the language of the Queen of Sciences if I did not know that of her handmaidens?

How, without Logic, could I know the general and particular rules by which the Sacred Scripture was written? Without Rhetoric, how should I understand its figures, tropes, and turns of speech? Without Physics, how might I penetrate so many questions of the nature of animals, of sacrifices, that have so many symbolic meanings, some declared and others hidden? And how might I know whether the healing of Saul by the sound of David's harp proceeded from the natural force and virtue of music or from a supernatural power that

God placed in David? Without Arithmetic, how should I comprehend the great Temple of Solomon, where God himself was the
master architect who drew up the specifications and the plan and the
Wise King was but the foreman who executed it — where there was
not a base without its mystery, not a column without its symbol, not
a cornice without an allusion or architrave without significance — and
so on in all its parts, so that even the smallest fillet not only served
to embellish but symbolized greater things? Without extensive knowledge of the rules and facts of History, how should one comprehend
the Historical Books? How, without ample knowledge of both
branches of the Law, could I understand the Legal Books? Without
vast erudition, how should I comprehend the many points of profane
history mentioned in the Sacred Scripture, so many pagan rites, customs, modes of speech? Without much reading of the Church Fathers,
how could one understand the obscure teaching of the Prophets? . . .

At one time my enemies persuaded a very saintly and guileless
prelate, who believed that study was a matter for the Inquisition, to
forbid me to study. I obeyed her (for the three months or so that
she had power over me) in what concerned my reading, but as for
the absolute ban on study, this was not in my power to obey, for
although I did not study in books, I studied everything that God
created, and all this universal machine served me as a textbook. I saw
nothing without reflecting upon it; everything I heard moved me to
thought. This was true of the smallest and most material things, for
since there is no creature, however lowly, in which one does not
recognize the *me fecit Deus* [God made me], so there is no object
that will not arouse thought, if one considers it as one should. Thus
I looked at and wondered about everything, so that even the people
I spoke to, and what they said to me, aroused a thousand speculations in me. How did such a variety of temperaments and intellects
come about, since we are all of the same species? What could be
the hidden qualities and traits that caused these differences? If I saw
a figure I would consider the proportion of its lines and measure it
in my mind and reduce it to other figures. Sometimes I would walk
about in the front part of a dormitory of ours (a very spacious
room); I noticed that although the lines of its two sides were parallel
and the ceiling was level, the lines seemed to run toward each other
and the ceiling seemed to be lower at a distance than it was close by —
from which I inferred that visual lines run straight but not parallel,
forming a pyramidal figure. And I speculated whether this could be
the reason that caused the ancients to wonder whether the world was a
sphere or not. Because although it appeared spherical, this might be an
optical illusion, presenting concavities where they perhaps did not
exist. . . .

This habit is so strong in me that I see nothing without reflecting

upon it. I noticed two little girls playing with a top, and I had hardly seen the movement and the object when I began, with my usual madness, to consider the easy motion of the spherical form — and how the impulse, once given, continued independently of its cause, for there was the top dancing at a distance from the girl's hand — the motive cause. Not content with this, I had some flour brought and strewn on the floor, in order to learn whether the top's motion described perfect circles or not; and I discovered that they were only spiral lines that gradually lost their circular character as the impulse diminished. Other children were playing at pins (which is the most infantile game known to children). I began to study the figures they formed, and seeing, by chance, that three pins formed a triangle, I set about joining one to the other, remembering that this is said to have been the figure of the mysterious ring of Solomon, in which were depicted some shadowy hints and representations of the most Sacred Trinity, by virtue of which it worked many miracles; it is said that David's harp had the same figure and that for this reason Saul was healed by its sound; the harps we use today have almost the same shape.

But what shall I say, my lady, of the secrets of nature that I have discovered while cooking? I observe that an egg coheres and fries in butter or oil but breaks up in sugar syrup; that to keep sugar fluid it is sufficient to pour on it a little water containing a quince or some other sour fruit; that the yolk and white of an egg are so opposed that each one separately will mix with sugar, but not both together. I shall not weary you with such trifles, which I mention only to give you an adequate notion of my character and which, I am sure, will make you laugh; but, my lady, what can we women know except kitchen philosophy? Lupercio Leonardo aptly said: "It is possible to philosophize while preparing dinner." And I often say, observing these trifles: "If Aristotle had been a cook, he would have written much more." . . .

Although I had no need of examples, I have nevertheless been aided by the many that I have read about, in both divine and profane writings. For I have seen a Deborah giving laws, both military and political, and governing a people in which there were so many learned men. I read of that sage Queen of Sheba, so learned that she dared to test with enigmas the wisdom of the wisest of men, and suffered no reproof for it but instead was made the judge of unbelievers. I observe so many illustrious women — some adorned with the gift of prophecy, like Abigail; others, with that of persuasion, like Esther; others with piety, like Rahab; others with perseverance, like Anna, mother of Samuel; and an infinite number of others, endowed with still other kinds of graces and virtues.

If I turn my gaze to the pagans, I first encounter the Sibyls, chosen by God to prophesy the principal mysteries of our faith, in

verses so learned and elegant that they arouse our wonder. I see the Greeks adore as goddess of learning a woman like Minerva, daughter of the first Jupiter and teacher of all the wisdom of Athens. I see a Bola Argentaria, who aided her husband Lucan to write the great "Battle of Pharsalia." I see a Zenobia, Queen of Palmyra, as wise as she was brave. An Aretea, the most learned daughter of Aristippus. A Nicostrata, inventor of Latin letters and most learned in Greek. An Aspasia of Miletus, who taught philosophy and rhetoric and was teacher of the philosopher Pericles. A Hypatia, who taught astronomy and studied for a long time in Alexandria. A Leontia, of Greek birth, who wrote against the philosopher Theophrastus and convinced him. A Jucia, a Corinna, a Cornelia, and finally all that multitude of women who won renown under the names of Greeks, Muses, Pythonesses and in the end were nothing more than learned women, regarded and venerated as such by the ancients. Not to mention an infinite number of others of whom the books tell, such as the Egyptian Catherine, who not only read but overcame in debate the wisest sages of Egypt. I see a Gertrude study, write, and teach. And there is no need to wander far afield, for I see a holy mother of my own order, Paula, learned in Hebrew, Greek, and Latin, and most skillful in interpreting the Scriptures — so much so, in fact, that her biographer, the great and saintly Jerome, declared himself unequal to his task. He said, in his usual serious, forceful way: "If all the members of my body were tongues, they would not be enough to proclaim the wisdom and virtue of Paula." He bestowed the same praise on the widow Blesilla and the illustrious virgin Eustoquio, both daughters of the same Paula; for her learning the latter won the name "Prodigy of the World." Fabiola, a Roman lady, was also most learned in the Sacred Scripture, Proba Falconia, a Roman matron, wrote an elegant work in Virgilian measures about the mysteries of our sacred faith. It is well known that our Queen Isabel, wife of Alfonso XII, wrote on astronomy. And . . . in our own time there flourishes the great Christina Alexandra, Queen of Sweden, as learned as she is brave and magnanimous, and there are also the excellent Duchess of Abeyro and the Countess of Vallambrosa.

3. THE MOVEMENT FOR EDUCATIONAL REFORM

In the eighteenth century the Enlightenment came to Spanish America. Foreign travelers and merchants helped to spread the new gospel of rationalism and progress, but much of the liberal impulse stemmed from Spain, where the Bourbon kings were engaged in a major effort at national reconstruction. From Spain came viceroys and intendants with "French" ideas, determined

to change the face of their provinces and the thinking of their backward subjects. To achieve this last aim they founded, or tried to found, printing presses, theaters, public libraries, and schools of a more useful and modern kind than the existing Church-controlled institutions. Typical of these men was Viceroy Manuel de Guirior of New Granada (1773–1776), whose recommendations for educational reform, it is worth noting, were rejected by the king's ministers, presumably because of clerical opposition.[3]

✠✠✠✠ The instruction of youth and the encouragement of the sciences and arts are among the fundamental principles of good government and are the source of the happiness and prosperity of a state. . . . Conscious of this fact, and of the zeal with which our prudent king and his government have worked to establish sound methods of instruction, I determined to make my contribution to the worthy project begun by his Excellency, my predecessor, of founding a public university. . . . By this means, at a small cost, the kingdom could make happy its young men, who at present are denied instruction in the useful sciences and the sound methods and good taste introduced by Europe in the study of belles-lettres, and are occupied in futile debate of the abstract questions posed by Aristotle.

Knowing that His Majesty had been informed of this project, and that a decision had been delayed by the opposition of the Dominican convent in this city, which at present enjoys the sole right of granting degrees, and wishing to put an end to this unhappy state of affairs before its evil effects become incurable, I determined in consultation with the illustrious prelate and the ministers who composed the *junta superior de aplicaciones* to commission the attorney of the *audiencia*, Don Francisco Antonio Moreno y Escandón, a man of sound training and one who had all the necessary qualifications for the task, to prepare a plan of study, adapted to local conditions, that might serve as a model for other educational establishments and help to eliminate existing abuses. After he had drawn up this plan, very intelligently and in entire conformity to the royal intentions, it was examined by the same *junta superior* and approved with universal acclaim and expressions of gratitude to Don Francisco for his zeal. It was also ordered that the plan should be carried out without delay, with the said Moreno acting as royal director of education, until such time as His Majesty . . . should make known his sovereign will.

Despite the opposition of some persons educated in the ancient fashion — notably that of the regular clergy (who were aggrieved be-

---

[3] "Relación del Excmo, Sr. de Guirior," in *Relaciones de los virreyes del Nuevo Reino de Granada*, edited by José Antonio Garcia y Garcia, New York, 1867, pp. 144–147. (Except translated by the editor.)

cause they had formerly monopolized education in their cloisters and were conscious of their inability to teach certain subjects which they would have to learn anew), a beginning was made with the new method in the two *colegios* of this city. . . . This has had such happy results that one year sufficed to demonstrate the progress made by the students in arithmetic, algebra, geometry, and trigonometry, and in jurisprudence and theology, whose true principles they found in the Church Councils, the ancient canons, Sacred Scripture, and the Church Fathers. . . . I am confident that your Excellency, moved by zeal in this cause, will not heed the appeals and clamors of the abovementioned convent, supported by the regular clergy, but will firmly insist that this reform be carried forward, demonstrating to His Majesty and the Royal Council of the Indies the advantages to the kingdom and monarchy of continuing this method and the urgent need for a university, a workshop in which could be formed heroes capable of making this nation happy. . . .

To this end, I have proposed to His Majesty that a beginning, at least, should be made of the university establishment, with the well-founded hope that time and circumstances will bring it to a state of greater perfection, meantime endowing it with many of the revenues of the Jesuit temporalities. . . . I have also informed His Majesty that all the books found in the *colegios* of the defunct Jesuit Society have been taken to form a public library in this capital, to which persons of literary tastes may come to obtain instruction in all subjects. A spacious room has been set apart for this worthy purpose. . . . In times to come this library can be enriched with new books, and with machines or instruments of which men of science will make profitable use.

4. THE RISE OF THE SCIENTIFIC SPIRIT

The intellectual atmosphere of the Spanish colonies was not conducive to scientific inquiry or achievement. As late as 1773 the Colombian botanist Mutis was charged with heresy for giving lectures on the Copernican system in Bogotá, and the prosecutor of the Inquisition asserted that Mutis was "perhaps the only man in Latin America to uphold Copernicus." In the closing decades of the eighteenth century, however, the growing volume of economic and intellectual contacts with Europe, as well as the patronage and protection of enlightened governors, created more favorable conditions for scientific activity. Science made its greatest strides in the wealthy province of New Spain, where the expansion of the mining industry stimulated interest in such fields as geology, chemistry, mathematics, and metal-

lurgy. In Mexico City arose a School of Mines, the first in the New World, a Botanical Garden, and an Academy of Fine Arts. The learned Humboldt had high praise for the state of scientific studies in New Spain at the opening of the nineteenth century.[4]

✠✠✠✠ No city of the new continent, without even excepting those of the United States, can display such great and solid scientific establishments as the capital of Mexico. I shall content myself here with naming the School of Mines, directed by the learned Elhuyar, to which we shall return when we come to speak of the mines; the Botanic Garden; and the Academy of Painting and Sculpture. This academy bears the title of *Academia de los Nobles Artes de México.* It owes its existence to the patriotism of several Mexican individuals, and to the protection of the minister Gálvez. The government assigned it a spacious building, in which there is a much finer and more complete collection of casts than is to be found in any part of Germany. We are astonished on seeing that the Apollo of Belvidere, the group of Laocoon, and still more colossal statues, have been conveyed through mountainous roads at least as narrow as those of St. Gothard; and we are surprised at finding these masterpieces of antiquity collected together under the torrid zone, in a table land higher than the convent of the great St. Bernard. The collection of casts brought to Mexico cost the king 200,000 francs. The remains of the Mexican sculpture, those colossal statues of basaltes and porphyry, which are covered with Aztec hieroglyphics, and bear some relation to the Egyptian and Hindoo style, ought to be collected together in the edifice of the academy, or rather in one of the courts which belong to it. It would be curious to see these monuments of the first cultivation of our species, the works of a semibarbarous people inhabiting the Mexican Andes, placed beside the beautiful forms produced under the sky of Greece and Italy.

The revenues of the Academy of Fine Arts at Mexico amount to 125,000 francs, of which the government gives 60,000, the body of Mexican miners nearly 25,000, the *consulado*, or association of merchants of the capital, more than 1500. It is impossible not to perceive the influence of this establishment on the taste of the nation. This influence is particularly visible in the symmetry of the buildings, in the perfection with which the hewing of stone is conducted, and in the ornaments of the capitals and stucco relievos. What a number of beautiful edifices are to be seen at Mexico! nay, even in provincial towns like Guanaxuato and Querétaro! These monuments, which frequently cost a million and million and a half francs, would appear

---

[4] Humboldt, *Political Essay on the Kingdom of New Spain,* I, pp. 212–223.

to advantage in the finest streets of Paris, Berlin, and Petersburg. M. Tolsa, professor of sculpture at Mexico, was even able to cast an equestrian statue of King Charles the Fourth; a work which, with the exception of the Marcus Aurelius at Rome, surpasses in beauty and purity of style everything which remains in this way in Europe. Instruction is communicated gratis at the Academy of Fine Arts. It is not confined alone to the drawing of landscapes and figures; they have had the good sense to employ other means for exciting the national industry. The academy labours successfully to introduce among the artisans a taste for elegance and beautiful forms. Large rooms, well lighted by Argand's lamps, contain every evening some hundreds of young people, of whom some draw from relievo or living models, while others copy drawings of furniture, chandeliers, or other ornaments in bronze. In this assemblage (and this is very remarkable in the midst of a country where the prejudices of the nobility against the castes are so inveterate) rank, colour, and race is confounded: we see the Indian and the Mestizo sitting beside the white, and the son of a poor artisan in emulation with the children of the great lords of the country. It is a consolation to observe, that under every zone the cultivation of science and art establishes a certain equality among men, and obliterates for a time, at least, all those petty passions of which the effects are so prejudicial to social happiness.

Since the close of the reign of Charles the Third, and under that of Charles the Fourth, the study of the physical sciences has made great progress, not only in Mexico, but in general in all the Spanish colonies. No European government has sacrificed greater sums to advance the knowledge of the vegetable kingdom than the Spanish government. Three botanical expeditions, in Peru, New Granada, and New Spain, under the direction of MM. Ruíz and Pavón, Don José Celestino Mutis, and MM. Sesse and Mocino, have cost the state nearly two millions of francs. Moreover, botanical gardens have been established at Manila and the Canary Islands. The commission destined to draw plans of the canal of los Guines was also appointed to examine the vegetable productions of the island of Cuba. All these researches, conducted during twenty years in the most fertile regions of the new continent, have not only enriched science with more than four thousand new species of plants, but have also contributed much to diffuse a taste for natural history among the inhabitants of the country. The city of Mexico exhibits a very interesting botanical garden within the very precincts of the viceroy's palace. Professor Cervantes gives annual courses there, which are very well attended. This savant possesses, besides his herbals, a rich collection of Mexican minerals. M. Mocino, whom we just now mentioned as one of the coadjutors of M. Sesse, and who has pushed his laborious excursions from the kingdom of Guatemala to the northwest coast or island of Vancouver and Quadra; and M. Echevería, a

painter of plants and animals, whose works will bear a comparison with the most perfect productions of the kind in Europe, are both of them natives of New Spain. They had both attained a distinguished rank among savants and artists before quitting their country.

The principles of the new chemistry, which is known in the Spanish colonies by the equivocal appellation of new philosophy (*nueva filosofía*), are more diffused in Mexico than in many parts of the peninsula. A European traveller cannot undoubtedly but be surprised to meet in the interior of the country, on the very borders of California, with young Mexicans who reason on the decomposition of water in the process of amalgamation with free air. The School of Mines possesses a chemical laboratory; a geological collection, arranged according to the system of Werner; a physical cabinet, in which we not only find the valuable instruments of Ramsden, Adams, Le Noir, and Louis Berthoud, but also models executed in the capital even, with the greatest precision, and from the finest wood in the country. The best mineralogical work in the Spanish language was printed at Mexico, I mean the *Manual of Oryctognosy*, composed by M. Del Rio, according to the principles of the school of Freyberg, in which the author was formed. The first Spanish translation of Lavater's *Elements of Chemistry* was also published at Mexico. I cite these isolated facts because they give us the measure of the ardour with which the exact sciences are begun to be studied in the capital of New Spain. This ardour is much greater than that with which they addict themselves to the study of languages and ancient literature.

Instruction in mathematics is less carefully attended to in the University of Mexico than in the School of Mines. The pupils of this last establishment go farther into analysis; they are instructed in the integral and differential calculi. On the return of peace and free intercourse with Europe, when astronomical instruments (chronometers, sextants, and the repeating circles of Borda) shall become more common, young men will be found in the most remote parts of the kingdom capable of making observations, and calculating them after the most recent methods. I have already indicated in the analysis of my maps the advantage which might be drawn by the government from this extraordinary aptitude in constructing a map of the country. The taste for astronomy is very old in Mexico. Three distinguished men, Velásquez, Gama, and Alzate, did honour to their country towards the end of the last century. All the three made a great number of astronomical observations, especially of eclipses of the satellites of Jupiter. Alzate, the worst informed of them, was the correspondent of the Academy of Sciences at Paris. Inaccurate as an observer, and of an activity frequently impetuous, he gave himself up to too many objects at a time. We have already discussed in the geographical introduction the merits of his astronomical labours. He is entitled to the real merit,

however, of having excited his countrymen to the study of the physical sciences. The *Gazetta de Litteratura*, which he published for a long time at Mexico, contributed singularly to give encouragement and impulsion to the Mexican youth.

The most remarkable geometrician produced by New Spain since the time of Siguenza was Don Joaquín Velásquez Cárdenas y León. All the astronomical and geodesical labours of this indefatigable savant bear the stamp of the greatest precision. He was born on the 21st July, 1732, in the interior of the country, at the farm of Santiago Acebedocla, near the Indian village of Tizicapan; and he had the merit, we may say, of forming himself. At the age of four he communicated the smallpox to his father, who died of them. An uncle, parish-priest of Xaltocan, took care of his education, and placed him under the instruction of an Indian of the name of Manuel Asentizio; a man of great natural strength of mind, and well versed in the knowledge of the Mexican history and mythology. Velásquez learned at Xaltocan several Indian languages, and the use of the hieroglyphical writings of the Aztecs. It is to be regretted that he published nothing on this very interesting branch of antiquity. Placed at Mexico in the Tridentine college, he found neither professor, nor books, nor instruments. With the small assistance which he could obtain, he fortified himself in the study of the mathematics and the ancient languages. A lucky accident threw into his hands the works of Newton and Bacon. He drew from the one a taste for astronomy, and from the other an acquaintance with the true methods of philosophising. While poor and unable to find any instrument even in Mexico, he set himself, with his friend M. Guadalaxara (now professor of mathematics in the Academy of Painting), to construct telescopes and quadrants. He followed at the same time the profession of advocate, an occupation which in Mexico, as well as elsewhere, is much more lucrative than that of looking at the stars. What he gained by his professional labours was laid out in purchasing instruments in England. After being named professor in the university, he accompanied the *visitador* Don José de Gálvez in his journey to Sonora. Sent on a commission to California, he profited by the serenity of the sky in that peninsula to make a great number of astronomical observations. He first observed there that in all the maps, for centuries, through an enormous error of longitude, this part of the new continent had always been marked several degrees farther west than it really was. When the Abbé Chappe, more celebrated for his courage and his zeal for the sciences than for the accuracy of his labours, arrived in California, he found the Mexican astronomer already established there. Velásquez had constructed for himself, in Mimosa planks, an observatory at St. Anne. Having already determined the position of this Indian village, he informed the Abbé Chappe that the moon's eclipse on the 18th June, 1769, would be visible in California. The French

astronomer doubted the truth of this assertion, till the eclipse actually took place. Velásquez by himself made a very good observation of the transit of Venus over the disk of the sun on the 3d June, 1769. He communicated the result, the very morning of the transit, to the Abbé Chappe, and to the Spanish astronomers, Don Vicente Doz and Don Salvador de Medina. The French traveller was surprised at the harmony between the observation of Velásquez and his own. He was no doubt astonished to meet in California with a Mexican, who, without belonging to any academy, and without having ever left New Spain, was able to observe as well as the academicians. In 1773 Velásquez executed the great geodesical undertaking, of which we have given some of the results in the geographical introduction, and to which we shall again return in speaking of the drain of the lakes of the valley of Mexico. The most essential service which this indefatigable man rendered to his country was the establishment of the Tribunal and the School of Mines, the plans for which he presented to the court. He finished his laborious career on the 6th of March, 1786, while first director-general of the *Tribunal de Minería*, and enjoying the title of *Alcalde del Corte honorario*.

After mentioning the labours of Alzate and Velásquez, it would be unjust to pass over the name of Gama, the friend and fellow-labourer of the latter. Without fortune, and compelled to support a numerous family by a troublesome and almost mechanical labour, unknown and neglected during his life by his fellow-citizens, who loaded him with eulogies after his death, Gama became by his own unassisted efforts an able and well-informed astronomer. He published several memoirs on eclipses of the moon, on the satellites of Jupiter, on the almanac and chronology of the ancient Mexicans, and on the climate of New Spain; all of which announce a great precision of ideas and accuracy of observation. If I have allowed myself to enter into these details on the literary merit of three Mexican savants, it is merely for the sake of proving from their example, that the ignorance which European pride has thought proper to attach to the Creoles is neither the effect of the climate nor of a want of moral energy; but that this ignorance, where it is still observable, is solely the effect of the isolation and the defects in the social institutions of the colonies.

5. COLONIAL JOURNALISM IN ACTION

Colonial newspapers and reviews played a significant part in the development of a critical and reformist spirit and a nascent sense of nationality among the educated creoles of Spanish America. They appeared in increasing number in the period after 1780.

Subjected to an oppressive censorship by Church and State, and beset by chronic financial difficulties, they generally had short and precarious lives. More important than the routine news items they carried were the articles they housed on scientific, economic, and social questions. The Semanario del Nuevo Reino de Granada, *edited between 1808 and 1811 by the distinguished Colombian scientist Francisco José de Caldas (1771–1816), was notable for the high quality of its contents. Caldas himself contributed many of the articles in the* Semanario, *including a brilliant essay on the geography of New Granada, from which the following excerpt is taken.*[5]

✤✤✤✤ Whether we look north or south, whether we examine the most populous or the most deserted places in this colony, everywhere we find the stamp of indolence and ignorance. Our rivers and mountains are unknown to us; we do not know the extent of the country in which we were born; and the study of our geography is still in the cradle. This capital and humiliating truth should shake us out of our lethargy; it should make us more attentive to our interests; it should draw us to every corner of New Granada to measure, examine, and describe it. This truth, engraved in the hearts of all good citizens, will bring them together in order to collect information, donate funds, and recruit men of learning, sparing neither labor nor expense to obtain a detailed reconnaissance map of our provinces. I am not speaking now of an ordinary map; reduced scales and economy must disappear from the minds of our countrymen. Two square inches, at least, should represent a league of terrain. Here should appear the hills, mountains, pastures, forests, lakes, marshes, valleys, rivers, their turns and velocities, straits, cataracts, fisheries, all settlements, all agricultural activities, mines, and quarries — in fine, everything above the surface of our land. These features, brought together, will produce a superb map, worthy of New Granada. The statesman, the magistrate, the philosopher, the businessman, will come to look at it to obtain information needed in the performance of their duties; the traveler, the botanist, the mineralogist, the soldier, and the agriculturist will see their concerns depicted in majestic strokes. . . . Each province will copy its own section and will guard it religiously. Our youth will be trained in the study of these sections, and in a few years we shall have men capable of conceiving and carrying out great plans. Everywhere we shall hear only of projects; projects of roads, navigation canals, new branches of industry, naturalization of foreign plants; the flame of patriotism will be lighted in every heart; and the ultimate result will be the glory of our monarch and the prosperity of this colony.

[5] Francisco José de Caldas, *Semanario del Nuevo Reino de Granada,* Bogotá, 1942, 3 vols., I, pp. 51–54. (Excerpt translated by the editor).

If a geographical-economic expedition were formed to survey the whole viceroyalty, composed of an astronomer, a botanist, a mineralogist, a zoologist, and an economist, with two or more draftsmen; if all the provinces contributed toward a fund set up by the wealthy, and especially by the landowners; if the merchants did the same in view of their financial interest in the project; if the Chamber of Commerce [*Consulado*] of Cartagena supported the enterprise as actively as it promotes other projects of the same nature; if the governmental leaders supported it with all their authority — there is no doubt that in a few years we would have the glory of possessing a masterpiece of geographical and political knowledge, and would have laid the foundations of our prosperity.

If this project presents difficulties, there remains no other recourse than to improve our educational system. If instead of teaching our youths trifles . . . , we gave them some acquaintance with the elements of astronomy and geography, and taught them the use of some easily-mastered instruments; if practical geometry and geodesy were substituted for certain metaphysical and useless subjects; if on finishing their courses they knew how to measure the earth, make a survey, determine a latitude, use a compass — then we would have reason to hope that these youths, dispersed throughout the provinces, would put into practice the principles they had learned in school, and would make a map of their country. Six months devoted to these interesting studies would qualify a young man to work on the great enterprise of the geography of this colony. I ask the persons responsible for our public education to consider and weigh whether it is more profitable to the State and Church to spend many weeks in sustaining airy systems and all that heap of futile or merely speculative questions than to devote this time to the study of the globe and the land that we inhabit. What do we care about the dwellers on the moon? Would it not be better to learn about the dwellers on the fertile banks of the Magdalena?

The religious orders who have in their charge the missions of the Orinoco, Caqueta, Andaquies, Mocoa, and Maynas should educate the young missionaries in these important subjects. These apostolic men would bring to the barbarians both the light of salvation and that of the useful sciences. Zealous imitators of Fathers Fritz, Coleti, Magnio, and Gumilla, they would leave us precious monuments of their activity and learning. Exact maps, geographical determination, descriptions of plants and animals, and important information about the customs of the savages whom they are going to civilize would be the fruits of these studies. They would serve them as a relief from the tedium and weariness that are inseparable from their lofty ministry.

The rudiments of arithmetic, plane geometry, and trigonometry, of which we possess good compendiums; the use of the graphometer,

the gnomon, the quadrant (with some knowledge of how to draw a meridian), and the use of the barometer and the thermometer qualify a young man to assist in the advance of our geographical knowledge.

We have two chairs of mathematics, and that of philosophy offers some instruction in these sciences; thanks to the wise and generous Mutis, we already have an astronomical observatory, where practical experience can be obtained in the use of certain instruments; we have books, and we lack nothing necessary to working for the good of our country. My love for the fatherland dictated these reflections. If they are useful to my countrymen, I am already rewarded for the labor they cost me; if not, they will pardon me, taking into account the purity of my intentions.

6. A COLONIAL FREETHINKER

The circulation and influence of forbidden books among educated colonials steadily increased in the closing decades of the eighteenth century and the first years of the nineteenth. In Mexico, writes Professor Jiménez Rueda, "Voltaire and the encyclopedists, Jean Jacques Rousseau and Montesquieu, were read by village curates, by canons of provincial cathedrals, and by lawyers in the capital. Pictures of Voltaire were even sold in the bookstalls by the Gate of the Augustine friars, and the books of all of them passed from hand to hand, although surreptitiously, because the Holy Office still kept watch." Encyclopedist influence is strongly evident in the work of the Mexican writer Fernández de Lizardi (1776–1827), whose stormy life spanned the declining years of the colony and the first years of its independence. His masterpiece, El periquillo sarniento (The Itching Parrot), the first true Spanish-American novel, depicted with harsh realism and biting satire the conditions of Mexican life in the late colonial period. First published in Mexico City in 1816, incomplete because of official censorship, it was later reprinted in its entirety. The following episode from The Itching Parrot, laid in Manila, illustrates Lizardi's emphatic dissent from social folly and prejudice of every kind.[6]

❖❖❖❖ I said before that a virtuous man has few misfortunes to relate. Nevertheless, I witnessed some strange affairs. One of them was as follows:

One year, when a number of foreigners had come from the

[6] José Joaquín Fernández de Lizardi, *El periquillo sarniento*, México, 1897, 2 vols., II(D), pp. 3–7. (Excerpt translated by the editor.)

port to the city for reasons of trade, a rich merchant who happened to be a Negro went down a street. He must have been bound on very important business, because he strode along very rapidly and distractedly, and in his headlong progress he inadvertently ran into an English officer who was paying court to a rich young creole lady. Such was the shock of the collision that if the girl had not supported him the officer would have fallen to the ground. As it was, his hat fell off and his hair was disheveled.

The officer's pride was greatly wounded, and he immediately ran toward the Negro, drawing his sword. The poor fellow was taken by surprise, and since he carried no arms he probably believed that it was all up with him. The young lady and the officer's companions restrained him, but he raged at the Negro for some time, protesting a thousand times that he would vindicate his injured honor.

So much abuse did he heap on the innocent black that the latter finally said to him in English: "Sir, be quiet; tomorrow I shall be waiting in the park to give you satisfaction with a pistol." The officer accepted, and there the matter rested.

I, who witnessed this incident and knew some English, having learned the hour and place assigned for the duel, took care to be there punctually to see how the affair would end.

At the appointed time both men arrived, each accompanied by a friend who acted as his second. As soon as they met the Negro drew two pistols, presented them to the officer, and said to him: "Sir, I did not intend yesterday to offend you; my running into you was an accident. You heaped abuse on me and even wished to wound or kill me. I had no arms with which to defend myself against you. I knew that a challenge to a duel was the quickest means of quieting you, and now I have come to give you satisfaction with a pistol, as I said I would."

"Very well," said the Englishman, "let's get on. It gives me no satisfaction to fight with a Negro, but at least I shall have the pleasure of killing an insolent rascal. Let's choose our pistols."

"All right," said the Negro, "but you should know that I no more intend to offend you today than I did yesterday. It seems to me that for a man of your position to decide to kill a man for such a trifle is not a matter of honor but a mere caprice. But if the explanation I gave you means nothing, and only killing will do, I don't propose to be guilty of murder or to die without cause, as must happen if your shot or my shot finds its target. So let luck decide who has justice on his side. Here are the pistols; one of them is loaded with two balls and the other is empty. Look them over, give me the one you don't want, and let us take our chances."

The officer was surprised by this proposal. The others said that it was highly irregular — that both must fight with the same weapons; and they offered other arguments that did not convince the Negro,

who insisted that the duel must take place on his terms, so that he might have the consolation of knowing that if he killed his opponent it was because Heaven had ordered it or especially favored him — and if he were killed, it would be no fault of his but pure chance, as when a ship is wrecked at sea. He added that since the arrangement favored neither party, since no one knew who would get the loaded pistol, refusal to accept his proposal could only be attributed to cowardice.

No sooner had the ardent young man heard this than he took up the pistols, selected one, and gave the other to the Negro.

The two men turned their backs to each other, walked a short distance, and then turned to face each other. At that moment the officer fired at the Negro — but in vain, for he had chosen the empty pistol.

He stood there as if stunned, believing with the others that he would be the defenceless victim of the Negro's wrath. But the latter, with the greatest generosity, said to the officer: "Sir, we have both come out with whole skins; the duel is over; you had to accept it with the conditions I imposed, and I could wage it on no other terms. I could fire at you if I wished, but if I never sought to offend you before, how could I do it now, seeing you disarmed? Let us be friends, if you consider yourself satisfied; but if only my death can appease you, take the loaded pistol and aim it at my breast."

Saying this, he presented the horrible weapon to the officer. The latter, moved by this extraordinary generosity, took the pistol and fired it in the air. Approaching the Negro with outstretched arms, he embraced him, saying with the greatest tenderness:

"Yes, friends we are and friends we shall be eternally; forgive my vanity and madness. I never believed that Negroes were capable of such greatness of soul." "That prejudice still has many followers," said the Negro, warmly embracing the officer.

We who witnessed this incident were eager to strengthen the bonds of this new friendship, and I, who knew them least of all, hastened to introduce myself to them as their friend, and to beg them to take a glass of punch or wine with me at the nearest coffeehouse.

17 ✢ The Revolt of the Masses

Innumerable servile revolts, large and small, punctuated the colonial period of Spanish-American history. Before Spanish rule had been firmly established the Indians rose against their new masters in many regions. The revolutionary wave subsided in the seventeenth century but rose again to great heights in the eighteenth, as a result of new burdens imposed on the common people.

The expansion of colonial economic life under the Bourbon dynasty failed to better the lot of the Indian and mestizo peasantry and artisans. On the contrary, Bourbon efforts to increase the royal revenues, by creating governmental monopolies and privileged companies, and by imposing new taxes, actually intensified the sufferings of the lower classes. This circumstance helps to explain the popular character of the revolts of 1780–1781, as distinct from the creole wars of independence of the next generation.

In November, 1779, José Gabriel Tupac-Amaru, a direct descendant of the last Inca, raised the standard of revolt in Peru by ambushing the hated *corregidor* Arriaga near the town of Tinta and putting him to death after a summary trial. By the first months of 1780 the southern highlands of the viceroyalty were aflame with rebellion. Although the various revolutionary movements lacked a uni-

fied direction, the rebel leaders generally recognized Tupac-Amaru as their chief, and they continued to invoke his name even after his death.

Tactical errors — such as the failure of Tupac-Amaru to attack Cuzco before the arrival of Spanish reinforcements, poor communications between the rebel forces, the superior arms and organization of the royalist armies, and divisions among the native nobility — doomed the rebellion to defeat. Despite some initial success, the rebel chieftain was soon completely routed. Tupac-Amaru, members of his family, and his leading captains were captured and put to death, in some cases with ferocious cruelty.

The revolt of the *Comuneros* in New Granada, like that in Peru, had its origin in intolerable economic conditions. The disturbances began in Socorro, an important manufacturing town in the north, and rapidly spread to other communities. Under the command of hesitant or unwilling creole leaders, a multitude of Indian and mestizo peasants and artisans marched upon Bogotá, capturing or putting to flight the small forces sent from the capital. An agreement reached on June 4, 1781, satisfied virtually all the demands of the rebels, and was sanctified by the archbishop by a special religious service. Secretly, however, the Spanish commissioners signed another document declaring the agreement void as obtained by force. The jubilant insurgents scattered and returned to their homes. Only José Antonio Galán, a young mestizo peasant leader, kept his small force intact and sought to keep the revolt alive.

Having achieved their objective of disbanding the rebel host, the Spanish officials prepared to crush the insurrection completely. The Viceroy Flores openly repudiated the agreement with the *Comuneros*. Spanish troops moved into the disaffected area and seized large numbers of prisoners. Galán, who vainly urged a new march on Bogotá, was seized by a renegade leader and handed over to the Spaniards, who put him to death by hanging on January 30, 1782. The revolt of the *Comuneros* had ended.

1. THE PLAN OF TUPAC-AMARU

The general causes of the great revolt in Peru are sufficiently clear. More obscure are the precise aims that the rebel leader, Tupac-Amaru, set for himself. It is difficult to believe that the well-educated José Gabriel, who had had years of experience in dealing with Spanish officialdom, seriously believed that he could obtain sweeping reforms from the crown by negotiation, even from positions of strength, especially after his execution of the

corregidor *Arriaga. More plausible is the view that his professions of loyalty to Spain represented a mask by means of which he hoped to utilize the still strong faith of the Indians in the mythical benevolence of the Spanish king and perhaps to soften his punishment in case of defeat. If this view is correct, it follows that his true object was the establishment of an independent Peruvian state, with himself as king or Inca. Such a state would have been essentially Spanish in religion and in political and social organization. The fiscal, or prosecuting attorney, of the viceroyalty of Buenos Aires offers a shrewd and convincing argument in favor of the thesis that the rebel leader aimed at independence.*[1]

❖❖❖❖ What is worthy of attention in this affair is not so much the pitiful death of the corregidor Don Antonio de Arriaga, the theft of his fortune, the seizure of the arms that he had in his house, or the outrages committed by the perfidious Tupac-Amaru, as the astuteness, the painstaking care, and the deceptions with which he managed to perform them and to subvert that and other provinces, preparing them to carry out his reprehensible secret designs.

It appears that in order to seize the corregidor Arriaga, in his own house, he arranged a banquet for his victim. In order to summon the military chiefs, caciques, and Indians of the province, he compelled the unhappy corregidor to issue or sign orders to that effect. In order to drag him to the gallows in the presence of the multitude with no disturbance, he published a decree, pretending that he acted on His Majesty's orders. On the same pretext, after this horrible deed, he departed for the neighboring province of Quispicanchi, in order to perpetrate similar atrocities on the corregidor and as many Spaniards as he could find, and as soon as he had returned to his town of Tungasuca issued orders to the caciques of neighboring provinces to imitate his example.

And although in the provinces of Azangaro and Carabaya, which belonged to this viceroyalty of Buenos Aires, his wicked designs failed to bear fruit, thanks to the loyalty with which his commissioner Don Diego Chuquiguanca (the cacique and governor of the town of Azangaro) and his sons turned over the dispatches, of which copies are found in the file on this case, the fact is that the province of Quispicachi, since the flight of Don Fernando Cabrera, its present corregidor, is under the sway of the rebel Tupac-Amaru; and he himself asserts in one of the papers written at Chuquiguanca that four more provinces obey his orders. And, knowing as he did the natives' great respect for

---

[1] "Vista del fiscal del virreinato de Buenos Aires, enero 15 de 1781," in: Manuel de Odriozola (ed.), *Documentos históricos del Perú*, Lima, 1863, pp. 132–133. (Excerpt translated by the editor.)

the orders of the king and their hatred of the corregidores and their European associates, he probably did not find it difficult to incite them to execute the supposed orders of the king.

But the essence of the careful planning and perfidy of the traitor Tupac-Amaru consists in this, that after speaking so often of the royal orders which authorized him to proceed against the corregidores and other Europeans, in his orders, letters, and messages, and in the edicts which he dispatched to Don Diego Chuquiguanca, in order to revolutionize that province and Carabaya, he now says nothing about the orders of the king, and proceeds as the most distinguished Indian of the royal blood and principal line of the Incas to liberate his countrymen from the injuries, injustices, and slavery which the European corregidores had inflicted on them, while the superior courts turned a deaf ear to their complaints. From which it follows that he repeatedly used the name of the king — in a vague way, not specifying our present ruler, Charles III — only to secure the acquiescence of the natives of those provinces in the violence done to Arriaga and to induce them to do the same to other corregidores. And considering these aims partially achieved, he transforms himself from a royal commissioner into a redeemer from injustices and burdens, moved only by pity for his compatriots, preparing the way for them to acclaim him as king, or at least to support their benefactor with arms, until they have raised him to the defunct throne of the tyrannical pagan kings of Peru, which is doubtless the goal of his contrivings.

Actually, he has already succeeded in assembling a large number of Indians, as noted by Colonel Don Pedro la Vallina (who was his prisoner) in a letter contained in the file on this case — and with their aid, it is stated, he defeated and slew some 300 men who came out to halt his advance on Cuzco, and took their weapons to arm the rebels who follow him. He took these first successful steps in his titanic enterprise after certain other things had occurred: the rising that took place in Arequipa as a result of the establishment of a customshouse; the rioting that with less cause broke out in the city of La Paz; the disturbances that occurred in the provinces of Chayanta for the same reason; and the rumors that the natives in other provinces were somewhat restless. When one considers that the rebel Tupac-Amaru, informed of these events, offers the natives freedom, not only from customshouse duties but from sales taxes, tributes, and forced labor in the mines, it must be admitted that he offers them a powerful inducement to follow him, and that there is imminent danger that the party of rebellion will progressively increase unless the most energetic effort is made to slay this insolent rebel, the prime mover of this conspiracy, so that others may be deterred from joining the rebellion and abandoning their loyalty to their legitimate monarch and natural lord, to the detriment of themselves and the commonwealth.

2. A HEROINE OF THE REVOLT

Micaela, the wife of Tupac-Amaru, played a leading role in the great revolt. From the first she was the rebel leader's principal adviser, and in his absence assumed full direction of the movement. After the initial victory over the small Spanish force sent from Cuzco, she strongly advised an immediate march on the city, to take advantage of the chaos and panic that reigned there. The capture of Cuzco, ancient capital of the Inca Empire and center of Spanish power in the highlands, would have been a stroke of the greatest moral and military significance. Tupac-Amaru decided instead to invade the provinces to the south, promising to return immediately and advance on Cuzco — a promise he failed to keep. By the time he returned, reinforcements had reached Cuzco from Lima, and the golden opportunity had vanished. The bitterness of Micaela's letter to José Gabriel reflects her appreciation of the immensity of his blunder. Despite these harsh reproaches, her letters to Tupac-Amaru contain "notes of profound and laconic tenderness." ("Chepe" was an affectionate nickname for her husband.)[2]

✠✠✠✠ Dear Chepe:

You are causing me mortal concern. While you saunter through the villages, wasting two days in Yauri, showing no sense of urgency, our soldiers are rightly becoming bored, and are leaving for their homes.

I simply cannot endure all this any longer, and I am ready to give myself up to the Spaniards and let them take my life when I see how lightly you regard this serious matter that threatens the lives of all of us. We are surrounded by enemies and constantly insecure; and on your account the lives of all my sons, and of all our people, are in danger.

I have warned you again and again not to dally in those villages, where there is nothing to do — but you continue to saunter, ignoring the fact that the soldiers are running short of food. They are receiving their pay, but the money will not last forever. Then they will all depart, leaving us to pay with our lives, because you must have learned by this time that they came only for reasons of self-interest, and to get all they could out of us. They are already beginning to desert; they are frightened by the rumor spread by Vargas and Oré that the Spaniards of Lampa, united with those of other provinces and Arequipa, are

---

[2] Micaela Bastidas to José Gabriel Tupac-Amaru, Dec. 6, 1780, in: Francisco A. Loáyza (ed.), *Mártires y heroínas,* Lima, 1945, pp. 48–51. (Excerpt translated by the editor.)

going to surround you, and so they want to get away, fearing the punishment that might befall them. Thus we will lose all the people that I have gotten together for the descent on Cuzco, and the forces at Cuzco will unite with the soldiers from Lima, who have been on the march for many days.

I must tell you all this, though it pains me. If you want to ruin us, continue to sleep and commit such follies as that of passing alone through the streets of Yauri, and even climbing to the church tower — actions certainly out of place at this time, and that only dishonor you and gain you disrespect.

I believed that you were occupied day and night with arranging these affairs, instead of showing an unconcern that robs me of my life. I am already a shadow of myself and beside myself with anxiety, and so I beg you to get on with this business.

You made me a promise, but henceforth I shall not heed your promises, for you did not keep your word.

I do not care for my life, but for the lives of my poor children, who need all my help. If the enemy comes from Paruro, as I suggested in my last letter, I am prepared to march to meet them, leaving Fernando in a secure place, for the Indians are not capable of acting by themselves in these perilous times.

I gave you plenty of warnings to march immediately on Cuzco, but you took them all lightly, giving the Spaniards time to prepare as they have done, placing cannon on Picchu Mountain, and devising other measures so dangerous that you are no longer in a position to attack them. God keep you many years. Tungasuca, December 6, 1780.

I must also tell you that the Indians of Quispicanchi are tired of serving as guards so long a time. In fine, God must want me to suffer for my sins. Your wife.

After I had finished this letter, a messenger arrived with the definite news that the enemy from Paruro is in Acos; I am going forward to attack them, even if it costs me my life.

3. THE DEATH OF TUPAC-AMARU

The rebel attack on Cuzco came too late. The strong resistance of the reinforced Spanish defenders and their Indian auxiliaries (the majority of combatants on both sides were natives), the superiority of the Spanish armaments, the constant desertions from Tupac-Amaru's undisciplined host, and the treason of the captured Spaniard who commanded the rebel artillery and systematically misdirected the fire of his pieces were among the

reasons for its failure. In January, 1781, Tupac-Amaru suddenly abandoned the siege and began a rapid withdrawal toward his base in the province of Tinta. The Spaniards soon launched a powerful offensive. The insurgent forces were defeated in fierce battles, and Tupac-Amaru evacuated Tinta, fleeing southward with the apparent intention of organizing a new resistance in the highlands around Lake Titicaca. During the disorderly retreat he, his wife, his sons, and a number of his captains were seized by treachery and handed over to the Spaniards. After a summary trial, on May 15, 1781, the visitador *Areche handed down sentences whose ferocity revealed how thin was the veneer of Enlightenment over the medieval mentality of Bourbon Spain. A contemporary account describes the death of Tupac-Amaru and other leaders of the rebellion.*[3]

✠✠✠ On Friday, May 18, 1781, the militia of Cuzco, armed with spears and some firearms, surrounded the public square, and the corps of mulattoes and Indians from Huamanga district, with fixed bayonets, surrounded the four-sided gallows. Then the following persons were brought forth: José Berdejo, Andres Castelu, the *zambo* Antonio Oblitas (the executioner of the corregidor Arriaga), Antonio Bastidas, Francisco Tupac-Amaru, Tomasa Condemaita, the woman cacique of Acos, Hipólito Tupac-Amaru, son of the traitor, his wife Micaela Bastidas, and the rebel leader himself. They were all brought out together in chains, in baskets of the kind they use to bring yerba maté leaves from Paraguay, and dragged along behind a harnessed horse. Accompanied by their guards and by priests who offered them spiritual consolation, they were brought to the foot of the scaffold, and there the executioners meted out the following deaths to them:

Berdejo, Castelu, the zambo, and Bastidas were simply hanged. Francisco Tupac-Amaru, the rebel's uncle, and his son Hipólito, had their tongues cut out before they were thrown down the steps of the gallows. The Indian woman Condemaita was strangled on a little scaffold provided with an iron screw made for this purpose, the first ever seen here. The Indian and his wife witnessed all these punishments, even that of their son Hipólito, who was the last to go to the gallows. Then Micaela went up to the scaffold, where, in the presence of her husband, her tongue was cut out and she was garroted, suffering infinite agony all the while because since her neck was very slender the screw could not strangle her, and the executioners had to dispatch her by tying ropes around her neck, each pulling in a different direction, and kicking her in the stomach and breast. Last to die was the rebel leader, José Gabriel. He was brought into the middle of the

[3] Odriozola, *Documentos históricos del Perú*, pp. 161–162. (Excerpt translated by the editor.)

square, and there the executioner cut out his tongue. Then they took off his chains and laid him on the ground. They tied four ropes to his hands and feet and attached the ropes to the girths of four horses, which four mestizos drove in four different directions. Cuzco had never before seen a spectacle of this kind. Either because the horses were not very strong or because the Indian was really made of iron, they simply could not tear him apart, although they tugged at him for a long time, while he dangled in the air like a spider. Finally the visitador Areche, moved by compassion, decided to end his suffering and sent an order from the Jesuit College, from whose windows he was watching these punishments, that the executioner should cut off his head, and so it was done. Then they laid his body under the gallows and cut off his arms and legs. They did the same to the women, and the heads of the others were cut off and sent to be displayed in various towns. The bodies of the Indian and his wife were borne to Picchu, where a great bonfire was made, into which they were thrown and reduced to ashes, which were thrown into the air and into the little river that runs through there. Such was the end of José Gabriel Tupac-Amaru and Micaela Bastidas, whose pride and arrogance reached such a pitch that they called themselves Kings of Peru, Chile, Quito, Tucuman, and other parts, even including the Grand Paititi, with other follies of the same kind.

A considerable number of people gathered on this day, but no one gave a cry or even spoke; many, and I among them, noted that there were no Indians in that multitude, at least not in their customary dress; if there were any there, they must have been disguised in cloaks or ponchos. Sometimes things happen as if the Devil had planned them to confirm these Indians in their abuses and superstitions. I say this because, although the weather had been very fine and dry, that day dawned with the sky heavily overcast, and at twelve o'clock, when the horses were tugging at the Indian, there arose a gust of wind followed by a downpour that forced all the people and even the guards to run for shelter. This has caused the Indians to say that the heavens and the elements were mourning the death of their Inca, whom the inhuman or impious Spaniards were putting to death with such cruelty.

4. A CHARTER OF LIBERTY

Although produced by the same causes, the rising of the Comuneros *in New Granada was a relatively peaceful affair by contrast with the vast upheaval in Peru. Its reformist spirit was reflected in the insurgent slogan:* Viva el rey y muera el mal gobierno (*Long live the king, and down with the rotten gov-*

ernment!) *But in view of its organization and its effort to form a common front of all colonial groups with grievances against Spanish authority (excepting only the Negro slaves), the revolt of the* Comuneros *marked an advance over the chaotic course of events to the south. A central committee, or* común, *elected in the town of Socorro by thousands of peasants and artisans from adjacent towns, directed the insurrection. Each of the towns in revolt also had a* común *and a captain chosen by popular election. The popular basis of the* Comunero *movement is evident from the terms which the rebel delegates presented to the Spanish commissioners, and which the latter signed and later repudiated. A number of important or typical articles follow.*[4]

❖❖❖❖ 1. The tax entitled Armada de Barlovento[5] must be abolished so completely that its name shall never again be heard in this kingdom. . . .

4. In view of the poverty of this kingdom, stamped paper shall circulate only in sheets of half *real*, for the use of ecclesiastics, religious, Indians, and poor people, and in sheets of two *reales* for the legal titles and lawsuits of persons of some wealth; and no other stamped paper shall circulate. . . .

5. The new tax on tobacco shall be completely abolished.

7. Considering the miserable state of all the Indians, who go about more poorly clothed and fed than hermits, and whose small knowledge, limited faculties, and meager harvests prevent them from paying the high tribute which the *corregidores* exact with such severity, not to mention the stipends assigned to their curates. The total annual tribute of the Indians shall be only four pesos, and that of mulattoes subject to tribute shall be two pesos. The curates shall not collect from the Indians any fee for the administration of holy oils, burials, and weddings, nor shall they compel them to serve as mayordomos at their saints' festivals. The cost of these festivals shall (except when some pious person offers to bear them) be borne by the brotherhood. . . . Furthermore, those Indians who have been removed from their towns but whose lands have not been sold or transferred shall be returned to their lands of immemorial possession; and all the lands which they at present possess shall be theirs, not only for their use but as their property, which they may use as the owners thereof. . . .

9. The *alcabala*, henceforth and forever, shall be two per cent of all fruits, goods, cattle, and articles of every kind when sold or exchanged. . . .

10. Since the cause of the widespread commotions in this king-

---

[4] Manuel Briceño, *Los comuneros*, Bogotá, 1880, Appendix, pp. 122–132. (Except translated by the editor.)

[5] This was a tax designed to strengthen the *armada de barlovento*, the Spanish squadron guarding the Windward Islands. B.K.

dom and in that of Lima has been the imprudent conduct of the *visita-dores*, who tried to squeeze blood out of stones and destroy us with their despotic rule, until the people of this kingdom, ordinarily so docile and submissive, were made desperate by their growing extortions and could no longer tolerate their tyrannical rule . . . , we demand that Don Juan Gutiérrez de Piñeres, *visitador* of the royal audiencia, be expelled from this kingdom to Spain, where our Catholic Monarch, reflecting on the results of his arbitrary conduct, shall do with him as he thinks best. And never again must officials be sent us who would treat us so severely and unwisely, for in such a case we shall again join together to repel any oppression that may be directed against us on any pretext whatever. . . .

18. All the officers on the present expedition, with the ranks of commander-general, captains-general, territorial captains, lieutenants, ensigns, sergeants, and corporals, shall retain their respective appointments, and shall be obliged to assemble their companies on Sunday afternoon of each week to train them in the use of arms, both offensive and defensive, against the event that an effort be made to break the agreements that we are now making in good faith, and also to aid His Majesty in resisting his enemies. . . .

21. In filling offices of the first, second, and third classes, natives of America shall be privileged and preferred over Europeans, who daily manifest their antipathy toward us . . . , for in their ignorance they believe that they are the masters and that all Americans of any kind are their inferiors and servants. And so that this irrational view may disappear, Europeans shall be employed only in case of necessity and according to their ability, good will, and attachment to the Americans, for since we are all subjects of the same king and lord we should live like brothers, and whoever strives to lord it over others and advance himself against the rule of equality must be removed from among us. . . .

32. The order greatly reducing the number of grocery stores has had the result that the stores licensed in each town are owned by the wealthiest or most favored individuals. We therefore ask, as a matter of public benefit, that the right to establish stores be granted to all inhabitants of the kingdom, as was formerly the case, without limitation as to their number.

5. TUPAC-AMARU AND THE COMUNEROS

The revolt of Tupac-Amaru had repercussions among the Indians of New Granada. In the eastern lowlands, where the powerful missions and their priests replaced the corregidors *as symbols of*

PART V

Spanish oppression, the news that a great king of their race had arisen was carried from town to town and caused wild rejoicing and revolts against Spanish authority among the Indians. In this region the popularly-chosen comúnes *pledged loyalty to the Inca. At Silos, in the district of Pamplona, where a great throng of Indians took an oath of allegiance to their distant king, the following decree of Tupac-Amaru was published.*[6]

✠✠✠✠ Don José I, by the grace of God Inca, King of Peru, Santafe, Quito, Chile, Buenos Aires, and the continents of the South Sea, Duke of the Superlative, Lord of the River of the Amazons, with dominion over the Grand Paititi, commissioner and distributor of the divine mercy. . . .

Whereas it has been determined by my council in prolonged sessions, on repeated occasions, both secret and public, that the Kings of Castile have usurped the crown and dominions of Peru, imposing an intolerable number of taxes, tributes, duties, excises, monopolies, tithes, fifths, viceroys, audiencias, corregidores, and other ministers, all equally tyrannical, who sold justice at auction. . . . ,

For these causes, and by reason of the cries which have risen up to heaven, in the name of Almighty God I order that henceforth no man shall pay money to any Spanish officer, excepting the tithe to priests and a moderate tribute and fifth to his natural King and Lord; and for the speedier observance of the abovesaid, I order that an oath of allegiance to my royal crown be taken in all the cities, towns, and villages of my dominions, and that I be informed without delay which vassals are faithful and loyal, so that I may reward them, and which ones are disloyal, so that I may mete out condign punishment to them.

[6] Briceño, *Los comuneros*, pp. 139–140. (Excerpt translated by the editor.)

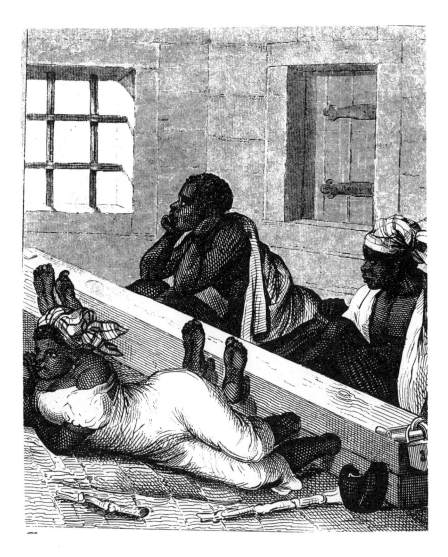

COLONIAL BRAZIL

Pedro Alvares Cabral, a Portuguese sea captain bound for India in the wake of Vasco da Gama's voyage, discovered Brazil in 1500. For several decades thereafter, Portugal's rulers neglected Brazil in favor of the Far East and its trade. However, as the profits of the Oriental spice trade declined, the Portuguese turned with increasing interest to the "Isle of Santa Cruz," as Brazil was then called. The export of brazilwood and the raising of sugar cane formed the principal economic activities of the early colonists. After 1550 large numbers of Negro slaves were imported to meet the needs of an expanding plantation economy.

French and Dutch invaders challenged Portuguese possession of Brazil in the sixteenth and seventeenth centuries but were beaten off by the colonists, practically unaided by the mother country. Meanwhile adventurous gold-seekers and slave-hunters from São Paulo pushed deep into the interior, far beyond the Line of Demarcation of 1494. In 1695 the Paulistas discovered gold in the region later called Minas Gerais — a timely find, for the first sugar cycle of the Northeast had about run its course as a result of competition from more efficient West-Indian producers. But the mineral cycle, marked by rapid and wasteful exploitation of the more accessible deposits of gold and diamonds, was of short duration. At the close of the colonial period

the Northeast, revived by a growing European demand for cotton, sugar, and other of Brazil's staples, again enjoyed economic primacy.

Like Spain, Portugal governed her empire with the aid of a royal council at home and an apparatus of viceroys, governors, judges, and inspectors overseas, but her administrative machinery for Brazil was less elaborate than that of the Spanish Indies. As in the Spanish colonies, the Church was under royal control but lacked the vast wealth and influence of its Spanish counterpart. The Jesuits led all other clergy in the work of converting the Indians, and in educational and humanitarian activities.

The nucleus of the social organization of the colony was the great estate, or fazenda, a self-sufficient patriarchal community centered about the Big House and its owner. Slavery cast a heavy shadow over every aspect of colonial life. One of its greatest evils was the resulting prejudice against labor — a prejudice that condemned to idleness or vagabondage many whites and free mixed-bloods who could neither aspire to be masters nor lower themselves by performing tasks ordinarily carried out by slaves.

Memo To: Professors Griffin, Kuzn

From: Goldie for NES

The sub-committee for Promot

meet on Wednesday, Sept. 29 at 2:

DEP

Reply:

18 ✤ The Formation of Colonial Brazil

Pedro Alvares Cabral, a Portuguese captain sent to follow up Gama's great voyage to India, accidentally discovered Brazil in 1500 and claimed it for his country. Projects of trade and conquest in the Far East claimed Portugal's chief attention at this time, but she did not completely neglect her new possession. Brazilwood, source of a valued red dye, was the first staple of the colony, but sugar soon established its economic leadership. Raids on Indian voyages and, after 1550, the importation of Negro slaves provided labor for the plantations and sugar mills.

The second half of the seventeenth century saw a crisis in the Brazilian sugar industry, which was faced with severe competition from newly-risen Dutch, English, and French sugar colonies in the West Indies. As the first economic cycle of colonial Brazil drew to a close, a second opened with the discovery of gold and diamonds in the regions of Minas Gerais, Goiaz, and Mato Grosso, lying west and south of Baía and Pernambuco. But the gold and diamonds were found in limited quantities, and production declined sharply after 1760.

As the interior provinces of Minas Gerais and Goiaz sank into decay, the Northeast enjoyed a revival based on the increasing European demand for sugar, cotton, and other semi-tropical products.

Between 1750 and 1800 Brazilian cotton production made large strides, but as rapidly declined in the face of competition from the more efficient cotton growers of the United States. The beginnings of the coffee industry, future giant of the Brazilian economy, also date from the late colonial period.

Until the decree of January 28, 1808, which opened the ports of Brazil to the trade of all nations, the commerce of the colony was restricted to Portuguese nationals and ships. A significant exception was made in the case of Great Britain, Portugal's protector and ally. By the Treaty of 1654, British merchants were permitted to trade between Portuguese and Brazilian ports. English ships frequently neglected the formality of touching at Lisbon, and plied a direct contraband commerce with the colony. The decree of free trade of 1808 only confirmed Great Britain's actual domination of Brazilian commerce.

I. THE BRAZILIAN INDIAN

At the time of the coming of the Portuguese, the Brazilian coast from the Amazon River to the Rio de la Plata was inhabited by a large number of Indian tribes closely related in language and culture. These tribes made their living by farming, hunting, and fishing, waged constant war against one another, and practiced ritual cannibalism. They generally accorded a friendly welcome to Europeans, until efforts to enslave them aroused their hostility. Pero de Magelhães, author of an important early chronicle of Brazil, describes the life and customs of the Brazilian Indian.[1]

✠✠✠✠ It is impossible to enumerate or to know the multitude of barbarous people which Nature has sown throughout this land of Brazil, because no one can safely travel through the *sertão*, nor travel overland without finding villages of Indians armed against all peoples; and as they are so numerous God granted that they are enemies one against the other, and that there is amongst them great hatred and discord, because otherwise the Portuguese would not be able to live in the land, nor overcome the great power of the inhabitants. There were many of these Indians on the coast near the Captaincies; the whole coast was inhabited by them when the Portuguese began to settle the country; but, because these Indians revolted against them and practised much treachery upon them, the Governors and Captains of the

[1] Pero de Magelhãs, *The Histories of Brazil*, translated and edited by John B. Stetson, Jr., New York, The Cortés Society, 1922, 2 vols., II, pp. 165-174.

land overthrew them little by little, and killed many of them; the others fled to the *sertão;* thus the coast remained unpopulated by the natives, near the Captaincies; however, some Indian villages, peaceful and friendly toward the Portuguese, were left.

All the people of the coast have the same language; it lacks three letters, namely, *f, l* and *r*, a fact worthy of wonder because they also have neither *F*aith, *L*aw, nor *R*uler; hence they live without justice and in complete disorder. The Indians go naked without any covering whatever, the males as well as the females; they do not cover any portion of their body, but all that Nature gave them goes uncovered. They all live in villages; there may be seven or eight houses in each. These houses are built long like rope-walks; and each one of them is filled with people, each of which has his stand on one side or the other, and the net in which he sleeps hung up there; thus they are all together, ranged in order, one after the other, and in the middle of the house there is an open aisle for passage. As I have said, there is among them no king nor justice, but in each village there is a head-man who is like a Captain, to whom they give voluntary obedience, but not through force; if this head-man dies, his son takes his place; he serves no other purpose than to go with them to war to take council with them as to the method they should employ in fighting, but he does not punish their wrong-doing, nor does he command them in any respect against their wills. This head-man has three or four wives; he has the greatest consideration for the first one and has more respect for her than for the others; they do this as a matter of position and dignity. They do not worship anything, nor do they believe that there is in another life glory for the good nor suffering for the wicked; they all believe that after this life ends their souls die with their bodies. Thus they live like beasts without thought, without regard and without restraint. These Indians are warlike and wage great wars, one tribe against the other; they are never at peace with one another, nor can they live on friendly terms, because one tribe fights against another, many are killed and so their hatred goes on increasing more and more [with each encounter], and they remain real enemies perpetually. The arms with which they fight are bows and arrows; whatever they aim at they hit; they are very accurate with this arm and much feared in war; they are expert in its use, and are much inclined to fight; they are very valiant and impetuous against their adversaries; and therefore it is a strange sight to witness two or three thousand naked men on opposite sides, shooting arrows at one another with shrieks and cries; all during this contest they are not still a moment, but leap from one place to another with much agility, so that the enemy can not aim at them nor shoot at any particular person: some of the old women are accustomed to gather up the arrows on the ground and serve them while they fight. This is

a very bold people which fears death but little; when they go to war, it always seems to them that victory is certain and that none of their company is to die; and when they leave they say, "We are going out to kill," without any other thought, nor do they believe that they themselves can be conquered.

They spare the life of none of their captives, but kill all and eat them, so that their wars are very perilous and should be considered seriously, because one of the reasons which have been the undoing of many Portuguese has been the great indifference with which they regarded fighting with the Indians, and the small concern which they felt for it; and so many of them have died miserably for not having prepared themselves as they should have; among them there have been disastrous deaths, and this is happening at each step in those regions. If at the time of their impetuous rush these Indians do not kill, but capture some of their enemies, they bring them alive to their villages, whether they be Portuguese or of some enemy Indian tribe. As soon as they arrive at their houses, they place a very thick rope about the neck of the captive in order that he may not flee; they hang up for him a net in which to sleep, and give him an Indian girl, the most beautiful and honoured in the village, to sleep with him; she is also charged with guarding him, and he goes nowhere unaccompanied by her. The Indian girl is charged with providing him well with food and drink; and after they have kept him in this way five or six months, or as long as they please, they decide to kill him. They celebrate great ceremonies and feasts in those days, and prepare much wine on which to get drunk; this is made of the root of a plant called *aypim* which is first boiled; after it is cooked, some Indian virgins chew it and spit the juice into large jars, and in three or four days they drink it. On the morning of the day on which they kill the captive, they take him to bathe in a stream, if there is one near the village, with much singing and dancing; when they arrive with him in the village they tie about his waist four cords, one stretching in each direction, with three or four Indians attached to each end; in this way they lead him to the middle of the plaza, and pull so much on each of these cords that it is impossible for him to move in any direction; they leave his hands free because they enjoy seeing him defend himself with them. The man who is designated to kill him first decks his whole body with parrot feathers of many colours; this executioner must be the most valiant and most honoured of the country. He carries in his hand a sword of very hard, heavy wood, with which they are accustomed to kill; and he comes up to the victim saying many things to him, threatening his entire posterity and his relatives: having insulted him with many injurious words, he gives him a heavy blow on the head which breaks his head in pieces and kills him on the spot. There is an old Indian woman by with a gourd in her hand who,

as soon as the victim falls, approaches very quickly and puts this
to his head, in order to catch the brains and blood. Finally, they cook
or roast and eat every part of him, so that none of him remains. This
they do more for the sake of vengeance than on account of hatred
or to satisfy their appetites. After they have eaten the flesh of these
enemies, they remain more confirmed in their hatred; because this
injury is felt keenly, they are always desirous of taking vengeance.
If the girl with whom the captive slept is pregnant, they kill the child
she bears, after it is weaned; they cook it and say that that child, boy
or girl, is verily their enemy, and therefore they are very desirous of
eating its flesh and taking vengeance upon it. And because the mother
knows the end destined for the child, often when she is pregnant she
kills the child in the womb and produces abortion. It sometimes happens that she falls so deeply in love with the captive and becomes so
enamoured of him that she flees with him to his country, in order
to save his life; hence there are living today some Portuguese who
have thus escaped. Many Indians have saved themselves in the same
manner, although some of them are so brutish that they do not wish
to flee after they have been taken. Once there was an Indian already
tied in the plaza to be killed, and they gave him his life; he did not
desire it, but wished them to kill him, for, said he, his relatives would
not consider him brave, and all of them would avoid him; hence it
comes about that they do not fear death; and when that hour arrives
they are imperturbable, and show no sadness in that pass. Finally,
those Indians are very inhuman and cruel; no piety moves them; they
live like brute beasts without the order or concord of men; they are
very dissolute and given to sensuality, yielding to vice as though they
lacked human reason; although they always have certain reserve, the
males and females in their congress, thereby manifesting a certain
sense of modesty. They all eat human flesh and consider it the best
of their dishes, not that of their friends with whom they are at peace,
but that of their enemies. These Indians have this quality, that whatever they eat, however small the quantity, they must invite all present
to share with them; this is the only charitable conception found among
them. They eat whatever insects grow in the country, rejecting none,
no matter how poisonous, except spiders. The male Indians have the
custom of pulling out all their beard, and do not allow hair to grow
on any part of the body except the head, and they pull it out even
from the lower part of this. The females pride themselves much on
their hair, and wear it braided with ribbons. The males are accustomed to wear the lips pierced and a stone placed in the hole for decoration; there are others who have the entire face full of holes, thereby
appearing very ugly and disfigured; this is done to them when they
are children. Some of these Indians also have the entire body painted
with a certain dye, in lines of many patterns; they always paint them-

selves with the same designs; they do not wear these designs unless they have performed some deed of valour. Moreover, the males as well as the females are accustomed to dye themselves with the juice of a fruit which is called *genipapo;* this is green when squeezed out, and after they have placed it on their bodies and it has dried, it turns very black; however much one bathes, it can not be removed for nine days; they do all this for adornment. The Indian women are faithful to their husbands and are very friendly with them, because adultery is not tolerated. Most of the men marry their nieces, the daughters of their brothers or sisters; these are their true wives, and the fathers of the women can not refuse their request. In these regions there are some Indian women who take an oath of chastity, and hence do not marry, or have commerce with men in any respect; nor would they consent to it, even if their refusal meant death. These give up all functions of women and imitate the men, pursuing the functions of the latter as though they were not women; they cut their hair, wearing it in the same way as the males, they go to war with their bows and arrows, and hunt; in a word, they always go in company with the men, and each one has a woman to serve her, who provides food for her as if they two were married. The Indian men live very much at ease; they think about nothing except eating, drinking, and killing people; for this reason, they grow very fat, and when anything worries them they become very thin; if any one is vexed at anything, he eats earth; and in this way many of them die like beasts. All are prone to follow the advice of the old women; their every suggestion is acted upon, and is believed to be true; hence it occurs that many inhabitants will not buy the old women [for slaves], so that these will not have an opportunity to cause their slaves to flee. When these Indian women give birth, their first act after birth is to wash themselves in a river, after which they are just as lusty as if they had not given birth. Instead of the woman, her husband remains in his hammock, and is visited and treated as though he were the one who had given birth. When one of these Indians dies, they are accustomed to bury him in a hole seated upon his feet, with the net in which he slept at his back, and then for the first few days they place something to eat over the grave.

2. THE PORTUGUESE COLONIZER

Unlike the Spanish conquistadores, who roamed through jungles and mountains in search of golden kingdoms, their Portuguese counterparts were content to remain on the fertile coast

of Northeast Brazil, where they established a plantation economy producing sugar for the world market. Yet the Portuguese colonizer could deal hard blows when necessity required, as shown by the story of Duarte Coelho, who undertook to settle the captaincy of Pernambuco. Gabriel Soares de Souza, a planter of Baía who wrote one of the earliest and most valuable accounts of colonial Brazil, tells of Duarte's exploits.[2]

✦✦✦✦ The town of Olinda is the capital of the captaincy of Pernambuco, which was settled by Duarte Coelho, a gentleman of whose courage and chivalry I shall not speak here in detail, for the books that deal with India are full of his deeds. After Duarte Coelho returned from India to Portugal to seek a reward for his services, he sought and obtained from His Highness the grant of a captaincy on this coast; this grant began at the mouth of the São Francisco River in the northwest and ran fifty leagues up the coast toward the captaincy of Tamaracá, ending at the Igaruçu River. . . . Since this brave captain was always disposed to perform great feats, he determined to come in person to settle and conquer this his captaincy. He arrived there with a fleet of ships that he had armed at his own cost, in which he brought his wife and children and many of their kinsmen, and other settlers. With this fleet he made port at the place called Pernambuco, which in the native language means "hidden sea," because of a rock nearby that is hidden in the sea. Arriving at this port, Duarte Coelho disembarked and fortified himself as well as he could on a high point free of any dominating peaks, where the town is today. There he built a strong tower, which still stands in the town square, and for many years he waged war against the natives and the French who fought at their side. Frequently he was besieged and badly wounded, with the loss of many of his people, but he courageously persisted in his aim, and not only defended himself bravely but attacked his enemies so effectively that they abandoned the neighboring lands. Later his son, of the same name, continued to wage war on them, harassing and capturing these people, called Cayté, until they had abandoned the whole coast and more than fifty leagues in the interior. In these labors Duarte spent many thousands of *cruzados* that he had acquired in India, and this money was really well spent, for today his son Jorge de Albuquerque Coelho enjoys an income of ten thousand *cruzados*, which he obtains from the retithe,[3] from his tithe of the fishing catch, and from the quit rent paid him by the sugar-

---

[2] Gabriel Soares de Souza, *Tratado descriptivo do Brazil em 1587*, São Paulo, 1938, pp. 27-29. (Excerpt translated by the editor.)
[3] The retithe was a tenth of all tithes collected by the king in his capacity of Master of the Order of Christ; it was paid to the donatory. B.K.

mills (fifty of these have been established in Pernambuco, and they produce so much sugar that the tithes on it yield nineteen thousand *cruzados* a year).

This town of Olinda must have about seven hundred house-holders, but there are many more within the limits of the town, since from twenty to thirty people live on each of these plantations, aside from the many who live on farms. Hence if it were necessary to assemble these people with arms, they could place in the field more than three thousand fighting men, together with the inhabitans of the town of Cosmos, which must have four hundred mounted men. These people could bring from their estates four or five thousand Negro slaves and many Indians. This captaincy is so prosperous that there are more than a hundred men in it who have an income of from one to five thousand *cruzados*, and some have incomes of eight to ten thousand *cruzados*. From this land many men have returned rich to Portugal who came here poor, and every year this captaincy sends forty to fifty ships loaded with sugar and brazilwood; this wood is so profitable to His Majesty that he has lately farmed out the concession for a period of ten years at twenty thousand *cruzados* a year. It seems to me that such a powerful captaincy, which yields this kingdom such a great store of provisions, should be better fortified, and should not be exposed for a corsair to sack and destroy — which could be prevented with little expense and less labor.

3. THE SLAVE-HUNTERS

The expanding plantation economy of the Brazilian Northeast required a steady supply of cheap labor. The Portuguese met the problem with raids on Indian villages, returning with trains of captives who were sold to plantation owners. These aggressions were the primary cause of the chronic warfare between the natives and the whites. Indian labor was quite unsatisfactory from an economic point of view, and after 1550 it began to be replaced by that of Negro slaves imported from Africa. But the supply of African slaves was often cut off or sharply reduced by the activities of Dutch privateers and other foreign foes, and Brazilian slave-hunters continued to find a market for their human prey throughout the seventeenth century. The men of São Paulo, lacking the sugar and brazilwood on which the prosperity of the Northeast was based, turned to slave-hunting as a lucrative occupation. The prospect of finding gold in the interior made their expeditions doubly attractive. As the coastal Indians were exterminated or fled before the in-

vaders, the bandeirantes, *the "men of the banner," pushed ever deeper south and west, expanding the frontiers of Brazil in the process. Almost the only voices raised against their predatory activities were those of the Jesuit missionaries. One of them, believed to be the famous Father Anchieta (1534–1597), describes the devastation wrought by the slave-hunters.*[4]

✠✠✠✠ The number of Indians that have been destroyed in this captaincy of Baía in the past twenty years passes belief; who would think that so many people could be destroyed in so short a time? In the fourteen churches maintained by the Fathers they had brought together 40,000 souls, by count, and even more, counting those who came after — yet today it is doubtful whether the three churches that remain have 3,500 souls together. Six years ago an honored citizen of this city, a man of good conscience and a city official at the time, said that in the two preceding years 20,000 souls, by count, had been brought from the back country of Arabó and that all of them went to the Portuguese plantations. These 20,000, added to the 40,000 of the churches, come to 60,000. Now for the past six years the Portuguese have been bringing Indians for their plantations, one bringing 2,000, another 3,000, some more, others less; in six years this must come to 80,000 souls or more. Now look at the sugar-mills and plantations of Baía, and you will find them full of Guinea Negroes but very few natives; if you ask what happened to all those people, they will tell you that they died.

In this way God has severely punished the Portuguese for the many offenses that they committed and still commit against these Indians, for they go into the interior and deceive these people, inviting them to go to the coast, where, they say, they would live in their villages as they did in their lands, and the Portuguese would be their neighbors. The Indians, believing this, go with them, and for fear they will change their minds the Portuguese destroy their gardens. On arrival at the coast they divide the Indians among themselves, some taking the women, others their husbands, and still others the children, and they sell them. Other Portuguese go into the interior and entice the Indians by saying that they will take them to the churches of the Fathers; and by this means they seduce them from their lands, for it is common knowledge in the backlands that only the Indians in the churches where the Fathers reside enjoy liberty and all the rest are captives. Matters reached such a point that a certain Portuguese, going into the back country in search of Indians, shaved his head like a priest, saying that he was a Father seeking Indians for the churches.

[4] *Cartas, Informaçoes, Fragmentos Históricos e Sermões do Padre Joseph de Anchieta, S. J. (1554–1594)*. Rio de Janeiro, 1933, pp. 377–378. (Excerpt translated by the editor.)

This happened at a time when Father Gaspar Lourenço was bound for the interior, and he found these people on the road. When they heard that the Father was going into the backlands they said: "How can that be, when he who brings us says that he is a Father, and that is why we go with him?" And the Portuguese with the shaven head hid himself, not wanting the priest to see him.

The Portuguese travel 250 and 300 leagues to find the Indians, for the nearest ones are by now a great distance away, and since the land is now depopulated most of them die on the road from hunger. There have been Portuguese who seized on the road certain Indians who were enemies of the ones they were bringing, killed them, and gave their flesh to their captives to eat. And when all these people arrive at the coast, seeing that the Portuguese do not keep the promises they made in the interior but separate them from each other, some flee into the forests, never to emerge again, and others die from grief and chagrin that they, who had been free men, should be made slaves.

4. AIMORÉ: WORD OF TERROR

The Brazilian Indian did not accept the loss of his land and liberty without a struggle. Indian resistance to white aggression was handicapped by the fatal propensity of the tribes to war against each other, a situation that the Portuguese utilized for their own advantage. Forced to retreat into the interior by the superior arms and organization of the whites, the natives often returned to make destructive forays on isolated Portuguese communities. As late as the first part of the nineteenth century stretches of the Brazilian shore were made uninhabitable by the raids of Indians who lurked in the forests and mountains back of the coast. "The coast from Espiritu Santo to Bahia was practically abandoned," says the historian Calogeras, "and even today reveals large gaps in its population as a consequence of these attacks." One tribe that never sought or granted a truce to the whites was that of the ferocious Aimorés. The chronicler Soares de Souza describes their mode of life and warfare.[5]

❖❖❖❖ It seems proper at this point to state what kind of people are those called Aimorés, who have done so much damage to this captaincy of Ilheos, as I have said. The coast of this captaincy used to

[5] Soares de Souza, *Tratado Descriptivo do Brasil*, pp. 56–60. (Excerpt translated by the editor.)

be inhabited by the Tupiniquins, who abandoned it from fear of these brutes and went to live in the back country; at the present time there are only two very small Tupiniquin villages, situated near the sugar mills of Henrique Luiz.

These Aimorés are descended from other people that they call Tapuias, from whom departed in olden times certain families that went to live in very rugged mountains, fleeing from a defeat inflicted on them by their enemies; and there they lived many years without seeing any other people; and their descendants gradually lost their language, and developed a new one that is not understood by any other nation in the whole country of Brazil. These Aimorés are so savage that the other barbarians consider them worse than barbarians. Some of these were taken alive in Porto Seguro and in Ilheos, and they would not eat, preferring to die like savages.

This people first came to the sea at the River Caravellas, hard by Porto Seguro, and roamed this countryside and the beaches as far as the River Camamú; from there they began to launch attacks near Tinharé, descending to the shore only when they came to make an attack. This people is of the same color as the others, but they are larger and of more robust build. They have no beards or any other hair except on their heads, because they pluck out the hairs on the other parts of their bodies. They fight with very large bows and arrows, and are such excellent bowmen that they never miss a shot; they are marvelously light on their feet, and great runners.

These barbarians do not live in villages or houses like other people, and so far no one has come across their dwellings in the woods; they go from one place to another through the woods and fields; they sleep on the ground on leaves; and if it rains they go up to the foot of a tree and squat there, covering themselves with leaves; no other furnishings have ever been found among them. These savages do not have gardens or raise any food; they live on wild fruit and the game they kill, which they eat raw or poorly roasted, when they have a fire. Both men and women cut their hair short, shearing it with certain canes of which they gather a great number; their speech is rough, projected from their throats with much force; like Basque, it is impossible to write down.

These barbarians live by robbing everyone they encounter, and one never sees more than twenty or thirty bowmen at one time. They never fight anyone face to face, but always employ treachery, for they attack in the fields and roads which they travel, waiting in ambush for other Indians and all other sorts of persons, each hidden behind a tree and never missing a shot. They use up all their arrows, and if the people turn on them they all flee in different directions, but if they see that their pursuers have dropped their guard they stop and find a place to hide until their pursuers have passed, when they

shoot them in the back with their arrows at will. They do not know how to swim, and any river that cannot be forded presents an adequate defense against them; but in order to find a crossing they will go many miles along the river in search of one.

These savages eat human flesh for sustenance — unlike the other Indians, who only eat it for the sake of revenge and in memory of their ancient hatreds. The captaincies of Porto Seguro and Ilheos have been destroyed and almost depopulated by fear of these barbarians, and the sugar mills have stopped working because all the slaves and the other people have been killed by them. The people on most of the plantations and those who have escaped from them have become so afraid of them that if they merely hear the word "Aimorés" they leave their plantations in search of refuge, the white men among them. In the twenty-five years that this plague has afflicted these two captaincies, they have killed more than 300 Portuguese and 3,000 slaves.

The inhabitants of Baía used to send letters to the people of Ilheos, and men traveled this road along the shore without danger. But when the Aimorés realized this they decided to come to these beaches to wait for the people who passed there, and there they killed many Portuguese and many more slaves. These bandits are such fleet runners that no one could escape them on foot, except those who take refuge in the sea; they dare not enter the ocean, but wait for them to come on shore until nightfall, when they retire. For this reason the road is forbidden, and no one travels it except at great risk of his life. If some means is not found to destroy these savages they will destroy the plantations of Baía, through which they roam at will. Since they are such intractable enemies of all mankind, it was not possible to learn more about their mode of life and customs.

5. THE DUTCH IN BRAZIL

The dyewood, the sugar, and the tobacco of Portuguese Brazil early excited the cupidity of foreign powers. For almost a century (1520–1615) the French, aided by friendly Indians, made sporadic efforts to establish themselves in the country. A greater threat to Portuguese sovereignty over Brazil came from the Dutch, who seized and occupied for a quarter of a century (1630–1654) the richest sugar-growing portions of the Brazilian coast. Under the administration of Prince Maurice of Nassau (1637–1644) Dutch Brazil, with its capital at Recife, was the scene of a brilliant scientific and artistic activity. But in 1654 the Dutch, weakened by revolt and war with England,

*were forced to evacuate the province, and before long almost
all trace of their presence had disappeared. Robert Southey
(1744–1843), author of a classic history of colonial Brazil, sums
up the achievements of the Dutch in Brazil.[6]*

✤✤✤✤ From the Potengi to the S. Francisco, the Dutch were in possession when the restoration of the Portuguese monarchy made them
apparently secure in their conquests. This portion of Brazil was then
called New Holland, in the maps; that appellation, however, was
destined to designate a more extensive country in a different part of
the world; and the New Holland of the West India Company, like
the Antarctic France of Villegagnon, soon became an empty name,
exemplifying the shortsightedness of presumptuous ambition. The
Dutch deserved to lose these possessions for the treachery with which
they attempted to extend their conquests during the truce, the baseness with which they sought to take advantage of the helpless state
of Portugal, their blind unfeeling avarice, and that brutal cruelty
which in all their foreign territories has characterized them: but they
were not without some redeeming qualities. Under Prince Mauritz
of Nassau great efforts were made for exploring the country, civilizing the Tapuyas, and improving the general condition of the people.
His bridges, his palace, and his city, remain monuments of his wise
and splendid administration; but they are not the only, nor the most
durable materials. He took out with him scholars, naturalists, and
draughtsmen. His actions were celebrated in Latin verse by Franciscus
Plante, and by Barlaeus in a Latin history worthy of the reputation
of its author. The work of Marcgraff and Piso is the first which appeared upon the natural history of Brazil; and the views in Barlaeus
were the first graphic representations of Brazilian scenery and manners.

Elias Herckmann was sent by Nassau into the interior of Pernambuco in search of mines. The attempt was unsuccessful; but he
discovered vestiges of some forgotten people who possessed the country before the present race of savages, and of whom not even the
most vague tradition had been preserved. He found two huge perfectly round stones, manifestly rounded by art, and placed by art one
upon another, the largest being uppermost; they were sixteen feet in
diameter, and the thickness such that a man standing on the ground
could scarcely reach to the middle: and on the following day he came
to some other stones, of such magnitude that it seemed impossible for
any human strength to have moved them; they were piled up like
altars, and Herckmann compares them to some monuments at Drent
in Belgium. . . .

[6] Robert Southey, *History of Brazil*, London, 3 vols., 1810–1819, II, pp. 651–659.

Great and commendable zeal was shown, not only under Nassau's administration, but as long as the Dutch continued in the country, for promulgating the reformed religion. There were Protestant ministers at Olinda, Itamaraca, Paraíba, Cape St. Augustines, and Serinhaem, and three at Recife. Some of them acquired the Tupi, and with what success they had labored among the Indians may be apprehended by the jealousy with which Vieyra regarded those who had been under their pastoral care. They laboured in civilizing as well as converting them. It has been seen, that in the Serra de Ibiapaba paper and sealing wax were in use, and that there were Indians there as well able to read and understand the laws as the Portuguese themselves. But although the government meant well toward the aboriginal inhabitants, and some of the clergy did their duty with eminent zeal and success, the conduct of the Dutch in general, both to the Indians and Negroes, was marked with that deep depravity which has characterized them in all their colonies. During the war their privateers seized all the Indians whom they found fishing, and kidnapped as many as they could catch on shore, and sold them to the Sugar Islands. Of six thousand four hundred imported Negroes, more than fifteen hundred died within a year and a half, and Nassau himself imputed this frightful mortality to their unwholesome or insufficient food on the voyage, and to their sufferings. It appears also that these wretched slaves frequently attempted to murder their inhuman masters, and when they failed in the attempt, delivered themselves by poison from a life of insupportable misery.

The conquerors introduced some improvements while they held the country. A people who were accustomed to such cleanliness at home could not tolerate the filth of a Portuguese city, and the streets of Recife under their government were regularly cleaned. They cultivated culinary herbs, which were soon propagated in every garden, and found their way into every kitchen; but the war put an end to horticulture, and this benefit seems to have been only transient. They reared vines with some success, procured a succession of grapes, and made a wine the excellence of which is expressed by saying that it was not inferior to the Cretan. The soldiers preferred mandioc to wheat, thinking it a stronger food. In other points the Dutch were more tenacious of old habits. Though the Brazilians, as it was said, dreamt of disease and death if they dwelt upon the lowlands, the Hollanders, with that obstinate attachment to swamps and standing water which has cost the lives of so many thousands at Batavia, built everywhere upon the plains and morasses. Such situations were suited to their mode of fortification, and they had need to fortify themselves. They experienced less injury than had been predicted, probably less than any other people would have done: their diet, which was more generous than that of the Portuguese, and their habit of

smoking, serving to counteract the pernicious effects of marsh exhalation, and their constitutions also being habituated to such an atmosphere. Their women, however, suffered greatly from the change of climate; for they neither drank nor smoked; and, as was the case at first with the Portuguese women, they reared very few children. They found it necessary to have Indian or Negress nurses, whose custom it was never to wean the infant until the end of the second year, and rarely so soon.

The whole country which they possessed, from the Potengi to the Lagoas, was cultivated only in patches. The cultivation usually extended from twelve to fifteen miles inland, seldom farther, and never more than one or two and twenty; but none of the Dutch settled more than eight miles from the coast, as much for fear of the savages and the Portuguese, as for the convenience of trade. Between one *freguezia* or parish, and another, there was usually a solitary track of ten or twelve miles, perhaps of greater extent. Salt works and fishermen's huts were sometimes found in these uncultivated parts, but all the rest was a wilderness, which the settled part of the inhabitants had never explored. The admirable industry of the Dutch had not time to display itself; and what branches of industry they found there suffered considerably during the war. A lucrative fishery upon the coast was entirely neglected after their conquest; they attempted to restore it during the truce, but the renewal of hostilities put an end to it. The Portuguese government permitted only ten thousand *quintaes* of Brazil to be felled yearly, that valuable wood being the property of the crown. The Dutch felled it without restriction, and cut down young trees as well as old: Nassau recommended that the Portuguese system should be observed, and that severe penalties should be inflicted upon those who destroyed the young trees. They were not acquainted with the process of making sugar when they arrived. When Vieyra argued for the cession of these provinces he urged their unskilfulness as a reason why the sugar trade would not be injured by it, that of the Portuguese captaincies bearing a better price and being in greater demand. But it is not possible that any nation can keep arts of this kind to itself, so as always to prevent other people, under circumstances equally favorable, from rivalling them. Under the expulsion of the Dutch they carried with them some Negroes who were perfectly acquainted with the management of an *Engenho;* these men instructed the French at Guadaloupe, and thus enabled them first to compete with the Portuguese sugar, and soon to supersede it in many of its markets.

Before the invasion Olinda was the most flourishing of all the colonial possessions of the Portuguese, and perhaps, it is said, the richest. Ships of all sizes were continually arriving and departing, yet there was scarcely tonnage to carry away the sugar, more of which

was raised at that time in Pernambuco than in Bahia. The ships from Peru which put back on their voyage, or which had evaded the duties in the port from whence they sailed, discharged the best part of their treasures here. Those who were not served in plate were regarded as poor. The women were not satisfied with wearing silks and satins, unless they were of the richest embroidery, and they were so profusely decked with jewels that it seemed, says F. Manoel do Salvador, as if pearls, rubies, emeralds, and diamonds had been showered upon them. Every new fashion in apparel, or in the furniture of swords and daggers, was instantly followed by the men, and the choicest delicacies of Portugal and the Western Islands were regularly imported for their tables. "The place," says the Friar, "hardly appeared like earth; it seemed rather an image of Paradise, as far as opulence and dissipation could make it so." The war proved fatal to this prosperity. "When first I beheld Olinda," says Vieyra, "the nobleness of her edifices, her temples and her towers, her valleys everywhere adorned, and her hills covered with green and loftiest palms, she seemed like a beautiful and most delicious garden, worthy of her name, and of being pictured that all the world might behold her. Now what is there but a desert, a solitude, a shapeless carcass, a dismal sepulchre without a name!" A flourishing city had risen at the port, but Recife had not succeeded to the splendor of its former capital. When Rennefort visited it in 1666 it contained, according to his computation, about three hundred indifferent houses, besides some others so wretchedly constructed that he seems to have considered them as hovels unworthy of being included in the account. They were all of only one floor. There were about an hundred more in S. Antonio, as Mauritias was now called, the founder having given place to the favorite saint of the Portuguese. But the works of that founder outlasted his name; the Governor resided in his palace; and the French traveler speaks with delight of the fragrance and beauty of the groves which Prince Mauritz had planted with such magnificence.

Though the Dutch were twenty-five years in the country, there had been very little intermixture of the two nations; the difference of religion was too great an obstacle, both parties being sincere, and regarding each other's religion with mutual contempt, mingled however, on the part of the Papists, with the fiercest and most intolerant abhorrence. The few intermarriages which occurred were with Portuguese women. Most of these would naturally follow their husbands upon their expulsion; but if the husbands chose to remain in the country among their new connections, if they did not conform themselves to the dominant superstition, their children fell into it of course, and in another generation no trace remained either of the religion, language, or manners of Holland. The ambitious struggle which the Dutch carried on so long, with such inhumanity, and such an expense

of treasure and blood, produced no other benefit than that of proving, as a warning for other powers, how impossible it is to effect a permanent conquest of Brazil. A people of such determined nationality as the Portuguese, in such a country, are invincible by any human force.

6. THE RISE AND FALL OF VILLA RICA

When the Dutch withdrew from Brazil they transferred their skills in sugar growing to their West Indian colonies. English and French planters in the Caribbean area also began to compete with Brazilian sugar producers. Thanks to their superior techniques and closer proximity to European ports, the West Indian growers were able to take over many of Brazil's best foreign markets. By the last decade of the seventeenth century the sugar cycle of the Northeast had about run its course. It was at this time of acute depression that the discovery of gold in Minas Gerais (1690) gave a new stimulus to Brazil's economic life, led to the first effective settlement of the interior, and began a major shift in the center of economic and political gravity from north to south. Like its predecessor, the mineral cycle was marked by rapid and superficial exploitation of the new sources of wealth, followed by an even swifter decline. The story of the rise and fall of the gold-mining center of Villa Rica is told by John Mawe (1764–1829), who visited it at the opening of the nineteenth century.[7]

The history of an establishment which, twenty years after its foundation, was reputed the richest place on the globe, was an object of considerable interest to me, and I made many inquiries respecting it from some of the best informed men on the spot. It appears that the first discovery of this once rich mountain was effected by the enterprising spirit of the Paulistas, who, of all the colonists in Brazil, retained the largest share of that ardent and indefatigable zeal for discovery which characterized the Lusitanians of former days. They penetrated from their capital into these regions, braving every hardship, and encountering every difficulty which a savage country, infested by still more savage inhabitants, opposed to them. They cut their way through impervious woods, carrying their provisions with them, and occasionally cultivating small patches of land to afford them food to retreat to, in case of necessity, as well as to keep up a communication with their city, St. Paul's. Every inch of ground was dis-

[7] John Mawe, *Travels in the Interior of Brazil*, London, 1815, pp. 171–177.

puted by the barbarous Indians, here called Bootocoodies, who were constantly either attacking them openly or lying in ambush, and but too frequently succeeded in surprising some of them, or their negroes, whom they immediately sacrificed to their horrible appetite for human flesh. They believed the negroes to be the great monkeys of the wood. The bones of the unfortunate sufferers were frequently found exposed, shocking testimonies of the barbarity of their murderers, whom the Paulistas, roused to revenge, invariably shot, wherever they met them. These examples of venegance answered their desired end; the Indians, terrified as well by the noise as by the fatal effect of the fire-arms, fled with precipitation, believing that the white men commanded lightning and thunder.

It does not appear that in exploring this territory they received any assistance whatever from the Aborigines; they followed the course of rivers, occasionally finding gold, of which they skimmed the surface, and continued to proceed until they arrived at the mountain which is our present subject. Its riches arrested their course; they immediately erected temporary houses and began their operations. The principal men of the party that first settled here, were Antonio Dias, Bartholomew Rocinho, Antonio de Ferrera (filho), and Garcia Ruis. It appears that they took the most direct way to the place, for the roads they then opened are the same which are still used. The fame of their success soon reached the city of St. Paul's; fresh adventurers arrived in great numbers, bringing with them all the negroes they had means to purchase. Other adventurers went from St. Paul's to Rio de Janeiro to procure more negroes, their own city being drained; and thus the news of the lately discovered gold-mountain being made known in the Brazilian capital, men of all descriptions went in crowds to this land of promise by the way of St. Paul's, which was the only route then known. The first settlers might have prevented the exposure of their good fortune, had they been able to moderate their joy, and consented to act in concert; but as gold was in such great abundance, every individual appropriated a lot of ground, and thus became a capitalist. Each strove which should make the most of his treasure in the shortest time, and thus there was a continual demand for more negroes, more iron, etc. and, in the general eagerness to obtain them, the secret which all were interested in keeping was disclosed. The Paulistas, independent in spirit, and proud of their wealth, were desirous of giving laws to the new-comers; but the latter determining to oppose this measure, formed themselves into a party under the guidance of Manuel Nuñez Viana, an adventurer of some consequence, who strenuously asserted their claim to equal rights and advantages. Disputes arose on both sides, and were at length aggravated into hostilities, which proved unfavourable to the Paulistas, the great part of whom fled to a considerable station of their own, and there

awaited reinforcements. Viana and his followers, without loss of time, went in pursuit of their foes, whom they found on a plain near the site of St. João del Rey. The two parties met on the borders of a river, and a sanguinary battle took place, which ended in the defeat of the Paulistas, who afterwards made the best terms they could. The slain were buried on the margin of the river, which, from that circumstance took the name of Rio dos Mortos.

The Paulistas, bent on revenge, but weakened by defeat, appealed to the sovereign, King Pedro, denouncing Viana and his followers as rebels who were attempting to take the district to themselves, and set up an independent government. The King's ministers, apprized of the state of affairs, and learning by report the immense riches of the country, immediately sent a chief, with a competent body of troops, to take advantage of the strife between the two parties; which, in a country tenable by a few men on account of its numerous strongholds, was a most fortunate circumstance. The name of this chief was Albuquerque; a man of enterprize and perseverance, in all respects qualified for the service on which he was sent. His appearance at first occasioned much confusion and discontent among both parties; and though he was not openly opposed, yet he was in continual alarm. The Paulistas now saw that the riches which they in conjunction with their rivals might have retained, were about to be seized by a third party which would reduce them both to subordination. Disturbances prevailed for some time, but reinforcements continually arriving from Government, tranquillity was at length perfectly established; and in the year 1711 a regular town began to be formed; a government-house, a mint, and a depot for arms were built. A code of laws was enacted for the regulation of the mines; all gold-dust found was ordered to be delivered to officers appointed for that purpose; a fifth in weight was taken for the King, and the remaining four parts were purified, melted into ingots at the expence of Government, then assayed, marked according to their value, and delivered to the owners, with a certificate to render them current. For the greater convenience of trade, gold-dust was likewise permitted to circulate for small payments. Notwithstanding these strict regulations, a considerable quantity of the precious metal in its original state found its way to Rio de Janeiro, Bahai, and other ports, clandestinely, without paying the royal fifth, until Government, apprized of this illicit traffic, established registers in various parts for the examination of all passengers, and stationed soldiers to patrol the roads. By these means, gold in immense quantities was seized and confiscated; the persons on whom any was found forfeited all their property, and, unless they had friends of great influence, were sent as convicts to Africa for life. The greatest disgrace was attached to the name of smuggler; and such was the rigour of the law against offenders of this description,

that every person quitting the district was obliged to take a certificate stating whither he was going, and what he carried with him. This regulation is still in force, and is rigorously observed.

Villa Rica soon enjoyed a considerable trade with Rio de Janeiro; the returns were negroes, iron, woollens, salt, provisions of various kinds, and wine, all which at that time bore amazingly high profits.

About the year 1713, when Dr. Bras de Silvia was appointed governor, the quantity of gold produced was so considerable that the royal fifth amounted to half a million sterling annually. The mountain became pierced like a honeycomb, as the miners worked every soft part they could find, and penetrated as far as they could, conveying the *cascalhão* which they dug out to a convenient place for washing. In rainy weather the torrents of water running down the sides of the mountain, carried away much earthy matter containing delicate particles of gold, which settled in the ground near its base. When the waters abated, this rich deposit gave employment to numbers of the poorer sort of people, who took it away and washed it at their convenience.

Antonio Dias, the person already mentioned as one of the leaders of the Paulistas, who discovered the place, having become extremely rich, built a fine church, and dying soon after, bequeathed to it considerable funds. It still bears his name. Five or six others were begun and soon finished, as neither wood nor stone was wanting, and the inhabitants were all ready to contribute a share of their property, and to employ their negroes in furtherance of these pious works. A law highly creditable to the wisdom of the Portuguese government was now enacted, to prohibit friars from entering the territory of the mines. What treasures were thus saved to the state, and what a number of persons were thus continued in useful labour, who would else have become burthensome to the community!

The town now underwent many improvements; its streets were more regularly built, and some parts of the side of the mountain were levelled to afford more convenient room for the construction of houses, and the laying out of gardens. Reservoirs were formed, from which water was distributed by means of conduits to all parts, and public fountains were erected in the most convenient and central situations. The mint and smelting-houses were enlarged, and rendered more commodious for the transaction of business. About this period the inhabitants amounted to twelve thousand or upwards; those who possessed mines were either the first settlers or their descendants, and as the best part of the district was occupied, the new adventurers who continued to arrive from time to time were obliged to enter into the service of the existing owners until they had learned their methods of working, after which they generally went in search of fresh mines,

proceeding along the water-courses and ravines, where they sometimes discovered new sources of wealth. Between the years 1730 and
1750 the mines were in the height of their prosperity; the King's fifth
during some years of that period is said to have amounted to at least
a million sterling annually.

The mines which produced this immense wealth at length became gradually less abundant; and, as the precious metal disappeared,
numbers of the miners retired, some to the mother-country, loaded
with riches, which tempted fresh adventurers, and many to Rio de
Janeiro and other sea-ports, where they employed their large capitals
in commerce.

Villa Rica at the present day scarcely retains a shadow of its
former splendour. Its inhabitants, with the exception of the shopkeepers, are void of employment; they totally neglect the fine country
around them, which, by proper cultivation, would amply compensate for the loss of the wealth which their ancestors drew from its
bosom. Their education, their habits, their hereditary prejudices,
alike unfit them for active life; perpetually indulging in visionary
prospects of sudden wealth, they fancy themselves exempted from
that universal law of nature which ordains that man shall live by the
sweat of his brow. In contemplating the fortunes accumulated by
their predecessors, they overlook the industry and perseverance which
obtained them, and entirely lose sight of the change of circumstances
which renders those qualities now doubly necessary. The successors
of men who rise to opulence from small beginnings seldom follow
the example set before them, even when trained to it; how then should
a Creolian, reared in idleness and ignorance, feel any thing of the
benefits of industry! His negroes constitute his principal property,
and them he manages so ill, that the profits of their labour hardly
defray the expences of their maintenance: in the regular course of
nature they become old and unable to work, yet he continues in the
same listless and slothful way, or sinks into a state of absolute inactivity, not knowing what to do from morning to night. This deplorable degeneracy is almost the universal characteristic of the
descendants of the original settlers; every trade is occupied either by
mulattoes or negroes, both of which classes seem superior in intellect
to their masters, because they make a better use of it.

19 ✤ Government and Church

The Portuguese crown first governed Brazil through donatories or lords proprietors who were given almost complete authority in their territories in return for assuming the responsibilities of colonization. In 1549, convinced that the system had failed to achieve its ends, the king issued a decree limiting the powers of the donatories and creating a central government for all of Brazil. The first captain-general of the colony was Thomé de Souza, and Baía was selected as his capital. Governors appointed by the king, and subordinate to the captain-general, gradually replaced the donatories as the political and military leaders of the captaincies.

During the period of the Spanish Captivity (1580–1640), Spain established a *Conselho da India* for the administration of the Portuguese colonies. After Portugal regained her independence, this body continued to have charge of Brazilian affairs. As the colony expanded, new captaincies or provinces were created. In 1763 the captain-general of Rio de Janeiro replaced his colleague at Baía as head of the colonial administration in Brazil, with the title of viceroy. In practice, however, his authority over the other governors was negligible.

Official inefficiency and corruption seem to have been as common in colonial Brazil as in the Spanish Indies. During the reform

administration of the Marquis de Pombal (1756–1777) the situation improved, but apparently without lasting effects.

The Brazilian Church lacked the immense wealth and influence of its counterpart in the Spanish Indies. By comparison with the Spanish monarchs, the Portuguese kings seemed almost niggardly in their dealings with the Church. But their control over its affairs was equally absolute.

In Brazil, as in the Spanish colonies, the Jesuits carried on intensive missionary work among the Indians. The priests aimed at the settlement of their Indian converts in villages completely isolated from the whites. Their efforts in this direction led to many conflicts with the Portuguese landowners, who wanted to enslave the Indians for work on their plantations. The clash of interests was most severe in São Paulo, whose halfbreed slave-hunters bitterly resented Jesuit interference with their operations.

Like their colleagues in the Spanish colonies, the Brazilian clergy — always excepting the Jesuits and some other orders — were often criticized for their worldly lives and indifference to their charges. Yet such educational and humanitarian establishments as existed were almost exclusively provided by the clergy, and from its ranks came most of the few distinguished names in Brazilian colonial science, learning, and literature.

1. THE ADMINISTRATION OF COLONIAL BRAZIL

The government of Portuguese Brazil broadly resembled that of the Spanish Indies in its spirit, its structure, and its vices. Henry Koster, an astute observer of Brazilian life in the early nineteenth century, describes the political and financial administration of the important province of Pernambuco.[1]

✦✦✦✦ The captaincies-general, or provinces of the first rank, in Brazil, of which Pernambuco is one, are governed by captains-general, or governors, who are appointed for three years. At the end of this period, the same person is continued or not, at the option of the supreme government. They are, in fact, absolute in power: but before the person who has been nominated to one of these places can exercise any of its functions, he is under the necessity of presenting his credentials to the *Senado da Câmara*, the chamber or municipality of the principal town. This is formed of persons of respectability in the place. The governor has the supreme and sole command of the

[1] Henry Koster, *Travels in Brazil*, London, 1816, 2 vols., I, pp. 46–50.

military force. The civil and criminal causes are discussed before, and determined by, the *Ouvidor* and *Juiz de Fora*, the two chief judicial officers, whose duties are somewhat similar: but the former is the superior in rank. They are appointed for three years, and the term may be renewed. It is in these departments of the government that the opportunities of amassing large fortunes are most numerous; and certain it is, that some individuals take advantage of them in a manner which renders justice but a name. The governor can determine in a criminal cause without appeal; but if he pleases, he refers it to the competent judge. The *Procurador da Coroa*, attorney-general, is an officer of considerable weight. The *Intendente da Marinha*, port admiral, is likewise consulted on matters of first importance; as are also the *Escrivão da Fazenda Real*, chief of the treasury, and the *Juiz da Alfândega*, comptroller of the customs. These seven officers form the *Junta*, or council, which occasionally meets to arrange and decide upon the affairs of the captaincy to which they belong.

The ecclesiastical government is scarcely connected with that above mentioned; and is administered by a bishop and a dean and chapter with his vicar-general etc. The governor cannot even appoint a chaplain to the island of Fernando de Noronha, one of the dependencies of Pernambuco; but acquaints the bishop that a priest is wanted, who then nominates one for the place.

The number of civil and military officers is enormous; inspectors innumerable — colonels without end, devoid of any objects to inspect — without any regiments to command; judges to manage each trifling department of which the duties might all be done by two or three persons. Thus salaries are augmented; the people are oppressed; but the state is not benefitted.

Taxes are laid where they fall heavy upon the lower classes: and none are levied where they could well be borne. A tenth is raised in kind upon cattle, poultry, and agriculture, and even upon salt; this in former times appertained, as in other Christian countries, to the clergy.[2] All the taxes are farmed to the highest bidders, and this among the rest. They are parcelled out in extensive districts, and are contracted for at a reasonable rate; but the contractors again dispose of their shares in small portions: these are again retailed to other persons: and as a profit is obtained by each transfer the people must be oppressed, that these men may satisfy those above them and enrich themselves. The system is in itself bad, but is rendered still heavier by this division of the spoil. The tenth of cattle, as I have already

2 When Brazil was in its infancy, the clergy could not subsist on their tithes, and therefore petitioned the government of Portugal to pay them a certain stipend, and receve the tenths for its own account: this was accepted: but now the tenths have increased in value twenty-fold, the government still pays to the vicars the same stipends. The clergy of the present day, bitterly complain of the agreement made by those to whom they have succeeded.

said, is levied in kind upon the estates in the interior of the country: and, besides this, a duty of 320 *reis per arroba* of 32 lbs. is paid upon the meat at the shambles, which amounts to about twenty-five *per cent.* Fish pays the tenth, to a duty of ten *per cent.* and moveables to five *per cent.* Besides these, there are many other taxes of minor importance. Rum, both for exportation and home consumption, pays a duty of 80 *reis per canada*,[3] which is sometimes a fourth of its value; but may be reckoned as from fifteen to twenty *per cent.* Cotton pays the tenth, and is again taxed at the moment of exportation 600 *reis per arroba*, of 32 lbs, or about 1¼ *d. per* lb. Nothing can be more injudicious, than this double duty upon the chief article of exportation from that country to Europe. The duties at the custom house are fifteen *per cent.* upon imports, of which the valuation is left in some measure to the merchant to whom the property belongs. Here, I think, ten *per cent.* more might be raised without being felt. A tax is paid at Pernambuco for lighting the streets of the Rio de Janeiro, whilst those of Recife remain in total darkness.

Now, although the expenses of the provincial governments are great, and absorb a very considerable proportion of the receipts, owing to the number of officers employed in every department, still the salaries of each are, in most instances, much too small to afford a comfortable subsistence. Consequently peculation, bribery, and other crimes of the same description, are to be looked for: and they become so frequent as to escape all punishment or even notice; though there are some men whose character is without reproach. The governor of Pernambuco receives a salary of 4,000,000 *reis*, or about 1000 £ *per annum.* Can this be supposed to be sufficient for a man in his responsible situation, even in a country in which articles of food are cheap? His honour, however, is unimpeached; not one instance did I ever hear mentioned of improper conduct in him. But the temptation and the opportunities of amassing money are very great, and few are the persons who can resist them.

2. LOCAL GOVERNMENT: THE CAPITÃO-MÔR

Away from the few large towns, local government in colonial Brazil in effect meant government by the great landowners or fazendeiros. *In the* câmaras, *or municipal councils, the power of*

[3] A great confusion exists in Brazil respecting measures. Every captaincy has its own, agreeing neither with those of its neighbours, nor with the measures of Portugal, though the same names are used invariably: thus a *canada* and an *alqueire* in Pernambuco represent a much greater quantity than the same denominations in Portugal, and less than in some of the other provinces of Brazil.

these rural magnates was sometimes checked by representatives of the crown or of urban interests, but on their vast estates they were absolute lords. To their personal influence the great planters often joined the authority of office, for the royal governors invariably appointed the capitães-môres, *or district militia officers, from among them. Armed with unlimited power to command, arrest, and punish, the* capitão-môr *(captain-major) became a popular symbol of despotism and oppression. The following selection from Koster's book illustrates his comment that "the whole aspect of the government of Brazil is military."*[4]

✤✤✤✤ I became acquainted and somewhat intimate with the *Capitão-môr* of a neighbouring district, from frequently meeting him, in my evening visits to a Brazilian family. He was about to make the circuit of his district, in the course of a few weeks, and invited one of my friends and myself to accompany him in this review or visit to his officers, to which we readily agreed. It was arranged that he should make us acquainted in due time with the day which he might appoint for setting out, that we might meet him at his sugar-plantation, from whence we were to proceed with him and his suite further into the country.

The *Capitães-môres*, captains-major, are officers of considerable power. They have civil as well as military duties to perform, and ought to be appointed from among the planters of most wealth and individual weight in the several *Termos*, boundaries or districts. But the interest of family or of relations about the Court, have occasioned deviations from this rule; and persons very unfit for these situations, have been sometimes nominated to them. The whole aspect of the government in Brazil is military. All men between the ages of sixteen and sixty, must be enrolled either as soldiers of the line, as militiamen, or as belonging to the body of *Ordenanças*. Of the regular soldiers, I have already spoken in another place. Of the second class, each township has a regiment, of which the individuals, with the exception of the major and adjutant, and in some cases the colonel, do not receive any pay. But they are considered as embodied men; and as such are called out upon some few occasions, in the course of the year, to assemble in uniform, and otherwise accoutred. The expense which must be incurred in this respect, of necessity, precludes the possibility of many persons becoming members of this class, even if the government were desirous of increasing the number of militia regiments. The soldiers of these are subject to their captains, to the colonel, and to the governor of the province. The colonels are either rich planters, or the major or lieutenant-colonel of a regiment of the line is thus promoted

4 Henry Koster, *Travels in Brazil*, I, pp. 252–255.

to the command of one of these; in this case, and in this case only, he receives pay. I am inclined to think, that he ought to possess some property in the district, and that any deviation from this rule is an abuse; but I am not certain that the law so ordains. The majors and the adjutants are likewise occasionally promoted from the line; but whether they are regularly military men or planters, they receive pay; as their trouble, in distributing orders, and in other arrangements connected with the regiment, is considerable.

The third class, that of the *Ordenanças*, consisting of by far the largest portion of the white persons, and of free mulatto men of all shades, have for their immediate chiefs, the *Capitães-môres*, who serve without pay: and all the persons who are connected with the *Ordenanças*, are obliged likewise to afford their services gratuitously. Each district contains one *Capitão-môr*, who is invariably a person possessing property in the part of the country to which he is appointed. He is assisted by a major, captains, and *alferes*, who are lieutenants or ensigns, and by sergeants and corporals. The duties of the *Capitão-môr* are to see that every individual under his command has in his possession some species of arms; either a firelock, a sword, or a pike. He distributes the governor's orders through his district; and can oblige any of his men to take these orders to the nearest captain, who sends another peasant forward to the next captain, who sends another peasant forward to the next captain, and so forth; all which is done without any pay. A *Capitão-môr* can also imprison for twenty-four hours, and send under arrest for trial a person who is accused of having committed any crime, to the civil magistrate of the town to which his district is immediately attached. Now, the abuses of this office of *Capitão-môr* are very many; and the lower orders of free persons are much oppressed by these great men, and by their subalterns, down to the corporals. The peasants are often sent upon errands which have no relation to public business; for leagues and leagues these poor fellows are made to travel, for the purpose of carrying some private letter of the chief, of his captains, or of his lieutenants, without any remuneration. Indeed, many of these men in place, seldom think of employing their slaves on these occasions, or of paying the free persons so employed. This I have witnessed times out of number; and have heard the peasants in all parts of the country complain: it is a most heavy grievance. Nothing so much vexes a peasant as the consciousness of losing his time and trouble in a service which is not required by his sovereign. Persons are sometimes confined in the stocks for days together, on some trifling plea; and are at last released without being sent to the civil magistrate, or even admitted to a hearing. However, I am happy to say, that I am acquainted with some men, whose conduct is widely different from what I have above stated; but the power given to an individual is too great, and the probability of being called to an

account for its abuse too remote, to insure the exercise of it in a proper manner.

The free mulattos and free negroes, whose names are upon the rolls, either of the militia regiments which are commanded by white officers, or by those of their own class and colour, are not, properly speaking, subject to the *Capitães-môres*. These officers, and the colonels of militia, are appointed by the supreme government: and the subaltern officers are nominated by the governor of each province.

3. CRUSADERS OF THE JUNGLE

The Jesuits, who enjoyed great influence in the Portuguese court until the middle of the eighteenth century, early established their leadership in the religious and educational life of Brazil. The first Fathers, led by Manoel de Nobrega, came in 1549 with the captain-general Thomé de Souza. Four years later the famous Father Anchieta arrived in Brazil. Far to the south, on the plains of Piratininga, Nobrega and Anchieta established a colegio or school for Portuguese, mixed-blood, and Indian children that became a model institution of its kind. Around this settlement gradually arose the town of São Paulo, an important point of departure into the interior for "adventurers in search of gold and missionaries in search of souls." The English historian Southey, whose bitter anti-Catholic bias did not blind him to the heroism and devotion of Anchieta and his colleagues, describes their apostolic labor.[5]

✱✱✱✱ When Thomé de Sousa had been Governor four years, he petitioned to be recalled, and D. Duarte da Costa was sent out to succeed him. Seven Jesuits accompanied the new Governor; among them were Luis da Gram, who had been Rector of the College at Coimbra, and Joseph de Anchieta, then only a Temporal Coadjutor, but destined to be celebrated in Jesuitical history as the Thaumatourgos of the New World. Loyola, the Patriarch, as he is called, of the Company, or more probably Laynez, by whose master-hand the whole machine was set in motion, had already perceived the importance of this mission, and delegated new powers to Nobrega, erecting Brazil into an independent Province, and appointing him and Luis de Gram joint Provincials. As neither of these Fathers had yet taken the fourth vow, which is the last and highest degree in the order, they were instructed now to take it before the Ordinary; and they were directed to choose out *Consultores*,

[5] Southey, *History of Brazil*, I, pp. 261–266.

or Advisers, from their companions, one of whom was to go with them upon all their journeys.

Nobrega's first act, after this accession of power, was to establish a College in the plains of Piratininga. Such an establishment was necessary because the Society was now numerous; they had very many children of both colours to support, and the alms upon which they subsisted were not sufficient to maintain them all in one place. The spot chosen was ten leagues from the sea, and about thirteen from St. Vicente, upon the great Cordillera which stretches along the coast of Brazil. The way was by a steep and difficult ascent, broken with shelves of level ground, and continuing about eight leagues, when a track of delightful country appeared in that temperate region of the air. Here were lakes, rivers, and springs, with rocks and mountains still rising above, and the earth as fertile as a rich soil and the happiest of all climates could render it. The best fruits of Europe thrive there, the grape, the apple, the peach, fig, cherry, mulberry, melon, and water-melon, and the woods abound with game.

Thirteen of the Company, under Manoel de Paiva, were sent to colonize here, where Nobrega had previously stationed some of his converts. Anchieta went with them as schoolmaster. Their first mass was celebrated on the feast of the Conversion of St. Paul, and from this, as from a good omen, they named their College after the Saint, a name which extended to the town that arose there, and has become famous in the history of South America. The plains of Piratininga had not yet been improved by European culture: nature indeed had fitted them for an earthly Paradise, but they were as nature left them, unassisted by human art. "Here we are," says Anchieta, in a letter written to Loyola, "sometimes more than twenty of us in a little hut of wicker work and mud, roofed with straw, fourteen paces long and ten wide. This is the school, this is the infirmary, dormitory, refectory, kitchen, and store-room. Yet we covet not the more spacious dwellings which our brethren inhabit in other parts, for our Lord Jesus Christ was in a straiter place when it was his pleasure to be born among beasts in a manger; and in a far straiter when he deigned to die for us upon the Cross." It was not however for want of room that Anchieta and his brethren and his pupils were thus crowded. They herded together in this way to keep themselves warm, for against the cold they were miserably provided. Fire indeed they had, but they had smoke with it, not having contrived a chimney; and sometimes cold was thought the more endurable evil of the two, and they studied in the open air. They slept in hammocks, and had no bed-clothes: for door there was a mat hung up at the entrance; their dress was calculated for a lower region; what little clothing it consisted of was cotton; they were barefooted, and without breeches. Banana-leaves served them for a table, and napkins, says Anchieta, may well be excused when there is nothing

to eat, for they had no other food than what the Indians gave them, sometimes alms of mandioc flour, and less frequently fish from the brooks, and game from the forest.

Many scholars, both Creoles and Mamalucos, came here from the nearest settlements. Anchieta taught them Latin, and learnt from them the Tupinamban, of which he composed a grammar and vocabulary, the first which were made. Day and night did this indefatigable man, whose life without the machinery of miracles, is sufficiently honorable to himself and to his order, labour in discharging the duties of his office. There were no books for the pupils; he wrote for every one his lesson on a separate leaf, after the business of the day was done, and it was sometimes day-light before this task was completed. The profane songs which were in use he parodied into hymns in Portuguese, Castilian, Latin, and Tupinamban; the ballads of the natives underwent the same travesty in their own tongue; how greatly should we have been indebted to Anchieta had he preserved them! In this language also he drew up forms of interrogations for the use of Confessors, suitable to all occasions, and wrote dialogues for the Catechumens, expounding the whole Christian, or rather Catholic faith. "I serve," says he, "as physician and barber, physicking and bleeding the Indians, and some of them have recovered under my hands when their lives were not expected, because others had died of the same diseases. Besides these employments, I have learnt another trade which necessity taught me, that is, to make *alpargatas*; I am now a good workman at this, and have made many for the brethren, for it is not possible to travel with leathern shoes among these wilds." The *alpargata* is a sort of shoe, of which the upper part is made of hemp, or any such substance — here they were of cordage from a species of wild thistle, which it was necessary to prepare for the purpose. . . . For bleeding he had no other instrument than a penknife; there was a scruple about this branch of his profession, because the clergy are forbidden to shed blood; they sent to ask Loyola's opinion, and his answer was, that charity extended to all things.

About three leagues from Piratininga, was a settlement called St. André, inhabited chiefly by Mamalucos. This breed, so far from being a link which should bind together the two races in friendly intercourse, was more desperately inimical to the natives than even the Portuguese themselves were. They hated the Jesuits for opposing the custom, as they termed it, of the land, and for interfering with what they called the liberty of making slaves. The conversion and civilization of the Indians was regarded by these wretches as measures necessarily destructive to their interests, and they devised an ingenious mode of prejudicing them against Christianity. Cowardice, they said, was the motive which induced them to be baptized; they were afraid to meet their enemies in battle, and so took shelter under the protection

of the Church. Of all reproaches, this was the most cutting which could be made to a savage; they added, that the Jesuits were a set of fellows turned out of their own country as idle vagabonds, and that it was disgraceful for men who could use the bow to be under their control. Some of the adjoining tribes, instigated by these ruffians, advanced to attack Piratininga, but were met and defeated by the converts. During the night they returned to the field to carry off the dead bodies of their enemies, and feast upon them. They found fresh heaps of earth, and concluding that the bodies which they sought were buried there, dug them up and carried them away in the darkness. At daylight, when they reached their settlements, they recognized the features of their own dead, and their expected feast was changed into lamentation.

4. THE JESUIT INDIAN POLICY

The Jesuits aimed at the settlement of their Indian converts in aldeas, *or villages, where they would live completely segregated from the white colonists, under the tutelage of the priests. The Jesuit Indian program led to many clashes with the Portuguese planters, who wanted to enslave the natives for work on their estates. In an angry protest to the* Mesa de Conciencia, *a royal council entrusted with responsibility for the religious affairs of the colony, the planters charged that the Indians in the Jesuit villages "were true slaves, who labored as such not only in the* colegios *but on the so-called Indian lands, which in the end became the estates and sugar mills of the Jesuit Fathers." Replying to these and other accusations, Father Anchieta explained the Jesuit Indian policy.*[6]

❖❖❖❖ Every day, in the morning, the Fathers teach the Indians doctrine and say mass for those who want to hear it before going to their fields; after that the children stay in school, where they learn reading and writing, counting, and other good customs pertaining to the Christian life; in the afternoon they conduct another class especially for those who are receiving the sacred sacraments. Daily the Fathers visit the sick with certain Indians assigned for this purpose, and if they have some special needs they attend to them, and always administer to them the necessary sacraments. All this they do purely for love of God and for no other interest or profit, for the Fathers get their food from the *colegio,* and they live with the Indians solely because of

[6] *Cartas . . . do Joseph de Anchieta,* pp. 381–382. (Excerpt translated by the editor.)

love of their souls, which have such great need of them. The Fathers make no use of them on plantations, for if the *colegio* needs them for certain tasks, and they come to help, they work for wages, . . . and not through force but of their own free will, because they need clothing or implements. For although it is their natural tendency to go about naked, all those who have been raised in the Jesuit schools now wear clothes and are ashamed to go about naked. It is not true, as some say, that the Fathers are the lords of the villages.

When the Portuguese come to the villages in search of Indian labor, the Fathers help them all they can, summoning one of the Indian headmen to take the Portuguese to the houses of the natives to show them the goods they have brought, and those who wish to go they permit to leave without impediment. If the Fathers object at times, it is because the Indians have not finished their farm work, and they have to do this for the sake of their wives and children. In other cases, the Indians are not getting along with their wives, and once they leave for the homes of the Portuguese they never return; such Indians the Father also restrains from going, so that they may continue living with their wives. . . .

The Indians are punished for their offenses by their own magistrates, appointed by the Portuguese governors; the only chastisement consists in being put in the stocks for a day or two, as the magistrate considers best; they use no chains or other imprisonment. If some Indian who went to work for the Portuguese returns before completing his time, the Father compels him to return to work out his time, and if the Indian cannot go for some good reason the Father arranges matters to the satisfaction of his employer.

The Fathers always encourage the Indians to cultivate their fields and to raise more provisions than they need, so that in case of necessity they might aid the Portuguese by way of barter; in fact, many Portuguese obtain their food from the villages. Thus one could say that the Fathers are truly the fathers of the Indians, both of their souls and of their bodies.

5. "YOU ARE ALL IN MORTAL SIN . . . !"

The clash of interests between Brazilian planters and slave-hunters, on the one hand, and the Jesuit missionaries, on the other, reached a climax about the middle of the seventeenth century, an era of great activity on the part of the bandeirantes *of São Paulo. In various parts of Brazil the landowners rose in revolt, expelled the Jesuits, and defied royal edicts proclaiming the freedom of the Indians. In 1653 the Jesuit Antonio Vieyra*

(1608–1679), a priest of extraordinary oratorical and literary powers, arrived in Brazil with full authority from the king to settle the Indian question as he saw fit. During Lent Vieyra preached a famous sermon to the people of Maranhão, in which he denounced Indian slavery in terms comparable to those used by Father Montesino on Santo Domingo in 1511. The force of Vieyra's tremendous blast was somewhat weakened by his suggestion that Indian slavery should be continued under certain conditions, and by the well-known fact that the Company itself had both Indian and Negro slaves. The following excerpt from Vieyra's sermon gives some notion of his burning eloquence.[7]

✦✦✦✦ Alexander and Caesar were lords of the world, but their souls are now burning in Hell, and will burn there for all eternity. Who will tell me now how to ask Caesar and Alexander what it profits them to have been masters of the world, and if they find that it has proved a good bargain to give their souls in exchange for it? Alexander! Julius! Was it good for you to have been masters of the world, and to be now where you are? They cannot answer me, . . . but answer me ye who can! Would any of you choose at this time to be Julius Caesar? God forbid that we should! How? Were they not masters of the world? They were so, but they lost their own souls. . . . Oh blindness! And it seems ill to you, for Alexander and for Caesar to have given their souls for the whole world, . . . and it seems well to you to give your own souls for what is not the world, nor hath the name of it! . . . At how different a price now . . . does the Devil purchase souls from that which he formerly offered for them — I mean in this country. The Devil has not a fair in the world where they go cheaper! In the Gospel he offers all the kingdoms of the earth for a single soul: he does not require so large a purse to purchase all that are in Maranhão. It is not necessary to offer cities, nor towns, nor villages; it is enough for the Devil to point at a plantation and a couple of Tapuyas, and down goes the man upon his knees to worship him. Oh what a market! A Negro for a soul, and the soul the blacker of the two! This Negro shall be your slave for the few days that you may have to live, and your soul shall be my slave through all eternity, as long as God is God; this is the bargain which the Devil makes with you! . . .

Do ye know, Christians, do ye know, nobles and people of Maranhão, what is the fast which God requires of you this Lent? It is that ye loosen the bands of injustice, and that you set those free whom you hold captives, and whom you oppress. These are the sins of Maranhão; these are what God commands me to announce; "Shew my people their transgression!" Christians, God commands me to un-

[7] Southey, *History of Brazil*, II, pp. 475–479.

deceive you, and I undeceive you on the part of God! You are all in mortal sin! you are all living and dying in a state of condemnation, and you are all going straight to Hell! Many are already there, and you also will soon be there with them, except you change your lives! Now mark the reasoning. Every man who holds another unjustly in servitude, being able to release him, is certainly in a state of condemnation. . . . . My brethren, if there be any who doubt upon this matter, here are the Laws, here are the Lawyers, let the question be asked. You have three Orders of Religioners in the State, and among them so many subjects of such virtue and such learning: ask them . . . examine the matter . . . inform yourselves. But Religioners are not necessary: go to Turkey, go to Hell, for there can neither be Turk so beturked in Turkey, nor Devil so bedeviled in Hell, as to affirm that a free man may be a slave. But you will say to me, this people, this republic, this state cannot be supported without Indians. Who is to bring us a pitcher of water or a bundle of wood? Who is to plant our mandioc? Must our wives do it? Must our children do it? In the first place, as you will presently see, these are not the straits in which I would place you: but if necessity and conscience require it, then I reply, yes! And I repeat it, yes! You and your wives and your children ought to do it! We ought to support ourselves with our own hands; for better is it to be supported by the sweat of one's own brow than by another's blood. O ye riches of Maranhão! What if these mantles and cloaks were to be wrung? They would drip blood!

20 ✤ Masters and Slaves

Race mixture played a decisive role in the formation of the Brazilian people. The scarcity of white women in the colony, the freedom of the Portuguese from Puritanical attitudes, and the despotic power of the great planters over their Indian and Negro slave women, all give impetus to miscegenation. Color lines were drawn, but less sharply than in the Spanish Indies, and in colonial Brazil the possession of wealth more easily expunged the taint of Negro blood.

Slavery played as important a role in the social organization of colonial Brazil as did race mixture in its ethnic make-up. The social consequences of the system were almost entirely negative. Slavery corrupted both master and slave, fostered harmful attitudes with respect to the dignity of labor, and retarded the economic development of Brazil. The virtual monopolization of labor by slaves sharply limited the number of socially acceptable occupations in which whites or free mixed-bloods could engage. This gave rise to a numerous class of vagrants, beggars, "poor whites," and other degraded or disorderly elements who would not or could not compete with slaves in agriculture and industry.

The nucleus of Brazilian social as well as economic organization was the large estate; this centered about the Big House and constituted a patriarchal community that included the owner and his family, his

chaplain and overseers, his slaves, and his *agregados*, or retainers — freemen of low social status who received the landowner's protection and assistance in return for a variety of services. In the sugar-growing Northeast the great planters became a distinct aristocratic class, possessed of family traditions and pride in their name and blood.

By contrast with the decisive importance of the *fazenda*, or large estate, most of the colonial towns were mere appendages of the countryside, dominated politically and socially by the rural magnates. But in a few large cities, such as Baía and Rio de Janeiro, were found other social groups that disputed or shared power with the great landowners: high officials of the colonial administration; dignitaries of the Church; wealthy professional men, especially lawyers; and the large merchants, almost exclusively peninsulars, who monopolized the export-import trade and financed the industry of the planters.

I. THE WORLD OF THE SUGAR PLANTATION

The Jesuit priest João Antonio Andreoni (1650–1715), who came to Brazil in 1667 and spent the rest of his life there, wrote a valuable account of the agricultural and mineral resources of the colony. His book, published in Lisbon in 1711, was promptly suppressed by the Portuguese government on the grounds that the information it contained might prove helpful to Portugal's European rivals. The following excerpts from Andreoni's book illustrate Gilberto Freyre's point that "the Big House completed by the slave shed represents an entire economic, social, and political system."[1]

❧❧❧❧ If the plantation owner must display his capacity in one thing more than another, it is in the proper choice of persons to administer his estate. . . .

The first choice that he must make with care, on the basis of secret information concerning the conduct and knowledge of the person in question, is that of a chaplain to whom he must entrust the teaching of all that pertains to the Christian way of life. For the principal obligation of the planter is to teach, or have taught, his family and slaves. This should be done not by some slave born in Brazil, or by some overseer who at best can only teach them their prayers and the laws of God and the Church by word of mouth, but by one who can explain to them what they should believe and what they must

[1] André João Antonil (João Antonio Andreoni), *Cultura e Opulencia do Brazil por Suas Drogas e Minas*, edited by Affonso de E. Tauny, São Paulo, 1923, pp. 77–83, 91–102. (Excerpts translated by the editor.)

do, and how they must do it, and how they are to ask God for what they need. And for this reason, if he must pay the chaplain a little more than is customary, the planter should understand that he could not put the money to better use. . . .

The chaplain should live outside the planter's house; this is best for both, because he is a priest and not a servant, a familiar of God and not of men. He should not have any woman slave in his house, unless she be of advanced years, nor should be trade in anything, either human or divine, for all this is opposed to his clerical state and is prohibited by various Papal orders.

It is customary to pay a chaplain, when he is free to say masses during weekdays, forty or fifty thousand *reis* a year, and with what he gains from the saying of masses during the week he can earn a respectable salary — and well earned too, if he does all the things described above. If he is expected to teach the children of the plantation owner, he should receive a just additional compensation. . . .

On the day that the cane is brought to be ground, if the plantation owner does not invite the Vicar, the chaplain blesses the mill and asks God to grant a good yield and to guard those who work in it from all misfortune. When the mill stops grinding at the end of the harvest, he sees to it that all give thanks to God in the chapel. . . .

The arms of the plantation owner, on which he relies for the good governance of his people and estate, are his overseers. But if each should aspire to be the head, it would be a monstrous government and would truly resemble the dog Cerberus, to whom the poets fancifully ascribe three heads. I do not say that the overseers should not possess authority, but I say that this authority must be well ordered and subordinate, not absolute, so that the lesser are inferior to the greater, and all to the master whom they serve.

It is fitting that the slaves should understand that the chief overseer has power to command and reprove them, and to punish them when necessary, but they should also know that they have recourse to the master and that they will be heard as justice requires. Nor must the other overseers suppose that their powers are unlimited, especially in what concerns punishment and seizure. The plantation owner, therefore, must make very clear the authority given to each, and especially to the chief overseer; and if they exceed their authority he should check them with the punishment that their excesses deserve — but not before the slaves, lest another time they rise against the overseer, and so that he may not bear the shame of being reproved before them and hence not dare to govern them. It will suffice if the master let a third party make known to the injured slave, and to some of the oldest slaves on the estate, that the master was much displeased with the overseer for the wrong that he had committed, and that if he did not amend his ways he would be immediately dismissed.

The overseers must on no account be permitted to kick slaves —
in particular to kick pregnant slave women in the belly — or to strike
slaves with a stick, because blows struck in anger are not calculated,
and they may inflict a mortal head wound on some valuable slave that
cost a great deal of money. What they may do is to scold them and
strike them a few times on the back with a liana whip, to teach them
a lesson. To seize fugitive slaves and any who fight and slash each other
and get drunk, so that the master may have them punished as they
deserve, is to show a diligence worthy of praise. But to tie up a slave
girl and lash her with a liana whip until the blood runs, or to place her
in the stocks or in chains for months at a time (while the master is in
the city) simply because she will not go to bed with him, or to do the
same to a slave who gave the master a faithful account of the overseer's disloyalty, violence, and cruelty, and to invent pretended offenses
to justify the punishment — this may not be tolerated on any account,
for it would be to have a ravening wolf rather than a well-disposed and
Christian overseer.

It is the obligation of the chief overseer of the plantation to
govern the people, and to assign them to their tasks at the proper time.
It is his duty to learn from the master who should be notified to cut
their cane, and to send them word promptly. He should have the
boats and carts ready to go for the cane and should prepare the forms
and fuel. He should apprise the master of everything that is needed to
equip the sugar-mill before the start of grinding, and when the season
is over he should put everything away in its place. He must see that
each performs his task, and if some distaster occurs he should hasten to
the scene to give what help he can. . . .

The slaves are the hands and feet of the plantation owner, for
without them you cannot make, preserve, and increase a fortune, or
operate a plantation in Brazil. And the kind of service they give depends on how they are treated. It is necessary, therefore, to buy a
certain number of slaves each year and assign them to the canefields,
the manioc fields, the sawmills, and the boats. And because they are
usually of different nations, and some more primitive than others, and
differ greatly in physical qualities, the assignments should be made with
great care. Those who come to Brazil are the Ardas, Minas, Congos,
others from S. Thomé, Angola, Cape Verde, and some from Mozam-
bique, who come in the India ships. The Ardas and Minas are robust.
Those who come from Cape Verde and S. Thomé are weaker. The
slaves from Angola, raised in Loanda, are more capable of acquiring
mechanical skills than those who come from the other regions that I
have named. Among the Congos there are also some who are quite
industrious, and good not only for work in the canefields but for
mechanical tasks and housework.

Some arrive in Brazil very barbarous and dullwitted, and con-

tinue so throughout their lives. Others in a few years become clever and skillful, not only in learning Christian doctrine but in mastering trades, and they can be used to handle a boat, carry messages, and perform any other routine task. . . . It is not well to remove a slave against his will from the plantation where he has been raised since childhood, for he may pine away and die. Those slaves who were born in Brazil, or were raised from infancy in the homes of whites, form an affection for their masters and give a good account of themselves; one of these who bears his captivity well is worth four slaves brought from Africa.

The mulattoes are even more apt for every task; but many of them, taking advantage of the favor of their masters, are haughty and vicious and swagger about, always ready for a brawl. Yet they and the mulatto women commonly have it best of all in Brazil, because the white blood in their veins (sometimes that of their own masters) works such sorcery that some owners will tolerate and pardon anything they do; not only do they not reprove them, but it seems that all the caresses fall to their share. It is hard to say whether the masters or the mistresses are more at fault in this respect, for there are some of both sexes who permit themselves to be ruled by mulattoes, and not those of the best sort, either, thus verifying the proverb that says that Brazil is the Hell of the Negroes, the Purgatory of the Whites, and the Paradise of the mulattoes — but let some distrust or feeling of jealousy change love into hatred, and it comes forth armed with every kind of cruelty and severity. It is well to make use of their capabilities, if they will make good use of them (as some do, to be sure), but they should not be treated with such intimacy that they lose respect, and from slaves turn into masters. To free mulatto women of loose habits is surely an iniquitous thing, because the money with which they purchase their freedom rarely comes out of any other mines than their own bodies, and is gained with repeated sins; and after they are freed they continue to be the ruination of many.

Some masters are opposed to the marriage of male and female slaves, and they not only are indifferent to their living in concubinage but consent and actually encourage them to live in that state, saying: "You, so-and-so, will in due time marry so-and-so"; and after that they permit them to live together as if they were already man and wife. It is said that the reason why masters do not marry such couples off is because they fear that if they tire of the match they may kill each other with poison or witchcraft, for among them there are notable masters of this craft. Others, after marrying off their slaves, keep them apart for years as if they were unwed, and this they cannot do in good conscience. Others are so negligent in what concerns the salvation of the slaves that they keep them for a long time in the canefields or at the sugar-mill without baptism. Furthermore, of those who have been

baptized, many do not know who is their Creator, what they should believe, what law they should observe, how to commend themselves to God, why Christians go to Church, why they adore the Church, what to say to the Father when they kneel before him and when they speak into his ear, whether they have souls and if these souls die, and where they go when they leave the body. . . .

In what concerns food, clothing, and rest from labor, clearly these things should not be denied them, for in all fairness the master should give a servitor sufficient food, medicine for his sicknesses, and clothing so that he may be decently covered and not go about half-naked in the streets; he should also regulate their labor so that it is not beyond their strength and endurance. In Brazil they say that the slaves must have the three P's, namely, a stick, bread, and a piece of cloth (*páo, pão, e panno*). And though they make a bad beginning, commencing with the stick, which stands for punishment, yet would to God that the bread and clothing were as abundant as the punishment! For it is frequently inflicted for some offense not wholly proved, or else invented, and with instruments of great severity (even if the crimes were proved), such instruments as are not used on brute beasts. To be sure, some masters take more account of a horse than of a half-dozen slaves, for the horse is cared for, and has a groom to find him hay, and wipe his sweat away, and a saddle, and a gilded bridle. . . .

Some masters have the custom of giving their slaves one day a week to plant for themselves, sometimes sending the overseer along to see that they do not neglect their work; this helps to keep them from suffering hunger or from daily milling about the house of the master to beg him for a ration of flour. But to deny them both flour and a day for planting, and to expect them to work in the fields by day, from sunrise to sundown, and in the sugar-mill by night, with little rest from labor — how shall such a master escape punishment before the Tribunal of God? If to deny alms to one who needs it is to deny it to Christ our Lord, as the Good Book says, what must it be to deny food and clothing to one's slaves? And how shall that master justify his conduct, who gives woolens and silks and other fineries to her who works his perdition and then denies four or five yards of cotton, and a few more of woolen cloth, to the slave who dissolves in sweat to serve him, and barely has time to hunt for a root and a crab-fish for his meal? And if on top of this the punishment is frequent and excessive, the slaves will either run away into the woods or commit suicide, as is their custom, by holding their breath or hanging themselves — or they will try to take the lives of those who do them such great evil, resorting, if necessary, to diabolical arts, or they will clamor so loudly to the Lord that he will hear them and do to their masters what he did to the Egyptians when they vexed the Jews with extraordinary labor, sending terrible plagues against their estates and sons, as we read in the Sacred Scripture. . . .

Not to punish their excesses would be a serious fault, but these offenses should first be verified, so that innocent people may not suffer. The accused should be given a hearing, and if the charges are proved the culprits should be chastised with a moderate lashing, or by placing them in chains or in the stocks for a short period. But to punish them overhastily, with a vengeful spirit, with one's own hand, with terrible instruments, and perhaps to burn them with fire or heated sealing wax, or to brand the poor fellows in the face — why, this is intolerable in barbarians, to say nothing of Christian Catholics. . . . And if, having erred by reason of their frailty, they themselves come to beg the master's pardon, or find sponsors (*padrinhos*) to accompany them, in such cases it is customary in Brazil to pardon them. And it is well for them to know that this will obtain them forgiveness, for otherwise they may one day flee to some fugitive-slave settlement (*mucambo*) in the forest, and if they are captured they may kill themselves before the master can lash them, or some kinsman will take it upon himself to avenge them by the use of witchcraft or poison. Completely to deny them their festivities, which are their only consolation in their captivity, is to condemn them to sadness and melancholy, to apathy and sickliness. Therefore masters should not object if they crown their kings and sing and dance decently for a few hours on certain days of the year, or if they amuse themselves in proper ways of an afternoon, after having celebrated in the morning the holiday of Our Lady of the Rosary, of Saint Benedict, and of the patron-saint of the plantation chapel. . . .

Since the management of a sugar plantation requires so many large outlays, as described above, it is plain that the owner must carefully watch the expenses of his household. . . .

It is a poor thing to have the reputation of being a miser, but it is no credit to bear the name of a prodigal. He who decides to assume the burdens of a plantation must either retire from the city, shunning its diversions, or maintain two houses — which is notably deleterious to the one from which he is absent and also doubly expensive. To keep one's sons on the plantation is to create country bumpkins who can only talk of dogs, horses, and cattle. To leave them in the city is to permit them to fall into vicious habits and contract shameful diseases that are not easily cured. To avoid both extremes, the best course is to place them in the household of some responsible and honorable relative or friend, where they will have no opportunity to make a false step — a friend who will faithfully keep the parent informed of their good or bad conduct and of their improvement or neglect of their studies. The lad's mother should not be permitted to send him money or to send secret orders for that purpose to the father's correspondent or cashier; nor must it be forgotten that money requested for the purchase of books can also be used for gambling. The father should therefore instruct his attorney

or agent not to give the boy anything without his order. For these young fellows can be very ingenious in their pleas for money, and can devise all manner of plausible reasons and pretexts, especially when they are supposed to be engaged in some course of studies. They are perfectly willing to spend three years of pleasant life at the expense of their father or uncle, who is in his sugar-cane fields and has no idea of what goes on in town. So when a father boasts that he has an Aristotle in the Academy, it may be that he really has an Asinius or an Apricius in the city. But if the father decides to keep his children at home, content to let them learn to read, write, and count, together with some knowledge of events or history, to enable them to converse in company, he should not fail to watch over them, especially when they reach a certain age. For the broad countryside is also a place of much freedom, and can breed thistles and thorns. And if one constructs a fence for cattle and horses to keep them from leaving the pasture, why should one not keep children within bounds, both inside and outside the house, if experience proves that it is necessary? . . . The good example of the father, however, is the best lesson in conduct; and the surest means of achieving peace of mind is to marry off the girls, and the boys as well, at the proper time. If they are content to marry within their station, they will find houses where they can make good matches and receive their rewards.

2. THE FREE POPULATION

Freemen and slaves formed the two great legal categories into which the Brazilian colonial population was divided. However, not all freemen belonged to the master class. Unable or unwilling to compete with slave labor in agriculture and industry, the majority maintained a precarious existence on the margins of a society dominated by the great landholding class. Perhaps the most hopeful feature of Brazilian colonial life was the gradual blurring of the color line through race mixture — a circumstance that gave free mulattoes and other mixed-bloods a greater social mobility than was possible in any other slave society of modern times.[2]

✣✣✣✣ In the Portuguese South American dominions, circumstances have directed that there should be no division of casts, and very few of those degrading and most galling distinctions which have been made by all other nations in the management of their colonies. That this was not intended by the mother country, but was rather submitted

[2] Koster, *Travels in Brazil*, II, pp. 167–187.

to from necessity, is to be discovered in some few regulations, which plainly show that if Portugal could have preserved the superiority of the whites, she would, as well as her neighbors, have established laws for that purpose. The rulers of Portugal wished to colonize to an unlimited extent: but their country did not contain a population sufficiently numerous for their magnificent plans. Emigrants left their own country to settle in the New World, who were literally adventurers; for they had not any settled plans of life, and they were without families. Persons of established habits, who had the wish to follow any of the ordinary means of gaining a livelihood, found employment at home; neither could Portugal spare them, nor did they wish to leave their native soil. There was no superabundance of population: and therefore every man might find occupation at home, if he had steadiness to look for it. There was no division in political or religious opinion. There was no necessity of emigration, save that which was urged by crimes. Thus the generality of the men who embarked in the expeditions which were fitted out for Brazil, were unaccompanied by females: and therefore, naturally, on their arrival in that country, they married, or irregularly connected themselves with Indian women, and subsequently with those of Africa. It is true that orphan girls were sent out by the government of Portugal: but these were necessarily few in number. In the course of another generation, the colonists married the women of mixed casts, owing to the impossibility of obtaining those of their own colour: and the frequency of the custom, and the silence of the laws upon the subject, removed all idea of degradation, in thus connecting themselves. Still the European notions of superiority were not entirely laid aside: and these caused the passing of some regulations, by which white persons were to enjoy certain privileges. Thus, although the form of trial for all casts is the same, in certain places only, can capital punishment be inflicted upon the favoured race. The people of colour are not eligible to some of the chief offices of government: nor can they become members of the priesthood.

From the mildness of the laws, however, the mixed casts have gained ground considerably. The regulations which exist against them are evaded, or rather they have become obsolete. Perhaps the heroic conduct of Camarão and Henrique Dias, the Indian and negro chieftains, in the famous and most interesting contest, between the Pernambucans and the Dutch, and the honours subsequently granted by the crown of Portugal to both of them, may have led to the exaltation of the general character of the much-injured varieties of the human species of which they were members. Familiarity between the chieftains of the several corps must be the consequence of their embarkation in the same cause, when the war is one of skirmishes, of ambuscades, of continual alarm, of assistance constantly afforded to

each other; a patriotic war, against a foreign invader, in which difference of religion exists, and each party mortally hates the other. On these occasions all men are equal; or he only is superior whose strength and whose activity surpasses that of others. The amalgamation of casts which is caused by this consciousness of equality could not have had a fairer field for its full accomplishment, than the war to which I have alluded: and the friendships which were formed under these circumstances would not easily be broken off. Although the parties who had been so united might have been in their situations in life very far removed from each other, still the participation of equal danger must render dear the companions in peril, and make the feelings, which had been roused on these occasions, of long duration; they would continue to act, long after the cessation of the series of occurrences which had called them forth.

The free population of Brazil at the present time consists of Europeans; Brazilians, that is, white persons born in Brazil; mulattos, that is, the mixed cast between the whites and blacks, and all the varieties into which it can branch; mamalucos, that is, the mixed casts between the whites and Indians, and all its varieties; Indians in a domesticated state, who are called generally Tapuyas; negroes born in Brazil, and manumitted Africans; lastly, mestizos, that is, the mixed cast between the Indians and negroes. Of slaves, I shall speak by and by more at large; these are Africans, creole negroes, mulattos, and mestizos. The maxim of the Civil law, *partus sequitur ventrem*, is in force here as well as in the colonies of other nations.

These several mixtures of the human race have their shades of difference of character as well as of colour. First we must treat of the whites. The Europeans who are not in office, or who are not military men, are, generally speaking, adventurers who have arrived in that country with little or no capital. These men commence their career in low situations of life, but by parsimony and continual exertion directed to one end, that of amassing money, they often attain their object, and pass the evening of their lives in opulence. These habits fail not, oftentimes, to give a bias to their dispositions, which is unallied to generosity and liberality. They look down upon the Brazilians, or rather they wish to consider themselves superior to them; and until lately the government took no pains to remove the jealousy which existed between the two descriptions of white persons; and even now, not so much attention is paid to the subject as its great importance seems to require.[3]

The Brazilian white man of large property, who draws his

---

[3] The majority of the clergy of Pernambuco, both regular and secular, are of Brazilian parentage. The governor is an European, and so are the major part of the chief officers, civil, military, and ecclesiastical but the bishop is a Brazilian, and so is the *ouvidor*.

descent from the first Donatory of a province, or whose family has for some generations enjoyed distinction, entertains a high opinion of his own importance, which may sometimes appear ridiculous; but which much oftener leads him to acts of generosity, — to the adoption of liberal ideas, — to honourable conduct. If he has been well educated and has had the good fortune to have been instructed by a priest whose ideas are enlightened, who gives a proper latitude for difference of opinion, who tolerates as he is tolerated, then the character of a young Brazilian exhibits much to admire. Surrounded by numerous relatives, and by his immediate dependents living in a vast and half-civilized country, he is endued with much independence of language and behaviour, which are softened by the subordination which has been imbibed during his course of education. That this is general, I pretend not to say. Few persons are instructed in a proper manner; and again, few are those who profit by the education which they have received; but more numerous are the individuals who now undergo necessary tuition, for powerful motives have arisen to urge the attainment of knowledge.

I have heard it often observed, and I cannot help saying, that I think some truth is to be attached to the remark, in the country of which I am now treating, that women are usually less lenient to their slaves than men: but this doubtless proceeds from the ignorant state in which they are brought up. They scarcely receive any education; and have not the advantages of obtaining instruction from communication with persons who are unconnected with their own way of life; of imbibing new ideas from general conversation. They are born, bred, and continue surrounded by slaves without receiving any check, with high notions of superiority, without any thought that what they do is wrong. Bring these women forward, educate them, treat them as rational, as equal beings, and they will be in no respect inferior to their countrymen. The fault is not with the sex, but in the state of the human being. As soon as a child begins to crawl, a slave of about its own age, and of the same sex, is given to it as a playfellow, or rather as a plaything. They grow up together: and the slave is made the stock upon which the young owner gives vent to passion. The slave is sent upon all errands, and receives the blame of all unfortunate accidents; — in fact, the white child is thus encouraged to be overbearing, owing to the false fondness of its parents. Upon the boys the effect is less visible in after-life, because the world curbs and checks them: but the girls do not stir from home, and therefore have no opportunities of wearing off these pernicious habits. It is only surprising that so many excellent women should be found among them, and by no means strange that the disposition of some of them should be injured by this unfortunate direction of their infant years.

As vegetation rapidly advances in such climates, so the animal sooner arrives at maturity than in those of less genial warmth; and here again education is rendered doubly necessary to lead the mind to new ideas, to curb the passions, to give a sense of honour, and to instil feelings of that species of pride which is so necessary to a becoming line of conduct. The state of society, the climate, and the celibacy of the numerous priesthood, cause the number of illegitimate children to be very great. But here the *roda dos engeitados*, and a custom which shews the natural goodness of the people, prevent the frequent occurrence of infanticide, or rather render it almost unknown. An infant is frequently during the night laid at the door of a rich person; and on being discovered in the morning is taken in, and is almost invariably allowed to remain: it is brought up with the children of the house (if its colour is not too dark to admit of this), certainly as a dependent, but not as a servant. However, a considerable tinge of colour will not prevent it from being reared with the white children. These *engeitados*, or rejected ones, as individuals who are so circumstanced are called, are frequently to be met with: and I heard of few exceptions to the general kindness with which they are treated. Public feeling is much against the refusing to accept and rear an *engeitado*. The owner of a house, who is in easy circumstances, and yet sends the infant from his own door to the public institution which is provided for its reception, is generally spoken of in terms of indignation. Sometimes a poor man will find one of these presents at his door: and he will generally place it at the landholder's threshold on the following night. This is accounted excusable and even meritorious; for at the Great House the child has nearly a certainty of being well taken care of.

I have observed that, generally speaking, Europeans are less indulgent to their slaves than Brazilians. The former feed them well: but they require from the poor wretches more labour than they can perform, whilst the latter allow the affairs of their estates to continue in the way in which they have been accustomed to be directed. This difference between the two descriptions of the owners is easily accounted for. The European has probably purchased part of his slaves on credit; and has, during the whole course of his life, made the accumulation of riches his chief object. The Brazilian inherits his estate: and as nothing urges him to the necessity of obtaining large profits, he continues the course that has been pointed out to him by the former possessors. His habits of quietude and indolence have led him to be easy and indifferent: and although he may not provide for the maintenance of his slaves with so much care as the European, still they find more time to seek for food themselves. That avaricious spirit which deliberately works a man or a brute animal until it is unfit for farther service, without any regard to the well-being of the

creature, which is thus treated as a mere machine, as if it was formed of wood or iron, is, however, seldom to be met with in those parts of the country which I visited. Instances of cruelty occur (as has been, and will yet be seen), but these proceed from individual depravity, and not from systematic, coldblooded, calculating indifference to the means by which a desired end is to be compassed.

Notwithstanding the relationship of the mulattos on one side to the black race, they consider themselves superior to the mamalucos. They lean to the whites; and from the light in which the Indians are held, pride themselves upon being totally unconnected with them. Still the mulattos are conscious of their connection with men who are in a state of slavery, and that many persons, even of their own colour, are under these degraded circumstances. They have therefore always a feeling of inferiority in the company of white men, if these white men are wealthy and powerful. This inferiority of rank is not so much felt by white persons in the lower walks of life: and these are more easily led to become familiar with individuals of their own colour who are in wealthy circumstances. Still the inferiority which the mulatto feels, is more that which is produced by poverty than that which his colour has caused; for he will be equally respectful to a person of his own cast, who may happen to be rich.[4] The degraded state of the people of colour in the British colonies is most lamentable. In Brazil, even the trifling regulations which exist against them, remain unattended to. A mulatto enters into holy orders, or is appointed a magistrate, his papers stating him to be a white man, but his appearance plainly denoting the contrary. In conversing on one occasion with a man of colour who was in my service, I asked if a certain *Capitão-môr* was not a mulatto man: he answered, "he was, but is not now." I begged him to explain, when he added, "Can a *Capitão-môr* be a mulatto man?" I was intimately acquainted with a priest, whose complexion and hair plainly denoted from whence he drew his origin. I liked him much. He was a well-educated and intelligent man. Besides this individual instance, I met with several others of the same description.

The regiments of militia, which are called mulatto regiments, are so named from all the officers and men being of mixed casts; nor can white persons be admitted into them. The principal officers are men of property: and the colonel, like the commander of any other regiment, is only amenable to the governor of the province. In the white militia regiments, the officers ought to be by law white men. But in practice they are rather reputed white men, for very little pains are taken to prove that there is no mixture of blood. Great

---

[4] The term of *Senhor* or *Senhora* is made use of to all free persons, whites, mulattos, and blacks: and in speaking to a freeman of whatever class or colour the manner of address is the same.

numbers of the soldiers belonging to the regiments which are officered by white men, are mulattos, and other persons of colour. The regiments of the line, likewise, (as I have elsewhere said) admit into the ranks all persons excepting negroes and Indians. But the officers of these must prove nobility of birth. However, as certain degrees of nobility have been conferred upon persons in whose families there is much mixture of blood, this proof cannot be regarded as being required against the mulatto or mamaluco part of the population. Thus an European adventurer could not obtain a commission in these regiments, whilst a Brazilian, whose family has distinguished itself in the province in former times, will prove his eligibility without regard to the blood which runs in his veins. He is noble, let that flow from whence it may.[5]

The late colonel of the mulatto regiment of Recife, by name Nogueira, went to Lisbon, and returned to Pernambuco with the Order of Christ, which the Queen had conferred upon him. A chief person of one of the provinces is the son of a white man and a woman of colour. He has received an excellent education; is of generous disposition; and entertains most liberal views upon all subjects. He has been made a colonel, and a degree of nobility has been conferred upon him; likewise the Regent is sponsor to one of his children. Many other instances might be mentioned. Thus has Portugal, of late years from policy, continued that system into which she was led by her peculiar circumstances in former times. Some of the wealthy planters of Pernambuco, and of the rich inhabitants of Recife, are men of colour. The major part of the best mechanics are also of mixed blood.

It is said that mulattos make bad masters: and this holds good oftentimes with persons of this description, who have been in a state of slavery, and become possessed of slaves of their own, or are employed as managers upon estates. The change of situation would lead to the same consequences in any race of human beings; and cannot be accounted peculiar to the mixed casts. I have seen mulattos of free birth, as kind, as lenient, and as forbearing to their slaves and other dependents, as any white man.

Marriages between white men and women of colour are by no means rare; though they are sufficiently so to cause the circumstance to be mentioned when speaking of an individual who has connected himself in this manner. But this is not said with the intent of lower-

---

[5] To this statement some explanation is necessary, owing to the regulations of the Portuguese military service. Privates are sometimes raised to commissions by the intermediate steps of corporals, quartermasters, and sergeants. These men gain their ensigncies without any relation to their birth: and though a decidedly dark-coloured mulatto might not be so raised, a European of low birth would. It is to enable a man to become a cadet, and then an officer without serving in the ranks, that requires nobility of birth.

ing him in the estimation of others. Indeed the remark is only made
if the person is a planter of any importance, and the woman is decidedly of dark colour; for even a considerable tinge will pass for
white. If the white man belongs to the lower orders, the woman is
not accounted as being unequal to him in rank, unless she is nearly
black. The European adventurers often marry in this manner, which
generally occurs when the woman has a dower. The rich mulatto
families are often glad to dispose of their daughters to these men,
although the person who has been fixed upon may be in indifferent
circumstances; for the colour of the children of their daughters is
bettered; and from the well-known prudence and regularity of this
set of men, a large fortune may be hoped for even from very small
beginnings. Whilst I was at Jaguaribe, I was in the frequent habit
of seeing a handsome young man, who was a native of the island of
St. Michael's. This person happened to be with me on one occasion
when the commandant from the Sertão was staying at my house. The
commandant asked him if he could read and write: and being answered in the negative, said, "then you will not do:" and turning to
me added, "I have a commission from a friend of mine to take with
me back to the Sertão a good-looking young Portuguese of regular
habits, who can read and write, for the purpose of marrying him to
his daughter." Such commissions (*encommendas*) are not unusual.

Still the Brazilians of high birth and large property do not like
to intermarry with persons whose mixture of blood is *very* apparent:
and hence arise peculiar circumstances. A man of this description
becomes attached to a woman of colour; connects himself with her;
and takes her to his home, where she is in a short time visited even
by married women. She governs his household affairs: acts and considers herself as his wife; and frequently after the birth of several
children, when they are neither of them young, he marries her. In
connections of this nature, the parties are more truly attached than
in marriage between persons who belong to two families of the first
rank; for the latter are entered into from convenience rather than
from affection. Indeed the parties, on some occasions, do not see
each other until a few days before the ceremony takes place. It often
occurs, that inclination, necessity, or convenience induces or obliges
a man to separate from the person with whom he is connected. In
this case, he gives her a portion; and she marries a man of her own
rank, who regards her rather as a widow than as one whose conduct
has been incorrect. Instances of infidelity in these women are rare.
They become attached to the men with whom they cohabit: and they
direct the affairs of the houses over which they are placed with the
same zeal that they would display if they had the right of command
over them. It is greatly to the credit of the people of that country,
that so much fidelity should be shewn on one side; and that this

should so frequently as it is, be rewarded by the other party, in the advancement of those who have behaved thus faithfully, to a respectable and acknowledged situation in society. It should be recollected too that the merit of moral feelings must be judged of by the standard of the country, and not by our own institutions. I have only spoken above of what occurs among the planters; for in large towns, man is pretty much the same everywhere.

The Mamalucos are more frequently to be seen in the Sertão than upon the coast. They are handsomer than the mulattos: and the women of this cast particularly surpass in beauty all others of the country. They have the brown tint of mulattos: but their features are less blunt, and their hair is not curled. I do not think that the men can be said to possess more courage than the mulattos. But whether from the knowledge which they have of being of free birth on both sides, or from residing in the interior of the country where the government is more loose, they appear to have more independence of character, and to pay less deference to a white man than the mulattos. When women relate any deed of danger that has been surmounted or undertaken, they generally state that the chief actor in it was a large mamaluco, *mamalucão;* as if they thought this description of men to be superior to all others. Mamalucos may enter into the mulatto regiments; and are pressed into the regiments of the line as being men of colour, without any regard to the sources from which their blood proceeds.

Of the domesticated Indians I have already elsewhere given what accounts I could collect, and what I had opportunities of observing. The wild Indians are only now to be met with at a great distance from the coast of Pernambuco: and although they are very near to Maranhão, and are dreaded neighbors, I had no means of seeing any of them.

I now proceed to mention that numerous and valuable race of men, the creole negroes; a tree of African growth, which has thus been transplanted, cultivated, and much improved by its removal to the New World. The creole negroes stand alone and unconnected with every other race of men: and this circumstance alone would be sufficient, and indeed contributes much to the effect of uniting them to each other. The mulattos, and all other persons of mixed blood, wish to lean towards the whites, if they can possibly lay any claim to relationship. Even the mestizo tries to pass for a mulatto, and to persuade himself and others, that his veins contain some portion of white blood, although that with which they are filled proceeds from Indian and negro sources. Those only who have no pretensions to a mixture of blood, call themselves negroes, which renders the individuals who do pass under this denomination, much attached to each other, from the impossibility of being mistaken for members of any

other cast. They are of handsome persons, brave and hardy, obedient to the whites, and willing to please. But they are easily affronted: and the least allusion to their colour being made by a person of lighter tint, enrages them to a great degree; though they will sometimes say, "a negro I am, but always upright." They are again distinct from their brethren in slavery, owing to their superior situation as free men.

The free creole negroes have their exclusive regiments, as well as the mulattos, of which every officer and soldier must be perfectly black. There are two of these regiments for the province of Pernambuco, which consists of indefinite numbers of men, who are dispersed all over the country. These regiments are distinguished from each other by the names of Old Henriques and New Henriques. The name of Henriques is derived from the famous chieftain, Henrique Díaz, in the time of the Dutch war. I have heard some of the most intelligent of those with whom I have conversed, speak in enthusiastic terms of the aid which he gave to the whites in that struggle. I have seen some portion of one of these regiments, in Recife, accompanying the procession of our Lady of the Rosary, the patroness of negroes. They were dressed in white cloth uniforms, turned up with scarlet: and they looked very soldier-like. They were in tolerable discipline; and seemed to wish to go through the duty of the day in the best manner that they were able. They acted with an appearance of zeal and the desire of excelling. Those of which I speak, formed a finer body of men than any other soldiers which I had an opportunity of seeing in that country. On gala days, the superior black officers in their white uniforms, pay their respects to the governor, exactly in the same manner that the persons of any other cast, holding commissions of equal rank, are expected to go through this form. These men receive no pay, so that their neat appearance on such occasions bespeaks a certain degree of wealth among them; neither are the privates nor any other persons belonging to these regiments paid for their services. Some of the whites rather ridicule the black officers, but not in their presence; and the laugh which is raised against them is caused perhaps by a lurking wish to prevent this insulted race from the display of those distinctions which the government has wisely conceded to them, but which hurt the European ideas of superiority. The old regiment of Henriques was, at the time that I resided in Pernambuco, without a colonel: and I heard much discussion on several occasions among the creole negroes, about the fittest person to be appointed to the vacant situation.

The creole negroes of Recife are, generally speaking, mechanics of all descriptions: but they have not yet reached the higher ranks of life, as gentlemen, as planters, and as merchants. Some of them have accumulated considerable sums of money; and possess many

slaves, to whom they teach their own trade: or these slaves are taught other mechanical employments by which they may become useful. They work for their owners, and render them great profits; for every description of labour is high, and that which requires any degree of skill bears a higher comparative value than the department of which a knowledge is more easily attained. The best church and image painter of Pernambuco is a black man, who has good manners, and quite the air of a man of some importance, though he does not by any means assume too much. The negroes are excluded from the priesthood; and from the offices which the mulattos may obtain through their evasion of the law, but which the decided and unequivocal colour of the negro entirely precludes him aspiring to. In law all persons who are not white, and are born free, class equally. Manumitted slaves are placed upon the same footing as persons born free. However, although the few exclusions which exist against the negroes, are degrading; still in some instances they are befriended by them. They are unable, owing to their colour, to serve in the regiments of the line, or in any regiments excepting those which are exclusively their own. But by means of this regulation they escape the persecutions under which the other casts suffer during the time of recruiting. The officers and men of the Henrique regiments are so united to each other, that the privates and subalterns are less liable to be oppressed by any white men in office even than the soldiers of the mulatto regiments. Of these latter, officers, having a considerable tinge of white, sometimes lean towards the wishes of the *capitão-môr*, or some other rich white officer, instead of protecting his soldiers.

The men whose occupation it is to apprehend runaway negroes, are, almost without exception, creole blacks. They are called *capitães-do-campo*, captains of the field; are subject to a *capitão-môr do campo* who resides in Recife; and receive their commissions either from the governor or from this officer. By these they are authorized to apprehend and take to their owners any slaves who may be found absent from their homes without their master's consent. Several of these men are to be found in every district, employing themselves in such pursuits as they think fit, when their services are not required in that calling which forms their particular duty. They are men of undaunted courage; and are usually followed by two or three dogs, which are trained to seek out, and, if necessary, to attack and bring to the ground those persons whose apprehension their masters are desirous of effecting. The men who bear these commissions can oblige any unauthorized person to give up to them an apprehended negro, for the purpose of being by them returned to his owner.

It is scarcely necessary to name the mestizos; for they usually class with the mulattos; nor are they to be easily distinguished from some of the darker varieties of this cast. A dark coloured man, of a

disagreeable countenance, and badly formed person, is commonly called a mestizo, without any reference to his origin.

3. NEGRO SLAVERY IN BRAZIL

At the close of the colonial period, according to the best available data, Negro slaves constituted one third of the total population of Brazil. On a base of Negro slave labor rested all the important large-scale economic activities of the colony: the cultivation of sugar cane, cotton, and tobacco. How the system functioned at the opening of the nineteenth century is told by Henry Koster with a wealth of factual detail.[6]

✦✦✦✦ The Indian slavery has been for many years abolished in Brazil: and the individuals who are now in bondage in that country are Africans, and their descendants on both sides, or individuals whose mothers are of African origin: and no line is drawn at which the near approach to the colour and blood of the whites entitles the child, whose mother is a slave, to freedom. I have seen several persons who were to all appearance of white origin, still doomed to slavery.

Slaves, however, in Brazil, have many advantages over their brethren in the British colonies. The numerous holidays of which the Catholic religion enjoins the observance, give to the slave many days of rest or time to work for his own profit: thirty-five of these, and the Sundays besides, allow him to employ much of his time as he pleases. Few masters are inclined to restrain the right of their slaves to dispose of these days as they think fit: or, at any rate, few dare, whatever their inclinations may be, to brave public opinion in depriving them of the intervals from work which the law has set apart as their own, that their lives may be rendered less irksome. The time which is thus afforded, enables the slave, who is so inclined, to accumulate a sum of money: however this is by law his master's property, from the incapability under which a slave labours of possessing any thing which he can by right call his own. But I believe there is no instance on record in which a master attempted to deprive his slave of these hard-earned gains. The slave can oblige his master to manumit him, on tendering to him the sum for which he was first purchased, or the price for which he might be sold, if that price is higher than what the slave was worth at the time he was first bought. This regulation, like every one that is framed in favour of slaves, is liable to be evaded, and the master sometimes does refuse to manumit a valuable slave: and no appeal is made by the sufferer, owing to the

[6] Koster, *Travels in Brazil*, II. pp. 189–215, 238–243.

state of law in that country, which renders it almost impossible for the slave to gain a hearing; and likewise this acquiescence in the injustice of the master proceeds from the dread, that if he was not to succeed, he would be punished, and that his life might be rendered more miserable than it was before. Consequently a great deal depends upon the inclinations of the master, who will, however, be very careful in refusing to manumit, owing to the well-known opinion of every priest in favour of this regulation, to the feelings of the individuals of his own class in society, and to those of the lower orders of people: and likewise he will be afraid of losing his slave. He may escape with his money: and the master will then run much risk of never seeing him again, particularly if the individual is a creole slave. In general, therefore, no doubts are urged, when application is made for manumission by a slave to his master; who is indeed oftentimes prepared for it by the habits of industry and regularity of his slave, and by common report among the other slaves and free persons upon the estate, that the individual in question is scraping together a sum of money for this purpose. The master might indeed deprive the slave of the fruits of his labours: but this is never thought of; because the slave preserves his money in a secret place, or has entrusted it to some person upon whom he can depend, and would suffer any punishment rather than disclose the spot in which his wealth lies concealed. A still more forcible reason than any other, for the forbearance of the master, is to be found in the dread of acting against public opinion: in the shame which would follow the commission of such an act; and perhaps the natural goodness which exists in almost every human being, would make him shun such gross injustice, would make him avoid such a deed of baseness.

A slave is often permitted by his owner to seek a master more to his liking; for this purpose a note is given, declaring that the bearer has leave to enter into the service of any one, upon the price which the master demands being paid by the purchaser. With this the slave applies to any individual of property whom he may wish to serve, owing to having heard a good report of his character towards his slaves, or from any other cause. This is a frequent practice; and at least admits the possibility of escape from a severe state of bondage to one that is less irksome.

A considerable number of slaves are manumitted at the death of their masters: and indeed some persons of large property fail not to set at liberty a few of them during their own lifetime. A deed of manumission, however simply it may be drawn out, cannot be set aside. A register of these papers is preserved at the office of every notary-public by which any distress that might be occasioned by the loss of the originals is provided against; for the copy, of course, holds good in law. A slave who has brought into the world, and has reared

ten children, ought to be free, for so the law ordains. But this regulation is generally evaded: and besides, the number of children is too
great for many women to be benefited by it. The price of a new-born
child is 5 £ (20,000 *mil-reis*) and the master is obliged to manumit the
infant at the baptismal font, on the sum being presented. In this manner,
a considerable number of persons are set at liberty; for the smallness
of the price enables many freemen who have had connections with
female slaves to manumit their offspring; and instances occur of the
sponsors performing this most laudable act. Not infrequently female
slaves apply to persons of consideration to become sponsors to their
children, in the hopes that the pride of these will be too great to allow
of their godchildren remaining in slavery. Thus by their own exertions, by the favour of their masters, and by other means, the individuals who gain their freedom annually, are very numerous.

The comforts of slaves in different situations are widely dis-
proportionate. Whilst some are doomed to an existence of excessive
toil and misery, from the nature of their occupations and the characters
of their masters, others lead a comparatively easy life. It is true, that in
countries of which the workmen are free, the daily labour is unequally
divided: but their wages are proportioned accordingly: and as each
man is a free agent, he seeks that employment to which his bodily and
mental powers are befitted. The slave is purchased for a certain purpose; and is to follow the line of life which his master has chalked out
for him.

He is not to be occupied in that which he would himself prefer,
or at any rate his wishes are not consulted upon the subject. The price
for which a slave is to be obtained, and the convenience of the purchaser are oftener consulted, than the fitness of his bodily strength to
the labour which it is his lot to be ordered to perform. Besides the
obligation of following an unsuitable trade, or at any rate of following
one which he has not chosen, he has to endure the still incomparably
greater grievance of bearing with a tyrannical, an inconsiderate, or a
peevish master, whose commands are not to be called in question, whose
will is absolute, and from whom the possibility of appeal is far removed, and that of redress placed at a still greater distance. Masters
are punished by the payment of fines, for cruelty to their slaves, if any
account of such behaviour should reach the ear of the Ouvidor of the
province. But I never heard of punishment having been carried farther
than this trifling manner of correction. The emoluments which proceed from this mode of chastising the offenders, weigh heavily in its
favour. The injury which the slave has received is not, I am afraid,
the only cause which urges the exaction of the stipulated penalty; of
this the slave does not receive any part.

All slaves in Brazil follow the religion of their masters; and notwithstanding the impure state in which the Christian church exists in

that country, still such are the beneficent effects of the Christian religion, that these, its adopted children, are improved by it to an infinite degree; and the slave who attends to the strict observance of religious ceremonies, invariably proves to be a good servant. The Africans, who are imported from Angola, are baptized in lots before they leave their own shores: and on their arrival in Brazil they are to learn the doctrines of the church, and the duties of the religion into which they have entered. These bear the mark of the royal crown upon their breasts, which denotes that they have undergone the ceremony of baptism, and likewise that the king's duty has been paid upon them. The slaves which are imported from other parts of the coast of Africa, arrive in Brazil unbaptized, and before the ceremony of making them Christians can be performed upon them, they must be taught certain prayers, for the acquirement of which one year is allowed to the master, before he is obliged to present the slave at the parish church. The law is not always strictly adhered to as to the time, but it is never evaded altogether. The religion of the master teaches him that it would be extremely sinful to allow his slave to remain a heathen: and indeed the Portuguese and Brazilians have too much religious feeling to let them neglect any of the ordinances of their church. The slave himself likewise wishes to be made a Christian; for his fellow-bondsmen will, otherwise, in every squabble or trifling disagreement with him, close their string of opprobrious epithets with the name of *pagão* (pagan). The unbaptized negro feels that he is considered as an inferior being: and although he may not be aware of the value which the whites place upon baptism, still he knows that the stigma for which he is upbraided, will be removed by it; and therefore he is desirous of being made equal to his companions. The Africans who have been long imported, imbibe a Catholic feeling; and appear to forget that they were once in the same situation themselves. The slaves are not asked whether they will be baptized or not. Their entrance into the Catholic church is treated as a thing of course: and indeed they are not considered as members of society, but rather as brute animals, until they can lawfully go to mass, confess their sins, and receive the sacrament.

The slaves have their religious brotherhoods as well as the free persons: and the ambition of the slave very generally aims at being admitted into one of these, and at being made one of the officers and directors of the concerns of the brotherhood. Even some of the money which the industrious slave is collecting for the purpose of purchasing his freedom, will oftentimes be brought out of its concealment for the decoration of a saint, that the donor may become of importance in the society to which he belongs. The negroes have one invocation of the Virgin (or I might almost say one virgin) which is peculiarly their own. Our Lady of the Rosary is even sometimes painted with a black face and hands. It is in this manner that the slaves are led to place

their attention upon an object in which they soon take an interest, but from which no injury can proceed towards themselves, nor can any through its means be by them inflicted upon their masters. Their ideas are removed from any thought of the customs of their own country; and are guided into a channel of a totally different nature, and completely unconnected with what is practised there. The election of a King of Congo by the individuals who come from that part of Africa, seems indeed as if it would give them a bias towards the customs of their native soil. But the Brazilian Kings of Congo worship Our Lady of the Rosary; and are dressed in the dress of white men. They and their subjects dance, it is true, after the manner of their creole blacks, and mulattos, all of whom dance after the same manner: and these dances are now as much the national dances of Brazil, as they are of Africa. The Portuguese language is spoken by the slaves: and their own dialects are allowed to lie dormant until they are by many of them quite forgotten. No compulsion is resorted to, to make them embrace the habits of their masters: but their ideas are insensibly led to imitate and adopt them. The masters at the same time imbibe some of the customs of their slaves; and thus the superior and his dependent are brought nearer to each other. I doubt not that the system of baptizing the newly imported negroes, proceeded rather from the bigotry of the Portuguese in former times than from any political plan: but it has had the most beneficial effects. The slaves are rendered more tractable. Besides being better men and women, they become more obedient servants. They are brought under the control of the priesthood: and even if this was the only additional hold which was gained by their entrance into the church, it is a great engine of power which is thus brought into action.

But in no circumstance has the introduction of the Christian religion among the slaves been of more service than in the change which it has wrought in the men regarding the treatment of their women, and in the conduct of the females themselves. . . .

The slaves of Brazil are regularly married according to the forms of the Catholic church. The banns are published in the same manner as those of free persons: and I have seen many happy couples (as happy at least as slaves can be) with large families of children rising around them. The masters encourage marriages among their slaves; for it is from these lawful connections that they can expect to increase the number of their creoles. A slave cannot marry without the consent of his master; for the vicar will not publish the banns of marriage without this sanction. It is likewise permitted that slaves should marry free persons. If the woman is in bondage, the children remain in the same state: but if the man is a slave, and she is free, their offspring is also free. A slave cannot be married until the requisite prayers have been learnt, the nature of confession be understood, and the Sacrament

can be received. Upon the estates the master or manager is soon made acquainted with the predilections of the slaves for each other; and these being discovered, marriage is forthwith determined upon, and the irregular proceedings are made lawful. In towns there is more licentiousness among the negroes, as there is among all other classes of men. The passion of love is suposed only to exist in a certain state of civilization, and this may be granted without at the same time declaring that negroes are incapable of lasting attachment, without supposing that the regard of each sex is mere animal desire, unconnected with predilection. That species of affection which is heightened until personal possession is almost forgotten, doubtless is not felt by human beings who are in a state of barbarism; but still a negro may be attached: he may fix upon one object in preference to all others. That this is the case, I can vouch. I have known and have heard of many instances in which punishments and other dangers have been braved to visit a chosen one; in which journeys by night have been made after a day of fatigue; in which great constancy has been shewn, and a determination that the feelings of the heart shall not be controlled.

The great proportion of men upon many of the estates, produce, of necessity, most michievous consequences. A supply is requisite to keep up the number of labourers. The women are more liable to misconduct, and the men imbibe unsettled habits. But if an adequate number of females are placed upon the estate, and the slaves are trained and taught in the manner which is practised upon well-regulated plantations, the negroes will be as correct in their behavior, as any other body of men: and perhaps their conduct may be less faulty than that of other descriptions of persons, who have less to occupy their time, though their education may be infinitely superior. That many men and many women will be licentious, has been and is still the lot of human nature, and not the peculiar fault of the much injured race of which I speak. . . .

As the voyage from the coast of Africa to the opposite shores of South America is usually short, for the winds are subject to little variation, and the weather is usually fine, the vessels which are employed in this traffic are generally speaking small, and not of the best construction. The situation of captain or master of a slave ship is considered of secondary rank in the Portuguese merchant-service: and the persons who are usually so occupied, are vastly inferior to the generality of the individuals who command the large and regular trading vessels between Europe and Brazil. The slave ships were formerly crowded to a most shocking degree; nor was there any means of preventing this. But a law has been passed for the purpose of restricting the number of persons for each vessel. However, I more than suspect, that no attention is paid to this regulation. . . . The rules of the port direct that they shall be disembarked, and taken to St. Amaro, which

is an airy spot, and sufficiently distant from the town to prevent the admittance of any infectious disorder, if such should exist among the newly-imported negroes; and yet the place is at a convenient distance for the purchasers. St. Amaro being situated immediately opposite to Recife, upon the island bank of the expanse of waters which is formed by the tide, on the land site of the town. However, like many others, this excellent arrangement is not attended to: and even if the slaves are removed for a few days to St. Amaro, they are soon conveyed back to the town. Here they are placed in the streets before the doors of the owners, regardless of decency, of humanity, and of due attention to the general health of the town. The small pox, the yaws, and other complaints have thus frequent opportunities of spreading. It is probable, that if the climate was not so very excellent, as it is, this practice would be discontinued; but if it was not put a stop to, and the country was subject to pestilential complaints, the town would not be habitable.

In the day-time, some of the streets of Recife are in part lined with miserable beings, who are lying or sitting promiscuously upon the footpath, sometimes to the number of two or three hundred. The males wear a small piece of blue cloth round their waists, which is drawn between the legs and fastened behind. The females are allowed a larger piece of cloth, which is worn as a petticoat: and sometimes a second portion is given to them, for the purpose of covering the upper parts of the body. The stench which is created by these assemblages is almost intolerable to one who is unaccustomed to their vicinity. . . . These people do not, however, seem to feel their situation, any farther than that it is uncomfortable. Their food consists of salt meat, the flour of the mandioc, beans, and plantains occasionally. The victuals for each day are cooked in the middle of the street in an enormous caldron. At night they are driven into one or more warehouses: and a driver stands to count them as they pass. They are locked in: and the door is again opened at daybreak on the following morning. The wish of these wretched creatures to escape from this state of inaction and discomfort is manifested upon the appearance of a purchaser. They start up willingly, to be placed in the row for the purpose of being viewed and handled like cattle: and on being chosen they give signs of much pleasure. I have had many opportunities of seeing slaves bought; for my particular friends at Recife lived opposite to slave-dealers. I never saw any demonstrations of grief at parting from each other: but I attribute this to the dread of punishment, if there had been any flow of feeling, and to a resigned or rather despairing sensation, which checks any shew of grief, and which has prepared them for the worst, by making them indifferent to whatever may occur: besides, it is not often that a family is brought over together; the separation of relatives and friends has taken place in Africa. It is among the

younger part of the assemblage of persons who are exposed for sale, that pleasure is particularly visible at the change of situation, in being removed from the streets of the town; the negroes of more advanced age do whatever the driver desires, usually with an unchanged countenance. I am afraid that very little care is taken to prevent the separation of relatives who may chance to come over in the same ship: and any consideration on this point lies entirely with the owner of the cargo. A species of relationship exists between the individuals who have been imported in the same ship. They call each other *malungos:* and this term is much regarded among them. The purchaser gives to each of his newly bought slaves a large piece of baize and a straw hat; and as soon as possible marches them off to his estate. I have often in travelling met with many parties going up to their new homes, and have observed that they were usually cheerful; — any thing is better than to sit at the door of the slave merchant in Recife. The new master, too, does every thing in his power to keep them in good humour at first, whatever his conduct may afterwards be towards them.

The slaves which are usually brought to Pernambuco, are known under the names of Angola, Congo, Rebolo, Anjico, Gabam, and Mosambique. These last have only been imported of late years, owing, I rather imagine, to the difficulty with which slaves have been obtained on the western coast of Africa, caused by the vigilance of the British cruisers in that quarter, and the vexations to which some of the slave ships have been liable from detention, although they were ultimately suffered to proceed on their voyages.

The Angola negroes make the best slaves. Many of them have been in bondage in their own country: and therefore to these the change is for the better. Some of them have even served the whites in the city of Loanda, which is the principal Portuguese settlement upon the coast of Africa. But others were free in Angola, and consequently to these is allotted a life of disappointment and vexation, whenever they remember their own country. The negroes from Angola are however usually tractable; and may be taught to perform the menial services of a house or stable without much pains being taken with them; and they often shew great attachment, fidelity, and honesty. The Angola negroes are those who most commonly exert themselves to purchase their own freedom. The Congo negroes partake much of the character of the Angolans, being equally tractable; but they are steadier, and are particularly adapted to the regular routine of field labour. They are less quick in their movements than the Angolans; and do not seem to be so spirited and courageous; they obtain in a short period a knowledge of the Portuguese language. The Rebolos can scarcely in persons be distinguished from the two former, being stoutly made, and not tall. They have a black skin; but it is not shining; and

the features are flat. They seem to be a branch of the Angolans and Congos: but they are more obstinate, and more subject to despond than the others. These three tribes appear to have belonged originally to the same nation; for many parts of their character are similar; their persons are of the same mould; and the dialects of each sufficiently resemble each other to be understood by all the three.

The Anjico negroes shew many marks of being of another nation. They make good slaves, if they are well treated, and are yet preserved under due control. They are difficult to train; and bear a heavy yoke impatiently. There is in them much independence of character, if they dared to shew it. There is also much cunning, and the desire and capability of over-reaching. Their persons are tall, and well formed. Their skins are of a glossy black; their eyes are expressive: and their countenances plainly denote, that it is not by their own will that they continue in slavery. They are not, however, numerous. Great neatness is shown by them in their household arrangements, and they often exert themselves to obtain money; but they are less careful and prudent than the nations of which I have already treated. All the Anjico negroes have three gashes on each cheek, which are cut in a circular form from the ear to the mouth.

The *Gabam*, or Gaboon negroes, have not been very long introduced: and from the well known general character of the nation, they are sold at a reduced price. I have heard many persons state that they are cannibals. They appear to be in a still more savage state than any of the former-mentioned nations; and are much given to despondency and consequent suicide. Indeed ten and even twenty that have been purchased together have, in some instances, in the course of a short period, all died from despair, or have put an end to their lives in a more summary manner. It is with difficulty that the Gaboons can be taught to perform any labour above that of the simplest description; and sometimes they remain for years unbaptized, from the great trouble which is required in making them articulate any sounds to which they have not been accustomed. Yet it is rather that they *will* not be taught, than they *cannot* learn; for I have heard many planters say, that if a Gabam negro can be made cheerful, and be induced to take an interest in those persons who are around him and his occupations, he becomes a most useful and intelligent slave. The *Gabam* negroes are tall and handsome: and their skins are very black and shining. The features of many of them are good, being much less flat and blunt than those of their countrymen in general.

The Mosambique negroes are a poor and ugly race of beings, languid and inactive, and subject to despondency. Their colour inclines to brown: but still they have completely the negro features. As the price of these slaves is much below that of any other description

of negroes, some of the planters have taken them on trial: but they are said to have many of the bad qualities of the Gaboons, without their hardiness.

A negro will sometimes tell his master, that he is determined to die, and too often the effects of his resolve begin shortly afterwards to be perceived. He becomes thin, loses his appetite, and dies almost a skeleton. One of the means which it is very generally said that these miserable beings employ for the purpose of destroying themselves, is that of eating considerable quantities of lime and earth, which either produces emaciation or dropsy. But it is strange that a habit of eating lime and earth should be contracted in some instances by African and likewise by creole children, and as frequently by free children as by those who are in slavery. This practice is treated as if it were a disorder: but it is accounted a habit, which, by attention from those who have the charge of the children — in watching and punishing them, may be conquered without the aid of medicine. I know of some instances in which no medical treatment was deemed necessary: but the individuals recovered by means of chastisement and constant vigilance. It is a subject upon which I was often led to converse: and I discovered that most of the free-born families were acquainted with the practice from experience among their own children, or those of their neighbours; and that they always considered it a habit and not as a disease. Among adults, however, slaves are infinitely more subject to it than free persons.

Pernambuco has never experienced any serious revolt among the slaves; but at Bahia there have been several commotions. I believe that Bahia contains fewer free people than Pernambuco in proportion to the number of slaves. But I cannot avoid attributing the quietude of the latter in some measure to the circumstance of a few of the Gold Coast negroes being imported into it, whilst at Bahia the principal stock of slaves is from that part of Africa. It is by the *Mina* negroes, in Bahia, that the revolts have been made, and by the *Koromanties*, in Jamaica, in 1760. These are, I believe, the same people under different names; and they are represented as possessing great firmness of mind and body, and ferociousness of disposition.

The Obeah-men, of the Columbian islands [the West Indies], and the *Mandingueiros* of Brazil, are evidently, from their practices, the same description of persons. The religion which the Brazilian slaves are taught, has likewise a salutary effect upon this point; for it tends to lessen or entirely remove the faith which was previously entertained by the Africans respecting the incantations of their countrymen. The superstitions of their native land are replaced by others of a more harmless nature. The dreadful effects of faith in the *Obeah*-men, which sometimes occur in the British colonies, are not experienced in Brazil from the *Mandingueiros*. Belief in their powers is certainly not

extinguished: and indeed even some or the creoles imbibe a notion of the efficacy of their spells: but the effects of these are not generally felt. . . .

From the vastness of the country, it might be supposed that if a slave escapes from his master, the chances would be against his return: but this is not the case. The Africans particularly are generally brought back. They are soon distinguished by their manner of speaking the Portuguese language; and if any one of them cannot give a good account of himself, he will not be allowed to remain long unmolested; for the profit arising from the apprehension of a runaway slave is considerable. Besides, the manumitted African generally continues to reside in the neighbourhood of the estate upon which he has served as a slave; so that when a man of this description, that is, an African, comes without being known, to settle in a district, suspicion immediately arises that he is not free. The manumitted creoles remove to where they are not known; because they do not wish that the state in which they were born should reach their new place of residence. An African must have been brought to Brazil as a slave: and therefore his situation of a freeman proves that his character is good, or he could not have obtained his liberty. But a creole may have been born free, and consequently his former state as a slave wishes to conceal. Creole slaves, and more especially mulattos, often do escape, and are never afterwards heard of by their masters: but even these are sometimes brought back. . . .

Some of the negroes who escape, determine to shun the haunts of man. They conceal themselves in the woods, instead of attempting to be received into some distant village as free persons. They form huts, which are called *mocambos*, in the most unfrequented spots; and live upon the game and fruit which their places of retreat afford. These persons sometimes assemble to the number of ten or twelve, and then their dislodgement is difficult; for their acquaintance with the woods around gives them the advantage over any party which may be sent to attack them. Sometimes a whole neighbourhood is disturbed by one of these communities, who rob the provision grounds, steal calves, lambs and poultry; and stories are told of the Gabam negroes stealing children.

The slaves of Maranhão are in a less favourable state than those of Pernambuco, on the whole. But the system which is followed respecting them is radically the same. Their food is usually rice, which is said to disagree with the most of the nations which come from Africa; and the treatment which they receive upon the estates in that part of the country, is said to be more rigorous; but of this I cannot myself speak, for I had no opportunities of judging.

Negroes who are decidedly of incorrigible character, are shipped from Pernambuco to Maranhão; and though the cause for which these transportations are made, is well known, they are often sold to great

advantage. Nothing tends so much to keep a slave in awe, as the threat of sending him to Maranhão, or to Pará.

That the general character of persons who are in a state of slavery should be amiable, and that goodness should predominate, is not to be expected. But we ought rather to be surprised at the existence of that degree of virtue which is to be found among those who are reduced to a situation of so much misery. Slaves are much inclined to pilfer, and particularly towards their masters this is very frequent. Indeed many of them scarcely think that they are acting improperly in so doing. Drunkenness is common among them. A direct answer is not easily obtained from a slave: but the information which is required is learnt by means of four or five questions put in various ways. The necessity for this is frequently caused by stupidity, or from ignorance of the language in which the slave is addressed, rather than from any wish to deceive. It is in their behaviour to their families and companions, that the good part of the human being is displayed: and natural enough it is that it should be so. The negroes shew much attachment to their wives and children, to their other relations if they should chance to have any, and to their *malungos* or fellow passengers from Africa. The respect which is paid to old age, it is extremely pleasing to witness. Superannuated Africans, upon the estates, are never suffered to want any comforts with which it is in the power of their fellow slaves to supply them. The old negroes are addressed by the term of pai and mai, father and mother. The masters likewise add this term to the name of their older slaves, when speaking to them. That the generality of the slaves should shew great attachment to their masters, is not to be expected: why should they? The connection between the two descriptions of persons, is not one of love and harmony, of good producing gratitude, of esteem and respect; it is one of hatred and discord, of distrust, and of continual suspicion; one of which the evil is so enormous, that if any proper feelings exist in those who are supposed to benefit from it, and in those who suffer under it, they proceed from our nature, and not from the system.

It will be seen from the above statement, that the slaves of those parts of Brazil which I have had opportunities of seeing, are more favourably situated than those of the Columbian islands [the West Indies]. But still they are slaves: and in this word is included, great misery, great degradation, great misfortune.

4. THE SOCIAL CONSEQUENCES OF SLAVERY

A forerunner of the Brazilian abolitionists of a later day, Luiz dos Santos Vilhena, regius professor of Greek in Baía from 1787

to 1798, boldly assailed the system of slave labor on which the sugar culture of his province was based. Slavery, and not an enervating tropical climate, he affirmed, was responsible for the dissolute manners and idleness of the Portuguese living in Brazil. The following exerpt from his book on Brazil, written in the form of letters to a Portuguese friend, illustrates the vigor and forthrightness of his attack.[7]

✵✵✵✵ The Negro women and a majority of the mulatto women as well, for whom honor is a delusion, a word signifying nothing, are commonly the first to corrupt their master's sons, giving them their first lessons in sexual license, in which from childhood on they are engulfed; and from this presently arises a veritable troop of little mulattoes whose influence on family life is most pernicious. But it often happens that those who are called the old masters, to distinguish them from their sons, are the very ones who set a bad example for their families through their conduct with their female slaves, giving pain to their wives and perhaps causing their death. Frequently their black favorites contrive to put the legitimate children out of the way, to avoid any difficulties in the event of the master's death.

There are other men who never marry, simply because they cannot get out of the clutches of the harpies in whose power they have been since childhood. There are ecclesiastics, and not a few, who from old and evil habit, forgetting their character and station, live a disorderly life with mulatto and Negro women, by whom they have sons who inherit their property; in this and other ways many of the most valuable properties of Brazil pass into the hands of haughty, arrogant vagabond mulattoes, to the great detriment of the State. This is a matter well deserving of His Majesty's attention, for if these sugar mills and great plantations are not prevented from falling into the hands of these mulattoes, who ordinarily are profligate and set little store by these splendid properties, having come by them so easily, in due time they will all fall into their hands and be ruined, as has happened to the greater part of those that came into the possession of such owners.

You must also know that the passion for having Negroes and mulattoes in the house is so strong here that only death removes them from the household in which they were born; there are many families that have sixty, seventy, and more superfluous persons within their doors. I speak of the city, for in the country this would not be remarkable. All this black brood, whether mulattoes or Negroes, are treated with the greatest indulgence, and that is why they are all vagabonds, insolent, bold, and ungrateful. . . .

[7] Luiz dos Santos Vilhena, *Recopilação de Noticias Soteropolitanas e Brasilicas,* edited by Braz do Amaral, 2 vols., Baía, 1921–1922, I, pp. 138–142. (Excerpt translated by the editor.)

The Negroes are harmful in still another way to the State of Brazil. For since all the servile labors and mechanical arts are in their charge, few are the mulattoes, and fewer still the white men, who will deign to perform such tasks. . . .

It has been observed that he who comes here as servant to some public official continues to be a good servant until he realizes that the work he does for his master is performed in other households by Negroes and mulattoes, whereupon he begins to plead with his master to find him some public employment not open to Negroes. Some masters yield to their entreaties, finding themselves so badgered and badly served that they are driven to distraction. But if they delay in finding them jobs, their servants leave them, preferring to be vagabonds and go about dying from hunger, or to become soldiers and sometimes bandits, to working for an honored master who pays them well and supports and cherishes them — and this only to avoid having to do what Negroes do in other households.

The same occurs with the serving women who accompany the ladies that come to Brazil. The same prejudice induces them to take to the streets; they prefer suffering all the resulting miseries to living in a home where they are honored and sheltered.

The girls of this country are of such disposition that the daughter of the poorest, most abject individual, the most neglected little mulatto wench, would rather go to the scaffold than serve a Duchess, if one were to be found in this country; that is the reason for the great number of ruined and disgraced women in this city.

The whites born in this land must either be soldiers, merchants, notaries, clerks, court officials, judges, or Treasury officials or else hold some other public occupation that is barred to Negroes, such as surgeon, apothecary, pilot, shipmaster or sea-captain, warehouse clerk (*caxeiro do trapiche*), and so forth. A few others are employed as sculptors, goldsmiths, and the like.

Many used to attend the school established by His Majesty in this city, a school that once boasted of excellent students who prepared for the Church and other learned professions. But when their fathers saw that the school was the fixed target at which the recruiting officers and soldiers aimed their shots, and that their sons were being snatched away for garrison duty, against which their immunities, privileges, and exemptions availed them nothing, they became convinced that the State had no further need of ecclesiastics or members of other learned professions . . . , and decided that they would not sacrifice their sons by exposing them to the enmity of autocratic and thoughtless soldiers. . . .

Is it not obvious that the inactivity of the whites is the reason for the laziness of the blacks? Why should a man not dig the ground in Brazil who in Portugal lived solely by his hoe? Why should one not

labor here who in Portugal knew nothing more than to put one hand to the plough-handle and another to the goad?

Why should a man go about here with his body upright who came here bent with labor?

Why should he who knows only obedience want only to command? Why should he who was always a plebeian strut about with the air of a noble?

How plentifully would these blessed lands produce, dear friend, if they were cultivated by other hands than those of savage Negroes, who do no more than scratch their surface!

What great profits they would yield if cultivated by sensible and intelligent men, and if sound views of political economy changed the prevailing system!

No land could boast of greater opulence and plenty than Baía if it were ruled wisely, and if henceforth admittance were denied to slaves, the causes of its backwardness and poverty.

THE INDEPENDENCE OF
LATIN AMERICA

Many factors combined to cause the Latin American Wars of Independence. The discontent of the creole class with Spanish restrictions on its economic and political activity, the influence of French and English liberal doctrines, the powerful example of the American and French Revolutions, and foreign interest in the liquidation of the Spanish Empire in America — all played a part in producing the great upheaval.

The immediate cause of the Spanish-American revolutions was the occupation of Spain by French troops in 1808. Napoleon's intervention provoked an uprising of the Spanish people, headed by *juntas*, or local governing committees. Creole leaders in the colonies soon took advantage of Spain's distresses. Professing loyalty to "the beloved Ferdinand VII," a prisoner in France, they forced the removal of allegedly unreliable Spanish officials and formed governing juntas to rule in the name of the captive king. Their claims of loyalty did not convince the Spanish authorities, and fighting soon broke out between patriots and loyalists.

Simón Bolívar led the struggle for independence in northern South America, and José de San Martín directed the military efforts of the patriots to the south. In 1822 the enigmatic San Martín resigned

command of his army, leaving to Bolívar the task of completing the conquest of Peru, the last Spanish stronghold in the New World. The battle of Ayacucho, won by Sucre, virtually ended the war. Brazil achieved a relatively peaceful separation from Portugal in 1822, under the leadership of Prince Pedro and his adviser José Bonifacio de Andrada.

The Mexican revolution, initiated in 1810 by the creole priest Miguel Hidalgo, was continued after his death by another liberal curate, José María Morelos. These men attempted to combine the creole ideal of independence with a program of social reform in behalf of the Indian and mixed-blood masses. The radicalism of Hidalgo and Morelos alienated many creole conservatives, who joined the royalist forces to suppress the revolt. Later, fearing the loss of their privileges as a result of the liberal revolution of 1820 in Spain, the same conservative coalition schemed to bring about a separation from the mother country. They found an agent in the ambitious creole officer Agustín de Iturbide. His Plan of Iguala offered a compromise solution temporarily acceptable to liberals and conservatives, to creoles and many Spaniards. Slight loyalist opposition was swiftly overcome, and in September, 1822, a national congress proclaimed the independence of the Mexican Empire.

21 ✢ The Background of the Wars of Independence

In the closing years of the eighteenth century a small number of Spanish-Americans began to dream of independence and even to work for the overthrow of Spanish rule. Most of them came from the wealthy and cultivated creole class, which had become increasingly resentful of Spanish restrictions on its economic and political activity.

From the writings of French and English philosophers enlightened creoles learned to regard the colonial system as unjust and irrational and to believe that all rightful authority derived from the people. The success of the North American and French Revolutions encouraged a few daring spirits to organize conspiracies, which were, however, easily discovered and crushed by the Spanish Government. Creole timidity and political inexperience and the indifference of the masses would probably have long delayed the achievement of Spanish-American independence if external factors had not hastened its coming.

British efforts to conquer new markets for England's expanding industry and commerce weakened Spain's hold on her American possessions. The British invasions of La Plata (1806–1807), defeated by the people of Buenos Aires without Spanish aid, placed arms in creole hands and inspired the *porteños* with confidence in their own powers. French attempts to dominate Spain influenced still more decisively

the fate of the Spanish colonies. In 1808 Napoleon forced the abdication of Charles IV and his son Ferdinand VII, and placed his brother Joseph on the Spanish throne. To these insults the Spanish people responded with a great insurrection against French occupation troops. Local juntas arose in the regions under patriot control. Later a central junta assumed leadership of the movement in the name of the captive King Ferdinand VII.

In the colonies the creole radicals watched the course of events in Spain with secret satisfaction. Confident that the French armies would crush all Spanish opposition, they prepared to take power into their own hands under the pretence of loyalty to Ferdinand. Early in 1810 news reached the colonies that French armies had overrun Andalusia and were threatening Cadiz, last stronghold of the Spanish cause. Swiftly the creole leaders moved into action. In Caracas, Buenos Aires, Bogotá, and Santiago they organized popular demonstrations that compelled the royal authorities to yield control to local juntas dominated by the creole element. But their hopes of a relatively peaceful transition to independence were doomed to failure.

1. THE CLEAVAGE WITHIN

By the close of the colonial period the creoles and peninsular Spaniards had become two mutually hostile castes, differing in their occupations and ideas. The Spaniards justified their privileged status by reference to the alleged indolence and incapacity of the natives. The creoles vented their spleen by describing the Europeans as mean and grasping parvenus. The pro-Spanish historian Alamán offers many revealing details of the cleavage within the colonial upper class in his classic History of Mexico.[1]

✦✦✦✦ The number of peninsular Spaniards who resided in New Spain in 1808 was in the neighborhood of 70,000. They occupied nearly all the principal posts in the administration, the Church, the judiciary, and the army; commerce was almost exclusively in their hands; and they possessed large fortunes, consisting of cash, which they employed in various lines of business and in all kinds of farms and properties. Those who were not officeholders had generally left their country at a very early age, belonged to poor but honest families, especially those who came from the Basque provinces and the mountains of Santander, and were for the most part of good character. Since they aimed to make their fortune, they were ready to gain it by every kind of pro-

[1] Alamán, *Historia de Méjico*, I, pp. 8-14. (Excerpt translated by the editor.)

ductive labor; neither great distances, perils, nor unhealthy climates frightened them. Some came to serve in the house of some relative or friend of the family; others were befriended by their countrymen. All began as clerks, subject to a severe discipline, and from the first learned to regard work and thrift as the only road to wealth. There was some relaxation of manners in Mexico City and Vera Cruz, but in all the cities of the interior, no matter how rich or populous, the clerks in each house were bound to a very narrow and almost monastic system of order and regularity. This Spartan type of education made of the Spaniards living in America a species of men not to be found in Spain herself, and one which America will never see again.

As their fortunes improved or their merits won recognition, they were often given a daughter of the house in marriage, particularly if they were relatives — or they might set up their own establishments; but all married creole girls, for very few of the women there had come from Spain, and these were generally the wives of officeholders. With financial success and kinship to the respectable families of the town came respect, municipal office, and influence, which sometimes degenerated into absolute dominance. Once established in this manner, the Spaniards never thought of returning to their country, and they considered that their only proper concerns were the furthering of their business affairs, the advancement of their communities, and the comfort and dignity of their families. Thus every wealthy Spaniard came to represent a fortune formed for the benefit of the country, a prosperous family rooted in Mexican soil, or, if he left no family, a source of pious and beneficial foundations designed to shelter orphans and succor the needy and disabled — foundations of which Mexico City presents so many examples. These fortunes were formed through the arduous labors of the field, the long practice of commerce, or the more risky enterprise of the mines. Although these occupations did not usually permit rapid enrichment, the economy practiced by these families, who lived frugally, without luxurious furniture or clothing, helped them to attain this goal. Thus all the towns, even the less important ones, included a number of families of modest fortunes, whose parsimony did not prevent the display of liberality on occasions of public calamity or when the needs of the state required it. . . .

The creoles rarely preserved these economical habits or pursued the professions that had enriched their fathers. The latter, amid the comforts that their wealth afforded, likewise failed to subject their sons to the severe discipline in which they themselves had been formed. Wishing to give their sons a more brilliant education, suitable to their place in society, they gave them a training that led to the Church or to the practice of law, or left them in a state of idleness and liberty that was deleterious to their character. Some sent their sons to the seminary of Vergara, in the province of Guipuzcoa in Spain,

after that institution had won renown as a school providing general instruction, and if this practice had become general it not only would have contributed greatly to the diffusion of useful knowledge in America but would have aided in formation of more durable bonds between Spanish America and the mother country. From the other and pernicious kind of rearing resulted this state of affairs: The European clerks, married to the master's daughters, carried on his business and became the principal support of the family, increasing their wives' inheritances, whereas the creole sons wasted their substance and in a few years were ruined — at which time they looked about for some trifling desk job that would barely keep them alive in preference to an active and laborious life that would assure them an independent existence.[2] The classical education that some of them had received, and the aristocratic manner that they affected in their days of idleness and plenty, made them scornful of the Europeans, who seemed to them mean and covetous because they were economical and active; they regarded these men as inferiors because they engaged in trades and occupations which they considered unworthy of the station to which their own fathers had raised them. Whether it was the effect of this vicious training or the influence of a climate that conduced to laxity and effeminacy, the creoles were generally indolent and negligent; of sharp wits, rarely tempered by judgment and reflection; quick to undertake an enterprise but heedless of the means necessary to carry it out; giving themselves with ardor to the present, but giving no thought to the future; prodigal in times of good fortune and resigned and long-suffering in adversity. The effect of these unfortunate propensities was the brief duration of their wealth; the assiduous efforts of the Europeans to form fortunes and pass them on to their children may be compared to the bottomless barrel of the Danaïdes, which no amount of water could fill. It resulted from this that the Spanish race in America, in order to remain prosperous and opulent, required a continuous accretion of European Spaniards who came to form new families, while those established by their predecessors fell into oblivion and indigence.

Although the laws did not establish any difference between these two classes of Spaniards, or indeed with respect to the mestizos born

---

[2] Hence the well-known proverb: "The father a merchant, the son a gentleman, the grandson a beggar," which characterized in a few words this transition from wealth gained by labor to idleness and prodigality, and from that to misery. This prodigality had a long history. Balbuena, in his *Grandeza mejicana*, a poem written in 1603, includes among the circumstances that made life in Mexico City pleasanter than anywhere else in the world,

> "That prodigal giving of every ilk,
> Without a care how great the cost,
> Of pearls, of gold, of silver, and of silk. . . ."

to either class by Indian mothers, a distinction came to exist between them in fact. With it arose a declared rivalry that, although subdued for a long time, might be feared to break out with the most serious consequences when the occasion should offer. As has been said, the Europeans held nearly all the high offices,[3] as much because Spanish policy required it as because they had greater opportunity to request and obtain them, being near the fountainhead of all favors. The rare occasions on which creoles secured such high posts occurred through fortunate coincidences or when they went to the Spanish capital to solicit them. Although they held all the inferior posts, which were much more numerous, this only stimulated their ambition to occupy the higher posts as well. Although in the first two centuries after the Conquest the Church offered Americans greater opportunities for advancement, and during that period many obtained[4] bishoprics, canonships, pulpits, and lucrative benefices, their opportunities in this sphere had gradually been curtailed. . . . The Europeans also dominated the cloisters, and in order to avoid the frequent disturbances caused by the rivalry of birth some religious orders had provided for an alternation of offices, electing European prelates in one election and Americans in the next; but as a result of a distinction introduced between the Europeans who had come from Spain with the garb and those who assumed it in America, the former were favored with another term, resulting in two elections of Europeans to one of creoles. If to this preference in administrative and ecclesiastical offices, which was the principal cause of the rivalry between the two classes, are added the fact that . . . the Europeans possessed great riches (which, though the just reward of labor and industry, excited the envy of the Americans . . .); the fact that the wealth and power of the peninsulars sometimes gained them more favor with the fair sex, enabling them to form more advantageous unions; and the fact that all these conditions combined had given them a decided predominance over the creoles — it is not difficult to explain the jealousy and rivalry that steadily grew between them, resulting in a mortal enmity and hatred.

[3] Of the one hundred and seventy viceroys who governed in America until 1813, only four had been born there — and that by chance, as the sons of officeholders. Three of them were viceroys of Mexico: Don Luis de Velasco, son of the Luis de Velasco who also held that office and died in Mexico in 1564; Don Juan de Acuna, Marquis of Casafuerte, born in Lima, who governed the viceroyalty between 1722 and 1734 and died there, being buried in the church of San Cosme de Mexico; and the Count of Revilla Gigedo, who was born in Havana while his father was captain-general of the island of Cuba, whence he was transferred to the viceroyalty of Mexico. The three were models of probity, capacity, and zeal. Of the six hundred and two captains general and presidents, fourteen had been creoles. . . .

[4] Of the seven hundred and six bishops who held office in Spanish America until 1812, one hundred and five were creoles, although few held miters of the first class. . . .

2. THE CRIME OF ANTONIO NARIÑO

Antonio Nariño (1765–1823), a cultivated and wealthy creole of Bogotá, incurred Spanish wrath when he translated and printed on his own press the French Declaration of the Rights of Man *(1789). For this subversive activity he was sentenced to imprisonment in Africa for ten years. He lived to become a leader and patriarch of the independence movement in New Granada, and to witness its triumph. The following excerpt is from an official report to the Spanish king on Nariño's trial.*[5]

✠✠✠✠ In the course of the search that was made among the papers of Nariño, one of the following tenor was found: "I have the idea of founding in this city a reading club along the lines of those to be found in some casinos of Venice; the members would meet in a spacious room, and after the expenses of lighting, etc., had been met, the rest would be spent for the purchase of the best newspapers, foreign journals, and other similar periodicals, according to the amount of the subscription. We would meet at certain hours, read the newspapers, criticize them, and converse about various matters, in this way passing some entertaining though useful hours. Members of the society might include Don José María Lozano, Don José Antonio Ricaurte, Don Francisco Zea, Don Francisco Tobar, Don Joaquín Camacho, Dr. Iriarte. . . ."

There was also found among his papers a plan for a study, with various inscriptions to Liberty, Reason, Philosophy, and others, among which the most notable is the following: "He snatched the lightning from the heavens, and the scepter from the hands of tyrants"; and above: "God, not Plato and Franklin," and a chain on a pedestal. Asked about this plan and the inscriptions, he said that it was all in his own handwriting; that the design was a rough sketch that he had made as a plan for his study, some seven or eight months previously; that the inscriptions to Philosophy, Reason, and Minerva were his work, and the others by the authors that he cited. . . .

Asked how he could think of placing in his study at the foot of the picture of Franklin the inscription which said: "He snatched the lightning from the heavens, and the scepter from the hands of tyrants," the second part of which was so scandalous and offensive to all legitimate monarchs, and consequently to Your Majesty, he replied that his attention had been caught by the first part of the inscription, which alluded to the electricity of the skies, in which his interest was well known; that he could see no reason for omitting the second part, knowing that it had been published in France without objection from the

[5] Eduardo Posada, ed., *El Precursor*, Bogotá, 1903, Appendix, pp. 607–609, 612–614. (Excerpt translated by the editor.)

royal government; and that he had never imagined that it might be censured as offensive to Your Majesty, whom he regarded as a most humane and just king.

He was asked how he could say this, when in his declaration Don Gabriel José Manzano . . . told how one day, when the accused was in Manzano's store for the purpose of buying a certain article, Manzano had said of its quality "that it was fit for a king," and Nariño had scornfully replied, "Drop that business of kings," which sounded very bad to Manzano, and made him believe . . . that the accused sustained sentiments and principles opposed to the legitimate authority of kings, and consequently to that of Your Majesty. He replied that the deposition on which the charge was based was false and calumnious, and that he had not the slightest recollection of the incident. . . .

On July 2, 1795, the prosecutors Berrio and Blaya, on the basis of the facts that emerged from the summary and his confession, charged Nariño and his accomplice Don Diego Espinosa with guilt in having published that seditious book, making most criminal use of the printing press, and demanded that both suffer the appropriate serious penalties which they had incurred under the laws and the royal dispositions. They pointed out that as far as the principal offense of publication was concerned, both had confessed and were convicted, offering no defense that might extenuate or lessen their offense or the malice with which they had committed it, for the sole aim of making five or six hundred pesos could not have moved Nariño to make this clandestine publication, since as treasurer of tithes he had many thousands at his disposal. The prosecutors also pointed out that the body of the offense, the cited book, was not attached to the proceedings, but a sufficient idea of its contents was given in the declaration of Don Francisco Carrasco, who had read it and had it in his possession, and who said that it contained a chapter that said or taught *that it was permissible for a man to do anything that did not injure his fellowmen; that it was permissible, in point of religion, for a man to think freely and express his thoughts, and that this was liberty;* that with respect to the power of kings, it stated *that since their power emanated from the people, the latter could set them up and remove them, and that their power was tyrannical,* and that this was the substance of this book. They said that even brief reflection on such expressions or phrases would show the extent of the crime committed here — they were contrary to the liberty of which they prated; they were subversive of all political order; they destroyed the union of men and aspired toward anarchy; they detached vassals from just obedience to their sovereign and denied his legitimate authority and rights; they tended directly against the very sovereignty of monarchs, and were anti-Catholic. . . . They further said that it was notable that this book was published at just the right time to assault

the minds of the unwary, when all Europe was threatened with seductions, calamities, and scenes of blood and slaughter, when perils besieged us on all sides, and when Your Majesty was engaged in saving his vassals from the most unheard-of barbarism, and from all the horrors of infidelity.

3. AN ABORTIVE CONSPIRACY

In 1797, three years after Nariño published the Declaration of the Rights of Man *in Bogotá, a conspiracy against Spanish rule was discovered in the town of La Guaira in Venezuela. The ringleaders fled to Trinidad, but one of them, José María España, having ventured to return to Venezuela, was seized and hanged. Among the papers of the conspirators was discovered a document of forty-four articles that embodied their program. French revolutionary influence is clearly evident in this document, which is considerably to the left of the constitution actually adopted by the Venezuelan revolutionists in 1811. Among its main provisions were the following.[6]*

✠✠✠✠ In the name of the Sacred Trinity and of Jesus, Mary, and Joseph, Amen:

The commanders of the provinces of Tierra Firme of South America, gathered in the place of N. to deal with and confer about the measures that should be adopted to restore to the American people their freedom, after a mature examination and long reflection, agreed, among other matters, that for the time being all the towns should observe the following articles:

1. All the inhabitants shall preserve union, constancy, and faith among themselves, and all shall form the firm resolution to die before abandoning this just cause.

2. Since this enterprise is of common interest, no one shall be permitted to regard it with indifference: the individual who holds back from this affair shall be immediately arrested, and such proceedings shall be taken against him as justice demands; whoever opposes it in any way shall be immediately punished as a declared enemy of the good of the Fatherland.

3. Whoever under cover of this revolution (daughter of reason, justice, and virtue) for private purposes sets fire to any buildings, commits any murder, strikes any person, perpetrates any robbery,

[6] Pedro Grases, *La conspiración de Gual y España y el ideario de la independencia*, Caracas, 1949, pp. 170–178. (Excerpt translated by the editor.)

treats any woman improperly, or steals any papers, shall be immediately and severely punished, without regard to his class.

4. The soldier or patriot who during the revolution distinguishes himself in any action shall be substantially rewarded, as will anyone who is disabled, and finally whoever has the misfortune to perish shall have his name immortalized and his family rewarded in proportion to his merit.

5. As soon as any town receives notice of this essential resolution, the townspeople will arm themselves as well as they can, and divided into various bands, each under the command of an elected head, shall proclaim in all the streets and squares: Long live the American people! They shall seize all offices and places where there are public moneys, papers, military stores, and foodstuffs, sealing their doors and leaving at each a sufficient number of soldiers and patriots for their custody, not permitting these doors to be opened or any papers, moneys, or any other effects to be moved without the express order of the Governing Junta or the military commander and Chief of the Revolution.

6. All officials presently employed in the Treasury or the army and in the administration of justice shall be immediately deposed by edicts, and the people shall be summoned to meet at a designated time and place for the election of an interim Governing Junta, the number of its members to be proportionate to the population and circumstances of each town. Only those landowners can be elected members of this Junta who have previously given unequivocal proof of their continued patriotism. . . .

11. All ecclesiastics, churches, and convents shall continue to receive their revenues as before the Revolution, but if any of them, against the divine doctrines of the gospel and the Sacred Books, should preach, exhort, disseminate papers, or commit any other action against the general welfare, stripping himself of his character of spiritual minister to become a defender of tyranny, he shall be treated as a traitor to the Fatherland and punished with the rigor of the laws. . . .

14. The cultivation and sale of tobacco shall be free, from the very beginning of the Revolution in each town; such foodstuffs as bread, rice, vegetables, roots, garden stuff, fruits, etc., shall also be free from all duty, but all other kinds of contributions and tributes shall remain on their present footing, reduced by one fourth, until the Junta General makes a decision. . . .

16. It shall be the care of the Governing Juntas to establish good order in their respective towns, to encourage by all possible means agriculture, industry, arts, and commerce, and more particularly the planting of all articles that are basic necessities, so that the towns and the army may not lack the essentials of daily living at any time. . . .

18. All our towns and harbors shall be open to all the nations of the world, preserving the greatest harmony with them and the most exact neutrality toward the belligerent powers. . . .

19. By these presents we proclaim the natural equality of all the inhabitants of the provinces and districts. The whites, Indians, mixed-bloods (*pardos*) and Negroes are advised to live in the greatest harmony, regarding each other as brothers in Jesus Christ and as made equal by God; they should seek to surpass each other only in merits and virtue, which are the only two true and real distinctions among men, and the only ones to exist in the future among the inhabitants of our republic.

33. By virtue of this equality the payment of Indian tribute — with which the tyrannical government insultingly stamped and oppressed the Indians, and which was imposed upon the lands that were forcibly usurped from them — is abolished; it shall be one of the cares of our government to insure their ownership of the lands that they possess, or of others that may be more useful to them, affording them the means to be as happy as other citizens.

34. Slavery is abolished as repugnant to humanity. By virtue of this provision, all masters shall present to the Governing Junta of their respective towns the number of their slaves with a sworn list of their names, country of origin, age, sex, employment, original cost, and number of years of service, together with a note of their conduct and indispositions, if any, in order that the Junta General may determine the amounts that should justly be paid to the respective owners out of the public funds. . . .

36. All these new citizens shall take an oath of loyalty to the Fatherland, and the able-bodied males shall serve in the militia until the liberty of the people is secured, or as long as the circumstances require. In the interim, so that agriculture may not suffer the least injury, the slaves employed in agriculture shall remain with their former masters, but on condition of receiving a just wage and proper treatment, and in order to avoid any excesses on either part, no slave or new citizen of this kind may leave his master without just cause, approved by one of the members of the Governing Junta, who shall be named by the judge in these cases.

37. When the liberty of the Fatherland is secured, these new citizens will be discharged and will receive all the aid that may be judged necessary for their regular establishment. . . .

43. In all the towns, from this very instant, the rights of men will be published for the intelligence and government of all. . . .

44. In token of the unity, harmony, and equality which should reign constantly among all the inhabitants of the Tierra Firme, the national device shall be a cockade of four colors, namely: white, blue, yellow, and red.

The significance of the four colors:
> The four colors of the united patriots, who are mixed-bloods (*pardos*), Negroes, whites, and Indians.
> The union of the four provinces that compose the State: Caracas, Maracaibo, Cumaná, and Guayana.
> The four foundations of the rights of men are equality, liberty, property, and security.

4. THE GREAT FORERUNNER

Of all the precursores *or forerunners of Spanish-American independence, none had a more remarkable history than Francisco de Miranda (1750–1816). A high point of Miranda's career was his effort to revolutionize Venezuela with the aid of North American volunteers — the ill-fated* Leander *expedition of 1806. On board the* Leander *as it headed toward the coast of Venezuela and disaster was one James Biggs, who later wrote the following sketch of Miranda.*[7]

✦✦✦✦ From this narrative, in connection with the prior history of General Miranda, you will receive an impression of his character not so favourable, as that entertained by many persons. I have related facts. They must be allowed to speak for themselves. His imagination and feelings were an overmatch for his judgment. He is more rash and presumptuous in projects, than dexterous in extricating himself from difficulties. In religion he is reputed skeptical; but in our hearing he never derided subjects of this nature. He used formerly to talk infidelity, to the offence of the serious; experience has taught him caution, or he has changed his sentiments. It is said upon good authority, that he partook the sacrament at Coro. He is too much of an enthusiast in his favourite objects to allow his means to be enfeebled by moral scruples. I am willing to believe he has as much conscience as the impetuous passions of such men generally admit.

I make a few remarks on his person, manners, and petty habits.

He is about five feet ten inches high. His limbs are well proportioned; his whole frame is stout and active. His complexion is dark, florid, and healthy. His eyes are hazel-coloured, but not of the darkest hue. They are piercing, quick, and intelligent, expressing more of the severe than the mild feelings. He has good teeth, which he takes much care to keep clean. His nose is large and handsome, rather of the English than Roman cast. His chest is broad and flat.

---

[7] James Biggs, *The History of Don Francisco de Miranda's Attempt to Effect a Revolution in South America*, Boston, 1808, pp. 288–291.

His hair is grey, and he wears it tied long behind, with powder. He has strong grey whiskers, growing on the outer edges of his ears, as large as most Spaniards have on their cheeks. In the contour of his visage, you plainly perceive an expression of pertinaciousness and suspicion. Upon the whole, without saying he is an elegant, we may pronounce him a handsome man. He has a constant habit of picking his teeth. When sitting, he is never perfectly still; his foot or hand must be moving to keep time with his mind, which is always in exercise. He always sleeps a few moments after dinner, and then walks till bedtime, which with him is about midnight. He is an eminent example of temperance. A scanty or bad meal is never regarded by him as a subject of complaint. He uses no ardent spirits; seldom any wine. Sweetened water is his common beverage. Sweetness and warmth, says he, are the two greatest physical goods; and acid and cold are the greatest physical evils in the universe.

He is a courtier and gentleman in his manners. Dignity and grace preside in his movements. Unless when angry, he has a great command of his feelings; and can assume what looks and tones he pleases. His demeanour is often marked by hauteur and distance. When he is angry he loses discretion. He is impatient of contradiction. In discourse, he is logical in the arrangement of his thoughts. He appears conversant on all subjects. His iron memory prevents his ever being at a loss for names, dates, and authorities.

He used his mental resources and colloquial powers with great address to recommend himself to his followers. He assumed the manners of a father and instructor to the young men. He spoke of the prospect of success, and of the preparations made for him, with great confidence. The glory and advantages of the enterprize were described in glowing colours. At another time, he detailed his travels, his sufferings and escapes, in a manner to interest both their admiration and sympathy. He appeared the master of languages, of science and literature. In his conversations, he carried his hearers to the scenes of great actions, and introduced them to the distinguished characters of every age. He took excursions to Troy, Babylon, Jerusalem, Rome, Athens and Syracuse. Men famed as statesmen, heroes, patriots, conquerors, and tyrants, priests and scholars, he produced, and weighed their merits and defects. Modern history and biography afforded him abundant topics. He impressed an opinion of his comprehensive views, his inexhaustible fund of learning; his probity, his generosity, and patriotism. After all, this man of blazoned fame, must, I fear, be considered as having more learning than wisdom; more theoretical knowledge than practical talent; too sanguine and too opinionated to distinguish between the vigour of enterprize and the hardiness of infatuation.

5. THE FORGING OF A REBEL

In his valuable brief autobiography, Manuel Belgrano (1770–1821), one of the Fathers of Argentine Independence, describes the influences and events that transformed a young creole of wealth and high social position into an ardent revolutionary. The French Revolution, disillusionment with Bourbon liberalism, the English invasions, and finally the events of 1808 in Spain all played their part in this process.[8]

✦✦✦✦ The place of my birth was Buenos Aires; my parents were Don Domingo Belgrano y Peri, known as Pérez, a native of Onella in Spain, and Doña María Josefa González Casero, a native of Buenos Aires. My father was a merchant, and since he lived in the days of monopoly he acquired sufficient wealth to live comfortably and to give his children the best education to be had in those days.

I studied my first letters, Latin grammar, philosophy, and a smattering of theology in Buenos Aires. My father then sent me to Spain to study law, and I began my preparation at Salamanca; I was graduated at Valladolid, continued my training at Madrid, and was admitted to the bar at Valladolid. . . .

Since I was in Spain in 1789, and the French Revolution was then causing a change in ideas, especially among the men of letters with whom I associated, the ideals of liberty, equality, security, and property took a firm hold on me, and I saw only tyrants in those who would restrain a man, wherever he might be, from enjoying the rights with which God and Nature had endowed him. . . .

When I completed my studies in 1793 political economy enjoyed great popularity in Spain; I believe this was why I was appointed secretary of the *consulado* of Buenos Aires, established when Gardoqui was minister. The official of the department in charge of these matters even asked me to suggest some other well-informed persons who could be appointed to similar bodies to be established in the principal American ports.

When I learned that these consulados were to be so many Economic Societies that would discuss the state of agriculture, industry, and commerce in their sessions, my imagination pictured a vast field of activity, for I was ignorant of Spanish colonial policy. I had heard some muffled murmuring among the Americans, but I attributed this to their failure to gain their ends, never to evil designs of the Spaniards that had been systematically pursued since the Conquest.

[8] Ricardo Levene, ed., *Los sucesos de mayo contados por sus actores*, Buenos Aires, 1928, pp. 60–71. (Excerpt translated by the editor.)

On receiving my appointment I was infatuated with the brilliant prospects for America. I had visions of myself writing memorials concerning the provinces so that the authorities might be informed and provide for their well-being. It may be that an enlightened minister like Gardoqui, who had resided in the United States, had the best of intentions in all this. . . .

I finally departed from Spain for Buenos Aires; I cannot sufficiently express the surprise I felt when I met the men named by the king to the council which was to deal with agriculture, industry, and commerce and work for the happiness of the provinces composing the vice-royalty of Buenos Aires. All were Spanish merchants. With the exception of one or two they knew nothing but their monopolistic business, namely, to buy at four dollars and sell for eight. . . .

My spirits fell, and I began to understand that the colonies could expect nothing from me who placed their private interests above those of the community. But since my position gave me an opportunity to write and speak about some useful topics, I decided at least to plant a few seeds that some day might bear fruit. . . .

I wrote various memorials about the establishment of schools. The scarcity of pilots and the direct interest of the merchants in the project presented favorable circumstances for the establishment of a school of mathematics, which I obtained on condition of getting the approval of the Court. This, however, was never secured; in fact, the government was not satisfied until the school had been abolished, because although the peninsulars recognized the justice and utility of such establishments, they were opposed to them because of a mistaken view of how the colonies might best be retained.

The same happened to a drawing school which I managed to establish without spending even half a real for the teacher. The fact is that neither these nor other proposals to the government for the development of agriculture, industry, and commerce, the three important concerns of the consulado, won its official approval; the sole concern of the Court was with the revenue that it derived from each of these branches. They said that all the proposed establishments were luxuries, and that Buenos Aires was not yet in a condition to support them.

I promoted various other useful and necessary projects, which had more or less the same fate, but it will be the business of the future historian of the consulado to give an account of them; I shall simply say that from the beginning of 1794 to July, 1806, I passed my time in futile efforts to serve my country. They all foundered on the rock of the opposition of the government of Buenos Aires, or that of Madrid, or that of the merchants who composed the consulado, for whom there was no other reason, justice, utility, or necessity than their commercial interest. Anything that came into conflict with that

interest encountered a veto, and there was nothing to be done about it.

It is well known how General Beresford entered Buenos Aires with about four hundred men in 1806. At that time I had been a captain in the militia for ten years, more from whim than from any attachment to the military art. My first experience of war came at that time. The Marqués de Sobremonte, then viceroy of the provinces of La Plata, sent for me several days before Beresford's disastrous entrance and requested me to form a company of cavalry from among the young men engaged in commerce. He said that he would give me veteran officers to train them; I sought them but could not find any, because of the great hostility felt for the militia in Buenos Aires. . . .

The general alarm was sounded. Moved by honor, I flew to the fortress, the point of assembly; I found there neither order nor harmony in anything, as must happen with groups of men who know nothing of discipline and are completely insubordinate. The companies were formed there, and I was attached to one of them. I was ashamed that I had not the slightest notion of military science and had to rely entirely on the orders of a veteran officer — who also joined voluntarily, for he was given no assignment.

This was the first company, which marched to occupy the *Casa de las Filipinas*. Meanwhile the others argued with the viceroy himself that they were obliged only to defend the city and not to go out into the country; consequently they would agree only to defend the heights. The result was that the enemy, meeting with no opposition from veteran troops or disciplined militia, forced all the passes with the greatest ease. There was some stupid firing on the part of my company and some others in an effort to stop the invaders, but all in vain, and when the order came to retreat and we were falling back I heard someone say: "They did well to order us to retreat, for we were not made for this sort of thing."

I must confess that I grew angry, and that I never regretted more deeply my ignorance of even the rudiments of military science. My distress grew when I saw the entrance of the enemy troops, and realized how few of them there were for a town of the size of Buenos Aires. I could not get the idea out of my head, and I almost went out of my mind, it was so painful to me to see my country under an alien yoke, and above all in such a degraded state that it could be conquered by the daring enterprise of the brave and honorable Beresford, whose valor I shall always admire.

[A resistance movement under the leadership of Santiago Liniers drives the British out of Buenos Aires. A second English invasion, commanded by General John Whitelocke, is defeated, and the entire British force is compelled to surrender. B.K.]

General Liniers ordered the quartermaster-general to receive

the paroles of the officer prisoners; for this reason Brigadier-General Crawford, together with his aides and other high officers, came to his house. My slight knowledge of French, and perhaps certain civilities that I showed him, caused General Crawford to prefer to converse with me, and we entered upon a discussion that helped to pass the time — although he never lost sight of his aim of gaining knowledge of the country and, in particular, of its opinion of the Spanish Government.

So, having convinced himself that I had no French sympathies or connections, he divulged to me his ideas about our independence, perhaps in the hope of forming new links with this country, since the hope of conquest had failed. I described our condition to him, and made it plain that we wanted our old master or none at all; that we were far from possessing the means required for the achievement of independence; that even if it were won under the protection of England, she would abandon us in return for some advantage in Europe, and then we would fall under the Spanish sword; that every nation sought its own interest and did not care about the misfortunes of others. He agreed with me, and when I had shown how we lacked the means for winning independence, he put off its attainment for a century.

How fallible are the calculations of men! One year passed, and behold, without any effort on our part to become independent, God Himself gave us our opportunity as a result of the events of 1808 in Spain and Bayonne. Then it was that the ideals of liberty and independence came to life in America, and the Americans began to speak frankly of their rights.

6. THE ECONOMIC FACTOR IN THE REVOLUTION

In the twilight years of the Spanish Empire in America, contraband trade with the Indies assumed vast proportions. Spain, locked in a desperate struggle with Napoleonic France, could not provide her colonies with the goods and shipping services that they must have. In August, 1809, two English merchants petitioned Viceroy Cisneros for permission to sell their cargoes in Buenos Aires. Cisneros called on representatives of various interests to give their opinions in the matter. Speaking for the cattle-raisers, the creole lawyer Mariano Moreno (1778–1811) came forward with a vigorous brief in favor of free trade. Faced with an empty treasury and creole military supremacy, the viceroy reluctantly sanctioned a limited free trade with allied and neutral nations. Moreno's slashing attack on Spanish

mercantilism foreshadowed the revolution that was less than one year away.[9]

✠✠✠✠ The resources of the Royal Treasury being exhausted by the enormous expenditure which has lately been required, your Excellency, on assuming the reins of Government, was deprived of the means of providing for the safety of the provinces committed to your charge. The only mode of relieving the necessities of the country, appears to be to grant permission to the English merchants to introduce their manufactures into the town, and to re-export the produce of the Interior, by which the revenue will be at once increased, and an impulse given to industry and trade.

Your Excellency possesses powers sufficient for the adoption of any measures that the safety of the country may require, but a natural desire to ensure the result of these measures, by adapting them to the peculiar situation of the viceroyalty, induced your Excellency to consult the Cabildo of this city, and the Tribunal of the Real Consulado, before any definitive resolution was taken.

The intentions of your Excellency had barely transpired, when several of the merchants manifested their discontent and dissatisfaction. Groups of European shopkeepers were formed in all the public places, who, disguising their jealousy and personal apprehensions under the most specious pretenses, affected to deplore, as a public calamity, the diminution of the profits, which they have hitherto derived from the contraband trade. At one time, with hypocritical warmth, they lamented the fatal blow which the interests of the Mother-country were about to receive, and at another, they predicted the ruin of the colony, and the total destruction of its commerce: others again announced the universal distress that the free exportation of the precious metals would bring upon us, and pretended to feel a lively interest in the fate of our native artisans (whom they have always hitherto despised), endeavouring to enlist in their cause the sacred name of religion, and the interests of morality.

Never, certainly, has America known a more critical state of affairs, and never was any European governor so well entitled as your Excellency to dispense at once with the maxims of past ages; for if, in less dangerous times, the laws have often been allowed to sleep, when their observance might have checked the free action of the Government, surely your Excellency cannot now be condemned for the adoption of a measure, by which alone the preservation of this part of the monarchy can be effected.

Those should be doomed to eternal infamy, who maintain that,

[9] "Extracts from a representation, addressed to the viceroy of Buenos Aires. . . ," in Henry G. Ward, *Mexico in 1827*, London, 1828, 2 vols., II, Appendix, pp. 479–483.

under present circumstances, it would be injurious either to Spain, or to this country, to open a free intercourse with Great Britain. But even supposing the measure to be injurious, still it is a necessary evil, and one which, since it cannot be avoided, ought at least to be made use of for the general good, by endeavouring to derive every possible advantage from it, and thus to convert it into a means of ensuring the safety of the state.

Since the English first appeared on our coasts, in 1806, the merchants of that nation have not lost sight of the Rio de la Plata in their speculations. A series of commercial adventures has followed, which has provided almost entirely for the consumption of the country; and this great importation, carried on in defiance of laws and reiterated prohibitions, has met with no other obstacles than those necessary to deprive the Custom-house of its dues, and the country of those advantages which it might have derived from a free exportation of its own produce in return.

The result of this system has been to put the English in the exclusive possession of the right of providing the country with all the foreign merchandise that it requires; while the Government has lost the immense revenues which the introduction of so large a proportion of foreign manufacturers ought to have produced, from too scrupulous an observance of laws, which have never been more scandalously violated than at the moment when their observance was insisted upon by the merchants of the capital. For what, Sir, can be more glaringly absurd than to hear a merchant clamouring for the enforcement of the prohibitive laws, and the exclusion of foreign trade, at the very door of a shop filled with English goods, clandestinely imported?

To the advantages which the Government will derive from the open introduction of foreign goods, may be added those which must accrue to the country from the free exportation of its own produce.

Our vast plains produce annually a million of hides, without reckoning other skins, corn, or tallow, all of which are valuable, as articles of foreign trade. But the magazines of our resident merchants are full; there is no exportation; the capital usually invested in these speculations is already employed, and the immense residue of the produce, thrown back upon the hands of the landed-proprietors, or purchased at a price infinitely below its real value, has reduced them to the most deplorable state of wretchedness, and compelled them to abandon a labour which no longer repays them for the toil and expense with which it is attended.

The freedom of trade in America was not proscribed as a real evil, but because it was a sacrifice required of the colonies by the Mother-country. The events which led to the gradual increase of this

exclusive commerce, till it became a monopoly of the Cadiz merchants, are well known.

Well informed men exclaimed in vain against a system so weak, so ruinous, and so ill judged; but inveterate evils are not to be cured at once. Minor reforms had paved the way for a system founded upon sounder principles, when the late extraordinary events, changing entirely the political state of Spain, destroyed by one unforeseen blow all the pretexts by which the prohibitory laws had been previously supported. — The new order of things which the Mother-country has proclaimed as the happy commencement of national prosperity, has completely changed the motives for the prohibitory system, and demonstrated, in their fullest extent, the advantages that must result to the country from a free trade. Good policy, therefore, and the natural wish to apply a remedy to pressing evils, are converted into a positive duty, which the first magistrate of the state cannot, in reason, or justice, neglect.

Is it just that the fruits of our agricultural labours should be lost, because the unfortunate provinces of Spain can no longer consume them? Is it just that the abundant productions of the country should rot in our magazines, because the navy of Spain is too weak to export them? Is it just that we should increase the distress of the Mother-country, by the tidings of our own critical and vacillating state, when the means are offered to us of consolidating our safety upon the firmest basis? Is it just, that, when the subjects of a friendly and generous nation present themselves in our ports, and offer us, at a cheap rate, the merchandize of which we are in want, and with which Spain cannot supply us, we should reject the proposal, and convert, by so doing, their good intentions to the exclusive advantage of a few European merchants, who, by means of a contraband trade, render themselves masters of the whole imports of the country? Is it just, that when we are entreated to sell our accumulated agricultural produce, we should, by refusing to do so, decree at the same time the ruin of our landed-proprietors, of the country, and of society together?

If your Excellency wishes to diminish the extraction of specie, which has taken place latterly to so great an extent, there is no other mode of effecting it than to open the ports to the English, and thus to enable them to extend their speculations to other objects. It is one of the fatal consequences of the contraband trade, that the importer is absolutely compelled to receive the value of his imports in the precious metals alone. His true interest, indeed, consists in exchanging them at once for articles that may become the objects of a new speculation; but the risks with which the extraction of bulky commodities must be attended, under a system of strict prohibition, induce him to sacrifice this advantage to the greater security which exports in

specie afford, and to deprive himself of the hope of new profits, and the country of the sale of its most valuable produce.

Yet the *apoderado* of the Cadiz monopolists maintains, "that a free trade will be the ruin of our agriculture." This luminous discovery is worthy of his penetration. The free exportation of the produce is declared to be detrimental to the interests of the producer! What, then, is to be the mode of encouraging him in his labours? According to the principles laid down by our merchants, the agricultural produce should be allowed to accumulate, — purchasers are to be deterred from entering the market, by the difficulties of exporting the articles bought up, to countries where they might be consumed; and this system is to be persevered in until, after ruining the landholders by preventing them from disposing of the fruits of their labours, the superfluous produce itself is to be disposed of, in order to fill up the ditches and marshes in the vicinity of the town.

Yes, Sir, this is the deplorable state to which our agriculture has been reduced during the last few years. The marshes around the town have been actually filled up with wheat; and this miserable condition, which forms a subject of lamentation with all true friends to their country, and scandalizes the inhabitants of the whole district, is the natural fate of a province, in which, as soon as an inclination is shown to apply a remedy to these evils, men are found daring enough to assert, "That by giving value, or in other words, a ready market, to the agricultural produce, agriculture will be ruined."

22 ✤ The Liberation of South America

Creole professions of loyalty to the "beloved Ferdinand," a prisoner in France, did not impress the Spanish authorities. Learning of the upheaval in Caracas, they declared the colony in revolt and proclaimed a blockade of its ports. Accordingly, in July, 1811, Venezuela declared its independence from Spain. Other provinces soon followed its example, although Argentina delayed the act of separation until 1816.

Simón Bolívar led the movement for independence in northern South America. A turning point in the northern war came when Bolívar routed a Spanish army at Boyacá, high in the mountains of New Granada (1819). The liberation of Venezuela and Ecuador soon followed. From the union of New Granada, Venezuela, and Ecuador arose a gigantic new state, Colombia, with Bolívar as its first president.

The austere figure of José de San Martín dominated the war for independence in southern South America. From its base in Buenos Aires the revolution flowed into the Banda Oriental (Uruguay) and other provinces of the old viceroyalty of La Plata, but was thrown back at the rugged borders of Upper Peru (Bolivia). San Martín's bold design for total victory proposed a march across the Andes to liberate Chile, followed by an attack on Lima from the sea.

San Martín planned and executed the campaign of the Andes

with consummate skill. The battle of Maipú (1818) ended Spanish rule in Chile. However, final victory in Peru escaped San Martín's grasp. In September, 1822, after a meeting with Bolívar that revealed serious political differences between the two men, he resigned his command; he soon afterwards departed for Europe. It remained for Bolívar to complete the work of continental liberation. In December, 1824, his lieutenant Sucre accepted the surrender of La Serna, the last Spanish viceroy in the New World.

Brazil made a fairly peaceful transition to independence. The flight of the Portuguese royal family to Brazil in 1808 as a result of the French invasion of the kingdom gave new importance and privileges to the colony. In 1820, after the fall of Napoleon, a jealous Portuguese *cortes* demanded the return of King João, and he reluctantly complied. But his son Pedro, supported by the Brazilian landed aristocracy, rejected a similar demand, issued the famous cry of "independence or death," and in December, 1822, was formally proclaimed constitutional Emperor of Brazil.

1. MAN OF DESTINY

There is no more controversial figure in Latin-American history than that of Simón Bolívar (1783–1830). To his admirers or worshippers he is the Liberator of a continent; Waldo Frank calls him "the culture hero of our hemisphere." To his critics he is the proverbial "man on horseback," an ambitious schemer who sacrificed San Martín to his passion for power and glory. Louis Peru de Lacroix, a French member of Bolívar's staff, wrote the following description of the Liberator in a diary that he kept during their stay at Bucaramanga in 1828.[1]

✦✦✦✦ The General-in-Chief, Simón José Antonio Bolívar, will be forty-five years old on July 24 of this year, but he appears older, and many judge him to be fifty. He is slim and of medium height; his arms, thighs, and legs are lean. He has a long head, wide between the temples, and a sharply pointed chin. A large, round, prominent forehead is furrowed with wrinkles that are very noticeable when his face is in repose, or in moments of bad humor and anger. His hair is crisp, bristly, quite abundant, and partly gray. His eyes have lost the brightness of youth but preserve the luster of genius. They are deep-set, neither small nor large; the eyebrows are thick, separated, slightly arched, and are grayer than the hair on his head. The nose

[1] Monseñor Nicolás E. Navarro, ed., *Diaria de Bucaramanga, estudia crítico*, Caracas, 1935, pp. 327, 329–331. (Excerpt translated by the editor.)

is aquiline and well formed. He has prominent cheekbones, with hollows beneath. His mouth is rather large, and the lower lip protrudes; he has white teeth and an agreeable smile. . . . His tanned complexion darkens when he is in a bad humor, and his whole appearance changes; the wrinkles on his forehead and temples stand out much more prominently; the eyes become smaller and narrower; the lower lip protrudes considerably, and the mouth turns ugly. In fine, one sees a completely different countenance: a frowning face that reveals sorrows, sad reflections, and sombre ideas. But when he is happy all this disappears; his face lights up, his mouth smiles, and the spirit of the Liberator shines over his countenance. His Excellency is clean-shaven at present. . . .

The Liberator has energy; he is capable of making a firm decision and sticking to it. His ideas are never commonplace — always large, lofty, and original. His manners are affable, having the tone of Europeans of high society. He displays a republican simplicity and modesty, but he has the pride of a noble and elevated soul, the dignity of his rank, and the *amour-propre* that comes from consciousness of worth and leads men to great actions. Glory is his ambition, and his glory consists in having liberated ten million persons and founded three republics. He has an enterprising spirit, combined with great activity, quickness of speech, an infinite fertility in ideas, and the constancy necessary for the realization of his projects. He is superior to misfortunes and reverses; his philosophy consoles him and his intelligence finds ways of righting what has gone wrong. . . .

He loves a discussion, and dominates it through his superior intelligence; but he sometimes appears too dogmatic, and is not always tolerant enough with those who contradict him. He scorns servile flattery and base adulators. He is sensitive to criticism of his actions; calumny against him cuts him to the quick, for none is more touchy about his reputation than the Liberator. . . .

His heart is better than his head. His bad temper never lasts; when it appears, it takes possession of his head, never of his heart, and as soon as the latter recovers its dominance it immediately makes amends for the harm that the former may have done. . . .

The great mental and bodily activity of the Liberator keeps him in a state of constant moral and physical agitation. One who observes him at certain moments might think he is seeing a madman. During the walks that we take with him he sometimes likes to walk very rapidly, trying to tire his companions out; at other times he begins to run and leap, to leave the others behind; then he waits for them to catch up and tells them they do not know how to run. He does the same when horseback riding. But he acts this way only when among his own people, and he would not run or leap if he thought that some stranger was looking on. When bad weather pre-

vents walking or riding, the Liberator rocks himself swiftly back and forth in his hammock or strides through the corridors of his house, sometimes singing, at other times reciting verses or talking with those who walk beside him. When conversing with one of his own people, he changes the subject as often as he does his position; at such times one would say that he has not a bit of system or stability in him. How different the Liberator seems at a private party, at some formal gathering, and among his confidential friends and aides-de-camp! With the latter he seems their equal, the gayest and sometimes the maddest of them all. At a private party, among strangers and people less well known to him, he shows his superiority to all others by his easy and agreeable ways and good taste, his lively and ingenious conversation, and his amiability. At a more formal gathering, his unaffected dignity and polished manners cause him to be regarded as the most gentlemanly, learned, and amiable man present. . . .

In all the actions of the Liberator, and in his conversation, as I have already noted, one observes an extreme quickness. His questions are short and concise; he likes to be answered in the same way, and when someone wanders away from the question he impatiently says that that is not what he asked; he has no liking for a diffuse answer. He sustains his opinions with force and logic, and generally with tenacity. When he has occasion to contradict some assertion, he says: "No, sir, it is not so, but thus. . . ." Speaking of persons whom he dislikes or scorns, he often uses this expression: "That (or those) c * * *." He is very observant, noting even the least trifles; he dislikes the poorly educated, the bold, the windbag, the indiscreet, and the discourteous. Since nothing escapes him, he takes pleasure in criticizing such people, always making a little commentary on their defects. . . .

I have already said that the Liberator can assume an air of dignity when among persons who do not enjoy his full confidence or with whom he is not on terms of familiarity; but he throws it off among his own people. In church he carries himself with much propriety and respect, and does not permit his companions to deviate from this rule. One day, noticing that his physician, Dr. Moore, sat with his legs crossed, he had an aide-de-camp tell him that it was improper to cross one's legs in church, and that he should observe how *he* sat. One thing that His Excellency does not know, when at Mass, is when to kneel, stand up, and sit down. He never crosses himself. Sometimes he talks to the person beside him, but only a little, and very softly.

The ideas of the Liberator are like his imagination: full of fire, original, and new. They lend considerable sparkle to his conversation, and make it extremely varied. When His Excellency praises, defends, or approves something, it is always with a little exaggeration. The

same is true when he criticizes, condemns, or disapproves of something. In his conversation he frequently quotes, but his citations are always well chosen and pertinent. Voltaire is his favorite author, and he has memorized many passages from his works, both prose and poetry. He knows all the good French writers and evaluates them competently. He has some general knowledge of Italian and English literature and is very well versed in that of Spain.

The Liberator takes great pleasure in telling of his first years, his voyages, and his campaigns, and of his relations and old friends. His character and spirit dispose him more to criticize than to eulogize, but his criticisms or eulogies are never baseless; he could be charged only with an occasional slight exaggeration. I have never heard his Excellency utter a calumny. He is a lover of truth, heroism, and honor and of the public interest and morality. He detests and scorns all that is opposed to these lofty and noble sentiments.

2. THE POLITICAL IDEAS OF BOLÍVAR

The political organization of the new Spanish-American states claimed much of Bolívar's attention. Rejecting a monarchical solution as unsuited to the conditions of the New World, he advocated a highly centralized republican government headed by a strong executive. Distrustful of the masses, he proposed to limit the suffrage and office-holding to the propertied and educated elite. The following excerpts from his celebrated message to the Congress of Angostura (1819), concerning a proposed new constitution for the Republic of Venezuela, illustrate his political views at that stage of his career.[2]

✠✠✠✠ Let us review the past to discover the base upon which the Republic of Venezuela is founded.

America, in separating from the Spanish monarchy, found herself in a situation similar to that of the Roman Empire when its enormous framework fell to pieces in the midst of the ancient world. Each Roman division then formed an independent nation in keeping with its location or interests; but this situation differed from America's in that those members proceeded to reëstablish their former associations. We, on the contrary, do not even retain the vestiges of our original being. We are not Europeans; we are not Indians; we are but a mixed species of aborigines and Spaniards. Americans by birth

---

[2] Vicente Lecuna, comp., and Harold A. Bierck, Jr., ed., *Selected Writings of Bolívar*, New York, Colonial Press, 1951, 2 vols., I, pp. 175–191. Reprinted by kind permission of the Banco de Venezuela.

and Europeans by law, we find ourselves engaged in a dual conflict: we are disputing with the natives for titles of ownership, and at the same time we are struggling to maintain ourselves in the country that gave us birth against the opposition of the invaders. Thus our position is most extraordinary and complicated. But there is more. As our role has always been strictly passive and political existence nil, we find that our quest for liberty is now even more difficult of accomplishment; for we, having been placed in a state lower than slavery, had been robbed not only of our freedom but also of the right to exercise an active domestic tyranny. Permit me to explain this paradox.

In absolute systems, the central power is unlimited. The will of the despot is the supreme law, arbitrarily enforced by subordinates who take part in the organized oppression in proportion to the authority that they wield. They are charged with civil, political, military, and religious functions; but, in the final analysis, the satraps of Persia are Persian, the pashas of the Grand Turk are Turks, and the sultans of Tartary are Tartars. China does not seek her mandarins in the homeland of Genghis Khan, her conqueror. America, on the contrary, received everything from Spain, who, in effect, deprived her of the experience that she would have gained from the exercise of an active tyranny by not allowing her to take part in her own domestic affairs and administration. This exclusion made it impossible for us to acquaint ourselves with the management of public affairs; nor did we enjoy that personal consideration, of such great value in major revolutions, that the brilliance of power inspires in the eyes of the multitude. In brief, Gentlemen, we were deliberately kept in ignorance and cut off from the world in all matters relating to the science of government.

Subject to the three-fold yoke of ignorance, tyranny, and vice, the American people have been unable to acquire knowledge, power, or [civic] virtue. The lessons we received and the models we studied, as pupils of such pernicious teachers, were most destructive. We have been ruled more by deceit than by force, and we have been degraded more by vice than by superstition. Slavery is the daughter of darkness: an ignorant people is a blind instrument of its own destruction. Ambition and intrigue abuse the credulity and experience of men lacking all political, economic, and civic knowledge; they adopt pure illusion as reality; they take license for liberty, treachery for patriotism, and vengeance for justice. This situation is similar to that of the robust blind man who, beguiled by his strength, strides forward with all the assurance of one who can see, but, upon hitting every variety of obstacle, finds himself unable to retrace his steps.

If a people, perverted by their training, succeed in achieving their liberty, they will soon lose it, for it would be of no avail to endeavor to explain to them that happiness consists in the practice of

virtue; that the rule of law is more powerful than the rule of tyrants, because, as the laws are more inflexible, every one should submit to their beneficent austerity; that proper morals, and not force, are the bases of law; and that to practice justice is to practice liberty. Therefore, Legislators, your work is so much the more arduous, inasmuch as you have to reëducate men who have been corrupted by erroneous illusions and false incentives. Liberty, says Rousseau, is a succulent morsel, but one difficult to digest. Our weak fellow-citizens will have to strengthen their spirit greatly before they can digest the wholesome nutriment of freedom. Their limbs benumbed by chains, their sight dimmed by the darkness of dungeons, and their strength sapped by the pestilence of servitude, are they capable of marching toward the august temple of Liberty without faltering? Can they come near enough to bask in its brilliant rays and to breathe freely the pure air which reigns therein? . . .

The more I admire the excellence of the federal Constitution of Venezuela, the more I am convinced of the impossibility of its application to our state. And to my way of thinking, it is a marvel that its prototype in North America endures so successfully and has not been overthrown at the first sign of adversity or danger. Although the people of North America are a singular model of political virtue and moral rectitude; although that nation was cradled in liberty, reared on freedom, and maintained by liberty alone; and — I must reveal everything — although those people, so lacking in many respects, are unique in the history of mankind, it is a marvel, I repeat, that so weak and complicated a government as the federal system has managed to govern them in the difficult and trying circumstances of their past. But, regardless of the effectiveness of this form of government with respect to North America, I must say that it has never for a moment entered my mind to compare the position and character of two states as dissimilar as the English-American and Spanish-American. Would it not be most difficult to apply to Spain the English system of political, civil, and religious liberty: Hence, it would be even more difficult to adapt to Venezuela the laws of North America. Does not *L'Esprit des Lois* state that laws should be suited to the people for whom they are made; that it would be a major coincidence if those of one nation could be adapted to another; that laws must take into account the physical conditions of the country, climate, character of the land, location, size, and mode of living of the people; that they should be in keeping with the degree of liberty that the Constitution can sanction respecting the religion of the inhabitants, their inclinations, resources, number, commerce, habits, and customs? This is the code we must consult, not the code of Washington! . . .

Venezuela had, has, and should have a republican government. Its principles should be the sovereignty of the people, division of pow-

ers, civil liberty, proscription of slavery, and the abolition of monarchy and privileges. We need equality to recast, so to speak, into a unified nation, the classes of men, political opinions, and public customs.

Among the ancient and modern nations, Rome and Great Britain are the most outstanding. Both were born to govern and to be free and both were built not on ostentatious forms of freedom, but upon solid institutions. Thus I recommend to you, Representatives, the study of the British Constitution, for that body of laws appears destined to bring about the greatest possible good for the peoples that adopt it; but, however perfect it may be, I am by no means proposing that you imitate it slavishly. When I speak of the British government, I only refer to its republican features; and, indeed, can a political system be labelled a monarchy when it recognizes popular sovereignty, division and balance of powers, civil liberty, freedom of conscience and of press, and all that is politically sublime? Can there be more liberty in any other type of republic? Can more be asked of any society? I commend this Constitution to you as that most worthy of serving as model for those who aspire to the enjoyment of the rights of man and who seek all the political happiness which is compatible with the frailty of human nature.

Nothing in our fundamental laws would have to be altered were we to adopt a legislative power similar to that held by the British Parliament. Like the North Americans, we have divided national representation into two chambers; that of Representatives and the Senate. The first is very wisely constituted. It enjoys all its proper functions, and it requires no essential revision, because the Constitution, in creating it, gave it the form and powers which the people deemed necessary in order that they might be legally and properly represented. If the Senate were hereditary rather than elective, it would, in my opinion, be the basis, the tie, the very soul of our republic. In political storms this body would arrest the thunderbolts of the government and would repel any violent popular reaction. Devoted to the government because of a natural interest in its own preservation, a hereditary senate would always oppose any attempt on the part of the people to infringe upon the jurisdiction and authority of their magistrates. It must be confessed that most men are unaware of their best interests, and that they constantly endeavor to assail them in the hands of their custodians — the individual clashes with the mass, and the mass with authority. It is necessary, therefore, that in all governments there be a neutral body to protect the injured and disarm the offender. To be neutral, this body must not owe its origin to appointment by the government or to election by the people, if it is to enjoy a full measure of independence which neither fears

nor expects anything from these two sources of authority. The hereditary senate, as a part of the people, shares its interests, its sentiments, and its spirit. For this reason it should not be presumed that a hereditary senate would ignore the interests of the people or forget its legislative duties. The senators in Rome and in the House of Lords in London have been the strongest pillars upon which the edifice of political and civil liberty has rested.

At the outset, these senators should be elected by Congress. The successors to this Senate must command the initial attention of the government, which should educate them in a *colegio* designed especially to train these guardians and future legislators of the nation. They ought to learn the arts, sciences, and letters that enrich the mind of a public figure. From childhood they should understand the career for which they have been destined by Providence, and from earliest youth they should prepare their minds for the dignity that awaits them.

The creation of a hereditary senate would in no way be a violation of political equality. I do not solicit the establishment of a nobility, for as a celebrated republican has said, that would simultaneously destroy equality and liberty. What I propose is an office for which the candidates must prepare themselves, an office that demands great knowledge and the ability to acquire such knowledge. All should not be left to chance and the outcome of elections. The people are more easily deceived than is Nature perfected by art; and, although these senators, it is true, would not be bred in an environment that is all virtue, it is equally true that they would be raised in an atmosphere of enlightened education. Furthermore, the liberators of Venezuela are entitled to occupy forever a high rank in the Republic that they have brought into existence. I believe that posterity would view with regret the effacement of the illustrious names of its first benefactors. I say, moreover, that it is a matter of public interest and national honor, of gratitude on Venezuela's part, to honor gloriously, until the end of time, a race of virtuous, prudent, and persevering men who, overcoming every obstacle, have founded the Republic at the price of the most heroic sacrifices. And if the people of Venezuela do not applaud the elevation of their benefactors, then they are unworthy to be free, and they will never be free.

A hereditary senate, I repeat, will be the fundamental basis of the legislative power, and therefore the foundation of the entire government. It will also serve as a counterweight to both government and people; and as a neutral power it will weaken the mutual attacks of these two eternally rival powers. In all conflicts the calm reasoning of a third party will serve as the means of reconciliation. Thus the Venezuelan senate will give strength to this delicate political structure,

so sensitive to violent repercussions; it will be the mediator that will lull the storms and it will maintain harmony between the head and the other parts of the political body.

No inducement could corrupt a legislative body invested with the highest honors, dependent only upon itself, having no fear of the people, independent of the government, and dedicated solely to the repression of all evil principles and to the advancement of every good principle — a legislative body that would be deeply concerned with the maintenance of a society, for it would share the consequences, be they honorable or disastrous. It has rightly been said that the upper house in England is invaluable to that nation because it provides a bulwark of liberty; and I would add that the Senate of Venezuela would be not only a bulwark of liberty but a bastion of defense, rendering the Republic eternal.

The British executive power possesses all the authority properly appertaining to a sovereign, but he is surrounded by a triple line of dams, barriers, and stockades. He is the head of the government, but his ministers and subordinates rely more upon law than upon his authority, as they are personally responsible; and not even decrees of royal authority can exempt them from this responsibility. The executive is commander in chief of the army and navy; he makes peace and declares war; but Parliament annually determines what sums are to be paid to these military forces. While the courts and judges are dependent on the executive power, the laws originate in and are made by Parliament. To neutralize the power of the King, his person is declared inviolable and sacred; but, while his head is left untouched, his hands are tied. The sovereign of England has three formidable rivals: his Cabinet, which is responsible to the people and to Parliament; the Senate [sic], which, representing the nobility of which it is composed, defends the interests of the people; and the House of Commons, which serves as the representative body of the British people and provides them with a place in which to express their opinions. Moreover, as the judges are responsible for the enforcement of the laws, they do not depart from them; and the administrators of the exchequer, being subject to prosecution not only for personal infractions but also for those of the government, take care to prevent any misuse of public funds. No matter how closely we study the composition of the English executive power, we can find nothing to prevent its being judged as the most perfect model for a kingdom, for an aristocracy, or for a democracy. Give Venezuela such an executive power in the person of a president chosen by the people or their representatives, and you will have taken a great step toward national happiness.

No matter what citizen occupies this office, he will be aided by the Constitution, and therein being authorized to do good, he can do no harm, because his ministers will cooperate with him only insofar

as he abides by the law. If he attempts to infringe upon the law, his own ministers will desert him, thereby isolating him from the Republic, and they will even bring charges against him in the Senate. The ministers, being responsible for any transgressions committed, will actually govern, since they must account for their actions. The obligation which this system places upon the officials closest to the executive power, that is to take a most interested and active part in governmental deliberations and to regard this department as their own, is not the smallest advantage of the system. Should the president be a man of no great talent or virtue, yet, notwithstanding his lack of these essential qualities, he will be able to discharge his duties satisfactorily, for in such a case the ministry, managing everything by itself, will carry the burdens of the state.

Although the authority of the executive power in England may appear to be extreme, it would, perhaps, not be excessive in the Republic of Venezuela. Here the Congress has tied the hands and even the heads of its men of state. This deliberative assembly has assumed a part of the executive functions, contrary to the maxim of Montesquieu, to wit: A representative assembly should exercise no active function. It should only make laws and determine whether or not those laws are enforced. Nothing is as disturbing to harmony among the powers of government as their intermixture. Nothing is more dangerous with respect to the people than a weak executive; and if a kingdom has deemed it necessary to grant the executive so many powers, then in a republic these powers are infinitely more indispensable.

If we examine this difference, we will find that the balance of power between the branches of government must be distributed in two ways. In republics the executive should be the stronger, for everything conspires against it; while in monarchies the legislative power should be superior, as everything works in the monarch's favor. The people's veneration of royal power results in a self-fascination that tends greatly to increase the superstitious respect paid to such authority. The splendor inherent in the throne, the crown, and the purple; the formidable support that it receives from the nobility; the immense wealth that a dynasty accumulates from generation to generation; and the fraternal protection that kings grant to one another are the significant advantages that work in favor of royal authority, thereby rendering it almost unlimited. Consequently, the significance of these same advantages should serve to justify the necessity of investing the chief magistrate of a republic with a greater measure of authority than that possessed by a constitutional prince.

A republican magistrate is an individual set apart from society, charged with checking the impulse of the people toward license and the propensity of judges and administrators toward abuse of the laws. He is directly subject to the legislative body, the senate, and the people:

he is the one man who resists the combined pressure of the opinions, interests, and passions of the social state and who, as Carnot states, does little more than struggle constantly with the urge to dominate and the desire to escape domination. He is, in brief, an athlete pitted against a multitude of athletes.

This weakness can only be corrected by a strongly rooted force. It should be strongly proportioned to meet the resistance which the executive must expect from the legislature, from the judiciary, and from the people of a republic. Unless the executive has easy access to all the [administrative] resources, fixed by a just distribution of powers, he inevitably becomes a nonentity or abuses his authority. By this I mean that the result will be the death of the government, whose heirs are anarchy, usurpation, and tyranny. Some seek to check the executive authority by curbs and restrictions, and nothing is more just; but it must be remembered that the bonds we seek to preserve should, of course, be strengthened, but not tightened.

Therefore, let the entire system of government be strengthened, and let the balance of power be drawn up in such a manner that it will be permanent and incapable of decay because of its own tenuity. Precisely because no form of government is so weak as the democratic, its framework must be firmer, and its institutions must be studied to determine their degree of stability. Unless this is done, we must plan on the establishment of an experimental rather than a permanent system of government; and we will have to reckon with an ungovernable, tumultuous, and anarchic society, not with a social order where happiness, peace, and justice prevail.

Legislators, we should not be presumptuous. We should be moderate in our pretensions. It is not likely that we will secure what mankind has never attained or that which the greatest and wisest nations have not acquired. Complete liberty and absolute democracy are but reefs upon which all republican hopes have foundered. Observe the ancient republics, the modern republics, and those of most recent origin: Virtually all have attempted to establish themselves as absolute democracies, and almost all have seen their just aspirations thwarted. The men who covet legitimate institutions and social perfection are indeed worthy of commendation. But who has told these men that they now possess the wisdom or practice the virtue that is so forcefully demanded by the union of power with justice? Only angels, not men, can exist free, peaceful, and happy while exercising every sovereign power.

The people of Venezuela already enjoy the rights that they may legitimately and easily exercise. Let us now, therefore, restrain the growth of immoderate pretensions which, perhaps, a form of government unsuited to our people might excite. Let us abandon the federal forms of government unsuited to us; let us put aside the triumvirate which holds the executive power and center it in a presi-

dent. We must grant him sufficient authority to enable him to continue the struggle against the obstacles inherent in our recent situation, our present state of war, and every variety of foe, foreign and domestic, whom we must battle for some time to come. Let the legislature relinquish the powers that rightly belong to the executive; let it acquire, however, a new consistency, a new influence in the balance of authority. Let the courts be strengthened by increasing the stability and independence of the judges and by the establishment of juries and civil and criminal codes dictated, not by antiquity nor by conquering kings, but by the voice of Nature, the cry of Justice, and the genius of Wisdom.

My desire is for every branch of government and administration to attain that degree of vigor which alone can insure equilibrium, not only among the members of the government, but also among the different factions of which our society is composed. It would matter little if the springs of a political system were to relax because of its weakness, so long as this relaxation itself did not contribute to the dissolution of the body social and the ruination of its membership. The shouts of humanity, on the battlefields or in tumultuous crowds denounce to the world the blind, unthinking legislators who imagined that experiments with chimerical institutions could be made with impunity. All the peoples of the world have sought freedom, some by force of arms, others by force of law, passing alternately from anarchy to despotism, or from despotism to anarchy. Few peoples have been content with moderate aims, establishing their institutions according to their means, their character, and their circumstances. We must not aspire to the impossible, lest, in trying to rise above the realm of liberty, we again descend into the realm of tyranny. Absolute liberty invariably lapses into absolute power, and the mean between these two extremes is supreme social liberty. Abstract theories create the pernicious idea of unlimited freedom. Let us see to it that the strength of the public is kept within the limits prescribed by reason and interest; that the national will is confined within the bonds set by a just power; that the judiciary is rigorously controlled by civil and criminal laws, analogous to those in our present Constitution — then an equilibrium between the powers of government will exist, the conflicts that hamper the progress of the state will disappear, and those complications which tend to hinder rather than unite society will be eliminated.

3. THE GREAT CAMPAIGN

A turning point in the struggle for independence in northern South America came in 1819, when Bolívar crossed the Colombian Andes with his army and attacked the Spanish forces in

New Granada from a completely unexpected direction. Victory on the field of Boyacá crowned one of the most daring and brilliantly executed campaigns in history. In the following selection Daniel F. O'Leary (1800–1854), Bolívar's English aide-de-camp and biographer, describes the epic campaign of 1819.[3]

✦✦✦✦ While Bolívar assembled his army in Tame, the royalist forces in New Granada, perfectly equipped and under the command of the ablest officers of the expeditionary army, were quartered in the following manner: Four thousand men garrisoned the northern frontier, separating the provinces of Cundinamarca and Tunja from the plains of Casanare; three thousand well disciplined and well paid men, Spaniards and Americans, guarded the city of Santa Fe and other towns of the interior and the littoral. The cavalry mounted excellent horses; the artillery was well operated and lacked nothing. Add to these resources, which alone were probably enough to defend the country, the natural obstacles presented by the terrain, and Bolívar's project must seem a fantasy. But he counted less on the material force of his army than on the resources of his own genius and on the iron will that made his name so dreaded by the enemies of his country.

From Tame to Pore, the capital of Casanare, the road was inundated. "The territory through which the army had to make its first marches was a small sea, rather than solid land," says Santander in his account of this campaign. On July 27 they encountered obstacles of another kind.

The gigantic Andes, which are considered uncrossable at this season, imposed a seemingly insuperable barrier to the march of the army. For four days the troops battled against the difficulties of these rugged roads — if precipices can be called roads.

The plainsmen regarded these stupendous heights with astonishment and terror, and marveled at the existence of a land so different from their own. As they ascended, each new elevation increased their surprise, for what they had taken for the last peak was only the beginning of other and still loftier mountains, from whose crests they could discern ranges whose summits appeared to lose themselves in the eternal clouds of the firmament. Men who on their plains were accustomed to cross torrential rivers, tame savage horses, and conquer in bodily combat the wild bull, the tiger, and the crocodile were frightened by the forbidding aspect of these strange surroundings. Losing hope of overcoming such stupendous difficulties, their horses already dead from fatigue, they decided that only madmen could persevere in the enterprise, in a climate whose temperature numbed their senses and froze their bodies. As a result, many of them deserted.

[3] Daniel F. O'Leary, *Bolívar y la emancipación de Sur-América*, Madrid, 1915, 2 vols., I, pp. 664–682. (Excerpt translated by the editor.)

The mules carrying the munitions and arms fell under the weight of their burdens; few horses survived the five days of marching; and the fallen animals of the forward division obstructed the road and increased the difficulties of the rear guard. It rained incessantly day and night, and the cold grew worse as they ascended. The cold water, to which the troops were not accustomed, caused diarrhea among them. It seemed as if sorcery had conjured up this accumulation of mishaps in order to destroy the hopes of Bolívar. He alone remained firm among reverses the least of which would have discouraged a weaker spirit. He inspired the troops with his presence and example, speaking to them of the glory that awaited them, and of the abundance that reigned in the country that they were going to liberate. The soldiers listened to him with pleasure and redoubled their efforts.

On the 27th the vanguard dispersed a royalist force of 300 men, advantageously posted in front of Paya, a town in the cordillera. This strong position could bar the passage of an army; the royalist detachment was more than sufficient to defend it against 6,000 men; but the timidity of the Spanish commander saved the army and opened to Bolívar the road to New Granada. . . .

After some days of rest, the army resumed its march on July 2. The royalist detachment which had been beaten at Paya retired to Labranza Grande, which was reached by a road that was considered the only passable one at that season of the year. There was another, across the *páramo* of Pisba, but it was so rough that it was hardly used even in the summer. The Spaniards considered it unusable and therefore neglected its defense; Bolívar selected it for precisely that reason. The passage of Casanare through plains covered with water, and that of the portion of the Andes which lay behind us, though rugged and steep was in every way preferable to the road which the army was to take.

At many points immense fallen rocks and trees, and slides caused by the constant rains that made walking dangerous and uncertain, completely obstructed its advance. The soldiers, who had received rations of meat and *arracacha* for four days, threw them away and kept only their rifles, for the climb presented enough difficulties without any burdens. The few surviving horses perished during this day.

As darkness fell the army reached the foot of the *páramo* of Pisba, where it passed a frightful night. It was impossible to have a fire, because there were no dwellings in the vicinity and a steady drizzle, accompanied by hail and a feezing wind, quenched the bonfires made in the open as quickly as they were lighted.

Since the troops were nearly naked, and the majority were natives of the burning plains of Venezuela, it is easier to conceive than to describe their cruel sufferings. The following day they reached

the *páramo* itself, a dismal and inhospitable desert, devoid of all vegetation because of its height. On that day the effect of the piercingly cold air was fatal to many soldiers; many fell suddenly ill while on the march and expired in a few minutes. Flogging was used, with success in some cases, to revive frozen soldiers; a colonel of cavalry was saved in this way.

During this day's march my attention was called to a group of soldiers who had stopped near where I had seated myself, overcome with fatigue. Seeing anxiety written on their faces, I asked one of them what was wrong; he replied that the wife of a soldier of the Rifles Battalion was in labor. The next morning I saw the same woman, her babe in her arms, and apparently in the best of health, marching in the rear guard of the battalion. After the birth she had walked for two leagues along one of the worst roads in that rough terrain.

One hundred men would have sufficed to destroy the patriot army while crossing the *páramo*. On the march it was impossible to keep the soldiers together because even the officers could barely stand the hardships of the road, much less attend to the troops. That night was more terrible than the preceding ones, and although the encampment was more sheltered and the rain less frequent, many soldiers died from the effects of their sufferings and privations. As the parties of ten or twenty men descended together from the *páramo*, the President [Bolívar] congratulated them on the approaching conclusion of the campaign, telling them that they had already conquered the greatest obstacles of the march.

On the 6th the division of Anzoátegui reached Socha, the first town in the province of Tunja; the vanguard had arrived there on the preceding day. The soldiers, seeing behind them the crests of the mountains, covered with clouds and mists, spontaneously vowed to conquer or die rather than retreat through those mountains, for they feared them more than the most formidable enemy. In Socha the army received a cordial welcome from the inhabitants of that place and its vicinity. Bread, tobacco, and *chicha*, a beverage made from corn and cane-juice syrup, rewarded the troops for their sufferings and inspired greater hopes for the future. But as the hardships of the soldier diminished, the cares of the general increased. . . .

Great was the royalist surprise to learn that they had unwelcome guests in the shape of an enemy army; it seemed incredible that Bolívar should have begun operations and overcome such great obstacles at a time of the year when few dared to undertake even the shortest journeys. . . .

Meanwhile the enemy remained in his positions, giving no sign that he wished to accept combat on the plain. After vain efforts to commit him to an action, Bolívar ordered a flank movement in an

effort to encircle his right wing. At dawn on the 25th of July, anniversary of the patron saint of Spain and the birthday of Bolívar, the army began to cross the Sogamoso River, which runs through the plains of Bonza.

At midday, as the army defiled through the swamp of Vargas, the enemy appeared on the heights in front.

Since nine in the morning Barreiro had observed the movement of the patriots and had speedily acted to counter it. Both armies immediately got ready for battle. The republicans were forced to occupy an unfavorable position, which Bolívar sought to improve by sending Santander with his division to the heights that dominated the left wing of the Army of Liberation, whose right wing was protected by a swamp.

Barreiro began the action by sending the first battalion *del Rey* against the left wing of the patriot army, to be followed by an attack on its shoulder. Seeing that this corps had seized the heights, where Santander offered very feeble resistance, Barreiro struck at the center of the line with such force that the Rifles and Barcelona battalions broke and gave way.

At that moment all seemed lost, but Bolívar flew to reunite the shattered corps, ordering Colonel Rook and his British Legion to dislodge the enemy from the heights that he had occupied. The fearless Englishman carried out his assignment with brilliant success.

Now the royalist general, fiery and tireless, made a second furious attack on the front of the patriot army. But he gained only a temporary advantage, for Bolívar, making judicious use of his small reserve, decided the fate of the battle with a magnificent cavalry charge.

One word or the efforts of a single individual have sometimes succeeded in calming an insurrection or gaining a triumph. At that critical moment, when everything seemed to favor the Spaniards, who already counted on the complete destruction of the patriot army, and when all — except Bolívar — despaired of victory, Rondón appeared with his squadron of *llaneros*. Bolívar shouted words of encouragement and cried to their leader: "Colonel, save the fatherland!" Rondón, followed by his brave soldiers, immediately hurled himself upon the advancing enemy squadrons and threw them back, with a heavy loss of life. The infantry imitated Rondón's feat, and the royalists could not withstand the impetus of the combined attack.

The night put an end to the bloody battle, whose outcome seemed doubtful at certain moments. Twice that day the Army of Liberation believed that all was lost.

Barreiro's communiqué pays tribute to the valor of our troops. "Desperation," he says, "inspired them with an unheard-of valor. Their infantry and cavalry left the gullies into which they had been hurled,

and rushed with fury up the heights which they had lost. Our infantry could not resist them. . . .

The bravery of Rondón and the calm bravery of the few British troops contributed substantially to victory, or rather to saving the liberating army of New Granada from destruction. In the general order published the next day, Bolívar acknowledged the merits of these brave foreigners by conferring on them the "Cross of Liberators," a distinction which they well deserved. . . .

Bolívar's activity and energy appeared to redouble even as his difficulties increased. He never showed himself more worthy of his reputation than after the battle of Vargas. General Páez had not lived up to his agreement to invade New Granada by way of Cúcuta, because he either could not or would not leave the plains of the Apure, so there was no longer any reason to hope for aid from that quarter. The army could rely only on the talents of Bolívar and the expedients that his genius might suggest. Actually, these were enough, as the course of events was to show. . . .

After the expected munitions and the convalescents from the hospital had arrived, and after the army had been augmented by numbers of patriotic volunteers, on August 3 the army began its advance on the enemy. Barreiro was forced to evacuate the town of Paipa, and as the patriots approached he withdrew his advance guards to the heights dominating the road to Tunja.

At nightfall the patriots crossed the Sogamoso River and encamped within half a league from the royalists. [The following day Bolívar recrossed the river, apparently returning to his former position at Bonza; but at nightfall he gave a counterorder, crossed the river once more, and, leaving the enemy behind, began a rapid march on Tunja by way of Toca. Ed.] At eleven in the morning he occupied the city and took as prisoners the few soldiers of the garrison, for the governor of Tunja had left that same morning for Barreiro's headquarters with the third *Numancia* battalion and an artillery brigade. The patriot army was received in Tunja with the same joyful demonstrations that had greeted it everywhere.

Bolívar's daring movement terrified the Spaniards and decided the fate of the campaign. The enemy learned of the movement only the next morning, when Barreiro set out for Tunja by the principal road. During the night he turned slightly to the right, and the next morning he entered Motavita, a village a short distance from the city.

A cavalry detachment which had followed his movements, stabbing at his rear guard, caused him a good deal of trouble during the night, and took all his stragglers as prisoners.

On the 7th, Barreiro continued his march, and as soon as Bolívar, by a personal reconnaisance, had assured himself of its direction, he

ordered the army to march toward the same point, with the intention of cutting the enemy off from Santa Fe.

At two in the afternoon the first royalists reached the bridge of Boyacá. They were passing over it when the patriot vanguard attacked their rear; simultaneously Santander's division appeared on the heights which dominated the position where Barreiro had drawn up his army.

The battle began with skirmishes between scouts. Meanwhile a column of royalist chasseurs crossed the bridge under the command of Colonel Jiménez and drew up in battle formation. But Barreiro, finding himself unable to do the same with the bulk of his army, ordered it to withdraw about three quarters of a mile from the bridge, and thereby gave the patriots time to cut him off from Santa Fe.

Bolívar immediately ordered Santander to force the bridge, and Anzoátegui simultaneously to attack the right wing and the center of the royalist position. The combat now became general; the Spanish infantry fought very bravely for some time, until Anzoátegui and his lancers enveloped their right wing and took the artillery on which the Rifles battalion had made a frontal attack; the fleeing cavalry was cut down, and when the infantry saw this they surrendered. A bayonet charge decided the day. Jiménez, who defended the bridge and was holding Santander's division in check, fell back when he saw Barreiro's plight, and the rout became general.

Sixteen hundred men laid down their arms. Barreiro, his second-in-command, Jiménez, and the majority of the chiefs and officers were taken prisoner. Artillery, munitions, arms, banners, money, and baggage fell into the hands of the victor. Bolívar personally pursued the fugitives as far as Venta Quemada, where he spent that night.

On the following morning an act of just retribution took place. Vinoni, the traitor, who had played a leading part in the uprising at and surrender of the castle of Puerto Cabello to the Spaniards, was recognized by Bolívar among the prisoners taken during the pursuit; he was immediately hanged.

4. THE ARMY OF THE ANDES

For Argentines the figure of José de San Martín has the same heroic and legendary quality that Bolívar possesses for the peoples of northern South America. Modest and reserved, San Martín was something of an enigma to his contemporaries, and we lack a description as revealing of the man as Peru de Lacroix's sketch of Bolívar. From the military point of view, San Martín's chief claim to greatness is his masterful campaign of the Andes,

*prelude to the decisive attack on Peru. To this day the standard
biography of San Martín is the classic life by Bartolomé Mitre
(1821–1906), distinguished Argentine soldier, historian, and
statesman. Mitre describes San Martín's painstaking preparations
for the passage of the Andes.*[4]

✠✠✠✠ San Martín tried to convince the enemy that he planned to invade Chile in the south, whereas he actually intended to strike in the center. This was a fixed major objective of his "war of nerves," and that is why he deceived friend and enemy alike with misleading communications and incomplete confidences, guarding his secret until the last moment. In order to confirm Marcó, the Spanish governor of Chile, in his mistaken views, he devised a new strategem, which, like all his ruses, bore the stamp of novelty and of a brain fertile in expedients.

Since 1814, San Martín, as governor of Cuyo, had cultivated friendly relations with the Pehuenche Indians, then masters of the eastern slopes of the cordillera south of Mendoza, in order to ensure the safe transit of his secret Chilean agents through the passes they dominated, and to have them on his side in case of an enemy invasion. At the time he assembled his army in the encampment of Plumerillo he decided to renew these relations, with the double object of deceiving the enemy with respect to his true plans, and of giving greater security and importance to the secondary operations which he planned to carry out by way of the southern passes. For this purpose he invited them to a general parley in the Fort of San Carlos, above the boundary line of the Diamond River, with the ostensible object of seeking permission to pass through their lands. He sent ahead trains of mules loaded with hundreds of barrels of wine and skins filled with aguardiente; with sweets, bright-colored cloths, and glass beads for the women; and, for the men, horse gear, foodstuffs of all kinds, and all the old clothes that the province could supply, in order to dazzle the allies. On the appointed day the Pehuenches approached the fort with barbaric pomp, blowing their horns, flourishing their long plumed lances, and followed by their women. The warriors were naked from the waist up and wore their long hair untied; all were in fighting trim. Each tribe was preceded by a guard of mounted grenadiers, whose correctly martial appearance contrasted with the savage appearance of the Indians. On approaching the esplanade of the fort, the women went to one side, and the men whirled their lances about by way of greeting. There followed a picturesque sham fight in Pehuenche style, with the warriors riding at full speed around the walls of the redoubt, from whose walls a gun fired a salvo every five minutes, to which the braves

[4] Bartolomé Mitre, *Historia de San Martín y de la emancipación sudaméricana,* Buenos Aires, 1944, 2 vols., I, pp. 319–334. (Excerpt translated by the editor.)

responded by striking themselves on the mouth and whooping with joy.

The solemn meeting that followed was held on the parade ground of the fort. San Martín asked permission to pass through the lands of the Pehuenches in order to attack the Spaniards through the Planchón and Portillo passes. The Spaniards, he told them, were foreigners, enemies of the American Indian, whose fields and herds, women and children, they sought to steal. The Colo-colo of the tribes was a white-haired ancient called Necuñan. After consulting the assembly and obtaining their opinions with suitable gravity, he told the general that with the exception of three caciques, with whom they could deal later, all accepted his proposals, and they sealed the treaty of alliance by embracing San Martín, one after another. In proof of their friendship they immediately placed their arms in the keeping of the Christians and gave themselves up to an orgy that lasted for eight consecutive days. On the sixth day the general returned to his headquarters to await the result of these negotiations, whose object he kept secret from even his most intimate confidants.

The creole diplomat had foreseen that the Indians, with their natural perfidy — or the dissident caciques, at any rate — would report his pretended project to Marcó, as actually happened. But just in case they should not do so, he hastened to communicate it to the Spanish leader directly by means of one of his characteristic ruses, in which he was aided by a coincidence that he had also foreseen. During the reorganization of his army he had cut the supposed communications of the Spaniards of Cuyo with Marcó, and the latter, ignorant of everything that was taking place east of the Andes, sent emissaries to obtain information from the individuals whom he believed to be his official correspondents. Such was San Martín's vigilance that for two years not a single royalist spy had been able to penetrate into Cuyo without being captured in the cordillera by patriot guards who had been warned by secret agents in Chile. The last letters of the Spanish governor met the same fate. With these letters in his possession, San Martín summoned the supposed correspondents to his presence, — among them was Castillo de Albo, — showed them the incriminating letters, and with pretended anger (it is said that he even threatened them with a pistol that he had on his desk) forced them to write and sign replies that he dictated. In these replies he announced that "about the 15th of October" a squadron was preparing to leave Buenos Aires for an unknown destination. It was "composed of a frigate, three corvettes, two brigantines, and two transports, all under the command of the Englishman Teler [Taylor]." "San Martín," they added, "has held a general parley with the Pehuenche Indians. The Indians have agreed to everything; we shall see how they carry out their pledges; caution and more caution; for lack of it our people have suffered imprisonment and spolia-

tions. Everything is known here." In another he said that a French engineer had left Mendoza in order to construct a bridge over the Diamond River. San Martín's letters, sent by an emissary who played the role of a double spy, were delivered to Marcó, who believed everything in them, lost his head entirely, and turned the whole province upside down to guard against a double invasion. At the same time San Martín informed the government of Buenos Aires that the purpose of the parley was to get the Indians "to assist the passage of the army with livestock and horses at the stipulated prices," while to his confidant, Guido, he wrote: "I concluded with all success my great parley with the Indians of the south; they not only will aid the army with livestock but are committed to take an active part against the enemy." As can be seen, San Martín was a well of large and small mysteries, with the naked truth hidden at the bottom.

Marcó, disheartened by the alarming news from his supposed correspondents in Cuyo, and by the simultaneous rising of the guerrillas of Manuel Rodríguez, who extended their excursions between the Maule and the Maipo and made armed assaults on villages in the very vicinity of the capital, dictated a series of senseless and contradictory measures that revealed the confusion in his mind and the fear in his heart. He ordered the ports to be fortified and attempted to convert some of them into islands with the object of preventing a disembarkation; at the same time he equipped a squadron to act against the imaginary fleet of Buenos Aires. He commanded that entrenchments should be thrown up in the pass of Uspallata, that the southern provinces of the kingdom should be mapped and that the entrances to the Maule and Planchón passes should be surveyed; but before these tasks had been completed he ordered strengthening of the guards at all the passes of the cordillera, from north to south. First he concentrated his troops and then he dispersed most of them again, moving them about in empty space. Finding no inspiration in himself, after jerking about like a puppet manipulated by San Martín, he finished by reproducing the man's very gestures, like a monkey; in imitation of the patriot general he held a parley with the Araucanian Indians, but failed to devise a rational plan of defense.

The objective of the astute Argentine leader was fulfilled: the captain-general of Chile sought to defend all its land and sea frontiers simultaneously; consequently he dispersed his army and thus became weak everywhere, never suspecting the point of the true attack. To crown his confusion, the spies he sent to obtain accurate information either did not return or served San Martín by bringing back false reports that led him to commit new errors. Some of his advisers urged him to take the offensive; others, that he persevere in his absurd waiting plan; and only one of them, his secretary, Dr. Judas Tadeo Reyes, the least knowledgeable in warfare, suggested the plan he should have

followed: concentrate the 50,000 veteran troops in the capital, disperse
the militia troops about the country, and await the invasion in that
posture. However, by this time Marcó was so distraught that good and
bad counsels were equally useless. He himself graphically depicted his
deplorable morale at this time (February 4, 1817): "My plans are reduced to continual movements and variations according to developments and news of the enemy, whose astute chief at Mendoza, kept informed of my situation by his innumerable lines of communication and
the disloyal spies who surround me, seeks to surprise me."

But it was not only the threat of impending invasion that made
Marcó uneasy. His resources were scanty, and as a result of the stupid
system of taxation established by Osorio and continued and intensified
by himself, the very sources of further contributions were exhausted.
In order to defray the public expenses he levied a tax on exports of
grain and flour and imports of wine and sugar; simultaneously he decreed a forced loan of 400,000 pesos to be collected from individuals
with an annual income of 1,000 pesos, not excluding civil and military
officers, and payable in cash. The sole result of these measures was the
spread of demoralization and discontent, which fanned the sparks of
insurrection lighted by the agents of San Martín, who announced his
immediate arrival at the head of a powerful liberating army. . . .

The situation was quite different in the encampment at Mendoza:
here there was a methodical activity, an automatic obedience coupled
with an enthusiasm born of understanding. A superior will, that knew
what it wanted and what it was doing, directed all, inspiring the soldiers
with the feeling that victory was certain. In Mendoza it was known
what Marcó did, thought, or was going to do, whereas Marcó did not
even know what he wanted to do. Everyone worked, each performing
the task assigned to him, and they all trusted in their general. Pack
mules and war horses were assembled; thousands of horseshoes were
forged for the animals; packsaddles were made for the beasts of burden;
fodder and provisions were stored; and herds of cattle were rounded
up for the passage of the cordillera. Leaders, officers, and soldiers devoted themselves to their respective duties and positions. The arsenal
turned out hundreds of thousands of cartridges. The forges blazed day
and night, repairing arms and casting projectiles. The indefatigable
Father Luis Beltran supervised the construction of new machines by
means of which, as he put it, the cannon would fly over the tops of the
mountains like condors. The ingenious friar had invented, or rather
adapted, a kind of narrow carriage (called *zorra*) of rude but solid
construction which, mounted on four low wheels and drawn by oxen
or mules, replaced the mounts of the cannon; the guns themselves
would be carried on the backs of mules along the narrow, tortuous
paths of the cordillera until they reached the plain on the other side. As
a precaution, long slings were made in which the carriages and cannon

would be hoisted over rough places between mules, as if in litters, one after the other; sleds of hide were also prepared in which heavy objects might be hauled up by hand or by a portable winch when the gradients were too steep for the mules.

Meanwhile the general-in-chief, silent and reserved, planned for everyone, inspected everything, and provided for all contingencies in the most minute detail, from food and equipment for men and beasts to the complicated machines of war, even seeing the cutting edge of his soldiers' sabres.

The army needed a healthful and nourishing food that would restore the soldiers' strength and would be suited to the frigid temperatures through which they must pass. San Martín found this in a popular dish called *charquican*, composed of beef dried in the sun, roasted, ground to powder, mixed with fat and chili pepper, and well pounded. A soldier could carry enough of this in his knapsack to last him eight days. Mixed with hot water and roasted maize meal it made a nutritious and appetizing porridge. . . . After providing for his soldiers' stomachs, San Martín took thought for their feet — the vehicles of victory. In order to obtain footwear without burdening the treasury, he asked the *cabildo* of Mendoza to collect and send to the camp the scraps of cowhide discarded every day by the slaughterhouses of the city. From these pieces he had the soldiers make *tamangos*, a kind of closed sandal often used by the Negroes. . . . He carried economy to extreme lengths in order to show, in his own words, that great enterprises can be accomplished with small means. An order of the day, made public to the sound of drums, asked the people to bring to special depots old woolen rags that could be used to line the *tamangos*, because, San Martín declared, "the health of the soldiers is a powerful machine that if well directed can bring victory; and our first concern is to protect their feet." The horns of slaughtered cattle were used to make canteens, necessary in crossing the waterless stretches of the cordillera. Another decree ordered all the cloth remnants in the stores and tailor shops of the city to be collected, and San Martín distributed them to the soldiers to make into straps for their knapsacks.

The sabres of the mounted grenadiers had lost their sharpness; San Martín had them given a razor-like edge and placed them in the hands of his soldiers, saying they were for cutting off Spanish heads. It was not enough to sharpen swords; arms had to be trained to use them; and martial instruments were needed to nerve the soldiers and to take the place of the officer's voice in battle. San Martín chose the trumpet, an instrument rarely used by American cavalry at that time. The army had only three trumpets. San Martín had some made out of tin, but they were mute. In his application to the government San Martín wrote: "The trumpet is as necessary for the cavalry as is the drum for the infantry. . . ."

The general gave the matter of horseshoes his closest attention. Before making a decision he held conferences with veterinarians, blacksmiths, and muleteers; after carefully listening to them, he adopted a model of a horseshoe which he sent to the government telling the officer who carried it to guard it as if it were made of gold and to present it to the Minister of War. . . . The army needed thirty thousand horseshoes with a double set of nails. In two months they were forged by artisans who toiled day and night in the shops of the arms factory in Buenos Aires and in the forges of Mendoza.

How was the army to cross the deep ravines and torrents that lay before it? How were the heavy materials of war to ascend and descend the steep slopes of the mountains? And finally, how were the carriages and their loads to be rescued from the depths into which they might fall? These were problems that had to be solved. For river passages a rope bridge of a given weight and length (60 *varas*) was devised, and the piece of cable which was to be shown to the government as a model was entrusted to an officer with the same solemnity as the horseshoe. "It is impossible to transport the artillery and other heavy objects over the narrow defiles and slopes of the cordillera, or to rescue material fallen from the path," wrote San Martín, "without the aid of two anchors and four cables, of a weight that can be transported on muleback." With this apparatus, moved by a winch, the difficulties of the passage were overcome. . . .

Amid this official correspondence concerning the movement of men, materials, and money, an exchange of letters of mixed character took place between the two protagonists of our story: General San Martín and Pueyrredón, Director of the United Provinces of La Plata. Passionately devoted to the same cause, they aided and comforted each other, until they and their mission became one. . . .

"You don't ask for much," the Director would write San Martín, "and I feel bad because I don't have the money to get these things for you; but I shall do my best, and by the beginning of October I shall have gotten together thirty thousand pesos for the use of the army." But hardly had Pueyrredón assumed direction of the government and began to make good his promises when there broke out in Córdoba a confused anarchical revolt that threatened to throw the entire Republic into chaos. . . .

When the brief uprising of Córdoba had been crushed, the general of the Andes renewed his insistent urging, as has been shown from the official correspondence. The Director provided everything, and when he had satisfied all demands he took up his pen and wrote with humorous desperation and comradely forthrightness: "I am sending official letters of thanks to Mendoza and the other cities of Cuyo. I am sending the officers' commissions. I am sending the uniforms you asked for and many more shirts. I am sending 400 saddles. I am send-

ing off today by post two trumpets — all I could find. In January I shall send 1387 *arrobas* of dried beef. I am sending the 200 spare sabres that you asked for. I am sending 200 tents or pavilions; that's all there are. I am sending the world, the flesh, and the devil! I don't know how I shall get out of the scrape I'm in to pay for all this, unless I declare bankruptcy, cancel my accounts with everyone, and clear out to join you, so that you can give me some of the dried beef I'm sending you. Damn it, don't ask me for anything else, unless you want to hear that they found me in the morning dangling from a beam in the Fort!" . . .

When everything was ready the general of the expedition asked for instructions concerning his military and political courses of action. The government, inspired by the same lofty aims as the general, drew up instructions infused with a broad, generous, and resolute spirit, in harmony with San Martín's continental plan; and formulated, in words which deeds were to make good, the liberation policy of the Argentine Revolution in respect to the other peoples of South America, on the basis of independence and liberty for each one of them. "The consolidation of American independence" (said Article I) "and the glory of the United Provinces of South America are the only motives of this campaign. The general will make this clear in his proclamations; he will spread it through his agents in every town, and will propagate it by every possible means. The army must be impressed with these principles. Care must be taken that not a word is said of pillage, oppression, conquest, or retaining possession of the liberated country." . . .

With these instructions in his portfolio, all decisions made, and the army poised at the eastern entrances to the Andes, San Martín, one foot already in the stirrup, wrote (January 24, 1817) his last letter to his most intimate confidant: "This afternoon I set out to join the army. God grant me success in this great enterprise."

5. THE INTERVIEW OF GUAYAQUIL

Historical controversy still rages in Latin America about the famous meeting between Bolívar and San Martín at Guayaquil, in July, 1822. One view is that San Martín came to Guayaquil in search of military aid from Bolívar, was rebuffed by the Liberator, and magnanimously determined to quit Peru, leaving the way open for Bolívar to complete the work he had begun. Other students deny that San Martín asked Bolívar for more troops at the conference; they say that San Martín's departure from Peru was motivated by personal reasons and had nothing

to do with the generals' discussion. The following account of this private conference was given by Bolívar to his secretary, J. G. Pérez.[5]

✠✠✠✠ General Headquarters, Guayaquil, July 29, 1822. The 12th [year].
My dear General Sucre:
I have the honor of informing you that on the 26th, at nine o'clock in the morning, His Excellency the Protector of Perú entered this city.

No sooner did the Protector see His Excellency the Liberator aboard the ship that had brought him than he expressed in the most cordial terms the sentiments that had heightened his desire to meet the Liberator, to embrace him, and to assure him of his true and lasting friendship. He congratulated His Excellency on his remarkable perseverance amidst the adversities that he had met with in defense of the cause of freedom and on the victory which had crowned his heroic achievements. Altogether, the Protector protested his friendship for His Excellency in terms of high eulogy and lavish praise.

His Excellency replied in the noble and gracious terms that propriety and gratitude demand in such circumstances.

The Protector opened the conferences in a most frank manner. The principal topics were as follows:

The situation recently experienced in this province, because of the ferment of political opinions, was discussed. Of his own accord the Protector told His Excellency that he had not interfered in the tangled affairs of Guayaquil, that he had not the slightest part in them, and that the fault was theirs, meaning the opposition. His Excellency replied that his desire to consult that city had been realized, for on the 28th the electors would meet, and that he was counting upon the will of the people and a plurality of votes in the assembly. The Protector thereupon changed the subject and went on to talk of military matters and of the expedition which is about to depart [for Perú].

The Protector complained a great deal about his command and, above all, about his comrades-in-arms who had recently abandoned him in Lima. He asserted that he was going to retire to Mendoza, that he had left a sealed note to be presented to the Congress, renouncing the Protectorate, that he would also refuse the election which he expected to win; and that, as soon as he had won the first victory, he would give up his military command and not await the war's end. But, he added, before retiring he would give thought to laying the foundations of the [Peruvian] government. He stated that this government should not be

[5] José Gabriel Pérez to General Antonio José Sucre, Guayaquil, July 29, 1822, in Lecuna and Bierck, *Selected Writings of Bolívar*, I, pp. 340–343. Reprinted by kind permission of the Banco de Venezuela.

democratic, as democracy did not suit Perú; and lastly he said that an independent, unattached prince should be brought from Europe to rule Perú. His Excellency replied that to invite European princes would please neither America nor Colombia, as they were extraneous to our people, and that for his part His Excellency would oppose them if he were able, yet without interfering in whatever form of government any country might desire. His Excellency set forth all his ideas on the nature of governments, repeating all that he had said in his speech to the Congress of Angostura. The Protector replied that the securing of a prince was a matter for the future.

It can be assumed that his plan is to erect a monarchy by offering the crown to several European princes, and finally to grant the throne to the one receiving the most popular support or having the strongest force to offer. If the Protector is sincere in what he says, no one is further than he from occupying such a throne. He appears to be convinced of the difficulties inherent in leadership.

The Protector applauded highly the federation of the American states as being the very foundation of our political existence. He regards Guayaquil as the most suitable place for the headquarters of such a federation. He believes Chile will have no objections to joining it, but that Buenos Aires, because of the lack of unity and method in that country, will refuse. He said that nothing was closer to his heart than to have the federation between Colombia and Perú continue, even in the absence of other states.

The Protector believes the enemy is weaker than he, and that the enemy's leaders, though daring and able, are not to be greatly feared. He will immediately open his campaign with a maritime expedition to Intermedios and from Lima, defending that capital by a frontal march on the enemy.

In their very first talks, the Protector, of his own accord, told his Excellency that the matter of boundaries between Colombia and Perú would be settled satisfactorily and without the slightest difficulty. He would undertake to sponsor it in the Congress, where he did not lack friends.

The Protector told His Excellency that he might ask anything he wished of Perú, as his answer would never be anything but yes, yes, yes; and that he hoped that Colombia would reciprocate. This offer of services and friendship is without qualification, and it displays a frankness and a sense of satisfaction that appear to be sincere. The Protector's visit to Colombia was not official in character; it was merely a visit to His Excellency the Liberator for no ulterior purpose, political or military. He did not so much as refer to the troops that Colombia is about to send to Perú.

Early yesterday morning the Protector departed. On taking

leave, he displayed the same cordiality, affection and sincerity toward His Excellency as at their first meeting.

6. AYACUCHO

The departure of San Martín from Peru left the country in the hands of weak and incompetent politicians. Threatened by a strong Spanish counter-offensive, the Peruvian leaders called on Bolívar to save the new state from destruction. Bolívar responded to their summons. The battle of Ayacucho, fought on December 9, 1824, was the last major action in the Spanish-American Wars of Independence.[6]

✦✦✦✦ Quinua, an Indian village, is on the western extremity of the plain of Ayacucho, the shape of which is nearly square, about a league in circumference, and flanked right and left by deep, rugged ravines. In the rear of the plain, or towards the west, is a gradual descent of two leagues to the main road from Guamanga to Guanta, which runs along the base of a mountain range, that rises like a wall with no apparent outlet. The eastern boundary of the plain is formed by the abrupt and rugged ridge of Condorkanki; which gigantic bulwark, running north and south, overlooks the field of Ayacucho. A little below the summit of this ridge was perched the royalist army.

The liberating army was drawn up on the plain, in front of the Spaniards, at an interval of about a mile, having Quinua in the rear, each corps being formed in close column, to await the attack of the royalists. . . .

During the night of the 8th, a brisk fire was maintained between the royalist and patriot outposts. It was the object of Sucre to prevent the royalists descending in the night. For this purpose the bands of two battalions were sent with a company near to the foot of the ridge, and continued playing for some time whilst a sharp fire was kept up. This feint had the desired effect, for the royalists did not stir from their lines.

The viceroy's position in the night of the 8th was very much exposed: his infantry, occupying the front of the ridge of Condorkanki, was within musket-range of the foot of the hill. The fire from two or three battalions, deployed into line, might have obliged the royalists to abandon their position. As it was, a lieutenant-colonel and two or three men, within the Spanish encampment, were killed,

[6] John Miller, *Memoirs of General Miller, in the Service of the Republic of Peru,* London, 1828, 2 vols., II, pp. 194–202.

as they sat round their fires, by chance balls from the patriot company at the foot of the hill.

The night of the 8th was one of deep and anxious interest. A battle was inevitable on the following day, and that battle was to decide the destinies of South America. The patriots were aware that they had to contend with twice their own numbers; and that nothing but a decisive victory could save them and their country from ignominious servitude. The patriot *soldier* might indeed expect to escape with *life*, reduced to the condition of a slave; but with the patriot generals and officers, it was only a choice between death and victory. They knew full well what would be the cruel policy of the Spaniards if they proved victorious. The viceroy was, it is true, a man of humane disposition, but the individual who counselled Monet to shoot two patriot officers in the pass of San Mateo, and the other man (if such he may be called) who ran his sword through the wounded and defenceless Major Gumer, on the field at Lea, were, with others, of a character equally sanguinary, amongst the advisers of La Serna; and it is extremely probable that unsparing executions would have been resorted to in the hope of destroying the very germ of future insurrection. Every one felt that the approaching battle was to have no common result.

The morning of the 9th dawned particularly fine. At first there was a chilliness in the air which seemed to influence the minds of the men, but when the sun rose above the mountain, the effects of its genial warmth became manifest in the renovated spirits of the soldiers. The men on both sides were observed rubbing their hands, and exhibiting every token of content and satisfaction. At nine A.M. the division of Villalobos began to descend. The viceroy, on foot, placed himself at its head; and the files wound down the craggy side of Condorkanki, obliquing a little to their left. The division Monet, forming the royalist right, commenced at the same time to defile directly into the plain. The cavalry, leading their horses, made the same movement, though with greater difficulty, between the infantry of each division. As the files arrived on the plain, they formed into column. This was a moment of extraordinary interest. It appeared as though respiration were suspended by feelings of anxiety, mingled with doubts and hope.

It was during this operation, which had an imposing effect, that Sucre rode along his own line, and, addressing a few emphatic words to each corps, recalled to memory its former achievements. He then placed himself in a central point, and, in an inspiring tone of voice, said, "that upon the efforts of that day depended the fate of South America;" then pointing to the descending columns, he assured his men, "that another day of glory was about to crown their admirable

constancy." This animating address of the general produced an electric effect, and was answered by enthusiastic "*vivas*."

By the time that rather more than half the royalist divisions, Monet and Villalobos, had reached and formed upon the arena, Sucre ordered the division Córdova and two regiments of cavalry to advance to the charge. The gallant Córdova placed himself about fifteen yards in front of his division, formed into four parallel columns with the cavalry in the intervals. Having dismounted, he plunged his sword into the heart of his charger, and turning to the troops, exclaimed, "there lies my last horse; I have now no means of escape, and we must fight it out together!" Then waving his hat above his head, he continued, "*Adelante, con paso de vencedores*" (Onward with the step of conquerors). These words were heard distinctly throughout the columns, which, inspired by the gallant bearing of their leader, moved to the attack in the finest possible order. The Spaniards stood firmly and full of apparent confidence. The viceroy was seen, as were also Monet and Villalobos, at the head of their divisions, superintending the formation of their columns as they reached the plain. The hostile bayonets crossed, and for three or four minutes the two parties struggled together, so as to leave it doubtful which would give way. At this moment the Colombian cavalry, headed by Colonel Silva, charged. This brave officer fell covered with wounds, but the intrepidity of the onset was irresistible. The royalists lost ground, and were driven back with great slaughter. The vice-king was wounded and taken prisoner. As the fugitives climbed the sides of Condorkanki, the patriots, who had deployed, kept up a well-directed fire, and numbers of the enemy were seen to drop and roll down, till their progress was arrested by the brush-wood, or some jutting crag.

Miller, who had followed up Córdova's division, perceiving its complete success, returned to the regiment of Úsares de Junín, which fortunately had been left in reserve.

At dawn of day, the royalist division Valdés commenced a detour of nearly a league. Descending the sides of Condorkanki on the north, Valdés had placed himself on the left of the patriots at musket-shot distance, separated by a ravine. At the important moment of the battle, just described, he opened a heavy fire from four field-pieces and a battalion in extended files. By this, he obliged two battalions of the Peruvian division La Mar to fall back. The Colombian battalion Bargas, sent to support the Peruvian division, also began to give way. Two royalist battalions crossed the deep ravine, already spoken of, on the left, and advanced in double quick time in pursuit of the retiring patriots. At this critical juncture, Miller took upon himself to lead the hussars of Junín against the victorious Spaniards,

and by a timely charge drove them back, and followed them across the ravine, by which time he was supported by the *granaderos a caballo* and by the division La Mar, which had rallied. The brave Colonel Plaza crossed the ravine at the head of the legion on the left. Lieutenant-Colonel Morán, at the head of the battalion Bargas, made a similar movement on the right of the cavalry. These two battalions and the cavalry, mutually supporting and rivalling each other in valour, repeated their charges with such resolution, that the division Valdés was broken; its artillery taken; its cavalry obliged to fly in disorder; and its infantry dispersed.

The royalists had now lost the battle, and fled to the ridge from which they had descended, in the morning, with so much confidence.

The action lasted an hour. Fourteen hundred royalists were killed, and seven hundred wounded, and they lost fifteen pieces of artillery.

The loss on the part of the patriots was three hundred and seventy killed, and six hundred and nine wounded.

The single piece of artillery belonging to the patriots did considerable execution on the royalist columns, and was of service also in attracting a heavy fire from their artillery, which if it had been directed upon the patriot columns, would have occasioned the loss to be more considerable.

The plan of the royalists was to wait until Valdés had outflanked the left of Sucre's position, from which having driven him, the whole army was to advance and complete the victory. The mistake of the viceroy in attacking at all, originated in suffering himself to be impelled to it by the eagerness of his troops. Their patience had been worn out, by the terrible marches, which appeared to them to be endless. At Guamanguilla, a system of pasquinading had been adopted. The tents of La Serna, Canterac, and others, had various lampoons pasted on them, and it may be fairly said that they were goaded by their own soldiers into a general action contrary to their own judgment.

The royalists, upon regaining the heights of Condorkanki, rallied as many of their defeated troops as they possibly could. The patriot divisions La Mar and Lara gained the summit of the heights at about 1 P.M. Before sunset Canterac sued for terms, and an hour afterward rode down to the tent of Sucre, where a capitulation was agreed upon. The Viceroy La Serna, Generals Canterac, Valdés, Carratala, Monet, Villalobos, Ferras, Bedoya, Somocursio, Cacho, Atero, Landazuri, García-Camba, Pardo, Vigil, and Tur; 16 colonels, 68 lieutenant-colonels, 484 officers, 3200 rank and file, became prisoners of war. The rest had dispersed.

The battle of Ayacucho was the most brilliant ever fought in South America. The troops on both sides were in a state of discipline which would have been creditable to the best European armies. The ablest generals and chiefs of either party were present, and it is difficult to say which army most panted for an appeal to the sword, as every man fought with undaunted bravery. What the patriots wanted in numbers was made up by enthusiasm, and by a perfect knowledge that, if beaten, retreat was utterly impracticable. It was not a victory of mere chance, but the result of the most determined valour, and of an irresistible onset, conceived and executed at the proper moment.

7. THE VISION OF BOLÍVAR

The most grandiose of Bolívar's political conceptions was that of a league of friendship and mutual assistance uniting all the Latin American states, under the leadership and protection of Great Britain. To achieve this project, Bolívar invited these and other nations to a congress, which was held at Panama in 1826. In the end this assembly proved an almost total failure. On the eve of the meeting Bolívar wrote down a statement of the advantages to be gained from the proposed confederacy. This document suggests that fear of the Holy Alliance, on the one hand, and of Negro and Indian insurrections, on the other, partly influenced Bolívar's decision to summon the Congress of Panama.[7]

✠✠✠ The Congress of Panama will bring together all the representatives of America and a diplomat-agent of His Britannic Majesty's government. This Congress seems destined to form a league more extensive, more remarkable, and more powerful than any that has ever existed on the face of the earth. Should Great Britain agree to join it as a constituent member, the Holy Alliance will be less powerful than this confederation. Mankind will a thousand times bless this league for promoting its general welfare, and America, as well as Great Britain, will reap from it untold benefits. A code of public law to regulate the international conduct of political bodies will be one of its products.

1. The New World would consist of independent nations,

[7] Lecuna and Bierck, *The Selected Writings of Bolívar*, II, pp. 561–562. Reprinted by kind permission of the Banco de Venezuela.

bound together by a common set of laws which would govern their foreign relations and afford them a right to survival through a general and permanent congress.

2. The existence of these new states would receive fresh guarantees.

3. In deference to England, Spain would make peace, and the Holy Alliance would grant recognition to these infant nations.

4. Domestic control would be preserved untouched among the states and within each of them.

5. No one of them would be weaker than another, nor would any be stronger.

6. A perfect balance would be established by this truly new order of things.

7. The power of all would come to the aid of any one state which might suffer at the hands of a foreign enemy or from internal anarchic factions.

8. Differences of origin and color would lose their influence and power.

9. America would have nothing more to fear from that tremendous monster who has devoured the island of Santo Domingo, nor would she have cause to fear the numerical preponderance of the aborigines.

10. In short, a social reform would be achieved under the blessed auspices of freedom and peace, but the fulcrum controlling the beam of the scales must necessarily rest in the hands of England.

Great Britain would, of course, derive considerable advantage from this arrangement.

1. Her influence in Europe would progressively increase, and her decisions would be like those of destiny itself.

2. America would serve her as an opulent domain of commerce.

3. America would become the center of England's relations with Asia and Europe.

4. British subjects in America would be considered the equals of American citizens.

5. The relations between England and America would in time become those between equals.

6. British characteristics and customs would be adopted by the Americans as standards for their future way of life.

7. In the course of the centuries, there might, perhaps, come to exist one single nation throughout the world — a federal nation.

These ideas are in the minds of many Americans in positions of importance who impatiently await the inauguration of this project at the Congress of Panama, which may afford the occasion to consumate the union of the new states and the British Empire.

8. A LETTER TO DOM PEDRO

Brazil made a swift and relatively bloodless transition to inde-
pendence. The immediate causes of separation were the efforts
of a jealous Portuguese cortes to revoke the liberties and con-
cessions won by Brazil since 1808 and to force the departure
of the prince regent, Dom Pedro, from Brazil. Messages of
support from juntas throughout the country, such as the fol-
lowing from the junta of São Paulo, encouraged the prince to
defy the Lisbon government and to issue his famous "fico" (I
remain).[8]

Sir,

✠✠✠✠ We had already written to your Royal Highness, before we
received the extraordinary gazette of the 11th instant, by the last
courier: and we had hardly fixed our eyes on the first decree of the
Cortes concerning the organization of the governments of the provinces of Brazil, when a noble indignation fired our hearts: because we
saw impressed on it a system of anarchy and slavery. But the second,
in conformity to which Your Royal Highness is to go back to Portugal, in order to travel *incognito* only through Spain, France, and
England, inspired us with horror.

They aim at no less than disuniting us, weakening us, and in
short, leaving us like miserable orphans, tearing from the bosom of the
great family of Brazil the only common father who remained to us,
after they had deprived Brazil of the beneficent founder of the kingdom, Your Royal Highness's august sire. They deceive themselves;
we trust in God, who is the avenger of injustice; He will give us
courage, and wisdom.

If, by the 21st article of the basis of the constitution, which
we approve and swear to because it is founded on universal and public right, the deputies of Portugal were bound to agree that the constitution made at Lisbon could then be obligatory on the Portuguese
resident in that kingdom; and, that, as for those in the other three
parts of the world, it should only be binding when their legitimate
representatives should have declared such to be their will: How dare
those deputies of Portugal, without waiting for those of Brazil, legis-
late concerning the most sacred interest of each province, and of the
entire kingdom? How dare they split it into detached portions, each
isolated, and without leaving a common centre of strength and union?
How dare they rob Your Royal Highness of the lieutenancy, granted
by Your Royal Highness's august father, the King? How dare they

[8] Maria Graham, *Journal of a Voyage to Brazil, and Residence There, During*
Part of the Years 1821, 1822, and 1823, London, 1824, pp. 174–177.

deprive Brazil of the privy council, the board of conscience, the court of exchequer, the board of commerce, the court of requests, and so many other recent establishments, which promised such future advantage? Where now shall the wretched people resort in behalf of their civil and judicial interests? Must they now again, after being for twelve years accustomed to judgment at hand, go and suffer, like petty colonists, the delays and chicanery of the tribunals of Lisbon, across two thousand leagues of ocean, where the sighs of the oppressed lose all life and all hope? Who would credit it, after so many bland, but deceitful expressions of reciprocal equality and future happiness!

In the session of the 6th of August last, the deputy of the Cortes, Pereira do Carmo, said (and he spoke the truth) that the constitution was the social compact, in which were expressed and declared the conditions on which a nation might wish to constitute itself a body politic: and that the end of that constitution is the general good of each individual who is to enter into that social compact. How then dares a mere fraction of the great Portuguese nation, without waiting for the conclusion of this solemn national compact, attack the general good of the principal part of the same, and such is the vast and rich kingdom of Brazil; dividing it into miserable fragments, and, in a word, attempting to tear from its bosom the representative of the executive power, and to annihilate by a stroke of the pen, all the tribunals and establishments necessary to its existence and future prosperity? This unheard-of despotism, this horrible political perjury, was certainly not merited by the good and generous Brazil. But the enemies of order in the Cortes of Lisbon deceive themselves if they imagine that they can thus, by vain words and hollow professions, delude the good sense of the worthy Portuguese of both worlds.

Your Royal Highness will observe that, if the kingdom of Ireland, which makes part of the United Kingdom of Great Britain, besides that it is infinitely small compared to the vast kingdom of Brazil, and is separated from England but by a narrow arm of the sea, which is passed in a few hours, yet possesses a governor-general or viceroy, who represents the executive power of the King of the United Kingdom, how can it enter the head of anyone who is not either profoundly ignorant, or rashly inconsiderate, to pretend, that the vast kingdom of Brazil, should remain without a centre of activity, and without a representative of the executive power; and equally without a power to direct our troops, so as that they may operate with celerity and effect, to defend the state against any unforeseen attack of external enemies, or against internal disorders and factions, which might threaten public safety, or the reciprocal union of the province!

We therefore entreat Your Royal Highness with the greatest

fervour, tenderness, and respect to delay your return to Europe, where they wish to make you travel as a pupil surrounded by tutors and spies: We entreat you to confide boldly in the love and fidelity of your Brazilians, and especially of your Paulistas, who are all ready to shed the last drop of their blood, and to sacrifice their fortunes, rather than lose the adored Prince in whom they have placed their well-founded hopes of national happiness and honour. Let Your Royal Highness wait at least for the deputies named by this province, and for the magistracy of this capital, who will as soon as possible present to Your Highness our ardent desires and firm resolutions; and deign to receive them, and to listen to them, with the affection and attention, which your Paulistas deserve from you.

May God preserve your Royal Highness's august person many years.

23 ✣ The War for
Mexican Independence

In Mexico, as in other Spanish-American colonies, news of the impending fall of Spain to French armies caused widespread agitation and inspired creole projects for separation from the mother country. In September, 1810, the patriot priest Miguel Hidalgo launched a revolt by calling on the Indians of his parish to rise against their Spanish rulers. After his first victories Hidalgo issued decrees abolishing slavery and personal tribute and ordering the restoration of their lands to the Indian communities. These measures gave the Mexican revolution a popular character that was largely absent from the movement for independence in South America. But they alienated many wealthy creoles who also desired independence — but without social revolution.

Hidalgo proved unable to weld his Indian hordes into a disciplined army, or to capitalize on his early victories. Less than one year after the revolt had begun, he was captured and executed by the royalists. Another capable priest, José María Morelos, assumed leadership of the revolutionary struggle. Morelos liberated a large part of Mexico, maintained order in the regions under his control, and summoned a congress that proclaimed Mexican independence and framed a republican constitution for the country. Morelos shared Hidalgo's

vision of the war as a social revolution, going beyond his master in his advocacy of agrarian reform. Like Hidalgo, Morelos had differences over policy with creole associates that seriously hampered him in his conduct of the war. In 1815 he was captured by the Spaniards, and after a speedy trial suffered the fate of Hidalgo.

After the death of Morelos, the revolution declined into a guerrilla war waged by many rival chiefs, some of whom were mere brigands. Royalist armies gradually extinguished the remaining centers of resistance. By 1820 only two patriot leaders — Vicente Guerrero and Guadalupe Victoria — were carrying on the struggle for independence.

At the opening of that year a revolution in Spain compelled Ferdinand VII to swear loyalty to the liberal Constitution of 1812. News of this development raised liberal hopes in Mexico and threw conservative churchmen and army officers into a panic. Fearing the loss of their privileges, they schemed to separate Mexico from the mother country. Their instrument was the creole officer Agustín de Iturbide, hitherto a merciless foe of the insurgents. His Plan of Iguala won the support of all creole monarchists and the temporary adherence of republican insurgents. Iturbide's "Army of the Three Guarantees" swiftly overcame scattered loyalist resistance. On September 28, 1821, the independence of the Mexican Empire was officially proclaimed, and eight months later a national congress elected Iturbide emperor of the new realm.

1. HIDALGO: TORCHBEARER OF THE REVOLUTION

Miguel Hidalgo (1753–1811), the scholarly white-haired priest of the town of Dolores and onetime rector of the college of San Nicolás at Valladolid, hardly seemed fitted by background and disposition to head a revolution. It was Hidalgo, nevertheless, who overcame the waverings of his associates when their conspiracy was discovered, and who transformed what had been planned as an upper-class creole revolt into a rising of the masses. Alamán, historian and bitter enemy of the revolution — who knew Hidalgo in the peaceful years before the great upheaval — describes the curate of Dolores.[1]

❖❖❖❖ Don Miguel Hidalgo, being neither austere in his morals nor very orthodox in his opinions, did not concern himself with the spiritual administration of his parish, which he had turned over, together

[1] Alamán, *Historia de Méjico*, I, pp. 352–354. (Excerpt translated by the editor.)

with half the income of his curacy, to a priest named Don Francisco
Iglesias. Knowing French — a rather rare accomplishment at that
period, especially among churchmen — he formed a taste for technical and scientific books and zealously promoted various agricultural
and industrial projects in his parish. He considerably furthered viti-
culture, and today that whole region produces abundant harvests of
grapes; he also encouraged the planting of mulberry trees for the
raising of silkworms. In Dolores eighty-four trees planted by him
are still standing, in the spot called "the mulberry trees of Hidalgo,"
as well as the channels that he had dug for irrigating the entire plantation. He established a brickyard and a factory for the manufacture
of porcelain, constructed troughs for tanning hides, and promoted a
variety of other enterprises.

All this, plus the fact that he was not only generous but lavish
in money matters, had won him the high regard of his parishioners
— especially the Indians, whose languages he had mastered. It also
gained him the esteem of all who took a sincere interest in the advancement of the country, men like Abad y Queipo, the bishop-elect
of Michoacán, and Riaño, the intendant of Guanajuato. It seems,
however, that he had little basic knowledge of the industries which
he fostered, and even less of that systematic spirit which one must
have to make substantial progress with them. Once, being asked by
Bishop Abad y Queipo what method he used for picking and distributing the leaves to the silkworms according to their age, and for
separating the dry leaves and keeping the silkworms clean — concerning which the books on the subject give such elaborate instructions —
he replied that he followed no particular order, that he threw down
the leaves as they came from the tree and let the silkworms eat as
they wished. "The revolution," exclaimed the bishop, who told me
this anecdote, "was like his raising of silkworms, and the results were
what might be expected!" Nevertheless, he had made much progress,
and obtained enough silk to have some garments made for himself and
for his stepmother. He also promoted the raising of bees, and brought
many swarms of bees to the hacienda of Jaripeo when he bought that
estate.

He was very fond of music, and not only had it taught to the
Indians of his parish, where he formed an orchestra, but borrowed
the orchestra of the provincial battalion of Guanajuato for the frequent parties that he gave in his home. Since his residence was a
short distance from Guanajuato, he often visited the capital and
stayed there for long periods of time. This gave me an opportunity
to see him and to know him. He was fairly tall and stoop-shouldered, of
dark complexion and quick green eyes; his head bent a little over his
chest and was covered by sparse gray hair, for he was more than

sixty years old.[2] He was vigorous, though neither swift nor active in his movements; short of speech in ordinary conversation but animated in academic style when the argument grew warm. He was careless in dress, wearing only such garb as small-town curates commonly wore in those days.

2. THE STORMING OF THE GRANARY

Hidalgo unleashed a storm of Indian revolt with his Grito de Dolores. *Under the banner of the Virgin of Guadalupe he led his peasant army to the liberation of Mexico. Some creoles joined him, but the majority recoiled before the elemental violence and radicalism of the movement. The spirit of the insurrection found expression in the first large-scale action of the war, in which Hidalgo's Indians and the miners of Guanajuato joined to storm the Alhóndiga de Granaditas, a large stone building used by the government for the storage of grain.*[3]

✤✤✤✤ A little before twelve a numerous rabble of Indians — a few armed with rifles, the majority with lances, clubs, slings, and bows and arrows — appeared in sight on the causeway of Our Lady of Guadalupe, which leads into the city from the Marfil road. The vanguard of this group passed over the bridge of the same name as the causeway and arrived in front of the barricade at the foot of Mendizábal hill. Don Gilberto de Riaño, to whom his father had entrusted command of that spot as the most dangerous one, ordered them to stop in the name of the king; as the multitude continued to advance, he gave the order to fire. A number of Indians were killed, and the rest retreated precipitately. On the causeway, a native of Guanajuato told them they should go to Cuarto hill, and he himself led them there.

Meanwhile Hidalgo's other foot soldiers, amounting to some 20,000 Indians, joined by the miners and the common people of Guanajuto, occupied the heights and all the houses fronting on the granary. The soldiers from Celaya, armed with rifles, took up positions there, while a cavalry corps of some 2,000 men, composed of dragoons of the regiment *de la reina*, and country people armed with lances, with Hidalgo at their head, ascended the road called *de la yerbabuena* as far as the place known as "the racetracks" and from there descended to the city. Hidalgo stopped at the barracks of the cavalry regiment

[2] Hidalgo was actually fifty-seven years old in 1810. B.K.
[3] Alamán, *Historia de Méjico*, I, pp. 425–433. (Excerpt translated by the editor.)

del príncipe, where he remained during the action. The column continued its march across the whole city, finally halting at the street *de Belén.* In their march the soldiery looted a candy store and released from jail all prisoners of both sexes, numbering between 300 and 400 persons, among them criminals guilty of grave offenses. The male prisoners were impressed into the insurgent ranks for the attack on the granary.

The intendant, noticing that the majority of the enemy were grouping in front of the barricade at the entrance to the street *de los Pozitos,* commanded by Captain Pedro Telmo Primo, decided it was necessary to reinforce that point with twenty infantrymen from the company of civilians attached to the battalion. With more daring than prudence, he himself led them to the position where they were needed; he was accompanied by his aide, Don José María Bustamante. He was returning, and was already on the stairs leading to the door of the granary, when he received a rifle bullet above his left eye and died immediately. The shot came from the window of one of the houses in the square of the granary, facing east; it was said that it had been fired by a corporal of the infantry regiment of Celaya. . . .

The mob gathered on Cuarto hill began to hurl stones, by hand and with slings, so thickly that they exceeded the heaviest fall of hail. The attackers were aided by swarms of Indians and their allies from Guanajuato, who continually brought up from the Cata River the round stones which cover the bed of that stream; so great was the discharge of stones during the short time that the attack lasted, that the roof of the granary was raised about eight inches above its ordinary level. It proved impossible to hold the barricades, and after withdrawing the troops that were defending them, Captain Escalera, who was guarding the entrance, closed the door. As a result the Europeans who occupied the hacienda of Dolores were cut off and had no recourse but to sell their lives dearly; the cavalry on the back of the River Cata were in the same or a worse plight. Nor could the roof be long defended, dominated as it was by the hills of Cuarto and San Miguel. . . . Notwithstanding the heavy casualties caused by the continuous fire of the troops stationed on the roof, the number of assailants was so great that the fallen were quickly replaced by others, and their loss was not felt.

As a result of the abandonment of the barricades and the withdrawal of the troops defending the roof, the mob poured in a confused mass down all the avenues to the foot of the granary; those in front were pushed forward by those behind them and thus could not retreat, like waves of the sea that force each other onward until they dash against the rocks. Courage could not display itself; cowardice could not impel to flight. The cavalry was completely swept away, having no opportunity to use its arms and horses. Captain Castilla was

killed; a number of soldiers died; the majority went over to the victors. Only the brave Don José Francisco Valenzuela, turning his horse about, rode three times up the slope, opening a way for himself with his sword. Torn from his saddle and suspended on the points of the lances of the mob about him, he managed to kill some of the men nearest to him before he received a mortal wound. He shouted "Long live Spain!" until he breathed his last. He was a native of Irapuato and a lieutenant of the company from that town.

On the corner of the streets of *los Pozitos* and *los Mandamientos* was a store which sold splits of torch pine to miners, who used them to light their way to their place of work. The mob broke in the doors and carried all this combustible material away, heaping it up at the door of the granary, after which they set fire to it; meanwhile skilled miners, protected by huge earthen jars, like Roman soldiers with the *testudo*, approached the rear of the structure and attempted to make a breach in order to dynamite it. The defenders hurled quicksilver flasks filled with powder through the windows on the mob; when they exploded they caused great havoc, but gaps in the crowd were immediately filled up, and the fallen were trampled underfoot and suffocated. This explains why so few attackers were wounded and so many killed. . . .

While Don Gilberto Riaño, thirsting to avenge his father, aided by Don Miguel Bustamante and others, was hurling quicksilver flasks or grenades on the assailants, the *asesor* of the intendency thrust out a white cloth as a flag of truce; but the populace, attributing to perfidy an act that was merely the result of the confusion prevailing among the defenders, renewed the combat with greater fury. Then the *asesor* had a soldier let down from a window to negotiate with the insurgents; the unhappy man was dead before he reached the ground. Father Martín Septiem, trusting in his priestly character and in an image of Christ that he carried, attempted to leave the building. A rain of stones shattered the image, but the father, using the cross which he held in one hand as an offensive weapon, managed, though badly wounded, to push his way through the multitude. Meanwhile some of the Spaniards, beside themselves with terror, threw money out the window in the hope of placating the mob; others clamored for surrender; and still others, persuaded that their last hour had come, threw themselves at the feet of the priests who were there, to receive absolution.

Berzábal, seeing the door in flames, assembled as many as possible of his soldiers and grouped them in front of the entrance. As the burning door collapsed, he ordered them to fire pointblank at the attackers. Many perished, but the momentum of those in the rear carried those in front over the bodies of the fallen and into the building, sweeping everything before them with irresistible force, and the

courtyard, stairs, and corridors of the granary were soon crowded with the Indians and the populace. Berzábal, retreating with a handful of surviving soldiers to a corner of the courtyard, defended the banners of the battalion with the standard-bearers Marmolejo and González. When both of them had fallen, he seized the banners; clutching them with his left hand, he defended himself first with his sword, and when that was broken, with a pistol, until, pierced by many lances, he fell still holding the banners he had sworn to defend. . . .

All resistance now ceased, and only an occasional shot was heard from some isolated defender, such as the Spaniard Ruymayor, who kept the Indians at bay until he had used up all his cartridges. The Europeans in the hacienda of Dolores tried to escape by a back door which opened on the wooden bridge spanning the Cata River. But they found that it had already been taken by the attackers, and so had to retreat to the draw-well, a high vantage point, where they defended themselves until their munitions gave out, causing heavy losses to the insurgents. It was said that Don Francisco Iriarte alone, the man who had warned the intendant from San Juan de los Llanos of the start of the revolution, and who was an excellent shot, killed eighteen. The few who remained alive fell or threw themselves into the well and drowned.

The taking of the granary of Granaditas was entirely the work of the populace of Guanajuato, joined by the numerous gangs of Indians led by Hidalgo. Hidalgo and his lieutenants could do no more than lead their people to the hills and begin the attack. Once it was begun, it was impossible to give any orders, since there was no one to receive orders and carry them out; there was no order in that confused mob, and no subordinate officers to direct it. The Indians, throwing themselves with extraordinary bravery into the first military action they had ever seen, could not turn back, for the mob, pressing upon those who went in front, compelled them to advance and instantly took the space left by the fallen. The resistance of the defenders, though courageous, lacked all order and plan, owing to the early death of the intendant, and the early end of the action must be attributed to this, for by four in the afternoon everything was over.

3. THE REFORMS OF HIDALGO

Hidalgo and Morelos attempted to combine the creole ideal of independence with a program of social justice for the oppressed classes of the Mexican population. The following decrees of Hidalgo, issued after his capture of Guadalajara, help

to explain why many conservative creoles fought on the Spanish side against the patriots.[4]

✠✠✠✠ Don Miguel Hidalgo y Costilla, generalissimo of America, etc. By these presents I order the judges and justices of the district of this capital to proceed immediately to the collection of the rents due to this day by the lessees of the lands belonging to the Indian communities, the said rents to be entered in the national treasury. The lands shall be turned over to the Indians for their cultivation, and they may not be rented out in the future, for it is my wish that only the Indians in their respective towns shall have the use of them. Given in my headquarters of Guadalajara, December 5, 1810. . . .

Don Miguel Hidalgo y Costilla, generalissimo of America, etc. From the moment that the courageous American nation took up arms to throw off the heavy yoke that oppressed it for three centuries, one of its principal aims has been to extinguish the multitude of taxes that kept it in poverty. Since the critical state of our affairs does not permit the framing of adequate provisions in this respect, because of the need of the kingdom for money to defray the costs of the war, for the present I propose to remedy the most urgent abuses by means of the following declarations. First: All slaveowners shall set their slaves free within ten days, on pain of death for violation of this article. Second: The payment of tribute by all the castes that used to pay it shall henceforth cease, and no other taxes shall be collected from the Indians. Third: In all judicial business, documents, deeds, and actions, only ordinary paper shall be used, and the use of sealed paper is abolished.

4. THE PLAN OF IGUALA

By a notable irony, the work begun by Hidalgo and Morelos was consummated by a creole officer, Agustín de Iturbide (1783–1824), who for nine years had fought the insurgents with great effectiveness. Behind Iturbide were conservative churchmen, army officers, and officials, who preferred separation from Spain to submission to the liberal Constitution of 1812, imposed on Ferdinand VII by his revolted army. Lorenzo de Zavala (1788–1836), a brilliant Mexican statesman, publicist, and historian, describes the origin and triumph of the Plan of Iguala.[5]

4 Alamán, *Historia de Méjico*, II, pp. 25–26. (Excerpt translated by the editor.)
5 Lorenzo de Zavala, *Ensayo histórico de los revoluciones de México*, México, 1918, 2 vols., I, pp. 69–79. (Excerpt translated by the editor.)

✠✠✠✠ The year 1820 was born among stormy portents. The gathering of troops on the island of León for dispatch to South America aroused no special interest, for experience had shown the futility of such expeditions. But the news of the first moves made by the army in the palm grove of the port of Santa María, under the orders of the Count of La Bisbal, to reëstablish the constitution of 1812, caused excitement in Mexico and inspired consternation in Viceroy Apodaca. He perceived that the seeming tranquillity of Mexico was an illusion, for the times were out of joint; he feared to lose in a moment the fruit of his labors and, above all, the glory he had acquired by bringing peace to Mexico — the result of a combination of circumstances that could produce only a momentary effect. The viceroy issued circulars announcing that the rumors being spread about the temper of the troops in Spain were false: *Never was the royal government more solidly established, or military discipline better; never did the king have greater proof of the love of his people and of his armies.* This was said in the government press, the only newspaper permitted to appear; the bishops and priests preached the same thing; but the only result of these measures was to increase alarm and to awaken hopes that were never extinguished. The very concern of the government, and its effort to discredit the news of this movement, only gave them greater currency. Commerce, that reliable index of developments and infallible barometer of political conditions, revealed more through its precautionary measures than any statements the government agents could make to conceal the situation from the public. The efforts of the unfortunate Lacy, in Cataluña, and of the martyred Porlier, in Galicia, were so many proofs that Spain had but temporarily accepted the yoke of an arbitrary power. . . . I shall now try to describe briefly and as exactly as possible the state of Mexican public opinion in these circumstances.

The upper clergy and the privileged classes, who saw the revolutionary principles of 1812 rising again to threaten their revenues and their benefices, united as if by instinct to oppose an insuperable barrier, as they thought, to the reestablishment of the Spanish constitution, which had so greatly weakened their influence. The first news of the cry of Riego in the town of Las Cabezas, on January 1, 1820, were received with terror by all those who lived on the credulity and ignorance of the people. Apodaca, a fanatical supporter of the royal power and of the abuses of superstition, formed the project of offering Ferdinand VII an asylum in Mexico against the enterprises of the constitutionalists, assuring him of a throne in a land to which the new doctrines would have no access. What a flattering prospect for the canons and aristocratic classes this was — to make Mexico the center of their power and to form a court that would dispense jobs and honors! The Mexican counts and marquises already saw them-

selves made grandees of the *first class*, raised to eminent titles and vying with the ancient Spanish nobility in pride, in wealth, and in ignorance! The project tended inevitably toward independence; to be sure, the Mexicans would have been glad to be independent, but it is very doubtful that they would have acquiesced to absolute power. Constitutional monarchy had become fashionable; the Mexicans would have wanted to keep in step with their peninsular fathers; the desire for a republic was not the plan of Apodaca and his advisers. In seeking to revive Napoleon's ancient project to transfer the royal family to Mexico, they only envisioned raising a throne for despotism and placing the immense barrier of the Atlantic between liberal ideas and the new monarchy. As if the example of the United States were not enough to excite new strivings on the part of the people! As if the progress made by the doctrines of anti-legitimacy and the sovereignty of the people among the Mexicans could be destroyed by this step! Futile efforts of a dying power, that only deceived itself with these illusions!

The rapidity with which the new revolution, headed by Riego, Quiroga, and other celebrated leaders, spread throughout Spain burst in a moment the bubble of Viceroy Apodaca. But from his plan there emerged another, in which the viceroy certainly had no part, no matter what may be said by some people who only judge by appearances and do not examine the background and causes of events. Frustrated in their first project, the clergy and the self-styled nobles decided that the moment had arrived to form a plan of independence which would assure a monarchy for Mexico and would summon a prince of the ruling house of Spain to occupy the throne. The idea was not new; the Count of Aranda had proposed it to Charles III fifty years before. It seemed to reconcile the interests of the different parties, it established independence, it made the monarchy secure, it gave guarantees to the Spaniards, and the people received a form of government best suited to their new needs and to their customs and habits. Amid these circumstances the elections of deputies for the Spanish *cortes* took place, and all those named for this mission agreed to present proposals to the assembly that harmonized with this solution. Amid this chaos of opinion and of parties, the viceroy was much perplexed. In April, 1820, arrived a royal order that required everyone to swear loyalty to the constitution. It was obeyed without resistance; the press began to speak freely once again; the dungeons opened to release prisoners held for political opinions; the Inquisition and the tribunal of public security disappeared; liberal ideas had triumphed in both worlds. New enterprises were set on foot — great projects that began under good auspices — and a man was needed, a man who would be valiant, active, energetic, enterprising. Where could he be found?

Popular revolutions present anomalies whose origin or causes are unknowable. Men who have followed one party, who have fought for certain principles, who have suffered for their loyalty to certain views or persons, suddenly change and adopt a completely different line of conduct. Who would ever have thought that the Mexican officer who had shed the blood of so many of his compatriots to maintain his country in slavery was destined to place himself at the head of a great movement that would destroy forever the Spanish power? What would have been thought of a man's sanity if in 1817 he had said that Iturbide would occupy the place of Morelos or would replace Mina? Yet the astonished Mexicans and Spaniards saw this happen.

Don Agustín de Iturbide, colonel of a battalion of provincial troops and a native of Valladolid de Michoacán, was endowed with brilliant qualities, and among his leading traits were uncommon bravery and vigor. To a handsome figure he united the strength and energy necessary to endure the great exertions of campaigning, and ten continuous years of this activity had fortified his natural qualities. He was haughty and domineering, and it was observed that to stay in favor with the authorities he had to remain at a distance from those who were in a position to give him orders. Every time that he came to Mexico City or other places where there were superiors, he gave indications of his impatience. . . . It is said that he was involved in a plan hatched at Valladolid in 1809 for the achievement of independence but withdrew because he was not placed in command, though his rank at the time did not qualify him for leadership. Be that as it may, there is no doubt that Iturbide had a superior spirit, and that his ambition was supported by that noble resolution that scorns dangers and does not retreat before obstacles of every kind. He had faced danger and difficulty in combat; he had learned the power of Spanish weapons; he had taken the measure of the chiefs of both parties — and one must confess that he did not err in his calculations when he set himself above all of them. He was conscious of his superiority, and so did not hesitate to place himself at the head of the national party, if he could only inspire the same confidence in his compatriots. He discussed his project with men whose talents would be useful to him in the political direction of affairs, and henceforth he threw himself heart and soul into forming a *plan* that would offer guarantees to citizens and monarchists and at the same time would remove all cause for fear on the part of the Spaniards.

Anyone who examines the famous Plan of Iguala (so called because it was made public in that town for the first time), bearing in mind the circumstances of the Mexican nation at the time, will agree that it was a masterpiece of politics and wisdom. All the Mexicans desired *independence*, and this was the first basis of that docu-

ment. The killings of Spaniards that had taken place, in reprisal for those that the Spaniards had committed during the past nine years, required a preventive, so to speak, to put an end to such atrocious acts, which could not fail to arouse hostility among the 50,000 Spaniards who still resided in the country. It was necessary to make plain the intentions of the new chief in this respect. Accordingly, he seized upon the word *union* as expressing the solidarity that should exist between creoles and Spaniards, regarded as citizens with the same rights. Finally, since the Catholic religion is the faith professed by all Mexicans, and since the clergy has a considerable influence in the country, the preservation of this church was also stated to be a fundamental basis, under the word *religion*. These three principles, *independence*, *union*, and *religion*, gave Iturbide's army its name of "the Army of the Three Guarantees." The representative monarchical system was established, and various articles stated the elementary principles of this form of government and the individual rights guaranteed to the people. Finally, the Spaniards were given freedom to leave the country with all their property. The expeditionary forces were offered the privilege of returning to Spain at the expense of the public treasury; those who chose to stay would be treated like Mexican soldiers. As can be seen, the plan reconciled all interests, and, raising New Spain to the rank of an independent nation, as was generally desired, with its immense benefits it silenced for the time being the particular aspirations of those who wanted the *republic* on the one hand and the *absolute monarchy* on the other. All the sons of the country united around the principle of *nationality*, putting aside for the moment their different ideals. We shall soon see the sprouting of these germs of ideas, as yet enveloped in mists or suppressed by the great matter of the common cause.

Don Agustín Iturbide made all these preparations in the greatest secrecy, and to conceal his projects more effectively he entered or pretended to enter the church of San Felipe Neri to take part in religious exercises. There, it is said, was framed the document I mentioned. This display of piety, and the prudence and reserve with which he managed the affair, inspired the viceroy, who also was devout, to entrust him with the command of a small division assigned to pursue Don Vicente Guerrero, whose forces had increased considerably after the arrival of the news of the Spanish revolution. At the end of the year 1820 Colonel Iturbide set out from Mexico City, charged with the destruction of Guerrero but actually intending to join him at the first opportunity to work with him for the achievement of national independence. A few days after his departure from the capital, Iturbide drew near to Guerrero's camp. The latter had routed Colonel Berdejo, also sent out in his pursuit, in a minor clash, and this provided Iturbide with an opportunity to send Guerrero a

letter inviting the patriot leader to abandon the enterprise that had
cost the country so much futile bloodshed: "Now that the King of
Spain has offered liberal institutions and confirmed the social guarantees of the people, taking an oath to support the Constitution of 1812,
the Mexicans will enjoy a just equality, and we shall be treated like
free men." He added: "The victories that you have recently gained
over the government forces should not inspire you with confidence
in future triumphs, for you know that the fortunes of war are mutable,
and that the government possesses great resources."

This letter was written very artfully, for at the same time that
it suggested a desire to enter into agreements and relations with the
insurgents it aroused no suspicion in the viceroy, who interpreted it
as reflecting the same policy that had been so useful to him in pacify-
ing the country. Presumably the persons employed by Iturbide to
deliver these letters carried private instructions explaining his intentions. General Guerrero replied, with the energy that he always
showed in defending the cause of independence and liberty, that he
was resolved "to continue defending the national honor, until victory
or death"; that he was "not to be deceived by the flattering promise
of liberty given by the Spanish constitutionalists, who in the matter
of independence [hold] the same views as the most diehard royalists;
that the Spanish constitution [offers] no guarantees to the Americans." He reminded Iturbide of the exclusion of the castes in the
Cadiz constitution; of the diminution of the American representatives;
and, finally, of the indifference of the viceroys to these liberal laws.
He concluded by exhorting Iturbide to join the national party, and
invited him to take command of the national armies, of which Guerrero himself was then the leader. The vigorous tone of this letter,
the sound observations that it contained, the convincing logic of its
judgments, produced an astounding effect upon the Mexicans. Iturbide needed no persuasion; we have seen him depart from Mexico
City with the intent of proclaiming the independence of the country,
and the only matter left unsettled was the precise method of beginning the work, with himself as the leader of the daring enterprise.

He received this letter in January, 1821, and replied to General Guerrero, in a few lines, that he wished to "confer with [him]
about the means of working together for the welfare of the kingdom"
and hoped that he (Guerrero) "would be fully satisfied concerning
his intentions." An agreement was reached for an interview between
the two men.[6] General Guerrero himself supplied me with details
of what took place at this meeting. The conference was held in a

6 Historians are not in agreement concerning the time of the first meeting between Iturbide and Guerrero. For a discussion of the controversy, see William
S. Robertson, *Iturbide of Mexico*, Durham, N.C., Duke University Press, 1952,
pp. 64–65. B.K.

town in the State of Mexico. . . . The two chiefs approached each other with some mutual distrust, although that of Guerrero was plainly the more justified. Iturbide had waged a cruel and bloody war on the independents since 1810. The Spanish leaders themselves hardly equaled this unnatural American in cruelty; and to see him transformed as if by magic into a defender of the cause that he had combated, would naturally arouse suspicions in men like the Mexican insurgents, who had often been the victims of their own credulity and of repeated betrayals. Nevertheless, Iturbide, though sanguinary, inspired confidence by the conscientiousness with which he proceeded in all matters. He was not believed capable of an act of treachery that would stain his reputation for valor and noble conduct. For himself, he had very little to fear from General Guerrero, a man distinguished from the beginning for his humanity and for his loyalty to the cause he was defending. The troops of both leaders were within cannonshot of each other; Iturbide and Guerrero met and embraced. Iturbide was the first to speak: "I cannot express the satisfaction I feel at meeting a patriot who has supported the noble cause of independence and who alone has survived so many disasters, keeping alive the sacred flame of liberty. Receive this just homage to your valor and to your virtues." Guerrero, who also was deeply moved, replied: "Sir, I congratulate my country, which on this day recovers a son whose valor and ability have caused her such grievous injury." Both leaders seemed to feel the strain of this memorable event; both shed tears of strong emotion. After Iturbide had revealed his plans and ideas to Señor Guerrero, that leader summoned his troops and officers, and Iturbide did the same. When both armies had been joined, Guerrero addressed himself to his soldiers, saying: "Soldiers: The Mexican who appears before you is Don Agustín de Iturbide, whose sword wrought such grave injury for nine years to the cause we are defending. Today he swears to defend the national interests; and I, who have led you in combat, and whose loyalty to the cause of independence you cannot doubt, am the first to acknowledge Señor Iturbide as the chief of the national armies. Long live independence! Long live liberty!" From that moment everyone acknowledged the new leader as general-in-chief, and he now dispatched to the viceroy a declaration of his views and of the step he had taken. Iturbide sent General Guerrero to seize a convoy of Manila merchants bound for the port of Acapulco with 750,000 pesos; he himself set out for the town of Iguala, forty leagues to the south of Mexico City, where he published the plan which I have outlined. The Spanish troops began to leave Iturbide's division, but the old patriot detachments began to reassemble everywhere to come to his aid.

All Mexico was set in motion by the declaration of Iguala. Apodaca immediately ordered General Liñán to march with a large

division against the new leader, to strangle in its cradle this movement of threatening aspect. But this was not the tumultuous cry of Dolores of 1810; the viceroy was not dealing with a disorderly mob of Indians armed with sickles, stones, and slings and sending up the confused cry "Death to the *gachupines*, long live Our Lady of Guadalupe!" He faced a chief of proven bravery, who, supported by the national will and followed by trained leaders, spoke in the name of the people and demanded rights with which they were well acquainted. . . . While this chief was making extraordinary progress in the provinces, the capital was in the greatest confusion. The Spaniards residing in Mexico City attributed the successes of Iturbide to the ineptitude of Apodaca, who a short time before, according to them, had been the peacemaker, the tutelar angel, of New Spain; now this same man suddenly turned into an imbecile incapable of governing. They stripped him of his command, replacing him with the Brigadier Francisco Novella. This fact alone suffices to give an idea of the state of confusion in which the last defenders of the Spanish government found themselves. Reduced to the support of the expeditionary forces, the dying colonial regime immediately revealed the poverty of its resources. . . . Of the 14,000 soldiers sent to defend the imaginary rights of the Spanish government, only 6,000, at the most, remained — and what could they do against the Mexican army, which numbered at least 50,000 men? Arms, discipline — everything was equal except morale, which naturally was very poor among troops suddenly transported to a strange land, two thousand leagues away from their country. . . . Was it surprising that they surrendered, in view of the situation? Thus, between the end of February, when Iturbide proclaimed his plan of Iguala, and September 27, when he made his triumphant entry into Mexico City, only six months and some days elapsed, with no other memorable actions than the sieges of Durango, Querétaro, Córdoba, and the capital. It was at this time that General Antonio López de Santa-Anna, then lieutenant-colonel, began to distinguish himself.

24 ✣ Spain's Work in America: For and Against

From the sixteenth century to the present, the Spanish record in America has been the subject of intense controversy. In our time the problem has acquired a new relevance because of its connection with the modern struggle of colonial peoples for independence. The West German editor of a 1969 edition of Las Casas's anticolonial tract, the *Very Brief Account of the Destruction of the Indies*, noted this connection when he drew a parallel between the Vietnam War and the Spanish wars of aggression that Las Casas attacked. "The headlines that we hear every morning on the broadcasts," he wrote, "signify that the destruction of the Indies continues. The *Very Brief Account* of 1542 is a backward look into our own future."

Las Casas has often been charged with responsibility for the so-called Black Legend of Spanish oppression and cruelty to the Indians. Certainly the *Very Brief Account*, translated into all the major European languages, helped to diffuse more widely the evil reputation that Spain had already acquired in Europe as a result of the Spanish Conquest and the conduct of Spanish soldiery in the Netherlands and elsewhere. But the "legend" had other sources. In 1565 the Italian Girolamo Benzoni published his *History of the New World*, a travel account that contained moving eyewitness descrip-

tions of Spanish cruelty in the Indies, and that was widely read. European critics of Spain's colonial policy even found material for their indictments in the writings of such staunch defenders of Spanish imperialism as the chroniclers López de Gómara and Oviedo.

Various motives inspired foreign attacks on Spain's colonial record in the sixteenth, seventeenth, and eighteenth centuries. Spain's colonial and commercial rivals—above all the English and Dutch merchant capitalists and their governments — used that record as a propaganda weapon in their efforts to wrest from Spain her colonies and colonial markets. But defenders of national independence, religious tolerance, and intellectual freedom — such men as the essayist Montaigne in the sixteenth century and the political philosopher Montesquieu in the eighteenth century — denounced Spanish imperialism not from the viewpoint of a narrow nationalism but in defense of the rights of man. In Spain the memory of Las Casas fell under a deep cloud after 1600. Yet sensitive Spaniards continued to criticize the Spanish Conquest and its aftermath as detrimental not only to the interests of the Indians but of the Spanish people. Typical is the comment of the intellectual reformer Fray Benito Feijóo in the early eighteenth century: "The gold of the Indies keeps us poor, and what is worse, it enriches our enemies. Because we mistreated the Indians, we Spaniards are now the Indians of other Europeans."

The Spanish-American Wars of Independence naturally inspired sharp rhetorical attacks on Spain's work in America. Bolívar, for example, claimed that Las Casas had seen America bathed "with the blood of more than twenty million victims." After independence the Spanish colonial legacy became a major issue in the political struggles of the new states. Liberals condemned Spanish tyranny, obscurantism, and backwardness and insisted on the need to liquidate the colonial heritage; conservatives, who often recalled the old social order with nostalgia, offered at least a partial defense of Spain's colonial rule.

By the last decades of the nineteenth century, however, Latin American historians had begun to modify their interpretations of the colonial era. As economic activity quickened with the growth of European trade and investments, with liberals and conservatives joining in pursuit of material prosperity and political stability, old party lines dissolved, and the liberal anti-Spanish arguments lost much of their raison d'être. After mid-century, moreover, the racist and biological-determinist theories of Spencer, Gobineau, and their disciples increasingly influenced Latin American thought. As a result, historians, whether liberal or conservative, now tended to justify the Spanish Conquest by the workings of a mysterious law of progress, and to shift much of the responsibility for the area's backwardness from Spain to the Indians and mixed-bloods, regarded as inherently inferior races.

A revisionist tendency emerged in United States historical

studies of colonial Latin America in the same period. The rise of Social Darwinism and America's new status as a colonial power after 1898 disposed United States historians to view the Spanish colonial experience with greater sympathy. A major work in this revisionist tradition was Edward G. Bourne, *Spain in America* (1904), which cleverly used the comparative method to put Spanish colonial policies in the best possible light. Bourne's influence permeated Lesley B. Simpson's influential *The Encomienda in New Spain* (1929), a book notable for its vitriolic attack on Las Casas. Beginning in the 1920's, such historians as Arthur Aiton, Irving Leonard, John Tate Lanning, and Lewis Hanke wrote important monographs that corrected errors and exaggerations in the writings of the traditional anti-Spanish school, but sometimes unduly embellished the Spanish colonial record.

In the Hispanic world this twentieth-century revisionism assumed an increasingly tendentious aspect as a result of the rise of acute political and social tensions in that area. In Spain, conservatives responded to a growing threat from the forces of liberalism and radicalism by developing a historical defense of the old order. This defense proclaimed, among other things, the grandeur of Spain's achievement in the New World and denounced Las Casas and other alleged detractors of Spain. A major anti-Lascasian work was Ramón Menéndez Pidal's violent attack on Las Casas, *El Padre Las Casas, su doble personalidad* (1963).

In Latin America, in the same period, conservative circles grew alarmed at the rise of *Indigenismo* and a variety of social revolutionary movements and identified themselves more closely with the Hispanic colonial past. A "White Legend" school of historiography which enjoyed considerable influence in some Latin American countries arose between 1930 and 1950. Its prominent exponents included the Mexican José Vasconcelos, the Argentine Rómulo D. Carbia, the Peruvian Raúl Porras Barrenechea, and the Chilean Francisco Encina.

In recent years a more critical and realistic appraisal of the Spanish colonial process has been developing among historians in the United States, Spain, and Latin America. Factors contributing to this trend include recent studies that confirm the traditional critique of Spanish labor and tribute systems as harshly exploitative, the anticolonialist temper of our time, and a growing awareness of the colonial roots of Latin American underdevelopment and neocolonialism.

1. THE NOBLE SAVAGE AND THE BLACK LEGEND

In the sixteenth, seventeenth, and eighteenth centuries the so-called Black Legend, the traditional critique of Spanish colonial policy as oppressive and obscurantist, was often joined to the

concept of the Noble Savage, of the American Indian regarded as a prime example of unspoiled humanity in the state of nature. The famous novel of Jean-François Marmontel (1723–1799), Les Incas (1777), illustrates this fusion of ideas. The story, pure fiction for the most part, relates the destruction of the Inca Empire; its characters include Las Casas, Pizarro (to whom Marmontel assigns great nobility of character), the "fanatical priest" Valverde, and the Inca Atahualpa. Marmontel, a typical Enlightenment figure, wrote the book to denounce the evils of fanaticism, not a unique Spanish wickedness. Indeed, he was careful to begin his preface with the words: "All nations have had their brigands and their fanatics, their times of barbarism, their fits of fury. The finest peoples are those which accuse themselves of their crimes. The Spaniards have this proud trait, worthy of their character." Typical of the spirit and style of Les Incas is the following episode, which describes the death of Atahualpa at the hands of the "perfidious priest" Valverde and his accomplices.[1]

✠✠✠✠ Atahualpa's family slept around him; their eyes were drained of tears, their hearts weary with sobbing. But the prince, filled with gloomy presentiments, could not shut his eyes. He heard the prison doors open. He saw Requelme enter; with him came three men wrapped in long cloaks which covered their faces up to their eyes; there was something frightful about their gaze. A sensation of terror seized Atahualpa; he rose and, overcoming his momentary weakness, stood before them.

"Inca," Requelme said to him, "let us leave this place; there is no need to awake these women and their children. Let the innocents rest in peace. Listen to us. You have been judged and condemned; you must burn at the stake according to the severe letter of the law. But you can save yourself from the flames; and this holy man will explain to you how it may be done."

The prince listened and grew pale. "I know," he said, "that the Council has judged me; but surely you must send me to the Spanish Court, reserving to your king a right that belongs to him alone." "Believe me," continued Requelme, "precious moments are passing; listen to this wise and virtuous man, who pities your misfortunes."

Valverde then spoke. "Do you not wish," he asked the Inca, "to adore the God of the Christians?" "Certainly," replied the unhappy prince, "if this God, as we are informed, is a beneficent God,

---

[1] Jean-François Marmontel, *Les Incas, ou la destruction de l'Empire du Perou*, Paris, 1777, 2 vols., II, pp. 347–350. (Excerpt translated by the editor.)

a powerful and just God, if Nature is his handiwork and the sun itself one of his benefactions, then I adore him together with Nature. What ingrate or madman could reject His love?" "And do you desire to be taught," continued the perfidious priest, "the holy truths that He has revealed to us, to know His cult, and to follow His law?" "I ardently desire it," replied the Inca, "I have already said so. I long to open my eyes to the light, to be instructed, and I shall believe." "God be thanked," exclaimed Valverde," he is as well disposed as I could hope. Down on you knees, then, and implore this God of goodness and mercy; receive from Him the healthful water that makes His children be born again." The Inca, with humble and meek spirit, knelt and received the holy water of baptism. "The Heavens are open," said Valverde, "and moments are precious." He immediately made a sign to his two henchmen, and the fatal rope stifled the last sighs of the Inca.

The pitiful cries of his children and their mothers spread the news of his death at daybreak. Some Spaniards shuddered at the news; but the multitude applauded the audacity of the assassins, and thought it was enough that they had spared the lives of the wives and children of the unhappy prince, henceforth abandoned to the pity of the Indians.

Pizarro, indignant but discouraged, weary of struggling against crime, after heaping curses on these unspeakable assassins and their fanatical partisans, withdrew to the City of the Kings [Lima], whose construction had begun. Licentiousness, robbery, furious rapacity, murder, and pillage raged unchecked; everywhere on the continent the Indian peoples fled, only to fall into the snares or under the swords of the Spaniards.

From the shores of Mexico arrived Alvarado, the friend of Cortés, that scourge of the two Americas. Rival of the new conquerors, he came to hurl himself upon their prey, to glut himself with gold and blood. The whole extent of that immense Empire was devastated. An innumerable multitude of Indians were slaughtered; almost all the rest, led away in chains to perish in the depths of mines, envied the fate of those who had been massacred.

2. THE FATAL LEGACY

In the decades after independence, Latin American leaders debated which road their countries should take to reach the goals of economic progress and political stability. Liberals looked to the United States, England, and France as models of dynamic advance; conservatives proposed to remain in the safe, familiar

way of their fathers and retain those features of the colonial regime not incompatible with the new republican order: the supremacy of the Catholic Church, clerical control of education, a hierarchical society with special privileges for the clergy and military, and the like. In 1844 two ardent liberals startled the staid aristocratic society of Santiago with their contributions to the debate. Francisco Bilbao (1823–1865) threw a bombshell with his famous essay on "The Nature of Chilean Society," in which he declared: "Slavery, degradation: that is the past. . . . Our past is Spain. Spain is the Middle Ages. The Middle Ages are composed, body and soul, of Catholicism and feudalism." Bilbao was tried and condemned for blasphemy, sedition, and immorality, he lost his university chair, and his book was officially burned by the public hangman. José Victorino Lastarria (1817–1888), more moderate and scholarly, caused a lesser stir with his address, "Investigations on the Social Influence of the Conquest and the Colonial System of the Spaniards in Chile." Despite an occasional factual error — such as the statement that Spain forbade the printing and sale of books of every kind in America — it remains an effective summary of the liberal case against the Spanish colonial regime.[2]

✦✦✦✦ It is well known that the Spaniards who conquered America drenched its soil in blood, not in order to colonize it but to acquire the precious metals it yielded so abundantly. Torrents of adventurers flowed over the New World; they were obsessed by the hope of gaining immense wealth at little cost, and to this end they directed all their activity, sparing no means or violence in order to achieve it. At last reality dispelled their illusions, and the conquistadors, convinced by their own experience that the fertility of the American mines was not as great as they had hoped, gradually abandoned their daring speculations and began to devote themselves to agricultural and commercial enterprises. But this new direction of their ambitions did not yield the benefits that might have been expected, given the potential wealth of the American soil, for they had neither the inclination nor the intelligence to exploit this new source of riches; and their government, for its part, with its absurd economic system, stopped up the very sources of economic progress.

When Spain established her colonies in America, she transplanted thither all the vices of her absurd system of government, vices that multiplied infinitely through causes that had their origin in the system itself. . . .

---

[2] José Victorino Lastarria, "Investigaciones sobre la influencia social de la Conquista i del sistema colonial de los españoles en Chile," in *Obras completas,* Santiago de Chile, 1909, Vol. VII, pp. 45–69. (Excerpt translated by the editor.)

A single leading idea dominated all the decisions of the Spanish Court and its agents in the colonies: this was the idea of maintaining America forever in a blind dependence on Spain, in order to exploit it exclusively, at the cost of the very existence and development of the colonies, and to extract from its possession all possible advantages. From this point of view, the metropolis had a system, a spirit that gave unity to its decisions and sanctified all means necessary to achieve those ends, no matter how unjust and unworthy they might be. For Spain the New World was a very rich mine that should be exploited and whose fruits should be consumed, no matter what devastation the process produced or what effects it might have on future productivity.

To this end Spain subjected the natives to the grossest, most humiliating servitude, declaring them slaves in certain cases and masking their slavery in others with a pretended, ironic respect for their liberty, even as it subjected them to the *mita*, the *repartimiento*, and other oppressive burdens. The tax laws were precisely calculated to benefit the royal treasury and to extract from the colonies all the wealth possible, even at the expense of the very elements of production. Commerce was monopolized for the benefit of Spain, manufacturing and agriculture were surrounded with a thousand restrictions and burdened with so many taxes that there clearly emerged the intention of impeding their further development. . . . Communication and commerce with foreign powers were forbidden so strictly that not only was it made a crime to maintain such relations but a pretended sovereignty of the seas was invoked, as in a royal cedula (1692) that ordered governors "to treat as an enemy ship every foreign ship sailing in American waters without license from this government, even if the vessel belongs to an allied nation."

For the rest, the laws and orders dictated to prevent the intellectual development of the Americans testify to the perverse intention of maintaining them in the most brutal and degrading ignorance, to make them perpetually bow their necks to the yoke of their *natural sovereign* and of all the governors who derived from him all their authority. It was forbidden under severe penalties to sell and print in America books of any kind, even books of devotion; and to introduce books a license was necessary from the Council of the Indies or some other authority anxious to prevent the light of intelligence from penetrating the New World. The few universities and colleges, established and regulated by law, were entirely designed to keep true knowledge from men; to use the happy expression of one American, they were "a monument of imbecility." Entirely subject to the rule of monks, intellectual and moral education was frustrated with the utmost diligence; care was taken to turn out only clergymen or, at most, lawyers and physicians, but all were taught false doctrines. They be-

came accustomed to juggle metaphysical subtleties and the most extravagant theories, and according to the formulas of their useless science they were made to adopt a grotesque and high-sounding style. Thus the Spanish government managed by means of its laws and orders to lead the minds of Americans astray and direct them into anti-social studies that subjected their minds to a perfect slavery and were designed to blind their reason so that they should see "in the king of Spain their absolute lord, who knew no superior or restraint on his power on the face of the earth, whose power derived from God Himself, a king whose person was sacred and in whose presence all should tremble."

In making this rapid survey of the colonial legislation with the aim of investigating its social influence, I must, however, prove my impartiality by noting that the tedium caused by perusal of this monstrous compilation is sometimes relieved by the reading of some provisions that prove the merciful sentiments of their authors. But only "merciful sentiments," mind you, for one does not discover in those provisions, any more than in the rest, that commonsense, that foresight, that result from philosophic analysis of the facts — qualities that are salient traits of the wise legislator. In effect, we note various laws designed to regulate the service of the natives in the mines, *encomiendas*, and *repartimientos* to which they were subject, and others that assessed their tributes so that they should not prove too burdensome. There are special laws designed to protect the liberty of the Chilean Indians and grant them more privileges and exemptions than were enjoyed by the Indians of other colonies, doubtless with the aim of attracting the Chilean Indians and ending their wars by means of these mild and protective measures. Undoubtedly these are the laws that have fascinated the defenders of the colonial legislation, who have assumed their good faith and deduced from them arguments to prove the wisdom of Spain and to eulogize the protection that she dispensed to her colonies. But if we recall what was said above concerning the spirit of that code and the system of the metropolis, what were those laws, at most, but the expression of an isolated goodwill, or perhaps a cover with which a corrupt and reactionary Court wished to mask its true intentions and opinions vis-à-vis the unhappy natives of the New World? Be that as it may, those protective laws were a mute and ineffective exception, a dead letter, since their execution, interpretation, and even the right to modify them were in the hands of the colonial governors. . . .

This was the dominant thought, the aspirations, the concentrated essence, of the civilization of the sixteenth-century Spaniard: his king and his interest, God, and the glory of war. . . .

That civilization, then, was the element that conditioned all the

exploits of that remarkable people; it was the origin of all its aberrations and determined the direction of its inclinations; it gave form to its customs. I believe, therefore, that when we examine the civil and political laws that moulded our society, we must consider them the logical result of that civilization and always keep in mind that the foundations of our social structure were laid by fanatical, warlike Spain; that the basis of the administrative system of our colony was the omnipotence of Charles V; and that our religion had for its base the terrorism of the Inquisition.

3. IN DEFENSE OF SPAIN

Conservative ideologists of the post-Independence period, who had lived under Spanish rule and sometimes participated in its overthrow, rarely offered an unqualified defense of the colonial regime. More often, conceding its errors and abuses, they countered the liberal attack by stressing its benefits: the long Pax Hispanica, *the relative mildness of Spanish rule, and the like. A review of Lastarria's "Investigations" by Andrés Bello (1781–1865), the distinguished Venezuelan scholar and educator who as rector of the National University of Chile gave Lastarria the opportunity to make his address, illustrates the thought of an enlightened conservative on the subject. Observe how Bello, conceding the cruelties of the Conquest, diminishes Spanish guilt by shifting responsibility for such acts to a flawed human nature, to a universal law by which the strong oppress the weak in all times and places. This line of defense has often been employed by apologists for Spanish imperialism and imperialism in general.*[3]

✤✤✤✤ Chapter 1 treats the Conquest and the prolonged struggle between the Chilean colonists and the indomitable Araucanian Indians, and is written with the rapid energy that the material demands. It would have been difficult, in such an outline sketch, for the author to give a more complete idea of those bitter hostilities that fathers passed on to sons generation after generation, and that even now only slumber under the appearance of a peace that is but a truce. Aside from one or another phrase that smacks more of exalted oratory than the moderate language of the historian, I do not find much reason to criticize as intemperate or passionate the account of the cruelty of the con-

---

[3] André Bello, review of Lastarria's "Investigaciones," in *Obras completas*, Caracas, 1957, Vol. XIX, pp. 161–166.

quistadors in this chapter. The historian is obligated to tell things as they happened, and we should not palliate them for fear of dishonoring the memory of the founders of Chile. Injustice, atrocities, perfidy in war, are not uniquely Spanish traits; they are common to all races of all times. If war between fraternal Christian nations in our own cultured, civilized times still assumes a character of savage, soulless cruelty, who should we marvel at murderous battles and the harsh results of victory in war between peoples for whom each other's customs, religion, aspect, or color were entirely alien and repugnant?

The vassals of Isabella, Charles I, and Philip II were the premier nation of Europe; their knightly spirit, the splendor of the Spanish Court, Spain's magnificent and proud nobility, the skill of its captains, the ability of its ambassadors and ministers, the bravery of its soldiers, their daring enterprises, momentous discoveries, and conquests, made Spain a target of detractors because it was an object of envy. The memoirs of that age present horrible scenes to our eyes. The Spaniards abused their power, oppressed, committed outrages, not impudently as Señor Lastarria claims — for one need not be impudent to do what everyone else does in the measure of his power — but with the same regard for humanity, the same respect for the rights of men, that powerful states have always displayed in their dealings with the weak, dealings of which our own moral and civilized time presents too many examples.

If we compare the practice, as opposed to theory, of international law in modern times with that of the Middle Ages and antiquity, beneath insubstantial differences of form and method we find a basic similarity. . . . Among the great masses of men that we call nations the savage state in which brute force rules has not ended. Men pay a superficial homage to justice by reference to the commonplaces of security, dignity, protection of national interests, and other equally vague clichés — premises from which a modicum of skill can derive all imaginable consequences. The horrors of war have been partly mitigated, not from greater respect for humanity but because material interests are better calculated, and as a result of the very perfection to which the art of destruction has been brought. It would be madness to enslave the conquered when there is greater profit in making them tributaries and forced suppliers of the conqueror's industry. The pillagers of old have been transformed into merchants, but merchants whose counters display the motto: *Vae victis* (woe to the vanquished). Colonization no longer brings death to the native inhabitants: why kill them, when it is enough to drive them from forest to forest, from prairie to prairie? In the long run deprivation and famine will achieve the work of destruction without noisy scandal. . . .

I do not accuse any nation, but rather human nature. The weak

invoke justice, but let them grow strong, and they will prove as unjust as their oppressors.

The picture that Señor Lastarria paints of the vices and abuses of Spain's colonial system he generally supports with documents of irrefutable authenticity and veracity: laws, ordinances, histories, the *Memorias Secretas* of Jorge Juan and Antonio de Ulloa. But profuse shadows appear in the picture; there is something about it that detracts from the impartiality required of the advocate, an impartiality not incompatible with the energetic tone of reproof with which the historian, advocate of the rights of man and interpreter of moral sentiments, should pronounce judgment on corrupting institutions.

To the dominant idea of perpetuating the tutelage of her colonies, Spain sacrificed not only the interests of her colonies but her own; in order to keep them dependent and submissive she made herself poor and weak. While American treasure inundated the world, the Spanish treasury grew empty and her industry remained in swaddling clothes. Colonies served to stimulate the growth of population and the arts in other countries; for Spain they were a cause of depopulation and backwardness. Spain displayed no industrial life or wealth, save in a few emporia that served as intermediaries in the trade between the two hemispheres, emporia in which the accumulated wealth of monopoly flaunted itself amid the general misery.

But we must be just: Spain's was not a *ferocious* tyranny. It chained the arts, clipped the wings of thought, stopped up the very sources of agricultural fertility, but its policy was one of obstacles and restraints, not of blood and torture. The penal laws were laxly administered. In punishing sedition it was not extraordinarily severe; it was as severe as despotism has always been, but no more, at least as concerns its treatment of the Spanish race and until the time of the Revolution that brought freedom to the Spanish dominions.

The prototype of Spanish despotism in America was that of the Roman emperors. There was the same ineffective benignity on the part of the supreme authority, the same pretorian arbitrariness, the same divinization of the Throne, the same indifference to industry, the same ignorance of the great principles that vivify and make fecund human associations, the same judicial organization, the same fiscal privileges. But to compensate for these negative qualities there were others of a different character. That civilizing mission which moves, like the sun, from east to west, and of which Rome was the most powerful agency in the antique world, Spain performed in a more distant, vaster world. No doubt the elements of this civilization were destined to amalgamate with others that should improve it, just as Roman civilization was modified and improved in Europe by foreign influences. Perhaps I deceive myself; but it seems to me that none of the nations that

emerged from the ruins of the Empire preserved a more pronounced stamp of the Roman genius: the very language of Spain preserves better than any other the character of that spoken by the masters of the world. Even in material things Spain's colonial administration displayed a touch of the imperial Roman style. To the Spanish government America owes all that is grand and splendid in its public buildings. Let us confess it with feelings of shame: we have hardly been able to maintain the structures erected under the viceroys and captains general. Remember, too, that Crown revenues were liberally spent for their construction, and that Spain did not impose the taxes and forced labors with which Rome burdened her imperial subjects for the building of roads, aqueducts, amphitheaters, hot baths, and bridges.

4. A REVISIONIST LANDMARK: BOURNE'S "Spain in America"

Side by side with "Black Legend" attitudes, kindlier attitudes toward the Conquest and Spanish colonial rule appeared in United States historical writings of the nineteenth century. William H. Prescott, for example, displayed a definite pro-Spanish bias in his monumental Conquest of Mexico. *Albert Gallatin, Hubert H. Bancroft, and Adolph Bandelier were other North American historians and social scientists who displayed some partiality for the Spanish colonial regime in this period. In the period 1898–1929 professional historians elaborated and synthesized the pro-Spanish elements in the writings of these men. The rise of this revisionist school coincided with the rise of an American empire in the Caribbean and the Pacific, and the new imperialist climate of opinion and America's new status as a colonial power undoubtedly disposed the revisionist historians to view the Spanish colonial experience with greater sympathy. A climactic work of this school was Edward Gaylord Bourne's* Spain in America *(1904). Its clear, simple style made it very readable; its professionalism, reasonableness, and apparent determination to maintain a just balance inspired confidence. Yet on close inspection Bourne's portrayal of Spain's Indian policy appears tendentious and idealized. Observe that he does not list exploitation of Indian labor in his enumeration of "the distinctive features of the Spanish Indian policy." Note, too, that he relies heavily on the Laws of the Indies for his description of the conditions of Indian life (although elsewhere Bourne showed that he was aware of the frequent divorce between colonial law and practice).[4]*

[4] Edward G. Bourne, *Spain in America, 1450–1580*, New York, 1962, pp. 256–262.

✢✢✢✢ The Indian legislation of the Spanish kings is an impressive monument of benevolent intentions which need not fear comparison with the contemporary legislation of any European country affecting the status of the working-classes.

The details of the history of the Spanish Indian policy are too voluminous for presentation in this survey of the population of Spanish America; yet they form an important and instructive chapter in the history of the contact of the "higher" and "lower" races, of which unfortunately only the tragic prologue has been made generally familiar through the wide diffusion of Las Casas' tracts on the Indian question. His *Breuissima Relacion de la Destruycion de las Indias*, a voluminous plea prepared to present to Charles V in 1540, was first published twelve years later. Translations into all the principal languages of Europe followed, and its pictures of terrible inhumanity, its impassioned denunciations of the conquerors, and its indictment of the colonial officials became the stock material of generations of historical writers.

It is forgotten that his book was the product of a fierce agitation, or that it was written before the Spaniards had been fifty years in the New World, where their empire lasted three hundred years. Two centuries of philanthropic legislation has been thrown into the background by the flaming words which first gave it impulse. Las Casas was the Lloyd Garrison of Indian rights; but it is as one-sided to depict the Spanish Indian policy primarily from his pages as it would be to write a history of the American Negro question exclusively from the files of the *Liberator;* or, after a century of American rule in the Philippines, to judge it solely from the anti-imperialistic tracts of the last few years. That the benevolent legislation of the distant mother-country was not, and probably could not be, wholly enforced will not seem strange to those familiar with our experience with federal legislation on the Negro question; but that a lofty ideal raised and maintained is as true of the Indian laws of Spain as of the Fifteenth Amendment.

All that can be attempted here is an outline sketch of the typical features of Indian society as reorganized by the conquest. The distinctive features of the Spanish Indian policy were the reduction of the Indians to village life, their conversion to the Christian religion, the suppression of their vices and heathen practices, and a training to industry and sobriety so that they should support themselves and contribute to meet the expenses of the colonial establishment. A portion of their labor was to belong either to their encomenderos or to the crown. On the other hand, they were to be protected from the struggle for existence in competition with the heterogeneous elements of a colonial population.

In pursuance of these aims the Indians were to live in villages

under their own magistrates. Each village, according to its size, had one or two alcaldes and from one to four regidores, who were annually elected by the residents in the presence of the cura, or pastor. These offices were not purchasable, as was the case in the Spanish towns. Each village must contain a church with a mission priest, the expense to be borne by the encomendero out of his tributes. No Indian could live outside his village, nor could any Spaniard, Negro, mestizo, or mulatto live in an Indian village; Spaniards could not tarry over one night, except merchants, who might stay two nights.

In these villages the Indian social life, their marriages, and the like were to be regulated in accordance with Christian principles; schools for teaching Spanish were to be opened; no wine could be sold there, and precautions were to be exercised that the native pulque should not be adulterated or fortified with spirits. Indians could not purchase or bear arms nor ride on horseback. In their religious relations they were exempt from the jurisdiction of the Inquisition. The caciques who had been the chiefs of the Indians before their conversion or reduction might retain that office, and it was recognized as hereditary. They exercised minor jurisdiction, but could not try capital offences. In case they were reported to be oppressive the Spanish officials were to look into their conduct.

The question of Indian tribute and labor was carefully regulated. All male Indians between eighteen and fifty were liable for an annual payment, which was payable in kind either to the crown or to the encomendero, as the case might be; but sometimes it could be commuted into money. The tribute was assessed by officials for the purpose, and protectors of the Indians were appointed to look after their interests. The amount of the tribute in money value was in the later period two or three pesos.

Slavery was absolutely prohibited; the caciques could not hold Indian slaves. In granting encomiendas the descendants of the conquerors, discoverers, and first settlers were to be preferred. Encomenderos could not be absentee landlords. They must provide for the religious instruction of the Indians and protect their rights. If negligent they were liable to forfeit their tributes. In the case of the larger encomiendas the tributes in excess of two thousand pesos were to be available for pensions of deserving persons. Encomenderos must not live in their Indians' villages, nor build houses there, nor allow their slaves to go thither, nor maintain stock-farms in the neighborhood of a village. They must marry within three years after receiving a holding, and could not leave their province without a license, or go to Spain except for some extraordinary emergency.

Many regulations safeguarding the good treatment of the Indians illustrate evils which needed correction. For example, no Spaniard of whatever station could be carried in a litter by Indians. The older

form of draughting Indians for labor had been prolific in abuses and was later abolished. Indians could be assigned by the proper officials to work for wages, and the same was done with idle Spaniards, mestizos, and Negroes; but it was forbidden that the Indians should be carried off against their will or kept overtime. If they demanded excessive wages the rate was to be settled by the officials. The absence of beasts of burden in New Spain, before they were introduced by the Spaniards, had necessitated all freight being carried by Indian porters; but the Indians were no longer to be compelled to carry burdens. Nor were Indian laborers to be apportioned to work in vineyards or olive groves, factories or sugar-mills. If, however, boys wished to work in a factory to learn the art of weaving it was permitted.

The required service of Indians in the mines was called the "mita." In Peru not more than one-seventh part of the Indians could be assigned on the "mita" at once; nor could an Indian be draughted again until all his fellow-villagers had completed their turn. In New Spain the "mita" drew only four from each hundred. For this as for all other services they received wages. They were not to be sent to poor mines, or employed in draining them of water.

One of the fullest pictures that we have of the conditions of Indian life in the middle of the colonial era is that of the English friar Thomas Gage, who was for several years stationed in Indian towns in Guatemala, and also served as a teacher of Latin in Chiapa and as lecturer on divinity in the University of Guatemala. After his return he became a Protestant, and his subsequent views in some respects colored his narrative. His incidental notices of Indian conditions impress the reader as indicating on the whole a status superior in its economic possibilities to that of the European peasantry of that day. His chapter devoted to a particular description of Indian life is darkly colored, but not more so than the average conventional picture of peasant life in France on the eve of the Revolution. Gage tells us that the apportionment of Indians as laborers was the occasion of much oppression, and that the wages were inadequate, being only about ten cents a day. Yet it does not appear that the system in Mexico was more oppressive than the French corvée.

5. A REPLY TO BOURNE

Bourne's Spain in America *gave a strong impetus to the reaction in the United States against what is now called the "Black Legend." A further stimulus to the revisionist movement was given by Lesley B. Simpson's* The Encomienda in New Spain *(1929), whose realistic, pragmatic stance went hand in hand*

with certain procolonialist premises, such as the premise that force or violence was necessary for the spread of civilization. Between 1920 and 1960 United States scholars published numerous monographs that served to rehabilitate Spain's colonial policies by demonstrating the industry and honesty of some colonial administrators, the relative laxity of Spanish controls over colonial culture, the high level of some colonial thought, and the "freedom of speech" that allegedly existed in sixteenth-century Spain and Spanish America. In recent years, however, other scholars have begun to view Spain's colonial record with more critical eyes. This reassessment reflects the social consciousness and anticolonialism of our times, concern with the welfare of the masses rather than elites, and understanding of the harmful effects of colonial survivals in Latin American life. By contrast with the traditional critique of Spanish colonialism, it draws its data from economic and social history rather than political history and is based on a sophisticated grasp of the complex mechanism of Spanish colonial rule. Stanley and Barbara Stein describe the "brutal exploitation of American masses."[5]

✠✠✠✠ The face of Iberian colonialism, of conquest, pacification, and evangelization may be seen in the basic administrative unit of Central Mexico and highland Peru of 1700, the corregimiento. There would be found the corregidor de indios or alcalde mayor, a literate Spaniard of generally limited legal training who had obtained appointment by purchase, family connection, or patronage. Since there was no regular promotional system at this bureaucratic level and salaries were low, the corregidor assumed his isolated post to maximize his one- to five-year tenure to accumulate a fortune. Moreover, the corregidor or alcalde mayor had undoubtedly borrowed from merchants at Madrid, Sevilla, Mexico, or Lima to cover outlays on bribes, on the tax of one-half the first year's salary (*media anata*), and on clothing, household goods, and travel. On arrival at his post, the corregidor was already integrated into an administrative, financial, and mercantile system whose infrastructure consisted of the Amerindian vassal, half-serf and half-peasant, and whose superstructure might be represented by an affluent ex-viceroy ensconced in his Madrid townhouse with dozens of retainers.

In the Central Andes the corregidor's major responsibility as district chief was to exact from caciques in Amerindian towns the annual quota of draftees for silver and mercury mines — in particular the dreaded mita de Potosí. Enforcement of the labor draft offered corregidores ample opportunity to accept bribes from Indians seeking

[5] Stanley J. Stein and Barbara H. Stein, *The Colonial Heritage of Latin America: Essays on Economic Independence in Perspective*, copyright © 1970 by Oxford University Press, Inc., pp. 77–81. Reprinted by permission.

to escape mine service or from estate owners and sweatshop entre-
preneurs seeking extra hands. Yet the most efficient way for such a
corregidor to amass a fortune was via unsanctioned but hallowed practice of forcing Amerinds to accept goods — wanted or unwanted, from
mules to mercury — whose quantities and prices he prescribed. The
colonial district chief or corregidor handled goods sent by merchants
in the viceregal capital, more than likely connected with Sevilla ex-
porters who had originally financed the corregidor's purchase of office.
In essence this was an important facet of the system of trade and
navigation between Spain and the Indies.

To the corregidor, miner, and merchant must be added another
representative of the colonial establishment, the parish priest in the
corregimiento de indios. Acquiring his position in the devious manner
of secular placement, his obligations were often taken lightly. The
curate had his commercial "rights" too: "gifts" of food and clothing,
religious fees, unremunerated household service. This, of course, is not
a comprehensive catalogue of the instruments of bureaucratic extortion
in Indian America around 1700: it is only to suggest the secular roots
of Amerindian fear of the European and the criollo and their mestizo,
mulatto, or cacique assistants.

These intimations of brutal exploitation of Amerindian masses
may seem unduly exaggerated. They have not been presented to
indict a people but a system. Obviously, only a minority of Iberians
profited from the overseas possessions while the mass of Iberians remained oblivious or powerlessly aware of colonial oppression. Nor is
it intended to overlook the fact that sensitive Spaniards and Portuguese
often denounced exploitation and inhumanity perpetrated by their
fellow Europeans in the American colonies. If the condition of the
lowest stratum of society in Spanish colonial America was generally
wretched, some will insist that the existence of west European peasants,
craftsmen, and miners in the sixteenth and seventeenth centuries was
equally wretched. This proposition in general is valid, and the difficulties inherent in calculating relative deprivation make criticism difficult unless one probes a bit further.

Were west Europeans forced into mines and kept there in the
seventeenth century without surfacing from Monday to Saturday?
Was there in operation in western Europe an annual labor draft which
forced unwilling laborers to move hundreds of miles to pitheads along
with their families, supplies, and pack animals? To change the scene,
were there west European occupations in which employers could
calculate with frightening accuracy that a worker's life would be
no longer than five to ten years in their employment — which the
Brazilian planters calculated for Negro slaves on sugar plantations in
the first half of the seventeenth century? Or, not to exhaust compari-
sons but to show their possibilities, could a high west European official

have returned from a post after four years of service with an income surplus of between 1 and 1.5 million silver pesos? For example, the Duque de Alburquerque in 1715 paid the Madrid government 700,000 silver pesos to avoid charges of gross malfeasance in office. If the answer to these questions is no, then the historian no matter how insensitive his skin must conclude that west Europeans from the Iberian peninsula utilized the right of conquest to exploit the subordinate peoples of America for personal profit beyond possibilities existing in the metropolis. Colonialism and uplift have always been antithetical.

A civil service invariably mirrors the matrix, metropolitan or colonial, in which it operates. By the end of the seventeenth century, the Spanish and Spanish colonial civil service reflected societies they were designed to administer. The rigidity of Spanish society, the inability or unwillingness to reshape the economy, the stagnation of Spain gave the elite and their wide circle of dependents by birth, marriage, or service few opportunities for employment other than in state service in the metropolis and especially in the colonies. To the colonies flowed a succession of viceroys chosen from the upper nobility and given wide discretion for enrichment. There they administered submissive colonial peoples in conjunction with the colonial audiencias. Beneath viceroys and audiencias came large numbers of Spanish placemen who had purchased preferment, indebted themselves to Spanish moneylenders, and who then proceeded to enrich themselves as corregidores or alcaldes mayores or their lieutenants in isolated Amerindian communities.

Thus by about 1700 the characteristic features of the colonial policy were already well established. Public office at all levels was seen as a legitimate instrument to further private interest over public weal. A monarchy extorting a share of a viceroy's spoils of office symbolized, indeed legitimized, venality, encouraged corruption and showed itself demonstrably incapable of controlling malfeasance in office. It is an ironic commentary on the effects of colonial rule that the very term "cacique" — originally applied to Amerinds who served the colonial elite to exploit the Amerindian masses — was to become in Spain the term for a local boss. Furthermore, the local colonial government of town officials, corregidores, and priests emerged as the core of political power that fused the interests of local elite of wealth, power, and prestige. It was expected that the colonial civil service armed with broad discretionary powers would work closely with local interests to enforce the *status quo* by manipulating the colonial law code. To the elite, law became a norm honored in the breach. To the unprivileged, law was arbitrary and alien, therefore without moral force.

Glossary of Spanish, Portuguese, and Indian Terms

ADELANTADO Commander of a conquering expedition; governor of a frontier or a recently conquered province.

ALCABALA Sales tax.

ALCALDE Magistrate of a Spanish or Indian town who in addition to administrative duties possessed certain judicial powers as a judge of first instance.

ALCALDE MAYOR Governor of a district or province.

ALFAQUÍ Moslem spiritual leader and teacher of the Koran.

ALGUACIL Constable.

AMAUTA An Inca sage.

AMIN A Jewish broth.

ANDÉN Agricultural terrace, widely used in Inca agriculture.

ARROBA Measure of weight (about 25 pounds).

ASESOR Assessor, adviser.

AUDIENCIA The highest royal court of appeals within a jurisdiction, serving at the same time as a council of state to the viceroy or captain general.

AYLLU Indian village community and kinship group in the Andean highlands.

CABILDO Municipal council.

CACIQUE Indian chieftain.

CAPITÃO-DO-CAMPO "Bush-captain," official charged with recapture of fugitive slaves in colonial Brazil.

CAPITÃO MÔR Commander-in-chief of the military forces of a province in colonial Brazil.

CARGA A measure of six and one-half bushels.

CASCALHÃO Alluvium containing gold or diamonds.

CHAPETÓN A disparaging name applied to European-born Spaniards in the South American colonies.

CHINAMPA A small artificially formed garden tract in a lake of the Valley of Mexico.

COLEGIO College; secondary school.

CONSULADO Colonial guild merchant and tribunal of commerce.

COROZA A peaked headdress.

CORREGIDOR Governor of a district.

CORREGIMIENTO Territory governed by a *corregidor.*

CRUZADO Ancient Portuguese gold coin.

DONATÁRIO Proprietor of an original land grant in colonial Brazil.

ENCOMENDERO Holder of an *encomienda.*

ENCOMIENDA Grant of allotment of Indians who were to serve the holder with tribute and labor.

ESTADO Measure of length (1.85 yards).

FANEGA A measure of grain (about 1.60 bushels).

FANEGADA A measure of land equal to one and one-tenth acres.

FISCAL Crown attorney.

FUERO Privilege or exemption.

GACHUPÍN A disparaging name applied to European-born Spaniards in New Spain.

GUACA *See* huaca.

GUAIPIL (*huipil*) Square, sleeveless blouse worn by Indian women in some parts of Mexico and Central America.

HIDALGO Nobleman.

HUACA (GUACA) Inca shrine or sacred object.

MAMELUCO (MAMALUCO) Mixture of white and Indian (Brazil).

MARAVEDÍ An old Spanish copper coin of the value of $.007 in U.S. pre-1934 gold dollars.

MESTIZO Mixture of white and Indian.

MITA Periodic conscription of Indian labor in the Spanish colonies.

MITIMAES Colonists sent by the Inca to consolidate control of newly-won territory.

MOCAMBO (MUCAMBO) Fugitive-slave settlement in Brazil.

OBRAJE Textile factory in the Spanish colonies.

OIDOR Spanish colonial judge, member of *audiencia*.

OREJÓN Inca noble.

OUVIDOR Portuguese colonial judge and administrative officer.

PARDO Mulatto or Negro.

PATRONATO REAL Right of the Spanish kings to dispose of all ecclesiastical benefices.

PESO Spanish coin and monetary unit.

PRINCIPAL Indian noble.

QUINTAL One hundred pounds.

QUIPU Inca counting device and memory aid.

REAL Spanish silver coin valued at 34 *maravedis*.

REGIDOR Councilman.

REPARTIMIENTO (1) An assignment of Indians or land to a Spanish settler during the first years of the Conquest; (2) the periodic conscription of Indians for labor useful to the Spanish community; (3) the mandatory purchase of merchandise by Indians from colonial officials.

RESIDENCIA Judicial review of a Spanish colonial official's conduct at the end of his term of office.

VARA Variable unit of length, about 2.8 feet.

VISITADOR GENERAL Official charged with the inspection or investigation of a viceroyalty or captaincy-general.

YANACONA Member of Inca and colonial servant or serf class.

ZAMBO Mixture of Indian and Negro.

PEOPLE AND ISSUES IN LATIN AMERICAN HISTORY